POLITICAL PARTIES OF THE AMERICAS, 1980s to 1990s

The Greenwood Historical Encyclopedia of the World's Political Parties

These volumes provide regional guides to the world's significant political parties from the beginnings of the party system in the eighteenth century to the present. Each guide provides concise histories of the political parties of a region and attempts to detail the evolution of ideology, changes in organization, membership, leadership, and each party's impact upon society.

Political Parties of the Americas: Canada, Latin America, and the West Indies
Edited by Robert J. Alexander (1982)

Political Parties of Europe
Edited by Vincent E. McHale (1983)

Political Parties of Asia and the Pacific
Edited by Haruhiro Fukui (1985)

Political Parties of the Middle East and North Africa
Edited by Frank Tachau (forthcoming)

Political Parties of Europe, 1980s to 1990s
Edited by Vincent E. McHale (forthcoming)

The Greenwood Historical Encyclopedia of the World's Political Parties

POLITICAL PARTIES
OF THE AMERICAS,
1980s TO 1990s
Canada, Latin America, and the West Indies

Edited by Charles D. Ameringer

GREENWOOD PRESS
Westport, Connecticut • London

Library of Congress Cataloging-in-Publication Data

Political parties of the Americas, 1980s to 1990s : Canada, Latin
    America, and the West Indies / edited by Charles D. Ameringer.
        p.   cm.
    Includes index.
    ISBN 0–313–27418–5 (alk. paper)
    1. Political parties—Canada. 2. Political parties—Latin
America. 3. Political parties—West Indies.   I. Ameringer, Charles
D., 1926–   .
JL195.P63   1992
324.27—dc20   92–3032

British Library Cataloguing in Publication Data is available.

Library of Congress Catalog Card Number: 92–3032
ISBN: 0–313–27418–5

First published in 1992

Greenwood Press, 88 Post Road West, Westport, CT 06881
An imprint of Greenwood Publishing Group, Inc.

Printed in the United States of America

The paper used in this book complies with the
Permanent Paper Standard issued by the National
Information Standards Organization (Z39.48–1984).

10 9 8 7 6 5 4 3 2 1

CONTENTS

PREFACE

This volume is intended to complement *Political Parties of the Americas: Canada, Latin America, and the West Indies*, edited by Robert J. Alexander and published by Greenwood Press in two volumes in 1982. Bob Alexander, whose work is part of the Greenwood Historical Encyclopedia of the World's Political Parties, described the work as a survey of all political parties of any importance in the nations and territories of the Western Hemisphere, excluding the United States. At Alexander's urging, because he wanted to devote his retirement years to his long-postponed biography of Norman Thomas, I agreed to take up this work where he and his collaborators left off, but I was determined to develop an approach that would combine an update with a free standing volume. The result is a volume that concentrates on new developments in the political parties of the Americas since 1980, presents fresh background data, and refers to related material in the Alexander work where appropriate, achieving backup without redundancy.

In order to achieve this result, each chapter is organized in a similar fashion. Each chapter, which covers the country or political unit in its title, comprises a general essay that summarizes essential background information and emphasizes political developments of the 1980s and the first years of the 1990s; a revised, updated bibliography; a list of active political parties, with a full description of each, highlighting recent changes; and a list of the historical political parties that ceased to exist before 1980, with a summary sketch of each.

Most of the contributors to this volume viewed the concept of the historical parties list skeptically, but they accepted it in the interest of preserving precious space for new material and with the understanding that readers would be referred to the Alexander volumes for more detailed descriptions of the parties in question. Fulfilling, this commitment, I wish to address the reader directly now: For a more detailed description of the parties treated in the "Political Parties—Historical" section included in most chapters, please consult Robert J. Alexander ed., *Political Parties of the Americas: Canada, Latin America, and the West Indies*, 2 vols. (Westport, Conn.: Greenwood Press, 1982).

Noting that this advisory contains the qualification, "most chapters," there are exceptions. In certain chapters, which treat countries where there are no historical parties—either no important party described in the related chapter in Alexander was defunct before 1980, or particular evolutionary factors link old parties with the new—the respective authors have preferred to draft a single "Political Parties" section for the sake of continuity. It should be noted that in all chapters there may be significant changes in the summary descriptions of historical parties, without affecting the advice to consult Alexander.

Similarly, one should consult Alexander for his appendices. I retained and updated only the first appendix "Chronology", but I omitted the second two ("Genealogy" and "Idealogical and Interest Group Parties"). Since change is the dominant theme of this volume, each chapter, in its essay and political parties sections, traces in detail the origin and orientation of each new political movement or event. It seemed more effective and efficient to integrate the material in this way than to set it apart in an appendix, the bulk of which is unchanged.

There are some new contributors to this volume, as well as some holdovers; the volume's goal of combining freshness with continuity extends to its authors. Each author in this volume is a productive scholar, who was invited to contribute because of her or his extensive research and travel experience in a particular country. The contributors are a diverse group of scholars and, aside from the agreed upon general format for each chapter, each has developed her or his own approach, particularly in the essay section, choosing to emphasize certain aspects of political affairs and the role of political parties, institutions, and leaders. However, cognizant that the volume is a component of the Greenwood Press Reference Guide series, each has written in a more factual than analytical mode. Nonetheless, each has particular insights and valuable contacts, and each is current in the most recent literature in English and in the appropriate foreign languages.

With reference to the political parties sections, a specific manner of formatting has been designed to accomodate the reader. Each political party is listed in alphabetical order by its name in English (original, or in translation) and is cross-listed by the name of the party in its local language, if other than English. The description of each party follows only the entry bearing the English name. Each contributor assumed the responsibility for translating party names into English, where appropriate, drawing upon experience and scholarship that combines accurate form with common usage.

I wish to thank the contributors for their patience and understanding in my efforts to achieve unity from diversity. I have tried to be as nonintrusive as possible, and I hope they are as pleased as I am with the results. Scholars may rebel against the restraints imposed in preparing a reference guide, but such impositions affect only format, not substance. And there is an important tradeoff in any case: The original scholarship contained in this volume will be disseminated to a wide audience, effectively linking specialists with a variety of readers, more so than usual.

Charles D. Ameringer

ABOUT THE EDITOR AND CONTRIBUTORS

ROBERT J. ALEXANDER received his B.A., M.A., and Ph.D. degrees from Columbia University and taught economics, political science, and history at Rutgers University from 1947 until his retirement in 1990. Professor Alexander is one of the most productive scholars in the field of Latin American studies, having written or edited twenty-nine books and scores of journal articles and papers during his lengthy career. He has contributed much to our knowledge, but his works dealing with Jorge Alessandri of Chile and Rómulo Betancourt of Venezuela and his studies of organized labor and communism in Latin America are particularly outstanding.

CHARLES D. AMERINGER received his Ph.D. degree from the Fletcher School of Law and Diplomacy. A specialist in the recent history of the Hispanic Caribbean and Central America, he is the author of numerous articles in professional journals and the following books: *The Democratic Left in Exile: The Antidictatorial Struggle in the Caribbean, 1945–1959*; *Don Pepe: A Political Biography of José Figueres of Costa Rica*; *Democracy in Costa Rica*; and *U.S. Foreign Intelligence: The Secret Side of American History*. Dr. Ameringer is Professor of Latin American History at Pennsylvania State University and served as head of the History Department from 1985 to 1990.

PATRICK BELLEGARDE-SMITH received his Ph.D. in international studies from American University in 1977. He is the author of two books, *In the Shadow of Powers: Dantes Bellegarde in Haitian Social Thought* and *Haiti: The Breached Citadel*, and of numerous articles on Haitian social history and socioeconomic development. Dr. Bellegarde-Smith is Associate Professor of Afro-American Studies at the University of Wisconsin-Milwaukee.

DAVID E. BLANK received his Ph.D. from Columbia University. He is the author of two books on Venezuelan political developments: *Politics In Venezuela* and *Venezuela: Politics in a Petroleum Republic*. He has also written about Mexican and Caribbean politics. Since 1969, he has been affiliated with the University of Louisville.

GARY BRANA-SHUTE received his Ph.D. in anthropology from the University of Florida in 1974. He is a specialist in the Anglophone Caribbean and Suriname and is currently the Deputy Director of Latin American and Caribbean Studies at the Foreign Service Institute, U.S. Department of State. He is the author of *On the Corner: Male Social Life in a Paramaribo Creole Neighborhood*, the editor of *Resistance and Rebellion in Suriname*, the coeditor of *Crime and Punishment in the Caribbean*, and a regular contributor to *Latin American and Caribbean Contemporary Record*, *Hemisphere: A Journal of Latin American and Caribbean Affairs*, and *Caribbean Review*.

ROSEMARY BRANA-SHUTE received her Ph.D. in history from the University of Florida in 1985. She is currently Associate Professor of History at the College of Charleston in South Carolina where she teaches Latin American and Caribbean history. She is the editor/compiler of *A Bibliography of Caribbean Migration and Immigrant Communities*, the coeditor of *Crime and Punishment in the Caribbean*, and a regular contributor to *Latin American and Caribbean Contemporary Record*.

JACQUELINE ANNE BRAVEBOY-WAGNER is a visiting scholar and consultant at the United Nations Institute for Training and Research (through 1991). She is Associate Professor at the City College and the Graduate School and University Center of the City University of New York. She has written numerous articles in books and journals, as well as the following books: *The Venezuela-Guyana Border Dispute: Britain's Colonial Legacy in Latin America*; *Interpreting the Third World: Politics, Economic and Social Issues*; and *The Caribbean in World Affairs: Foreign Policies of the English-Speaking Caribbean*. She also has forthcoming *The Caribbean in the Pacific Century* (with collaborators) and *The Role of the Military in the Newer Caribbean*. She has been editor of the *Newsletter* of the Caribbean Studies Association and is the association's vice president and president-elect (1991–1993).

EUGENIO CHANG-RODRÍGUEZ received his Ph.D. from the University of Washington and an honorary doctorate from the National University Federico Villareal of his native Peru, which also later awarded him the Congressional Medal and the Order of Merit. He is Professor of Romance Languages at Queens College of the City University of New York, editor of *Word* and *Boletín* of the North American Academy of the Spanish Language, corresponding member of the Spanish Royal Academy, and Professor *honoris causa* at San Marcos University of Peru. He was President of the International Linguistics Association, Chairman of the Columbia University Seminar on Latin America, cultural attaché at the Embassy of Peru in Washington, D.C., and member of the Joint Committee on Latin-American Studies of the Social Science Research Council and Council of Learned Societies. He has authored, coauthored, and edited eighteen books—published in the Americas, Europe, and China—including, *La literatura política de González Prada, Mariátegui y Haya; Frequency Dictionary of Spanish Words; Poética e ideologia en Mariátegui;* and *Opciones políticas peruanas.*

HAROLD D. CLARKE received his Ph.D. from Duke University and is Professor of Political Science, University of North Texas. He is the coauthor of several books, including *Political Choice in Canada, Citizen Politicians—Canada, Representative Democracy in the Canadian Provinces, Absent Mandate: Interpreting Change in Canadian Elections, How Voters Change: The 1987 British Election Campaign in Perspective,* and *Citizens and Community: Political Support in a Representative Democracy.* His articles have appeared in numerous journals, including the *American Journal of Political Science,* the *American Political Science Review,* the *British Journal of Political Science,* the *Canadian Journal of Political Science,* the *European Journal of Political Research,* the *European Journal of Political Economy,* and the *Journal of Politics.* His research focuses on the dynamics of political support in Anglo-American democracies.

ANN L. CRAIG received her Ph.D. in political science from the Massachusetts Institute of Technology in 1978. She has been teaching at the University of California at San Diego since 1980, where she is currently an associate professor in the Department of Political Science. She is the author of *The First Agraristas: An Oral History of a Mexican Agrarian Reform Movement,* coeditor (with Joe Foweraker) of *Popular Movements and Political Change in Mexico,* and coauthor (with Wayne A. Cornelius) of several book chapters and monographs on Mexico.

JOHN T. DEINER received his Ph.D. from Rutgers University and he is Associate Professor of Political Science and International Relations at the University of Delaware. He has written widely on Latin American politics. His publications include numerous articles on Paraguayan and Argentine political leaders and political party activity. He has also written on the cyclical nature of Argentine politics, the politics of the Argentine Catholic Church, and the Argentine trade union movement. Other publications include articles on the politics of literacy and the politics of fishing and fisheries resources in Latin America and the Caribbean.

CHARLES GILLESPIE was Assistant Professor of Political Science at the University of Wisconsin-Madison before his recent untimely death. He received his undergraduate degree from Oxford University and his Ph.D. from Yale University. His many publications on Uruguay include chapters in *Transitions from Authoritarian Rule* (Guillermo O'Donnell et al., eds.) and *Democracy in Developing Countries* (with Eduardo Gonzalez, Larry Diamond et al. eds.); he coedited and contributed to *Uruguay y la democracia.*

HOWARD HANDELMAN is Professor of Political Science at the University of Wisconsin-Milwaukee. He received his B.A. from the University of Pennsylvania and his Ph.D. from the University of Wisconsin-Madison. His publications include *Struggle in the Andes: Peasant Political Mobilization in Peru, Military Rule and the Road to Democratic Government in South America* (with Thomas Sanders), *The Politics of Agrarian Change in Asia and Latin America*, and *Paying the Costs of Austerity in Latin America* (with Werner Baer).

ALLAN KORNBERG received his Ph.D. from the University of Michigan. He is Norb F. Schaefer Professor and Chairman of the Department of Political Science at Duke University. He is the former editor of the *Journal of Politics*, a former president of the Southern Political Science Association, and the current Chairman of the Legislative Studies Section of the International Political Science Association. A native of Winnipeg, he is author of *Canadian Legislative Behavior* and coauthor of *Influence in Parliament—Canada, Citizen Politicians— Canada*, and of *Representative Democracy in the Canadian Provinces*. He also is coauthor and editor of *Legislatures in Developmental Perspective, Legislatures in Comparative Perspective, Minorities and the Canadian State*, and *The Resurgence of Conservatism in Anglo-American Democracies*. He has contributed articles to numerous journals, including the *American Journal of Political Science*, the *American Political Science Review*, the *Journal of Politics, Social Forces*, the *British Journal of Political Science*, and the *Canadian Journal of Political Science*. He was the 1989 recipient of the American Political Science Association's Samuel Eldersveld Award for Lifetime Achievement in political parties and organizations and the 1990 recipient of the Mentoring Award from Womens' Caucus, American Political Science Association.

SHELDON B. LISS is Professor of Latin American History and Politics at the University of Akron. He received his Ph.D. in 1964 from American University and, since then, has specialized in Latin American political and social thought and inter-American relations. He has traveled throughout and conducted research in Mexico, the Caribbean, and Central and South America. He serves as coeditor of the monograph series *Latin American Issues*, and he is the author of dozens of articles and reviews. His numerous books include *Radical Thought in Central America, Roots of Revolution: Radical Thought in Cuba, Marxist Thought in Latin America*, and *Diplomacy and Dependency: Venezuela, the United States, and the Americas*. He is currently completing a study of the political and social thought of Cuban leader Fidel Castro.

JOHN D. MARTZ is Distinguished Professor of Political Science and Head of the Department of Political Science at Pennsylvania State University. He received his Ph.D. at the University of North Carolina, where he taught prior to moving to Penn State. One of the most productive and respected scholars in the Latin American field, he is the author or editor of over fifteen books and more than 100 articles, reviews, monographs, and chapters. He was formerly the editor of the *Latin American Research Review* and currently (since 1988) is serving as the editor of *Studies in Comparative International Development*.

CHRISTOPHER MITCHELL is Associate Professor of Politics and Director of the Center for Latin American and Caribbean Studies at New York University. With B.A. and Ph.D. degrees from Harvard University, he is the author of *The Legacy of Populism in Bolivia* and the editor of *Changing Perspectives in Latin American Studies* and *Western Hemisphere Immigration and United States Foreign Policy* (forthcoming). He has published articles in *Comparative Politics*, *International Migration Review*, and other journals.

TOMMIE SUE MONTGOMERY is Associate Professor of Latin American Studies at Agnes Scott College in Decatur, Georgia. She received her Ph.D. in politics from New York University. She has been the recipient of two Fulbright grants, most recently to study Salvadorean refugees in Belize. She is the author of *Revolution in El Salvador: Origins and Evolution* and the editor of *Mexico Today*. She has published numerous articles on El Salvador, the churches in Central America, and on U.S. policy in the region.

DAVID J. MYERS received his Ph.D. from the University of California at Los Angeles and is Associate Professor of Political Science at Pennsylvania State University. He has traveled extensively throughout South America, the Caribbean Basin, and Western Europe. He has been a visiting professor at the Central University of Venezuela, the *Instituto de Estudios Superiores de Administración*, in Caracas, Venezuela, and the U.S. Military Academy at West Point. He has published numerous articles and book chapters on Latin American politics, regional international relations, and comparative urban politics; he is also the author of two books and the editor and coeditor of three others. His most recent work is *Regional Hegemons: Threat Perception and Strategic Response*.

WILLIAM JAVIER NELSON received his B.A. from South Carolina State College, M.A. from Tufts University, and Ph.D. from Duke University, all in sociology. An export consultant in Raleigh, North Carolina, he specializes in the Dominican Republic. He is the author of *Almost a Territory: America's Attempt to Annex the Dominican Republic* and of numerous articles which have appeared in *Phylon*, *The Americas*, and *Revista de Historia de América*.

NEALE J. PEARSON, Professor of Political Science at Texas Tech University, in Lubbock, received his Ph.D. from the University of Florida. He has published chapters or articles in fourteen books, including *Latin American Peasant Movements*, *Latin American Labor Organizations*, *Biographical Dictionary of Latin American and Caribbean Political Leaders*, and *Rural Change and Public Policy (Latin America, Eastern Europe and Australia)*. He has been a regular contributor to the *Annual Yearbooks* of the *Encyclopedia Americana* and the *World Book Encyclopedia*, and he has published numerous articles and book reviews in professional journals. He has been a frequent visitor to Central and South America; most recently he visited Costa Rica, Guatemala, and Nicaragua.

DIÓMEDES PÉREZ, who collaborated with William Javier Nelson on the Dominican Republic chapter, is a native of the Dominican Republic. He recently entered professional school in the United States and has extensive, ongoing contact with Dominican political leaders.

SERGIO G. ROCA completed his undergraduate work at Drew University and received his Ph.D. from Rutgers University. He is Professor of Economics at Adelphi University, Garden City, New York. His area of interest is Latin American economic development, and much of his work has centered on Cuba. His numerous publications include *Cuban Economic Policy and Ideology: The Ten Million Ton Sugar Harvest*. He served as a member of a Council on Foreign Relations panel on Cuba. He has lectured at universities in the United States, Canada, England, Cuba, and the Dominican Republic. He is currently writing about the management of state enterprises in socialist Cuba. His most recent book, *Socialist Cuba*, has been widely praised in scholarly reviews.

J. MARK RUHL is Professor of Political Science at Dickinson College in Carlisle, Pennsylvania. He received his Ph.D. from the Maxwell School, Syracuse University in 1975. He has written extensively on Latin American politics, with special attention to Honduras and Colombia. He is the coauthor (with R. H. McDonald) of *Party Politics and Elections in Latin America* and the author of *Colombia: Armed Forces and Society*. His articles have appeared in *Western Political Quarterly, Latin American Research Review, Journal of Interamerican Studies and World Affairs, Estudios Sociales Centro-americanos, Latin American and Caribbean Contemporary Record*, and several other journals and collections.

RICHARD E. SHARPLESS, who received his M.A. and Ph.D. degrees from Rutgers University, teaches Latin American and U.S. history at Lafayette College in Easton, Pennsylvania. He is the author of *Gaitán of Colombia* and *The Kingdom of Coal* and of numerous articles treating Latin American and U.S. politics, immigration, and labor. He resided in Colombia and Puerto Rico for several years and has traveled widely throughout Latin America and the Caribbean.

MARIANNE C. STEWART received her Ph.D. in political science from Duke University. She is an Associate Professor of Government, Politics, and Political Economy at the University of Texas at Dallas. Her research on citizen attitudes and political participation in contemporary democracies appears in such journals as the *American Journal of Political Science, American Political Science Review, Electoral Studies, European Journal of Political Economy*, and *Journal of Politics*, as well as in edited books. She is the coeditor of *Economic Decline and Political Change: Canada, Great Britain, the United States* and the coauthor of *Current Controversies in Political Economy* (forthcoming).

ROBERT H. TRUDEAU, Professor and Chair of the Political Science Department and Director of the Latin American Studies Program at Providence College, earned his Ph.D. degree from the University of North Carolina. He has specialized in the study of Central American politics since the 1960s, and he has contributed to several major edited volumes on the region, including *Confronting Revolution* (edited by Morris Blachman, William LeoGrande, and Kenneth Sharpe), *Elections and Democracy in Central America* (edited by John Booth and Mitchell Seligson), and *Handbook of Political Science Research on Latin America* (edited by David Dent). He is the author of a forthcoming book on Guatemalan politics.

W. MARVIN WILL, Associate Professor of Political Science at the University of Tulsa, received his Ph.D. degree from the University of Missouri. He is past president of the Midwest Association of Latin American Studies as well as a founder and past board member of the Caribbean Studies Association. The author of numerous articles, he coedited *The Restless Caribbean* and has just coauthored a book manuscript comparing the Pacific and Caribbean basins. He has been awarded a 1991–1992 Fulbright Fellowship to conduct research in the Caribbean.

ALMA H. YOUNG is Professor of Urban and Public Affairs and director of the doctoral program in urban studies at the University of New Orleans. She received her Ph.D. in political science from the Massachusetts Institute of Technology. She is a past president of the Caribbean Studies Association. She is the coeditor of *Militarization in the Non-Hispanic Caribbean* and has written widely on political developments in the English-speaking Caribbean.

POLITICAL PARTIES OF THE AMERICAS, 1980s to 1990s

INTRODUCTION

Much has changed about politics in the Americas since the publication of Robert J. Alexander's *Political Parties of the Americas* in 1982. But much has stayed the same. For example, Alexander asked the question, "What is a political party?" and answered by citing a definition given by the Bahamian leader, Sir Randol Fawkes in *The Faith That Moved the Mountain* (Nassau, 1979), to wit: "A political party consists of a group of persons united in opinion or action, more or less permanently organized, which attempts to bring about the election of its candidates to public offices and by this means to control or influence the actions and policy of government. Its long-range goal is to put into effect its political, social, and economic philosophy" (211). Although Alexander was not completely satisfied with Fawkes's definition, observing that no hard and fast definition could be made, it suited his purposes then and it generally serves ours today.

Much of the insightful geographic and historical background that Alexander provided is unchanged and needs no repetition or revision here. The Western Hemisphere, by definition half of the earth, comprises a tremendous variety of topographical features, resources, and climatic conditions that have influenced the patterns of human settlement and have determined the relationships among the primarily three races of people who inhabit its space. The only common thread in this diverse half sphere, at least in the last 500 years, is its colonial experience.

Beginning early in the sixteenth century, the states on Europe's Atlantic edge—England, France, Holland, Portugal, and Spain—established their dominion over what they called the New World. For 300 years, the colonial powers exercised exclusive authority for the purpose of economic exploitation and fought among themselves for spoils, frequently exchanging territory because there was "no peace beyond the line." Depending upon the abundance of precious metals or the presence of an indigenous or imported work force in bondage, the nature of colonial government varied from benign neglect to absolute control. Spain practiced the most aristocratic and authoritarian form of government in its overseas empire, but the other powers also maintained a monopoly of power where their interests were strong. With the possible exception of England's North American colonies (and the United States experience is not under specific discussion here) and Brazil, the imperial states were not good models for the kinds of governments that eventually emerged in the Americas after independence.

The nations of the Americas achieved independence at different times in different ways. Brazil, Canada, and the English, Dutch, and French possessions of the circum-Caribbean, taken together, began the process early in the nineteenth century and are now in the final stages. For most of these countries, the separation has been bloodless (Haiti is a major exception), with the former colonial powers generally facilitating the transition and encouraging the retention of their respective governmental forms. Brazil is an exception in this case inasmuch as it changed its form of government from monarchy to republic after seventy years.

In the case of Spain's American territories, the achievement of independence was hard-fought and bitter, and the legacy of Spanish rule hindered the development of political parties. During the first half of the nineteenth century, two groups of elites competed for power, usually by force of arms: the conservatives, who, idolizing Spain's Golden Age, fought to preserve authoritarian rule and the primacy of the Catholic Church; and the liberals, who, accepting Spain's decline, tried to impose systems copied from the prevailing laissez-faire states, England and France, and the up-and-coming United States. A little past the midcentury mark, having exhausted themselves in internecine struggle, they settled on positivism as an approach. The positivist philosophy, with its watchwords order and progress, had something that both conservatives and liberals sought. It preserved elitist rule, but now for the loftier goal of national development. Both elements anticipated that it would resolve their respective concerns about the subjugated races, but the construction of railroads and the addition of street lighting alone did not do the job.

The economic activity at the end of the nineteenth century created the conditions for the emergence of political parties in many parts of Latin America at the beginning of the twentieth century. Liberal elites, satisfied with the progress being made, sensed the need to reform the aging order, and leaders of a new, urban proletariat agitated for workers' rights. Though they had some success in Argentina, Chile, and Uruguay, they failed in Mexico. In Mexico, the reformers offering effective suffrage and no reelection were swept aside by the demand of dispossessed peasants for land and liberty and industrial workers for a socialist state. The Mexican Revolution, along with those occurring in China and Russia, set standards for popular parties throughout Latin America on the basis of economic and social activism. The New Deal in the United States also provided a model—one that offered a democratic framework. By midcentury, three types of political parties competed on the left side of the political spectrum: Christian democratic, Communist, and social democratic.

In the three decades after World War II, these parties achieved a certain vitality and where they were able to function attempted ambitious programs of economic development and social progress. They exhibited certain common features, namely, central planning, state ownership or regulation of natural resources and essential services, and public responsibility for education, health, and housing. They expressed common themes that linked them to broad, Third World movements (including those of the new states of the Caribbean) and protested against colonialism, imperialism, and dependency. Among the more successful were the Christian democratic parties in Chile and Venezuela and the social democratic parties in Costa Rica (National Liberation), the Dominican Republic (Dominican Revolutionary), Jamaica (People's National), Puerto Rico (Popular Democratic), and Venezuela (Democratic Action). But in virtually all countries of Latin America similar parties struggled to lead and some even managed to achieve power when free elections occurred, such as the National Revolutionary Movement in Bolivia and the Christian Democratic Party in El Salvador.

Even where and when these parties were outlawed and banished, they strongly influenced the economic, political, and social environment. In certain important countries, such as Argentina, Brazil, Chile, Peru, Uruguay, and Venezuela, the armed forces kept political parties on a short tether and intervened directly in political affairs when they decided it was necessary. They viewed most civilian politicians as corrupt and ineffcent, but most of all as weak and vacillating before the challenge of communism, particularly that of the Cuban Revolution after 1959, inviting violence and instability. Nonetheless, the military regimes generally continued on the path toward economic development, keeping in place many of the state institutions and control over economic resources that they found when they took over.

In the case of Brazil and Argentina, though democratic left parties were factors, the large role of the state in the economy owed its existence to the earlier corporatism and economic nationalism of Getulio Vargas and Juan Perón, respectively. In Peru, a populist military regime coopted the agrarian reform and anti-imperialist state programs of the American Popular Revolutionary Alliance (APRA), even nationalizing the country's major foreign enterprise in 1969, the International Petroleum Corporation (IPC). Similar situations, with variations, existed in Bolivia and Panama. Only in those places where personalist dictators or racist oligarchies clung to power with lethal persistence were political parties that advocated the social reform model of development nonexistent or without influence (though even in one of these countries—El Salvador—the Christian Democratic Party took root).

If part of the definition of a political party is that it exists to get its candidates for office elected, then the actual holding of free elections is vital to political party development. In this regard, the decade of the 1980s has been a time unlike any other in Latin America. Democracy has been busting out all over; the armed forces in all major countries literally have fled the government palace and have returned to the barracks. A number of factors caused this to happen, most of them beyond the control of Latin Americans themselves. In the 1970s, the worldwide energy crisis ravaged some Latin American economies and encouraged reckless borrowing by others, leaving all burdened with an enormous foreign debt, and U.S. President Jimmy Carter pursued a vigorous human rights policy that helped undo Latin American governments of force. In the 1980s, two men in business suits, Ronald Reagan and Mikhail Gorbachev, achieved counterrevolutions, wiping out the regulatory and the socialist states, respectively. In more specific cases, the miscalculation of the General Leopoldo Galtieri government in the 1982 Falklands/Malvinas war restored civilian rule to Argentina, and U.S. military and covert operations gave democracy a controversial helping hand in toppling the New Jewel Movement in Grenada in 1983 and Manuel Noriega in Panama in 1989 and in opposing the Sandinistas in Nicaragua and the Farabundo Marti National Liberation Front in El Salvador.

The 1980s, with the achievement of democratic government virtually everywhere in Latin America and the Caribbean, witnessed the flowering of political parties. But democratization saddled with debt was a hollow victory. Ironically, though political parties were more influential than ever in determining who held office, they appeared to lose relevance to the issues confronting their societies. The political parties that survived the long winter of military rule, especially, were not attuned to the problems of overwhelming debt, soaring crime, AIDS, drugs, the environment, and population growth. As a result, during the 1980s in Latin America, new parties and coalitions appeared and succeeded in capturing the presidency with candidates who were relatively young.

In Argentina and Brazil, the winning parties supported candidates who looked good on television and engaged in negative campaigning. In Chile, the Christian Democratic Party made a comeback, but as part of a coalition whose main purpose was to avoid extremism in order to keep the military in camp. In Costa Rica and Venezuela, the National Liberation and Democratic Action parties abandoned their former platforms, cutting social programs and returning state enterprises to the private sector. In Uruguay, the Blancos, reorganizing after a period of oppressive military rule and pledging to trim the welfare state, achieved a rare victory over the once unbeatable Colorados. In Nicaragua, in one of the decade's most dramatic turnabouts, the ruling Sandinista National Liberation Front lost an election and relinquished power to a coalition of political forces that could agree only to be democratic and to be different. Even in Mexico, the dominant Institutional Revolutionary Party (PRI) had a scare and toyed with the idea of privatization. It was the same almost everywhere; the collapse of communism caused not just Marxist parties to fade, but deflated social democratic and like-spirited national revolutionary and social Christian parties as well. The United States was exorcised of its bogey of Moscow intervention, but its ideas for Latin American development were limited to the promotion of free trade and a free-market economy, though packaged with some development assistance in Ronald Reagan's Caribbean Basin Initiative and George Bush's Enterprise for the Americas Initiative.

The general pragmatism and lack of ideological commitment on the part of most political parties in Latin America today may provide democracy with the breathing spell it needs to take root and eventually thrive. In the 1950s through the 1970s, democracy was the victim of its own ambition, and those parties that set the most idealistic goals in the economic and social spheres were the ones most shattered when they failed to deliver. If democracy can survive on its own terms as a guarantor of individual freedom and orderly process for the transfer of political power, then the future holds promise for the development of political parties that are not obliged to stretch their goals beyond reasonable limits. The prevailing international situation helps by reducing the temptation for rightist coups or leftist insurgencies.

But the economic and social problems are still there, and they are mounting. The new/old solutions being tried by the democratic managers to reduce indebtedness and restore growth will in time have to stand the test of economic and social advance. This standard will not go away. Many of today's presidents— Carlos Saúl Menem (Argentina), Fernando Collor de Mello (Brazil), Patricio Aylwin (Chile), Rodrigo Borja (Ecuador), Carlos Salinas de Gortari (Mexico), Alberto Fujimori (Peru), Luis Alberto Lacalle (Uruguay), and Carlos Andrés Pérez (Venezuela)—seem strangers in contrast to the pre–1980 political leaders, even though some have been around awhile and represent established parties. Only Jamaica's Michael Manley remains as an example of the old-style charismatic leader, and even he is following a course more moderate than before.

These "political entrepreneurs," to borrow David Myers's phrase, and their bureaucracies collect taxes and provide services, but they are pragmatic; they engage in coalition politics; and they employ teams of technicians instead of party loyalists. Almost uniformally, they have sought to get out of debt by adopting austerity, balance-of-payments, and monetary stabilization plans devised by the International Monetary Fund and the U.S. Agency for International Development (AID). They have slashed the public payroll, cut social services, sold off state enterprises, reduced subsidies to public services, and relaxed restrictions on private foreign investment. If these actions control inflation and restore economic growth, the cost of the "lost decade" of the 1980s may be redeemed, and Latin American political parties will continue to crowd the center. But if the quality of life continues to deteriorate in Latin America's cities and its countryside remains unprotected, nasty events such as the street riots in Venezuela that took 300 lives in February–March 1989 will recur as reminders of discontent. Already pressure groups representing labor and business and professional groups, among others, are challenging political parties as principal actors in Latin American politics, and a substantial alternate political economy exists maintained by urban gangs and narcotics production and trade.

These matters are discussed in detail, country by country, in the following chapters. These fascinating accounts of nations in flux have been written by scholars with specialized knowledge of particular countries. Though this introduction does not refer to Canada specifically, the chapter on Canada provides both unique features and those in common with the rest of the hemisphere. In the same way, the chapters on the states of the West Indies and Caribbean coast deal more effectively with distinct characteristics, but the states themselves are an integral part of the Latin American experience (which only emphasizes the need for a more appropriate term). The future of political parties as they have been defined here depends on the health of democracy, and democracy in turn may depend on the ability of political parties to respond to the needs of the people. At the present time in Latin America, democracy is not getting the kind of help it needs.

ANGUILLA

Anguilla is the most northerly of the Leeward Islands, a low-lying island approximately 3 miles wide by 16 miles long, located 65 miles north of Saint Kitts and 150 miles east of Puerto Rico but only 5 miles from the Dutch and French island of Saint Martin (Sint Maarten). Together with several offshore islets or cays, its total size is 60 square miles and its population is just over 7,000. Named by the Spaniards—probably because of its eel-like shape—it has been a British colony since the mid-seventeenth century. Although often tied administratively to nearby but much larger Saint Kitts and, after the 1950s, to the joint colony of Saint Kitts-Nevis, the communities developed quite separately, and Anguilla today remains culturally distinct from its larger neighbors. The current populations of both entities are dominated by the descendants of nineteenth-century slaves, although Anguilla, with its poorer cultivation conditions and its tendency toward small plots, does not share the Kittitian legacy of sugar plantation agriculture, the cycle of labor riots and elite reactions of the 1930s, or the resultant formation of labor parties.

When Britain sought to incorporate Anguilla as part of the associated state of Saint Kitts-Nevis and Anguilla in 1967, after failure of two attempts at federation of the West Indian colonies, a most uneasy association was predictable. Almost immediately following announcement of the tripartite consolidation, an Anguillian-sponsored plebiscite indicated that popular support for the three-unit state was not present in Anguilla. The limited support that did exist had almost totally collapsed by 1969, as demonstrated by another plebiscite in which just 4 Anguillians voted for association with Saint Kitts and Nevis and 1,739 opposed such an affiliation.

This plebiscite was immediately followed by the formal secession of Anguilla in the famous "mouse that roared" independence move which was aborted only by intervention of the British military. Later that year, Anguilla returned to a de facto separate dependency status with the United Kingdom. This recolonization status was formalized in 1971 although Anguilla's legal break with Saint Kitts-Nevis did not culminate until 19 December 1980.

Political History

Political party development in particular and political organization in general have never been strong in Anguilla. This is due primarily to the small size of this colony and also to the previously noted distinct cultural development of this island which, in the words of Bonham C. Richardson, is manifested as "solidarity among most Anguillians [but] . . . interpreted as clannishness by most other West Indians" (Richardson 1982, 46). Until now, Richardson continues, the Anguillian culture "ha[s] had little political expression." This appears especially applicable to its orientation toward labor party politics.

Despite the relative unpopularity of the Saint Kitts-Nevis-Anguilla Labour Party in Anguilla, David Lloyd from Anguilla was elected to the parliament of the West Indies Federation (1958–1962) under this label. In 1967 Peter Adams was elected as the island's representative to the statehood talks and as the lone Anguillian representative to the Saint Kitts-Nevis-Anguilla legislature under the label of another Saint Kitts-based party, the anti-Labour People's Action Movement (PAM).

Current Electoral Politics: The Dominance of Personality

Elections and politics in Anguilla during the 1980s and 1990s have persistently reflected a high level of personal dominance over institutional development. This pattern is readily evident in the political career of J. Ronald Webster, identified as the father of Anguillian separation for his role as the acknowledged leader of the uprising against Saint Kitts at the end of the 1960s.

By the 1970s, Webster had become head of the Progressive People's Party (PPP), which had been "formed in time for the assembly elections of 1976." Webster and his personalist party won that election, but they were replaced by Emile Gumbs and his Anguilla National Alliance (ANA) within a year as the result of a no-confidence vote. Webster then became head of the Anguilla United Party (AUP), later known as the Anguilla United Movement (AUM). In May 1980, the AUP won six of seven seats in the Anguilla legislature; the remaining seat went to Gumbs's ANA. This AUP/AUM victory allowed Webster to replace Gumbs as chief minister. By June 1981, however, the Webster government had fallen, and Webster was expelled from the AUP/AUM over the dismissal of one minister and the sympathy resignation of a second.

Webster then formed the Anguilla People's Party (APP) and retrieved his position as chief minister when he and his new group won five of seven seats in the June 1981 balloting to replace his just-collapsed government. The ANA won two seats in this election and the AUP/AUM, now headed by Edison Hughes, was shut out although just a year earlier it had won seven seats. Webster retired in 1984 following an electoral defeat. Gumbs again became chief minister of Anguilla.

Gumbs and his ANA retained parliamentary leadership in the February 1989 general election, although they secured only three seats in the seven-seat Anguillian legislature, by acquiring the support of the lone elected independent, M. Osbourne. The AUP currently holds two seats, and the Anguilla Democratic Party (ADP) holds one seat. The newly formed Party for Anguilla's Culturation and Economy (PACE) received a mere 6.2 percent of the electoral vote (235 votes) in the 1989 balloting and did not win a seat.

The formal power of Emile Gumbs, current chief minister of Anguilla, has increased due to the implementation of a new constitution in 1989. It is felt this could increase political stability in Anguilla, at least in the perception of Gumbs's backers.

Conclusion

Differentiation and program emphasis are minimal among the personalist political parties in Anguilla, although the last general election (1989) in this island state directed attention to such major issues as jobs and joblessness, the pros and cons of tourism, and how to address crime—particularly how to diffuse the impact of the 1988 murder of two tourists, which placed a considerable damper on what had been an expanding tourist industry. Despite this, however, politics in Anguilla remains poorly institutionalized and dominated by personality.

Bibliography

Rosemary Brana-Shute and Gary Brana-Shute. "The Anglophone Eastern Caribbean and British Dependencies," in Abraham F. Lowenthal, ed., *Latin America and Caribbean Contemporary Record*, vol. 6, 1986–1987 B449–50, Holmes and Meier, New York, 1989.

Jerome L. McElroy and Klaus de Albuquerque. "The British Caribbean," in Jack W. Hopkin ed., *Latin America and Caribbean Contemporary Record*, vol. 3, 1983–1984, 687–93. Holmes and Meier, New York, 1985.

John Paxton, ed. "Anguilla," in *The Statesman's Yearbook*. St. Martin's Press, New York. 1990.

C. L. Perry. *Anguilla: Where There's a Will, There's a Way*. [The Valley], Anguilla; n.p., 1984.

Bonham C. Richardson. "Anguilla," in Robert J. Alexander, ed., *Political Parties of the Americas* vol. 1, 44–46. Greenwood Press, Westport, Conn., 1982.

M. M. Kateri Scott-McDonald. "The British Caribbean," in James M. Malloy and Eduardo A. Gamarra, eds., *Latin America and Caribbean Contemporary Record*, vol. 7, 1987–1988, B365–68, Holmes and Meier, New York, 1990.

Political Parties—Active

ANGUILLA DEMOCRATIC PARTY (ADP). The ADP developed out of a split in the Webster-dominated Anguilla People's Party. It holds one seat in the Anguillian parliament as a result of the 1989 general election. (*See* Anguilla People's Party.)

ANGUILLA NATIONAL ALLIANCE (ANA). Emile Gumbs and the ANA gained island attention in the late 1970s when Gumbs replaced J. Ronald Webster as chief minister of Anguilla as the result of a no-confidence vote in 1977, before losing the post in 1980. Although Gumbs and the ANA suffered an electoral defeat in 1981, Gumbs was again chief minister just four years later when he and his party scored electoral victories. The ANA won three seats in the February 1989 general election, a bare plurality in the three-party race for the seven-seat Anguillian legislature. Control of the government was achieved through support of the lone independent parliamentarian, M. Osbourne, formerly a member of the Anguilla People's Party. Gumbs currently heads the Anguillian crown colonial government as chief minister.

ANGUILLA PEOPLE'S PARTY (APP). The APP was formed in 1981 by J. Ronald Webster after his Anguilla United Party (AUP) government fell and he was expelled from the AUP/AUM over the dismissal of a minister and the sympathy resignation of a second. Webster retrieved his position as chief minister of Anguilla when his newly formed APP won five of seven seats in the June 1981 balloting. Webster retired in 1984 following an electoral defeat that returned Emile Gumbs to the office of chief minister. (The APP is still listed as a current party by M. M. Kateri Scott-McDonald although it had no electoral success in the 1989 election.)

ANGUILLA UNITED PARTY (AUP). The AUP was headed by J. Ronald Webster in the late 1970s after his Progressive People's Party was removed from office by a no-confidence vote. By May 1980 the highly personalist AUP, later also known as the Anguilla United Movement (AUM), won six of seven legislative seats and Webster, the father of Anguillian separation, reclaimed the office of chief minister. This government fell by 1981, and Webster was expelled from the AUP/AUM. The AUP, currently headed by Edison Hughes, holds two seats in the Anguillian parliament as a result of the 1989 general election. (*See* Anguilla United Movement.)

PARTY FOR ANGUILLA'S CULTURATION AND ECONOMY (PACE). The PACE, formed just in time to contest the 1989 election, received 235 votes (6.2%) in the balloting, an insufficient show of support to secure a parliamentary seat. Last minute formation of political parties and equally rapid changes in leadership are not uncommon in Anguillian politics.

Political Parties—Historical

ANGUILLA UNITED MOVEMENT (AUM). The AUM is one of the titles used by the pro-Webster Anguilla United Party in the early 1980s. (*See* Anguilla United Party.)

PEOPLE'S ACTION MOVEMENT (PAM). The Saint Kitts-based movement, the PAM, was an anti-Labour party that was somewhat active in Anguilla prior to Anguilla's separation from Saint Kitts-Nevis. Under the PAM banner, Peter Adams was elected in 1967 as Anguilla's representative to the statehood (Associated State) talks and as the lone Anguillian representative to the short-lived Saint Kitts-Nevis-Anguilla legislature. The PAM now governs Saint Kitts-Nevis. (*See* People's Action Movement in the Saint Kitts-Nevis chapter.)

PROGRESSIVE PEOPLE'S PARTY (PPP). The PPP was formed in 1976 by J. Ronald Webster, just in time to challenge the election of that year. Webster and the PPP won that election, but they were replaced by Emile Gumbs and the Anguilla National Alliance within a year as the result of a no-confidence vote. By the next elections, 1980–1981, Webster had shifted to another party label, the Anguilla United Party, which was also known as the Anguilla United Movement. (*See* Anguilla United Party.)

SAINT KITTS-NEVIS-ANGUILLA LABOUR PARTY (SKNALP). The Saint Kitts-Nevis-Anguilla Labour Party was the first party to function in Anguilla following its founding in 1940 subsequent to the labor unrest in Saint Kitts. Although the party garnered minimal support in Anguilla, David Lloyd from Anguilla was elected to the parliament of the short-lived West Indies Federation parliament (1958–1962) under the SKNALP banner. This party was not active in Anguilla after this island severed its administrative ties with Saint Kitts-Nevis in the late 1970s. (For additional historical details of this party, which is still active in Saint Kitts, *see* Saint Kitts-Nevis Labour Party in the Saint Kitts-Nevis chapter).

W. Marvin Will

ANTIGUA AND BARBUDA

The state of Antigua and Barbuda 112 square miles in size, located about 260 miles east of Puerto Rico, comprises three islands in the Leeward group in the northern part of the Lesser Antilles. Named and claimed by Christopher Columbus in 1493, Antigua was colonized by Britain in 1632. Barbuda, situated 25 miles north of Antigua, was colonized from Antigua in 1661 and currently has only approximately 1,500 of this state's 80,000 inhabitants (1986). Redonda, the uninhabited third island that makes up this state, is located 25 miles southwest of Antigua. Barbudans, who seldom are celebratory regarding their linkage with Antigua, alternate between perceptions of inordinate manipulation by a paternal Antiguan government and feelings of being ignored or slighted, particularly in public policy outlays by the larger island. As a result, Antigua and Barbuda join Saint Kitts-Nevis and Trinidad and Tobago in finding national integration problematic. Political parties, with the potential to divide or integrate, often have a significant impact on this problem.

From Multifunctional Union to Party Development in Antigua

In Antigua, as in other West Indian states, political parties had their genesis in the labor movements of the 1930s and 1940s. With the founding of the Antigua Trades and Labour Union (ATLU) in 1939, the foundation was laid to expand the representation of working-class Afro–West Indian Antiguans in the government. By 1944 the Antigua Labour Party (ALP) had evolved from the political committee of the ATLU although, as in Grenada, there was little to separate the party from the union structure for a number of years (1968).

Vere C. Bird, Sr., who has served as the leader of the ATLU since 1943, was elected to the Legislative Council of Antigua under the ALP banner in 1945. A second ATLU-ALP leader joined Bird two years later. The combined pressure of these elected representatives reinforced a responsive Britain which was now reacting positively to the recently published Moyne Report recommendations for metropolitan adaptation in the aftermath of the West Indian insurrections of the 1930s. (*See* also the Barbados chapter.) Thus, by 1952, suffrage gates were lowered in Antigua, and in 1956 a semi-ministerial government was introduced. These changes increased the appeal of the ALP, and the ALP remains the governing party in Antigua and Barbuda in the early 1990s. Bird continues to serve as its leader and also as the sitting prime minister.

The Rise of Labour Opposition

The colony of Antigua and Barbuda became a separate dependency in 1956, following the abrogation of the Leeward Islands federation. In 1967, the joint state of Antigua and Barbuda was awarded associate state status with domestic sovereignty and a Labour-controlled, full ministerial government and house of representatives. At the same time, George Walter, a leader within the ATLU, organized an anti-Bird rebellion among middle-level leaders of the ATLU and formed an opposition union, the Antigua Workers Union (AWU). Of greater importance here, he also formed and led an opposition political party, the Progressive Labour Movement (PLM). The PLM captured the Antiguan government in the general election of 1971 by winning thirteen of seventeen parliamentary seats; the remaining four seats were won by the ALP.

This displacement of the Bird regime—Vere Bird, Sr., and two of his sons who have served as governmental ministers—was the only time the Birds have been out of power in the history of the state of Antigua and Barbuda despite the country's reputation as one of the most corrupt and least open regimes in the Commonwealth Caribbean. Tony Thorndike underscores the latter point by entitling his 1991 article on Antigua, published in *Corruption and Reform*, "Avarice in the Aviary." Lester Bird, a governmental minister perceived to be the Bird family member least involved in corruption, seems to corroborate these charges in a statement he recently wrote to his father, declaring that they needed to put their own house in order, or the government and Labour Party would be blown away by a gale-force wind of change. The opposition parties certainly hope so.

The failure of an opposition to mount a sustained challenge to the Bird regime is in large part the result of a plethora of small, often squabbling, personalist parties which mushroomed after the George Walter–led rebellion against Bird leadership in the late 1960s. These factors, reinforced by an ideological component, have produced an opposition that is too splintered to be viable. As early as 1979 Patrick A. M. Emmanuel divided the multitude of Antiguan parties into three often warring groups: the left-leaning Antigua Caribbean Liberation Movement (ACLM), which usually campaigns alone; the ALP and its allies in the ATLU; and the various parties associated with George Walter, such as the current United National Democratic Party (UNDP), plus the AWU. In 1985–1986, there were six parties in Antigua; that number has now decreased by one.

In 1976, for example, the ALP won eleven to six despite receiving a minority of votes. The 1980 general election, called a year early because of pending independence, was swept by the ALP fourteen to three, and the ALP again easily defeated a much-divided opposition in 1984, winning all but the lone Barbudan seat, which went to an independent candidate. Despite serious divisions in "Birdland," and several high-placed investigations for alleged wrongdoing by governmental ministers, the ALP won the last general election (March 1989) by a margin of fifteen to two, losing one seat to a candidate from the UNDP and, as usual, the lone Barbudan seat. The refusal of the two major opposition groups in 1989, the ACLM and the UNDP, to work in concert scuttled any chances of an opposition victory.

It should be noted that considerable political support for the establishment flows from the general support expressed for the Antiguan government by the U.S. government, including the U.S. decision to expend US$1.5 million per annum as rental payment for a naval station in Antigua and a scheduled additional $8 million to convert the station into a school–training camp in survival, evasion, resistance, and escape. Even with such external assistance, the aged Vere Bird cannot long endure, and the considerable intragovernment friction that now exists will probably continue to grow. Recently, the elder Bird was even asked to resign by his own cabinet—before several members were induced not to honor their own resolve and signatures, that is. And Lester Bird has warned his father's government, that either reform must be initiated or the ALP will be destroyed. With a viable opposition, one could expect one of these options to be exercised by the 1994 or 1999 election, but at the present time a coalesced opposition does not exist, and the expectation of major restructuring may not currently be waiting in the wings.

Bibliography

Robert J. Alexander. "Antigua," in Robert J. Alexander, ed., *Political Parties of the Americas*, vol. 1, 47–51. Greenwood Press, Westport, Conn. 1982.

"Are the Birds Coming or Going?" *Caribbean Contact* 18, 5 (March/April), pp. 1, 7. 1991.

Gary Brana-Shute and Rosemary Brana-Shute. "The Organization of Eastern Caribbean States," in James M. Malloy and Eduardo A. Gamarra, eds., *Latin America and Caribbean Contemporary Record*, vol. 7, 1987–1988, B501–04. Holmes and Meier, New York, 1990.

———"The Anglophone Eastern Caribbean and British Dependencies," in Abraham Lowenthal, ed., *Latin America and Caribbean Contemporary Record*, vol. 6, 1986–1987, B440–43. Holmes and Meier, New York, 1989.

Patrick A. M. Emmanuel. *General Elections in the Eastern Caribbean*. Letchworth Press, Ltd. for Institute of Social and Economic Research, University of the West Indies, Barbados, 1979.

Percy C. Hintzen and W. Marvin Will. Biographies of Antiguan political leaders, in

Robert J. Alexander, ed., *Biographical Dictionary of Latin American and Caribbean Political Leaders*, 57–59, Greenwood Press, Westport, Conn. 1988.

Charles H. Kunsman, Jr. "The Origins and Development of Political Parties in the British West Indies." Ph.D. diss., University of California, Berkeley, 1963.

Tony Thorndike. "Avarice in the Aviary: The Sad Story of Corruption in Antigua and Barbuda" *Corruption and Reform*, December, 1991.

W. Marvin Will. Personal interviews with Antigua Labour Party and opposition leaders. 1981–1983.

Political Parties—Active

ANTIGUA CARIBBEAN LIBERATION MOVEMENT (ACLM). Under leader-founder Tim Hector, the ACLM has been labeled the Antiguan Marxist or "leftist" party by U.S. business magazines and by personnel from the Antiguan and U.S. governments. These labels notwithstanding, the primary goals of the ACLM are to promote community development (something of a cross between Lloyd Best's Tapia House project in Trinidad and the Acorn groups in the United States), to act as the key Antiguan voice against the corruption of the Bird regime, and to serve as a driving force for Antiguan and Caribbean dignity. Hector concluded that the latter, at times, requires harsh rhetoric against U.S. imperialism. One reason for the anti–U.S. posture on the part of the ACLM is the strong U.S. support extended to the Bird government.

The Outlet, a publication of the ACLM, is instrumental in pursuing and achieving the goals of the ACLM. Ironically, *The Outlet* is not only the most widely read opposition newspaper on the island, but it also has the widest circulation of any newspaper in Antigua. Hector does not advance his cause with his positive nods toward Cuba, nor in his support for the 1979–1983 revolutionary government in Grenada, a regime that was not popular with the average Antiguan citizen. The net result is a situation somewhat akin to the status of the Maurice Bishop Patriotic Movement in Grenada: a highly visible party that is labeled leftist, to which cautious Antiguans seldom give more than 1 percent of their votes. This also means that other opposition parties in this two-island state are hesitant to ally with Hector against the Bird regime.

ANTIGUA LABOUR PARTY (ALP). The ALP began as the political arm of the Antigua Trades and Labour Union (ATLU). The union was registered in 1940 to represent Antiguan workers, primarily those in the sugar industry, and Vere C. Bird, Sr., was elected president in 1943. By 1944 the ALP came into separate existence, also under the Bird presidency, but the party and union remained relatively undifferentiated until the late 1960s, partially as a result of the joint presidency. The aged Bird, continues in the ALP leadership position in the early 1990s.

Throughout its history, the ALP has lost control of the Antiguan government but once. This occurred in the general election of 1971 when the Progressive

Labour Movement (PLM) came to power. Although edged in popular votes by the PLM in the 1976 election, in which there was 95 percent electoral participation, the ALP was returned to power (eleven to five to one). Throughout the 1980s and early 1990s, Labour (ALP) has rolled up a large popular vote and parliamentary seat majorities. In essence, critics note, the Bird-led government has built a playpen for the Bird family and their associates who have apparently profited handsomely from international arms and influence peddling. Various investigatory committees have accused the Bird regime of contravening the arms embargo against South Africa and of consorting with Colombian drug merchants, while the United States has accused the Bird government of selling immigration documents and Antiguan passports. All of this activity is condoned on the principle of "Who knows of or cares about Antigua?" Many, including the prime minister's son Lester, warn that the abuses of the Bird machine must be ended or the ALP itself could be destroyed. Party realignment could easily occur, were there a more united and responsive party opposition in place.

BARBUDA PEOPLE'S MOVEMENT (BPM). As its name suggests, the BPM is a local party on the island of Barbuda. The BPM attempts to reflect Barbudan needs and to direct attention to abuses by the government, especially those of the Bird machine. It opposed joint independence with Antigua and has advocated secession. In local government elections in 1981, it won all nine seats to the Barbudan legislature. The leader of the BPM is Hilbourne Frank, who presided over a predecessor group, the Barbuda Democratic Movement, in the early 1960s.

ORGANISATION FOR LOCAL RECONSTRUCTION (OLR). The OLR is a relatively new but weak party that was shut out in the 1989 election. Arthur Gibbs serves as leader of the OLR.

UNITED NATIONAL DEMOCRATIC PARTY (UNDP). The UNDP is led by a surgeon, Dr. Ivor Heath. Formed in 1986, it is made up of former members of the Progressive Labor Movement, organized by George Walter, and Heath's own National Democratic Party. The UNDP's electoral chances are minimal in the early 1990s because the party is neither associated with a particular platform nor appeals to a particular constituency; rather it functions as the primary group in which Antiguans can express their anti–Antigua Labour Party (ALP) and anti-Bird positions as well as the lack of an acceptable alternative. It is most difficult to make corruption an election issue in a society that has been effectively hardened by years of continuous exposure to corruption. As a result, the UNDP was able to win but one seat in the 1989 balloting. Still, this was an improvement over the shutout it suffered in the 1984 election in which the ALP won all parliamentary seats except the lone Barbudan seat. (*See* Progressive Labour Movement.)

Political Parties—Historical

ANTIGUA AND BARBUDA DEMOCRATIC MOVEMENT (ABDM). More than an individual party, the ABDM was a coalition of parties during the 1960s. It included the Antigua Democratic Labour Party, which Emmanuel says hardly deserves the appellation "party," and the Barbuda Democratic Movement. It fielded a full slate of candidates in 1965 without securing a single victory. Robert Hall served as the leader of the ABDM. In 1968, it joined with George Walter's rebels from the Antigua Labour Party and with the Antigua Progressive Movement to form the Progressive Labour Movement. (*See* Progressive Labour Movement.)

ANTIGUA DEMOCRATIC LABOUR PARTY (ADLP). *See* Antigua and Barbuda Democratic Movement.

ANTIGUA PROGRESSIVE MOVEMENT (APM). The APM contributed to the formation of the Progressive Labour Movement prior to the 1971 general election. (*See* Progressive Labour Movement.)

BARBUDA DEMOCRATIC MOVEMENT (BDM). The BDM, founded by Hilbourne Frank, was the party under which Frank sought election in the early 1960s. In 1965 it worked in a coalition with the Antigua and Barbuda Democratic Movement. (*See* Antigua and Barbuda Democratic Movement.)

NATIONAL DEMOCRATIC PARTY (NDP). The small NDP was headed by Dr. Ivor Heath until it merged into the United National Democratic Party in 1986. (*See* United National Democratic Party.)

PROGRESSIVE LABOUR MOVEMENT (PLM). The Progressive Labour Movement was founded after a schism occurred within the Antigua Trades and Labour Union (ATLU) in 1967. This schism led to the departure of George Walter, the ATLU general secretary, due to an unresolved conflict with Vere Bird, Sr., over union and party leadership. Many individuals from the ATLU and the Antigua Labour Party (ALP), who joined in the walkout, consolidated efforts with groups such as the Antigua and Barbuda Democratic Movement and the Antigua Progressive Movement to form the PLM, led by Walter. The new party contested the February 1971 general election and captured thirteen of seventeen seats to gain control of the government and hand the Bird-led ALP the only defeat it has ever suffered.

The PLM again outpolled the ALP (49.9% to 49%) in 1976 but lost the election on the basis of parliamentary seats (eleven to five). By 1980, the vote count for the PLM, now called the Progressive Labour Party (PLP), had declined to 40 percent and it won only three parliamentary seats. The PLM was unable to generate this type of support in future elections, although it was one of the two main opposition parties to the ruling ALP in 1984. Cooperation between the opposition parties faltered as the result of interparty bickering and accusations. This failure, together with the popular support for the military cooperation by the Antiguan government in the 1983 intervention in Grenada, was instrumental in a sweeping victory by the ALP.

Although the recent volume of the *Latin America and Caribbean Contemporary Record* (Brana-Shute and Brana-Shute 1990) still lists the PLM as an active party under the leadership of Robert Hall, in reality it has split and generally has faded away. Many of its members have moved to the United National Democratic Party, as have some of its former leaders. Several former leaders of the PLM have been jailed by a vengeful Bird government. Although he was later freed on appeal, Walter was convicted and imprisoned by the ALP government for alleged corruption during his 1971–1976 term. It is not easy to oppose the ALP. (*See also* United National Democratic Party.)

PROGRESSIVE LABOUR PARTY (PLP). *See* Progressive Labour Movement.

UNITED PEOPLE'S MOVEMENT (UPM). The UPM was a minor party that unsuccessfully contested the 1984 general election.

W. Marvin Will

ARGENTINA

Argentina, with a 1990 population of 31.5 million, occupies most of the southern third of South America. The country was an outpost of the Spanish empire, with little economic importance. It declared independence from Spain on 9 July 1816.

The early days of independence witnessed a struggle between leaders in Buenos Aires and those in the interior of the country. Juan Manuel de Rosas gained power in 1829 and united the country from above, eliminating or coopting regional leaders and ruling with little regard for democratic practices. His ouster in 1852 was followed by a short period of civil war.

In 1862, General Bartolomé Mitre gained the presidency, beginning a fifty-year period during which Argentina's economy and society were transformed. From 1862 to 1916 Argentina became one of the world's great grain and meat producers and exporters. The vast pampas were divided among a small number of very large landowners who dominated national economic and political affairs. Julio A. Roca's inauguration in 1880 produced a strong presidency which represented the political and economic interests of the rural landholding elite. National political parties had little importance, provincial parties supported the government, and fraudulent electoral practices were widespread.

Industrialization had started by the beginning of World War I, particularly in Buenos Aires and surrounding areas. It accelerated during the 1930s despite lack of government support, as Argentina was forced to become self-sufficient by the Great Depression. Despite the growth of industrialization, later supported by Presidents Arturo Frondizi and Juan Perón, agriculture remained the nation's leading export earner.

Until 1916, the national government was controlled by conservative landholding interests. The Radical Civic Union (UCR) had boycotted elections to protest fraud and dishonesty. A 1912 law mandated secret balloting, and in 1916 UCR candidate Hipólito Yrigoyen won the presidency in the first national election contested by the party. The Radicals, appealing primarily to middle-class interests, ruled from 1916 to their ouster by the military in 1930. They established electoral honesty, but they brought few fundamental economic or social changes to Argentina.

Yrigoyen's ouster in 1930 marked the entry of an autonomous military into politics. The military relinquished control to civilian conservatives who ruled from 1931 until the military coup of 1943. Following a short period of internal struggle, Colonel Juan D. Perón emerged as the governmental strongman, and he was elected president in 1946.

Perón ruled from 1946 to 1955. He and his wife Evita transformed Argentine politics. They mobilized workers and the poor, and they called for active state intervention to industrialize and modernize the economy. They emphasized social and economic programs, with lesser regard for individual political rights. Their emotional and nationalistic appeal polarized the nation into Peronists and anti-Peronists. After Perón's ouster in a 1955 coup, the trade unions became the backbone of the Peronist movement, enabling it to survive continual attacks by Radical and military governments during the decade from 1955 to 1966.

Recent Political History

A coup in 1966 led to the banning of political parties. Military rulers were unable to bring about the development they had promised. Economic instability, accompanied by political unrest and increasing violence after 1969, led the military to withdraw from office. An aging Juan Perón returned from exile and was elected president in 1973. He was briefly able to halt both the violence and the inflationary spiral plaguing the country, but once it was clear that Perón represented the conservative interests within Peronism, both guerrilla violence and inflation resumed.

Perón died in 1974, and he was succeeded by his vice presidential wife "Isabelita." Violence and economic deterioration worsened during her two years in power. Finally, in 1976, the military under General Jorge Videla took power in a coup.

The military banned all political parties and political organizations. Their violent antiguerrilla campaign was destructive of human rights. Kidnappings and torture resulted in the death of some 9,000 Argentines during the military's "dirty war" against subversion. By 1979 guerrilla activity had been virtually eliminated, but economic problems remained unsolved.

Following a series of internal changes in the military government, General Leopoldo Galtieri took power. Soon after, in 1982, Argentina invaded the Malvinas islands and claimed a nationalist victory in recapturing the islands from the British. Several months later, when Argentine forces were driven from the islands, it was a crushing defeat for the military. Pressure mounted for them to get out of politics. They had been politically and economically inept, abusive of human rights, and incompetent at warfare.

Elections held in 1983 resulted in a victory for UCR candidate Raúl Alfonsín, who gained 52 percent of the presidential vote. He campaigned mainly on the issue of reducing military influence and returning liberal democracy to Argentina. His Peronist opponent, Italo Luder, was weakened by factionalism in the Peronist movement, but he still managed to get over 40 percent of the presidential popular vote. The election marked the first defeat for Peronists when they were allowed to compete in a national election. The new government faced two major problems: the military and the economy. Alfonsín adopted a number of measures designed to reduce military influence. He retired a number of generals, put a civilian in charge of the armed forces, reduced the military budget, and sought trials for those officials deemed responsible for human rights violations during the dirty war. Some major leaders of the preceding military governments, such as General Videla, were convicted and sentenced to jail, but as time went on Alfonsín was forced to back down on his policies. Disgruntled military men pressured him to halt the trials of their fellow officers. Three small military uprisings were attempted in opposition to the government's efforts to punish rights violators.

Alfonsín had little success on the economic front. Argentina's international debt grew despite all efforts to reduce it. Efforts to obtain debt renegotiation or debt relief achieved limited success, but at the cost of difficult austerity programs. Attempts to privatize found few buyers for inefficient government-run industries. Various austerity programs, wage and price freezes, and even a change of currency all had momentary stabilizing effects on the economy, but the problems always resurfaced. Inflation reached more than 1000 percent at times, and the value of the Argentine currency, the austral, dropped as much as 20 percent overnight. By the time of the 1989 election, the economic situation was so dismal that UCR candidate Eduardo Angeloz had to call for the resignation of his own party's economic team during his campaign.

Probably the greatest triumph of the Alfonsín government was that it endured. Elections were held in 1989, and for the first time in many years one elected government was able to turn power over to another elected government. Peronist Carlos Saúl Menem, a flamboyant former governor of La Rioja province, got 47.4 percent of the vote in leading the Partido Justicialista to victory. During his campaign, Menem promised to regain the Malvinas for Argentina, to reinvigorate the economy, to halt payment on the country's debt for five years, and to provide sweeping wage increases. He denied charges that he had made a deal with the military regarding amnesties for those accused of human rights violations. Angeloz, his UCR opponent, campaigned mainly on the UCR record of restoring liberal democracy to Argentina.

Once elected, President Menem did an about-face on many of his promises. He instituted a severe austerity program, raised prices of government services, dismissed large numbers of government employees, and aggressively pursued a policy of privatization of the governmental interests in utilities, transportation, and energy. Menem also tried to placate international lenders, promising debt payments while seeking debt renegotiations. He made particular efforts to improve relations with the United States.

Like Alfonsín, President Menem faced pressure from the military. The *carapintadas*, a group of nationalist military leaders, staged a brief, but bloody, uprising in December 1990. Their leader, former Colonel Seineldín, had previously led a 1988 uprising, demanding an end to military trials and calling for government recognition of the military's fight against subversion. Although Menem pardoned those convicted of rights violations, including former President Videla, his actions did not satisfy the nationalists. On the opposite side, human rights advocates protested the pardons given to military and guerrilla leaders. Leftist Peronist leaders protested the government's economic austerity policies, calling Menem a traitor to Peronism. Despite Menem's efforts, economic stability remained elusive.

In addition to economic, labor, and military problems, the president also had personal difficulties. At one point Menem secured a court order barring his estranged wife from the presidential residence. Later, rumors circulated that a military uprising aimed at ousting the president would begin when she gave the signal. Other Menem family members and in-laws were accused of cocaine smuggling and of soliciting bribes. Speculation about President Menem's personal and family problems filled Argentina's gossip magazines.

Political Parties

Argentina has a rich political party history. The nation's parties began to take their modern form in the late 1800s. During the last 100 years they have vied with the military for control of the country. Although hundreds of political parties have been active in the twentieth century alone, the majority have been small, and many have been of only regional interest.

Argentina's nationally important political parties can be categorized into several groups: Conservatives, Radicals, Socialists, Communists, Trotskyists, Christian Democrats, Peronists, and others. Since 1946, Radicals and Peronists have dominated national party politics. Their combined votes totaled nearly 95 percent of the total in the 1983 presidential election, and in 1989 they totaled almost 85 percent of the presidential vote and over 80 percent of the votes for national legislators. The Union of the Democratic Center, third largest party, attained only 6 percent of the popular presidential vote in 1989; the remaining vote was shared among about a dozen tiny parties, none of which had any realistic chance of gaining national power.

In addition to the trend toward a two-party system, Argentine party politics is characterized by factionalization. Factions forming around policies, ideologies, and personalities have led to the creation of splinter groups across the political spectrum. Factional struggles have been bitter and at times violent.

Conservatives held power from the time of Rosas until 1916 and again from 1931 to 1943. They operated through local and regional parties which generally represented the interests of large landowners. Once the UCR began to gain strength, conservatives attempted to form a single national party (Unión Nacional, 1912; Concentración Nacional, 1922; Partido Demócrata Nacional, 1931–1958; and, in the 1980s, the Unión del Centro Democrático), but they have been frustrated by divisions caused by local issues.

Conservative parties supported free trade and development based on agricultural exports. They opposed state intervention in the economy and were against aid for industrialization. Out of power after 1943, Argentina's conservatives continued to be influential through agricultural (the Sociedad Rural) and journalistic (*La Prensa* and *La Nación*) connections and ties to banking and financial sectors.

Socialists became active in the nineteenth century in Argentina. Initially, they struggled with anarchists and syndicalists for labor dominance, and later with communists. The rise of Peronism virtually destroyed socialist strength in labor, and the UCR eclipsed them as a national political party alternative to conservative rule. Socialists also suffered from a large number of internal splits. After 1958 they were reduced to a very minor, and fragmented, position in Argentine politics.

Argentina's Communist Party formed from a dissident group of socialists soon after the formation of the Communist International. They remained a minor force in labor and national politics until the late 1930s. Peronism thereafter ended their influence among trade unionists. Communists, like the socialists, have been weakened by a large number of splits. These splits have given rise to dissident communist groups, including some Trotskyist and Maoist revolutionary factions.

The Christian Democrats were latecomers to Argentine politics. Their parties achieved some moderate electoral successes after 1955, but they have since suffered greatly from the splintering and fragmentation so common among the nation's parties.

The Radicals

The UCR was Argentina's largest party from its formation in the 1890s to the emergence of Peronism in the 1940s. Radicals have either won or been the leading opposition party in every presidential election in which they have competed.

The Radicals represent a centrist position in Argentina. Although much of their support lies in the middle class, their appeal goes beyond narrow class limits. The strong personalities of some Radical leaders, such as Yrigoyen, Frondizi, and Arturo Frondizi Ricardo Balbín, have led to party fragmentation. Ideological and tactical questions have also caused splits. The Unión Cívica Radical Intransigente (UCRI), the Unión Cívica Radical del Pueblo (UCRP), the Movimiento de Integración y Desarrollo (MID), and the Partido Intransigente (PI) are some of the major offshoots of the UCR. Despite their differences, Radicals have constantly championed honesty in elections, civilian supremacy, and the basic individual rights of liberal democracy. These principles contributed strongly to their 1983 electoral victory. Radical leaders were strong advocates for human rights in the years after 1976.

Peronism

Peronism is unique to Argentina. The movement derives from the actions of Juan D. Perón and his wife Evita. Perón participated as a colonel in the 1943 coup, became the strongman in the government, was elected president in 1946, and then ruled until he was overthrown and exiled in 1955. He continued to command the loyalty of his followers while in exile, even though Peronist political activity was legally banned during most of the time between 1955 and 1973. Perón returned from exile to be elected president again in 1973. He died in 1974 and was succeeded in the presidency by his wife, Vice President María Estela Martínez de Perón (Isabelita). She ruled until overthrown by the military in 1976. When political party activity resumed in 1983, Peronist candidate Italo Luder placed second in the presidential elections. In 1989 Peronist Carlos Saúl Menem was elected president. Since their formation, the Peronists have been Argentina's largest political group.

Although Peronism includes a diverse group of people and ideologies, its main source of strength is the organized trade union movement. Peronists, along with other political sectors in Argentina, have often been divided and fragmented. Peronist ideology and policies, though sometimes vague, are generally nationalistic. Peronists have historically supported industrialization, national control of the economy, and governmental intervention to bring about economic and social justice. They have at times valued what they considered national needs over individual political rights. Peronist trade union disputes have frequently been violent, and some extremist Peronists have supported violent guerrilla and youth activities. Since the early 1970s, Peronists have been represented by the Justicialist Party (Partido Justicialista).

Bibliography

Robert J. Alexander. *Communism in Latin America.* Rutgers University Press, New Brunswick, N.J., 1957.

Ramón Andino and Eduardo J. Paredes. *Breve historia de los partidos políticos argentinos.* Alzamor, Buenos Aires, 1974.

Alberto Ciria. *Partidos y poder en la Argentina moderna 1930–46.* Alvarez, Buenos Aires, 1964.

John T. Deiner. "Argentina," in Robert J. Alexander, ed., *Political Parties of the Americas: Anguilla-Grenada,* 52–89. Greenwood Press, Westport, Conn., 1982.

Gabriel del Mazo. *El radicalismo: El movimiento de intransigencia y renovación 1945–1957.* Editora Gure, Buenos Aires, 1958.

Donald C. Hodges. *Argentina 1943–1976: The National Revolution and Resistance.* University of New Mexico Press, Albuquerque, 1976.

Ronald H. McDonald and J. Mark Ruhl. *Party Politics and Elections in Latin America.* Westview Press, Boulder, Colo., 1989.

Ciaran O. Maolain. *Latin American Political Movements.* Facts On File Publications-Longman Group, Oxford, England, 1985.

Rodolfo Puiggros. *Las izquierdas y el problema nacional.* Cepe, Buenos Aires, 1973.

David Rock. *Argentina 1516–1987: From Spanish Colonization to Alfonsín.* University of California Press, Berkeley, 1987.

James D. Rudolph, ed. *Argentina: A Country Study.* Area Handbook Series. U.S. Government, Washington, D.C., 1986.

Peter H. Smith. *Argentina and the Failure of Democracy: Conflict among Political Elites, 1904–1955.* University of Wisconsin Press, Madison, 1974.

Peter G. Snow. *Political Forces in Argentina.* Praeger, New York, 1979.

Peter G. Snow and Gary Wynia. "Argentina: Politics in a Conflict Society," in Harvey F. Kline and Howard J. Wiarda, eds., *Latin American Politics and Development,* 129–56 Westview Press, Boulder, Colo., 1990.

Carlos Waisman. *Reversal of Development in Argentina.* Princeton University Press, Princeton, N.J., 1987.

Gary Wynia. *Argentina: Illusions and Realities.* Holmes and Meier, New York, 1986.

Political Parties—Active

ALIANZA DEMÓCRATA SOCIALISTA. *See* DEMOCRATIC LEFTIST FRONT.

ALIANZA DE LA IZQUIERDA UNIDA. *See* UNITED LEFT ALLIANCE.

ALIANZA FEDERAL. *See* FEDERAL ALLIANCE.

ALIANZA SOCIALISTA. *See* SOCIALIST ALLIANCE.

ARGENTINE COMMUNIST PARTY (PARTIDO COMUNISTA ARGENTINO—PCA). The PCA was founded by a Marxist faction of the Socialist Party. It has generally supported the international policy of the Communist Party of the Soviet Union. Banned in 1966, it was later legalized and held congresses in 1973 and 1975. In 1982, it supported formation of the Multipartidaria alliance. The PCA was legalized the following year, and it chose to cooperate with the Peronists. There was some internal opposition to such cooperation. Party membership is estimated at from less than 75,000 to 300,000. Athos Fava was general secretary in the mid-1980s.

ARGENTINE SOCIALIST CONFEDERATION (CONFEDERACIÓN SOCIALISTA ARGENTINA—CSA). This is a small fragment of the socialist movement.

AUTHENTIC PERONIST PARTY (PARTIDO PERONISTA AUTÉNTICO—PPA). The PPA was formed in March 1975 by Dr. Oscar Bidegain, former governor of Mendoza province, and other leftist Peronists. Shortly thereafter, in April, this group was expelled from the mainstream Peronist movement (FREJULI-Partido Justicialista) and was banned in December 1975. In April 1977 it merged with Mario Firmenich's Montonero guerrilla movement. Bidegain had fled the country, but he returned from exile (along with fellow leader Ricardo Obregón Cano) in December 1983 to try to reestablish the PPA as a legal political party. He was soon arrested on charges of incitement and illegal association. The PPA was on the violent left of the Peronist movement. It called for worker control of the national economy, denounced the 1973–1976 Peronist government's compromise with imperialism, and actively opposed the military government from 1976 to 1983.

AUTHENTIC SOCIALIST PARTY (PARTIDO SOCIALISTA AUTÉN-TICO—PSA). This small leftist socialist faction supported the Peronists' 1989 electoral platform.

AUTONOMOUS LIBERAL PACT (PACTO LIBERAL AUTÓNOMO—PLA). This provincially based party held both Corrientes' Senate seats in the 1980s.

CHRISTIAN DEMOCRATIC PARTY (PARTIDO DEMÓCRATA CRISTIANO—PDC). The party, organized in 1954 by progressive Roman Catholics, initially followed the lines of European Christian Democracy. It later adopted nationalistic economic positions and worked closely with Peronists in the 1960s. It suffered severe fragmentation after first supporting, and then breaking with, the Onganía government. One breakaway faction, the Popular Christian Party, supported FREJULI in 1973; another sector, under Horacio Sueldo, formed the Christian Revolutionary Party, which supported Oscar Alende's Popular Revolutionary Alliance.

In the 1980s, the party was affiliated to the Christian Democratic International. It won one seat in the 1983 Chamber of Deputies. In 1989, the Christian Democrats supported the views of Frejupo, the Peronist electoral alliance.

CHRISTIAN DEMOCRATIC UNION. See UNION OF THE DEMOCRATIC CENTER.

CHRISTIAN REVOLUTIONARY PARTY. See CHRISTIAN DEMO-CRATIC PARTY.

CONCENTRACIÓN DEMOCRÁTICA. See DEMOCRATIC CONCEN-TRATION.

CONFEDERACIÓN SOCIALISTA ARGENTINA. See ARGENTINE SO-CIALIST CONFEDERATION.

DEMOCRACIA SOCIAL. *See* SOCIAL DEMOCRACY.

DEMOCRATIC CONCENTRATION. *See* FEDERAL ALLIANCE.

DEMOCRATIC INTEGRATION PARTY (PARTIDO DE INTEGRACIÓN DEMOCRÁTICA—PID). This conservative party was founded in January 1983, amid speculation (denied by both the government and the party) that it was sponsored by the military government.

DEMOCRATIC LEFTIST FRONT (FRENTE DEMOCRÁTICO DE LA IZ-QUIERDA—FDI, also known as the ALIANZA DEMÓCRATA SOCI-ALISTA). This center-left alliance of the Progressive Democratic Party (PDP) and the Democratic Socialist Party was formed in June 1983. Rafael Martínez Raymonda (the PDP leader), its 1983 presidential candidate, polled approximately 92,000 votes.

DEMOCRATIC SOCIALIST PARTY (PARTIDO SOCIALISTA DEMO-CRÁTICO—PSD). The PSD was created in a 1958 split in the Socialist Party. Maintaining an uncompromisingly hardline position against Peronism and Communism, it became increasingly conservative in the 1960s and 1970s. It even supported the military government after 1976. The PSD remained headed by longtime leader Américo Ghioldi in the 1980s. In 1983, the PSD left the Unión del Centro Democrático to join the Progressive Democratic Party in forming the Frente Democrático de la Izquierda. The PSD had about 40,000 members in the 1980s.

FEDERAL ALLIANCE (ALIANZA FEDERAL—AF). This rightist party was formed by four parties (Partido Federal, Concentración Democrática, Fuerza Federalista Popular, and the Movimiento Línea Popular) in June 1983 to back Francisco Manrique's presidential candidacy. Manrique was a former military man and populist leader who had held positions in the Lanusse government. Many of the same parties had also participated in the Alianza Popular Federalista coalition which had backed Manrique in 1973. The Federal Alliance supported a free market, but mainly called for more provincial autonomy. After getting only 80,000 votes in 1983, it virtually disappeared, although some of the coalition's parties remained important in their provinces.

FEDERAL PARTY (PARTIDO FEDERAL—PF). Existing to support Francisco Manrique's candidacy, the PF was the leading party in the Alianza Federal coalition.

FRENTE DE IZQUIERDA POPULAR. *See* POPULAR LEFTIST FRONT.

FRENTE DEMOCRÁTICO DE LA IZQUIERDA. See DEMOCRATIC LEFT-IST FRONT.

FUERZA FEDERALISTA POPULAR. See POPULAR FEDERALIST FORCE.

INDEPENDENCE PARTY (PARTIDO DE INDEPENDENCIA—PI). This small, center-right party formed in late 1982.

INTRANSIGENCIA Y MOVILIZACIÓN PERONISTA. See PERONIST IN-TRANSIGENCE AND MOBILIZATION.

INTRANSIGENT PARTY (PARTIDO INTRANSIGENTE—PI). The PI emerged from a 1963 split in the Intransigent Radical Civic Union (UCRI), which left Oscar Alende as the UCRI leader. Alende finished second in the 1963 presidential election to Arturo Illia of the Radical Civic Union of the People (UCRP). In 1965, the UCRI's vote dropped significantly. In 1972, the party changed its name to the Intransigent Party after election officials gave the traditional Unión Cívica Radical title to the UCRP. In the March 1973 elections, Alende ran as the candidate of the Popular Revolutionary Alliance (Alianza Revolucionaria Popular) (made up of the PI, sectors of the Union of the Argentine People (UDELPA), the Communist Party, and the Christian Revolutionary Party) and gained 8 percent of the popular vote. After 1976, the party moved to the left, defining itself as a non-Marxist, social democratic alternative. Oscar Alende, the Intransigent Party's presidential candidate, got 2.3 percent of the vote in the 1983 elections, and the party won two seats in the lower house. The party called for nationalization of banking and restrictions on multinationals. The party won three deputy seats in the 1985 by-elections, and six in the 1987 by-elections. It also elected one senator in 1987. In 1989, the party voted with the Peronists.

IZQUIERDA DEMÓCRATA POPULAR. See POPULAR DEMOCRATIC LEFT.

JUSTICIALIST PARTY (PARTIDO JUSTICIALISTA—PJ). The Justicialist Party is the official name of the Peronist Party. It is the successor to the 1946–1955 Partido Peronista and the 1973 Justicialist Liberation Front (FREJULI) coalition which elected Héctor Cámpora as president. The PJ was formed to support Perón's return to Argentina, and he won the presidency in 1973 as the Justicialista Party candidate. Vice President Isabelita Perón succeeded to the presidency when her husband died in 1974, and she ruled until she was overthrown in 1976. Along with other parties, the PJ was banned after the 1976 military coup.

Between 1976 and the 1983 elections, Peronism was divided into a number of factions. One group, led by Italo Luder, was loyal to Isabelita. Peronist unionism was further divided into two factions. The majority faction was led by Saúl Ubaldini and Lorenzo Miguel. A competing faction, militantly opposed to the military government, was related to the Juventud Peronista. It was led by Vicente Saadi. There were also provincial Peronist organizations.

As the 1983 elections approached, a struggle for control of Peronism developed between the "verticalists" (unionists and others who demanded loyalty to party leadership) and the "anti-verticalists," who wanted to democratize the party. The verticalists, led by Herminio Iglesias (Buenos Aires province party leader), Miguel, and Luder, gained control of the party. They named Luder as presidential candidate, with Antonio Cafiero as vice presidential nominee. Union leadership, spearheaded by Miguel, refused to accept Cafiero, and they forced his replacement with Iglesias as the vice presidential candidate. Consequently, Peronism and the Partido Justicialista were weakened in the 1983 elections. Presidential candidate Luder ran second, receiving 40.2 percent of the vote. The party won 111 of the 254 seats in the Chamber of Deputies and was the leading vote-getter in Senate and governor races, winning half of each.

Peronism remained divided after the election. The verticalist (oficialista) faction led by Miguel worked to broaden their labor base and gained control of the party at a 1985 meeting.

By 1987, the Justicialista Party had three factions: a reformist wing was headed by Carlos Saúl Menem and Cafiero; Iglesias led a second faction, the Movimiento Nacional 17 de Octubre; and the third faction, the Oficialistas, was led by Miguel.

The party united behind candidate Menem in the 1989 presidential election, and he won, with 47 percent of the popular vote and over half the electoral votes. Menem campaigned on a nationalistic platform that was pro-worker and defiant of international financial pressure for Argentina to implement austerity programs. Almost immediately after becoming president, however, Menem reversed his campaign policies. His government sought foreign investment and pardoned all those convicted of human rights violations. Faced with skyrocketing inflation, he imposed limits on wage increases, aggressively tried to privatize the economy, worked to increase tax revenues, and began massive dismissals of public sector employees.

During 1990 Menem faced opposition from both within and outside the Justicialist Party. He put down a brief, but bloody, military uprising in early December, led by nationalist factions loyal to former Colonel Seineldín. He encountered civilian criticism because of his pardons to those involved in the dirty war and because of the deteriorated economy. Some opposition came from the Justicialist Party itself, which was divided into three factions: those loyal to Menem, the renewalist faction headed by Cafiero, and a leftist trade union faction led by Saúl Ubaldini, the head of the rebel CGT (General Confederation of Labor–Confederación General de Trabajo).

Cafiero was forced to resign as Justicialist Party president after losing a plebiscite which would have allowed him to continue as Buenos Aires province governor. With Cafiero's resignation, Menem became the party president. He quickly solidified his control by installing Menem family members into all top party leadership posts. Menem countered Ubaldini's threat of a general strike by signing a decree limiting strikes by workers in essential public services.

At the end of 1990, the Partido Justicialista remained Argentina's largest party, with over 3,000,000 members. President Menem controlled the party, but his reversal of traditional Peronist policies since coming to office, coupled with a very troubling economic situation, suggested that he would continue to face challenges to his leadership.

MOVEMENT OF INTEGRATION AND DEVELOPMENT (MOVIMIENTO DE INTEGRACIÓN Y DESARROLLO—MID). Led by Arturo Frondizi, Rogelio Frigerio, and Antonio Salonia, the MID was formed in a 1964 break from the Intransigent Radical Civic Union (UCRI). It supported former President Frondizi's developmentalist ideas and sought to cooperate with the Peronists. The party initially outpolled the UCRI, but later became more of a personalist vehicle for Frondizi rather than a continuer of Radicalism. The MID supported the FREJULI coalition of Héctor Cámpora in the 1973 presidential election. It later was strongly critical of Isabelita Perón and supported her overthrow by the military. In 1983, its own unsuccessful presidential candidate was Frigerio. In general, the party has supported increased industrialization, foreign investment, and the widest possible participation in national political life. Its specific policy positions have usually reflected those of Frondizi. Membership was estimated at about 140,000 during the 1980s. The MID supported the Justicialist Party candidate in 1989, and Salonia was named to Carlos Saúl Menem's cabinet.

MOVEMENT TO SOCIALISM (MOVIMIENTO AL SOCIALISMO—MAS). The Trotskyist MAS had its origins in the Socialist Workers' Party, which was formed in 1971. Active among dissident trade unionists, especially transport workers, MAS attacked both the Peronist trade union bureaucracy and the Alfonsín government as being controlled by U.S. imperialism. After 1989 it attacked the economic and political policies of President Carlos Saúl Menem and represented itself as being the leftist alternative to Peronism.

MOVIMIENTO AL SOCIALISMO. See MOVEMENT TO SOCIALISM.

MOVIMIENTO DE INTEGRACIÓN Y DESARROLLO. See MOVEMENT OF INTEGRATION AND DEVELOPMENT.

MOVIMIENTO LÍNEA POPULAR. See POPULAR LINE MOVEMENT.

MOVIMIENTO POPULAR NEUQUEN. See NEUQUEN POPULAR MOVEMENT.

NATIONAL CENTER PARTY (PARTIDO NACIONAL DEL CENTRO—PNC). Founded in 1980, this conservative party, led by Raúl Rivanera Carles, remained active through the 1980s.

NEUQUEN POPULAR MOVEMENT (MOVIMIENTO POPULAR NEU-QUEN—MPN). This provincial party won both of Neuquen's senate seats in the 1980s.

PACTO LIBERAL AUTÓNOMO. *See* AUTONOMOUS LIBERAL PACT.

PARTIDO BLOQUISTA DE SAN JUAN. *See* SAN JUAN BLOC PARTY.

PARTIDO COMUNISTA ARGENTINO. *See* ARGENTINE COMMUNIST PARTY.

PARTIDO COMUNISTA REVOLUCIONARIO. *See* REVOLUTIONARY COMMUNIST PARTY.

PARTIDO CONSERVADOR POPULAR. *See* POPULAR CONSERVATIVE PARTY.

PARTIDO DE INDEPENDENCIA. *See* INDEPENDENCE PARTY.

PARTIDO DE INTEGRACIÓN DEMOCRÁTICA. *See* DEMOCRATIC IN-TEGRATION PARTY.

PARTIDO DEMÓCRATA CRISTIANO. *See* CHRISTIAN DEMOCRATIC PARTY.

PARTIDO DEMÓCRATA PROGRESISTA. *See* PROGRESSIVE DEMO-CRATIC PARTY.

PARTIDO FEDERAL. *See* FEDERAL PARTY.

PARTIDO INTRANSIGENTE. *See* INTRANSIGENT PARTY.

PARTIDO JUSTICIALISTA. *See* JUSTICIALIST PARTY.

PARTIDO NACIONAL DEL CENTRO. *See* NATIONAL CENTER PARTY.

PARTIDO OBRERO. *See* WORKERS' PARTY.

PARTIDO PERONISTA AUTÉNTICO. *See* AUTHENTIC PERONIST PARTY.

PARTIDO REVOLUCIONARIO DE LOS TRABAJADORES. *See* REVO-LUTIONARY PARTY OF THE WORKERS.

PARTIDO SOCIALISTA AUTÉNTICO. *See* AUTHENTIC SOCIALIST PARTY.

PARTIDO SOCIALISTA DEMOCRÁTICO. *See* DEMOCRATIC SOCIAL-IST PARTY.

PARTIDO SOCIALISTA POPULAR. *See* POPULAR SOCIALIST PARTY.

PARTIDO SOCIALISTA UNIFICADO. *See* UNIFIED SOCIALIST PARTY.

PERONIST INTRANSIGENCE AND MOBILIZATION (INTRANSIGEN-CIA Y MOVILIZACIÓN PERONISTA—IMP). Led by Nilda Gares and Vi-cente Leonidas Saadi, this leftist faction of the Peronist movement called for more state control and industrialization.

POPULAR CONSERVATIVE PARTY (PARTIDO CONSERVADOR POP-ULAR—PCP). This small conservative party was active in the mid-1980s.

POPULAR DEMOCRATIC LEFT (IZQUIERDA DEMÓCRATA POPU-LAR—IDP). The IDP was part of the United Left Alliance in 1989.

POPULAR FEDERALIST FORCE. *See* FEDERAL ALLIANCE.

POPULAR LEFTIST FRONT (FRENTE DE IZQUIERDA POPULAR—FIP). Headed by Jorge Abelardo Ramos, the Trotskyist FIP did not accept the class struggle doctrine, nor did it call for socialization of the means of production. The front supported Justicialist Party candidate Italo Luder in 1983 but ran its own candidates for other offices, getting less than 0.1 percent of the popular vote.

POPULAR LINE MOVEMENT. *See* FEDERAL ALLIANCE.

POPULAR SOCIALIST PARTY (PARTIDO SOCIALISTA POPULAR—PSP). Founded in October 1982, in cooperation with the Confederación So-cialista Argentina and the provincial Partido Socialista del Chaco, the PSP supported the Peronist candidate for president in 1983, and gained 30,000 votes in the congressional races. It has sought to merge with other small socialist groups. It numbered many intellectuals among its estimated 50,000 members.

POPULAR UNION (UNIÓN POPULAR—UP). Headed by Antonio Cafiero, a former minister of the economy, this Peronist center-left organization was formed in September 1985. It was supported by the Grupo de los 25, a trade union alliance tied to the *renovador* movement in Peronism. (*See also* historical parties.)

PROGRESSIVE DEMOCRATIC PARTY (PARTIDO DEMÓCRATA PROGRESISTA—PDP). The PDP was founded by Lisandro de la Torre in 1916 as an alternative to the Radical Civic Union. It had strength in Santa Fe province, but it deteriorated after de la Torre's death in 1939. Horacio Thedy became the party's main leader after de la Torre's death, and later he brought the party into alliance with the Union of the Argentine People. Thedy was Pedro Aramburu's unsuccessful running mate in 1963. By the 1973 election, the party was weakened by internal defections.

The PDP joined the Unión del Centro Democrático in 1980, and later joined the Democratic Socialist Party in 1983 to form the Frente Democrático de la Izquierda, with PDP leader Rafael Martínez Raymonda as its presidential candidate. It represented the interests of small farmers and had some strength among professionals in Santa Fe province.

RADICAL CIVIC UNION (UNIÓN CÍVICA RADICAL—UCR). The UCR's origins date back to 1890, when Bartolomé Mitre and Leandro Alem formed various groups to oppose the conservative governments. After several splits, Alem's faction established the Radical Civic Union. The UCR, led by Alem and later by Hipólito Yrigoyen, boycotted elections and attempted unsuccessful uprisings in 1893 and 1905. They called for honest elections and government, with broader political participation. After the 1912 introduction of the secret ballot, Yrigoyen entered and won the 1916 presidential election. The Radicals became Argentina's largest party.

The Yrigoyen government introduced no major economic or social reforms. Its numerous interventions in the provinces increased the power of the central government. Radical policy toward labor was inconsistent; sometimes it supported organizational efforts, at other times it used force against demonstrators.

Once in power, the UCR began to suffer from fragmentation. The Antipersonalist faction's leader, Marcelo T. de Alvear, was elected president in 1922. Yrigoyen and the Personalists were reelected in 1928 and then overthrown by a coup in 1930. Antipersonalists participated in the conservative governments that ruled the country in the 1930s. Factionalism continued until a unified Radical Civic Union was reestablished in the early 1940s.

The Radicals split again in 1945, this time over relations with Peronists. Arturo Frondizi and Ricardo Balbín formed the Movement of Intransigence and Renovation (MIR) faction. By 1951, the Intransigents controlled the UCR organization. Presidential candidate Balbín, with Frondizi his vice presidential running mate, lost in the 1951 election against Juan Perón.

UCR fragmentation continued following Perón's 1955 overthrow. Intransigents sought support from Peronists, while Unionists were arch anti-Peronists.

When Frondizi was named UCR candidate for president in 1956, Balbín's followers left and combined with the Unionist faction to form the (Radical Civic Union of the People (UCRP). Frondizi's majority group became the Intransigent Radical Civic Union (UCRI). Finally, just before the 1973 election, the UCRP was awarded the party's traditional name, Radical Civic Union, and it has continued to use that name since. The UCRI became the Partido Intransigente, and Frondizi's group left to become the Movement of Integration and Development.

The UCR remained fragmented during the Peronist and military governments from 1973 to 1982. Balbín remained the party's principal spokesman, although his leadership was challenged by Raúl Alfonsín. By 1981 the UCR was composed of three factions: a *línea nacional* group; the *renovación y cambio* faction, headed by Alfonsín; and a Movimiento de Afirmación Yrigoyenista faction.

When Balbín died in 1981, it became possible to reunite the factions. Alfonsín formed an alliance with Víctor Martínez, the UCR leader in Córdoba. The Alfonsín/Martínez ticket then won the presidency in 1983 with 52 percent of the vote. The UCR also won 129 out of 254 seats in the lower house of the legislature, 16 of 48 senate seats, and 7 of 24 provincial governorships. Some internal party divisions remained, especially in relation to economic policy. The UCR's vote declined slightly in the 1985 and 1987 by-elections.

The 1983 election results were a vote against the military as much as a vote for Alfonsín. He confronted difficult economic and military-related issues during his presidency. He attempted to limit military influence by abolishing compulsory military service, reducing the military budget, and changing the military justice system. Some senior officers, including General Videla and other junta members, were convicted and imprisoned for human rights violations committed during the dirty war. Eventually, though, military pressure (including three uprisings) forced the government to end its prosecution of suspected human rights violators. Alfonsín needed to placate the military in order to remain in office.

Economic problems proved unsolvable. The $46 billion debt inherited from the military grew to almost $60 billion by 1989. Austerity measures aimed at dealing with the debt caused social unrest. Hyperinflation ravaged the country. Privatization efforts failed to attract buyers. By 1989, voters had lost faith in the Radicals' possibilities for economic success.

Eduardo Angeloz, the governor of Córdoba who was the UCR candidate in the 1989 presidential election, was unable to distance himself from the government's failed economic policies. He managed to get 32.8 percent of the vote, five times more than the third place candidate, but well behind the victorious Peronist Carlos Saúl Menem. The UCR also finished well behind the Peronists in congressional races. In mid-March 1990, in the middle of his own economic emergency, Menem offered Angeloz a cabinet post, in hopes of showing unified civilian support for the government, but Angeloz refused.

Raúl Alfonsín remained the leader of the UCR after he left the presidency. He strongly criticized the Menem government about the influence of US Ambassador Terence Todman. The UCR remained the nation's second largest party, with an estimated membership of 1,500,000, in 1990.

REVOLUTIONARY COMMUNIST PARTY (PARTIDO COMUNISTA RE-VOLUCIONARIO—PCR). This Maoist offshoot of the Argentine Communist Party was formed in the 1970s.

REVOLUTIONARY PARTY OF THE WORKERS (PARTIDO REVOLU-CIONARIO DE LOS TRABAJADORES—PRT). A small Trotskyist group headed by Nahuel Moreno had consistently opposed Peronists in the 1940s and 1950s. In January 1965, this group established the Revolutionary Party of the Workers. Following the 1969 *Cordobazo*, the uprising of students and workers in Córdoba, the PRT split. The pro-violence wing of the PRT became the political wing of the better known Ejército Revolucionario del Pueblo (ERP) guerrillas. The ERP was very active from 1972 until July 1976, when its leaders were killed. The PRT became a fairly active exile organization, but it had little influence inside Argentina after 1976. The antiguerrilla faction of the PRT, led by Moreno, affiliated with a splinter of the Argentine Socialist Party to establish the Partido Socialista de los Trabajadores, which supported Juan Carlos del Coral in the 1973 presidential elections.

SAN JUAN BLOC PARTY (PARTIDO BLOQUISTA DE SAN JUAN—PB DE SJ). This provincial party elected both national senators from San Juan province in the 1980s.

SOCIAL DEMOCRACY (DEMOCRACIA SOCIAL—DS). The DS, a right-ist, nationalist group led by Admiral (ret.) Emilio Massera, defended the military's fight against terrorism and supported extremist rightist interests.

SOCIALIST ALLIANCE (ALIANZA SOCIALISTA—AS). This small leftist group, active in the 1980s, elected the mayor of Rosario in 1989.

UNIFIED SOCIALIST PARTY (PARTIDO SOCIALISTA UNIFICADO—PSU). This small leftist faction was active in the 1980s.

UNIÓN CÍVICA RADICAL. *See* RADICAL CIVIC UNION.

UNIÓN CRISTIANA DEMÓCRATA. *See* CHRISTIAN DEMOCRATIC UNION.

UNIÓN DEL CENTRO DEMOCRÁTICO. *See* UNION OF THE DEMO-CRATIC CENTER.

UNION FOR THE NEW MAJORITY (UNIÓN PARA LA NUEVA MAY-ORÍA—UNM). Led by José Antonio Romero Feris, this small rightist-center party was formed in 1986.

UNION OF THE DEMOCRATIC CENTER (UNIÓN DEL CENTRO DE-MOCRÁTICO—UCÉDE). This centrist-conservative party, led by Alvaro Alsogaray, continued many of the ideas of the former Partido Cívico Independiente, which had been established in the early 1960s by Alsogaray and his brother General Julio Alsogaray. The UCéDe was formed in 1980 by a coalition of eight small parties, including the Unión Cristiana Demócrata, the Progressive Democratic Party, and the Democratic Socialist Party. It supported Alsogaray's monetarist views, calling for a complete ending of state intervention in the economy. It elected two members to the Chamber of Deputies in 1983 and slightly increased its percentage of the popular vote in the 1985 and 1987 by-elections, getting 18 percent of the votes in Buenos Aires province. It had support among conservative intellectuals and banking circles. It stated that its goal was to end the monopoly of politics by populist parties.

By 1989, the UCéDe was the nation's third largest party. Its presidential candidate, Alsogaray, polled 6.4 percent of the total vote, and the UCéDe got nine seats in the Chamber of Deputies. Alsogaray was named the government's foreign debt negotiator; he resigned from that position in early 1991.

UNIÓN PARA LA NUEVA MAYORÍA. See UNION FOR THE NEW MAJORITY.

UNIÓN POPULAR. See POPULAR UNION.

UNITED LEFT ALLIANCE (ALIANZA DE LA IZQUIERDA UNIDA—AIU). This group, formed on 24 October 1988, brought together the Argentine Communist Party, the Movement towards Socialism, the Popular Democratic Left, and the Intransigent Party. Its presidential candidate in 1989 was Nestor Vicente. The alliance hoped to form a unified left position, proposing land reform, nationalization of the banks, and nonpayment of the foreign debt.

WORKERS' PARTY (PARTIDO OBRERO—PO). This Trotskyist party, with an estimated 60,000 members, was founded in 1982. Gregorio Flores, the party's candidate in the 1983 presidential elections, got less than 1 percent of the vote. Other leaders were Jorge Altamira and Christian Rath. The PO called for socialization of the means of production and for replacement of the armed forces with a popular militia. PO influence was limited to fringe elements of the labor movement.

Political Parties—Historical

ALIANZA POPULAR FEDERAL. See FEDERAL POPULAR ALLIANCE.

ALIANZA REPUBLICANA FEDERAL. *See* FEDERAL REPUBLICAN ALLIANCE.

ANTIPERSONALIST RADICAL CIVIC UNION (UNIÓN CÍVICA RADICAL ANTIPERSONALISTA—UCRA). The UCRA split from the Radical Civic Union to oppose Hipólito Yrigoyen's leadership. It supported the 1930 Justo coup and formed part of the National Concentration government which ruled until the 1943 coup. The UCRA was led by Justo and Marcelo T. de Alvear.

ARGENTINE REPUBLICAN PARTY (PARTIDO REPUBLICANO ARGENTINO—PRA). The PRA was created in 1964 by conservatives who opposed the Illia government. It strongly supported private enterprise.

ARGENTINE SOCIALIST PARTY (PARTIDO SOCIALISTA ARGENTINO—PSA). Led by Alfredo Palacios, the first Argentine Socialist Party broke away from the Socialist Party in 1915 to support Palacios's Argentine nationalism. It lasted only a few years.

ARGENTINE SOCIALIST PARTY (PARTIDO SOCIALISTA ARGENTINO—PSA). The second Argentine Socialist Party split from the Socialist Party in 1958 when PSA leaders desired some cooperation with Peronists. It suffered numerous splits in the 1960s and 1970s over issues of support for Peronists, Fidel Castro, and Trotskyists.

CHRISTIAN DEMOCRATIC FEDERAL UNION (UNIÓN FEDERAL DEMÓCRATA CRISTIANA—UFDC). A Catholic nationalist party, formed in 1956, the UFDC received 2 percent of the votes in the 1957 elections. Most UFDC leaders supported Arturo Frondizi in 1958. It called for a corporatist state, emphasized Catholic values, and praised the Hispanic values of the Franco government in Spain.

CIVIC LEGION (LEGIÓN CÍVICA). *See* CONSERVATIVE NATIONALISTS.

CIVIC UNION (UNIÓN CÍVICA—UC). Established on 13 April 1890, the Civic Union lasted only about a year before it divided into two factions: the National Civic Union, headed by Bartolomé Mitre; and the Radical Civic Union, headed by Leandro Alem.

CONSERVATIVE NATIONALISTS. Argentina has had many nationalist groups on the far right, none of which has had significant voter support. Examples of such groups include the Argentine Anti-Communist Alliance (AAA), Federal Union (Unión Federal), Civic Legion (Legión Cívica), Legion of May (Legión de Mayo), Nationalist Alliance (Alianza Nacional), Party of Nationalist Action (Partido de Acción Nacionalista), and the Republican League (Liga Republicana).

FEDERACIÓN NACIONAL DE PARTIDOS CONSERVADORES. *See* NATIONAL FEDERATION OF CONSERVATIVE PARTIES.

FEDERAL POPULAR ALLIANCE (ALIANZA POPULAR FEDERAL—APF). This coalition of small rightist parties was formed to sponsor Francisco Manrique's 1973 presidential candidacy.

FEDERAL REPUBLICAN ALLIANCE (ALIANZA REPUBLICANA FEDERAL—ARF). This coalition of provincial conservative parties polled 3 percent in the March 1973 presidential elections.

FREJULI. *See* JUSTICIALIST LIBERATION FRONT.

FRENTE JUSTICIALISTA DE LIBERACIÓN. *See* JUSTICIALIST LIBERATION FRONT.

INDEPENDENT CIVIC PARTY (PARTIDO CÍVICO INDEPENDIENTE—PCI). Led by economist Alvaro Alsogaray and his brother General Julio Alsogaray, this party advocated private enterprise. Formed in the early 1960s, it supported the 1966 coup, and in 1973 it supported the heavily financed Nueva Fuerza coalition.

INDEPENDENT PARTY (PARTIDO INDEPENDIENTE—PI). The smallest of the three parties organized to support Juan Perón's candidacy, it merged with the other two (Labor Party and Renovating Radical Civic Union) after Perón's 1946 election.

INDEPENDENT SOCIALIST PARTY (PARTIDO SOCIALISTA INDEPENDIENTE—PSI). The PSI represented the right wing, more anti–Hipólito Yrigoyen faction of the Socialist Party when it split off in 1928. It outpolled the Socialists in 1928, supported the 1930 coup against Yrigoyen, and disappeared by the end of the 1930s.

INTERNATIONALIST SOCIALIST PARTY (PARTIDO SOCIALISTA INTERNACIONALISTA—PSI). The Communist Party began in Argentina in 1918 as the Partido Socialista Internacionalista. When the Communist International was created, it accepted the PSI, which then changed its name to become the Communist Party.

INTRANSIGENT RADICAL CIVIC UNION (UNIÓN CÍVICA RADICAL INTRANSIGENTE—UCRI). The UCRI resulted from a 1957 split in the

Radical Civic Union. Led by Arturo Frondizi, it advocated cooperation with Peronists, national control of natural resources, and industrialization. Frondizi won the 1958 presidential election as the UCRI's candidate, but he was ousted by the military in 1962. Following Frondizi's ouster, Oscar Alende (who opposed close cooperation with Peronists) gained control of the UCRI and ran second to Arturo Illia in the 1963 presidential election. Frondizi's faction left to form the Movement of Integration and Development. In 1972, the UCRI changed its name to Partido Intransigente (see Intransigent Party); it is still headed by Alende.

JUSTICIALIST LIBERATION FRONT (FRENTE JUSTICIALISTA DE LIB-ERACIÓN—FREJULI). FREJULI was an electoral alliance formed by the Justicialist Party, the Movement of Integration and Development, and several extralegislative groups as a vehicle for the successful candidacy of Peronist Héctor Cámpora in the 1973 presidential race. Cámpora resigned shortly thereafter and called for new elections in which Juan Perón himself could run. Perón was then elected president.

LABOR PARTY (PARTIDO LABORISTA—PL). The Labor Party was organized by trade union leaders to support Juan Perón's candidacy in 1946. After the election, Perón merged the party into an organization that eventually became the Peronist Party, whereupon the Labor Party effectively disappeared.

LEGIÓN CÍVICA (CIVIC LEGION). See CONSERVATIVE NATIONALISTS.

LEGION OF MAY (LEGIÓN DE MAYO). See CONSERVATIVE NATIONALISTS.

LIBERAL PARTY (PARTIDO LIBERAL—PL). The Liberal Party was established immediately after the overthrow of Juan Manuel de Rosas in 1852. Its leaders, Bartolomé Mitre, Domingo F. Sarmiento, and Nicolas Avellaneda ruled from 1862 to 1880, but their disagreements split the party, and it had disappeared by 1880.

MOVIMIENTO REVOLUCIONARIO PERONISTA. See PERONIST REV-OLUTIONARY MOVEMENT.

NATIONAL AUTONOMIST PARTY (PARTIDO AUTONOMISTA NA-CIONAL—PAN). The PAN was formed in 1879 by Domingo F. Sarmiento, Hipólito Yrigoyen, Luis Sáenz Peña, Leandro Alem, Bartolomé Mitre, and others to fight the presidential candidacy of General Julio A. Roca. When Roca triumphed and established a strong personalist presidency, the party disappeared.

NATIONAL DEMOCRATIC PARTY (PARTIDO DEMÓCRATA NA-
CIONAL—PDN). Established soon after the 1930 coup, the PDN was the
single largest party in the conservative coalitions which governed until the 1943
coup. It favored large landowners' interests and opposed industrialization. Although greatly weakened, it voiced opposition to Juan Perón before it disappeared by the time of Perón's 1955 overthrow.

NATIONAL FEDERATION OF CONSERVATIVE PARTIES (FEDERA-
CIÓN NACIONAL DE PARTIDOS CONSERVADORES—FNPC). The anti-
Peronist FNPC succeeded the Partido Demócrata Nacional as the principal
conservative party in 1958. It supported free enterprise and particularly opposed
intervention in agriculture.

PARTIDO AUTONOMISTA NACIONAL. See NATIONAL AUTONO-
MIST PARTY.

PARTIDO CÍVICO INDEPENDIENTE. See INDEPENDIENTE CIVIC
PARTY.

PARTIDO DEMÓCRATA CONSERVADOR POPULAR. See POPULAR
CONSERVATIVE DEMOCRATIC PARTY.

PARTIDO DEMÓCRATA NACIONAL. See NATIONAL DEMOCRATIC
PARTY.

PARTIDO INDEPENDIENTE. See INDEPENDENT PARTY.

PARTIDO LABORISTA. See LABOR PARTY.

PARTIDO LIBERAL. See LIBERAL PARTY.

PARTIDO PERONISTA. See PERONIST PARTY.

PARTIDO PERONISTA FEMENINO. See PERONIST WOMEN'S PARTY.

PARTIDO POPULAR CRISTIANO. See POPULAR CHRISTIAN PARTY.

PARTIDO REPUBLICANO. See REPUBLICAN PARTY.

PARTIDO REPUBLICANO ARGENTINO. See ARGENTINE REPUBLI-
CAN PARTY.

PARTIDO SOCIALISTA. See SOCIALIST PARTY.

PARTIDO SOCIALISTA ARGENTINO. *See* ARGENTINE SOCIALIST PARTY.

PARTIDO SOCIALISTA DE LOS TRABAJADORES. *See* SOCIALIST PARTY OF THE WORKERS.

PARTIDO SOCIALISTA INDEPENDIENTE. *See* INDEPENDENT SOCIAL-IST PARTY.

PARTIDO SOCIALISTA INTERNACIONALISTA. *See* INTERNATION-ALIST SOCIALIST PARTY.

PARTIDO SOCIALISTA OBRERO. *See* SOCIALIST WORKERS' PARTY.

PARTIDOS PROVINCIALES POPULARES. *See* PROVINCIAL POPULAR PARTIES.

PERONIST PARTY (PARTIDO PERONISTA—PP). Following the 1943 coup, Colonel Juan Perón developed widespread support among trade unionists. They formed the backbone of supporters who elected him to the presidency in 1946. He was elected as the candidate of three hastily formed parties. Once in the presidency, Perón merged his followers into the Partido Peronista and created the Partido Peronista Femenino when women got the vote a few years later. When Perón was overthrown in 1955, the Peronist parties were outlawed, and ensuing Radical and military governments attempted to destroy the Peronist movement. Peronism, centered largely on its trade union base, however, re-mained strong.

In 1971, the military legalized political activity, but barred the use of Perón's name. Widely varying Peronist groups formed the Justicialist Party (Partido Justicialista) to work for his return. Since then, the Peronist party at the national level has been known as the Justicialist Party. In 1973, they elected Héctor Cámpora as president. He soon resigned so that Perón himself could run for, and win, the presidency in September 1973. When Perón died in office on 1 July 1974, he was succeeded by his wife, Vice President Isabelita Perón. She was overthrown by a military coup which outlawed all political parties. When party politics resumed after Argentina's 1982 defeat in the Malvinas, the Pe-ronists were still organized in the Justicialist Party. They ran second in the 1983 presidential elections and won the presidency in 1989 with Carlos Saúl Menem as the Justicialist candidate.

PERONIST REVOLUTIONARY MOVEMENT (MOVIMIENTO REVOLU-CIONARIO PERONISTA—MRP). The MRP, led by Andrés Framini, split from the Unión Popular to call for more revolutionary action. It was dissolved by the 1966 Onganía government.

PERONIST WOMEN'S PARTY (PARTIDO PERONISTA FEMENINO—PPF). The PPF was formed as an adjunct to the Partido Peronista when women gained the vote during the first Perón government. The PPF was headed by Evita Perón during her lifetime.

PERSONALIST RADICAL CIVIC UNION (UNIÓN CÍVICA RADICAL PERSONALISTA—UCRP). The UCRP represented those Radicals who supported Hipólito Yrigoyen in the mid-1920s split in the Radical Civic Union. They were slightly more leftist than the opposing faction. Banned from the 1932 election, the Personalist Radicals reunited with the anti-personalist faction in 1943 to again form a single Unión Cívica Radical.

POPULAR CHRISTIAN PARTY (PARTIDO POPULAR CRISTIANO—PPC). A social Christian group, led by José Antonio Allende, it supported the 1973 FREJULI coalition.

POPULAR CONSERVATIVE DEMOCRATIC PARTY (PARTIDO DE-MÓCRATA CONSERVADOR POPULAR—PDCP). Although the PDCP represented conservatives, it joined the 1973 FREJULI coalition. PDCP leader Vicente Solano Lima was actually elected vice president as Héctor Cámpora's FREJULI running mate. They both resigned office shortly thereafter, allowing the reelection of Juan Perón. The PDCP soon disappeared.

POPULAR UNION (UNIÓN POPULAR—UP). Formed in 1955 under Juan Bramuglia, the UP was completely loyal to Juan Perón. It was barred from the 1958 elections and was dissolved by the military after the 1966 coup.

PROVINCIAL POPULAR PARTIES (PARTIDOS PROVINCIALES POP-ULARES—PPP). The PPP bloc represented provincial parties which elected pro-Peronist congressional candidates in the years after 1955. Their victories in ten provincial elections in 1962 stimulated the military coup that overthrew Arturo Frondizi.

RADICAL CIVIC UNION OF THE PEOPLE (UNIÓN CÍVICA RADICAL DEL PUEBLO—UCRP). The UCRP was formed in 1957 from three factions in the Radical Civic Union (UCR) that were opposed to the presidential candidacy of Arturo Frondizi and his overtures to the Peronists. In 1958, Ricardo Balbín, leader of the UCRP, lost the presidential race to Arturo Frondizi and the Intransigent Radical Civic Union. After Frondizi was overthrown, Arturo Illia, the UCRP's candidate, won the presidency in 1963. He in turn was overthrown in 1966. Ricardo Balbín, head of one of its factions, then became the spokesman for the UCRP. Prior to the 1973 election, the party was allowed to change its name to Unión Cívica Radical, and its candidate, Balbín, ran second to the Peronists with 21 percent of the vote. Since 1973, the UCRP has been known as the UCR.

RENOVATING RADICAL CIVIC UNION (UNIÓN CÍVICA RADICAL RENOVADORA—UCRR). This party was formed by Hortensio Quijano (Juan Perón's vice presidential candidate) and Juan Guillermo Cooke to support Perón's presidential candidacy in 1946. It represented a very small minority of Radical leaders and it ended in 1946, when all three parties that had supported Perón were merged into what would become the Partido Peronista.

REPUBLICAN LEAGUE (LIGA REPUBLICANA—LR). See CONSERVATIVE NATIONALISTS.

REPUBLICAN PARTY (PARTIDO REPUBLICANO—PR). The PR resulted from an alliance between ex-President Bartolomé Mitre and Adolfo Alsina. It existed for almost a decade before merging with other groups to form the National Autonomist Party in 1879.

SOCIALIST PARTY (PARTIDO SOCIALISTA—PS). The Socialist Party was formed in 1896. Socialists were frequently elected to congress and were influential in the labor movement until the rise of Peronism in the 1940s. The Socialist Party strongly opposed Juan Perón and in return was persecuted by the military government after the 1943 coup, and by Perón thereafter. Throughout their history, the socialists had many splits and factions. The leadership's hardline opposition to Peronism caused a final split in 1957 which ended the Socialist Party as a significant actor. One faction formed the strongly anti-Peronist Democratic Socialist Party, and the second faction became the Argentine Socialist Party, which sought cooperation with some elements of the Peronist movement.

SOCIALIST PARTY OF THE WORKERS (PARTIDO SOCIALISTA DE LOS TRABAJADORES-PST). See REVOLUTIONARY PARTY OF THE WORKERS.

SOCIALIST WORKERS' PARTY (PARTIDO SOCIALISTA OBRERO—PSO). This Trotskyist group was formed in 1971. It was succeeded by the Movement towards Socialism.

UNIÓN CÍVICA. See CIVIC UNION.

UNIÓN CÍVICA RADICAL ANTIPERSONALISTA. See ANTIPERSONALIST RADICAL CIVIC UNION.

UNIÓN CÍVICA RADICAL DEL PUEBLO. See RADICAL CIVIC UNION OF THE PEOPLE.

UNIÓN CÍVICA RADICAL INTRANSIGENTE. *See* INTRANSIGENT RADICAL CIVIC UNION.

UNIÓN CÍVICA RADICAL PERSONALISTA. *See* PERSONALIST RADICAL CIVIC UNION.

UNIÓN CÍVICA RADICAL RENOVADORA. *See* RENOVATING RADICAL CIVIC UNION.

UNIÓN DEL PUEBLO ARGENTINO. *See* UNION OF THE ARGENTINE PEOPLE.

UNIÓN FEDERAL DEMÓCRATA CRISTIANA. *See* CHRISTIAN DEMOCRATIC FEDERAL UNION.

UNION OF THE ARGENTINE PEOPLE (UNIÓN DEL PUEBLO ARGENTINO—UDELPA). UDELPA was formed in January 1963, primarily to support ex-President Pedro Aramburu as the leader of conservative anti-Peronism. He ran third in the 1963 presidential elections, with 7 percent of the vote. UDELPA disappeared after Aramburu's May 1970 assassination.

UNIÓN POPULAR. *See* POPULAR UNION.

John T. Deiner

ARUBA

Aruba, a small island near the coast of Venezuela, 75 square miles in size with a population of 67,000, was until 1 January 1986 a part of the Netherlands Antilles. On that date, it became a separate part of the Kingdom of the Netherlands, together with the Netherlands itself and the Netherlands Antilles. It is scheduled to become an independent nation in 1996, although a referendum on the matter will be held in 1994.

For about sixty years, until 1985, the principal economic activity of the island was petroleum refining. This industry was established in the 1920s by oil companies with operations in Venezuela which feared possible political problems in that country. The industry was responsible for Aruba's having one of the highest per capita incomes in the Caribbean. However, in 1984, it was announced that the last refinery, that of Exxon, would close in the following years. As a consequence, some 3,000 workers have left Aruba for the Netherlands, Venezuela, and the United States. But they may return, because of an agreement reached in late 1989 between the government and the Coastal Oil Company of Texas to renovate part of the former Exxon refinery and begin operations in 1991, with a capacity of 150,000 barrels of petroleum daily.

Agriculture is virtually nonexistent in Aruba because of the island's arid soil. Recent governments have encouraged the establishment of small-scale assembly industries, and offshore financial operations have also constituted an appreciable segment of the economy. The upshot of all this has been that tourism, which had been a modestly growing segment of the economy before the mid-1980s, has become the principal center of economic activity.

Aruba has a somewhat heterogeneous population. Arawak Indians survived there longer than in most of the rest of the West Indies, and many of the present-day Arubans have at least some Arawak ancestry. Virtually all also have some African heritage, and some either came from Venezuela to work in the oil industry or their forebears did.

The Arubans are multilingual. They are taught in Dutch in primary school, then they learn Spanish and English. The common language of the people is papiamento. Because of this multiplicity of language, different political parties in Aruba use different languages for their names, and the following entries appear in the form used by the organization, as well as in English.

Political parties in Aruba were first organized during and following World War II, when the Netherlands began the processes of self-government and popular elections. The oldest of these appears to have been the Aruban Patriotic Party, which for many years was aligned with the Democratic Party of Curaçao, which between 1944 and 1969 largely dominated the politics of the Netherlands Antilles.

However, there developed a widespread feeling in Aruba that it was being exploited by the largest island of the Netherlands Antilles, Curaçao. In 1971 the Electoral Movement of the People (MEP) was founded to attain separation of Aruba from the Netherlands Antilles and ultimately to win independence for the island. Largely due to the efforts of the MEP, separation was achieved in 1986, with a commitment to independence a decade later.

In 1981, after the MEP withdrew from the Netherlands Antilles government, negotiations, among the governments of the Netherlands, the Netherlands Antilles, and Aruba, culminated in an agreement, which was signed in March 1983, providing for the separation of Aruba from the Netherlands Antilles. It was also agreed that the Netherlands would be responsible for foreign and defense affairs until 1996 and that a cooperative arrangement would be established between Aruba and the Netherlands Antilles on economic and monetary issues.

During the 1980s, two changes of government occurred. The MEP won the election in 1983, but when the government had to adopt an economic austerity program in the wake of the announcement of the closing of the last oil refinery, the party lost popularity. As a consequence, the MEP lost the 1985 election to the Aruban People's Party, which formed a coalition government. At the beginning of 1989, the MEP returned to power—again at the head of a coalition government.

Bibliography

The Europa World Year Book 1990. Europa Publications Ltd., London.
Facts on File. Facts on File, New York, 1980s.
Keesings Record of World Events. New York, 1980s.
Personal contacts of the author.

Political Parties

ACCIÓN DEMOCRÁTICO 86. *See* DEMOCRATIC ACTION 86.

ACCIÓN DEMOCRÁTICO NACIONAL. *See* NATIONAL DEMOCRATIC ACTION.

ARUBAN DEMOCRATIC PARTY (PARTI DEMOCRÁTICO ARU-BANO—PDA). The PDA was founded in 1983 under the leadership of Leonard Berlinski. In the 1985 election, it won two seats in the Staten and participated in the coalition government headed by J.H.A. (Henry) Eman. However, the party lost both of its deputies in the 1989 election.

ARUBAN PATRIOTIC PARTY (PARTI PATRIÓTICO ARUBANO). The Aruban Patriotic Party was the first party to be established in Aruba, in 1949. Because of its close association with the Democratic Party of Curaçao, as a result of which it often participated in the Netherlands Antilles cabinet, in its earlier years it is sometimes referred to as the Aruban Democratic Party (Parti Democrático Arubano). Its principal leader is Leo Chance.

For many years the Aruban Patriotic Party strongly supported independence of a united Netherlands Antilles. As a consequence, it opposed the drive of the Electoral Movement of the People (MEP) for separation of Aruba from the Netherlands Antilles. Even after the separation became a reality, the party continued to oppose the ultimate achievement of Aruban independence.

The Aruban Patriotic Party won two of the twenty-one seats in the Aruban legislature in the 1985 election, and it participated in the coalition government established after that election, which was led by the Aruban People's Party. In the following election, in 1989, it elected one additional member. In spite of having participated in the previous administration, it again was represented by one member in the cabinet that was formed under the leadership of the MEP.

ARUBAN PEOPLE'S PARTY (ARUBANSE VOLKSPARTIJ—AVP). The second largest party in Aruba, the AVP supported the move to separate Aruba from the Netherlands Antilles, a move that originally had been promoted by the Electoral Movement of the People (MEP). Because of an austerity program undertaken by the MEP-dominated government, parties opposed to that government won the November 1985 election. The AVP, as the largest opposition party, with seven members in the Staten, formed a new government, under party leader J.H.A. Eman. The AVP leader thus became the first prime minister of the Aruban government after it had separated from the Netherlands Antilles. Eman's government was a coalition of his party and the Aruban Democratic Party, the Aruban Patriotic Party, and the National Democratic Action. The Eman government put major emphasis on trying to develop economic alternatives to oil refining which, before it disappeared from Aruba, had provided 40 percent of the island's gross national product.

However, in the election of February 1989, the government of Prime Minister Eman was defeated, even though the AVP won eight seats in the Staten, instead of the seven that it had held in the previous legislature. A new government was formed under the leadership of the MEP.

ARUBANSE VOLKSPARTIJ. *See* ARUBAN PEOPLE'S PARTY.

DEMOCRATIC ACTION 86 (ACCIÓN DEMOCRÁTICO 86). A new party established in 1986 under the leadership of Arturo Oduber, it is one of the country's minor parties.

ELECTORAL MOVEMENT OF THE PEOPLE (MOVIMENTU ELECTORAL DI PUEBLO—MEP). Established in 1971, as the result of a split in the Aruban Patriotic Party, the MEP is oriented toward social democracy. From its inception, the MEP became the principal advocate of separation of Aruba from the Netherlands Antilles and of eventual attainment of independence.

The MEP was part of a coalition government of the Netherlands Antilles after 1979, and it pressed there for concessions leading to the independence of Aruba. In 1981, it withdrew from the Netherlands Antilles government. In March 1983, its objectives of separation and independence were achieved during negotiations held among the governments of the Netherlands, the Netherlands Antilles, and Aruba.

In April 1983, in Aruban elections, the MEP won thirteen of the twenty-one seats in the Aruba Staten. Gilberto (Bertico) Croes, the founder of the MEP, became the leader of the government of Aruba. However, a program of austerity adopted by the Croes government to deal with the coming closing of the island's last oil refinery, generated considerable discontent. As a consequence, the MEP was defeated in the November 1985 elections, in which it won only eight seats in the island legislature.

As an ironic consequence of this defeat, it was not an MEP government that led the island into its separate status on 1 January 1986; during the next three years, the MEP constituted the major opposition party.

In January 1989, the MEP increased its seats in the Staten in new elections from eight to ten. After the election, another member of the legislature joined the MEP, giving the party a majority. A new coalition government was formed under the leadership of the MEP, with six cabinet members, and one each from the Aruban Democratic Party and the Aruban Patriotic Party. However, Bertico Croes did not become the leader of the new MEP government. Croes suffered what proved to be a fatal automobile accident, and he died several weeks after the MEP returned to power. Nelson Oduber became the new MEP prime minister.

Although the MEP had campaigned for immediate independence for Aruba, it did not press the issue after the election, although it did announce that a referendum on the question would be held before the next election in 1994. Prime Minister Oduber announced that he favored a continuing association with the Netherlands in a Dutch Commonwealth, and that he hoped that, even after independence, the Netherlands would continue to be responsible for the defense of the island.

MOVIMENTU ELECTORAL DI PUEBLO. See ELECTORAL MOVEMENT OF THE PEOPLE.

NATIONAL DEMOCRATIC ACTION (ACCIÓN DEMOCRÁTICO NACIONAL—ADN). The ADN was founded in 1985, under the leadership of John Bool. In the election of that year, the ADN placed two members in the Staten and was represented thereafter in the coalition government of Prime Minister J.H.A. Eman. In the subsequent election of February 1989, the ADN increased its members of the Staten to three. It was given one post in the coalition cabinet organized by the leader of the Electoral Movement of the People, Nelson Oduber.

NEW PATRIOTIC PARTY (PARTI PATRIÓTICO NOBO). Founded in the late 1980s as a split from the Aruban Patriotic Party, the party is led by Eddy Werlenan. It is one of the island's smaller parties.

PARTI DEMOCRÁTICO ARUBANO. See ARUBAN DEMOCRATIC PARTY.

PARTI PATRIÓTICO ARUBANO. See ARUBAN PATRIOTIC PARTY.

PARTI PATRIÓTICO NOBO. See NEW PATRIOTIC PARTY.

Robert J. Alexander

THE BAHAMAS

Popularly known as the Bahamas, the Commonwealth of the Bahamas, an archipelago comprising 2,700 islands, cays, and reefs, is the insular state closest to the United States, just fifty miles east, southeast of Florida at its nearest point. With more than 10 percent of its approximately 225,000 population of Caucasian descent, the Bahamas has one of the highest percentages of creole Europeans among Commonwealth Caribbean states, partly as a legacy of the heavy immigration of exiled British to Abaco during the American Revolution. It is routinely accepted that the Bahamas archipelago, allegedly named for its shallow sea (*baja mar*), was the first American territory to be discovered by Europeans, since Watling Island (San Salvador) was the island on which Christopher Columbus landed on his maiden voyage of discovery in 1492. The Bahamas was also one of the first territories to have its native population eradicated and replaced by imported Africans. The archipelago was eventually colonized by Britain in 1629; the initial settlers came from Bermuda. It was one of the earliest of Britain's Caribbean colonies to be incorporated into its expanding empire, preceded only by Saint Kitts-Nevis and Barbados.

Political History and the Development of Political Parties

The Bahamian House of Assembly was developed in 1729 and, like Bermuda and Barbados, it never agreed to the Crown Colony option in lieu of its cherished "old representative system" of home-ruled governance. But, also like Bermuda and Barbados, that governance was dominated by wealthy white males, who clung to political and economic power well into the present era. Hume Wrong (1923) says that 1843 was the first date "men of color" were elected but, according to Paul Albury (1975), four black representatives were elected to the local parliament as early as 1834, the first year that Afro-Bahamians could vote. Their number increased to seven by 1910. This number remained fairly static, however, and 1950 still saw political leadership, even for the out islands, coming largely from the Nassau business district on New Providence Island, especially the Bay Street group.

The Bahamas experienced unionization and some major labor-management clashes between 1936 and 1942, but it was not until the 1950s that political parties developed, and an antidiscrimination resolution was bulldozed through the local assembly. It was not until 1967–1968 that the white business community, the so-called Bay Street Boys, lost an election to the newly empowered popular forces. Elite power was maintained and the workers' suffrage restrained, despite more relaxed property requirements compared to other islands, according to Robert J. Alexander (1982), by a system of multiple votes sometimes extended to owners of multiple properties and businesses, with eventual concentration of this power in the capital, Nassau. Another factor was a conservative, fragmented Bahamian culture that was partially controlled by opinion leaders on the many islands.

The vehicle by which national mass participation finally was realized, and by which national independence was won in 1973, was the emergence of mass political parties in the early 1950s. Still, it was not until the late 1960s, when the so-called quiet revolution began to overturn the Bahamian political culture, that blacks or Afro-Bahamians from the over-the-hill area of Nassau and the outlying islands won control of the government for the first time.

Contemporary Political Parties and Elections

The institutional leader of the quiet revolution, which opened the political process and served as a harbinger of expanded suffrage and civil rights for Afro-Bahamians, was the Progressive Liberal Party (PLP). It was founded in 1953, largely through the efforts of William Cartwright, but it was the return of the charismatic Lynden Pindling from legal studies in Britain that energized the party. Pindling quickly assumed leadership of the PLP. A party newspaper helped spread the message to the masses and throughout the family of islands.

The initial election contested by the PLP took place in 1956, and it won six of the then twenty-nine seats in the House of Assembly. The following year it won four additional seats in by-elections to fill four newly created districts. Expectations were high for an electoral takeover in 1962, especially since major suffrage reforms had been legislated. After years of agitating, women had finally secured the vote, and no longer was there a property qualification. The PLP was badly disappointed, however. With gerrymandering still alive and well and hard-to-change patterns implanted in the local culture, the old guard had one last hurrah in 1962. Despite winning a majority of the popular votes, the PLP captured only eight seats and suffered a decisive loss to the United Bahamian Party (UBP).

The quiet revolution overturned the Bay Street establishment and changed Bahamian politics forever in the general election of 1967, albeit by a one-vote margin that was achieved only with coalition support from Randol Fawkes of the recently formed Labour Party, plus an independent member of parliament. The quiet revolution was solidified the following year when the PLP called an early election and saw its parliamentary seats expand from eighteen to twenty-eight of the then thirty-eight seats. There was a repeat of the 1968 electoral victory in 1972 and, with the coming of independence the following year, there was also a new title for the PLP leader, that of prime minister.

Each election since 1972 has been easily won by the Pindling-led PLP. In the 1982 balloting, for example, the PLP won thirty-two parliamentary seats; eleven were won by the ten-year-old Free National Movement (FNM), historically the party of opposition as well as the more business- and establishment-oriented party. That election also was notable in marking a victory for the first female member of the Bahamian House of Assembly.

An expanded House of Assembly was at stake in the 1987 general election. This time the PLP captured thirty-one seats; sixteen went to the FNM and two to independent candidates. The victory margin was surprising to many in view of the cloud of impropriety hanging over the Pindling regime, including suspected drug trafficking by Pindling, who allegedly evaded arrest by a Miami sting operation only because of pressure from Washington, D.C. Voter concern was no doubt surmounted by the buoyant Bahamian economy which, although generally flat for the past three years, has risen to a gross domestic product of more than U.S. $10,000 per capita, the highest among independent states in geopolitical Latin America.

In short, Prime Minister Pindling and the PLP continue to have firm control of the Bahamian government in the early 1990s. There has been no relinquishment of power and, in fact, support continues from the electorate despite questions of improprieties and even serious corruption. Perhaps an equally serious problem has been the inability of the opposition FNM thus far to ever win more than half the number of seats secured by the PLP. The net result is that no other Commonwealth Caribbean state has experienced such a low level of governmental turnover. Even Trinidad's once-indomitable People's National Movement government has suffered electoral defeat. Guyana's still marginally open government (People's National Congress) has a new leader, Desmond Hoyte, since 1985 and is focusing on a more open electoral process in its upcoming elections. Only the Bahamanians have changed neither their government nor their leader. Not so ironically, of these three members of the Caribbean Community's "big five," only the Bahamas has maintained a growth economy, although even that has been less robust in recent years.

Bibliography

Paul Albury. *The Story of the Bahamas*. Macmillan Education, Ltd., London, 1975.
Robert J. Alexander. "The Bahamas," in Robert J. Alexander, ed., *Political Parties of the Americas*, 90–95. Greenwood Press, Westport, Conn., 1982.

"The Bahamas," in *The Europa World Year Book 1990*, vol. 1, 418. Europa Publications, Ltd., London, Ltd. 1991.

Rosemary Brana-Shute and Gary Brana-Shute. "The Anglophone Eastern Caribbean and British Dependencies," in Abraham F. Lowenthal, ed., *Latin America and Caribbean Contemporary Review*, vol. 6, 1986–1987, B443–45. Holmes and Meier, New York, 1989.

————. "The Anglophone Eastern Caribbean and British Dependencies," in Abraham F. Lowenthal, ed., *Latin America and Caribbean Contemporary Review*, vol. 5, 1985–1986, B438–39. Holmes and Meier, New York, 1988.

Dean W. Collingwood. "The Bahamas," in *Latin America and Caribbean Contemporary Review*, Jack W. Hopkins, ed., vol. 1, 1981–1982, 496–501. Holmes and Meier, New York, 1983.

Dean W. Collingwood and Steve Dodge. *Political Leadership in the Bahamas*. Occasional Papers, Series No. 1, The Bahamas Research Center, Nassau, 1987.

Patrick A. M. Emmanuel. *General Elections in the Eastern Caribbean*. Institute of Social and Economic Research, University of the West Indies, Cave Hill, Barbados, 1979.

Percy Hintzen and W. Marvin Will. Biographical Essays of Political Leaders from the Bahamas, in Robert J. Alexander, ed., *Biographical Directory of Latin American and Caribbean Political Leaders*, 223–24,ff. Greenwood Press, Westport, Conn., 1988.

Michael A. Symonette. *The New Bahamians*. Bahamas International Publishing Co., Ltd, Nassau, the Bahamas, 1982.

W. Marvin Will. Observations of Bahamian election and interviews with leaders of the participating parties, 1982.

Hume Wrong. *Government of the West Indies*. Negro Universities Press, New York, 1923.

Political Parties—Active

FREE NATIONAL MOVEMENT (FNM). The Free National Movement, currently the official opposition party in the Bahamas, was founded in 1971 by a group of eight former Progressive Liberal Party (PLP) members of the House of Assembly led by Cecil Wallace-Whitfield, a former PLP official, who were now members of the one-year-old Free Progressive Liberal Party (FPLP). Claiming that the Pindling-led PLP was abandoning party principles, the FPLP group merged with remnants of the United Bahamian Party (UBP) to form the FNM.

The initial FNM leader was Wallace-Whitfield. Leadership soon passed to prominent Afro-Bahamian barrister Kendal Isaacs of Nassau, who held the position through the mid-1980s. Wallace-Whitfield then reassumed leadership of the FNM until his death in 1990. The FNM currently is led by Hubert Ingraham. The FNM has traditionally been the party that is closest to business interests. Because of this legacy from the UBP, some feel that the FNM is incapable of being a truly viable alternative to the PLP, thus contributing to one-party governance in the Bahamas. (*See also* United Bahamian Party, Progressive Liberal Party, and Free Progressive Liberal Party.)

PEOPLE'S DEMOCRATIC FORCE (PDF). The People's Democratic Force was founded in 1989 by Fred Mitchell, who is the current party leader, in anticipation of the 1992 general election.

PROGRESSIVE LIBERAL PARTY (PLP). The PLP was founded in 1953 largely through the efforts of William Cartwright. He was soon joined by Lynden Pindling, who returned from legal studies in Britain shortly after the party's initiation. The charismatic Pindling quickly assumed the leadership reins of the PLP and currently continues as its president. Although not a labor party per se, the PLP won close support from the working class by its support of strike actions, including a major strike in 1958.

In 1956 the PLP contested its first election and won six of twenty-nine seats in the House of Assembly. In 1960 it secured four additional seats in by-elections to fill four newly created districts. With expectations of an electorial takeover in 1962, the year in which suffrage was substantially expanded, the PLP was badly disappointed when the party won only eight seats despite receiving a majority of the popular vote. The PLP was victorious in the election of 1967, however, capturing eighteen seats and the assistance of two coalition partners. This victory marked a significant step of success for the so-called quiet revolution over the Bay Street establishment.

The realization that many of the seats secured by the United Bahamian Party in 1967 were won by extremely narrow margins led the PLP to dissolve the government the following year and call an early election, which saw its eighteen seats expand to twenty-eight of the thirty-eight-seat total. In 1972 there was a repeat victory for the PLP. With the advent of independence one year later, Pindling gained the new title of prime minister. The PLP has been successful in each election subsequent to 1972. In the 1987 general election, for example, the PNP garnered thirty-one seats to sixteen for the Free National Movement and two for independent candidates. This large margin was forthcoming despite a cloud of suspicion hanging over Pindling and key aids regarding fiscal impropriety and suspected drug trafficking. Voter concern was no doubt surmounted by the region-leading growth economy of the Bahamas. But prospects are less bright for 1992 because of continuing suspicion of impropriety and an economic slowdown.

VANGUARD NATIONALIST AND SOCIALIST PARTY (VNSP). The Vanguard Party is the most left-oriented party in the Bahamas. It fights valiant but losing battles in most general elections. In one election it received only fifty votes nationwide. Founded in 1971, the longtime leader of the VNSP was John McCartney, who has been a professor of political theory at Purdue University. He was recently replaced by Lionel Carery.

WORKERS PARTY (WP). Little information is available on the Workers Party; however, it did nominate and run a number of candidates in the 1987 general election.

Political Parties—Historical

BAHAMIAN DEMOCRATIC PARTY (BDP). The Bahamian Democratic Party was formed in 1976 by rebels from the Free National Movement. In the 1977 general election, the BDP won six seats in the House of Assembly, seats formerly held by the United Bahamian Party including the traditional "white" seats. It became the official opposition party at this time.

COMMONWEALTH PEOPLE'S PARTY (CPP). The Commonwealth People's Party was formed by Holland Smith, who had been expelled from the Progressive Liberal Party in 1965. The CPP took a strong stand against the move for independence in 1973.

FREE PROGRESSIVE LIBERAL PARTY (FPLP). The Free Progressive Liberal Party was the party label adopted by eight defectors from the Progressive Liberal Party (PLP) during 1970–1971 prior to the formation of the Free National Movement (FNM). The FPLP was led by Cecil Wallace-Whitfield, a former PLP official and soon-to-be leader of the FNM. (See Free National Movement.)

LABOUR PARTY (LP). The Labour Party was founded in 1957 by Randol Fawkes, later Sir Randol, who had won a house seat the previous year. In 1967 the party nominated but four candidates including Fawkes, president of the Bahamas Labour Union (BLU). Fawkes was victorious and joined with one independent to form a coalition with the Progressive Liberal Party (PLP). This election marked the first victory by black and progressive forces over the Bay Street Boys.

Fawkes served as minister of labour in the first Pindling government. Although he was reelected in 1968 with no PLP opposition, Fawkes was not again appointed to the cabinet. Sir Randol, a well-respected unionist and attorney, was also a noted advocate of civil rights. His BLU strike actions attracted considerable support from the PLP, with whom he continued to maintain good relations.

SOCIAL DEMOCRATIC PARTY (SDP). According to Michael A. Symonette (1982), the Social Democratic Party "represented residual UBP [United Bahamian Party] support in the country." The SDP collapsed in the wake of allegations against its leader, Norman Solomon, by the press and the Free National Movement. Solomon was defeated in the election of 1982 and the party ceased to exist.

UNITED BAHAMIAN PARTY (UBP). The United Bahamian Party was established in 1958. According to Albury (1975), as out islanders increasingly moved to Nassau where they could represent both their home island and their Nassau business or businesses, the country's political elite became focused on Bay Street and the informal organization of the Bay Street Boys. With the advent of the Progressive Liberal Party (PLP) in 1953, and with it a more competitive political environment, stricter party discipline was required and, thus, the more formal UBP with its business and establishment orientation was created.

The UBP won the 1962 election decisively, and in 1964 its leader, Sir Roland Symonette, became the first premier of the Bahamas. In the general election of 1967, the UBP tied with the PLP, who formed a coalition and assumed control of the government, relegating the UBP to the status of official opposition. The UBP suffered an overwhelming defeat to the PLP in 1968, and in 1971 it joined with disenchanted former members of the PLP, who had formed the short-lived Free Progressive Liberal Party, to forge the Free National Movement. (*See* Free National Movement.)

W. Marvin Will

BARBADOS

Barbados, the only Commonwealth Caribbean state that was continuously under British control from its colonization (1625–1627) to its independence (1966), is well known for its gradualistic approach to change. Since 1985, however, the transition in prime ministers in this, the most easterly of the Caribbean islands, has been most rapid. Tom Adams and Errol Barrow, both internationally prominent leaders, died during their terms in office, and Bernard St. John was defeated in the 1986 general election following his initial term as prime minister. This election saw the Democratic Labour Party (DLP) hand the incumbent Barbados Labour Party (BLP) the most massive defeat in Barbadian history (twenty-four to three). Another political rarity in Barbados, during this same period, was the initiation of a new political party, the New Democratic Party (NDP), led by Dr. Richard Haynes. Due to the BLP's sparse electoral victories in 1986, plus some defections from the party, the newly formed NDP actually replaced the BLP as the official opposition for a time, but its appeal appears to be short lived. The NDP was shut out in the 1991 general election in which the DLP was again victorious, although the BLP made a strong return.

That the DLP, led by Erskine Sandiford, retained a solid parliamentary majority in 1991 was a surprise to some observers in view of Barbados's worsening economy and a soaring national debt. The political future of Barbados therefore appears mixed. Although the Barbadian legacy of two competing middle-of-the-road labor parties appears to be back on the competitive track established over a period of four decades, the mounting economic difficulties could produce discord. The last time the economy and debt burden reached such negative levels in Barbados, during the pre–World War II depression era, it produced an insurrection that led directly to near revolutionary political change with the birth of labor unions and political parties.

The Violent 1930s and the Birth of West Indian Parties

From Dismal Labor Conditions to Insurrection

The bad times of the 1930s brought labor violence and even insurrection throughout the region, from Belize and Saint Kitts to Trinidad and Barbados. Although Barbados was then and still remains the least radical and most orderly state in the Caribbean, it too experienced radicalization of its black masses. Serious rioting took place in 1937. The riots triggered development of the one institution of governance absent in more than three centuries of British transferrals, the mass political party. The competitive party system that ultimately evolved in Barbados was a harbinger of a continuing process that, by 1980, according to Jamaica's Carl Stone, made the Barbadian political economy the envy of the region.

The catalyst for the Barbadian insurrection in the 1930s was the arrival of Clement Payne, a follower of Uriah Butler, the leader of the highly inflammatory labor insurrection in Trinidad. British naval forces eventually were required to quell the insurgent Trinidadian workers. Payne, minister of propaganda from Trinidad's Youth League, sought to export the confrontation message to the Barbadian workers. He stirred the populace of Bridgetown in seventeen meetings in which he railed at the "lackeys of employers," according to F. A. Hoyos (1963), and described the police as "dogs of the capitalists." Perhaps of even greater long-term concern were the efforts of his subordinates to encourage mass participation and the development of political organizations in Barbados.

Payne, who was born in Trinidad of Barbadian parents, was arrested on the technicality that he had made a false declaration of his place of birth. Following his release from custody, after an effective legal defense by Grantley Adams, an Oxford-educated barrister and an aggressive legislative member, a rally to protest Payne's legal harassment was held in the heart of the principal working-class area in Bridgetown. This, in turn, induced a march to Government House. "Because he opening we eyes," some were heard to say, "de tryin to lock him up." (Hoyos 1963) Payne was again incarcerated and ordered deported. His aroused supporters, bolstered by rumors of police brutality (including an allegation that police had killed the child of his female companion), surged through the city on the night of 27 July 1937. The insurrection spread to the surrounding countryside during the following two days. Strong police force was exercised, resulting in approximately 50 wounded, more than 500 arrested, and 14 fatalities—more than one-third of the total fatalities for the entire riot-torn Commonwealth Caribbean. The violence in Barbados was particularly unsettling in view of the diminutive size of the island as well as the Barbadian reputation for order.

Labor conditions in Barbados, among the worst in the area, were a responsible factor in the insurrection. With nearly no non-sugar-related industry, the Barbadian work force was divided roughly among the agriculture, commerce and sugar processing, and domestic sectors. All sectors provided extremely low wages, even in comparison with neighboring Caribbean areas. Despite their common head-of-household responsibilities, women encountered the worst treatment. Many worked as common manual laborers, typically carrying seventy-two-pound loads on their heads. As domestic servants, they generally received no board or sick leave and earned from six to twelve shillings per week for from six to nine daily hours of hard labor—an amount that declined to as little as one shilling, six pence per week if food was included. Female employees in the smaller shops labored long hours for sixteen shillings per month. Conditions were indeed grim.

Restrictive Political Conditions

Although Crown Colony status had been imposed on most of British America by the mid-nineteenth century, Bermuda, the Bahamas, and Barbados retained their old representative government, a system dominated by the white plantation and commercial elites. Of these, the Barbadian system was not the least open nor the least efficient, concluded the Moyne Report. Its legislature consisted of a nine-member Legislative Council appointed by the Crown and a twenty-four-member House of Assembly which was elected annually—albeit with a very restrictive property qualification for voting. The executive role was vested in a Council appointed by the Crown which included four members nominated by the governor from the House of Assembly. Most crucial, all money votes were introduced in the legislature and all government measures were initiated there by, and with the advice of, the Executive Committee, but the executive had no means of ensuring passage of legislation nor for providing funds. The elected House of Assembly could bar passage of any legislation and had complete freedom to withhold the provision of money votes moved by the executive. The governor's program was not the only one frustrated, so was much social legislation and many of the services needed by the working masses.

To vote in Barbados one was required to be a taxpaying male property owner, or one who lived well in a house valued at £50 or rented for £15, or one who had an English university degree or a profession. Most common laborers were excluded from suffrage by the minimum income requirement of £50 per annum for nonproperty holders. Such restrictions contributed to an unbelievably low registration of only 3.3 percent in January 1938 (just 6,359—only half the percentage of low-participation Trinidad). Even more shocking to those positively socialized in favor of mass politics, fewer than 300 voters were registered in each of eight Barbadian parishes which accounted for sixteen members and a crucial two-thirds of the legislature. Eligibility for election to the House of Assemby was even more discriminatory. In economic language, the white elite possessed an oligopoly. According to Francis Mark (1965),

Centuries of habit made the whole elective process a casual, almost informal affair. . . . Electoral campaigning had been the exception rather than the rule, public meetings had been unknown, and contested elections were so infrequent that their occurrence took on the character of a breach of established convention.

From the First Stirrings of Party Democracy to Formation of the Democratic League

Important pre-party organizations formed by the early nineteenth century chipped away at the socially frozen process. Following the end of slavery, this effort was bolstered by the election to parliament of several "free coloureds," led by Samuel Jackman Prescod. Prescod not only served several terms in office but also advanced a Liberal Party, a loosely structured, biracial cadre organization, primarily urban based, that pursued goals of honest government and liberalization of suffrage during the three or four decades following the late 1830s.

Probably the most important pre-party political group to form in Barbados prior to the 1937 crisis was the Democratic League organized in October 1924. Formed largely through the motivation of West Indian–American black power advocate Marcus Garvey, and organized locally by a black, socialist medical doctor, Charles Duncan O'Neale, the Democratic League was primarily a liberal, middle-class cadre group. This group provided a major impetus to political organization in Barbados for more than a decade, promoting socialistic principles and the importance of expanded political activism.

Although the league elected three of its members to the Barbadian House of Assembly between 1924 and 1932, including O'Neale himself, the principal function of the organization and its leader was to arouse and politicize the middle sectors. This was risky activity for such progressivism was perceived as a threat to society, and any attempt at political organization was considered seditious. When O'Neale died just one year before the 1937 riots, his fragile structural legacy was unable to survive. A new organization—the mass political party—was needed to mobilize and organizationally enlist the workers.

The Rise of Labor Party Politics in Barbados

The Barbados Progressive League

The Barbados Progressive League (BPL) had been formed by October 1938, slightly more than a year after the riots that occurred in the summer of 1937. This multifunctional institution became the parent of both of Barbados's major labor parties—the BLP and, after the mid-1950s, the breakaway (DLP)—as well as the island's premier labor union, the Barbados Workers' Union (BWU). The guiding principle of the BPL was that the popular forces in Barbados must organize in order to open the system and then that these forces must work within that system. Before there could be a truly mass political party in Barbados, however, a sufficient broadening of suffrage rules was imperative. Since suffrage in Barbados was still severely limited by an economic test, the first order of business for the BPL was to promote higher wages through union organization. In the ongoing depression of the 1930s, there was also a serious need for social welfare and inexpensive insurance for Barbadians. The multifaceted Barbados Progressive League served all these needs: political, economic, and social.

More than any other Barbadian institution, the BPL was a product of Barbadian initiative that was built on the crisis mobilization produced by the Great Depression and the 1937 violence. As stated in 1944 by this umbrella organization's own publication, *Past Present and Future: Policy and Programme*, its immediate raison d'être was "to mobilise and direct the upsurge of political enthusiasm and energy released as a result of the disturbances of 1937 and the announcement of the appointment of the Royal Commission." If there were ever a time to build a mass organization, this was it. Only strong leadership was a questionable factor.

Organization and the Problem of Leadership

Following a nearly universal pattern, initial organizational stimulation for the BPL came from middle-class elites who quite frequently had been exposed to metropolitan politicization. Hope R. Stevens, a New York attorney and former West Indian (from Tortola) who was touring the Caribbean in spring 1938, was the lone individual with legal training directly involved when the BPL constitution was drafted. In Barbados he had attracted the support of W. A. Crawford, a politician and publisher who had been influenced by the mass parties and unions of North America.

The initial planning meeting for the league, as related to this author in personal interviews, was called in the home of C. Edwa Talma, a labor leader who had gained valuable organizational experience in the petroleum industries of Venezuela and the Dutch island of Aruba. In this four-hour meeting, the primary need and goal articulated was the development of a multifunctional mass political party, but it was felt that the organization's activities should not be limited to party politics. The aims and objectives of the organization were further polished at a subsequent meeting held in the home of J. D. Martineau, a prominent political labor leader and past associate of O'Neale. By October 1938, after three months of arduous debate and planning, the Barbados Progressive League was formed and officers were elected. C. A. Braithwaite, a veteran booster of the Democratic League, was selected president; Talma was chosen general secretary; Martineau, treasurer; and barrister-politician Grantley Adams, vice president. Adams was at that time reeducating himself to the realities of West Indian labor politics following exposure to active party politics while a student in England during the 1920s. Herbert Seale, who had gained experience as an assistant secretary to the noted Jamaican leader Marcus Garvey, and who was instrumental in early BPL recruitment efforts, served as assistant to General Secretary Talma before he assumed that office during the league's

debut year. Many of the lower echelon officials in the BPL, such as field secretaries and field organizers, had political or trade union experience either in
the United States or in other Caribbean areas. The BPL officialdom, fortunately,
was not an association of amateurs.

The league's timeliness and dynamic, experienced leadership, especially that
of its promotional wizard Herbert Seale, were reflected in a soaring membership,
which grew to between 20,000 to 30,000 adherents within approximately one
year. Despite the lack of a dues-paying tradition, and the current economic
depression which made regular payment of the six-cent (rural) or twelve-cent
(urban) monthly dues impossible for many, a bankroll of about $10,000 was
raised by November 1939 to facilitate the purchase of a much-needed building
for permanent headquarters for the BPL. Aggressive, high-caliber leadership
does not guarantee consensual relations in any society or organization, however,
and particularly not in a relatively impoverished and very small society where
relationships are personal in the extreme. It could be expected that clashes
rooted both in personality and in program differences would divide the BPL.

Major leadership fissures occurred during the league's first year, and these
divisions involved the organization's stalwarts: Braithwaite, Adams, Martineau,
and, eventually and most bitterly, Crawford. The genesis of these conflicts
involved both ideology and personality differences. Adams was regarded as too
conservative by some, and, in turn, he eschewed the direct confrontational
politics advocated by Seale. Personal ambition was also a divisive element.

Despite his late conversion to progressivism, Adams was easily the movement's
most charismatic leader. The masses called him "Moses . . . who led us from the
wilderness to the promised land!" Institutional expansion and legitimization,
especially that of the mass party, can benefit most positively from a charismatic
leader—if the leader sets limits on his or her behavior. Adams was a positive
contributor to the institutionalization process in Barbados because he did set
limits on both his personal integrity and his quest for power. He was also
extremely ambitious and frequently was neither flexible nor subtle in his relationships. Hilton Vaughan personally informed this author in 1970 and 1971
that Adams had been ideologically linked to the old school but that he
changed for the best and that he possessed a great feel for local values. "One
must be of extraordinary mettle to grow younger politically as one ages," Vaughan
concluded.

As reported in Hoyos (1963), Adams once told a large crowd of workers in
Bridgetown,

You are being told the Progressive League [is] too slow, [you should] form a procession
and go to Government House. Well, the procession that went to Government House
[in 1937] was the beginning of the last riot. I ask you, instead . . . to come and tell us
every single grievance and let the procession be that of the Progressive League to a seat
at a conference table.

Adams eventually became general secretary of the BPL and led the BWU until 1954 when he was afforded the opportunity to head the BLP–led government of Barbados. He resigned the Barbadian premiership in 1958 when he left the island to become premier of the West Indies Federation. Relinquishing union leadership upon assuming the reins of the BLP was instrumental in permitting differentiation between union, party, and government—a developmental process never fully realized by Grenada's Eric Gairy, Guyana's Forbes Burnham, nor Antigua's Vere Bird.

The Barbados Workers' Union: A Case in Sector Differentiation

At the outset, little real distinction was made between sectors of the BPL because party, union, and "friendly society" had a common board of directors and a common financial pool. But the need to enlarge the working-class electorate, plus passage of pro-union legislation in 1939–1940, led the BWU to be independently registered in 1941. The BWU, with a membership in excess of 20,000, purchased a separate union hall and by 1949 had established an existence separate from the BPL. As noted earlier, Adams aided the differentiation process by stepping aside as secretary general of the BWU in 1954, and Frank Walcott assumed the office. Independence of the BWU was further assured the following year (1955) when the Barbados Labour Party split into two parties: the BLP and the DLP. The BWU remains one of the region's most independent unions today.

The Barbados Labour Party: Labour Party Politics and the Rise of Self-Government

By 1940, the BPL political council had published a party platform, or manifesto, for the general election that year. This platform was beneficial in the election of five of the BPL's six candidates to the Barbadian House of Assembly. It was the first time in Barbadian history that a party with a declared policy had gained electoral support for its team of candidates. The BPL's impact on the house was enormous. By 1942, almost every candidate for public office in Barbados professed to have adopted some or all of the league's manifesto. It was also the beginning of the end for independent parliamentary candidates. The percentage of independents declined steadily, election by election, until by the 1970s non-party-related candidates were practically nonexistent. When the league won a by-election in 1941, J.T.C. Ramsay became the first member of the Barbadian working class to secure a seat in the House of Assembly, where he joined league parliamentarians who were middle-class attorneys, educators, and other professionals. As a symbol of working-class pride, Ramsay marked the occasion by wearing his work clothing to the parliamentary session.

But numbers counted far more than such symbols. After 1943–1944, with British support (through the governor), the franchise gates were slowly opened.

By 1944, eight members of the BPL had gained parliamentary seats, and eight members of Crawford's labor-oriented West Indian National Congress Party were also victorious, resulting in the first Barbadian majority for progressive parties. No longer would a mere 6,000 electors choose the twenty-four representatives for this colony of more than 200,000 people. The gates were indeed opening. And open they must. Governor Sir Grattan Bushe was fond of saying that if there is no opening in the political sluice gates, the dam will break and wash away all that lies before it. Lessons from Britain's North American experience seem to have registered. Britain had learned to adapt.

Parties in Passage: The Demise of the Conservatives and the Rise of the Democratic Labour Party

By 1954, the suffrage gates were opened not only in Barbados but throughout the British West Indies in general, a region now being pushed toward federation and eventual independence by war-impoverished Britain. In Barbados the coming of universal suffrage spelled the end of elitist parties, such as the Electors Association, a primarily white commercial-planter conservative party that had organized in reaction to the rise of labor parties in an attempt to maintain control of the island's government. By 1960 the Electors Association had been renamed the Barbados National Party (BNP), and by 1970 this last bastion of the conservative cause had ceased to exist. The new era ushered in labor governments led by either the BLP or, after its 1955 schism, the DLP. The DLP, a Young Turk offshoot party, was led by F. G. Smith from 1955 to 1959, at which time Errol Barrow assumed leadership of the DLP and served in that capacity until his death on 1 June 1987. Personality differences between Barrow, just back from service in World War II, and Grantley Adams were instrumental in the party split although questions of economic policy were also a factor.

From the first experimentation with semi-cabinet government in Barbados in 1946, and especially after 1954 when full cabinet government was installed, one or the other of the labor parties ruled. Until the 1986 general election, in which the DLP was victorious, there had in fact been a pattern of three BLP governments, three DLP governments. The expansion of competitive mass parties, garnering more than 80 percent of the vote as they do, also contributes to the legitimization of government, especially Westminster-modeled parliamentary government. The league planning meetings held in 1939 were now paying genuine political dividends.

Electoral Stability

Despite extreme economic dependence and the paramount importance of economically related domestic issues in the electoral politics in Barbados, competitive electoral politics in this island state—and in the subregion in general—have experienced amazing stability. The gradual institutionalization that has occurred is all the more noteworthy in view of the relatively brief half-century history of party politics in Barbados, as well as the high electoral support often given to personal leadership.

A remarkably strong two-party system has evolved in Barbados for which one measure of popular support is the relatively high percentage of the electorate that exercises the voting privilege. This percentage increased steadily in Barbados from the initiation of full suffrage in 1950 until it reached 82 percent in 1971, despite the inclusion of the eighteen-year-old vote in that election. Percentages declined to 62 percent in 1991, however, a postindependence low. Perhaps Barbados has begun to experience some apathy and voter turnoff, which have been so problematic in North America. Furthermore, in a region where the independent candidate is a common reality, the party share of total vote in Barbados has increased steadily in the two decades following the introduction of mass suffrage until by the 1970s it reached the 99th percentile. It continues at this level.

Third Party Politics

Despite a grim economy during the bulk of the 1980s and despite recent reversals in the political leadership of Barbados, the two-party system appears to be as well accepted in Barbados as in any country in the Caribbean region. There is complete legal freedom for third party candidates to file for office and to conduct a campaign—as well as a truly free press and support from the parliamentary system itself—but minor party candidates rarely garner sufficient support to salvage their filing fee. The massive electoral defeat of the NDP in the 1991 general election perpetuated this pattern. Despite the massive BLP loss in 1986, the cycle of two-to-three general elections won, two-to-three lost has been maintained from 1951 to the present.

The partisan alignment of this island state's electoral districts has remained remarkably constant despite several redistrictings. These have included a major one-person, one-vote redistricting just prior to the 1971 general election, which broke up the time-honored Barbadian pattern of two parliamentary seats per parish; expansion of the number of electoral districts from twenty-four to twenty-seven in 1981; and expansion again in 1990 when the parliamentary districts were expanded by one seat.

The Potential for Multiterm Governance by the DLP

The general election landslide in 1986 saw DLP percentages vis-à-vis the BLP increase in all but one electoral district as the DLP achieved a record vote swing of nearly 12 percent. This produced a DLP gain of fourteen house seats for an overwhelming twenty-four-to-three majority (89 percent), as well as the required two-thirds majority for implementing constitutional alterations. A vote swing of these massive proportions presents the likelihood of a new multiterm alignment in favor of the DLP such as previously occurred for the DLP in 1961 and for the BLP in 1976. This prediction was borne out in the 1991 general election, as the Sandiford–DLP team again won control of the government (eighteen to ten), albeit with a much-reduced popular vote margin (49 percent to 43 percent). The reduced margin of victory, both in seats and votes, was due largely to the reestablishment of the balance of Barbados' two-party system and also, not insignificantly, to concern over escalating governmental debt, atypical mounting crime levels, and electoral frustration arising from loss of confidence in political promises and possibly in the state itself. Today, perhaps more than at any other period in history, governments must compete for investment dollars and corporate placement and, indeed, to restrain qualified citizens from emigrating. Voter frustrations are not far behind.

Although the wildly fluctuating electoral swings of 1986–1987 had moderated by 1991, one must take risks to predict that the swings will continue to moderate in upcoming electoral contests. The sheer weight of Barbadian tradition (including the Barbadian love of liberty and the fear of one-party dominance) has a balancing aspect not found in most new nations, but the "misbehaving" economies in Barbados and the region, plus the recent tragic losses in Barbadian political leadership, invoke the need for predictive sobriety. The Barbadian party system, a time-honored stabilizing influence since its creation following the crisis of the 1930s, will certainly be tested in the next two or three general elections.

Bibliography

Robert J. Alexander, ed. *Political Parties of the Americas*. 2 vols. Greenwood Press, Westport, Conn., 1982.

———. "Barbados" *Advocate News* 9 February, 1973.

Barbados Progressive League. *Past Present and Future: Policy and Programme*. Barbados Progressive League, Bridgetown, Barbados, 1944.

Hilary McD. Beckles. *A History of Barbados*. Cambridge University Press, London, 1990.

W. A. Beckles. *The Barbados Disturbances, 1937*. [Advocate Press], Bridgetown, Barbados, 1937.

Neville C. Duncan. "Barbados," in James M. Malloy and Eduardo A. Gamarra, eds., *Latin America and Caribbean Contemporary Record*, vol. 7, 1987–1988, B353–62. Holmes and Meier, New York, 1990.

Patrick A. M. Emmanuel. *General Elections in the Eastern Caribbean*. Letchworth Press, Ltd., for ISER (EC) of the University of the West Indies, Barbados, 1979.

Percy Hintzen and W. Marvin Will. Caribbean essays in Robert J. Alexander, ed., *Biographical Directory of Latin American and Caribbean Political Leaders*. Greenwood Press, Westport, Conn., 1988.

F. A. Hoyos. *The Rise of West Indian Democracy: The Life and Times of Sir Grantley Adams*. Advocate Press. [Bridgetown, Barbados], 1963.

———. *The Story of the Progressive Movement: Achievements of a Decade*. Beacon Printery, [Bridgetown, Barbados], 1948.

Harold Hoyte. "Will Erskine Sandiford Find That Errol Barrow and Tom Adams Are Tough Acts to Follow?" *Caribbean Affairs* 1, July–September, 1988, p. 96.

William Knowles. *Trade Union Development and Industrial Relations in the British West Indies.* University of California Press, Berkeley, 1959.

Francis Mark. *The History of the Barbados Workers' Union.* Advocate Press, [Bridgetown, Barbados], 1965.

"Moyne Report." See U.K. Colonial Office. *West India Royal Commission Report, 1938– 39.* 1945.

Carl Stone. *Power in the Caribbean Basin: A Comparative Study of Political Economy.* Inter-American Politics Series, vol. 5. Institute for the Study of Human Issues, Philadelphia, Pa., 1986.

W. Marvin. Will, "Democracy, Elections and Public Policy in the Eastern Caribbean." *The Journal of Commonwealth & Comparative Politics* 27, 3, November 1989, pp. 321–46.

———. "Mass Political Party Institutionalisation in Barbados." *The Journal of Commonwealth & Comparative Politics* 19, 2, July 1981, pp. 134–56.

———. Election observations and personal interviews with most Barbadian political leaders, 1970–1990.

Political Parties—Active

BARBADOS LABOUR PARTY (BLP). Founded as the political wing of the Barbados Progressive League in 1938, the BLP is the third oldest, active mass party in the Commonwealth Caribbean. By 1946, when it became known as the BLP, it won its first plurality by out-polling both the West Indies Congress Party (with which it had just served a term as coalition partners) and the conservative Barbados Electors Association. The reward to the BLP and Grantley Adams was leadership of the semi-cabinet government being constituted in Barbados by Governor Sir Grattan Bushe. By 1954, full home rule, also controlled by the BLP and Premier Adams, had come to Barbados. The BLP also won the federal election for the 1958–1962 West Indies Federation, in association with the West Indies coalition of federal labor parties, and sent Sir Grantley Adams, its leader, to be the first and only premier of the federation. However, he gave up local party leadership.

In 1955, the somewhat less business-oriented wing of the BLP broke away to form the Democratic Labour Party (DLP). By 1961, this new party was able to defeat the then poorly led BLP in the first of three general elections. The BLP, under the leadership of J.M.G.M. "Tom" Adams, regained control of the government in 1976 and again in 1981. Barbadians were shocked by the death of Prime Minister Tom Adams on 11 March 1985. BLP leadership and the position of prime minister passed to Bernard St. John, who lacked much of the charisma and strong leadership qualities of Adams. In 1986 only three BLP candidates survived an electoral onslaught by the DLP. In this record defeat, even Prime Minister St. John failed to carry his constituency. In the January 1991 general election, the BLP resurged somewhat, securing ten of twenty-eight seats; however, its popular vote of 43 percent to less than 50 percent for the DLP suggests a reestablishment of the two-party balance that has characterized the last four decades of Barbadian politics. The BLP, under the leadership of Henry Forde, former attorney general and foreign minister, is currently the "loyal" opposition party. (See Barbados Progressive League.)

DEMOCRATIC LABOUR PARTY (DLP). The Democratic Labour Party, led by F. G. Smith until 1959 and then by Errol Barrow, former RAF pilot and graduate of the London School of Economics, was formed in April 1955 as a breakaway faction of the Barbados Labour Party (BLP). By 1961, Barrow and his "Dems" were able to defeat the BLP and gain control of the Barbadian government. The DLP, with Barrow at the helm, retained governmental control until 1976. The DLP and Barrow were returned to power in 1986 in a massive defeat (twenty-four to three) of the incumbent BLP and were again victorious in 1991, although the margin of victory declined. The DLP, along with the BLP, has contributed significantly to the smooth and uncomplicated transition of party administrations in each of the three elections that have brought about a change in government in this island state.

By virtue of the DLP victory in the independence election in 1966, Barrow became the first prime minister of Barbados. Following his death on 1 June 1987, Erskine Sandiford assumed leadership of the Barbadian government and the DLP. Educated at the University of the West Indies, Sandiford is the first prime minister of Barbados to be educated in the Caribbean. Serving as the fourth prime minister of Barbados, Sandiford is an able former educator, but he lacks the charisma of either Barrow or Tom Adams and he faces one of the worst economic crisis periods in the island's history. (See Barbados Progressive League and Barbados Labour Party.)

NEW DEMOCRATIC PARTY (NDP). Formed primarily by defectors from the 1986 Barbados Labour Party (BLP) government, the New Democratic Party is led by Richard Haynes, a medical doctor who was an unsuccessful contender to replace Errol Barrow at the helm of the Democratic Labour Party in the early 1980s. The NDP replaced the BLP as the official opposition party in Barbados from 1986 to 1991. Some thought the replacement could be permanent, but Barbados's two-party precedent proved too strong. In the 1991 general election, the NDP's popular vote dropped to just 6.8 percent, and the party retained no parliamentary seats. Its future is therefore clouded.

Political Parties—Historical

BARBADOS ELECTORS ASSOCIATION (BEA). The Barbados Electors Association, which dates back to 1941, is often referred to simply as the Electors Association or the conservatives. Initially this group was a significant electoral force but gradually lost its impact under the onslaught of Labour politics. The conservatives sponsored eighteen candidates in the election of 1951, thirteen in 1956, and twelve in 1961 before ceasing to exist in 1970. (*See* Barbados National Party.)

BARBADOS NATIONAL PARTY (BNP). The BNP family of political parties is replete with name changes. From the rise of the Barbados Labor Party (BLP) and allied workers parties, the white elite, which gradually incorporated conservative individuals of color as well, grouped themselves under varied party banners, all of which were basically the same party. The Barbados Electors Association, according to Patrick A. M. Emmanuel (1979), was formed in 1941, was renamed the Progressive Conservative Party in 1956, and by 1960 had become known as the Barbados National Party. Robert J. Alexander (1982), on the other hand, adds the following to this progression of name changes: Voters Association, Conservative Electors Association, and Progressive Electors' Association.

The electoral success of this family of parties dwindled with the expansion of suffrage and the rise of the two labor parties. In 1940, this elite group, then informally called the Voters Association, won all parliamentary seats except the five seats won by Labour. Four years later, as the conservative Barbados Electors Association, it won eight seats under the leadership of F. C. Goddard. By 1956, now under the label of the Progressive Electors Association and headed by a black man, E. D. Mottley of Bridgetown, the party secured but six seats. In the federal election of 1958, Florence Daysch won a seat in the federal parliament under the label Barbados National Party. Her election was ironic for, as a result of losses by the Federal Labour Party coalition in 1960, Premier Grantley Adams, the nemesis of the Barbadian conservative forces, was impelled to rely on Daysch's largely independent vote in the severely weakened federal government.

In the December 1961 balloting, with the BLP in disarray, the BNP won four seats in Barbados House of Assembly in an election that was won by the breakaway Democratic Labour Party. The BNP urged voters in this election to support the DLP in races where it did not field a candidate. By 1966, the National Party elected but one candidate, Mottley. By 1970 the party was over for the BNP family of parties. Mottley's son, however, won a parliamentary seat under the BLP banner—an example of the adaptability of Barbadian conservatives.

BARBADOS PROGRESSIVE LEAGUE (BPL). Officially launched in October 1938 as a multifunctional umbrella institution (labor union, political party, and insurance and welfare association), the Barbados Progressive League evolved into the Barbados Workers Union and the Barbados Labour Party (BLP) by the 1940s. Officers selected at its organizational meeting were C. A. Braithwaite, president; C. Edwa Talma, general secretary; J. D. Martineau, treasurer; and Grantley Adams, vice president. Herbert Seale, a former assistant secretary to Marcus Garvey, served as assistant to Talma and within a year became the BPL general secretary. It was Seale who was responsible for much of the great success in the league's recruitment efforts, attracting as many as 30,000 adherents within a year despite the Barbadian lack of a dues-paying tradition and the serious economic depression encompassing the island. Adams eventually emerged as president of the league.

By 1939, the BPL was financially able to procure a handsome new office building, and in 1940 it won five of the six House of Assembly seats for which it competed. This began a gradual evolution toward mass democracy in Barbados and toward mass party status for the BPL's partisan successor, the BLP. In 1944, while still functioning under the BPL label, this party formed a coalition government with the West Indian National Congress Party. (See Barbados Labour Party.)

DEMOCRATIC LEAGUE. Organized in October 1924, the Democratic League was probably the most important of the pre-mass-party cadre groups in Barbados. It was founded by Charles Duncan O'Neale, a middle-class, black medical doctor, who used his organization to educate and uplift as much as to elect candidates. The league died with its founder in 1936, on the eve of the 1937 riots and the emergence of Labour politics (1938).

ELECTORS ASSOCIATION. The Electors Association, officially titled the Barbados Electors Association, dates back to 1941. It was an early label under which those opposed to the Barbados Progressive League and the Barbados Labour Party assembled to seek office. (See Barbados National Party and Barbados Electors Association.)

PEOPLE'S POLITICAL ALLIANCE (PPA). The People's Political Alliance was a coalition of the People's Democratic Movement, formed in 1975, and the People's Pressure Group, organized to halt perceived governmental restrictions on civil liberties by the Democratic Labour Party regime. The PPA only contested the 1956 election, in which all PPA candidates lost their filing fees.

PEOPLE'S PROGRESSIVE MOVEMENT (PPM). The People's Progressive Movement was a short-lived party that fielded candidates only in the election of 1956.

PROGRESSIVE CONSERVATIVE PARTY (PCP). The Progressive Conservative Party was renamed the Barbados National Party in 1958. (See Barbados National Party.)

WEST INDIAN NATIONAL CONGRESS PARTY (CP). The Congress Party, officially named the West Indian National Congress Party, was founded and led by W. A. Crawford after his split from the Barbados Progressive League (BPL) largely over personal differences between leadership principals. In its first contested election in 1944, the Congress Party won eight seats, which permitted formation of a coalition government with Grantley Adams and the BPL which also held eight seats. By the 1946 elections, the CP had dropped to third rank with seven seats to eight for the Electors Association and nine for the Barbados Labour Party (BLP).

The record number of seats for the progressive forces in 1944 and 1946 (sixteen of twenty-four) followed passage of a suffrage law in 1943 that reduced overall property qualifications for voting from £50 to £20 and granted women the right to vote. The conservative forces would never again control the Barbadian government, nor would the Congress Party again reach parity with the BLP. The Congress Party soon passed from the scene but not before it contributed significantly to the emergence of working-class identity and Barbadian democratization.

W. Marvin Will

BELIZE

Belize, a former British colony known until 1973 as British Honduras, obtained its independence in 1981. Like most of the English-speaking Caribbean, to which it has been drawn historically, Belize is a constitutional monarchy. Although independent, Belize retains a governor-general who represents the queen of England, the titular head of state. Located on the Caribbean coast, east of Guatemala and south of Mexico's Yucatan, Belize, with approximately 190,000 residents, is Central America's least populated nation. Its 8,867 square miles makes the country slightly larger than El Salvador. It is a nation of exceptional ethnic heterogeneity, with the two largest groups being creoles of West Indian heritage and mestizos, traditionally from Mexico and Guatemala.

The Spanish never occupied and settled the area of present-day Belize; instead, the country developed from the British pirate and smuggler settlements that grew up among the secluded bays of the uninhabited coast. By 1638 the British settlement had become a major provider of logwood and mahogany, but Britain, not wishing to offend Spain, did not accept it as a British colony until 1862.

From 1862 until 1936, Belize was an old-style Crown Colony, in which the governor held virtually unlimited power. Constitutional changes beginning in 1936 were limited, and Britain's slow pace led to considerable political discontent in the 1930s and 1940s. The decolonization movement began in earnest in 1950, shortly after the governor used his reserve powers to devalue the local currency. In September 1950, the People's United Party (PUP) became the country's first effective political party. In 1954 the PUP was victorious in the first election held under universal adult suffrage, and George Price became the acknowleged leader of the nationalist movement. By 1961 the British had agreed to the decolonization process for Belize. In January 1964, Belize received full internal self-government, with the governor responsible only for defense, foreign affairs, internal security, and the civil service. The country's significant constitutional changes, including independence, were achieved with the PUP at the helm and George Price as its leader. For thirty years, Price's major emphasis was on gaining independence for Belize.

While the PUP controlled the government and politics in pre-independence Belize, other parties and political factions did exist: most of them opposed the PUP's call for independence. Most of the opposition feared that independence would only increase the country's economic and territorial insecurity. The opposition has gone through various changes, starting in 1956 when several members broke away from the PUP to form the Honduras Independence Party (HIP). In 1958 the HIP merged with a smaller party to form the National Independence Party (NIP), which remained the dominant opposition party until the 1970s. Philip Goldson, the head of NIP and a former PUP stalwart, became the leader of the opposition, a position he held for almost twenty years. In 1969 younger leaders of the NIP split to form the People's Democratic Movement (PDM), with Dean Lindo as leader. In 1972 another group, made up mostly of pro-business elements within the NIP, formed itself into the Liberal Party, with Manuel Esquivel as one of its leaders. In September 1973, the NIP, the PDM, and the Liberal Party together formed the United Democratic Party (UDP), with Lindo soon to be its leader. In the 1974 general elections, the PUP polled only 51.3 percent of the vote, its lowest ever, and the UDP, with 38.1 percent of the vote, gained five seats, unprecedented for a party opposed to the PUP.

The 1979 election was the first time that eighteen-year-olds had the right to vote. The UDP's major campaign issue was that it was "time for a change"; it also demanded that independence be delayed for at least ten years. The PUP based its campaign on the attainment of independence and the increased development that would result. The election attracted a great deal of voter interest; 90.7 percent of the registered electors voted. The PUP won 51.8 percent of the votes and thirteen seats; the UDP gained five seats with 46.8 percent of the vote, the highest ever gained by a single opposition party. Theodore Aranda was elected as party leader and leader of the opposition; however, Aranda was never really accepted by the party as leader, and his stormy tenure came to an end in 1983, when he resigned from the party. Shortly thereafter, in a hotly contested election, Esquivel defeated Goldson to become the party leader. In the next two years, Esquivel proceeded to cement the organization of the party and to prepare for the elections expected in 1984.

The 1980s witnessed the full development of the two-party system in Belize. Voters changed governments twice, in 1984 and again in 1989, and did so peacefully. The 1980s began with Belize's being granted its independence from Great Britain. After more than seventeen years as a self-governing colony, Belize gained its independence on 21 September 1981. Amid the celebration and the excitement, Belize prepared to face the greatest challenge to its nationhood— neighboring Guatemala's claim to the territory. Because the territorial dispute has never been settled, Guatemala does not recognize Belize's sovereignty.

The framework for a settlement of the dispute was signed by Britain and Guatemala, with Belize signing as a witness, on 11 March 1981, but discussions to flesh out the document, known as the Heads of Agreement, broke down in the summer of 1981. Led by the opposition UDP and the Public Service Union

(PSU), Belizeans denounced the agreement, charging that its provisions violated the territorial integrity of the country. When the opposition's demands for a referendum on the agreement were not accepted by the government, riots broke out throughout the country and the PSU engaged in paralyzing strikes. The British governor declared a state of emergency on 2 April 1981 and sent out local and British troops to end the disturbance. Once calm returned, the opposition continued to campaign against the Heads of Agreement and against independence "without a suitable defense guarantee."

By 1981, through lobbying efforts of the Price government, international support for the independence of Belize was virtually unanimous. Because of such support from the international community and with the consent of the British government, Price decided in July 1981 to proceed to independence and to continue efforts to settle the dispute with Guatemala. The British agreed to continue to defend the country against a possible Guatemalan incursion by keeping 1,600 British troops in Belize for "an appropriate period" and to provide more intensive training for the Belize Defense Force. This defense guarantee effectively foreclosed the opposition's position against independence; however, the opposition refused to be a party to independence negotiations with Britain.

On 14 December 1984, in the first general elections held since independence, Belizean voters swept the PUP from office. Perhaps more significant, Price, the "father of the country," lost his parliamentary seat. Besides Prime Minister Price, five other ministers lost their seats. The UDP won twenty-one of the twenty-eight seats in the House. The PUP took the remaining seven seats. The UDP, led by Esquivel, ran well in every region of the country, and in rural (the traditional stronghold of the PUP) as well as in urban areas.

Several factors accounted for the PUP defeat in 1984. The first factor was the split within the PUP between the conservative element, which was strongly pro–United States, and the left wing, which was in favor of a more broadly based economic and foreign policy. Price walked a tightrope between the two elements for several years, but after the PUP lost all nine seats of the Belize City Council to the UDP in the December 1983 elections, the conflict escalated and led to public squabbling. The infighting was the target of UDP criticism throughout the campaign.

The second factor was the state of the economy. During the first years of independence, Belize faced a weakening economy, largely because of lower prices for export commodities and insufficient investment capital. Sugar, the mainstay of the economy since the 1970s, suffered from a shrinking market and low prices. Cash-flow problems were severe at times, resulting in late salary payments to civil servants and late crop payments to small farmers. During the 1984 campaign, the UDP promised to diversify the economy by reducing the nation's dependence on sugar exports and by promoting foreign investments more aggressively.

The expansion of the House of Representatives from eighteen to twenty-eight seats was the third major factor in the election. Price stunned the UDP by changing the boundaries of all but one of the electoral constituencies and adding ten new ones just weeks before the general elections. Confusion was rampant. The UDP called it gerrymandering, and the charges resulted in a groundswell against the PUP.

Perhaps the major reason for the PUP's defeat was that the party had lost its reason for being. For thirty years, the PUP had fought for independence. The euphoria of independence soon evaporated, and the stagnating economy made it very difficult for the governing party to meet the pent-up expectations of its citizens. The changing political fortunes were reflected in the results of the 1981 and 1983 Belize City Council elections. In December 1981, the PUP wrested control of the council away from the opposition for the first time in twenty years. But the December 1983 City Council elections resulted in a total rout of the PUP, and all nine seats went to the UDP. It was the worst defeat the PUP had ever suffered. The PUP was unable to regain voter confidence and thus ended up losing, for the first time, a general election.

The UDP, under the leadership of Prime Minister Esquivel, proclaimed itself the party of free enterprise and moved away from the PUP's mixed economy policy. To stimulate economic growth and increase employment, the new government welcomed foreign investment and accorded high priority to agriculture, agro-industries, and tourism. The UDP policy was tested in October 1985, when the government facilitated the sale of more than 600,000 acres in northern Belize (one-eighth the land area of the country) to private investors in the United States. Part of the land was to be used by Coca-Cola's subsidiary, Minute Maid, to develop a citrus nursery and processing plant. However, due to pressure from U.S. citrus growers and international environmentalists, Coca-Cola decided not to go forward with its project, and no plans have been announced for the remainder of the land.

During their first two years in office, the UDP government succeeded in turning around the ailing economy by maintaining strict fiscal discipline in the public sector, achieving a high level of infrastructural development, and providing a climate of economic stability in order to encourage increased foreign and domestic private sector investment. Much of this success stemmed from the close relationship established between the Esquivel government and the United States. Between 1981 and 1987, the U.S. government provided U.S. $60 million in aid to Belize; this aid outstripped that from all other sources. In 1985 the United States's $14.5 million balance-of-payments support loan, which complemented a U.S. $7 million International Monetary Fund (IMF) standby credit, was the predominant factor in pulling Belize out of foreign debt arrears and improving the country's short-term financial situation. In less than two years, the IMF ended its standby program, applauding Belize for its successful compliance with IMF demands. During the 1980s, the U.S. strategy in Belize was designed to create a stable ally in a country with one foot in Central America and one foot in the Caribbean, and the Esquivel government was more than willing to assume that role.

For the UDP, as it had been for the PUP, the most important foreign policy issue remained its troubling relationship with Guatemala. The coming to power in 1986 of a civilian administration in Guatemala, after almost thirty years of military rule, did much to ease the tensions. Guatemala's Vinicio Cerezo proved to be more accommodating and more conciliatory in his statements than had his military predecessors. The UDP, now in power, was also more interested in finding a solution to the dispute. Thus, in May 1988, the Belize government initialed a joint accord with Guatemala to create a Belize–Guatemala permanent commission, with Britain as observer, to work out a compromise to the conflict. Both countries have agreed to present any treaty proposal to the voters before signing it into law. The commission has met several times, and it appears that progress is being made. Guatemala also consented to Belize's becoming a member of the Organization of American States (OAS) in December 1990.

After its defeat in the 1984 general elections, the PUP worked hard to reorganize itself as a party. The results of its efforts were apparent when, in the town board elections held in March 1988, the PUP gained control of four of the seven town boards, winning twenty-nine seats to the governing UDP's twenty seats. The PUP's confidence as a party was also bolstered by a growing factionalism in the UDP. Esquivel attempted to consolidate his power at the May 1988 UDP national convention by supporting Energy Minister Derek Aikman for chairmanship of the party against the incumbent, Agriculture Minister Lindo, a former leader of the party. After the PUP settled into its role as opposition, its attacks on the government were measured but constant. The PUP criticized the government for its lenient attitude toward foreign business interests, charging that the government had sharply increased the country's indebtedness by borrowing abroad to help private sector investment. The PUP also criticized the government's foreign policy, which it said tilted too heavily toward a pro–U.S. stance, rather than a nonalignment stance.

These charges, coupled with the PUP's effective organizing nationwide, helped the PUP to win a surprise victory in the September 1989 general elections. In a neck-and-neck race, with a 73-percent voter turnout, the PUP won fifteen seats (50.02 percent of the vote) to the UDP's thirteen seats (48.2 percent of the vote), giving George Price a political comeback. The election results were a surprise because most political analysts thought that the strength of the economy was enough for the UDP to win again. In fact, Esquivel had called the elections several months earlier than expected to take advantage of the seasonal upswing in the economy. However, the UDP was not able to counter the PUP's charge that the party leadership had lost touch with the people and had become "too arrogant."

The PUP also charged that the economy was too fast paced and too open. The PUP promised to put "Belizeans first" and continued its historic theme of being the party of the impoverished and the dispossessed. Immediately after the elections, the PUP began to change the style of government, making it more accessible and down to earth, and to slow the pace of development. In the

Belize City Council elections held in December 1989, the PUP won all nine seats.

While the UDP lost the 1989 general elections, Esquivel kept his seat in the House. For the first time in its history, Belize has a former head of government on the opposition side of the House. With so many former ministers in opposition, also a first for Belize, the level of debate in the House should be much improved. The close elections of 1989 seem to ensure that compromises will have to be worked out and that a greater degree of cooperation will be necessary for the passage of legislation. The 1989 elections clearly suggest that the two-party system in Belize is intact.

Bibliography

Belize Independence Secretariat. *The Road to Independence.* Government of Belize, Belmopan, Belize, September 1981.

Belize Today: A Society in Transformation. Sunshine Books, Belize City, 1984.

Belizeans First with the People's United Party, 1989–1994. PUP Manifesto '89. People's United Party, Belize City, 1989.

O. Nigel Bolland. *Belize, a New Nation in Central America.* Westview Press, Boulder, Colo., 1986.

Government and People Building a Better Belize. UDP Manifesto '89. United Democratic Party, Belize City, 1989.

C. H. Grant. *The Making of Modern Belize: Politics, Society and British Colonialism in Central America.* Cambridge University Press, Cambridge, 1976.

A History of Belize: Nation in the Making. Sunshine Books, Belize City, 1983.

Assad Shoman. *Party Politics in Belize, 1950–1986.* Cubola Productions, Belize, 1987.

———. "The Birth of the Nationalist Movement in Belize, 1950–54." *Journal of Belizean Affairs* 2, December 1973, pp. 3–40.

Tony Thorndike. "Belizean Political Parties: The Independence Crisis and After." *Journal of Commonwealth and Comparative Politics* 21, 2, 1983, pp. 195–211.

Alma H. Young. "Belize," in *Latin America and Caribbean Contemporary Record*, vols. 1–8. Holmes and Meier, New York, 1983–1990.

Alma H. Young and Dennis H. Young. "The Impact of the Anglo-Guatemalan Dispute on the Internal Politics of Belize." *Latin American Perspectives* 15, 2, Spring 1988, pp. 6–30.

Political Parties—Active

BELIZE POPULAR PARTY (BPP). The BPP was formed in 1988 by two members of the PUP's right wing, Fred Hunter and Louis Sylvestre, who had resigned, charging that the party had become too leftist in orientation. The party was active in the San Pedro district in northern Belize during the 1988 town board elections and in the 1989 general election, but neither of its candidates won. The party is now all but moribund.

PEOPLE'S UNITED PARTY (PUP). The PUP has been the dominant party in Belizean politics since its establishment in September 1950. All other parties established since then have been organized as opponents of the PUP.

The PUP led the fight for self-government in Belize. Against open opposition from the governor, the PUP won the 1954 general election and became members of the executive council. By that time, George Price had become the acknowledged leader of the PUP and of the nationalist movement. In the late 1950s, the PUP suffered two splits, both times over the question of what the relationship of Belize should be to Guatemala and to Central America. In time, those who split the party in the 1950s would go on to form the National Independence Party, the major source of opposition to the PUP during the nationalist era.

The PUP kept up constant pressure for changes in the constitution. These culminated in 1964 with the establishment of full internal self-government. The final move to independence was held up for seventeen years by continuing claims of Guatemala to Belize and fear of a Guatemalan invasion if British troops were removed following independence. Independence was finally achieved in September 1981 after the PUP government had won international support for its sovereignty and after Great Britain agreed to keep 1,600 troops in independent Belize for an unspecified period of time as guarantors of the country's independence.

The ideology of the PUP has never been very precise, except for its commitment to independence. Although basically social-democratic in practice, the PUP has been open to those of the left—and thus it has proclaimed the importance of a mixed economy and economic democracy—as well as to those of the right. In its 1979 manifesto, for instance, the party cautioned against both unbridled communism and unbridled capitalism.

Once independence was achieved in 1981, the party had a difficult time governing the country. The stagnating economy made it very hard for the governing party to meet the pent-up expectations of its citizens. The lack of a coherent ideology led to public disputes among the three wings of the party— left, center, and right. By the time of the 1984 general elections, the party was too fractured to counter the charge made by the United Democratic Party (UDP) that the country needed a change. For the first time in PUP history, the party lost a general election, winning only seven seats to the UDP's twenty-one seats. Price lost his seat, as did five other ministers.

During the late 1980s, the base of the party moved steadily toward the center, and its right and left wings weakened or broke away. The right wing, led by Louis Sylvestre and Fred Hunter, resigned from the party in 1984 and subsequently formed the now all but moribund Belize Popular Party. One of the leaders of the left wing, Assad Shoman, left the party shortly before the 1984 elections to do grassroots education through the Society for the Promotion of Education and Research (SPEAR). In 1988 the PUP incorporated Theodore Aranda's center-right Christian Democratic Party, which represented the southern district of Stann Creek, as well as Alejandro Vernon's Toledo Popular Party, which represented the southern district of Toledo.

During its period in opposition, Price worked hard to unify disparate regional and ideological factions and to organize the party nationwide. In the National Assembly, the PUP challenged the UDP government on a number of significant issues, always appealing to nationalist sentiments. When the UDP called elections in September 1989, the PUP was ready. Winning by a swing vote of about 5 percent, the PUP got fifteen seats to the UDP's thirteen seats. Back in office, the PUP appears to be adhering to its faith in a mixed economy as opposed to the free-market principles praised by the UDP. The PUP's promise to put "Belizeans first" will be challenged as never before by the strong parliamentary opposition—a situation that places a premium on party unity. For this reason, every elected PUP representative was given a role in a ministry, as either a full minister or a deputy minister.

UNITED DEMOCRATIC PARTY (UDP). The UDP became the major opposition party in 1973, when it was formed by a merger of the National Independence Party, the People's Democratic Movement, and the Liberal Party. It has proven to be the most successful of any opposition party in Belizean history. It had its first victory in 1974, when it captured control of the Belize City Council, a victory repeated three years later. In the 1974 general elections, it won five of the eighteen seats in the House of Representatives. It won the same number of seats in 1979; however, the UDP had been expected to win that national election.

Its defeat in 1979 brought about a considerable shakeup in the UDP leadership. Among those defeated in the 1974 election was Dean Lindo, the party leader. Theodore Aranda, a U.S.–educated man of Garifuna descent, replaced Lindo as party leader. However, the party continued to be plagued by internal disputes, weak support outside Belize City, and the failure to back the independence movement. Aranda resigned from the party in 1983, amid charges of arrogance and incompetence. In a hotly contested election, Manuel Esquivel defeated Philip Goldson to become party leader. Esquivel had been party chairman since 1976, and in 1979 he had been appointed to the Senate. In the next two years, Esquivel proceeded to cement the organization of the party and to prepare for the elections expected in 1984.

No longer simply the opposition to the People's United Party (PUP), the UDP under Esquivel offered voters a platform based on free enterprise, with significant support from the business community. The voters chose the UDP, which won the 1984 elections with 53.4 percent of the vote and twenty-one of the twenty-eight seats in the House. The UDP gave Belizeans a more conservative government and one tied more closely to Washington, D.C. As prime minister, Esquivel saw the government's main task as that of rescuing the economy, and he set about attracting foreign investment, much of it from the United States.

In preparation for the 1989 elections, the UDP carried out a primary election contest that badly divided the party among its political factions. When Esquivel called for a snap election in September 1989, many observers expected the UDP to win based on the country's positive economic performance. However, the party was unable to counter the PUP's charges that the UDP had grown too arrogant and had left the country too open to foreign influences. The UDP narrowly lost to the PUP, winning thirteen seats to the PUP's fifteen. Thus the UDP once again assumed its old role as the opposition party.

Political Parties—Historical

CHRISTIAN DEMOCRATIC PARTY (CDP). The CDP was formed in 1958, when Nicholas Pollard, the veteran trade union leader, was expelled from the People's United Party. After unsuccessfully contesting the 1961 general elections, the CDP disappeared through merger with the National Independence Party.

CHRISTIAN DEMOCRATIC PARTY (CDP). The second CDP was formed in 1983 shortly after Theodore Aranda resigned from the United Democratic Party. Mainly a regional party, Aranda established it in his southern district of Stann Creek. In 1988 the CDP merged with the PUP in preparation for the 1989 general elections. (Aranda's CDP had no connection to Nicholas Pollard's CDP of the 1960s.)

COROZAL UNITED FRONT (CUF). This regional party was established in the northern region of Corozal in 1973 after the People's United Party (PUP) representative resigned from the party amid allegations that the region's interests were being ignored by PUP. After unsuccessfully contesting the 1974 general elections, the party disappeared.

COROZAL UNITED PARTY (CUP). This regional party was formed by People's United Party (PUP) dissidents in 1956. The party joined forces with the PUP in the 1957 elections and did not survive as a separate party after that.

DEMOCRATIC PARTY (DP). The first party organized to oppose the People's United Party (PUP), it disappeared with the creation of the National Party, the PUP's major opponent in the early 1950s.

HONDURAS INDEPENDENCE PARTY (HIP). The HIP was established in 1956, when two of the leading founders of the People's United Party broke with George Price over his opposition to Belize's participating in the proposed West Indian Federation. The HIP unsuccessfully contested the 1957 general elections, and shortly afterward it merged with the National Party to form the National Independence Party.

LIBERAL PARTY. The Liberal Party was established in 1970 by a group of young men with close ties to the Chamber of Commerce. The party contested the 1970 Belize City Council elections as part of a coalition opposed to the People's United Party (PUP), but the coalition was badly beaten by the PUP. The Liberal Party merged in 1973 with the National Independence Party and the People's Democratic Movement to form the United Democratic Party.

NATIONAL INDEPENDENCE PARTY (NIP). The NIP was formed by a merger of the National Party and the Honduras Independence Party in mid-1958, and, for most of its existence, it was headed by Philip Goldson, a former stalwart of the People's United Party. After winning two seats in the 1965 elections, the NIP chose Goldson as the leader of the opposition, a position he held for many years. Throughout the 1960s, the NIP was the major opposition party. In 1973 the NIP joined with the People's Democratic Movement and the Liberal Party to form the United Democratic Party.

NATIONAL PARTY (NP). The National Party was organized in 1951, with the encouragement of the British colonial authorities, to confront the rising nationalist movement represented by the People's United Party (PUP). The NP was the first opposition party to denounce the PUP for having pro-Guatemala sympathies. Except for the 1952 Belize City Council elections, the party was not very successful at the polls, and by mid-1958 it had merged with the Honduras Independence Party to form the National Independence Party.

PEOPLE'S DEMOCRATIC MOVEMENT (PDM). The PDM was established in 1969 as a result of a split in the National Independence Party (NIP) led by several young leaders who felt that the NIP concentrated too exclusively on opposition to the PUP and on hostility toward Guatemala. Led by Dean Lindo, the party competed unsuccessfully at the polls. In 1973 the PDM merged with the Liberal Party and the NIP to form the United Democratic Party.

PEOPLE'S GROUP. The People's Group was a loosely organized party, composed largely of business and professional men, which functioned in the 1930s. It can be seen as a precursor of the nationalist movement of the 1950s.

POLITICAL ACTION COMMITTEE (PAC). The PAC, established in 1968 under the leadership of three young men recently returned from British universities, denounced the growing cultural and economic domination of the country by U.S. interests. In late 1969, the PAC merged with the United Black Association for Development to form the Revolitical Action Movement. This group disbanded shortly thereafter when two of the young men, Said Musa and Assad Shoman, left to join the PUP; by the mid-1970s, they were members of George Price's cabinet.

PROGRESSIVE PARTY. One of the precursors in the 1930s and 1940s of the Belizean nationalist movement, the party took a lead in the campaign in the early 1930s for the introduction of elected members in the legislative council, which was successful in 1935. It is unclear when the Progressive Party disappeared, but it certainly did not survive after the People's United Party was formed in 1950.

REVOLITICAL ACTION MOVEMENT (RAM). The RAM was formed in 1969 as the result of the merger between the Political Action Committee and the United Black Association for Development. The leaders of the RAM expressed total dissatisfaction with the decolonization process and called on Belizeans to develop their own political system. The party was disbanded four months later when two of its leaders, Said Musa and Assad Shoman, joined the People's United Party.

TOLEDO POPULAR PARTY (TPP). *See* Toledo Progressive Party.

TOLEDO PROGRESSIVE PARTY (TPP). The TPP, a regional party in the southern district of Toledo, was formed in the early 1970s under the leadership of Alejandro Vernon, after his expulsion from the People's United Party (PUP). Its major distinction in the 1970s was that it was the only party in the country that advocated annexation to Guatemala. Vernon denied charges that he was an agent of Guatemala. The party did very poorly in the elections it contested in the late 1970s. Reconstituted in the early 1980s as the Toledo Popular Party, Vernon downplayed his sympathies for Guatemala and highlighted the need for the southern district to be more fully integrated into the nation. In preparation for the 1989 general elections, the TPP merged with the PUP.

UNITED BLACK ASSOCIATION FOR DEVELOPMENT (UBAD). The UBAD, organized in 1968, began as a social and cultural organization modelled loosely on the black power movement in the United States. The chief figure in the UBAD was Evan X Hyde, who had recently returned from completing his studies at Dartmouth College. By 1969 the UBAD had become more overtly political, and it merged with the Political Action Committee to form the Revolitical Action Movement in October. When four months later the RAM was disbanded, the UBAD was reconstituted and Hyde ran unsuccessfully in municipal elections in 1970 and in general elections in 1974. Shortly thereafter, the UBAD disbanded as a political party. Since then, Hyde has been the publisher and editor of Belize's only "independent" newspaper.

Alma H. Young

BERMUDA

Bermuda is a small cluster of subtropical islands in the Atlantic Ocean off the coast of North Carolina. With a land area of some nineteen square miles, the almost totally tourist-based economy supports a population of 60,000, making the island one of the most densely populated countries in the hemisphere. Bermuda enjoys one of the highest per capita incomes in the world at U.S.$23,000.

Similar to other British possessions, the executive branch of government is composed of the British monarch, the appointed governor and deputy governor, the elected premier and deputy premier, and the elected Executive Council, which acts as a cabinet. The legislative branch includes a bicameral parliament composed of an appointed upper house or Senate and a forty-member lower house or House of Assembly, elected by universal adult suffrage. Queen Elizabeth II, the head of state, is represented in Bermuda by Governor Sir Desmond Langley (since 1988). The head of government is Premier John William David Swan who led the United Bermuda Party (UBP) to victory in both the 1985 and 1989 elections. In fact, since the establishment of a new constitution in 1968 and under Swan's predecessors, the UBP has exercised the role of governing party.

In winning the 1968 elections, the UBP, a business-oriented and centrist party, immediately confronted the pressing political problem of racial tension between the small white elite and the majority black population. The confrontation was spawned by the pan-Caribbean black power movement that appealed to the black masses in what was at the time a decidedly white-dominated colonial polity. There were race riots in 1972, during which time the governor was assassinated, and again in 1977, when the British declared a state of emergency and sent troops to the island. In the 1976 elections, the UBP maintained power but lost ground to the pro-independence, democratic-socialist Progressive Labour Party (PLP).

Although the UBP won the 1980 elections by a small majority, it went on to experience an upswing in electoral fortunes by mid-1980. David Gibbons, who had held the positions of premier and UBP chief of party since 1976, relinquished both posts to John Swan in 1982, reacting to the formation of the National Liberal Party (NLP) in the same year by dissident members of the business community. An early election was held in 1985, and Swan led the UBP to a decisive victory, winning thirty-one seats to seven for the PLP and two for the NLP. In the election of 1989, the UBP fell back to twenty-three seats; the PLP gained fifteen, but the NLP dropped to one. An independent won the remaining seat in 1989.

At present, there is no political independence movement, as the main parties see their fortunes tied to continuing British foreign aid. The economy, which is tourist driven, remains the major policy issue, with rival political parties differing little in their philosophies.

Bibliography

Robert J. Alexander. "Bermuda," in Robert J. Alexander, ed., *Political Parties of the Americas*. Greenwood Press, Westport, Conn. 1982.

Central Intelligence Agency. *The World Factbook, 1990.* Central Intelligence Agency, Washington, D.C., 1990.

Frank Manning. *Bermudian Politics in Transition: Race, Voting and Public Opinion.* Island Press, Hamilton, 1978.

————. *Black Clubs in Bermuda: The Ethnography of a Play World.* Cornell University Press, Ithaca, N.Y., 1974.

Political Parties

NATIONAL LIBERAL PARTY (NLP). The NLP was formed in 1982 under the leadership of Gilbert Darrell, who represented business interests dissatisfied with the programs of the dominant United Bermuda Party. It captured two seats in the forty-member Assembly in 1985 but achieved only one seat four years later.

PROGRESSIVE LABOUR PARTY (PLP). Organized in 1963, the PLP is Bermuda's oldest active political party. It has never served as the governing party, but since its founding it has been the principal opposition party. From its beginning, it has been an overwhelmingly black party, although its position on many social issues moderated during the 1980s, reflecting the improved status of Bermuda's black majority, and it has all but abandoned its former stand in favor of independence. Under the leadership of Frederick Wade, its number of seats in the House of Assembly has fluctuated from a high of eighteen in 1980 to a low of seven in 1985, with a strong recovery in 1989 to fifteen.

UNITED BERMUDA PARTY (UBP). Established in 1964, as a direct response to the formation of the Progressive Labour Party (PLP), the leadership of the

UBP has come from the traditional aristocratic politicians. However, under the astute guidance of its founder Sir Henry "Jack" Tucker, the UBP largely stole the thunder of the PLP and achieved the support of a large portion of black voters by promoting desegregation, free secondary education, and universal adult suffrage. These achievements, plus the implementation of important social programs, have continued during the 1980s under party leader and Premier John William David Swan, who led the UBP to a thirty-one-seat majority in 1985. More difficult economic times caused the UBP's total to decline in the 1989 election, when the party captured only twenty-three seats.

Gary Brana-Shute
Rosemary Brana-Shute

BOLIVIA

In Bolivia's more than 165 years of independence, political parties have seldom exerted crucial influence over political events. More often, parties have served as instruments for social classes or regional interests whose fortunes rose and fell in accord with economic and international developments. Perhaps paradoxically, few Bolivian parties have been able to establish stable public followings, which would be loyal to party programs through good political times and bad. Bolivian party life did not basically break with these well-established patterns during the decade of the 1980s, although certain significant changes in the parties and in the party system should be noted.

Sometimes periods occur in public life when one part of the political spectrum is naturally favored, and adherents of other viewpoints can at most take defensive measures. In Bolivia, the 1980s were almost symmetrically divided between a Moment of the Left (1980–1985) and a Moment of the Right (1985–1990). At the start of the decade, the murderousness and corruption of General Luis García Meza's dictatorship (1980–1981) marked the exhaustion (for the time being) of the military as a hegemonic conservative force in national politics. In 1982 a transitional military government belatedly inaugurated the overwhelming winner of the 1980 presidential election, Hernán Siles Zuazo, at the head of a left-populist alliance, the Democratic and Popular Union (UDP).

Almost immediately, however, the UDP was undermined by its inability to discipline its own supporters or to command a congressional majority, while under pressure from the worst depression since the 1930s. Bolivia's gross domestic product per capita shrank by more than 30 percent during the 1980s, and the UDP followed at best a meandering policy course in seeking to confront the nation's growing domestic improverishment and international bankruptcy. Inflation reduced the Bolivian peso's value from 250 to the dollar to nearly one million to the dollar during the UDP's tenure, and the Bolivian state showed itself to be woefully weak in the face of strikes, lockouts, and constant demonstrations.

In the 1985 presidential election, President Siles's party polled less than 5 percent of the vote, and a more conservative coalition of the Nationalist Rev-olutionary Movement (MNR) and the Nationalist Democratic Action (ADN) gained control of the presidency and a congressional majority. President Víctor Paz Estenssoro (elected for the fourth time in his career) almost immediately issued the strongly deflationary Decree 21060, which sought to cut employment by the state, free most prices from government controls, and end the system of artificial exchange rates with the dollar. Within a year, Bolivia had one of Latin America's most stable currencies. The politics, if not the economics, of this new economic policy (NPE) were bolstered by the 1985 drop of over 60 percent in the international price of tin, until then Bolivia's principal export commodity. More than 75 percent of the miners employed by the state mining corporation (COMIBOL) were discharged, effectively breaking the power of the nation's strongest, most militant labor union. The Paz Estenssoro administration also marked a historic retreat by the state from many forms of economic intervention and provision of social services, which had been staples of government policy since the National Revolution of 1952.

It has often been said that the Bolivian party system includes the expression of all possible political ideologies, from Trotskyism and Maoism to pro-Franco falangism. This array of parties tried to adapt, usually in predictable ways, to the sharply changing political winds of the 1980s. Parties with some centrist elements sought to appear progressive in the decade's first half and then tried to move to the right after 1985. One fast-growing party, the Movement of the Revolutionary Left (MIR), managed to ally itself first with Siles in 1982 and then with right-wing General Hugo Banzer Suárez in 1989 and tried to capture the presidency in 1989. While the political right was definitely in the ascendant after 1985, the nation's continuing poverty and backwardness offer important potential advantages to left-wing parties if they are well led and coherent in their ideas.

Little was achieved in the 1980s to correct the prevailing isolation of Bolivian parties and politicians from the concerns of (much less control by) the nation's citizenry. In part, this failure is traceable to the marginal national role now assigned to the peasantry, to the caste-like interests of the legal and economic elite, and to the near impossibility of responding to popular needs in South America's poorest nation. Efforts were made with limited success after 1980 to reduce the participation of mini-parties in presidential races, and in recent elections there has been a drift toward a system of three major parties—ADN, MIR, and MNR—plus fringe contenders. However, politicians have thus far been unwilling to end the conspicuous indirectness of presidential selection. The constitution requires an absolute majority for popular election, failing which the newly elected Congress selects the president. The most squalid and cynical backroom negotiations are encouraged by this system, which in 1985 gave the presidency to the second most popular candidate, and in 1989 to the third. A simple constitutional reform to create a runoff election would almost certainly encourage centrist concentration among Bolivian parties, while perhaps bolstering public confidence in political leadership and reversing a 9 percent decline in voting participation between 1985 and 1989.

Bibliography

Robert J. Alexander, ed. *Political Parties of the Americas: Canada, Latin America, and the West Indies*. Greenwood Press, Westport, Conn., 1982.

James Dunkerley. "Political Transition and Economic Stabilisation: Bolivia, 1982–1989," University of London Institute of Latin American Studies *Research Papers*, no. 22 London, 1990.

Eduardo Gamarra. "Mass Politics and Elite Arrangements: Elections and Democracy in Bolivia," in Jerry Ladman and Juan Antonio Morales. eds., *Bolivia after Hyperinflation*. Arizona State University Center for Latin American Studies, Tempe, 1991.

Kevin Healy. "The Rural Development Role of the Bolivian Peasant *Sindicatos* in the New Democratic Order." Paper presented at the Twelfth International Congress of the Latin American Studies Association, Albuquerque, N.M., April 1985.

Herbert S. Klein. *Bolivia: The Evolution of a Multi-Ethnic Society*. Oxford University Press, New York, 1982.

Jerry Ladman, ed. *Modern Day Bolivia: Legacy of the Revolution and Prospects for the Future*. Arizona State University Center for Latin American Studies, Tempe, 1982.

James M. Malloy and Eduardo Gamarra. *Revolution and Reaction: Bolivia 1964–1985*. Transaction Books, New Brunswick, N.J., 1988.

Political Parties—Active

ACCIÓN DEMOCRÁTICA NACIONALISTA. *See* NATIONALIST DEMOCRATIC ACTION.

AUTHENTIC REVOLUTIONARY PARTY (PARTIDO REVOLUCIONARIO AUTÉNTICO—PRA). This splinter party from the Nationalist Revolutionary Movement (MNR) has essentially rejoined its parent. In the 1989 election, PRA leader Walter Guevara Arze was the candidate for vice president on the MNR ticket.

BOLIVIAN COMMUNIST PARTY (PARTIDO COMUNISTA BOLIVIANO—PCB). During the 1980s, this Moscow-line Communist party went from its only taste of high office to near breakdown. As a member of the 1982–1985 ruling coalition known as the Democratic and Popular Union (Unión Democrática y Popular, or UDP), the PCB held several cabinet posts. However, when labor unions, which represented the party's core constituents, opposed the UDP's efforts at fiscal austerity, the PCB suffered internal splits and left the ruling coalition. In 1989, the PCB backed the United Left (Izquiera Unida, or IU) ticket, which placed a poor fifth in the presidential election.

BOLIVIAN SOCIALIST FALANGE (FALANGE SOCIALISTA BOLI-VIANA—FSB). Although this was the first conservative party in Bolivia to show itself willing to adapt to the era of mass political participation after 1952, the FSB was driven from the field during the 1980s by the competition of the Nationalist Democratic Action (ADN). In 1985 its candidate, David Añez Pedraza, captured only 1.2 percent of the national vote, and the party did not field a candidate or join a coalition in 1989.

CHRISTIAN DEMOCRATIC PARTY (PARTIDO DE LA DEMOCRACIA CRISTIANA—PDC). This very small party was rooted in the continent-wide vogue for Christian democracy in the 1960s, and its reformism has come to represent a conservative political position in Bolivia. The PDC survives primarily to bolster the electioneering of stronger forces which have a chance of capturing congressional seats or the presidency. In 1983–1984, the PDC held cabinet posts in the Democratic and Popular Union Coalition administration. In 1985 PDC candidate Luis Ossio Sanjinés took 1.4 percent of the presidential vote, and in 1989 the PDC backed the candidacy of General Hugo Banzer Suárez, of the Nationalist Democratic Action (ADN). The Christian Democrats won an unexpected dividend in the latter year: The complex postelection negotiations leading to the ADN's support of Jaime Paz Zamora (of the Movement of the Revolutionary Left) as president included the choice of Ossio Sanjinés for the position of vice president.

CONCIENCIA DE PATRIA. See CONSCIENCE OF THE FATHERLAND.

CONSCIENCE OF THE FATHERLAND (CONCIENCIA DE PATRIA—CONDEPA). This party, founded in the late 1980s, centered in La Paz, has a highly eclectic ideological stance. It combines elements of traditional conservatism, populism, and even leftist sentiments, and it includes a group of leaders with a similar patchwork of previous experience in other parties. The central goal of the party might be described as aggressive constituent service, which was initially carried out via television by the party's founder and dominant personality, Carlos Palenque. During the early and mid-1980s, this entrepreneur and former folksinger became a sort of electronic godfather to paceños through his television and radio stations, earning the affectionate nickname of compadre by offering short-term individual solutions to the numberless problems of urban marginals.

CONDEPA carried the city of La Paz easily in 1989, giving the party a role in the postelection elite bargaining over the presidency. If the party can extend its appeal beyond the respectable 11 percent (fourth place) it garnered nationwide in 1989, it will become a significant new populist force, taking advantage of the public disillusionment with traditional parties and politicians.

DEMOCRATIC AND POPULAR UNION (UNIÓN DEMOCRÁTICA Y POPULAR—UDP). Not a political party as defined, the UDP was the ruling coalition of President Hernán Siles Suazo, 1982 to 1985. It was comprised of the Nationalist Revolutionary Movement of the Left, the Movement of the Revolutionary Left, and the Bolivian Communist Party.

FALANGE SOCIALISTA BOLIVIANA. See BOLIVIAN SOCIALIST FALANGE.

MIR-BOLIVIA LIBRE. See MIR-FREE BOLIVIA.

MIR-FREE BOLIVIA (MIR-BOLIVIA LIBRE—MBL). This party, led by Antonio Araníbar Quiroga, which seceded from the Movement of the Revolutionary Left, seeks to express the original left-wing thrust of that party. By 1989 the MBL was able to lead the United Left (IU) coalition in presidential voting, which won 7.2 percent of the national tally. The IU lost credibility in the public mind by seeking to gather support among coca growers in the Chapare region near Cochabamba.

MOVEMENT OF THE REVOLUTIONARY LEFT (MOVIMIENTO DE LA IZQUIERDA REVOLUCIONARIA—MIR). At its inception in 1970, the MIR was a youth-oriented populist party of the left, created by dissident members from the Christian Democratic Party. During the 1980s, the MIR enjoyed a successful if somewhat opportunistic odyssey. It formed part of President Hernán Siles Zuazo's leftist Democratic and Popular Union coalition, and MIR leader Jaime Paz Zamora served as the nation's vice president. In late 1984, however, Paz Zamora resigned as vice president, and the MIR withdrew from the UDP; it had been critical of President Siles's occasional concessions to the International Monetary Fund's demands for policies of fiscal austerity. The party placed third in the 1985 elections, with 8.9 percent of the vote. During the 1985–1989 presidency of Víctor Paz Estenssoro, the MIR carved a niche for itself as a critic of government policy from the left, while, at the same time, it distanced itself from the UDP's record of chaotic administration.

In the 1989 election campaign, however, the MIR did not take fundamental issue with the policy of draconian free-market stabilization initiated under Decree 21060 of 1985. Thus adroitly positioned, the MIR once again took third place in the 1989 popular voting for president, more than doubling its tally to 19.6 percent. In the postelection maneuvering that took place in Congress, Paz Zamora benefitted from the poor judgment of Gonzalo Sánchez de Lozada, the candidate of the Nationalist Revolutionary Movement, who had won the popular contest by a 5,000-vote margin. Sánchez de Lozada had so alienated the backers of the Nationalist Democratic Action (ADN) candidate Hugo Banzer Suárez that they threw their support to the MIR candidate in Congress, and Paz Zamora was elected president. In this alliance, however, the MIR received fewer and less powerful cabinet positions than the ADN did, and Banzer enjoyed potentially greater practical influence than Paz Zamora. The twists and turns of the party's record during the decade encouraged a number of defections by members dedicated to socialist priorities, most significantly from the MIR-Free Bolivia (MIR-Bolivia Libre, or MBL).

MOVIMIENTO DE LA IZQUIERDA REVOLUCIONARIA. See MOVEMENT OF THE REVOLUTIONARY LEFT.

MOVIMIENTO NACIONALISTA REVOLUCIONARIO. See NATIONALIST REVOLUTIONARY MOVEMENT.

MOVIMIENTO NACIONALISTA REVOLUCIONARIO DE IZQUIERDA. See NATIONALIST REVOLUTIONARY MOVEMENT OF THE LEFT.

NATIONALIST DEMOCRATIC ACTION (ACCIÓN DEMOCRÁTICA NACIONALISTA—ADN). Founded in 1978 by then-outgoing President (and retired General) Hugo Banzer Suárez, the ADN has solidly established itself as Bolivia's strongest conservative party. Its ideological position has evolved from a developmentalist nationalism, which implicitly looked to the state to aid and protect private business interests, to a laissez-faire faith in the free market. ADN planners pioneered many of the ideas behind President Víctor Paz Estenssoro's shock-treatment Decree 21060 of 1985. Partly through its close alliance with the Bolivian Private Businessmen's Confederation, ADN has recruited a group of technocratic civilian leaders whose role suggests that the party may outlast Banzer's personalistic dominance. The ADN has shown itself adept at coalition politics, cooperating with the Nationalist Revolutionary Movement from 1985 until early 1989, before switching to assist in the congressional choice of Jaime Paz Zamora (Movement of the Revolutionary Left) as president for 1989–1993. In 1985, the ADN polled more popular votes than any other party (28.6 percent) and virtually tied for first (23 percent) in 1989. However, if Bolivia were to institute a runoff system in presidential elections, the ADN's relative weakness with rural voters might hinder its advance to the national majority following that would be needed to win the presidency.

NATIONALIST REVOLUTIONARY MOVEMENT (MOVIMIENTO NACIONALISTA REVOLUCIONARIO—MNR). This most important of Bolivia's mass populist parties proved its durability and vigor once again during the 1980s. At the start of the decade, it was deeply factionalized between Hernán Siles Zuazo's Nationalist Revolutionary Movement of the Left (MNRI) and Víctor Paz Estenssoro's Historical MNR (MNRH). The Paz faction opposed the MNRI from a strong position in Congress, advocating a more conservative policy line. With the discredit of the Siles administration in 1983 and 1984, the Paz Estenssoro group achieved the presidency through a combination of a strong second-place showing in the 1985 popular voting (26.4 percent) and an alliance with the Movement of the Revolutionary Left in the constitutionally mandated choice of the president by Congress.

Within weeks of taking office, Paz Estenssoro took full advantage of the extreme disarray into which the left had fallen. The deflationary new economic policy (NPE) succeeded in ending the nation's hyperinflation and in returning the economy to an (anemic) growth rate of 2 percent of gross domestic product in 1988. The *Movimiento* was able to withstand the resulting furious reaction by the labor movement, partly through an alliance made in late 1985 with former President Hugo Banzer Suárez's Nationalist Democratic Action (ADN). This "Pact for Democracy" guaranteed what Siles Zuazo had not enjoyed: a reliable congressional majority to pass legislation and fend off parliamentary censure.

The MNR also scored a conspicuous electoral success in the late 1980s era of laissez-faire new conservatism in Bolivian politics. In the 1989 campaign, the party managed to escape the fate at the polls of similar groupings in Peru and Ecuador, which were decisively rejected during the 1980s following single terms in office. The MNR candidate Gonzalo Sánchez de Lozada, chief implementer of Decree 21060 and other deflationary measures, actually won the 1989 popular vote (23 percent), but he missed the presidency largely because the ADN had been alienated by his harsh personal campaign style and by the breakup of the Pact for Democracy which Banzer Suárez had hoped would assure him of MNR backing to achieve the presidential sash in 1989.

NATIONALIST REVOLUTIONARY MOVEMENT OF THE LEFT (MOVIMIENTO NACIONALISTA REVOLUCIONARIO DE IZQUIERDA— MNRI). Hernán Siles Zuazo created this splinter from the MNR as the core of the Democratic and Popular Union coalition which won the 1980 elections and brought him to the Presidential Palace in 1982. The MNRI combined the traditional populist stance of the Nationalist Revolutionary Movement with socialist programs and alliances with the Bolivian Labor Confederation (COB); this stance took full advantage of the left-wing moment in Bolivian politics at the start of the 1980s. Severely weakened in popular standing, however, by the hyperinflation and labor turmoil experienced in Siles's three years in office, the MNRI attracted less than 5 percent of the vote for its candidate Roberto Jordán Pando in 1985. It is no longer a significant force in national politics.

PARTIDO COMUNISTA BOLIVIANO. *See* BOLIVIAN COMMUNIST PARTY.

PARTIDO DE LA DEMOCRACIA CRISTIANA. *See* CHRISTIAN DEMOCRATIC PARTY.

PARTIDO OBRERO REVOLUCIONARIO. *See* REVOLUTIONARY WORKERS PARTY.

PARTIDO REVOLUCIONARIO AUTÉNTICO. See AUTHENTIC REVO-
LUTIONARY PARTY.

PARTIDO SOCIALISTA. See SOCIALIST PARTY.

REVOLUTIONARY VANGUARD OF APRIL 9 (VANGUARDIA REVOL-
UCIONARIA–9 DE ABRIL—VR-9). The VR-9 is one of the few splinters of
the Nationalist Revolutionary Movement to retain tactical political influence
after 1985. VR-9 leader Carlos Serrate Reich is a former minister of education
who has used his ownership of the popular La Paz newspaper *Hoy* to build a
following among voters in the countryside of that department. VR-9 staked out
a leftist position in coalition with the Movement of the Revolutionary Left
(MIR) in 1989, and the party's refusal to cast its congressional votes for Hugo
Banzer Suárez helped give the presidency to Jaime Paz Zamora of the MIR.

REVOLUTIONARY WORKERS PARTY (PARTIDO OBRERO REVOLU-
CIONARIO—POR). Bolivia's long-standing Trotskyist party, the POR, succumbed in the 1980s to the disarray of the trade union movement and the
pressure in the 1980 electoral law against very small parties. POR *jefe* Guillermo
Lora's 1985 candidacy for president garnered less than 1 percent of the national
vote, and the severe weakening of the mine workers' union later deprived the
party of most of its small, traditional following. The continuing political respect
for Lora is based on his personal and ideological rectitude.

SOCIALIST PARTY (PARTIDO SOCIALISTA—PS-1). This independent
party of the left continues to suffer from a lack of leadership which could project
it as a major national spokesman for the interests of workers and peasants. Since
the assassination of the party's cofounder Marcelo Quiroga Santa Cruz by the
Luis García Meza dictatorship in 1980, the PS-1 has played only a minor role.
In 1985 the party polled 2.2 percent of the national vote for its candidate
Ramiro Velazco Romero; four years later it tallied 2.5 percent. One of its
principal leaders is Roger Cortez.

UNIÓN DEMOCRÁTICA Y POPULAR. See DEMOCRATIC AND POPU-
LAR UNION.

VANGUARDIA REVOLUCIONARIA–9 DE ABRIL. See REVOLUTION-
ARY VANGUARD OF APRIL 9.

Political Parties—Historical

The following parties were significant in Bolivian politics before 1980, but
they are now inactive. For a full discussion, see Robert J. Alexander, ed., *Political*

Parties of the Americas, vol. 1, *Anguilla–Grenada* (Westport, Conn.: Greenwood Press, 1982), 129–46.

CONSERVATIVE PARTY (PARTIDO CONSERVADOR). This traditional elite party last held the presidency in 1899.

LIBERAL PARTY (PARTIDO LIBERAL). This party represented private tin-mining interests. It dominated national politics from 1899 to 1920.

MARXIST-LENINIST COMMUNIST PARTY (PARTIDO COMUNISTA MARXISTA-LENINISTA—PCML). This Beijing-oriented Communist party was established in 1964.

MOVIMIENTO POPULAR CRISTIANO. *See* POPULAR CHRISTIAN MOVEMENT.

NATIONALIST PARTY (PARTIDO NACIONALISTA). This party was made up of young intellectuals during the 1920s.

PARTIDO COMUNISTA MARXISTA-LENINISTA. *See* MARXIST-LENINIST COMMUNIST PARTY.

PARTIDO CONSERVADOR. *See* CONSERVATIVE PARTY.

PARTIDO DE LA IZQUIERDA REVOLUCIONARIA. *See* PARTY OF THE REVOLUTIONARY LEFT.

PARTIDO DE LA UNIÓN REPUBLICANA SOCIALISTA. *See* PARTY OF THE REPUBLICAN SOCIALIST UNION.

PARTIDO LIBERAL. *See* LIBERAL PARTY.

PARTIDO NACIONALISTA. *See* NATIONALIST PARTY.

PARTIDO REPUBLICANO. *See* REPUBLICAN PARTY.

PARTIDO REVOLUCIONARIO DE LA IZQUIERDA NACIONALISTA. *See* REVOLUTIONARY PARTY OF THE NATIONALIST LEFT.

PARTIDO SOCIAL DEMÓCRATA. *See* SOCIAL DEMOCRATIC PARTY.

PARTY OF THE REPUBLICAN SOCIALIST UNION (PARTIDO DE LA UNIÓN REPUBLICANA SOCIALISTA—PURS). This party was the last conservative party to rule prior to the Bolivian National Revolution of 1952.

PARTY OF THE REVOLUTIONARY LEFT (PARTIDO DE LA IZQUIERDA REVOLUCIONARIA—PIR). This Moscow-line Communist party was discredited when it backed a conservative coup against President Gualberto Villarroel in July 1946.

POPULAR CHRISTIAN MOVEMENT (MOVIMIENTO POPULAR CRISTIANO—MPC). This party was the principal electoral vehicle for President René Barrientos Ortuño (1966–1969).

REPUBLICAN PARTY (PARTIDO REPUBLICANO). This urban-based party was active from 1914 to 1935.

REVOLUTIONARY PARTY OF THE NATIONALIST LEFT (PARTIDO REVOLUCIONARIO DE LA IZQUIERDA NACIONALISTA—PRIN). This party, the electoral vehicle of labor union leader Juan Lechín Oquendo, was founded in 1963.

SOCIAL DEMOCRATIC PARTY (PARTIDO SOCIAL DEMÓCRATA—PSD). This party constituted a small conservative elite, including President Luís Adolfo Siles Salinas, who served for five months in 1969.

Christopher Mitchell

BRAZIL

Portuguese-speaking Brazil is big, dynamic, and diverse. With a population of 152.5 million (1990) and an area of 3,285,618 square miles, Brazil is the fifth-largest country in the world. Given this enormous territory (encompassing 47 percent of South America), population density is low. People are distributed unevenly; pulsating cities with millions interrupt vast empty expanses. Ninety percent of Brazilians reside in three regions—the northeast, southeast, and south—but these three account for only 35 percent of the total national territory. A fourth region, the vast Amazonian north, encompasses 42 percent of the national territory; however, the north contains only 5 percent of the national population. Finally, the emerging agricultural center-west region boasts just over one-fifth of Brazil's land area and 6 percent of its people. Regions and states are important in Brazil's politics, for Brazilians identify strongly with their area of origin.

Brazil has experienced dramatic socioeconomic transformations since the Great Depression of the 1930s, and the change accelerated after World War II. For centuries Brazil's economy depended on exporting a small number of primary products. After 1950 a large and diversified industrial sector became economically pivotal. The contribution of industry to gross domestic product rose from not quite 20 percent in 1947 to about 38 percent in the mid-1980s. During the same years, cities grew exponentially, with the proportion of urban Brazilians increasing from 30 percent to 75 percent. However, these achievements did not transform Brazil into an industrial society. From the perspective of most Brazilians, the quality of life continued at the levels prevailing among countries categorized as "developing" or "Southern."

Fallout from the second oil shock at the beginning of the 1980s shaped the remainder of the decade. Brazilians experienced declining living standards as inflation outpaced wages. Raw materials and manufactured goods were exported in record amounts to service Brazil's external debt. The military's incompetence in responding to the second oil shock created irresistible demands that the generals return to the barracks. Thus, in 1984, the armed forces stood aside as the governing party they had created, the Democratic Socialist Party (PDS), fragmented and lost control of the presidential succession. Military commanders subsequently entered into broad-ranging negotiations that culminated with the opposition-controlled Congress electing civilian Trancredo Neves as president on 15 January 1985. Although Neves died before he could be inaugurated, his vice president, José Sarney, presided over a transitional government that gave way to a party-based electoral democracy. In late 1989 Fernando Collor de Mello, the young scion of a northeast political dynasty, captured the presidency in a two-round direct election. Seven months after his inauguration, Brazilians voted, again in two rounds, for congressmen, senators, governors, and state legislators. During late February 1991, when President Collor addressed the newly installed Congress, individuals chosen in free and open elections occupied the executives and legislatures of Brazil's state and national governments for the first time in twenty-seven years.

Brazil is governed under the constitution promulgated on 5 October 1988. It divides power at the national level among a president, a legislature, and a judiciary. The president, chosen by direct popular vote, serves a five-year term. If no candidate obtains a majority, the victor is chosen in a runoff election between the two first-round candidates receiving the most votes. The vice president is elected on the same slate as the president. Between 1967 and 1988, the military-imposed constitution stipulated that the president be elected indirectly, by an electoral college made up of members of the national Congress and delegates appointed by the state legislatures. Until the government of João B. Figueiredo (1979–1985), the president possessed a wide range of arbitrary powers which were frequently wielded through the issuing of decree laws or "institutional acts." The executive used these powers to govern, often without consulting Congress or submitting decisions to the Supreme Court. Most of the decree laws were allowed to expire in late 1979, and throughout the 1980s Brazil became more democratic. The 1988 constitution seeks to strengthen Congress in its dealings with the executive, and the judicial system in its capability to safeguard civil rights.

The national Congress has two houses: a Senate composed of 81 members, and a 503-member Chamber of Deputies. Each of the twenty-six states, as well as the Federal District, is entitled to three senators. Senators are elected directly, with only a part of the Senate being up for election at one time. The 503 members of the Chamber of Deputies are allocated among the states and the Federal District on the basis of population. In Brazil's system of proportional representation, parties do not control the order by which individual representatives are elected. Parties present a lengthy list of candidates for state and federal deputy and for *vereador* (municipal councilman). Citizens cast only one vote for federal and state deputies and *vereador*, and they cast it for a specific individual. Seats are allocated first according to the number of votes each party receives. The intraparty order of seats depends exclusively on the number of individual votes each candidate wins. This means that, in order to get elected, candidates compete with their own party members as much as with the candidates of other parties.

Other electoral laws, including the timing of elections, were in flux throughout the 1980s. This will be less true as Brazil's fledgling "New Republic" develops in the 1990s. The 1990s began with senators being elected for eight years, with half of the senate up for renewal every four years. Deputies enjoyed four-year terms, and the entire Chamber of Deputies faced the electorate at four-year intervals. Municipal councilmen served for five years. Presumably, there will be adjustments after the 1993 plebiscite. At that time, voters will be required to choose between the existing presidential system, a parliamentary system, and a constitutional monarchy. A Constituent Assembly will follow the plebiscite. Public opinion polls in early 1991 revealed substantial support for each of the three alternatives. Even if voters opt for the presidential system, delegates to the Constituent Assembly are likely to fine-tune provisions of the 1988 constitution.

Brazilian political parties in the 1980s, like the political regime itself, evolved rapidly. The decade began with the military government's dismantling the two-party system that the army had imposed on Brazil in 1965. It drew to a close with twenty-two political parties offering candidates in the first round of the November 1989 presidential elections. In that contest, no candidate secured more than 29 percent of the total vote, and seven candidates received over 4 percent. In the congressional and gubernatorial elections of the following year, the political party of the winning presidential candidate was not a major factor. This underscores that, by comparison with political parties in more established Latin American democracies, those of Brazil's New Republic are frail. They are also clientalistic, precariously rooted in civil society, and, except for the militantly leftist Workers' Party (Partido dos Trabalhaldores, or PT), dependent on the personal popularity and power base of politicians who switch partisan affiliation with surprising ease and frequency.

The following discussion analyzes how Brazil's party system evolved in the 1980s and why Brazilian political parties failed to grow stronger. It begins by examining the authoritarian regime's final effort to frustrate consolidation of the Brazilian Democratic Movement (MDB) as a unified opposition party capable of defeating progovernment politicians in free elections. Subsequently the focus turns to negotiations among the military, progovernment, and antigovernment party leaders over the terms under which political parties would be empowered to manage the transition to direct electoral democracy. The initial success (in dominating the party system) and the subsequent decline of the "opposition turned government" Democratic Alliance is the third central focus. Attention is then turned to the dynamics of party competition following the return of full electoral democracy. These dynamics raise significant doubts about whether Brazilian political parties can develop the capabilities that will allow them to consolidate the embryonic democratic system. The last section profiles Brazil's important political parties during the 1980s.

Military Response to the Threat of a Dominant Opposition Party

The 1970s drew to a close with Brazil's military rulers scrambling to disassemble the two-party system that they had imposed fifteen years earlier. At that time, in 1965, regime strategists had hoped that the official government party (the National Renovating Alliance, or ARENA) might come to dominate Brazil as the Revolutionary Institutional Party (Partido Revolucionario Institucional, or PRI) dominated Mexico. To the extent that voting for ARENA was a plebiscitary expression of backing for the regime, election returns during the Costa e Silva government (1967–1969) and early in the Medici presidency (1970) suggested that a majority of Brazilian voters supported the regime. The early 1970s brought unprecedented economic growth. Thus, in their preparation for the elections of November 1974, President Ernesto Geisel and his advisors radiated confidence; they even relaxed controls over the media. Political dissidents, deprived of their civil and political rights, appeared demoralized and without influence. The urban poor had been subjected to "intelligence community" terrorism, but their concerns were not perceived as being widely shared. The *Planalto* (President Geisel and his staff) and the Army high command calculated that once again the electorate would endorse their policies. Great was their surprise when the opposition MDB received a majority of the vote cast for senators and effectively tied ARENA in the contests for federal deputies and state legislators. While this result did not immediately threaten ARENA's control over Congress, it did convince the military that ARENA was not going to evolve into a Brazilian PRI.

Despite ARENA's disappointing electoral performance, the *Planalto* was not prepared to abandon it as a vehicle for controlling the presidential succession. During April 1977, President Geisel introduced changes intended to prolong ARENA domination. These included continued indirect elections of governors (through ARENA-controlled state electoral colleges), continued indirect election for one-third of the Senate, changes in the size of the state delegations to the Chamber of Deputies (discriminating against the larger states, where opposition support was strongest), a simple congressional majority for passage of constitutional amendments, extension of censorship, a one-year extension of the next president's term, and a postponement of the proclamation of the new president by the electoral college to October 1978. An angry MDB viewed these changes as a *Planalto* subterfuge to secure a new lease on life for the regime. They doomed President Geisel's efforts to enlist the opposition in planning for the transition to democracy.

The *Planalto* and military high command, while favoring democratization, envisioned a measured, gradual transition. Opposition politicians were to be barred from the presidency until the 1990s. Geisel's tinkering with the rules for electoral college selection appeared to ensure this scenario, for the regime-supporting ARENA was able to eke out an electoral college majority in the

1978 elections. General João B. Figueiredo, President Geisel's choice, became president for the 1979–1985 constitutional period. However, the narrowness of ARENA's victory confirmed that liberalization was undermining the *Planalto*'s ability to shape electoral outcomes. The government party could provide only a rural-based electoral machinery that was dominant in the more backward states. The MDB, with growing support among workers and the urban poor, was positioned to dominate the 1980s.

Figueiredo's first year in office saw implementation of a political party system reorganization intended to cripple the capability of the MDB to compete effectively with the government party. Presidential strategy was to preserve the government party (under a new name) and promote the creation of multiple parties within the opposition. Regime strategists calculated that this would allow them, either by splitting the opposition vote or by forming a coalition with conservative elements of the opposition, to retain control. A bill to accomplish this purpose was sent to Congress and passed in November 1979. By the end of the year, new parties had been formed. ARENA returned as the PDS, and much of the former MDB coalesced in the Brazilian Democratic Movement Party (Partido do Movimento Democrático Brasileiro, or PMDB).

Planalto strategy was vindicated, at least in the short run, by the appearance of other opposition parties. Leonel Brizola, the most prominent leader of the outlawed Brazilian Labor Party (Partido Trabalhista Brasileiro, or PTB), immediately sought the historic name of this working-class party. It was seen as bestowing an advantage in organizing the left. However, with *Planalto* encouragement, electoral authorities awarded it to Ivete Vargas, a minor politician who was a grandniece of former president Getúlio Vargas. Brizola subsequently designated his party the Democratic Labor Party (Partido Democrático Trabalhista, or PDT). More militantly leftist than either of these parties was the PT, led by Luis Inácio da Silva (Lula), president of the metalworkers union in São Paulo. Rounding out the field was the Popular Party (Partido Popular, or PP), a conservative opposition group led by bankers. It merged with the PMDB in November 1981.

The recast party system's rules of organization and voting were designed to encourage crystallization of limited forces (four or five parties) rather than an inoperably large number of small parties. The *Planalto* hoped this would end the plebiscitary nature of the two-party system, replacing it with one that was basically centrist and conducive to evolutionary change. The net effect, labeled *Abertura*, was to create more options on the left.

As new players, leftist parties faced greater difficulties than the official PDS. They had to expend more energy in rapidly attracting a constituency and in organizing and differentiating themselves from each other, as well as from the government party. Thus leftists grudgingly accepted President Figueiredo's postponement of municipal elections from 1980 to 1982, including an extension of the mandate of the officials already in office. In this way, the *Planalto* succeeded in engaging as participants, in its post-1979 party system, the new elites formed during the recent development process. Political figures returning under the unconditional amnesty also were incorporated. These successes gave the regime breathing space during which it hoped to arrange for control over the 1985 presidential succession.

The Military Regime Loses Control of the Party System

President Figueiredo and his advisors grew apprehensive as Abertura's intensification diminished their ability to influence events. Again the Planalto tinkered with the electoral system, loading the dice even more in favor of the PDS. While this brought qualified success at the polls, subsequent maneuvering opened a rift between Planalto strategists and the PDS leadership. President Figueiredo appeared unprepared for the give and take of party politics in an open democracy. When he attempted to deal, he was clumsy and ineffective. Thus, the government managed to snatch defeat from the jaws of victory; the PDS split, opening the way for the electoral college to elevate Neves, the PMDB candidate, to the presidency. Although Neves's unanticipated death opened the way for Vice President Sarney, a longtime regime collaborator, to assume the presidency, the generals had lost their capability to dominate the party system.

The November 1981 modifications to the reformed party system were a victory by regime hard-liners opposed to Abertura. They sought to counteract opposition strengths and bolster the PDS: Multiparty alliances were forbidden; straight ticket voting was required; and aspiring parties were forced to submit candidates for all posts within a state in order to present a slate. Because the newly crystallizing opposition parties lacked infrastructure in many of the over 4,000 municípios (unlike the PDS and PMDB), they were effectively barred from competing for offices in a number of localities where they had support. For the small, probusiness PP, the burden became so impossible that its leaders rejoined the PMDB (from which many had come).

Planalto strategists also imposed a more complicated ballot without party and candidate names, requiring voters themselves, still within the straight ticket, to write in all their candidates (a possible total of six) separately by name or number. The chief intent of this voto vinculado (tied vote) was to increase the potential for well-known local candidates or patronage givers, most of whom supported the PDS, to pull in the top of the ticket with them. Finally, Constitutional Amendment 22, which went into effect on 22 June 1982, was yet another measure to improve the government's position in the election and during the remainder of President Figueiredo's term. It overrepresented, throughout the electoral system but especially in the enlarged Chamber of Deputies, the less-populated and less-developed states in which PDS strength lay. Urbanized states in the south and southeast, with their opposition political cultures, were disadvantaged.

Balloting in November 1982 configured the transition to civilian rule. Thus the stakes were enormous. Because local elections had been postponed from

1980 until 1982, voters were being asked to choose at every level but the presidential. For the first time since 1965, governors were to be elected directly. All governors and the one-third of the federal senators up for election were to be chosen by simple majorities, and all the federal deputies and state legislators by proportional representations. Table 1 summarizes the electoral results and profiles the partisan alignment in the electoral college that would choose a new president on 15 January 1985.

Brazilian political scientist David Fleischer observed of the 1982 voting, "As has been the case with Brazil's long history of electoral law manipulations, the witchcraft returned to plague the witch" Initially, *Planalto* witchcraft, while not an unqualified success, appeared to have preserved regime control over the political infrastructure. The progovernment PDS secured a majority in the presidential electoral college, retained control of the federal Senate, and elected more members of the Chamber of Deputies than any other political party. On the other hand, imposition of *voto vinculado* balloting in hopes of "localizing" the election of federal office holders and producing a "reverse coattail" effect backfired. Outside of the traditional northeast, the opposition prevailed and local PDS candidates went down to defeat. The opposition won in ten of the twenty-three states, a group accounting for nearly 70 percent of Brazil's population, gross national product, and tax base.

Analysis of the 1982 voting returns suggests that once the political constraints of authoritarian rule on information and competition were lowered, mass belief systems evolved in ways the regime could not control. Brazilians began behaving like voters in other mass democracies. They demanded substantive democracy in both political and economic manifestations. Political campaigning became critical in organizing public opinion, and, outside of the traditional northeast, the electorate found regime policies wanting. In other words, authoritarian political rules of the game had forfeited their legitimacy because they could no longer manage tensions between politics based on appeals to substantive justice and the political and economic constraints imposed by the government.

President Figueiredo reacted badly to the PDS failure to do as well as expected. He refused to include representatives from the diverse PDS factions in his cabinet, and he wielded patronage in a bumbling attempt to displace independently minded PDS leaders. In late July 1983, the president went to Cleveland, Ohio, for coronary bypass surgery, which was followed by two months of convalescence. Following his return to the *Planalto*, in October, Congress rejected two decree laws submitted for approval by the executive. This was the first such rejection of regime legislation since the 1967 constitution went into effect. It marked the beginning of an inglorious descent into defeat by President Figueiredo and the PDS.

Throughout 1984, President Figueiredo barely concealed his lack of confidence in the PDS. In January, he initiated a three-month campaign to pressure Congress into amending the constitution so as to select the next president by direct and immediate elections. While public opinion and the opposition, as well as

Table 1
Results of the November 15, 1982 Elections and Composition of the January 15, 1985 Electoral College (by political party)

	PDS	PMDB	PDT	PTB	PT	TOTAL
VOTES (%)[a]	43.2	43.0	5.8	4.5	3.5	100.0
GOVERNORS[b]	13	9	1	---	---	23
SENATORS[c]	45	22	1	1	1	69
FEDERAL DEPUTIES	235	200	23	13	8	479
DELEGATES ELECTORAL COLLEGE[d]	81	51	6	---	---	138
ELECTORAL COLLEGE COMPOSITION[e]	361	273	30	14	8	686

SOURCE: Compiled from preliminary election statistics reported by the Superior Electoral Court (TSE), Diario de Justicia, November 28, 1983, pp. 18,630-18,686; reproduced in a more complete form in Wayne E. Selcher, ed., Political Liberalization in Brazil (Boulder, CO.: Westview Press, 1986), p. 127.

Note:

[a]Election for Federal Deputy (excludes 5,286,684 blank and 2,058,459 void ballots).

[b]Only twelve PDS governors were elected directly, Rondônia appointed through 1987.

[c]Includes forty-four senators elected in 1978(twenty-two "bionics") and three new seats elected from Rondônia.

[d]Six delegates representing the majority party in each of the twenty-two State assemblies. Due to a tie in Mato Grosso do Sul, the PDS and PMBD each got three delegates.

[e]Met on January 15, 1985. Included senators, federal deputies, and delegates.

elements within the PDS, favored direct presidential elections, there was apprehension because of President Figueiredo's interest in running for reelection. This led to a congressional imbroglio in which the "Direct Elections Now" amendment failed to gain the two-thirds quorum in the Chamber of Deputies. Yet another time, the *Planalto's* occupant would be chosen by the military-designed electoral college.

Tensions between President Figueiredo and the PDS intensified following defeat of the "Direct Elections Now" amendment. The PDS divided. Vice President Aureliano Chaves, together with Senator Sarney (ex-PDS president) and other PDS leaders, especially from the northeast, created the autonomous Liberal Front. In August, the Liberal Front entered into a coalition with the PMDB. The resulting Democratic Alliance offered a presidential ticket of Minas Gerais governor Neves (PMDB), and northeasterner Sarney. The rump PDS countered with Paulo Salim Maluf, a deputy and former governor of São Paulo. Maluf, the PDS leader President Figueiredo most detested, received lukewarm support from the *Planalto* and the military high command. However, Maluf's personal wealth gave him ample financial resources which he marshaled in an ill-fated attempt to influence individual PDS members of the electoral college. This strategy antagonized PDS state bosses, especially in the traditional northeast. They viewed this use of Maluf's fortune as a challenge to the patronage on which their power rested. Ironically, many in the military regime now saw the opposition PMDB as more attractive than the PDS.

The electoral college met on 15 January 1985, in a climate of full liberty, with abundant national and international news coverage. Democratic Alliance candidate Neves crushed Maluf, receiving 480 votes out of a possible 686. The Neves-Sarney slate collected 309 votes from the four opposition parties combined, 35 short of a majority. Another 171 came from electors chosen in 1982 on the PDS slate. Of these, 113 had affiliated with the Liberal Front, now constituted as an official party, the Partido da Frente Liberal (PFL). Neves, Brazil's first civilian chief executive in more than two decades, owed his victory not only to forces that had opposed the post-1964 military revolution, but also to important elements of the regime itself.

While conservative forces anticipated playing a major role in the Neves government, their influence was magnified by the sudden illness and passing of the president-elect. Vice-President Sarney's elevation to the presidency on 23 April 1985 brought to the *Planalto* a northeasterner whose career had been based largely on support for the military regime. In most respects, his PFL represented what had been the more traditional wing of the PDS. Eminently acceptable to the military, his major problem was the PMDB. The long-suffering opposition party was devastated by the death of its popular leader, stunned by its loss of control over the *Planalto*, and distrustful of a president who, as Senate leader of the ARENA party, had introduced measures that restricted political rights and handicapped efforts to restore free electoral competition.

The Frustration of Consolidation: The 1986 Elections and Their Aftermath

During the Sarney administration (1985–1990), elections continued to display the plebiscitary cast they had taken on during the military regime. The president's policies, style of wielding patronage, and widely oscillating personal popularity channeled party system evolution. Voting for either partner in the PFL/PMDB coalition signaled approval of the government, even though PMDB leaders displayed little enthusiasm for Sarney's "accidental presidency." During implementation of the 1986 Cruzado Plan, when *Planalto* policies appeared to have restored economic growth and tamed inflation, the PMDB and PFL achieved an unprecedented popular mandate. They added to their strength in Congress, captured all of the governorships, and dominated the Constituent Assembly that wrote the constitution of 1988. Subsequently, when economic reverses strengthened perceptions that the *Planalto* was inept and corrupt, the fortunes of the PMDB and PFL declined. Voters turned to the opposition, especially the PT and PDT. As President Sarney's term drew to a close, leftist forces were not only electing large numbers of municipal councilmen, they had become competitive for the upcoming direct presidential elections.

During his first year and a half as president, Sarney's performance exceeded the expectations of even his most ardent supporters. After unifying a grieving and skeptical nation, he seized the high ground on electoral reform and inaugurated a far-reaching plan to restore economic growth and tame inflation. On the matter of electoral reform, Congress first took the initiative, modifying legislation governing party organization and elections during May and June 1985. These modifications abolished the regulations that required deputies and senators to vote as directed by the party caucus (*sublegenda*), loosened procedures for organizing new parties, unfettered 202 municipalities from national security legislation, and regulated the direct election of their mayors, which took place on 15 November 1985. During the military presidencies, electoral reform of this magnitude would have originated in the *Planalto*.

Sarney attempted to reassert his leadership by shaping provisions dealing with political succession and constitutional reform. On 28 June 1985, he submitted to Congress a proposal that would restore direct presidential elections, without specifying the next date. This shielded his government from proposals that would have shortened its mandate, a course also opposed by the military. Nevertheless, many congressmen, especially from the PT and PDT, pressed for direct elections in 1986. The majority Democratic Alliance could not make up its mind. Congress came to an impasse.

On 15 November 1985, municipal elections were held in those cities that had not elected mayors and councilmen in 1982. The PT won in one capital (Fortaleza) where it had captured less than 1 percent of the vote in 1982, and it barely lost to the PMDB in Goiânia. The PDT won significant victories in Rio de Janeiro and Pôrto Alegre and garnered at least 10 percent of the vote in eight other capitals. Taken as a whole, the 1985 municipal returns revealed a fragmenting party system, with the PMDB and PFL losing support. This moved the PFL/PMBD majority in Congress to pass Sarney's proposal in toto. The legislation provided for the election of the next president by an absolute majority, with a runoff, if necessary, to be held thirty days later between the two most voted candidates. It was essentially the system of France's Fifth Republic. This legislation also deferred the questions of length of presidential mandate and election date to a Constituent Assembly which would meet in early 1987 to amend the constitution, thus postponing direct presidential elections for at least three years. Success in this matter enhanced President Sarney's leadership within the Democratic Alliance.

Once demands that democratization continue, albeit at a measured pace, were assuaged, economic matters occupied center stage. It was self-evident that popular support for the Sarney *Planalto*, and for the parties of the Democratic Alliance, would be conditioned by perceptions of how well the economy was being managed. The 1981 recession ended during 1985, but during early 1986 the rate of inflation began to climb. Thus, on 28 February 1986, President Sarney announced the Cruzado Plan, a program intended to kill inflation in a dramatic blow. The Cruzado Plan's most important components included a general freeze on the prices of final goods, the freezing of wages and mortgage payments following an initial readjustment, the prohibition of indexation clauses for contracts of less than one year, and the introduction of a new currency, the *cruzado*, which replaced the old *cruzeiro* (CZ$1 equalled Cr$1,000).

The immediate results of the Cruzado Plan were spectacular both from the economic and from the political points of view. The monthly inflation rate, as measured by the general price index, declined from 22 percent in February 1986 to −1 percent in March, rose to −0.6 percent in April, and to +0.5 percent in June. Industrial production accelerated as increased purchasing power, derived from the plan's initial upward wage adjustments, was used by consumers to purchase long-delayed big-ticket items. The Cruzado Plan's expansionary thrust also maintained downward pressure on interest rates. The Brazilian economic miracle of the 1970s appeared to be returning. President Sarney's popularity soared, and leaders of the PMDB/PFL coalition prepared to reap the electoral dividends.

The elections held on 15 November 1986 shaped not only the final transition to a full electoral democracy but also the initial rules of the game for the New Republic. Voting set the partisan alignment of the Chamber of Deputies and the Senate; together these institutions were to serve as the National Constituent Assembly. Also at stake in the 15 November balloting was control over all twenty-two state governments. The electoral regulations for selecting state and national officials were those approved early in the Sarney government. In contrast to earlier electoral laws, which sought to limit the number of partisan contenders, these provided unprecedented opportunities for small political parties to gain representation. Federal and state deputies were to be elected by a system of proportional representation with the largest remainders method. In these contests, the entire state constituted an electoral district, and each state had from eight to sixty federal deputies and from twelve to eighty-four state deputies. There was no national threshold, and the state threshold (namely, the electoral quotient, i.e., the number of votes divided by the number of seats) was low. In a large state, such as São Paulo, this allowed a party or coalition to secure representation in the Federal Chamber of Deputies with 1.67 percent of the vote. State governors, in contrast, were to be elected by an absolute majority, with a runoff authorized between the two candidates having the most support should none receive an absolute majority in the first round of voting.

Balloting in November 1986 failed to confirm either the party system fragmentation or the increased support for leftist forces that had surfaced in the preceding year's municipal elections. The plebiscitary impulses that had characterized voting during most of the military regime persisted, and the Sarney government's Cruzado Plan received a ringing endorsement. The PMDB captured twenty-two state governorships, and the PFL won the other (Sergipe); furthermore, the PMDB won thirty-six of the forty-nine Senate seats up for grabs, and the PFL won eight, the PDS, two, and the Brazilian Socialist Party (PSB), PDT, and PTB, one each. This all added up to a 61-percent PMDB majority in the Senate. In the Chamber of Deputies, the PMDB gained 257 seats (a 53-percent margin), and the PFL, the other Democratic Alliance partner, boasted 120. The combined opposition strength in the Chamber was 110. Opposition party leaders voiced concern that the executive's ability to craft policy was leading to domination by a single party or coalition.

Before all of the ballots had been counted, President Sarney backed away from the Cruzado Plan policies that the voters had endorsed so overwhelmingly. Economic factors intervened to force decisions that were politically damaging. Indeed, serious problems with the Cruzado Plan had surfaced five months prior to the November voting. In July 1986, demand for consumer goods began to exceed supply, and Brazil's international balance-of-payments surplus slipped into deficit. Producers commenced withholding goods from the market, claiming that retail prices no longer covered the costs of production. Nevertheless, President Sarney responded to entreaties from the Democratic Alliance that he maintain the price freeze. It symbolized the success of his Cruzado Plan. This success barred the way to leftist candidates and strengthened the appeal of the PMDB and PFL.

Postelectoral adjustments to the Cruzado Plan were intended to cool consumption and stimulate exports. They also revived inflation, and the price of many previously accessible goods rose to where most consumers could not afford them. Adoption of policies with these consequences within days of the Democratic Alliance's electoral sweep discredited President Sarney's leadership. It also led to cynicism toward the PMDB and PFL. Subsequently, both parties distanced themselves from the government.

Following revision of the Cruzado Plan, the focus of Brazilian politics shifted to the Constituent Assembly. The Assembly remained in session from February 1987 to October 1988. In their conduct of Constituent Assembly business, political parties appeared quarrelsome and feckless. Ulysses Guimarâes, president of the majority PMDB, was elected to preside over the Assembly; however, he could not shape his party into a cohesive bloc. Consensus became contingent on negotiations surrounding each article of the new constitution. These negotiations confirmed the personalistic tenor of Brazilian political parties, as well as their lack of ideological and organizational coherence.

Brazilian political party leaders have always acted as political entrepreneurs. Their flexibility can be observed from the magnitude of parachuting into the PMDB during the early 1980s. It was so great that, in the 1987 Constituent Assembly, the largest group, in terms of 1977 political affiliations, was not the PMDB. That honor belonged to the precursor of the promilitary regime PDS, ARENA, with 217 members. The more original or authentic PMDB had but 212. Of the 298 PMDB members on whom data are available, 40 were from the PDS of 1983 and another 42 were from ARENA of 1979. Thus, rather than a majority of 54 percent in the Assembly, the PMDB could count only 40 percent once these latecomers from the right were excluded. This made the Assembly more conservative and fragmented than would be inferred by merely abstracting from the November 1986 electoral returns.

The constitution promulgated on 5 October 1988 reflected and reinforced the political process of its delineation. Struggle to reduce centralized authoritarianism took shape in a weakening of executive powers in relation to Congress and of national government powers in relation to other levels of authority. The constitution included provisions for substantial improvements in human rights and social guarantees, with incredibly detailed sections on everything from censorship to maternity leave. It also sought to diminish what many civilian politicians saw as the dominant economic influence gained by multinational corporations during the military regime. Thus, the overall tone of the 1988 constitution was nationalistic, populistic, and statist. It contained something for everyone, except the peasants. By exempting productive land, even if not fulfilling a social function, from expropriation, the constitution reversed the 1965 agrarian reform of President Humberto Castelo Branco.

The dynamics of formulating the constitution did nothing to strengthen political parties. Instead, they confirmed a lack of party discipline that cast doubt on the ability of the strengthened Congress to exercise its powers responsibly. Without changes in the electoral law, local bosses retained the flexibility that enabled them to operate in Brasilia with scant regard for party discipline. Measures which might have strengthened party organization, such as a movement to a district system of representation, did not even emerge as pertinent issues in the Constituent Assembly. Even the highly unrepresentative number of deputies imposed by the military remained largely intact. Lobbies of all imaginable variations, from religious associations to ecological groups to business interests, exercised greater influence than party leaders. By one estimate, one-half of the members of the Assembly were representatives of lobbies. Thus, political parties were weaker and less well organized than many interests, especially the state bureaucracy, the military, and organized labor.

On the eve of the return to full electoral democracy, Brazil's party system was unsettled. The PMDB and PFL were so divided that they could not agree on a presidential candidate. Unable to articulate coherent positions in the Constituent Assembly, they seemed confused and captive to special interests. The PMDB and PFL appeared to have squandered their historic opportunity. Nevertheless, their leaders enjoyed access to patronage, and they controlled powerful local machines. The ability of these traditional machines to deliver votes, despite growing challenges on the left, remained formidable.

Leftist parties also had serious problems. They were experiencing difficulties in outgrowing the constraining spatial and class appeals which gave them birth. On the other hand, a leftist coalition of the PT and PDT, which reached out to emerging forces, such as the Brazilian Social Democratic Party (PSDB), could present a unity candidacy capable of making a serious run at the *Planalto*. Given that presidential elections were likely to go into a second round, such an alliance was highly probable. This led conservatives to search for a fresh and charismatic face. Thus, the contest to choose Brazil's first popularly elected president in three decades came to center around jerry-built alliances of weak parties which were little more than personalistic followings, local patronage machines, and narrow ideological movements.

Full Electoral Democracy and the Frustration of Hope

Two years were needed to complete the transition to full electoral democracy. Most of 1989 was taken up with the first campaign in almost three decades to elect a president popularly. The following year witnessed the inauguration of the new chief executive, Fernando Collor de Mello, Collor's initial efforts at taking charge, and a second election campaign. At stake in the second election was control of the national congress, state governorships, and state legislatures. Early in 1989, with an eye to influencing this transition, President Sarney had crafted a final initiative to tame inflation and reactivate economic growth. Failure dissipated what little prestige the outgoing administration retained. On the other hand, there was great anticipation that popularly elected leaders in the New Republic, especially the president, would do away with the vestiges of authoritarianism and set the economy to rights. When President Collor de Mello, however, achieved disappointing results after administering painful economic medicine, disillusionment set in. With nowhere else to turn, the electorate opted for the familiar. The same political parties that had dominated in the Constituent Assembly won seats in the new Congress. Only now Congress was even more factious. In early 1991, the hope that had marked presidential campaigning gave way to cynicism and frustration.

President Sarney unveiled his "Summer Plan" in mid-January 1989. He aimed to duplicate the initial success of the Cruzado Plan by again freezing prices and wages. One month after the plan's inauguration, the president assured his countrymen, in a televised broadcast, that it was working; inflation, which exceeded 30 percent in January, would be 5 percent in February. Congress, however, resisted passing important provisions of the Summer Plan. Earlier failures and the abrupt termination of the first Cruzado Plan after the November 1986 elections had destroyed government credibility. Even Sarney's own PFL treated the Summer Plan gingerly. Pressure on Congress from unions opposed to the plan was intense. Labor leaders charged that its timing of wage and price freezes had robbed workers of their purchasing power. The unions also vented their anger in mid-March by paralyzing the economy with a two-day general strike. Inflation picked up, and on 20 April the government resurrected indexation. This was followed by the lifting of price controls, which further fueled inflation. By October, the monthly rate of inflation had soared to 37.6 percent. With President Sarney appearing powerless to enforce his will, there were suggestions that he resign early. These were rejected. No aspirant to the *Planalto* seemed in a great hurry to take responsibility for an economy that had undermined the credibility of three administrations in less than a decade.

The human carnage created by rising prices, high rates of unemployment, and downward middle-class mobility set the stage in 1989 for Brazil's presidential election to unfold as a resounding vote of no confidence in the Sarney government and the Democratic Alliance parties (PMDB and PFL). Leftist leaders, who had seen their candidates routed in 1986, believed they would ride this wave of discontent to victory. Foremost among the leftist presidential hopefuls were Luís Inácio (Lula) da Silva (PT) and Leonel Brizola (PDT). Brizola was Brazil's most charismatic politician: the PT boasted a string of impressive victories in the municipal elections of 1988. Mario Covas's recently formed PSDB appealed to the hard-pressed middle class; Covas also cast a long shadow on the left. At the beginning of 1989, it appeared that, although no contender would secure an absolute majority in the first round of presidential voting, the two candidates of the second round would emerge from among Brizola, da Silva (Lula), and Covas.

Conservative forces, which had supported the military regime and had controlled the transition, were appalled at a choice among Brizola, Lula, and Covas. High-profile conservative politicians, however, were discredited. Thus, the establishment began a frantic search for someone who was trustworthy and electable. They settled upon Collor, the governor of the small northern state of Alagoas. Collor's family, on his father's side, had long been a politically dominant force in Alagoas. His maternal grandfather, the author of labor legislation during the *Estado Novo* of Getúlio Vargas, added a progressive touch. Collor himself was the epitome of an antiparty, conservative populist. He entered politics under the banner of the progovernment PDS, was elected governor in 1986 as the PMDB candidate, and had broken with President Sarney over the allocation of patronage within Alagoas.

Governor Collor de Mello's clash with President Sarney made him a national celebrity, casting the Alagoas governor as a champion of honesty and the enemy of unfair bureaucratic privilege. His crusade became a battle against civil servants whose custom of drawing more than one salary enabled them to live opulently in a time of austerity. Collor's "hunt for the Maharajahs" made him the kind of electable populist needed by the conservatives. He quickly became the preferred option of *Rede Globo* television and its powerful president, Roberto Marinho. Skillful media packaging, coupled with widespread antipathy toward established political parties and politicians, enabled Collor to take and hold the lead in public opinion polling throughout most of the campaign. His closest rivals were on the left: Brizola and Lula. As expected, the candidates of the Democratic Alliance parties (Guimarães of the PMDB and Chaves of the PFL) trailed far behind.

Balloting in the first round of November failed to produce an absolute majority for any candidate. Collor de Mello, as expected, finished first, but he had only 28.5 percent of the total vote. A last minute surge propelled Lula past Brizola and into the runoff. Events between the first and second round of the presidential election confirmed the wisdom of conservative strategists in searching out a new face. The left did coalesce behind Lula's candidacy and mounted a formidable challenge. The margin of victory was just under 5 percent. However, the contest never became a plebiscite on Sarney's stewardship. Lula enjoyed great success in Rio de Janeiro and Rio Grande do Sul; he also carried Pernambuco and ran close races in Santa Catarina, Bahia, and Rio Grande do Norte. Collor, however, won the election with strong showings in São Paulo, Paraná, Minas Gerais, and the northeast. On 15 March 1990, Brazil inaugurated its first popularly elected president since the military ousted President João Goulart.

President Collor moved decisively to shape economic events. His multidimensional *Plano Novo Brasil* promised cost-cutting administrative reforms, tough fiscal measures, and a temporary price freeze, to be followed by price and wage adjustments based on official estimates of inflation. The plan also envisioned an end to subsidizing state corporations, the liberalization of imports, and introduction of a new currency. However, these and other measures were overshadowed by the stunning proposal to sequester temporarily some U.S. $100 billion (30 percent of Brazil's total gross domestic product) from bank and savings accounts and overnight deposits. Given that 90 percent of Brazilians lacked such financial instruments, the impact of the policy proved to be highly selective. Thus, while criticism surfaced over the authoritarian style of policy-making, even left-wing politicians conceded that Collor appeared to be carrying out his campaign promise "to fight inflation with the wallets of the rich."

The *Plano Novo Brasil* set Brazilians on yet another journey of hope; it was to end again in frustration. Initially, the economy came to a standstill. Unemployment rose, but the mood turned optimistic when the monthly rate of inflation plunged from 84.3 percent in March to just 3.2 percent in April. Inflation, however, began seeping back into the economy. During October it passed 14 percent, and, with the November rise, it approached 19 percent. Other bad news surfaced when, at the end of the year, the respected, London-based *Latin American Weekly Report* calculated that during 1990 industrial production had fallen 7.5 percent. During the same period, the gross domestic product had contracted by 4.6 percent.

Brazilians had waited long for the return of electoral democracy, and they pinned great hopes on the new president. Had it been otherwise, the disastrous economy of 1990 would probably have led to a repudiation of the government in the October and November elections. The results, in fact, were ambiguous. Collor, the archetypical antiparty entrepreneur, decided against making a major effort to popularize his fledgling National Reconstruction Party (PRN). He left the field to the parties that had emerged prior to the 1989 presidential campaign, although, as the campaign progressed, his tilt toward the right increased. Rightist and center-right congressional candidates generally did well in the first-round elections of 3 October although Collor's PRN failed to emerge as a major force. Gubernatorial candidates favored by the president, and not forced into the November runoff, had great success. However, in the fifteen gubernatorial contests decided in runoff elections, Collor's candidates fared badly. Especially disappointing to the new president were the defeats sustained in the populous states of São Paulo, Minas Gerais, and Rio Grande do Sul. Table 2 compares results from the 1990 elections with those of November 1986.

The 1990 elections brought change; they also confirmed the persistence of historic traits. From the perspective of cadre renewal, the composition of the first Congress of the New Republic was striking. Less than 40 percent of those who had served during the transition were present on 1 February 1991 when the new Congress was sworn in. Also, ideological differences received less attention than they had during the transition. With command economies in Eastern Europe shorn of their luster and with Brazilian state enterprises running large deficits, party spokesmen on both the left and right stressed that their organizations were progressive or renewalist. Cynics argued that this superficial agreement reflected the lack of a working majority on the part of any party or coalition and that congressmen of all persuasions stood ready to trade votes for patronage.

The same political parties that had dominated the transitional Congress reappeared in the newly elected chambers, but Congress was more fragmented. Leftist or "progressive" parties, although still a minority, had greater representation. While a broad coalition of "renewalist" (or establishment) parties could theoretically dominate Congress, greater parity in the size of the party delegations increased the difficulties of holding any specific coalition together for very long. Collor, the antiparty president, did not hesitate to negotiate ad hoc majorities for each major piece of legislation he desired from Congress. It had the makings of the situation that had helped to discredit President Sarney.

Results in the state elections confirmed the failure of truly national parties to crystallize, as well as the continuing power of local patronage machines. The

Table 2
Results of Legislative Elections in 1986 and 1990 (by political party)

PARTY	SENATE		CHAMBER OF DEPUTIES		GOVERNORS
	(1987)	(1991)	(1987)	(1991)	1991*
PMDB	45	26	259	108	7
PFL	15	14	116	87	9
PSDB	- -	10	- -	37	1
PDT	2	5	24	47	3
PDS	5	4	32	43	1
PRN	- -	4	- -	40	1
PTB	1	6	18	35	2
PT	- -	1	16	35	- -
PDC	1	3	5	22	- -
PL	1	- -	6	14	- -
PSB	1	2	1	11	- -
PST	- -	1	- -	2	- -
PRS	- -	- -	- -	4	1
PCdeB	- -	- -	5	5	- -
PCB	- -	- -	3	3	- -
PSC	- -	- -	- -	6	- -
PTR	- -	- -	- -	2	2
OTHERS**	1	5	2	2	- -
TOTAL	72	81	487	503	27

SOURCE: Folha De São Paulo, October 29, 1990; Latin American Regional Reports Brazil (RB-91-01), 10 January 1991, p. 2.

Note: * Following the November 1986 elections, the PMDB controlled all governorships, except Sergipe. In 1990, fifteen governorships were decided in the second round of voting.
     ** Independents and assorted microparties.

PFL and PMDB, both catchall alliances of state and regional bosses, captured sixteen of the twenty-seven governorships. PFL governors controlled most state-houses in the traditional northeast and the north. States electing PMDB governors were a heterogeneous lot. They ranged from the populous São Paulo to the vast, largely vacant Amazonas. Brizola's PDT, the only other party to control three or more governorships, added Espírito Santo to its historic strongholds in Rio de Janeiro and Rio Grande do Sul. Thus, the mosaic of party control over the twenty-six state governments resembled the fragmentation and imperviousness to change apparent in the new Congress. Both situations fostered immobilism and frustration with political parties.

Conclusion

Brazilian political parties multiplied during the 1980s, but they failed to grow stronger. The previous decade ended with the military regime's dissolving the artificial two-party arrangement it had imposed in 1965. Critical in this context was recognition that an antiregime majority had crystallized within the Brazilian electorate. Each of the four political parties that emerged in place of the MDB, the catchall opposition party, was deemed too weak to challenge for national power. This strategy misfired in 1984, when the progovernment PDS broke up and lost control of the succession process. The new president was chosen in an electoral college that gave the PDS candidate only 26.2 percent of the total vote.

The 1980s drew to a close with the first popular elections held for president in twenty-nine years. The victor, Collor de Mello, was an antiparty populist. His inauguration was followed by state and local elections in which the new president supported individual candidates for governor and stood aloof from his own antiparty movement, the PRN. When results were tabulated, Collor's candidates had lost the most important governorships; the aspiring senators and deputies who had latched on to his PRN constituted less than 10 percent of the new Congress. Thus, the 1990s began with Brazil's government in the hands of such a diverse lot that no single party or coalition could be held responsible for the success or failure of public policy. Despite the weakening of executive powers in the 1988 constitution, politics remained personalist and presidential.

Important characteristics of Brazilian politics during the 1980s have negative implications for the strengthening of political parties. First, success in presidential politics came to depend on an aspirant's ability to forge a broad multiparty alliance. This favored independents, who once elected had few incentives to disseminate patronage to any single party. On the contrary, the executive exchanged favors for the passage of legislation, and almost every new request required inducements to an ad hoc coalition in Congress. Second, as discussed in the introduction, the combination of proportional representation and an open list has encouraged individualism among politicians and has helped undermine parties. Third, during the military regime and the 1989 presidential election campaign, television enabled candidates to bypass parties and to reach out directly to the electorate. Fourth, as Scott Mainwaring (1990) pointed out, from the perspective of "spaces" occupied in the political system, expansion of the state apparatus during the military regime encouraged interest groups to lobby bureaucracies directly. Whatever the fate of President Collor's plans to privatize, the 1990s began with the bureaucracy as the focal point of political action. Finally, the low level of information, awareness, and interest of the Brazilian electorate has retarded the formation of strong political parties.

The economy remains critical in crafting strong parties. Economic reverses can undo any party or political leader, as well as the democratic regime itself. The 1980s were for Brazil, as for most of Latin America, a lost decade in terms of economic development. Inflation, unemployment, and negative economic growth discredited Presidents Figueiredo and Sarney, sent the parties of the Democratic Alliance into eclipse, and diminished President Collor's influence within a year of his inauguration. In the city of São Paulo, this syndrome also undercut the PT government of Mayor Luiza Erundina do Souza. The PT in São Paulo, like the national parties in Brasilia, fell out of favor when it was forced to bear the brunt of huge budget deficits, hyperinflation, and declining living standards. This raises the question as to whether any political party can grow and become an object of popular support while governing, until the economy stabilizes and recovers.

The beginning of the 1990s finds Brazil's party system fragmented and its political parties weak. These conditions confirm the precarious and feckless state of New Republic democracy. Still, the present configuration of forces is likely to continue in the short term, through the scheduled 1993 plebiscite. After that, the outlook becomes murky for individual political parties, for the party system, and for popular government.

Bibliography

Werner Baer. *The Brazilian Economy: Growth and Development.* Praeger, New York, 1989.

Fernando H. Cardoso and Bolívar Lamounier, eds. *Os partidos e as eleicões no Brasil.* Paz e Terra, Rio de Janeiro, 1975.

Julian M. Chacel, Pamela S. Falk, and David V. Fleischer, eds. *Brazil's Economic and Political Future.* Westview Press, Boulder, Colo., 1988.

Youssef Cohen. *The Manipulation of Consent: The State and Working Class Consciousness in Brazil.* University of Pittsburgh Press, Pittsburgh, Pa., 1989.

Daniel Herz. *A história secreta da REDE GLOBO.* Editoria Tchê, Porto Alegre, 1987.

Bolívar Lamounier. "Authoritarian Brazil Revisited: The Impact of Elections on the Abertura," in Alfred Stepan, ed., *Democratizing Brazil: Problems of Transition and Consolidation.* Oxford University Press, New York, 1989.

Bolívar Lamounier and Rachel Meneguello. *Partidos politicos e consolidacão democrática.* Brasiliense, Sâo Paulo, 1986.

Frank D. McCann and Michael L. Conniff. *Modern Brazil: Elites and Masses in Historical Perspective.* University of Nebraska Press, Lincoln, 1989.

Scott Mainwaring. "Brazil: Weak Parties, Feckless Democracy." Paper presented at the 1990 Annual Meeting of the American Political Science Association.

Wayne A. Selcher. "A New Start Toward a More Decentralized Federalism in Brazil?" *Publius: The Journal of Federalism* 19,3, Summer 1989, pp. 176–93.

Wayne A. Selcher, ed. *Political Liberalization in Brazil: Dynamics, Dilemmas, and Future Prospects.* Westview Press, Boulder, Colo., 1986.

Golbery do Couta e Silva. *Conjunctura política nacional, o poder executivo e geopolitica do Brasil.* Editôra Universidade do Brasilia, Brasilia, 1981.

Alfred Stepan. *Rethinking Military Politics: Brazil and the Southern Cone.* Princeton University Press, Princeton, N.J., 1988.

Kurt Von Mettenheim. "The Brazilian Voter in Democratic Transition, 1974–1982." *Comparative Politics* 23,1, October 1990, pp. 23–44.

Jordan Young. "Brazil," in Robert J. Alexander, ed., *Political Parties of the Americas*, vol. 1, 147–86. Greenwood Press, Westport, Conn., 1982.

Political Parties

ALIANÇA RENOVADORA NACIONAL. *See* NATIONAL RENOVATING ALLIANCE.

BRAZILIAN COMMUNIST PARTY (PARTIDO COMUNISTA BRASILEIRO—PCB). On 25 March 1922, in Rio de Janeiro, the Brazilian Communist Party was organized by representatives of small groups from Pôrto Alegre and Rio de Janeiro. A major figure in founding the party was Atrojildo Pereira. Unlike many of the anarchist revolutionaries of the period who had first been attracted by the Bolshevik revolution but had lost confidence in it by 1922, this small group led by Pereira continued to think of themselves as Bolsheviks and so established the party. The PCB has always followed the Moscow line.

The legal existence of the PCB was brief. When the July 1922 *tenente* rebellion occurred in Rio de Janeiro, the government declared a state of siege and the party went underground. In Robert J. Alexander, ed., *Political Parties of the Americas* (1982), Jordan Young analyzes the fortune and strategies of the PCB from the party's founding through the Figueiredo reforms of November 1979. At the time of the reforms, various leaders of the Brazilian Communist Party, including Luis Carlos Prestes, returned to Brazil. Soon afterward, the PCB leadership became involved in a severe internal conflict. In May 1980, Prestes was removed as secretary general, a post he had held since 1945, and Giocondo Gervasi Dias, a sixty-seven-year old member of the Central Committee, was chosen to succeed him. The major issue between Prestes and the majority of the Central Committee was the committee's desire to form a kind of popular front alliance with other groups opposed to the military regime and Prestes's advocacy of a narrower alliance with far-left groups.

The PCB, weakened and dispirited, remained peripheral to the process of *abertura* during the 1980s. In the 1990 legislative elections, the Brazilian Communist Party obtained three deputies, one each from the Federal District, Rio de Janeiro, and Pernambuco.

BRAZILIAN DEMOCRATIC MOVEMENT (MOVIMENTO DEMOCRÁTICO BRASILEIRO—MDB). The MDB was the official opposition party organized after the military regime of President Humberto Castelo Branco outlawed in 1965 all parties then in existence. The party reform bill introduced by President Figueiredo in October 1979, and passed by Congress shortly afterward, presaged the extinction of the two-party system established fourteen years before. As a result of that law, the MDB officially went out of existence on 30 November 1979.

BRAZILIAN DEMOCRATIC MOVEMENT PARTY (PARTIDO DO MOVIMENTO DEMOCRÁTICO BRASILEIRO—PMDB). The PMDB was the largest opposition group to emerge from the 1979 party reform. Like its predecessor, the Brazilian Democratic Movement, the PMDB has remained an extremely heterogeneous and personalist political party. Its dominant orientation is centrist, although beginning in the mid–1980s many conservatives flocked to its banner.

Elation over the 1985 victory of PMDB presidential candidate Trancredo Neves was short lived, when the president-elect died before he could be inaugurated. Subsequently, as part of the Democratic Alliance with the Liberal Front Party, the PMDB provided critical support in Congress for the government of José Sarney.

Although the PMDB dominated the 1987–1988 Constituent Assembly, it remained a collection of political luminaries and regional bosses. After a bitter nominating battle, many local leaders backed away from the party's 1989 presidential candidate, Ulysses Guimarães. With 4.4 percent of the total first-round presidential vote, Guimarães finished a disappointing seventh. In 1990, while the PMDB failed to repeat its sweep of 1986, it elected the largest delegation to the national Congress and retained seven governorships. Governors in wealthy São Paulo and Paraná provide powerful bases from which to challenge for power in the future. The PMDB boasts support throughout the entire country, although its 1990 showing in Rio de Janeiro was surprisingly anemic.

BRAZILIAN LABOR PARTY (PARTIDO TRABALHISTA BRASILEIRO— PTB). This predominantly center-right party was established in 1979 but traces its origin back to 1945, when President Getúlio Vargas ordered his labor minister to form a political party that would attract working-class voters. Funding was supplied indirectly by the national government, and most of the early officials of the PTB were employees of the Labor Ministry. From 1945 to 1961, the party grew slowly and was viewed by many as merely a vote-getting machine aimed at workers in the major cities. Vargas used the PTB as a vehicle to capture the presidency in 1951, and the party went into eclipse after his 1954 suicide.

In 1960 João Goulart of the PTB was elected vice president. When President Jânio Quadros resigned unexpectedly, Goulart was catapulted into the presidency. During Goulart's administration, Governor Leonel Brizola of Rio Grande do Sul, the president's charismatic brother-in-law, emerged as a national PTB leader. Soon after the April 1964 ouster of President Goulart, the military government abolished the PTB.

Following the party reform of 1979, Brizola and Ivete Vargas, grandniece of Getúlio Vargas, sought to assume the historic mantle of the PTB. The military feared Brizola and hoped to disadvantage his bid for power from the left. Thus the PTB label's symbolism was passed to Ivete Vargas. The new PTB cooperated with the progovernment Democratic Socialist Party (PDS) until the PDS lost control of Congress and the political succession process in 1984.

The PTB, after a dreadful performance in the 1989 presidential race—Affonso Camargo received only 0.5 percent of the first-round vote—made a surprising recovery in the 1990 elections. The PTB captured governorships in Matto Grosso do Sul and Roraima and elected six senators and thirty-five deputies from twelve different states.

BRAZILIAN SOCIAL DEMOCRATIC PARTY (PARTIDO SOCIAL DE-MOCRÁTICO BRASILEIRO—PSDB). In 1988, thirty-eight deputies and seven senators of the Brazilian Democratic Movement Party opposed to the policies of President José Sarney split off and formed a new party, the PSDB. Mario Covas, one of those founding senators, finished fourth in the 1989 presidential elections. He remains his party's best known leader. The PSDB appeals to the urban middle class. In the 1990 congressional and gubernatorial elections, it was most successful in São Paulo, Ceará, and Minas Gerais.

BRAZILIAN SOCIALIST PARTY (PARTIDO SOCIALISTA BRASI-LEIRO—PSB). This independent leftist party was founded in 1985 by dissidents from the Brazilian Democratic Movement Party. The PSB is strongest in the northeast, especially in the state of Pernambuco, where former governor Miguel Arraes received the greatest proportional vote of any congressman in the 1990 elections.

CHRISTIAN DEMOCRATIC PARTY (PARTIDO DEMÓCRATA CRIS-TÃO—PDC). The PDC, a doctrinal reformist party, was organized in 1945. At various times in its short career, it attracted some of the most respected and prominent politicians in Brazil, including the old *tenente* leader Juárez Távora, who served for many years as its secretary-general. The Christian Democratic Party went out of existence in October 1965, as a result of Institutional Act 2. No serious effort was made to keep the party going clandestinely.

The PDC was reestablished in 1986. In contrast to Christian Democratic parties in many countries, the Brazilian party is on the right end of the political spectrum. PDC strength is greatest in the center-west (Tocantins) and north (Maranhão) regions, although it has some following in Rio de Janeiro.

COMMUNIST PARTY OF BRAZIL (PARTIDO COMUNISTA DO BRASIL-PC DO B). The PC do B coalesced in 1961, around a splinter group which separated from the Brazilian Communist Party (PCB). Subsequently, until Deng Xiaoping set China on a more moderate course (during the middle 1970's), the

PC do B sided with Beijing in the Sino-Soviet controversy. Those who formed the party were a group of men who had controlled the PCB in the 1947–1957 period during which Secretary-General Luis Carlos Prestes was forced underground. After the Kubitschek government withdrew the charges levelled against Prestes, and he was allowed to take over leadership of the PCB once again, those who had been running the party chafed over being relegated to subordinate status. They also disagreed with Prestes' unshakable loyalty to Moscow. Best known among the founding PC do B leaders were Mauricio Grabois and João Amazonas.

With only a meager following, the PC do B had little impact on the national scene, although during the Goulart presidency it did have some small influence in the new agricultural workers' unions then being organized. During the military regime, the party worked to set up rural *focos* of armed resistance, but with little success.

By 1980 the PC do B had been alienated by the trends of Chinese policy. After the death of Mao Tse-tung, they aligned themselves internationally with the leadership of the Albanian Communist Party. Legalized during the Sarney government, the PC do B participated in the 1990 legislative elections and was marginally more successful than the PCB. In addition to support in São Paulo and Rio de Janeiro, the PC do B has a small but dedicated following in the cities of the northeast.

DEMOCRATIC LABOR PARTY (PARTIDO DEMOCRÁTICO TRABAL-HISTA—PDT). This populist party, founded in 1979, centered on Leonel Brizola, the governor of Rio de Janeiro. The PDT traces its lineage to Getúlio Vargas and the pre-1964 Brazilian Labor Party. The PDT also has strong ties with the international Social Democratic Movement.

After Brizola finished third in the 1989 presidential election, he threw PDT support in the runoff behind the unsuccessful candidacy of Luis Inácio (Lula) da Silva, of the Workers' Party (PT). In 1990 the PDT won victories in the gubernatorial races of Rio Grande do Sul, Rio de Janeiro, and Espírito Santo. The PDT also enjoyed greater success in congressional races than its leftist rival, the PT. This reestablished the PDT as the most important party on the left. An important weakness of the PDT remains its lack of support in the populous states of Minas Gerais and São Paulo, where the PT has its greatest following.

DEMOCRATIC SOCIALIST PARTY (PARTIDO DEMOCRÁTICO SO-CIAL—PDS). The PDS emerged from the party reform of 1979 as the successor to the proregime National Renovating Alliance. In 1982 President João Figueiredo's manipulation of electoral rules allowed the PDS to win control of the electoral college that would select the president three years later. However, the candidacy of Paulo Salim Maluf cooled military support for the PDS. It also alienated many northeastern political bosses who had backed the military regime since its inception. Widespread opposition to Maluf cleared the way for Trancredo Neves, of the Brazilian Democratic Movement Party, to sweep the electoral college in January 1985.

The PDS remains a significant actor in the New Republic. Although Maluf was defeated in the 1989 runoff election for governor of São Paulo, the party sent important delegations to Congress from the states of Acre, Rio Grande do Sul, Santa Catarina, and São Paulo.

LIBERAL FRONT PARTY (PARTIDO DA FRENTE LIBERAL—PFL). Created in 1984 by dissidents from the Democratic Socialist Party opposed to the presidential candidacy of Paulo Salim Maluf, the PFL is a conservative party with a strong rural constituency. PFL leader José Sarney negotiated a pact with the Brazilian Democratic Movement Party in 1984 which led to the electoral college's selection of Trancredo Neves as president. Sarney, the vice president, became president upon the death of Neves.

In the 1989 presidential election, the PFL candidate, Aureliano Chaves, suffered from identification with the discredited Sarney government. The failure of Chaves to stake out an independent identity caused PFL leaders to back away in mass from his candidacy. The 1990 congressional and state elections were a different story. The party elected nine governors, more than any other party, and boasted the second largest delegation of senators and deputies. The PFL is strongest in the north and northeast regions and weakest in the south, especially in São Paulo and Rio Grande do Sul.

LIBERAL PARTY (PARTIDO LIBERAL—PL). A conservative party, founded in 1986, the PL is known for its antistatist discourse. The PL gained a high profile when its 1989 presidential candidate, Guilherme Afif Domingos, performed well in the televised presidential debates. Afif is prominent in the commercial sector of São Paulo, which along with neighboring Minas Gerais is the center of greatest support for the PL.

MOVIMENTO DEMOCRÁTICO BRASILEIRO. See BRAZILIAN DEMOCRATIC MOVEMENT.

NATIONAL RECONSTRUCTION PARTY (PARTIDO RENOVADOR NACIONAL—PRN). This movement was created in 1989 by Fernando Collor de Mello to coordinate his run for the presidency. Roberto Marinho, president of the Globo Group, who gave Collor unlimited access to television, portrayed him as a populist who would not pander to leftist ideologues. In the 1990 legislative elections, local politicians in the northeast and Minas Gerais used the party with some success as a vehicle for their own personal ambitions.

NATIONAL RENOVATING ALLIANCE (ALIANÇA RENOVADORA NACIONAL—ARENA). ARENA, the official government party from 1966 to 1979, was established after the military regime had dissolved all then existing parties, in October 1965.

As a result of a party reform bill, submitted to Congress in October 1979 by President João Figueiredo, which suppressed both ARENA and its opponent, the Brazilian Democratic Movement, ARENA came to an end. It was officially dissolved by decree on 30 November 1979.

POPULAR PARTY (PARTIDO POPULAR—PP). This conservative offshoot of the Brazilian Democratic Movement Party (PMDB) was short lived. It was reabsorbed into the PMDB after the Figueiredo government tampered with electoral laws to discriminate against smaller political parties.

PARTIDO COMUNISTA BRASILEIRO. See BRAZILIAN COMMUNIST PARTY.

PARTIDO COMUNISTA DO BRASIL. See COMMUNIST PARTY OF BRAZIL.

PARTIDO DA FRENTE LIBERAL. See LIBERAL FRONT PARTY.

PARTIDO DEMÓCRATA CRISTÃO. See CHRISTIAN DEMOCRATIC PARTY.

PARTIDO DEMOCRÁTICO SOCIAL. See DEMOCRATIC SOCIALIST PARTY.

PARTIDO DEMOCRÁTICO TRABALHISTA. See DEMOCRATIC LABOR PARTY.

PARTIDO DO MOVIMENTO DEMOCRÁTICO BRASILEIRO. See BRAZILIAN DEMOCRATIC MOVEMENT PARTY.

PARTIDO DO TRABALHADOR REVOLUCIONARIO. See REVOLUTIONARY WORKERS' PARTY.

PARTIDO DOS TRABALHADORES. See WORKERS' PARTY.

PARTIDO LIBERAL. See LIBERAL PARTY.

PARTIDO POPULAR. See POPULAR PARTY.

PARTIDO RENOVADOR NACIONAL. See NATIONAL RECONSTRUCTION PARTY.

PARTIDO REVOLUCIONARIO SOCIALISTA. *See* REVOLUTIONARY SOCIALIST PARTY.

PARTIDO SOCIAL CRISTÃO. *See* SOCIAL CHRISTIAN PARTY.

PARTIDO SOCIAL DEMOCRÁTICO. *See* SOCIAL DEMOCRATIC PARTY.

PARTIDO SOCIAL DEMOCRÁTICO BRASILEIRO. *See* BRAZILIAN SOCIAL DEMOCRATIC PARTY.

PARTIDO SOCIALISTA BRASILEIRO. *See* BRAZILIAN SOCIALIST PARTY.

PARTIDO TRABALHISTA BRASILEIRO. *See* BRAZILIAN LABOR PARTY.

REVOLUTIONARY SOCIALIST PARTY (PARTIDO REVOLUCIONARIO SOCIALISTA—PRS). This centrist party, from the state of Minas Gerais, competed in 1990 as part of a slate which included the Brazilian Labor Party and the Liberal Party. In the second round of elections, the PRS candidate for governor, Hélio Garcia, defeated his Collor-supported, National Reconstruction Party rival. The party elected four members to the national Chamber of Deputies.

REVOLUTIONARY WORKERS' PARTY (PARTIDO DO TRABALHADOR REVOLUCIONARIO—PTR). This small leftist grouping has its strength in the Federal District and in Rio de Janeiro.

SOCIAL CHRISTIAN PARTY (PARTIDO SOCIAL CRISTÃO—PSC). This small centrist Christian party has its strength in the north and northeastern states, as well as some strength in Alagoas.

SOCIAL DEMOCRATIC PARTY (PARTIDO SOCIAL DEMOCRÁTICO—PSD). This small conservative party is centered in Goiás. Its single deputy, Ronaldo Caiado, founded and oversees the lobby in Brasilia for rural landowners, the Uniâo Democrática Ruralista. The contemporary Social Democratic Party has no connection with the middle class–based party of the same name which dominated Brazilian politics between 1956 and 1964.

WORKERS' PARTY (PARTIDO DOS TRABALHADORES—PT). A heterogeneous leftist party, the PT was founded in 1979 by the then president of the São Paulo metalworkers union, Luis Inácio (Lula) da Silva. The PT continues to be linked with the Central Unica dos Trabalhadores, the country's most aggressive labor union. PT militants range from Marxist revolutionaries, through liberation theology Christians, to social democrats. After a disappointing show-ing in the elections of 1982 and 1986, the PT won a string of impressive victories in the municipal elections held in November 1988. Its most stunning success came in the city of São Paulo, where Luiza Erundina do Souza was elected mayor.

PT presidential candidate Lula was runner-up in the first round of the 1989 presidential election. He lost a close contest in the second round to Fernando Collor de Mello. PT identification with the command economies of Eastern Europe, at the very moment Communist regimes in the region were crumbling, contributed to Lula's loss. In the 1990 balloting, the PT did worse than expected; it secured no governorships and elected only one senator. Its greatest strength remains among the poor of São Paulo, Minas Gerais, Rio Grande do Sul, and in the north.

David J. Myers

BRITISH VIRGIN ISLANDS

The British Virgin Islands are an archipelago comprising more than fifty islands, including a land area of almost 53 square miles, and supporting a population of nearly 12,500. The population resides on the four main islands of Jost van Dyke, Tortola, Virgin Gorda, and Anegada. The terrain is hilly and thus more appropriate for livestock raising than agriculture. The tourist industry and the licensing of offshore businesses and banks provide the majority of the colony's revenue and a per capita income of U.S.$8,200.

The executive branch is composed of the British monarch who is represented locally by a British-appointed governor responsible for defense and internal security, external affairs, and administration of the judiciary. There is also the Executive Council, with the governor as chairperson, joined by the attorney general, the chief minister (the leader of the elected members of the legislature), and three other members appointed by the governor on the advice of the chief minister. Finally, there are nine members of the Legislative Council, elected by universal adult suffrage. Queen Elizabeth II, the head of state, has been represented locally since 1986 by Governor John Mark Ambrose. The head of government is Chief Minister H. Lavity Stoutt, who has been in office since the 1986 elections for the Legislative Council.

The British Virgin Islands have a very stable democratic system which has been characterized by tranquility and an orderly transfer of power. There is little ideological or social difference among the three political parties now functioning on the islands.

Stoutt, the leader of the Virgin Islands Party (VIP), became the islands' first chief minister when the British Virgin Islands achieved a degree of self-government under a new constitution in 1967. In the 1975 election, with the VIP winning three of the then seven seats and the United Party (UP) also gaining three seats, an independent by the name of Willard Wheatly won the remaining seat and was able to form a coalition government and serve as chief minister, with Stoutt as his deputy. In the 1979 elections (following the expansion of the Legislative Council to nine seats), independents won five seats, and Stoutt's VIP won four, thus enabling Stoutt to again assume the chief ministership. In the 1983 elections, both the VIP and the UP, then headed by Willard Wheatly, won four seats, and an independent named Cyril B. Romney formed a coalition government and became chief minister. In 1986, Stoutt's VIP returned to power with five seats.

Political parties here differ insignificantly in their basic philosophies. Policy concern focuses on the stability of the tourist-driven economy. There is no independence movement; the citizenry prefers to maintain ties with, and financial assistance from, the United Kingdom.

Bibliography

Central Intelligence Agency. *The World Factbook, 1990*. Central Intelligence Agency, Washington, D.C., 1990.

Sandra Meditz and Dennis Hanratty, eds. *Islands of the Commonwealth Caribbean: A Regional Study*. Area Handbook Program, U.S. Government Printing Office, Washington, D.C., 1989.

Additional information can be gleaned from the following newsletters: *Caribbean Monitor, Latin American and Caribbean Contemporary Regional Reports—Caribbean*, and *Caribbean Insight*.

Political Parties

INDEPENDENT PEOPLE'S MOVEMENT (IPM). This new party captured one seat in the 1983 elections, enabling its leader, Cyril B. Romney, to take advantage of the four-four split between the two main parties to form a coalition government and to serve as chief minister from 1983 to 1986. The IPM currently holds two seats in the nine-member Legislative Council, which is dominated by the Virgin Islands Party.

UNITED PARTY (UP). Formed in the early 1970s under the leadership of Conrad Maduro, the UP has yet to be the governing party. It tied with the Virgin Islands Party (VIP) on two occasions, but each time an independent member, with the swing vote, formed a coalition government with the VIP. In 1986, it won only two seats.

VIRGIN ISLANDS PARTY (VIP). Established in 1969 under the leadership of the then chief minister, H. Lavity Stoutt, the VIP has been the islands' most successful political party and the best organized one. It currently holds five seats in the Legislative Council, and Stoutt is again chief minister, a post he has held on and off since 1967.

Gary Brana-Shute
Rosemary Brana-Shute

CANADA

Canada is a country of immense size. Its approximately 3.8 million square miles, extending from the North Pole to the Great Lakes, make it the world's second largest state. It currently has a population of over 26 million, the majority of whom reside in metropolitan areas located in a relatively narrow band north of the Canadian border with the United States.

The country was initially settled by French colonists who established two major outposts (Quebec City, 1608, and Montreal, 1642) in what is now the province of Quebec. Periodic eighteenth-century conflicts between England and France and clashes between French and British colonists in North America culminated in Canada's becoming a British possession in 1763.

Representative government and a legislature were introduced by British authorities in 1791. Basic political institutions and processes, such as the cabinet form of responsible government, an independent judiciary, the rule of law, nascent political parties, competitive elections, and peaceful transitions of executive power, were firmly established and legitimized by the time the provinces of Ontario, Quebec, Nova Scotia, and New Brunswick became a federal union in 1867 by an act of the British parliament, the British North America Act. The provinces of Manitoba and British Columbia entered the union in 1870 and 1871, respectively, and Prince Edward Island joined in 1873. The provinces of Alberta and Saskatchewan were carved out of the west in 1905, and Newfoundland voted in a referendum to join Canada and became the country's tenth province in 1949.

Demography

Similar to the United States, Canada's current population is derived from a polyglot of ethnic groups, the largest of which is the Anglo-Scottish-Irish. About 26 percent of the population is of French descent, and approximately 80 percent of them reside in the province of Quebec and are Francophones. The cleavage between English- and French-speaking Canadians is arguably the most important characteristic of Canadian society. It has its origins in the aforementioned British conquest of Quebec. The British authorities did not try to assimilate the local population. Instead, the French were allowed to retain their language, Catholic religion, system of education, and civil law code. The legitimacy of a distinctly French-Canadian culture thus was recognized, and the socialization opportunities inherent in its ecclesiastically dominated educational system enabled it to be sustained. Also of importance for French-Canadian "survivance" has been a high birth rate—so high, in fact, that although immigration from France essentially ceased after 1760, the proportion of Canada's population that is French remained relatively constant for over 200 years. In the past two decades, however, the birthrate of Francophone Quebecers has declined precipitously, heightening their fears of becoming culturally assimilated by Canada's Anglophone majority.

Party Origins and Development

In their suggestive essay, Joseph LaPalombara and Myron Weiner (1966) observe that there are both "inside" and "outside" explanations of the origins and development of political parties. In some instances, parties have their origins in legislative bodies, beginning as factional groupings loosely organized around charismatic individuals. Factional lines begin to harden, internal organizations develop, and cohesive group actions increase when one or more major issues, whose resolution can extend over a generation or more, arise. Concomitant with the democratization of the electorate, the losing side(s) in such controversies (the "outs") generally begin to develop ties with supporters in the electorate in an effort to become the "ins." They gradually expand and develop these ties into ongoing electoral organizations and, since organization generally stimulates counterorganization, twentieth-century political parties in democratic political systems are characterized by institutionalized patterns of communication and interaction between their legislative and extralegislative components. Outside parties, in contrast, begin not as factional groupings within legislatures, but as mass social movements responding to social and economic dislocations, such as those associated with industrialization and urbanization. Some of these mass social movements solidify, develop organizational structures, and institutionalize procedures that enable them to recruit candidates and elect them to public offices. The inside and outside explanations account for the origins and development of Canada's national political parties. The two "major" national parties, the Liberal and Progressive Conservative (formerly the Conservative), are inside parties. Their beginnings are rooted in early nineteenth-century legislative struggles to achieve responsible government in the then British colonies. Most other parties, such as the New Democratic Party (formerly the Cooperative Commonwealth Federation) and Social Credit, are outside parties.

The Party System(s)

Three points about the Canadian party system are especially noteworthy. First, it is exceedingly complex. Indeed, one could reasonably argue that the country really does not have a one-party system, but several. In part, this is a consequence of the important role the provinces play in the federal system. Also, in part, it is a function of strong regional feelings based upon economic and social-cultural particularisms that characterize Canadian political life. Whatever the reasons, the reality is a party struggle in which both the identities of the contestants and the patterns of competition between and among them can vary sharply from province to province. Moreover, within individual provinces, party competition at one level of government often seems to be almost hermetically sealed from competition at another.

Consider some examples. Interparty competition in the provinces of Nova Scotia, Manitoba, and British Columbia is of the classic two-party variety. The identities of the contesting parties, however, differ as one moves from east to west. In Nova Scotia, the electoral struggle is waged between the old-line center-left and center-right parties, the Liberals and the Conservatives (throughout this chapter, the labels "Conservative," "Progressive Conservative," and "PC" are used interchangeably). In Manitoba, the fight is between the Conservatives and the social-democratic New Democratic Party (NDP), and in British Columbia, it is between the NDP and their professed ideological foes, Social Credit. In Quebec, two parties—the Union Nationale and the Parti Québécois (PQ)— do not even compete in federal elections, but they have governed the province during 58 percent of the postwar period. However, the Liberal Party has also been successful at the provincial level in Quebec; it has won six elections since 1960, and it has dominated federal politics in the province until recently. In sharp contrast, the Conservative Party was a nonstarter at both the federal and provincial levels in Quebec for many years. Although this remains true provincially, in the two most recent federal elections (1984 and 1988), it gained 50 percent plus of the popular vote and captured three-fifths of Quebec's seats in the national parliament. In Ontario, patterns of party competition are different again. The Liberals did not win a single Ontario provincial election from the late 1930s to the mid-1980s but, with the exception of 1984, they frequently have fared quite well in federal elections. The Conservatives governed the province continuously between 1943 and 1985 and lost badly in the 1987 and 1990 provincial elections, but the party has been a formidable force in the federal arena since the late 1970s. The NDP also has electoral support in Ontario and, although the party typically has run behind its Conservative and Liberal rivals in federal and provincial elections, in 1990 it swept the Liberals from power to become the first NDP government in the province's history.

Second, although Canada has multiple national parties, for much of the post–World War II era the federal political arena has tended toward one-party dominance; the Liberal Party has governed the country for approximately thirty-two of the thirty-nine years between 1945 and 1984. The hegemony that the party long enjoyed in federal politics rested in large part on its aforementioned success in Quebec. In the thirteen national elections held between 1945 and 1980, the party captured, on average, over half (54 percent) of the Quebec vote, a considerably larger share than it received in the Atlantic provinces, in Ontario, and, in particular, in the west. The distortion produced by the first-past-the-post electoral system also worked in favor of the party. In ten of these thirteen national elections, the Liberals' share of parliamentary seats has exceeded its share of the vote, and on five occasions a minority of the popular vote gave the party a majority of parliamentary seats (compare Figures 1 and 2). Also, although many Canadians do not have strong, stable psychological attachments to political parties, during the era of Liberal dominance opposition parties had little success in developing electoral strategies capable of attracting the preponderance of those with flexible party ties. Rather, the pattern of voter movement between elections frequently has been a crosscutting one which has had little net effect on Liberal vote totals.

The tendency toward domination by a single party also is evident at the provincial level. There are numerous examples. In Ontario, the Tory "Big Blue Machine" governed continuously from 1943 to 1985. Newfoundland was governed for twenty-two years (1949–1971) by the provincial Liberals led by Joey Smallwood. In Saskatchewan, the provincial NDP governed without interruption for twenty years (1944–1964), and Social Credit was in power in Alberta for thirty-six years before being defeated by the Conservatives in 1971, who, in turn, have been in power continuously since then. In British Columbia, Social Credit has formed the provincial government for all but three years since 1952. In Quebec, the Liberals were in power for thirty-nine years without interruption early in the country's history, and between 1936 and 1960 the Union Nationale governed for nineteen years.

Third—tendencies toward one-partyism notwithstanding—there is a curious periodicity to party fortunes. A party may enjoy years of electoral success and then rapidly fall from grace. For example, Liberal candidates captured 65 percent of the parliamentary seats in the 1953 federal election, 40 percent in 1957, and only 19 percent in 1958—a decline of more than 40 percent in a five-year period. The Conservatives won almost 80 percent of the seats in the 1958 election but won only 36 percent six years later. More recently, the Liberals governed for all but nine months between 1963 and 1980, and they captured 147 of the 282 seats in the 1980 federal election. Four years later, however, the party suffered a crushing defeat, electing only 40 of 295 MPs. The tendency has manifested itself equally strongly at the provincial level. To illustrate, after governing for a generation, the Liberal Party of Newfoundland and the Social Credit Party of Alberta virtually disappeared from their respective provincial legislatures during the 1970s. In Ontario, the long-dominant Conservatives saw their seat totals drop from 56 percent to 42 percent to 12 percent in three provincial elections held between 1981 and 1987. These sharp swings in party

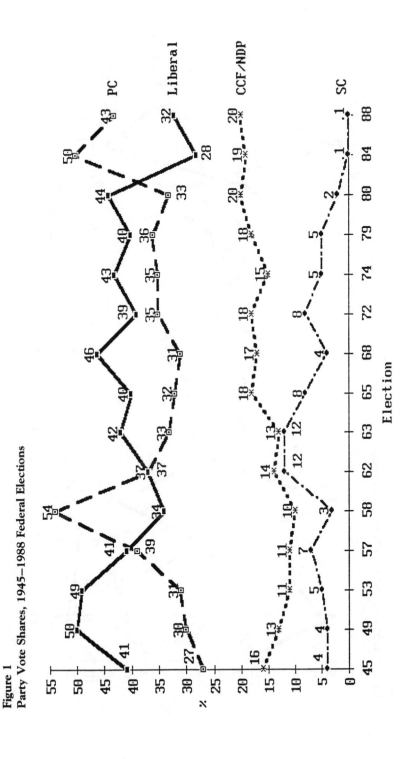

Figure 1
Party Vote Shares, 1945–1988 Federal Elections

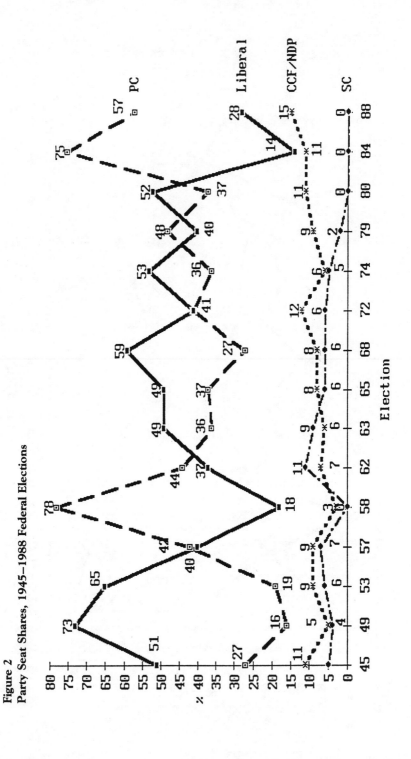

Figure 2
Party Seat Shares, 1945–1988 Federal Elections

fortunes are at least partially the result of the aforementioned fact that many Canadians have weak and unstable party identifications. Further, the pattern whereby a party within a particular province fares much better in federal than in provincial elections, or vice versa, is related to the tendency of many voters to "split" their partisan attachments: to identify with party "A" at one level of the system and with party "B" at the other.

Parties in Parliament

The institution of parliament and virtually all of the procedures initially adopted were transported from Great Britain via the legislative bodies of the four provinces that united in 1867 to form a new Canadian state. In the more than 120 years since then, the membership of the House of Commons has changed from loose factions into disciplined, cohesive parties that focus many of their activities on either supporting or opposing government-initiated legislation. As has been the case in other representative democracies with British-model parliamentary government, parliament's membership has increased significantly (in Canada from 100 to 295); at the same time, formal procedures have been implemented to limit the opportunities available to private members to participate in the process of drafting and evaluating legislation. The reasons for these developments are complex. In brief, however, they may be viewed as consequences of societal growth and modernization. The argument is that, if their parliaments are to be representative, their compositions must reflect both the increases and the geographic distributions of their populations. If they are also to be effective instruments for governing a complex industrial society, the political parties that have won elections must have the opportunity to implement their policies and programs.

In Canada, successive governments have tried to carry out their perceived mandates in four related ways:

1. By enlarging the cabinet, organizing it into committees, and supplying it with appropriate expert staff assistance

2. By ensuring that the consideration of cabinet legislation takes calendar and time precedence over private-member legislative proposals

3. By limiting the opportunities available to private members either to initiate legislation or to participate in its evaluation

4. By officially recognizing the role that opposition parties play in the policy process and by providing them with the expert staff required to function effectively.

The principal mechanism employed to achieve cohesive action is the party caucus. Each party generally caucuses weekly during a parliamentary session, and the two major parties also make use of regional and subregional caucuses. A caucus performs the following functions: It provides a party's members of parliament (MPs) with an opportunity to discuss the strategies and tactics that will be employed in evaluating current legislation in plenary and committee sessions; it enables MPs to hammer out party positions on policy issues; it provides backbench MPs with a means to express grievances or complaints to party leaders and to exchange information about the distribution of grass-roots opinions in their constituencies; it socializes MPs to accept a division of labor in which party leaders play the principal role in legislative debates while backbenchers give their time and attention to the performance of services on the behalf of constituents.

A recurring observation and a frequent complaint of students of Canadian politics is that the Liberals and Conservatives (the only two parties that have governed at the national level) have similar values and ideological perspectives, recruit the same kinds of people as parliamentary candidates, and generate similar policies when in office. The late John Porter's version of this argument is perhaps the most widely known, but variations on this theme can be found in the work of many other political scientists and historians. A longitudinal analysis of the legislative outputs of Canada's first twenty-eight parliaments (1867–1972) tends to support Porter's claim regarding the relative similarity of the policy outputs of the two parties. Although Liberal governments have passed more redistributive legislation and more foreign affairs bills and have expended a larger proportion of the budget on defense, it can be argued that such differences between Liberals and Conservatives are time related. The Liberals have held office for most of the twentieth century, whereas the period of Conservative hegemony was the nineteenth century when the issues confronting parliament were less complex and the scope of desired governmental activity was more restricted.

With respect to leadership differences, an in-depth study of the distribution and correlates of influence in a reasonably typical parliament (the twenty-eighth, 1968–1972) indicates that both the parliamentary and preparliamentary careers, as well as the values and perspectives, of Liberal cabinet ministers and Conservative front-benchers differed. Although the two groups were drawn largely from the same population pool, the Conservative leaders tended to be older (eight years on average), were more apt to be native Canadians and Protestants, and more frequently had an Anglo-Celtic and Northern European heritage; Liberal cabinet ministers were more frequently French Canadians as well as university and professional school graduates, especially in law.

There is also evidence that, although the policy outputs of Liberal and Conservative governments have not differed greatly over the years, MPs in the two parties view themselves as occupying different ideological positions on important policy issues. This is the case as well for Social Credit and NDP MPs. The public also perceives differences among the four parliamentary parties' policy positions, although these differences are not as great as the MPs believe them to be. Analysis reveals that a left-right ideological dimension most often underlies MPs' perceptions of their own and their parties' positions on policy issues, whereas the public most often sees the parties in terms of government-opposition, major-minor, and French–non-French dimensions. Other studies have indicated that provincial legislators also take significantly different positions on left-right ideological scales. Although no evidence is currently available, it seems reasonable to assume that the public perceives the policy positions of provincial parliamentary parties in much the same way as they view federal parties.

Regardless of which positions the public sees parties occupying in issue space, a more important question is whether Canadian parties effectively perform the kinds of functions that we normally ascribe to them. The observation that there really is no single-party system suggests that the integrative function has been performed with less than conspicuous success over the years. In a thoughtful essay, party scholar John Meisel (1975) indicts the parties for their failure in this area and argues that their ability to perform functions, such as political mobilization, interest aggregation, and policy formulation, also has declined markedly since World War II. He attributes this decline to a number of long-term factors. Included are the rise of a bureaucratic state, increased interest-group activity, incipient corporatism, the growth of executive federalism, the rise of electronic media and investigative journalism, the influence of economic interests, and, until the mid-1980s, the domination of federal politics by the Liberal Party.

A governing party's ability to formulate policy has been the area in which decline has been most severe. Concomitant with the increased scope of governmental activity in the post–World War II period has been a vast increase in the size and power of the federal bureaucracy. Upper-echelon bureaucratic officials (that is, deputy and assistant deputy ministers in traditional line departments together with central agency officials) formulate the bulk of public policy because they structure and limit the range of policy alternatives from which their political masters in cabinet choose, and they also marshall the supporting data that assist ministers in making their choices. Before any important policy decision is made, there customarily is an intense period of consultation among cabinet ministers, their principal bureaucratic subordinates, and representatives of the interests that are likely to be affected. The consultation process has been institutionalized through the appointment of advisory committees and other bodies that ensure that government officials are continuously apprised of the positions of the organized group interests. However, a more recent tendency has been to carry on these consultations *without* the presence of ministers.

Another reason that parliamentary parties have become minor and segmental participants in the policy process is that many major policies are hammered out through the mechanisms of executive federalism which feature periodic federal-provincial ministerial conferences involving the prime minister, the several provincial premiers, and their respective platoons of bureaucratic advisors. The advisors work out the details involved in implementing policy decisions in the multitude of meetings of committees, task forces, and working groups which take place annually. During the post–World War II era, the exercise of bureaucratic power over policy formulation and administration was facilitated by successive Liberal governments which seemed to have an affinity for bureaucrats and vice versa. Given the virtually continuous hegemony that the party exercised over federal politics in this period, it is argued that the line between the federal bureaucracy and the Liberal Party became blurred: In fact, the party's entire platform in one national election supposedly was written by a group of high-level civil servants.

The ability of parliamentary parties to mobilize public opinion has been seriously affected by the rise of electronic media (particularly television) and the tendency of media figures to ascribe to themselves the role of "official opposition" to the government of the day, thereby usurping one of the principal roles of opposition parties. Legislative party leaders make statements and engage in other activities that are intended to attract the electronic media and, through them, the attention of the millions who watch television and listen to radio. In order to appeal to the media, party leaders have had to accommodate them-selves to media demands and needs. The principal concern of the media, ac-cording to Meisel, is to *entertain* the widest possible audience. Consequently, with the active collaboration of party leaders, the media present political events to the public in ways that will maximize their attractiveness. For example, federal and provincial elections are cast as kinds of athletic contests in which the comings, goings, performance, and personality of the star player of each team (that is, the party leader) are the principal attractions. Although these tactics may result in short-term gains for parties that "package" their leaders in appealing ways, their long-term effect seems to contribute to the cynical and negative attitudes toward parties and their leaders that have characterized Ca-nadian public opinion throughout the past two decades.

Extraparliamentary Party Organizations

In the United States, one consequence of the reliance of political parties on electronic media to convey their messages to the electorate has been a decline in party organizations, in general, and a diminution in the importance of their roles in election campaigns, in particular. There is reason to believe that this also may be the case in Canada. Studies of extraparliamentary party organizations indicate that Canadian party officials are very much attuned to and make use of the latest American campaign technology. This is especially true of the Liberal and Conservative parties, but other parties have also adopted these election-eering strategies. The Liberals took the lead in building rudimentary extrapar-liamentary organizations in the nineteenth century. However, as late as 1880, only about 50 percent of the federal constituencies had even paper party asso-ciations. The Liberals did not hold their first national convention until 1893 and did not establish a national office until 1912. The Conservatives lagged behind the Liberals in both areas (for example, their first national leadership convention was held in 1927). Not until the 1920s did either party make concerted, systematic attempts to organize their supporters into viable extra-parliamentary organizations. Their efforts were spurred by the expansion of the electorate that occurred at the time and the need to mobilize the support of the newly enfranchised groups. The Social Credit and the Cooperative Commonwealth Federation (CCF)-NDP followed the lead of the two older parties.

Extraparliamentary organizations have been controlled historically by people whose primary goals have been to select and elect candidates for public office. These goals have taken precedence over other objectives. The tasks associated with the performance of the recruitment-election function have been virtually monopolized by the constituency-level units of extraparliamentary party organizations. They are the most active in hierarchies that are generally skeletal, decentralized, and loosely articulated. It is true that federal parties have national and, in some provinces, provincial offices. The offices of the Liberal, Conservative, and New Democratic parties have minimum staffs that are expanded immediately before elections, but the Social Credit party lacks even this level of organization. Central party offices provide financial assistance, speakers, campaign materials, and other forms of assistance to constituency organizations and their candidates. These forms of support are welcomed since, under certain conditions, they may provide the margin between electoral success and failure. Despite this assistance, and the occasional "parachuting" of candidates into constituencies, the aforementioned tasks of candidate recruitment and electioneering are usually firmly in the hands of constituency party leaders.

The organizational form of most constituency parties tends to be a truncated pyramid. The more elaborately organized parties in metropolitan areas have multiple layers (for example, poll, area, zone, constituency), but the less fully organized generally dispense with the two intermediate ones. In some areas, party workers are paid either directly or indirectly for their services. In most cases, however, these payments are very modest and are almost entirely restricted to individuals holding positions at the bottom level of the organizational hierarchy. An overwhelming majority of a party's activists in upper-echelon positions are unpaid. Thus, constituency organizations are populated almost entirely by amateurs. Since most constituency-level party officials do not receive material rewards for their services, when a conflict occurs between the demands of party work and other obligations, the latter usually take precedence. The potential for conflict is heightened by the episodic nature of most party work, which is oriented toward periodic elections. Since the interims between active campaigns can be quite lengthy, local parties may experience morale problems, and the organizations are characterized by high rates of personnel turnover.

Democratic norms, customary practice, and party constitutions usually require that the parties adhere to an open-door recruitment policy. Although they are not legally required to admit anyone, the need to maintain and broaden their base of support is a strong inducement for party leaders to accept and actively recruit or coopt representative members from a broad spectrum of social groups, including those that do not traditionally support their respective parties. Given the distinctive features of party organizational structures and functions, recruitment is not an easy task. Party officials proceed with the business of acquiring new members much as do other voluntary organizations. People sometimes are coopted, personal friendships are traded on, and when these do not suffice, the prospect of holding a high party position or engaging in interesting and exciting work is held out as an inducement to join. Even so, a considerable number of those recruited by these means join primarily as a convenience to current officials. If recruits of this kind rarely develop a great desire to become contenders for public offices or organizational powers, they also do not expect to devote too much time or effort to party affairs, as many candidates for parliamentary or for provincial legislative seats have found to their sorrow.

Types of Party Officials

Three types of local party officials may be distinguished. The first, the "stalwarts," occupy middle-level positions of the truncated structures of constituency parties. A second group, the "insiders," hold high-level positions in the party hierarchy, and their principal tasks are to coordinate and supervise the work of stalwarts. They also engage in a variety of routine record-keeping tasks, and they apprise top position-holders and candidates for elected office of partisan sentiments among voters and policy concerns on the basis of information collected in face-to-face canvassing and other interactions with the public. Insiders not only coordinate the work of stalwarts, they also perform some of the same tasks. However, they generally have performed them longer and more effectively. "Elites," the third group, frequently occupy the highest organizational positions and they, more often than the others, are a party's standard-bearers in an electoral contest or are its appointees to nonelective public offices. Most important, they are the most influential people in party affairs. Although the exact proportions vary somewhat by party, approximately 60 percent of the officials of every party may be classified as stalwarts, about 30 percent as insiders, and the rest as elites.

Analyses indicate that elites, more frequently than insiders or stalwarts, come from high-status backgrounds. In many cases, these initial socioeconomic status advantages are maintained and even enhanced over time. Political socialization differences also characterize the three types. Elites, more often than insiders or stalwarts, report that they were reared in politicized childhood and adolescent environments. In many cases, their parents were politically active; as a result, elites tend most frequently to report steadily increasing political interest and involvement prior to joining a party.

The three types of party officials are further differentiated by varying levels of commitment to party work and by their attitudes toward their organizations and themselves. Elites report doing more work, working longer for their parties than insiders or stalwarts, and holding more positions generally and more high-level positions in particular. Such differences are reflected in the reactions of the three types to their experiences. Elites and insiders, more frequently than stalwarts, derive a sense of accomplishment from their party activities and are more likely to view party work as leading to public office opportunities. Finally, the three groups have different self-images; elites are the most and stalwarts are the least likely to think of themselves in political terms.

Although there is evidence that the situation is slowly changing, women historically have been a minority in extraparliamentary parties, and they have tended to occupy the lower ranks of the parties' organizations. By way of illustration, a study of local party organizations in Winnipeg and Vancouver showed that the ratio of stalwarts to elites among male officials was approximately 3:1 but that there were almost fourteen times as many stalwarts as elites among women. Since political activity in Canada has traditionally been seen as a male role, it is not surprising that the women who do rise to the top of party organizations have many of the socioeconomic attributes (extensive formal education, high incomes, prestigious occupations) that are associated with the political success of men. Perhaps in reaction to the difficulties they face in achieving political success, such women tend to manifest higher levels of psychological commitment to party work and to devote more time to party activities than do their male counterparts.

Since there are so few layers in a constituency party hierarchy through which officials can move upward, the pinnacle of a "successful" party career for both men and women officials is (1) selection as the party's candidate in a federal or provincial election, (2) appointment to a federal or provincial judgeship, or (3) appointment to one of the numerous boards, commissions, and advisory groups which are such integral parts of federal and provincial bureaucracies. These positions, rather than direct monetary compensation, are the principal payoffs to middle- and upper-middle-class individuals for their work in party organizations.

Parties in the Electorate

Only a small percentage of Canadians are actively involved in party organizations. For the vast majority, party affiliations are psychological rather than behavioral. The pervasiveness of these psychological attachments to political parties is illustrated by the fact that, in sixteen national surveys conducted over the past quarter century, the number of citizens expressing some sense of attachment to a federal political party has averaged 86 percent (see Table 1). It should be noted, however, that many Canadians do not have strong party attachments to federal or provincial parties. On the average, fewer than one person in four has a "very strong" sense of identification with a federal party; an equal number indicate that their feelings are either "not very strong" or that they merely feel a "little closer" to a party. Also, the strength of party identification waxes and wanes, increasing in response to the stimulus provided by elections and decreasing in the interim between them (see Figure 3).

Regarding the direction of party ties, four points are noteworthy. First, consistent with their dominant position in federal politics between 1965 and 1980,

Table 1
Direction of Federal Party Identification in Canada, 1965–1989

Federal Party Identification	1965[a]	1968[a]	1974[a]	1979[a]	1979[b]	1980[a]	1981[b]	1983[c]	1984[a]	1984[c]	1985[c]	1986[c]	1987[c]	1988I[c]	1988II[c]	1989[c]
Liberal	43%	50%	49%	42%	41%	45%	45%	37%	34%	32%	33%	36%	36%	33%	32%	38%
Progressive Conservative	28	25	24	29	26	28	28	36	41	40	30	25	24	37	40	28
New Democratic Party	12	11	11	13	13	15	13	10	14	15	16	12	19	16	16	16
Social Credit/ Crediste	6	5	3	3	4	1	2	2	1	1	1	1	1	1	1	2
No Party Identification	11	9	13	13	16	10	13	15	9	12	20	27	20	12	11	16
(N=)	(2615)	(2706)	(2411)	(2604)	(2837)	(1761)	(2792)	(2013)	(2965)	(1876)	(1660)	(1698)	(1759)	(2051)	(1939)	(1549)

Note: a - National Election Study
b - Social Change in Canada
c - Political Support in Canada
d - missing data and "other" party identifiers removed

Figure 3
Percentage of "Very Strong" Federal Party Identifiers, 1965–1989

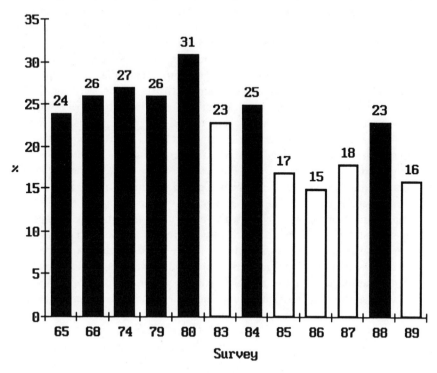

Note: unshaded bars are non-election years

the Liberals have the largest number of party identifiers in this era. In six national surveys, Liberals, on the average, had the allegiance of 46 percent of the electorate, whereas the percentages identifying with the Conservative, NDP, and Social Credit parties averaged 27 percent, 13 percent, and 4 percent, respectively (Table 1). Second, although the proportions identifying with the four major federal parties did not fluctuate greatly prior to 1983, since then large changes have occurred. Conservative partisanship has varied sharply over brief time intervals, with the percentage of this party's identifiers increasing from 28 percent in 1981 to 40 percent in 1984. Its cohort of identifiers then plummeted to 24 percent in 1987 before rebounding to 40 percent immediately after the 1988 election and then falling again to 28 percent in 1989. Although short-term variations in the percentages identifying with the other federal parties have not been as large, an overall decline in Liberal partisanship is readily apparent— the average percentage of Liberal identifiers in the 1983–1989 surveys is only 35 percent, some 11 points less than that for the 1965–1980 period. Third, the figures given in Table 1 mask large regional and provincial differences in patterns of party identification, which are consistent with the notion that Canada has not one but several party systems. Illustrative are findings from the 1988 preelection survey in which the percentage of federal Liberal identifiers varied from a high of 42 percent in the Atlantic provinces to a low of 21 percent in the Prairies and British Columbia. Similarly, the percentage of Conservative identifiers ranged from 49 percent in the Prairies to 33 percent in Ontario and British Columbia, and the percentage of New Democrats ranged from 33 percent in British Columbia to 12 percent in Quebec.

Finally, in a number of provinces, the percentages of identifiers with parties competing at the provincial level are very different from the percentages identifying with the same parties when they compete in federal elections. The 1988 preelection survey data illustrate this point: 40 percent of British Columbia residents identified with the Social Credit in provincial politics but only 4 percent did so federally. Even more dramatic is the Quebec case where 31 percent identified in provincial politics with the Parti Québécois, which does not even compete in federal politics. This does not mean that supporters of the Parti Québécois, which is dedicated to a politically sovereign Quebec, do not identify with one of the national parties. In the 1970s, nearly two-fifths of them were federal Liberal identifiers. In the 1980s, they continued to identify with federal parties, although their allegiances shifted strongly toward the Conservatives. In the runup to the 1988 election, for example, 52 percent of the provincial *Péquistes* were federal Conservatives, and only 9 percent were federal Liberals.

Studies of the relationships between socioeconomic and demographic variables and party identification consistently have shown that, in addition to region, religion and ethnicity correlate with partisanship. In federal politics, Roman Catholics tend to be Liberals, and this normally has been the case among French Canadians as well. However, in the 1984 and 1988 elections, large numbers of Québécois supported the Conservatives and, since the vast majority of French Canadians reside in Quebec, this had the effect of reversing the typically positive relationship between French-Canadian ethnicity and Liberal partisanship. Protestants and those of Anglo-Celtic origins divide their loyalties more evenly between the Liberals and the Progressive Conservatives. Supporters of the NDP tend to be drawn from those with no formal religious affiliations and persons of other than French-Canadian origin. Over time, Social Credit partisanship has shifted so that the party's main base of support in federal politics is composed of Roman Catholic Québécois rather than Protestants residing in the western provinces.

The relationship between social class and partisan identification long has been much weaker in Canada than it has been in such other countries as Australia, Great Britain, and many continental European democracies. Indeed, national-level studies using data gathered since the 1940s consistently show that objective and subjective measures of social class have little statistical ability to explain voters' partisan attachments. Somewhat stronger correlations can be found within particular regions or provinces. For example, Donald E. Blake (1985), Martin Robin (1978), and others have pointed to the existence of persistent class divisions in the British Columbia electorate in both federal and provincial politics. Similarly, John Wilson (1974) has argued that class divisions are sharpening in Ontario and Manitoba. Overall, however, Robert R. Alford's argument (1963) that the class basis of party politics is weaker in Canada than in many other democracies continues to receive strong empirical support.

More generally, the weakness of social class is only the most extreme example of the inability of sociodemographic variables to account for differences in Canadians' partisan attachments. In 1988, for example, age, education, ethnicity (French-other), gender, income, and region collectively explained less than 10 percent of the variance in Conservative, Liberal, and NDP party identifications. Analyses of data gathered in earlier years tell the same story—party identification is substantially decoupled from the kinds of societal cleavages that have done much to structure political conflict in many other Western countries. Canadians' feelings about political parties are strongly affected by highly mutable short-term forces specific to particular political contexts.

Split and Unstable Party Attachments

It was observed above that a sizeable minority of Canadians divide or split partisan attachments. Nationally, 26 percent of those interviewed in the 1988 preelection survey reported different federal and provincial party identifications, 8 percent maintained an identification at one level only, and 6 percent did not have a party identification at either level. The 1988 case is typical—since 1974, an average of 23 percent of those participating in national surveys have stated that they identify with different parties at the two levels of government. As might be expected, levels of congruence between federal and provincial identifications differ markedly across provinces (see Table 2). In 1988, for example, in the Atlantic provinces, 10 percent identified with different parties at the federal and provincial levels, whereas the percentages doing so in Quebec and British Columbia were 49 percent and 46 percent, respectively. High levels of split partisanship in these two provinces are apparent in earlier surveys as well. Research in other federal systems, such as Australia and the United States, has failed to reveal large numbers of split identifiers, suggesting that this aspect of the linkage between citizens and parties may well be unique to Canada.

There also is evidence that the ties between the electorate and parties may be less stable in Canada than in other relatively similar societies. There are two

Table 2
Federal and Provincial Party Identification by Region, 1988 National Preelection Survey

Patterns of Federal and Provincial Party Identification

Region	(N)	Same	Different	Federal Only	Prov. Only	No Party Identifi- cation
Atlantic	(187)	79%	10	2	2	7
Quebec	(507)	29%	49	5	10	7
Ontario	(763)	74%	12	2	5	7
Prairies	(348)	74%	17	1	4	4
British Columbia	(248)	44%	46	3	4	3
Canada	(2047)	60%	26	3	5	6

types of data on this point: recalled changes in party identifications and changes that are measured with the use of panel data. Regarding the former, Canadian figures are consistently higher than those of Great Britain or the United States. In the 1979 and 1984 national election surveys, for example, 32 percent and 34 percent, respectively, said they had changed their federal party identifications one or more times in the past. Comparable figures for the United States and Great Britain range from 20 to 26 percent.

A more accurate measure of the rate of change in party identification is provided by panel surveys in which the same respondents are interviewed at different points in time. Data from such surveys indicate that partisan instability is greater in Canada than in other Anglo-American democracies. Over the 1974–1979 period, 34 percent of the Canadian panel respondents either switched their federal party identifications or moved between identification and noni-dentification (see Table 3). The comparable figure for provincial party identi-fications was 38 percent. Similar changes were reported by 20 percent of American (1972–1976) and 22 percent of British panels (1970–1974) conducted during this period. The high incidence of individual-level partisan instability in Canada is not unique to the 1970s. In the 1980–1984 and 1984–1988 national panels, 33 percent and 30 percent, respectively, had unstable party identifica-tions. Partisan change over very brief time intervals also is substantial. In the nine months separating the 1979 and 1980 federal elections, 24 percent man-ifested unstable party ties, and 23 percent did so during the even shorter period separating the pre- and postelection interviews of the 1988 panel study.

Two additional observations may heighten the reader's appreciation of the theoretical significance of the relatively high rates of partisan instability in Canada. The first concerns the forces which encourage persons to change their party identifications. It appears that Canadians are willing to shift their partisan allegiances in response to short-term forces that are part and parcel of the normal

Table 3
Stability and Change in Federal Party Identification, 1974–1988 National Panel Surveys

	Panel Surveys				
	74-79	79-80	80-84	84-88I	88I-88II
Stable Identification	62%	72%	63%	66%	73%
Switched Parties	16	12	21	19	12
To/From Nonidentification	16	12	12	11	11
Stable Nonidentification	5	4	4	5	5
N	1,299	1,690	600	794	1,429

Note: 88I = 1988 pre-election survey
       88II = 1988 post-election survey

political process. When requested to specify the reasons for shifting their federal party identifications, 25 percent of respondents in the 1974 national election study mentioned party leaders, 31 percent cited issues, 16 percent referred to the parties' performance, and 30 percent cited local or personal matters. Data from this study also reveal that 31 percent of those who had changed reported doing so during the 1974 election campaign itself, and an additional 51 percent cited the 1967–1973 period, which also was characterized by politics as usual. Data regarding the time of changes in provincial partisan attachments are quite similar.

Second, since partisan change frequently is a function of the short-term forces of normal politics, party identification is very strongly correlated with voting behavior. Thus, in the 1979 federal election, the percentages of Liberal, Conservative, and NDP partisans casting ballots for "their" parties were 86 percent, 97 percent, and 90 percent, respectively. Nine years later, at the time of the 1988 election, the pattern persisted; 71 percent cast ballots for the Liberal Party, 86 percent, Conservative, and 85 percent, NDP. These extremely high figures suggest that changes in party identification and voting behavior travel together more frequently in Canada than in some other political systems, such as the United States and Great Britain. Comparative analyses of panel data for the three countries demonstrate that this is, in fact, the case.

Significance of Party Identification

The strong relationship between party identification and voting, coupled with high levels of partisan instability, suggest the limited explanatory power of party identification for understanding individual voting behavior and electoral outcomes. To reiterate, the properties of party identification and their relationship to electoral choice indicate that many Canadians lack long-term, firmly rooted, psychological ties to political parties. For many persons, a particular vote decision and a current partisan allegiance *both* reflect the operation of short-term electoral forces. As a result, election outcomes are very difficult to forecast. If short-term forces operate such that parties exchange relatively equal numbers of identifiers, the balance of partisan forces will be undisturbed. However, when shifts in partisan attachments are asymmetric, a governing party may be forced from office. The 1984 and 1988 elections are cases in point. The former resulted in the defeat of a majority Liberal government and a sweeping triumph by the Conservatives, whereas the latter witnessed the Conservatives' return to office, albeit with a reduced majority. Over the 1980–1984 period, panel data indicate that 14 percent abandoned an identification with the governing Liberals while only 5 percent shifted to them. The victorious Conservatives, in contrast, gained 16 percent but lost only 5 percent. Between 1984 and 1988, the pattern of partisan shifts was very different—the Liberals lost over 8 percent but gained over 7 percent of the electorate, and Conservative losses and gains were perfectly balanced at slightly less than 10 percent.

Dramatic disturbances in the balance of partisan forces also occur at the provincial level. As noted earlier, Social Credit dominated provincial politics in Alberta from 1935 to 1971, but less than a decade later (in 1979), only 5 percent of Albertans identified with the party. In Quebec, the Union Nationale, the governing party in 1970, now claims the partisan allegiance of less than 3 percent of the electorate. In contrast, the Parti Québécois was formed in 1967, gained power in 1976, and currently claims the loyalties of over 30 percent of the electorate. In Ontario, the once mighty Conservatives, in power as late as 1985, claimed the identification of less than one-third of the electorate in 1988, whereas 44 percent were Liberal partisans and only 13 percent were New Democrats. Less than two years later, however, the governing Liberals were swept from office in an election that saw the New Democrats obtain 38 percent of the popular vote and 74 of the 130 seats in the Ontario legislature.

The case of the Parti Québécois illustrates a third element that may affect levels of public support for political parties. Studies conducted in the 1970s consistently showed that support for the Parti Québécois is strongly age related. In 1979, for example, the percentage of PQ identifiers decreased monotonically from 53 percent among persons in the age bracket from 18 to 25 to 14 percent among those 56 years and older. An opposite pattern emerged for the Quebec Liberals, who had more partisans among older-age cohorts. These patterns have persisted throughout the 1980s. Such stable party identification–age correlations suggest that long-term demographic processes operate hand in hand with shorter term forces to structure the configuration of party systems at particular points in time. Moreover, the perpetuation of such age-related patterns may have long-term consequences for the balance of partisan forces—as older voters exit and younger ones enter the electorate, significant changes in the party system are possible. In Canada, however, parties pinning their hopes on inexorable demographic forces run a significant risk of disappointment. The effects of electoral replacement may be repeatedly deflected by a changing mix of short-term factors operating in a system where weak and unstable partisan attachments characterize federal and provincial electorates alike.

Scholars have pointed to this volatility of the Canadian electorate and have argued that it illustrates the failure of the parties to integrate the polity by, for example, formulating issues whose attractiveness could transcend provincial and regional cleavages and the particularities on which they rest. These and other criticisms of the performance of the parties are not without merit. However, it is doubtful that the parties could exercise the powerfully independent and transformative effects on the political system that some critics desire. Indeed, given the historic skewness in the numerical and ethnic-religious distributions of the population across the several provinces, the incompatibility of federal and parliamentary forms of government, persistent regional economic disparities, and other centrifugal forces in Canadian society, what may be most notable about the parties is that they have been able to exercise more than a modicum of influence on the political system's operation over the years. They are unlikely to become powerful and independent factors in the future.

Bibliography

Robert R. Alford. *Party and Society: The Anglo-American Democracies*. Rand McNally, Chicago, 1963.

Keith Archer. *Political Choices and Electoral Consequences*. McGill-Queen's University Press, Montreal, 1989.

Sylvia B. Bashevkin. *Toeing The Lines: Women and Party Politics in English Canada*. University of Toronto Press, Toronto, 1985.

Donald E. Blake. *Two Political Worlds: Parties and Voting in British Columbia*. University of British Columbia Press, Vancouver, 1985.

Janine Brodie and Jane Jenson. *Crisis, Challenge and Change: Party and Class in Canada Revisited*. Carleton University Press, Ottawa, 1988.

Harold D. Clarke. "The Parti Québécois and Sources of Partisan Realignment in Contemporary Quebec." *Journal of Politics* 44, 1983, pp. 63–85.

Harold D. Clarke, Jane Jenson, Lawrence LeDuc, and Jon H. Pammett. *Absent Mandate: Interpreting Change in Canadian Elections*, 2d ed. Gage Educational Publishing Company, Agincourt, Ont., 1991.

———. *Political Choice in Canada*. McGraw-Hill Ryerson, Toronto, 1979.

Harold D. Clarke, Richard G. Price, Marianne Stewart, and Robert Krause. "Motivational Patterns and Differential Participation in a Canadian Party: The Ontario Liberals." *American Journal of Political Science* 22, 1978, pp. 135–51.

Harold D. Clarke and Marianne C. Stewart. "Partisan Inconsistency and Partisan Change in Federal States: The Case of Canada." *American Journal of Political Science* 31, 1987, pp. 383–407.

———. "Short-Term Forces and Partisan Change in Canada: 1974–80." *Electoral Studies* 3, 1985, pp. 15–36.

John C. Courtney. *The Selection of National Party Leaders in Canada.* Macmillan, Toronto, 1973.

Frederick C. Englemann and Mildred A. Schwartz. *Canadian Political Parties: Origins, Character, Impact.* Prentice-Hall, Scarborough, Ont., 1975.

Frank Feigert, *Canada Votes: 1935–1988.* Duke University Press, Durham, N.C., 1989.

Alain G. Gagnon and Brian Tanguay, eds. *Canadian Parties in Transition.* Nelson Canada, Scarborough, Ont., 1989.

John A. Irving. *The Social Credit Movement in Alberta.* University of Toronto Press, Toronto, 1959.

Allan Kornberg and William Mishler. *Influence in Parliament: Canada.* Duke University Press, Durham, N.C., 1976.

Allan Kornberg, William Mishler, and Joel Smith. "Political Elite and Mass Perceptions of Party Locations in Issue Space: Some Tests of Two Positions." *British Journal of Political Science* 5, 1975, pp. 161–85.

Allan Kornberg, Joel Smith, and Harold D. Clarke. *Citizen Politicians—Canada: Party Officials in a Democratic Society.* Carolina Academic Press, Durham, N.C., 1979.

Joseph LaPalombara and Myron Weiner, eds. *Political Parties and Political Development*, chap. 1. Princeton University Press, Princeton, N.J., 1966.

Lawrence LeDuc, Harold D. Clarke, Jane Jenson, and Jon H. Pammett. "Partisan Instability in Canada: Evidence From a New Panel Study." *American Political Science Review* 78, 1984, pp. 470–84.

Seymour Martin Lipset. *Agrarian Socialism: The Cooperative Commonwealth Federation in Saskatchewan.* Anchor Books, New York, 1968.

C. B. Macpherson. *Democracy in Alberta: Social Credit and Political Crisis.* University of Toronto Press, Toronto, 1962.

Kenneth McRoberts. *Quebec: Social Change and Political Crisis*, 3d ed. McClelland and Stewart, Toronto, 1988.

John Meisel. *Working Papers on Canadian Politics* 2d enl. ed. McGill-Queen's University Press, Montreal, 1975.

William Morton. *The Progressive Party in Canada.* University of Toronto Press, Toronto, 1963.

Norman Penner. *The Canadian Left: A Critical Analysis.* Prentice-Hall, Scarborough, Ont., 1977.

George Perlin. *The Tory Syndrome.* McGill-Queen's University Press, Montreal, 1980.

Maurice Pinard. *The Rise of a Third Party: A Study in Crisis Politics.* Prentice-Hall, Englewood Cliffs, N.J., 1971.

John Porter. *The Vertical Mosaic: An Analysis of Social Class and Power in Canada.* University of Toronto Press, Toronto, 1965.

Herbert F. Quinn. *The Union Nationale: A Study in Quebec Nationalism.* University of Toronto Press, Toronto, 1963.

Escott M. Reid. "The Rise of National Parties in Canada." *Papers and Proceedings of the Canadian Political Science Association* 4, 1932, pp. 187–200.

Martin Robin. *Canadian Provincial Politics: The Party Systems of the Ten Provinces*, 2d ed. Prentice-Hall, Scarborough, Ont., 1978.

David E. Smith. *The Regional Decline of a National Party: The Liberals on the Prairies.* University of Toronto Press, Toronto, 1981.

Michael Stein. *The Dynamics of Right-Wing Protest: Social Credit in Quebec.* University of Toronto Press, Toronto, 1973.

Frank Underhill. *In Search of Canadian Liberalism.* University of Toronto Press, Toronto, 1960.

Joseph Wearing. *The L Shaped Party: The Liberal Party of Canada 1958–1980.* McGraw-Hill Ryerson, Toronto, 1981.

Joseph Wearing, ed. *The Ballot and Its Message: Voting in Canada.* Copp Clark Pitman, Toronto, 1991.

Reginald Whitaker. *The Government Party.* University of Toronto Press, Toronto, 1977.

John Wilson. "The Canadian Political Cultures: Toward a Redefinition of the Nature of the Canadian Political System." *Canadian Journal of Political Science* 7, 1974, pp. 438–83.

Conrad Winn and John McMenemy. *Political Parties in Canada.* McGraw-Hill Ryerson, Toronto, 1976.

Walter Young. *The Anatomy of a Party: The National C.C.F., 1932–1961.* University of Toronto Press, Toronto, 1969.

Leo Zakuta. *A Protest Movement Becalmed: A Study of Change in the CCF.* University of Toronto Press, Toronto, 1964.

Political Parties—Active

BLOC QUÉBÉCOIS. This nascent party is led by Lucien Bouchard, a former cabinet minister in the Mulroney government. It consists of a faction of Quebec MPs whose deep dissatisfaction with the failure of the Meech Lake Accord prompted their departure from the Conservative Party caucus and their advocacy of Quebec separatism.

COMMUNIST PARTY. Always small in numbers, the Communist Party became a very minor actor on the Canadian political stage after World War II as postwar affluence, the cold war, and rigid adherence to an unimaginative Stalinist orthodoxy doomed it to irrelevance. Although the party continues to exist, and even to offer candidates in several large urban areas, it has no impact on Canadian political life.

CONSERVATIVE PARTY. *See* PROGRESSIVE CONSERVATIVE PARTY.

LIBERAL PARTY. The ancestors of the present Liberal Party were rural and small-town, nonestablished church, and moderate reform groups in Ontario, and antibusiness, anticlerical, relatively radical reform elements in Quebec. Under the leadership of Alexander Mackenzie, the "Grits," as they then were termed, were able to oust Sir John A. Macdonald and his Tory colleagues in the election of 1874. Defeated in 1878, the party returned to office in 1896 under the leadership of Wilfrid Laurier. A combination of Laurier's political skills, economic prosperity, and the chauvinism generated by the inclusion of the new western provinces of Saskatchewan and Alberta kept his Liberal administration in office until its defeat in the 1911 election. The party's downfall at that time reflected the alienation of isolationist elements within Quebec and disaffection within the Ontario business community, which opposed the Liberals' proposal for limited reciprocal free trade with the United States.

The party was deeply divided during World War I over the issue of conscription for overseas service. Laurier retired at the end of the war, and, in a leadership convention held in 1919, William Lyon Mackenzie King was elected leader. By 1921 he was prime minister of a minority Liberal government. King, who was to serve as prime minister for nearly a quarter of a century, viewed the party primarily as a mechanism for mediating and resolving intergroup conflicts and only secondarily as a vehicle for generating and implementing public policy. Even if King's style was to react rather than to innovate, the foundation of Canada's welfare state was laid during his tenure as prime minister. Such social programs, together with other redistributive measures and policies intended to broaden the industrial base of the Canadian economy, were pursued by King's successor, Louis St. Laurent, during the years from 1948 to 1957. St. Laurent retired after the party lost the 1958 election, and he was succeeded by Lester B. "Mike" Pearson. Pearson—although he enjoyed great popularity with party regulars—was unable during the ten years he led the party to translate his personal popularity into a majority victory at the polls. After Pearson retired in 1968, the party chose Pierre Elliot Trudeau as its new chieftain.

Liberal fortunes fluctuated during Trudeau's stewardship of the party. A smashing victory in the 1968 election was followed by near defeat and reduction to minority government status in 1972. Another solid victory in 1974 was followed by the progressive erosion of his own and his government's popularity and electoral defeat in 1979. Although Trudeau resigned after losing this election, when the minority Conservative government unexpectedly lost a vote of confidence on its first budget in December 1979, he heeded the pleas of party elites and returned as Liberal leader. In this capacity, he led his party to a majority victory in the 1980 election.

Upon regaining the reins of power, the Liberals embarked on an ambitious program of constitutional and economic reform. The former culminated in an agreement on a new constitution which was put in place in 1982. The latter, spearheaded by the government's National Energy Program (NEP), produced bitter reaction from Alberta and other energy-producing provinces. Federal-provincial disputes over the NEP and the severe recession of the early 1980s effectively scuttled the Liberals' economic policy initiatives and led to a sharp decline of public support. Faced with mounting discontent in his party and in the country at large, Trudeau resigned in early 1984. The party chose former Liberal cabinet minister, John Turner, as his replacement.

Turner's selection as party leader was accompanied by a surge in public support for the Liberals which, in turn, led him to call an election for September 1984. The result was an outright disaster for the party, which elected only forty members of parliament. Influential elements within the party blamed Turner for the debacle and made widely publicized attempts to oust him. Although these efforts proved unsuccessful, Turner's difficulties continued as the Liberals were defeated again in the 1988 election. In the wake of two successive losses, he resigned. His replacement, Jean Chretien, a longtime cabinet minister in the Trudeau years, is faced with the task of rebuilding the party organization and developing policies that will refurbish its severely tarnished image. Whether he will be able to do so is problematic.

NEW DEMOCRATIC PARTY (NDP). Formed in 1932, the Cooperative Commonwealth Federation (CCF), the predecessor of the NDP, was at once a "party" and a "movement." In the Regina Manifesto, drafted at the party's first convention in 1933, the CCF declared its adherence to the principles of democratic socialism. As a vehicle of political protest, the party quickly claimed the support of many of the groups (mainly farmers and workers) who had been attracted to the Progressive Party in the 1920s. Led by J. S. Woodsworth, the CCF contested elections at the federal level in several provinces during the 1930s and 1940s. Although not able to effect dramatic electoral breakthroughs in national politics, the party established itself as a prominent feature on the political landscape. Provincially, the CCF fared considerably better, particularly in Saskatchewan where it captured power in 1944. Postwar prosperity, the cold war, and continuing frustration at the ballot box led the party to moderate its ideological pronouncements and electoral platforms, a trend culminating in the 1956 Winnipeg Declaration, in which the party agreed to accept and support a "mixed" private-public economy.

Ideological stagnation and the lengthy series of electoral disappointments finally produced a reconstruction of the party in 1961 as the NDP. In founding the NDP, CCF leaders attempted to broaden their political base in central Canada by uniting with major labor unions in the Canadian Labor Congress (CLC). Under the guidance of the longtime CCF premier of Saskatchewan, Tommy Douglas, the NDP tried to present itself as a viable alternative to the two older centrist parties—the Liberals and the Conservatives. Throughout the 1960s and 1970s, the NDP was able to capture an average of twenty-three seats in successive federal elections. In the 1980s, it fared somewhat better, particularly in 1988 when forty-three New Democrats were elected. However, even the latter figure represents only 20 percent of all parliamentary seats.

While remaining a third force in federal politics, the party has had some major successes at the provincial level. Over the past three decades, it has formed governments in Manitoba, Saskatchewan, and British Columbia. Most recently, it scored a dramatic victory in the 1990 Ontario election, when it became the first NDP government in the history of that province. However, the party has been unable to make significant headway in provincial politics in the Maritimes or Quebec. The same is true federally in these regions, although the party occasionally has shown some meaningful electoral muscle at the federal level in Newfoundland, and it has made a few strong showings in public opinion polls in Quebec in recent years.

Ideologically, the NDP has continued to tread a cautious path characteristic of the CCF in its declining years. This tendency has found strong support from "pragmatic" labor leaders in the CLC who occupy positions of considerable influence in the party. At the same time, however, the NDP's ideological stance periodically has been subjected to vigorous criticism from within by a number of academics and intellectuals. The most widely publicized critiques occurred in the late 1960s and early 1970s when an intraparty group (dubbed the "Waffle Movement") called for a return to basic socialist principles coupled with a strident Canadian nationalism. Although disbanded as an organizational element within the party, ex-Waffle members and sympathizers have continued to argue that neither the NDP nor Canada will achieve its full potential until the present course of ideological moderation is abandoned. These arguments gained new vigor at the time of the 1988 federal election when the issue of free trade with the United States heightened the salience of questions about Canada's economic, political, and cultural sovereignty.

At present, the NDP's future is uncertain. Successive national party leaders Douglas (1961–1971), David Lewis (1971–1975), Ed Broadbent (1975–1990), and Audrey McLaughlin (1990–present) have maintained a low ideological profile and have eschewed the more radical economic nationalism favored by some party activists. This was perhaps most evident in the 1988 election campaign when the party failed to take the lead in opposing the free-trade pact with the United States. As a result, many of those who would have worked vigorously within the party to defeat free trade organized themselves as a nonparty force, the Pro Canada Network, to make their voices heard. Perhaps the party's best hope for success at the national level is provided by the serious problems experienced by the Liberals in recent years. These difficulties give the NDP a meaningful opening to establish an image in the public mind as the "real opposition" and, hence, a viable alternative to the governing Progressive Conservatives. Although a genuine national breakthrough is problematic as long as the party remains weak east of the Ontario border, the party's periodic strength in public opinion polls gives its activists grounds for hope.

Provincially, the party remains a force in several western provinces (British Columbia, Manitoba, and Saskatchewan), and its 1990 victory in Ontario represents a major achievement. The fact that the party has been able to gain power in Canada's largest province may enable it to command continuing commitment from party activists who see it as the logical vehicle for implementing socialism in Canada. However, faced with mounting economic difficulties, the new Ontario NDP government, led by Bob Rae, shows no signs of embracing a radical program of social and economic reform. This, in turn, could disappoint hitherto faithful New Democrats and prompt increasing reliance on alternative organizational vehicles, such as the Pro Canada Network, for achieving cherished ideological goals.

PARTI CRÉDITISTE. *See* SOCIAL CREDIT PARTY.

PARTI QUÉBÉCOIS (PQ). Formed in 1968 under the leadership of René Lévesque, a former cabinet minister in the quiet revolution government of Liberal Premier Jean Lesage, the Parti Québécois rallied disparate separatist elements in Quebec, including members of small parties, such as the Rassemblement pour L'Indépendance National (RIN) and the Ralliement National (RN). The RIN and RN differed regarding the future of Quebec; the RIN called for complete independence, and the RN opted for associate-state status. In addition, the RN espoused a brand of political and social conservatism quite similar to that of the Social Credit Party, whereas the RIN tended to take positions on the left of the ideological continuum. Such ideological and stylistic differences did not prevent these groups from offering enthusiastic support to the Parti Québécois. Under the dynamic leadership of Lévesque, the PQ quickly came to the forefront of Quebec provincial politics. The party's meteoric rise to power culminated in November 1976, with the election of a majority PQ government (69 of 110 seats, 41 percent of the popular vote). Avowedly dedicated to the establishment of a sovereign Quebec, the PQ in power plunged Canada into a constitutional crisis.

During their rise to power, the *Péquistes* were unanimous in viewing sovereignty for Quebec as the sine qua non for the realization of Québécois economic, political, and cultural aspirations. In this respect, the party differs from early Quebec nationalist parties such as the Bloc Populaire (a short-lived nationalist party formed during World War II to oppose conscription) or the Union Nationale, which were content, or at least resigned, to trying to *defend* the interests of Québécois within the framework of Canadian federalism. In emphasizing the positive role of the Quebec state as the vehicle for achieving nationalist goals, the PQ has completed the ideological reorientation in Quebec political thought first manifested in the quiet revolution of the 1960s. This reorientation was twofold. In addition to a commitment to transform Quebec into an economically and technically advanced urban, secular society, it defined the province as the true "homeland" of the Québécois "nation." *Only* within a sovereign Quebec, it was argued, could French Canadians achieve the quiet revolution's goal of becoming *maîtres chez nous*.

In striving to attain sovereignty, the PQ has consciously pursued a strategy of *étapisme*, that is, it has proceeded in a step-by-step fashion. This strategy frankly recognized that a majority of the Quebec population did not favor independence. However, PQ leaders calculated that public opinion would swing in their favor if they could allay fears regarding Quebec's ability to survive and prosper as an independent entity. To this end, the party stressed two principal themes. First, it developed the concept of *sovereignty association* which, if implemented, would make Quebec a sovereign state with economic ties to Canada. By retaining such an economic relationship, the PQ hoped to assuage the fears of those concerned about the viability of an independent Quebec. Second, the party has tried to present an image of competence and rationality: to demonstrate that it has the ability to govern a modern industrial state. Indeed, some *Péquiste* leaders have rationalized their moderate social policies in terms of the need to avoid a radical image that would frighten away much-needed foreign capital and throw the Quebec economy into a tailspin for which the party would be blamed.

To establish its "good government" image and to propagate the wisdom of a sovereign Quebec, the PQ has deferred its promised referendum on sovereignty association for nearly four years. Even this was not enough. On 20 May 1980, voters denied the PQ a mandate to negotiate sovereignty association by a decisive margin (60 percent voted no). After the referendum defeat, both its *étapiste* strategy and the PQ itself were in disarray. Although the party was able to retain power in the 1981 election, it was defeated in 1985 by the resurgent Liberals led by Robert Bourassa. Battles concerning both strategies for achieving independence and even the validity of the goal itself flared within the PQ. These disputes occasioned the exit from the party of a number of prominent prosovereignty figures, including high-ranking officials in the Lévesque government. However, after effectively abandoning sovereignty and fighting the 1985 election under the charismatic moderate Pierre-Marc Johnson, the party gradually moved back toward an openly proindependence stance, a movement that culminated in the selection of a former PQ cabinet minister, Jacques Parizeau, as leader in 1988.

Although the PQ was defeated again in the 1989 election, the party's dream of an independent Quebec was given a major boost by the failure of the Meech Lake Constitutional Accord in June 1990. The accord, initiated by the Conservative federal government of Prime Minister Brian Mulroney, was designed to satisfy Quebec's constitutional aspirations in a federalist framework; if approved, it would have given the province "special status" within the confederation. The heated debates surrounding the accord and the bitter recriminations that followed in the wake of its failure seemingly have convinced large numbers of Québécois of the validity of the PQ's arguments that independence is the only viable solution. Public opinion polls show that upward of two-thirds of Quebecers now are prepared to embrace the party's option. Although the rancor engendered by Meech Lake may fade over time and opinion may shift back in a profederalist direction, the Parti Québécois now would seem to have the ammunition needed to fight a renewed stuggle for an independent Quebec.

PROGRESSIVE CONSERVATIVE PARTY. The Progressive Conservative Party grew out of an 1854 coalition of business-professional and Established Church (Anglican) elites who held sway in Ontario, and ultramontane French-Catholic and Anglo-Scottish business and financial oligarchies in Quebec. Sir John Alexander Macdonald, the architect of this coalition, became Canada's first prime minister in 1867 and, except for a five-year hiatus, remained the head of government until 1891. The Conservative government's decision to execute Louis Riel, a Francophone Catholic Métis who was the leader of an aborted rebellion in Saskatchewan in 1885, put severe strains on the Quebec segment of the Conservative coalition. The party's support in Quebec was eroded further because of the government's waffling on the issue of provincial government financial support for Catholic schools. These issues and the death of Macdonald resulted in the Conservatives' defeat in the 1896 federal election. The party remained in the political wilderness until 1911 when its new leader, Sir Robert Borden, mobilized a combination of anti–free trade and anti-American sentiment in Ontario and isolationism in Quebec to oust the Laurier Liberals.

This alliance dissolved during the conscription crisis of 1917. The bitterness of French Canada over Borden's insistence on conscripting men for overseas service in World War I was not dispelled when he retired, and, lacking support in Quebec, the party was defeated in the election of 1921. It remained out of office until it won the 1930 election under the leadership of R. B. Bennett. In power during the worst of the Great Depression, the party was soundly defeated in 1935. Despite subsequent efforts to broaden its base of support by—among other actions—changing its name to Progressive Conservative, the party remained in opposition until 1957 when John Diefenbaker, a small-town Saskatchewan lawyer, led it to a minority government victory. The next year, largely as a result of his personal charisma, the PCs swept into power with a huge majority. However, they were reduced to minority government status in the next (1962) election and were defeated outright in 1963.

Serious intraparty divisions over the quality of Diefenbaker's leadership led to the "Chief's" replacement by Robert L. Stanfield in 1967. Stanfield, unable to oust the Liberals in the 1968, 1972, and 1974 elections, retired under pressure in 1976, and Joe Clark was elected leader in a hotly contested national leadership convention. After three years as opposition leader, Clark led the party to a narrow victory in the May 1979 election and formed a minority government. His tenure as prime minister was short lived. In December 1979, his finance minister, John Crosbie, introduced a controversial austerity budget in the House of Commons. To the surprise of many observers, the House declared its lack of confidence in the government. In the ensuing February 1980 election, the Liberals returned to office.

The swift fall of the Clark government led to renewed bickering within the party, and Clark himself came under heavy fire for permitting the party to lose power so quickly after sixteen years in opposition. These disputes prompted the party to hold a leadership convention in 1983, and Clark was defeated by Brian Mulroney, a former lawyer and the president of the Iron Ore Company of Canada. Although Mulroney had never held a seat in the House of Commons when he was chosen party leader, he promised that, as a Quebecer, he could lead the party to power by bringing his native province into the Tory camp. In the 1984 federal election, he did just that and much more besides. The Conservatives crushed the Liberals in every region of the country.

Once in office, the PCs quickly fell from public favor as a series of scandals involving high-ranking cabinet ministers rocked the new Mulroney government. All was not lost, however, and, assisted by a series of internecine disputes concerning John Turner's leadership of the Liberals, the PCs were able to win a second consecutive victory in 1988. Since then, the constitutional crisis engendered by the failure of the Meech Lake Accord and the Mulroney government's insistence on proceeding with a highly unpopular goods and services tax (the GST) have prompted a dramatic decline in Conservative support in all parts of the country. Whether the party will be able to recover remains to be seen.

REFORM PARTY. This protest party, established in 1987, is based in Calgary, Alberta, and is led by Preston Manning, a businessman and the son of a former Social Credit leader and Alberta premier. His efforts have focused on attracting members, raising money, developing constituency and university organizations, and advancing the party's agenda at the national, rather than the provincial, level. This agenda would reduce government expenditure, increase government accountability, and foster free enterprise, individual equality, and regional fairness through Senate reform. The party currently has one senator, and one MP from a 1989 by-election in an Alberta riding. Its public support is approximately 7 percent at the national level but much higher in the western provinces. The ability to vend the party's program and to capitalize on public discontent with the Mulroney government may result in its winning several seats, particularly from the Conservatives, in the next federal election.

RHINOCEROS PARTY. A comic interloper on the political scene, the Rhinoceros Party long has provided satirical commentary on Canadian elections. Although the party never has elected a member of parliament, it regularly runs candidates in several Quebec ridings, and does so in a handful of ridings in other provinces as well. Despite, or perhaps because of, its humorous bent, some Canadians vote for its candidates. In 1988, for example, over 50,000, approximately 0.4 percent of all voters, did so.

SOCIAL CREDIT PARTY. Similar to the Cooperative Commonwealth Federation (CCF), Social Credit began in 1933 as a result of the political protests of the depression era. Unlike the CCF, however, the intellectual roots of Social

Credit reside not in democratic socialism, but rather in a mixture of prairie populism and the curious economic theories of the eccentric British engineer, Major Douglas. Social Credit doctrine, with its emphasis on the fundamental flaws of modern capitalism and the ineptitude of parliamentary government, echoed the long-standing grievances of many in the western provinces who blamed eastern financial interests and their allies in the Liberal and Conservative parties in Ottawa for the plight of prairie farmers.

Although prevailing social, economic, and political conditions laid the groundwork for the development of the Social Credit movements in the west, the crucial catalyst was provided by the propagation of Social Credit ideas by the evangelist high school principal, William "Bible Bill" Aberhart. Broadcasting from his Prophetic Bible Institute in Calgary, Alberta, Aberhart's heady mixture of fundamentalist Christianity and Social Credit theory attracted a vast and receptive audience. Aberhart quickly converted this doctrinal appeal into a potent political force and succeeded in electing fifty-six MLAs to the sixty-three member Alberta legislature in 1935. After the late 1930s, Alberta Social Credit evolved into a relatively orthodox conservative government which remained in power until 1971. Defeated by the Progressive Conservatives in the provincial election of that year, the party's strength diminished rapidly to the point that it currently holds no seats in the provincial legislature. Although Social Credit shows no signs of revitalization in the province, some of its former members are playing leading roles in the new Reform Party.

Outside of Alberta, Social Credit's major successes have been in British Columbia and Quebec. Social Credit came to power in British Columbia in 1952. Under the leadership of W.A.C. "Wacky" Bennett, Social Credit promised "to oppose equally as strongly the forces of monopoly and the forces of socialism." In fact, however, the party has received strong and continuing support from corporate leaders who perceive it as the only viable free-enterprise option in British Columbia politics. This support, and the party's ability to attract the votes of all those opposing the CCF and the New Democratic Party (NDP), enabled the British Columbia Social Credit Party under Bennett's leadership to remain in office from 1952 to 1972. Since returning to office in 1975, the party has continued to present itself as the alternative to the socialist NDP, a tactic that has proved remarkably successful in a province where class cleavages are relatively important by Canadian standards. Victorious in 1979 and 1983 under the leadership of William Bennett, the son of the former premier, and in 1986, under the leadership of William Vander Zalm, the party has avoided the political sclerosis afflicting Social Credit elsewhere in the country.

In Quebec, Social Credit (le Parti Créditiste) has been successful primarily at the federal level. Although active in the province since the 1940s, it was not until 1962 that the party achieved a significant electoral breakthrough by capturing twenty-six seats in parliament. Essentially a vehicle of political protest, the Créditistes' success at that time can be attributed largely to the ability of their charismatic leader, Réal Caouette, who expressed the frustrations of those persons who suffered from the social and economic dislocations produced by the modernizing forces unleashed by Quebec's quiet revolution. Although the party elected twenty MPs in the 1963 election, it subsequently went into decline. It failed to win a single parliamentary seat in the three federal elections held in the 1980s.

Provincially, party prospects are also dim. During the mid-1960s, the Créditistes entered an abortive alliance with the right-wing nationalist party, the Ralliement National (RN). After the RN's total failure in the 1966 provincial election, the Social Crediters decided to contest the 1970 election under their own banner. Although thirteen Créditiste MNAs were successful in 1970, they won only two seats in 1973, and they failed to elect a single candidate in the 1976, 1981, 1985, and 1989 elections. A casualty of the ongoing battle between the federalist Liberals and the separatist Parti Québécois, the Parti Créditiste is unlikely to play any meaningful role in Quebec politics in the 1990s.

UNION NATIONALE. Formed in Quebec in 1936 by Conservatives and dissident Liberals (the Action Liberale Nationale), the Union Nationale employed a combination of economic discontent and charges of corruption to sweep the Liberals from office in Quebec City after the latter had held power continuously for thirty-nine years. The Union Nationale quickly established itself as the dominant party in Quebec provincial politics and, under the leadership of Maurice Dupléssis, the party governed for nineteen of the next twenty-four years.

Although the Union Nationale in the Dupléssis era received strong support from the farmers and the urban working class, it could not be characterized as a left-of-center party. Indeed, Dupléssis opposed state intervention in the economy and actively resisted trade union activity. To appeal to workers and farmers, Dupléssis cultivated the party's populist image as the defender of *les petits* against *la haute bourgeoisie*, and he presented the party as the defender of French-Canadian cultural interests threatened by federal governments dominated by Anglophone Canadians. The party's success also rested on Dupléssis's ability to use patronage and the pork barrel to build an extensive network of patron-client relationships, particularly in rural areas that were disproportionately favored by the electoral system.

Profound changes in Quebec society in the 1950s and 1960s eroded the party's appeal. To the extent that the Union Nationale's strength rested on its reputation as the defender of French-Canadian culture, societal transformations during the quiet revolution set in motion a reorientation of Québécois nationalist ideology which tended to make the Union Nationale appear irrelevant. Under Dupléssis, the party had attempted to minimize state intervention in society. In contrast, first the Liberals during the 1960s and then the Parti Québécois in the 1970s relied heavily on state action to advance the socioeconomic and cultural interests of Québécois. Although Daniel Johnson led the party back to power in 1966, in retrospect this victory appears to have been "a last hurrah." In the 1970s, the party captured a total of only twenty-eight seats in three provincial elections, and in the 1980s, no Union Nationale MNAs were elected. Over the past two decades, the party has been ground between the opposing forces of federalism and separatism, and the resulting polarization of political options has largely obliterated its support.

Political Parties—Historical

ACTION LIBERALE NATIONALE. See UNION NATIONALE.

BLOC POPULAIRE. See PARTI QUÉBÉCOIS.

COOPERATIVE COMMONWEALTH FEDERATION (CCF). See NEW DEMOCRATIC PARTY.

LABOR PROGRESSIVE PARTY. See COMMUNIST PARTY.

PROGRESSIVE PARTY. The Progressives constituted the first third party to challenge the Liberal-Conservative duopoly. The product of rural discontent, the party gained its initial impetus when the United Farmers of Ontario were swept into power in the 1919 Ontario provincial election. This stimulated the development of the Progressive Party, which elected sixty-five MPs to Ottawa in 1921. In the mid-1920s, a number of Progressive MPs joined the Liberals, thereby making the party a spent force in federal politics. The party remained important in the Prairies until the 1940s.

RALLIEMENT NATIONAL. See PARTI QUÉBÉCOIS.

RASSEMBLEMENT POUR L'INDÉPENDANCE NATIONAL. See PARTI QUÉBÉCOIS.

UNITED FARMERS OF ONTARIO. See PROGRESSIVE PARTY.

Allan Kornberg
Harold D. Clarke
Marianne C. Stewart

CAYMAN ISLANDS

The Cayman Islands consist of three tropical islands—Grand Cayman, Little Cayman, and Cayman Brac—with an area of roughly 100 square miles and a population of about 28,000. The economy, which relies almost entirely on tourism and offshore licensing and banking facilities, yields a per capita income of approximately U.S.$14,000 per year. The Cayman Islands were dependencies of Jamaica under the governor of Jamaica until 1959, when they became a separate dependency under the British Crown. By any measure, the Cayman Islands demonstrate prosperity and political stability. However, a recent wave of financial scandal in the offshore banking sector, particularly the Cayman-based International Bank of Credit and Commerce (known by its French acronym as BCCI), has placed the islands under increased international scrutiny.

The islands do not have political parties as they are conventionally known. Political preference at the polls is demonstrated by voting for individual candidates who represent, for lack of a better term, political clubs or, as they are known locally, "teams." There is no central or hierarchical political party machinery coordinating voter mobilization.

As a Crown Colony, the Cayman Islands have a British governor who governs with an Executive Council and a Legislative Assembly. The governor, who is responsible for defense and external affairs, wields immense local power and influence. The Executive Council, which administers the colony, is chaired by the governor and comprises three governor-appointed members, plus four additional members elected by the Legislative Assembly from within its own ranks. There is also a chief minister, who conventionally is the candidate of the winning team. The Legislative Assembly numbers twelve elected members and three ex-officio members appointed by the governor. Queen Elizabeth II, the head of state, is represented locally by Governor Alan James Scott, who has served in that position since 1987. Benson Ebanks, representing the Dignity Team, is chief minister in something of a turnabout from the beginning of the 1980s.

The 1980 elections saw the Unity Team, led by Jim Bodden, win eight seats to only two for Ebanks's Dignity Team; the remaining two went to independents.

The 1984 elections demonstrated a dissatisfaction with the Unity Team and, amid accusations of a drug scandal and impropriety in government, it won no seats; independents secured nine seats, and the remaining three went to the Dignity Team. Ebanks was able to form a working coalition and become chief minister. This outcome was repeated in the 1988 elections.

There is no political independence movement in island politics; however, a major scandal broke in mid-1991 when the Cayman-based BCCI collapsed. The BCCI allegedly had devious financial relationships with international figures, including heads of state, terrorists, narcotics traffickers, and the espionage community. The repercussions and subsequent closer monitoring of island banks by U.S. and British agents may have a dampening effect on future banking, legal or otherwise.

Bibliography

Robert J. Alexander. "Cayman Islands," in Robert J. Alexander, ed., *Political Parties of the Americas.* Greenwood Press, Westport, Conn., 1982.

Central Intelligence Agency. *The World Factbook, 1990.* Central Intelligence Agency, Washington, D.C., 1990.

Ulf Hanertz. *Cayman Islands Politics.* University Press, Stockholm, 1976.

Sandra Meditz and Dennis Hanratty, eds. *Islands of the Commonwealth Caribbean: A Regional Study.* Area Handbook Program, U.S. Government Printing Office, Washington, D.C., 1989.

Political Parties

There are no political parties in the Cayman Islands but rather what are known locally as "teams," which are simply groups of people who vote for the same candidate. Previously, during the 1960s, two parties, the Christian Democratic Party and the National Democratic Party, functioned, but disappeared.

DIGNITY TEAM. The leader of the Dignity Team is Benson Ebanks, who is the current chief minister. The Dignity Team currently has three seats in the Legislative Council; independents occupy the other nine elective seats.

UNITY TEAM. Led by Jim Bodden, the Unity Team's fortunes have slipped from winning eight seats in the Legislative Council in 1980 to none in 1984 and 1988. The team was first shut out in the 1984 elections amid accusations of a drug scandal and impropriety in government.

Gary Brana-Shute
Rosemary Brana-Shute

CHILE

After the military coup of September 1973, led by General Augusto Pinochet, all political parties were in effect made illegal in Chile. Immediately, the Pinochet regime outlawed the six parties which had been part of the Popular Unity (Unidad Popular), the coalition which had supported the regime of deposed (and deceased) President Salvador Allende, that is, the Socialist Party of Chile (PSCh), the Communist Party of Chile (PCCh), the Radical Party, the Christian Left (IC), the Popular Independent Action (API), and the United Movement of Popular Action (MAPU), as well as the Movement of the Revolutionary Left (MIR), a Fidelista-type party outside of the Unidad Popular. About a month later, the Pinochet regime "suspended" the activities of all other parties, and ultimately outlawed them as well.

In fact, this did not mean the total disappearance of all political parties. Only the MIR, which from the beginning had been an insurrectionist group, was almost totally obliterated by the armed forces and police of the dictatorship. The National Party (Partido Nacional), the principal right-wing party of the Frei-Allende period, declared its voluntary dissolution. Most of the rest of the parties tried to maintain some kind of underground organization.

However, during the early years of the Pinochet regime, the only two parties that were able to function with some effectiveness were the Christian Democratic Party (PDC) and the Communist Party of Chile. The Communists had a well-established underground organization, which was never totally abandoned even after the party was relegalized in the late 1950s. The Christian Democrats also were able to maintain a more or less well-functioning underground organization, perhaps because of their association with the Roman Catholic Church.

Considerable numbers of the country's major political figures, particularly those of parties associated with the Allende administration, spent much of the Pinochet period in exile. There they maintained functioning units of their groups, pending the possibility of returning home.

Political party leaders of the pre-1973 period did not play a significant role in the government of General Pinochet, with a few exceptions. Sergio Onofre

Jarpa, a coming figure in the pre-1973 National Party, served as head of Pinochet's cabinet for some time, and a few other leaders of that party served the regime as ambassadors. William Thayer and Juan de Dios Carmona of the PDC, both of whom had played a significant role in the government of President Eduardo Frei, also became strong supporters of Pinochet, which resulted in their expulsion from the PDC. Thayer was named by Pinochet to be an appointed member of the Senate at the end of the dictatorship. By and large, however, politicians did not play a major role in the Pinochet administration, which was made up largely of military men and technocrats.

With the relaxation of the tyranny of Pinochet in the mid-1980s, the parties began to reorganize. By the time of the 1989 elections, which brought about the end of the dictatorship, there were more than twenty functioning parties, but most of them disappeared after the elections because of their poor showing.

With the reestablishment of democratic government in 1990, the panorama of Chilean political parties, with one major exception, was to a remarkable degree what it had been before the 1973 coup; however, the relative strength of the parties was somewhat different from what it had been before the Pinochet dictatorship. The principal Chilean parties continued to be the PDC, the successor to the National Party—the National Renovation (RN)—the PSCh, the radicals of various stripes, and the PCCh. The small, left-wing MAPU and the IC also persisted. The major innovation was a new party of the far right, the Independent Democratic Union (UDI), led by relatively young people who had played significant roles in the Pinochet administration, although Pinochet himself was not a member of that party or of any party.

The end of the Pinochet dictatorship came as the result of two electoral exercises. In 1988, the president submitted to a plebiscite an authorization for him to stay on as chief executive for several more years. That move was strongly defeated, and as a result, the alternative that had been provided for if Pinochet did not receive a majority of yes votes, a general election, took place in December 1989.

Both for the plebiscite and the general election, a broad coalition was formed against the Pinochet administration and its supporters. This coalition, La Concertación de los Partidos por la Democracia, usually referred to as La Concertación, included seventeen different parties and political groups. For the general election, the coalition supported a single presidential candidate and common lists of nominees for the Senate and Chamber of Deputies. Although there was agreement in La Concertación that their presidential nominee would be a Christian Democrat, since the PDC certainly represented the largest contingent in the coalition, there was considerable discussion about who that nominee should be. Agreement was finally reached on Patricio Aylwin, who had led the campaign for a no vote in the plebiscite the year before. In addition to the support of La Concertación, Aylwin had the backing of the PCCh and the MIR, neither of which had yet been legalized. Aylwin was faced with two competitors in the presidential election: Hernán Buchi, favored by the Pinochet administration, had support from both major right-wing parties, the RN and the UDI, and Francisco Javier Errazuriz, a businessman, was an independent rightist candidate.

Four different elements competed in the congressional election. La Concertación was by far the largest, the RN was the second largest, and the UDI, the third. The fourth element was an alliance formed by the PCCh (which was not yet relegalized), the *Obrero y Campesino* (worker and peasant) faction of MAPU, the IC, and the faction of the Radical Party led by Anselmo Sule. This coalition, known for electoral purposes as the Authentic Party of the Socialist Left (Partido Auténtico de la Izquierda Socialista), did rather poorly; the Communists, in particular, did not elect a single candidate.

The election resulted in a substantial triumph for La Concertación. Aylwin won with 53.8 percent of the total vote, followed by Buchi with 28.7 percent and Errazuriz with 15 percent. The rest of the ballots were blank or mutilated. In the Chamber of Deputies, La Concertación won seventy-two posts and the combined right opposition, forty-eight; in the Senate, La Concertación seated twenty-two against sixteen for the two right-wing parties. However, because of the existence of nine other senators appointed by outgoing President Pinochet, the winning coalition lacked a majority in the upper house.

When President Aylwin took office, he formed a cabinet consisting of members of the parties of La Concertación: ten Christian Democrats, six Socialists, two Radicals, and one each from the Social Democracy Party and the Pact of Alliance of the Center.

Although the newly elected government took over on 11 March 1990, the constitution which President Pinochet had decreed in 1980, and under which the elections were held, had a number of features which were bothersome for the political parties. These included the right of General Pinochet to continue as commander of the army for an additional eight years, the presence of nine appointed senators whom he had named, the continuation of appointed rather than elected mayors of the country's principal urban areas, and a freezing in place of all governmental employees holding office when Pinochet left the presidency.

Although there seemed to be an agreement between La Concertación and the RN that all of these clauses of the constitution, with the possible exception of the tenure of General Pinochet, should be removed, impediments to their abolition arose during the first year of the Aylwin administration. When the Aylwin government introduced a constitutional amendment to provide for elected mayors, the two right-wing opposition parties, the RN and the UDI, apparently concluded that they would suffer severe setbacks in any new mayoral elections. As a consequence, they joined forces with the appointed senators to block the amendment.

This action, of course, immediately raised the issue of the continuation of the appointed senators. However, the Aylwin government and the parties supporting it decided that, rather than raise a possible constitutional crisis over these two issues, they would let time resolve the problem. When the terms of the mayors ran out, new appointments would be made by President Aylwin, and they certainly would not come from the right-wing parties. Also, when it came time for President Aylwin, as one of his last duties in office, to name nine new appointed senators for the Congress, who would take office with the administration following his, he would name people who were aligned with him and his supporters. Hence, in time, presumably these issues would be resolved to the satisfaction of La Concertación.

Politics in post-Pinochet Chile differ fundamentally in one regard from politics before the 1973 military coup. Before 1973, politics was to a large degree a zero-sum game, where each of the three elements in national politics, the right, the left, and the center, was determined in one way or another to undermine and even destroy the others. In contrast, by the time of the reestablishment of democracy in 1990, there was a wide degree of consensus among all of the country's major political forces.

This consensus had several aspects. First, virtually all of the civilian political leaders, as well as most military leaders, were determined not to allow any situation to develop that might lead to a new military coup. Second, both of the parties represented in the Aylwin government, as well as those in the opposition—except, perhaps, the left-wing Socialists, the Communists, and some left-wing fringe groups—were agreed on broad lines of economic and social policy. There was agreement to maintain the market-oriented, basically private enterprise economy, which had been established in the latter half of the Pinochet dictatorship, and to maintain the emphasis on the development and growth of new exports for the world market. No significant party—again with the probable exception of the Communists and left-wing Socialists—sought to return to the very high degree of government ownership and management of the economy that had developed after World War II.

This consensus was reflected in common positions taken by all of the significant parties in the period leading up to the end of the dictatorship. Thus, virtually all parties agreed that the Communist Party of Chile should be legalized along with the others and that the National Security Council should have no more than an advisory role in the democratic regime. That body consists of the four military commanders, the president of the Supreme Court, the president of the Senate, the president of the Republic, and one other civilian. General Pinochet had proposed that it have a virtual veto power on the democratically elected government, but in the face of the opposition of all of the parties, he backed down on that as well as on the issue of legalization of the Communist Party. At the beginning of the democratic regime, there was also agreement by all parties to a list of presiding officers of the Senate, in which La Concertación did not have a majority because of the presence of the nine appointed members of that body.

Bibliography

Keesings Record of World Events.
Personal contacts of the writer.

Various Chilean newspapers and magazines.
Weekly Latin American Report, London.

Political Parties

ACCIÓN POPULAR INDEPENDIENTE. See POPULAR INDEPENDENT ACTION.

AUTHENTIC PARTY. See COMMUNIST PARTY OF CHILE.

CHRISTIAN DEMOCRATIC PARTY (PARTIDO DEMÓCRATA CRIS-TIANO—PDC). For thirty years, the PDC has been the largest party in Chile. It was established in June 1957 as the result of a merger of three groups: the National Phalanx (Falange Nacional), the majority element of the Social Christian Conservative Party (Partido Conservador Social Cristiano), and a dissident group from the National Christian Party (Partido Nacional Cristiano). Then, in the 1961 parliamentary elections, the PDC won four seats in the Senate and twenty-three in the Chamber of Deputies, which made it the nation's largest party.

In 1964, the candidate of the Christian Democratic Party, Eduardo Frei, was elected president of the Republic, and in the following year, in parliamentary elections, the PDC succeeded in winning a majority in the Chamber of Deputies, the first time any party had done so in 100 years. It remained the largest party in the Senate, although it did not gain an absolute majority there.

Under President Frei, substantial reforms were carried out. A large land redistribution program was launched; the country's key mining firms were "Chileanized," being coordinated under the Copper Corporation of Chile (CODELCO); a more equitable tax system was established; and a massive program to expand the educational system was carried out.

In spite of the accomplishments of the Frei administration, the party lost the presidency in 1970 in a three-way race, in which Salvador Allende, supported by the Popular Unity (Unidad Popular) coalition, triumphed. During the Allende administration, the Christian Democrats were in the opposition, and in several by-elections and in the 1973 congressional election, they joined with the right-wing opposition party, the National Party (Partido Nacional), to form joint slates. On three different occasions, when the Christian Democrats sought to reach an agreement with President Allende on the enactment of elements of his program by Congress, where the opposition had the majority, they were frustrated by the opposition of the Socialist Party leadership under Senator Carlos Altamirano.

When General Augusto Pinochet seized power, he first suspended the activities of the PDC and then officially outlawed the party. The PDC continued to function illegally, however, holding regular meetings of its central authorities and maintaining contact with its regional and local groups. Undoubtedly, the sympathy of much of the hierarchy of the Roman Catholic Church was an important factor in the PDC's ability to continue. Nevertheless, the party suffered substantial persecution in the early years of the dictatorship; some of the PDC leaders were exiled, and many secondary leaders and rank and filers were jailed for varying periods of time, where some were tortured.

In the underground, the Christian Democrats emerged as the largest single force in the organized labor movement, in which the party had made substantial progress even during the Allende years. The PDC also took the lead in mounting demonstrations against the regime in 1983.

With the relaxation of the Pinochet dictatorship in the mid-1980s, the PDC took the lead in organizing a broad coalition of all opposition forces to the regime. This led to the establishment of La Concertación de los Partidos por la Democracia (La Concertación), which conducted the campaign for a no vote in the plebiscite of 1988 to decide whether President Pinochet should continue in power. With the victory of La Concertación in that poll, the Christian Democrats joined to form common lists of candidates for the 1989 election.

All elements of La Concertación agreed that the coalition's presidential candidate should be a Christian Democrat since the PDC was the largest party in the country. After considerable controversy both within the party and within La Concertación, the candidate chosen was Patricio Aylwin, who had led the campaign for a no vote in 1988. Aylwin won the election with a clear majority among the three candidates. In the congressional race, the PDC received the highest number of members of both houses of Congress. In the Senate, the PDC won 13 of the 36 elected seats; in the Chamber of Deputies, the PDC won 38 out of the 120 seats. When President Aylwin took office, he appointed a coalition cabinet in which the PDC had half of the posts.

The PDC is a widely based party. Although the party's founders came from the middle and upper classes, from the 1950s the party paid particular attention to organizing in the shantytowns of Santiago and other cities. They emerged after the dictatorship as the single most important political group in the organized labor movement. The agrarian reform and rural unionization program of the Frei administration had won them wide support in the rural areas, even though the Pinochet dictatorship subsequently reversed the land reform. Judging that both the economic and the social conditions in the countryside had altered substantially in the previous two decades or more, the PDC-led government of Patricio Aylwin made no move to reinstigate land redistribution.

Unlike some of the other parties, the PDC did not go through a massive change of leadership during the years of the Pinochet dictatorship. Although President Frei died during that period, most who had been party leaders in 1973 were still leading the party in 1990. The only new face of major significance was Eduardo Frei, Jr., who emerged as the most popular candidate for the Senate in the Santiago area, but he remains a relatively untested figure.

CHRISTIAN LEFT (IZQUIERDA CRISTIANA—IC). The IC was formed in 1971 as the result of the second split of that period in the Christian Democratic

Party. It participated in the Unidad Popular coalition backing President Salvador Allende, who included some representatives of the party in his various cabinets. After the September 1973 military coup, the IC virtually disappeared for some years; however, with the move back toward a democratic regime, it reappeared under the leadership of Luis Naira.

Izquierda Cristiana did not become part of La Concertación, the major co-alition against the Pinochet dictatorship. Rather, in the 1989 election, it was part of the Communist-led Partido Auténtico de la Izquierda Socialista and was able to elect some members to the Chamber of Deputies.

At the time of the reunification of the Socialist Party of Chile in December 1989, a faction of IC, under the leadership of Sergio Bitar, participated in that process. Bitar was also a member of the leadership of the Party for Democracy.

Almost a year later, in November 1990, the first congress of the reunited Socialists agreed to accept within its ranks another faction of the IC, led by Naira, and a majority of the political commission of that party. Naira became an adjunct vice president of the Partido Socialista, and his group of ex-Izquierda Cristiana members were given six of the nearly 100 seats in the central committee.

Another faction of the Christian Left, headed by Subsecretary General Rob-erto Celedon, rejected merger with the Socialists, and kept the Izquierda Cris-tiana in existence.

CHRISTIAN SOCIAL MOVEMENT (MOVIMIENTO SOCIAL CRIST-IANO). The Christian Social Movement was established in 1984 by Juan de Dios Carmona, a former leader of the Christian Democratic Party (PDC) who broke with the PDC to support the Pinochet dictatorship. The party's secretary general is Manuel Rodriguez. The Christian Social Movement is one of the country's smaller parties.

COMMUNIST PARTY OF CHILE (PARTIDO COMUNISTA DE CHILE— PCCh). The second oldest Chilean political party still in existence, it was established before World War I as the Socialist Labor Party (Partido Obrero Socialista). In 1922, when it joined the Communist International, it assumed its present name.

The Communist Party was a major part of Unidad Popular, the coalition which elected President Salvador Allende in 1970 and supported his adminis-tration thereafter. During the Allende government, the party, one of the more moderate elements in the administration, was particularly critical of the extre-mist role played by the Socialist Party of Chile, led by Carlos Altamirano.

The Communists suffered considerably less than some of the other Unidad Popular parties from the persecution of the Pinochet dictatorship. Illegal for a decade in the late 1940s and the 1950s, the party did not entirely give up its underground organization when it was relegalized. Thus, even in the worst days of the Pinochet dictatorship, although its principal leaders had been arrested or had fled abroad, the party was able to maintain a substantial organizational structure. During the first years of the Pinochet administration, virtually its only serious rival in the underground was the Christian Democratic Party.

With the relaxation of the Pinochet dictatorship in the mid-1980s, the Partido Comunista adopted a particularly hard line in 1983, known as the strategy of the "popular rebellion of the masses." For this purpose, it organized the Frente Patriótico Manuel Rodríguez, a paramilitary group, which carried out various attacks on the police, soldiers, and others. When the Frente split in 1988, one faction declared its independence from the Communist Party and its determination to continue its insurrectional activities at all costs.

The faction of the Frente that stayed loyal to the Partido Comunista announced early in 1989 that it was suspending its armed activities temporarily. However, a congress of the party early in 1989 reasserted support for the insurrectionist line and elected hard-liner Volodia Teitelbaum as secretary general. It was not until 28 January 1990 that the Communist Party, on the occasion of the sixty-eighth anniversary of its assuming that name, formally renounced its "popular rebellion of the masses" strategy. Even then, it did not repudiate the Frente Manuel Rodríguez.

Because of its support of armed insurrection against the Pinochet regime, the Communist Party was completely separated from the efforts of the other parties to work within the political framework established by General Pinochet as the preferred means of defeating the dictatorship, efforts which culminated in the elections of 1989 and in the assumption of office by President Patricio Aylwin in March 1990. Although it sought to become a member of the anti-Pinochet coalition, La Concertación, which led the campaign for a vote in the 1988 plebiscite against the continuance of Pinochet in power, and joined forces to oppose the regime in the 1989 election, all of the parties belonging to La Concertación rejected Communist membership because of the party's refusal to abandon its insurrectionist strategy.

During 1988 and 1989, when other parties were seeking legal recognition from the Pinochet regime, the Communist Party did not do so, although it had been agreed that it could be granted such status if it fulfilled the requirements for a party to obtain legality. For the purposes of the 1989 election, the Communists organized a coalition, the Partido Auténtico de la Izquierda Socialista, with a faction of the MAPU, the IC, and a small faction of the Radical Party. That coalition did very poorly in the election; for the first time since its establishment, the Communist Party failed to elect a single deputy or senator.

This disastrous showing, together with the collapse of Communist regimes in Eastern Europe and the turmoil in the Soviet Union in 1989 and 1990, had a grave impact on the Communist Party of Chile, which had a reputation as being one of the Latin American parties most loyal to Moscow. This led to several splits in the party during 1990. First, a group of party members led by Patricio Hales quit the party and joined the Party for Democracy. A little later, fourteen of the fifty full members of the central committee of the Communist youth group resigned in protest of the party's policies. At the same time, a group calling itself Pro Vocación Democritica (sic), formed within the Communist Party's top leadership, headed by ex-deputy Luis Guastavino, Augusto Samamego, José Antonio Leal, Manuel Fernando Contreras and ex-Senator Toro, announced its opposition to the current party leadership.

On 8 August 1990, Guastavino was "separated" from the Communist Party by its leadership. In December the party's secretary of international affairs, Leal, publicly resigned from the party in a letter denouncing its continued support for "all forms of struggle," including insurrection, and accusing it of failure to undergo a process of "renovation." During the later months of 1990, scores of leading figures in the party, including many of its intellectuals, former members of parliament, and trade union and student leaders, publicly resigned from the party.

In spite of the party's poor electoral showing, its political isolation, and its defections, the Communists remain a significant factor in the country's political life. They continue to have extensive organizations in the shantytowns of Santiago and other cities, as well as considerable influence in the Central Unitaria de Trabajadores (CUT) and its affiliated unions. In the CUT, they tend to be allied with members of that segment of the Socialist Party who follow the leadership of Clodomiro Almeyda, which provides the Communists considerably more influence than they would have on their own. However, the Communists and their allies remain a distinct minority in the leadership of the CUT.

Shortly after the inauguration of the Aylwin government, the Communist Party was granted legal recognition as a political movement; however, it took the Communists much longer than expected to gather the 35,000 signatures needed to register as a political party. It was not until October 1990 that they finally achieved such recognition.

FALANGE NACIONAL. See CHRISTIAN DEMOCRATIC PARTY.

FRENTE NACIONAL DEL TRABAJO. See NATIONAL RENOVATION.

GREEN PARTY (PARTIDO VERDE). A new environmentalist party, modeled on those in Europe the Green Party was part of the anti-Pinochet La Concertación coalition in the 1989 election. It received a few secondary positions in the administration of President Patricio Aylwin.

HUMANIST PARTY (PARTIDO HUMANISTA). A party formed in the last months of the Pinochet dictatorship, it was part of the La Concertación coalition in the 1989 election. Its president, Laura Rodríguez, was elected to the Chamber of Deputies. The Humanist Party has connections with some political factions in Argentina.

INDEPENDENT DEMOCRATIC UNION (UNIÓN DEMOCRÁTICA INDEPENDIENTE—UDI). This new party was formed at the end of the Pinochet dictatorship. Although it traces its origins back to student politics at the Catholic University of Santiago in the late 1960s, it is notable mainly for being the principal party of the far right and for being led mainly by people who were closely associated with the Pinochet regime. A number of these are among the "Chicago Boys," the people who drew up and applied the extreme laissez-faire policies of the dictatorship between 1974 and 1982.

The party leaders define themselves as not wanting to change much of anything in the economic and social fields accomplished during the Pinochet regime. They also profess to be for representative government, "with reservations." Among those reservations is support for the maintenance of the nine members of the Senate appointed by the president of the republic. The UDI is the only party who avowedly supports this.

The UDI won two seats in the Senate and thirteen in the Chamber of Deputies in the 1989 election. The party made a particularly good showing in the shantytown *poblaciones* in Santiago.

Among the leaders of the UDI are Jaime Guzmán, who, a one-time political and economic adviser to General Augusto Pinochet, was elected senator in 1989, and Julio Ditborn Cordua, president of the party, who is a one-time Chicago Boy.

IZQUIERDA CRISTIANA. *See* CHRISTIAN LEFT.

IZQUIERDA RADICAL. *See* SOCIAL DEMOCRACY PARTY.

MOVEMENT OF THE REVOLUTIONARY LEFT (MOVIMIENTO DE IZ-QUIERDA REVOLUCIONARIA—MIR). Originally organized by left-wing dissidents from the Socialist Party of Chile in the mid-1960s, it was an overtly insurrectionist or terrorist group. During the Frei administration, the MIR carried out a number of spectacular robberies, which resulted in a number of its members serving jail sentences. President Salvador Allende pardoned those MIR members, and, during Allende's administration, the party was particularly active in organizing takeovers of rural properties, urban factories, and other enterprises. They often did so in conjunction with members of the Socialist Party, and there were undoubtedly a number of people who held dual membership in both groups.

After the 1973 coup, the MIR was a particular target for the armed forces, which organized a veritable expeditionary force to uproot the MIR from the land the party had seized in the Temuco area. Clashes between armed members of the MIR and units of the army and police also occurred elsewhere. Some of its leaders and members fled abroad, and others were killed. The MIR was to a large degree physically destroyed.

With the move toward the reestablishment of a democratic regime in the 1980s, the MIR was able to regenerate itself to some degree. It did not seek or receive legal recognition from either the Pinochet administration or its successor.

It supported the Communist-led Partido Auténtico de la Izquierda Socialista in the 1989 election.

The principal leader of the MIR is Andrés Pascal Allende.

MOVIMIENTO ACCIÓN POPULAR UNIDO. See UNITED MOVEMENT OF POPULAR ACTION.

MOVIMIENTO DE IZQUIERDA REVOLUCIONARIA. See MOVEMENT OF THE REVOLUTIONARY LEFT.

MOVIMIENTO SOCIAL CRISTIANO. See CHRISTIAN SOCIAL MOVEMENT.

NATIONAL CHRISTIAN PARTY. See CHRISTIAN DEMOCRATIC PARTY.

NATIONAL FRONT OF LABOR. See NATIONAL RENOVATION.

NATIONAL PARTY. See NATIONAL RENOVATION.

NATIONAL PHALANX. See CHRISTIAN DEMOCRATIC PARTY.

NATIONAL RENOVATION (RENOVACIÓN NACIONAL—RN). The RN is a virtual reincarnation in the post-Pinochet period of the National Party, which had been established in 1965 with the merger of the traditional Liberal and Conservative parties. However, it differs in several respects from the National Party. The RN was established by the merger of the National Front of Labor (Frente Nacional del Trabajo), led by Angel Fantuzzi, and the National Union (Unión Nacional), headed by Andrés Allemand.

The National Renovation seems to have a somewhat broader constituency than the National Party did. In the 1989 election, it received approximately the same percentage of votes that the National Party had received in the late 1960s and early 1970s. However, it did so in the face of the existence of another party on the right (and to its right), the Independent Democratic Union (UDI), which had not existed in the earlier period. Furthermore, although some of the pre–1973 leaders of the National Party, such as Sergio Onofre Jarpa, are among the leaders of National Renovation, the most outstanding figures in the RN are younger people, who had not played any significant role—if any at all—in politics before the Pinochet dictatorship. Among the most important of these new members are Andrés Allemand, the party's national secretary, and Sebastian Pinera.

Renovación Nacional defines itself as being a party of the center right. Internationally, it is aligned with the International Democratic Union, which includes among its members the Conservative Party of Great Britain, the Republican Party of the United States, and the Unión del Pueblo of Spain.

In the election of 1989, National Renovation came in second, behind the La Concertación coalition. It won eleven seats in the Senate and twenty-nine in the Chamber of Deputies. It constitutes the largest part of the opposition to La Concertación in Congress.

NATIONAL UNION. *See* NATIONAL RENOVATION.

PACT OF ALLIANCE OF THE CENTER (PACTO DE ALIANZA DEL CENTRO). This new, post-Pinochet party, consists principally of people who before 1973 would have belonged to the right-wing National Party. It was part of the La Concertación coalition during the final years of the Pinochet regime and thereafter; one member of the cabinet formed by President Patricio Aylwin, when he came into office, came from this party. One of Chile's smaller parties, it is a member of the Liberal International. Germán Riesco is its principal leader.

PACTO DE ALIANZA DEL CENTRO. *See* PACT OF ALLIANCE OF THE CENTER.

PARTIDO AUTÉNTICO DE LA IZQUIERDA SOCIALISTA. *See* COMMUNIST PARTY OF CHILE.

PARTIDO COMUNISTA DE CHILE. *See* COMMUNIST PARTY OF CHILE.

PARTIDO CONSERVADOR SOCIAL CRISTIANO. *See* CHRISTIAN DEMOCRATIC PARTY.

PARTIDO DEMÓCRATA CRISTIANO. *See* CHRISTIAN DEMOCRATIC PARTY.

PARTIDO HUMANISTA. *See* HUMANIST PARTY.

PARTIDO NACIONAL. *See* NATIONAL RENOVATION.

PARTIDO NACIONAL CRISTIANO. *See* CHRISTIAN DEMOCRATIC PARTY.

PARTIDO POR LA DEMOCRACIA. *See* PARTY FOR DEMOCRACY.

PARTIDO SOCIALDEMOCRACIA. *See* SOCIAL DEMOCRACY PARTY.

PARTIDO SOCIALISTA DE CHILE. *See* SOCIALIST PARTY OF CHILE.

PARTIDO SOCIALISTA OBRERO. *See* COMMUNIST PARTY OF CHILE.

PARTIDO VERDE. *See* GREEN PARTY.

PARTY FOR DEMOCRACY (PARTIDO POR LA DEMOCRACIA—PPD). A new party, the PPD was formed in the last phase of the Pinochet dictatorship as an electoral vehicle for the Socialists before they had united or gained legal recognition. Its principal leader at the time of its formation was Ricardo Lagos, who was also a principal figure in the moderate element among the Socialists. Its president was Ernesto Schanke, son of one of the principal founders of the Socialist Party of Chile and a former leader of the Socialist left wing. Most, although not all, of the members of the PPD also belong to the Socialist Party.

The PPD was part of La Concertación, the major coalition opposing the Pinochet regime. With the victory of La Concertación in the 1989 election and the inauguration in March 1990 of President Patricio Aylwin, the PPD was officially represented in the government of the new president among the Socialist Party members of the cabinet. In the middle of 1990, a dissident element, led by Patricio Hales, broke away from the Communist Party of Chile and entered the PPD.

Although the PPD was originally established as an electoral vehicle for the Socialists, with the presumption that it would disappear once the various Socialist factions were reunited and received legal recognition as a party, the PPD took on a life of its own. It recruited an appreciable number of people who were not members of the Socialist Party, including some ex-Communists. The question of dual membership in the Socialist Party and the PPD remained an issue in both groups.

When dual membership was debated at the November 1990 congress of the Socialist Party, it was decided that such membership should be ended by the next Socialist Party congress, scheduled in two years. It was also decided that no one could hold official positions of leadership in both parties at the same time. Meanwhile, the PPD made clear its absolute opposition to any future alliance with the Communist Party, an alliance favored by the left wing of the Socialists.

POPULAR INDEPENDENT ACTION (ACCIÓN POPULAR INDEPENDIENTE—API). The API, a minor left-wing party, participated in the Popular Unity coalition of Salvador Allende.

POPULAR UNITY. *See* COMMUNIST PARTY OF CHILE.

RADICAL DEMOCRACY. *See* RADICAL PARTY.

RADICAL LEFT. *See* SOCIAL DEMOCRACY PARTY.

RADICAL PARTY (PARTIDO RADICAL). This party, the oldest party still in existence in Chile, was established in 1857. In its earlier decades it was noted particularly for its strong anticlericalism. In the first decade of the twentieth century, it experienced an extended internal debate between those who wanted to commit it to a rather ill-defined socialism and those opposed to the idea; the former group won. The Radical Party participated in the reform administration of President Arturo Alessandri, between 1920 and 1924, whose first prime minister, Pedro Aguirre Cerda, was a Radical.

In the 1930s and 1940s the Radical Party was the principal representative of the Chilean middle class, including white-collar workers (particularly government employees), small businessmen, and small landholders. In that period, the party occupied the center of Chilean politics, although it participated in the Popular Front of 1936–1941, together with the Socialist Party of Chile, the Communist Party of Chile, and several other smaller groups. During the 1930s and 1940s, it provided the country with four presidents: Juan Esteban Montero (1931–1932), Pedro Aguirre Cerda (1938–1941), Juan Antonio Rios (1941–1946) and Gabriel González Videla (1946–1952).

Subsequent to the González Videla administration, the Radical Party fared poorly in elections and eventually became part of Unidad Popular, the left-wing coalition which elected President Salvador Allende in 1970. It served in his government and was immediately outlawed by President Augusto Pinochet when he seized power. In the 1960s, the Radical Party joined the Socialist International, to which it still belongs.

In the late 1960s and early 1970s, the Radical Party underwent two splits. A more conservative group broke away to form the Radical Democracy (Democracia Radical), which went out of existence during the Pinochet regime. During the Allende presidency, another group broke away to form the Radical Left (Izquierda Radical), which was renamed the Social Democracy Party (Partido Socialdemocracia) and still exists.

With its revival in the last years of the Pinochet regime, the Radical Party became part of the La Concertación coalition which elected President Patricio Aylwin in 1989, although it was not one of the major members of that alliance. President Aylwin named a member of the party as his first foreign minister.

The president of the Radical Party is Enrique Silva Cimma; the secretary general is Ricardo Navarrete.

RENOVACIÓN NACIONAL. See NATIONAL RENOVATION.

SOCIAL CHRISTIAN CONSERVATIVE PARTY. See CHRISTIAN DEMOCRATIC PARTY.

SOCIAL DEMOCRACY PARTY (PARTIDO SOCIALDEMOCRACIA). This post-dictatorship party is a reincarnation of the Radical Left (Izquierda Radical), which had been formed by a group that broke away from the Radical

Party during the Allende regime, under the leadership of Luis Bossay. In August 1973, shortly before the coup led by General Augusto Pinochet, Izquierda Radical had changed its name to Partido Socialdemocracia.

With its resurgence in the last phase of the Pinochet regime, the party was under the leadership of Eugenio Velasco, a pre-1973 leader of the organization. However, its leadership and members consisted principally of younger people, who had entered politics in the latter part of the struggle against the Pinochet dictatorship. They had considerable influence among the university students of Santiago and Valparaíso.

The Partido Socialdemocracia became part of the La Concertación alliance which backed the presidential candidacy of Patricio Aylwin. It elected several members of parliament and received one post in the cabinet of President Aylwin.

SOCIALIST LABOR PARTY. *See* COMMUNIST PARTY OF CHILE.

SOCIALIST PARTY OF CHILE (PARTIDO SOCIALISTA DE CHILE— PSCh). The party was originally established in 1933 by leaders of the trade unions that had been organized and legalized under the Labor Code enacted in the previous decade and by the leaders and members of several small socialist parties which had emerged after the ouster of the dictatorship of General Carlos Ibáñez del Campo (1927–1931). Ever since its founding, the PSCh has been one of the country's major parties. However, almost since its inception, it has been peculiarly prone to bitter internal conflicts and splits, a characteristic it apparently did not abandon with the end of the Pinochet dictatorship and the reestablishment of democracy.

The PSCh was, of course, the axis of the government of President Salvador Allende, who himself belonged to the party. However, during the Allende years, the party organization was controlled by a group of very young men, led by the somewhat older Carlos Altamirano. This group constituted the extremist fringe of the coalition supporting the Allende government. The party encouraged widespread illegal seizures of property, both urban and rural, and many of the members worked closely with the Fidelista Movimiento de Izquierda Revolucionaria. They did much to provoke the uprising that finally overthrew the Allende government.

With the seizure of power by the armed forces under General Augusto Pinochet in September 1973, the Socialist Party undoubtedly suffered more than any other major Chilean party at the hands of the Pinochet dictatorship. Although many of its leaders had talked extensively about seizing total power, the party in fact had little or no underground or paramilitary organization. It was totally unprepared for the severe persecution to which it was subjected by the Pinochet regime. There were instances in which local military commanders ordered the execution of all members of the party's local and regional committees.

During the years of the dictatorship, the Socialists, both inside Chile and in exile, split into a number of competing groups. At the end of the dictatorship, there were at least six of these factions. The two most important were those led by Clodomiro Almeyda and by Carlos Altamirano.

During his years in exile, Almeyda, who had held several cabinet posts in the Allende administration, allied himself closely with the Communists, and with the return of democracy, he and his followers still tended to favor some kind of reconstitution of the Unidad Popular alliance with the Communist Party of Chile.

In contrast, Altamirano, in reconsidering his and his party's actions during the Allende period, came to the conclusion that they had been fundamentally mistaken in pressuring Allende to adopt extremist positions. In a letter to the November 1990 congress of the Socialist Party, he declared that "Leninism, as a theory on which to base 'the revolution' and the 'revolutionary party' has been overturned . . . and Marxism is to say the least, in great crisis."

In December 1989, six Socialist factions joined together to reestablish the Partido Socialista de Chile. There also participated in this unification one part of the United Movement of Popular Action and a segment of the Christian Left led by Sergio Bitar.

Even before unification, the various Socialist factions participated in the anti-Pinochet coalition, La Concertación, which had conducted the no-vote campaign in the 1988 plebiscite and had joint tickets in the 1989 election. With the formation of the government of President Patricio Aylwin, the Socialist Party was given six seats in the new cabinet and various other posts in the new administration, drawn from the party's two more moderate factions.

Eight months after reunification, the Socialist Party held elections by the membership for a new central committee, in which approximately 22,000 of the 57,000 members cast their votes. In this voting, three distinct factions—each with subgroups—emerged. The "orthodox" group, still proclaiming firm belief in Marxism-Leninism and headed by Clodomiro Almeyda's brother Manuel, received the largest number of votes, 33 percent. The most moderate faction, headed by Ricardo Lagos, received 24 percent. The third group, also proclaiming itself (like Lagos's group) for a "renovation" of the party, headed by Isabel Allende and supporting outgoing party secretary general Jorge Arrate, received 28 percent.

In the first post-dictatorship convention of the party—named in honor of Salvador Allende and held a few weeks after the central committee election—the three factions were also present. Although there were clearly sharp differences of opinion among the three factions, all sought to avoid any kind of break in the unity of the party, and all sought to reach resolutions that could be supported by all three factions.

In terms of basic ideology, the Almeyda faction clearly favors adherence to the Marxism-Leninism that characterized the party in the 1960s and early 1970s. The other two groups seek some degree of renovation, emphasizing the maintenance of political democracy and a pluralistic society.

The attitudes of the three factions toward the government of President Patricio

Aylwin and the La Concertación coalition that support him also differed. The Almeyda group tends to be strongly critical of the government, although it does not want to break with it. The Arrate faction is also critical, but it puts more emphasis on maintaining the stability of the regime. The Lagos group rejects any public criticism of the regime, arguing that "either you are in it or you are not."

The factions also follow different policies in the newly reorganizing trade union movement. Within the Central Unitaria de Trabajadores, the principal labor organization, the Almeyda faction continues generally to work with the Communists; the other two tend to work against the Communists within the labor movement and to be more or less in alliance with the Christian Democrats.

Finally, clearly different views on the problem of the Party of Democracy (PPD) were aired at the congress and since then. Originally established as an electoral vehicle of the Socialist Party before their unification and legal recognition as a party, the PPD continued in existence after the elections. Ricardo Lagos, leader of the most moderate faction of the Socialists, has been its principal figure. His group favored continuing indefinitely the possibility of people holding membership in both groups simultaneously; the Almeyda group favored ending that situation immediately; and Jorge Arrate and his followers indicated a desire to end it but to do it more slowly. At the Salvador Allende Congress, it was decided that full separation of the two parties would be undertaken before the next Socialist Party congress, scheduled to be held two years later and that, in the meanwhile, no one should be able to hold a leading position in both parties at the same time.

The heterogeneous nature of the Socialist Party of Chile was reflected in the invitations to foreign parties to send fraternal delegates to the Salvador Allende Congress. These invitations ranged from the Radical Party of Argentina to the Socialist parties of France, Spain, Belgium, Sweden, and various other countries, to the Aprista Party of Peru, the government party of Mexico (the PRI), and the Communist parties of Italy and Cuba.

UNIDAD POPULAR. *See* COMMUNIST PARTY OF CHILE.

UNIÓN NACIONAL. *See* NATIONAL RENOVATION.

UNITED MOVEMENT OF POPULAR ACTION (MOVIMIENTO ACCIÓN POPULAR UNIDO—MAPU). Formed in the late 1960s as the result of the first of two left-wing splits in the Christian Democratic Party, the MAPU became part of the Unidad Popular, the coalition that elected and backed Salvador Allende as president. Near the end of the Allende regime, it split, and the more radical of the factions took the name MAPU Obrero y Campesino. With the movement to return to a democratic regime, the more moderate faction supported the candidates of La Concertación; the MAPU Obrero y Campesino took part in the Partido Auténtico de la Izquierda Socialista, which was organized by the Communist Party of Chile for the 1989 election.

Immediately after the 1989 election, with the unification of the forces of the Socialist Party, the more moderate faction of MAPU, led by Oscar Guillermo Garreton, joined in forming the new Partido Socialista de Chile. The other faction maintained an independent MAPU, but it remained one of the smaller of the country's parties. It won no representation in parliament in the 1989 election.

Robert J. Alexander

COLOMBIA

The republic of Colombia, comprising an area of 440,000 square miles, is located in the northwestern corner of the South American continent. It borders the Caribbean Sea in the north and the Pacific Ocean in the west, and has land frontiers with Panama in the northwest and with Venezuela, Brazil, Peru, and Ecuador to the east and south. The hot coastal lowlands and river valleys, the vast eastern plains, and the three ranges of the Andes mountains, with their high plateaus, endow the country with a richly varied topography and climate.

Colombia's population is slightly more than 30 million. Approximately 70 percent of the people live in rapidly growing urban areas. Ten cities in Colombia have populations in excess of 250,000; four of these (Bogotá, the national capital, Medellín, Cali, and Barranquilla) have several million inhabitants each.

The ethnic composition of the population is complex. About 58 percent are mestizo; 20 percent, white; 14 percent, mulatto; 4 percent, African; 3 percent, African-Indian; and 1 percent, Indian. These groups are spread throughout the national territory, although mestizos and whites are more numerous in the highlands, and people of African descent are concentrated in the coastal areas and the Magdalena and Cauca river valleys. Small Indian communities are scattered throughout the country.

Nineteenth-Century Politics

Two parties, the Liberal and Conservative, have dominated the country's political history. Both parties have their roots in the 1830s and 1840s, when regional elites contended for power in the aftermath of the war against Spain for independence. The nineteenth-century political elites, primarily large land-owners and their allies, including professionals, commercial groups, artisans, and members of the higher clergy, struggled over economic issues and about the structure and direction of the new state. They mobilized the majority of the population—the tenants, sharecroppers, small landowners, and the urban groups who were dependent on them—as followers and partisans in the political conflicts, uprisings, and civil wars that characterized politics throughout the century. Both Liberals and Conservatives thus emerged as multiclass parties controlled by small but powerful regional leaderships, with masses of adherents whose loyalties were cemented by dependent relationships and "hereditary hatreds" conditioned by interparty violence. As a result, families, villages, towns, and even regions were indelibly labeled as either Liberal or Conservative.

Neither party was able to establish complete dominance over the other, although for several decades after 1850 the Liberals achieved ascendancy in the national government and were able to forward their agenda. National administrations changed hands frequently, often as a result of splits and realignments among and between the parties and party factions.

In reaction to the political turmoil, Rafael Núñez was elected president in 1880 with the slogan of "Regeneration." Though nominally a Liberal, he was supported by a coalition of moderates from both parties. He dominated Colombian politics until 1894.

Liberal uprisings against the government occurred in 1884–1885 and again in 1899–1902. Both failed, but the latter marked a turning point in Colombian politics. Known as the War of the Thousand Days, the 1899–1902 civil war resulted in 100,000 deaths and so weakened the country that it was unable to respond to the secession of Panama encouraged by the United States. In the war's aftermath, the elites of both parties reached an agreement to end their destructive partisan struggles by guaranteeing the minority party—in this case, the Liberals—some representation in the national government. This arrangement provided the precedent for future agreements between the political elites during periods of crisis.

Twentieth-Century Politics

During the three decades of Conservative hegemony to 1930, Colombia experienced significant socioeconomic change. The country was integrated into the international capitalist market. The development of such export products as coffee, bananas, and petroleum was accompanied by the building of a modern economic infrastructure. Industrialization began in Antioquía and several other regions. The growth of cities and towns was spurred. In them, new middle sectors and working classes appeared. The elites of both parties shared in the new wealth; their old differences began to fade in the new economic atmosphere.

The benefits of economic growth, however, were not distributed equitably. In large measure, the lower classes were excluded. By the 1920s, the middle sectors, workers, students, and intellectuals began to clamor for change. After 1922, the Liberal Party reoriented its programs in order to attract these groups. When the economic crisis at the end of the decade contributed to a split in the Conservative leadership, the Liberals came to power.

Following a transitional administration, the Liberal Party dominated the government until 1946. Known as the Liberal Republic, it was an era—especially during the Alfonso López presidency (1934–1938)—of social, economic, educational, and governmental reforms intended to provide more benefits and increased participation in the system for the middle sectors and working classes. The state also assumed a greater role in economic development. The Liberal programs, though limited in practice, were enough to arouse the apprehensions of elements among both parties' elites. The most vociferous opposition came from the Conservative Party leader, Laureano Gómez.

Indeed, a Liberal politician, the populist firebrand Jorge Eliécer Gaitán, a longtime champion of the lower classes, argued that the Liberal reforms had not gone far enough. His candidacy for the presidency in 1946 split the Liberal Party and resulted in the election of a minority Conservative government.

Over the next decade Colombia, a politically divided, class-ridden, highly stratified society, with gross inequities of wealth, experienced the most savage conflict in its history. It began at the time of the 1946 election, when Conservative partisans attempted to reduce Liberal majorities through intimidation and terror in several rural departments. Then, Gaitán, who had captured the leadership of the Liberal Party, was assassinated in April 1948. His murder set off massive uprisings in towns and cities throughout the country. Though these were put down, conflict intensified in large areas of the countryside. Known as La Violencia, the civil war claimed 200,000 lives before it subsided in the late 1950s. The national political elites remained intact, but the threat to the country forced them to turn to the military. A coup ousted the Conservative administration of Gómez in 1953.

Just as they had during previous times of national crisis, the party elites came together. General Gustavo Rojas Pinilla, the military dictator who had dealt with the worst of the violence, was ousted by his colleagues in 1957 after threatening to circumvent the traditional parties. Although La Violencia clearly illustrated the need for significant socioeconomic reforms and a more open, democratic political system, Liberal and Conservative leaders opted instead for another political arrangement designed to preserve their power. This was called the National Front. All political power and offices would be shared equally between the two parties from 1958 through 1974. Other political parties would be excluded.

The National Front governments succeeded in reestablishing peace between the two parties. Colombian politics, however, at the highest levels remained the province of a relatively small group of notables; at the regional and local levels, party bosses and their clients dominated. National Front administrations were increasingly characterized by governmental stalemates, policy half measures, and party factionalism. Politics appeared ever more remote to the concerns of the average Colombian; this was reflected in widespread voter apathy.

Challenges to the National Front came from various directions. In the mid-1960s several Marxist guerilla groups appeared, thus adding a class-based dimension to Colombian politics. The largest, the Colombian Revolutionary Armed Forces (FARC), with links to the Colombian Communist Party and roots in the era of *La Violencia*, operated mostly in southern departments of the country. The Fidelista-oriented National Liberation Army (ELN) and the Maoist Popular Army of Liberation (EPL) organized in the northeastern and northern areas of the country, respectively. Though these groups achieved some limited success in recruiting followers, controlling rural areas, and withstanding army offensives, they posed no immediate threat to the system. Nevertheless, their continued survival remained an irritant and a source of instability.

Politically, the National Front was attacked from within by two movements in the late 1960s and early 1970s. The nominally Conservative former dictator, General Rojas Pinilla, mounted an electoral challenge with his populist National Popular Alliance (ANAPO) which narrowly missed winning the presidential election of 1970 (his followers claim that he was denied the election by fraud). ANAPO disintegrated after Rojas's death later in the decade, but leftist elements from it formed the core of an urban-based revolutionary movement, the 19th of April Movement—Democratic Alliance (ADM 19), which became increasingly active after 1974. Within the Liberal Party, Alfonso López Michelsen formed a dissident, reformist group called the Liberal Revolutionary Movement, which provided the base of support for López's successful drive to capture the nomination of his party as presidential candidate in 1974.

Beyond the National Front

The ban on competition at the national level between the Liberals and Conservatives ended prior to the 1974 election, but as a result of a 1968 constitutional amendment presidents were required to give "adequate and equitable" representation in the government to the majority party not occupying the executive. This, in effect, assured the continued domination of the two traditional parties; administrations until the mid-1980s honored the arrangement. Yet the pact that ended the violent competition between the major parties had the effect of widening the gap between what Gaitán had called the "political country" and the vast majority of people in the "national country." One of the results was growing social unrest.

In 1974 López Michelsen won the first post–National Front "free" election by a wide margin over his Conservative opponent Alvaro Gómez Hurtado. The fact that both candidates were the sons of former presidents illustrated the exclusive nature of the political system. López, like his father before him, had campaigned as a reformer. Unlike his father, he was unable to achieve substantial reforms. The weakness of guaranteed political power sharing, with entrenched interests and the lack of the need for accountability, plus no decisive majority for either party, doomed any sweeping efforts to deal with the country's acute problems. The result was political bickering, widespread corruption, and regression to reliance on *caciques*, or political bosses. Ideological differences between the parties almost disappeared.

The López administration, which began with high expectations, proved to be a disappointment. Public disenchantment was demonstrated by the fact that the Liberal Party, which claimed a majority of the registered voters, only barely managed to get Julio César Turbay Ayala (son of the 1946 regular Liberal candidate) elected to the presidency in 1978. Turbay was an old-line politician who offered no real new directions for the country. In addition to the usual political maneuvering, his administration was beset with growing unrest. Not only had the various revolutionary groups intensified their activities but increasing violence occurred as a result of the activities of the drug cartels now operating in the country. The preoccupied Turbay administration responded with draconian measures. A state of siege was declared, and the expanded military and police forces were unleashed. Despite widespread repression—and charges of human rights violations—guerrilla activity grew. Polls at the time indicated mounting public sympathy for the revolutionary movements.

Economic conditions also worsened during the final years of the administration. The coffee and drug "booms" of the 1970s ended. By the early 1980s, the balance of payments had slipped into deficit and the foreign debt grew dramatically. As the international economy contracted at the same time, Colombian exports also declined. The country slipped into recession, registering both negative growth rates and growing unemployment by 1982–1983. Many Colombians felt that a critical juncture had been reached as the Turbay administration limped to its end.

The 1980s: The Politics of Crisis

Colombian had changed significantly by the 1980s. It was now an urban country with 70 percent of its people living in towns and cities. In large measure this was due to the growth and diversification of the economy, primarily in the larger urban centers, which attracted rural migrants. Successive National Front governments had fostered growth, though worldwide economic expansion in the 1960s and 1970s certainly was a contributing factor. Programs such as import substitution in industry, encouragement of nontraditional export crops, development of oil and coal reserves, and generally conservative fiscal policies contributed to growth rates of up to 5 percent annually for many of the years between 1961 and 1982. Inflation, in Latin American terms, generally was kept at manageable levels. Foreign investment was modest; repatriation of profits did not represent a serious capital drain. In the 1970s, the country enjoyed a bonanza due to high world coffee prices and profits from the illicit drug trade. For many Colombians, especially the urban middle classes, economic growth was accompanied by improved standards of living. Indices for nutrition, life expectancy, infant mortality, and literacy registered steady gains.

Yet not all Colombians benefitted. Ownership and control of wealth remained highly inequitable. Per capita income in 1985 was still around U.S. $1200. Underemployment in the cities affected 20 percent or more of the working population, thus marginalizing many. Creation of jobs did not keep up with the numbers of young Colombians attaining working age. Social welfare programs reached only a small proportion of the population. Organized labor, which constituted a "privileged" sector of the working class, did not include a majority of workers. Millions of poor in the cities lived in substandard housing, with inadequate sanitation and other public services. Public health care and educational facilities were woefully inadequate. In the countryside, despite limited efforts at agrarian reform, 4 percent of all landholdings occupied 67 percent of the arable land; 73 percent of farms were less than ten hectares in size but constituted only 7.2 percent of arable land. Some 1.5 million families, half the rural population of nine million, owned no land at all.

The "demonstration effect" of economic growth and prosperity in the cities, with visible affluence and a richly modern life-style for some, undoubtedly had an impact on the majority excluded from higher education, rewarding employment, and the fruits of the consumer society. With a closed political system that offered little hope of meaningful change, it was no wonder that many turned to alternative political movements or even armed opposition. Some young lower and lower-middle class Colombians sought their opportunities in the lucrative drug trade.

Colombians began the large-scale cultivation of marijuana for export, mostly to North America, in the mid-1970s. Cocaine was added later in the decade. Laboratories and production facilities were set up in various, often remote, parts of the country, and a sophisticated international transport, distribution, and marketing network was established. Though estimates vary widely as to the value of the trade, by the early 1980s it probably was contributing 2 to 3 billion dollars annually to the economy.

Violence accompanied the growth of the drug trade as various groups fought for control of it. Eventually two cartels emerged, one centered in Medellín, the other in Cali. Drug capital was invested in urban real estate, land, and legitimate enterprises. Public officials, including police and members of the judiciary, were bribed and suborned; the uncooperative were threatened or simply eliminated. The drug "lords" even boasted that they had representatives in the national legislature. Cooperation between guerrillas and drug groups occurred, though they also fought each other. The drug "mafia" was able to recruit its own private armies and equip them with sophisticated weapons.

The attitude of the Liberal administrations of the 1970s toward the drug trade was ambivalent. On the one hand, the illicit money pouring into the country was a boon to the economy. The national Bank of the Republic set up a special mechanism, known as the *ventanilla siniestra* (sinister window), in which hard currency could be exchanged with no questions asked. On the other hand, as violence and corruption related to the drug trade mounted, the administrations, especially Turbay's, cracked down. By the early 1980s, however, drugs were merely one of the country's serious concerns. The activities of the various revolutionary groups intensified. At the same time, economic conditions worsened.

As happened in the past, elements of the Colombian political elite responded with a certain imagination. The Conservative Party supported as its candidate in the 1982 presidential election Belisario Betancur, head of a minority faction within the party and an unsuccessful presidential candidate in 1978. As Betancur himself acknowledged, the minority Conservatives picked him again because they recognized that his ability to attract support from some Liberals and even from some Communists provided the best hope of winning the election.

Betancur was not the usual "oligarch" so typical of high-level national politics. He came from a working-class family; his affiliation with the Conservative Party was the result of his family's traditional loyalty rather than ideological affinity. In fact, he worked to convert the Conservatives into a modern Christian Democratic party with social concerns and programs.

Betancur organized the National Movement, a coalition of Conservatives and Liberals disenchanted with their party, and mounted a populist campaign that promised programs for the country's poor. He also pledged to take new approaches in dealing with the guerrillas and drug cartels. Once elected, he appointed young members of both parties to important government positions and shifted the economic strategy toward dealing with domestic development.

In his speeches and writings, Betancur frequently expressed the view that the poverty and backwardness associated with underdevelopment was the primary cause of violence in Latin American societies. His administration moved on two fronts to attack these problems simultaneously. First, in order to "open" the political system, efforts were made to provide access to political groups excluded by the existing bipartisan arrangement. A lenient amnesty law covering guerrillas was passed in 1982; this was followed by truces with three of the four main revolutionary organizations, including the FARC and the ADM-19. A package of reforms was proposed, including the popular election of departmental and local officials and measures designed to enlarge and enhance the fiscal capabilities of local governments. Finally, a promised national dialogue with opposition groups began in late 1984 between those who had accepted the truce and members of the administration and national legislature.

The second of the administration's initiatives was an attack on poverty, especially in rural areas affected by guerrilla activity. A National Rehabilitation Plan was devised to carry out agrarian reform, create employment, extend social services and programs, and establish credit facilities, all efforts to improve living conditions generally. Members of the opposition were appointed to direct implementation of the plan.

Another—surprising—new direction taken by the administration was in foreign policy. Betancur took Colombia into the association of nonaligned nations, a move in keeping with his belief that Third World countries were better able to deal with their problems themselves. He played an active role in the Contadora group of nations that sought a solution to the conflicts in Central America. His call for an end to superpower competition and arms buildups in the region, in addition to his efforts to bring the opposing sides together in Central

America, placed Colombia in a position somewhat independent of its traditional close relationship with the United States.

In dealing with the *narcotraficantes* (drug dealers), the administration took a hard line. Responding to evidence that drug money was influencing and corrupting broad sectors of society, the government mounted a strong antidrug campaign that included raids on cocaine-processing facilities and seizures of the drug cartels' properties, capital, and arms. After Justice Minister Rodrigo Lara Bonilla was assassinated in 1984, allegedly by gunmen in the employ of drug lords, the campaign was intensified. Efforts by the cartels to arrange a truce with the government were rejected; it appeared that success was finally being achieved in the long war on the narcotics business.

The hopes raised by the initiatives and programs of Betancur, however, failed to be realized. A severe economic recession—the worst since the 1930s—afflicted the country from the earliest days of the administration. The recession, largely a result of the policies of the previous Liberal governments, was combined with a worldwide economic downturn. Exports fell, the national debt soared to U.S. $15 billion, and unemployment in the cities reached 14 percent. Faced with a declining growth rate and serious balance-of-payment and public sector deficits, the administration initiated an austerity program and other measures to deal with the situation. By the mid-1980s the economy had begun to recover, but the ambitious plans to attack poverty and underdevelopment were crippled. This, in turn, contributed to undermining the peace process. Further, the opposition of entrenched interests in both traditional parties to Betancur's political "opening" stymied his efforts to democratize the political system.

Frustrated by economic recession and political intransigence, the administration could not maintain its national dialogue with the armed opposition. By 1985 two of the three truces with the guerrillas had failed; in November, M-19 dealt the peace process a mortal blow when it occupied the Palace of Justice in Bogotá. Despite efforts of the administration to negotiate with the revolutionaries, the military launched an assault on the building. Eleven Supreme Court justices, forty militants, and others were killed. The smoldering ruin of the Palace of Justice symbolized the fate of Betancur's reforms. What remained were only an uneasy truce with the FARC, whose new civilian political entity, the Unión Patriótica (UP), agreed to participate in the 1986 election, and a plan to provide for the popular election of mayors.

In 1986 the Liberals once again won the presidency. Virgilio Barco, an American-trained engineer, former ambassador to the United States, and longtime politician, scored a decisive victory over the Conservative candidate, Alvaro Gómez Hurtado. Barco's election by the biggest majority (58 percent to 36 percent for Gómez) of any post–World War II presidential candidate revealed the voters' desires for a new course. Violence by guerrillas, drug traffickers, and common criminal elements were reaching alarming levels. In response, the security forces stepped up repressive measures, but an ominous new factor was in play: Right-wing death squads were striking at perceived liberal and leftist opponents. Colombia appeared to be edging ever closer to anarchy.

Barco reversed the previous administration's conciliatory approach by promising to take a tough stand against the guerrillas and *narcotraficantes*. Budget and personnel for the armed forces and police were increased. Though Barco did speak of the need for negotiating with the armed opposition, it was clearly to be within the context of pacification by government forces. In any case, since the attack by M-19 on the Palace of Justice, the military increasingly seemed to be operating outside of civilian control.

Like his predecessor, Barco believed that only significant socioeconomic reforms could undercut the causes of endemic violence. In addition to retaining Betancur's National Plan for Rehabilitation, Barco developed a Plan against Absolute Poverty (PAA) to provide employment and services for the 40 percent of Colombians living below the poverty line. Though well intentioned, the administration refused to allocate the funds necessary to make a significant impact; the plan, like others before it, merely raised the level of public frustration with the government.

Meanwhile, the violence continued unabated. In October 1987, the UP's leader, Jaime Pardo Leal, was assassinated. He had taken the lead in protesting the government's failure to crack down on rightist death squads who were targeting not only militants of the UP, but peasant and labor leaders, Marxists, and government critics, as well. Then, in early 1988, during a wave of terrorist actions, Attorney General Carlos Mauro Hoyos Jiménez was kidnapped and killed. The administration responded by expanding the powers of the security forces and vastly increasing the number of judicial positions.

These new measures failed to have the desired effect. By midterm the administration was beset on all sides by increasingly bold guerrilla activities, killings and terrorism by drug traffickers, rightist paramilitary murders, and kidnappings and other crimes by common criminal elements. In addition, the UP's ranks were decimated as hundreds of its leaders, candidates for office, and followers were killed. Colombia's international reputation suffered accordingly; foreign investment declined sharply, several international petroleum companies suspended operations, and Amnesty International condemned human rights violations by the security forces. Relations with neighboring Venezuela, already strained by a dispute over petroleum rights in the border region, deteriorated further when that country took measures to prevent a spillover of guerrilla activities along the common frontier.

In an effort to reach a peace agreement with the armed opposition, the Barco administration elaborated a complicated plan in 1988 designed to provide for a ceasefire, amnesty, and incorporation of the rebels into civil society. This was to be accompanied by an end to the state of siege and constitutional amendments allowing for political and social reforms. For dealing with the drug traffickers, the administration proposed a new extradition treaty with the United States, similar to a 1979 treaty that had been declared void by the Supreme Court, which provided for prompt dispatch of captured drug dealers out of the country.

Nothing, however, came of these initiatives. Liberals, Conservatives, and the UP attacked the peace plan as being either too complex or as a disguised form of surrender by the rebels. The *Coordinadora Nacional Guerrillera*, the main revolutionary coordinating body, denounced the plan as merely a military solution. The military, for its part, advocated exactly that course. As for the extradition treaty, it remained a highly divisive political issue. The administration refused to take a firm course, or even to cooperate in an international campaign against the drug trade organized by the United States and several European and Latin American countries. Domestic politics ruled out any decisive international action against the *narcotraficantes*.

The one positive political achievement of the Barco years was the holding of the first popular elections of mayors and local officials in March 1988. Though the elections confirmed the national majority of the Liberal Party, the violence-crippled UP did participate and scored some victories. Further efforts to democratize the political system through constitutional reforms, including an end to a guaranteed role for the majority opposition party, failed when the Liberal and Conservative leaders refused to surrender their monopoly of political power. This political deadlock occurred despite the fact that the Barco administration was the first since the formation of the National Front to govern without sharing power with the opposition.

As the end of the Barco administration neared, the violence that had claimed 15,000 lives since 1986—and almost 80,000 since the beginning of the decade—touched the highest political levels of the country. In August 1989, the leading Liberal candidate for president, Luis Carlos Galán, was assassinated, allegedly by gunmen of the Medellín drug cartel. Before the May 1990 election, two other presidential candidates, Bernardo Jaramillo Ossa of the UP, and Carlos Pizarro Leóngómez of the ADM-19, also were killed. For the UP, the death of Jaramillo marked the culmination of an elimination campaign that claimed approximately 1,400 of its adherents over the years, deaths that seriously weakened the party. Though government officials blamed the *narcotraficantes* for the murders, others, including the new Liberal candidate, César Gaviria Trujillo, accused previous administrations that had allowed rightist paramilitary groups to operate and ally themselves with the drug cartels.

Shocked Colombians went to the polls in May 1990, in an election that revealed not only the alienation of the citizenry, but also the splintering of the traditional two-party system. Gaviria won 48 percent of the vote against a leftist and two Conservative candidates. Significantly, however, 60 percent of the electorate abstained from voting. An overwhelming majority of those who did vote supported the proposal for a constituent assembly, thus indicating a deep desire for change.

As a minority president, the forty-three year-old Gaviria organized a coalition administration that included Liberals, Conservatives, and the former guerrilla and M-19 leader, Antonio Navarro Wolff. The new president promised to spur the lagging economy by increasing incentives for investments and exports—the "internationalization" of the economy—while encouraging "social development" through meeting the demand for jobs, fair wages, and investment in public works and services.

Gaviria recognized the need for political and social reforms that included the further democratization of the system and restructuring of the country's administration of justice and reorganization of the security forces. He therefore supported the election of a constituent assembly. While promising a new approach in dealing with drug traffickers and paramilitary groups, he also offered new initiatives in reaching peaceful accommodation with the guerrilla groups.

By early 1991, the Gaviria administration had achieved some success in dealing with Colombia's seemingly intractable problem of violence. A pact with the M-19 and EPL insurgents resulted in their laying-down of arms; efforts toward a negotiated peace with the FARC and ELN went forward. Negotiations also were held with the drug traffickers, based on a policy of no extradition and judicial leniency if they surrendered and submitted to Colombian justice. Leniency was offered also to the paramilitary groups.

Perhaps the most significant political development was the constituent assembly elections held in December 1990. Although 75 percent of the voters abstained, the elections delivered a devastating blow to Liberal-Conservative bipartisan politics. The ADM-19 emerged with 27 percent of the vote against only 28 percent for several Liberal factions and even fewer votes for the equally divided Conservatives. It was the first time in Colombia's history that a left-of-center party—and a former guerrilla organization, at that—won a major place in the political system.

Although writing a new constitution with a factious constituent assembly and questionable legitimacy will prove to be difficult, it offers a glimmer of hope that the tortured country eventually may achieve peace and more open, democratic politics.

Bibliography

Bruce Bagley, Francisco Thoumi, and Juan Tokatlían, eds. *Beyond the National Front: State and Society in Contemporary Colombia.* Westview Press, Boulder, Colo., 1987.
Olga Behar. *Las guerras de la paz.* Planeta Colombiana Editorial, Bogotá, 1985.
Robert H. Dix. *The Politics of Colombia.* Praeger, New York, 1986.
Donald Herman, ed. *Democracy in Latin America: Colombia and Venezuela.* Praeger, New York, 1987.
Harvey F. Kline. *Colombia: Portrait of Unity and Diversity.* Westview Press, Boulder, Colo., 1983.

Political Parties—Active

COMMUNIST PARTY (PARTIDO COMUNISTA—PCC). Founded by a group of left-wing intellectuals in 1930, the Communist Party, which has experienced periods of both persecution and toleration, is the longest surviving third party in Colombia. It has managed this by following a strategy that combines participation in electoral politics with support for the Revolutionary Armed Forces of Colombia (FARC), the country's largest existing guerrilla organization.

In the 1980s, the Moscow-oriented PCC (estimated to have about 20,000 members) maintained its strength in the labor movement, with its unions representing perhaps 20 percent of organized workers, and among peasants in rural areas where the party has been dominant for about half a century. The party also counts adherents in the larger cities, especially Bogotá.

The PCC historically has provided at least conditional support for what it considers "progressive" programs of the two traditional parties. During the 1980s, the party encouraged the various efforts of the Conservative Betancur and the Liberal Barco administrations to broaden political participation and seek peaceful resolution of the violence wracking the country. The party influenced the FARC to enter into truces with the government, acted as intermediary with guerrilla groups, and supported Betancur's multiparty National Movement which helped gain him the presidency in 1982.

The PCC's limited electoral appeal, however, has forced it into alliances with other leftist movements over the past two decades. In 1984, responding to the political "opening" encouraged by the Betancur administration, it was instrumental in organizing the Unión Patriótica (UP), which provided an electoral vehicle for the FARC and smaller armed groups, such as the urban-based Workers' Self-Defense (Auto-Defensa Obrera—ADO). While enjoying limited success at the polls, the PCC also has suffered from the rightist paramilitary terror that decimated the UP's ranks in the late 1980s.

With the collapse of the Soviet bloc and the disarray in international communism, the party has been forced into a period of critical self-evaluation. Burdened by a past that includes opportunism, clientelism, alliances with corrupt Liberal Party bosses, and ongoing ties to revolutionary groups, the party has yet to define its future role in Colombian politics.

CONSERVATIVE PARTY (PARTIDO CONSERVADOR). *See* SOCIAL CONSERVATIVE PARTY.

LIBERAL PARTY (PARTIDO LIBERAL). The populist Liberal politician Jorge Eliécer Gaitán once remarked that the Liberal people were more advanced than their leaders. The results of Colombia's elections in 1990 appeared to verify that observation. The party scored substantial victories in municipal, departmental, and congressional elections, and presidential candidate César Gaviria Trujillo won 48 percent of the vote against several other contenders. In the December 1990 constituent assembly election, however, various Liberal factions came in well behind the first place leftist 19th of April Movement—Democratic Alliance (ADM 19) and runner-up Alvaro Gómez Hurtado's right-wing Conservative breakaway National Salvation Movement. Liberal voters obviously were willing to support their party's candidates when choices were limited, but they abandoned the party when reformist alternatives were available. This pattern goes back at least to the 1960s, when Alfonso López Michelsen's dissident Liberal Revolutionary Movement attracted significant support with a platform that advocated widespread social and economic reforms.

The elections—other than for the constituent assembly—verified what had been fact since the 1930s: the Liberal Party is the country's major political organization. It continues to attract voters from a broad spectrum of the electorate, especially the urban working and middle classes who formed its twentieth-century base. But its status as the largest party does not always guarantee victory. Political compromises resulting from liberalism's longtime, bipartisan association with the Conservatives, bossism, and intense factionalism have undermined the party's programs and have caused widespread voter disaffection. Furthermore, the monopoly of the national leadership by a rather tired political elite, which only reluctantly went along with limited "democratization" of the political system in the 1980s, has also alienated voters. The party, like its traditional opponents, the Social Conservative Party, entered the 1990s in disarray and uncertain of its future in a country at a critical political juncture.

That Liberal voters were willing to support promised systemic reforms was borne out repeatedly in the 1970s and 1980s. López Michelsen won handily in 1974, as the National Front ended at the presidential level. Despite his disappointing administration, Liberals were able to elect Julio César Turbay by a narrow margin in 1978. But disenchantment with their party's inability to deal with national problems caused many to support the progressive Conservative Belisario Betancur in 1982. Betancur admitted that his election was due to his reformist platform's attractiveness to Liberals. Then, in 1986, the Liberal candidate Virgilio Barco, campaigning on a platform promising a hard line on violence combined with support for a political "opening", won by the largest margin in history.

Throughout this period, Liberals also dominated congress and most departmental offices. In 1988, in the country's first elections for mayors and city councillors, an electoral reform supported by Barco, the Liberals with almost 3 million votes won 427 offices against the Social Conservative Party's 2.1 million votes and 412 mayorships. The 1990 elections saw the Liberals increase their margins. They won almost twice as many congressional seats as the Social Conservatives, seventeen of twenty-two departments, and over half of the 1,000-plus mayoralties in the country.

Consistent electoral majorities, however, have not been translated into significant programs dealing with such severe national problems as the more than 40 percent of Colombians living in poverty, the half of the rural population that is landless, or the violence that is endemic to the country. Liberal rhetoric, in fact, has far outdistanced action, even more than is usual in politics. It remains to be seen whether President Gaviria, the youngest chief executive in the nation's history, can provide the vigorous leadership necessary not only to deal with the national crisis, but also to restore the Liberal Party to its twentieth-century promise as the party of reform.

LIBERAL REVOLUTIONARY MOVEMENT (MOVIMIENTO REVOLU-CIONARIO LIBERAL). *See* LIBERAL PARTY.

MOVIMIENTO 19 DE ABRIL—ALIANZA DEMOCRÁTICA. *See* 19TH OF APRIL MOVEMENT—DEMOCRATIC ALLIANCE.

MOVIMIENTO REVOLUCIONARIO LIBERAL. *See* LIBERAL PARTY.

19TH OF APRIL MOVEMENT—DEMOCRATIC ALLIANCE (MOVI-MIENTO 19 DE ABRIL—ALIANZA DEMOCRÁTICA-ADM-19). The party is named for the date in 1970 when former dictator and National Popular Alliance (ANAPO) leader, General Gustavo Rojas Pinilla, narrowly missed winning a controversial presidential election against the candidate of the National Front. Rojas had organized ANAPO as a nationalist and populist alternative to the existing bipartisan arrangement between the Liberal and Conservative parties.

M-19 was formed in the mid-1970s, when ANAPO's militant wing, ANAPO-Socialista, split off over disagreements with the party leadership, notably María Eugenia Rojas de Moreno, the general's daughter and a 1974 presidential candidate. A founder and early leader of M-19 was former congressman Carlos Toledo Plata, whose Marxist formulations laid the basis for the movement's socialist platforms.

M-19's initial adherents generally were university students, intellectuals, professionals, artists, and so on. Later the movement expanded to include, for example, members of the urban poor. Though primarily based in the cities, it eventually also initiated rural guerrilla warfare.

In its first decade, M-19 carried out a series of highly visible actions, including hijacking milk for distribution to poor children, kidnapping wealthy business-men, and making assaults on military arsenals. Official repression followed, and M-19, now under the influence of former Communist youth leader Jaime Bate-man Cayón, reacted with terrorism and sought to make alliances with other guerrilla groups. In November 1985, M-19 launched a spectacular raid on the national Palace of Justice in Bogotá. The occupation of the palace resulted in an army counterattack that left eleven Supreme Court justices and over forty M-19 militants dead.

Despite the death and imprisonment of many of its original leaders and followers, M-19 continued to survive as one of Colombia's most important revolutionary groups. It demonstrated considerable flexibility by agreeing to truces with both the Betancur and Barco administrations. In 1989 it was incorporated into civilian politics when over 800 members laid down their arms.

The M-19—Democratic Alliance was formed in 1990 as the result of a fusion of the main organization and several smaller "new left" groups. The coalition presented candidate lists for the national elections in May of that year. Although ADM-19's presidential aspirant, Carlos Pizarro Leóngómez, became the third presidential candidate to be assassinated prior to the elections, the party decided to remain within the electoral process and named another former guerrilla leader, Antonio Navarro Wolff, to run. Navarro subsequently placed third with a surprising 12.7 percent of the vote, the highest ever for a leftist presidential candidate. In recognition of ADM-19's new political importance, Navarro was named minister of health in the cabinet of incoming Liberal President César Gaviria Trujillo. Otty Patiño was then named party head.

ADM-19 continued to broaden its political appeal in the December 1990 constituent assembly election. The party's list, headed by Navarro, won 27 percent of the vote, outpolling several Liberal and Conservative factions and making it the single largest political group. The ADM-19's nineteen seats in the assembly assure it an important role in the writing of Colombia's new constitution. Further, it is altogether possible that the party will break the traditional Liberal-Conservative hold on political power if its popularity continues to grow.

PARTIDO COMUNISTA. See COMMUNIST PARTY.

PARTIDO CONSERVADOR. See SOCIAL CONSERVATIVE PARTY.

PARTIDO CONSERVADOR SOCIAL. See SOCIAL CONSERVATIVE PARTY.

PARTIDO LIBERAL. See LIBERAL PARTY.

PATRIOTIC UNION (UNIÓN PATRIÓTICA—UP). Formed in 1984 at the instigation of the Communist Party during a period of truce between the Conservative Betancur administration and the guerrilla groups, the UP became, in effect, the political arm of the Revolutionary Armed Forces of Colombia (FARC). It constituted a broad-based, leftist, political alternative to the traditional parties, and it included Communists and small groups such as Workers' Self-Defense (Auto-Defensa Obrera).

Under its founder and first leader, Jaime Pardo Leal, the UP formulated a nationalist and reformist program, with special emphasis on agrarian reform and improving conditions of Colombia's poor through state-sponsored social and economic development. Its primary bases of support lie in those areas of the country under FARC control, notably in the south and the northwestern banana region of Uraba. The UP also has been willing to enter into alliances with local Liberal political bosses.

In its first foray into national politics in 1986, the UP's presidential candidate, Pardo Leal, won only 4.5 percent of the vote, but the party did elect several congressmen. In the first popular elections of mayors and local officials in 1988, the party gained fifteen mayoralties and numerous municipal council seats.

The UP's electoral effectiveness was limited from the outset by intimidation and violence, which the party leadership blamed on the security forces and right-wing paramilitary death squads. Pardo Leal was assassinated in 1987 and twenty-nine of eighty-seven mayoral and over one hundred municipal candidates were killed prior to the 1988 elections. By 1990 more than 1,400 party leaders, candidates, and militants had fallen to assassins' bullets, including the UP's second presidential candidate, Bernardo Jaramillo Ossa. The impact of the repression was felt in the elections of that year, when the UP lost several congressional and mayoral seats, and was partly eclipsed as a party of the left by the newly emerging M-19—Democratic Alliance.

SOCIAL CONSERVATIVE PARTY (PARTIDO CONSERVADOR SO-CIAL—PCS). Known until 1987 as the Conservative Party, the addition of the word Social in its title indicates the efforts of at least its majority faction to give this "historic collectivity" an orientation similar to that of modern Christian Democratic parties.

The Conservatives, along with their principal rivals in the Liberal Party, have dominated Colombian politics since the postindependence period of the 1840s. Traditionally, the party counted its greatest strength in the countryside, which to some extent is still the case. This allowed the Conservatives to control successive national administrations, for example, through the first third of the twentieth century. The rapid urbanization of the country, however, accompanied by the mass movement of people to the cities, eroded the Conservatives' electoral base. Further, the long period of collaboration with the Liberals in the bipartisan National Front blurred the Conservatives' ideological image. The party is now struggling to define itself in an era of diminishing political loyalties and deep voter alienation with both traditional parties.

In the 1980s, the PCS managed to overcome its minority status vis-à-vis the Liberal Party to elect one of its own candidates to the presidency. But the election of Belisario Betancur (1982–1985) was the result not only of the candidate's uncharacteristic—for Conservatives—populist appeal, but also of his willingness to enter into an electoral alliance with progressive, dissident Liberals. Subsequent efforts by Betancur and others to remold the party achieved only partial success; the hold of old-line politicians and rural *caciques*—party bosses— with their practices of patronage and clientelism remained strong. Also, party factionalism in the national leadership was reflected at regional and local levels.

The roots of the principal current division are planted in the quarter-century-old conflict between two late presidents: the centrist, Mariano Ospina Pérez, (1946–1950), and the right-wing idealogue, Laureano Gómez Hurtado (1950–1953). Despite this rivalry, the latter's son, Alvaro Gómez Hurtado, was twice selected party candidate for president, in 1974 and 1986 (in both instances, he lost by large margins).

Party chief Misael Pastrana has long advocated cooperation between the major parties; his protegé, Betancur, practiced it during his administration. They both to some extent have redirected the party away from the paternalism of the past to support for economic and social development programs, especially for the country's poor. Policies such as these have raised criticism from traditionalists, who claim that they diminish even more the differences between Liberals and Conservatives. Nevertheless, the PCS's efforts to attract social strata such as the urban lower classes reaped some dividends. In the first mayoral elections held in the country in 1988, Social Conservative candidates won in Bogotá and Medellín, the two largest cities and longtime Liberal strongholds.

The ongoing debate over the direction of the party and continued factionalism, however, weakened the PCS in the 1990 elections. Liberals outpolled Social Conservatives almost two to one in congressional races and won all but five of twenty-two departmental capitals, including Bogotá and Medellín. The party also lost substantially in mayoralty races. Gómez Hurtado, angered by the selection of the *Pastranista* Rodrigo Lloreda Caicedo as the party's presidential candidate, bolted to run for the office with the dissident far-right National Salvation Movement. The PCS suffered further humiliation when Gómez Hurtado finished second with 24 percent of the vote behind Liberal winner César Gaviria Trujillo. Lloreda came in a weak fourth with only 12 percent of the vote.

The December 1990 constituent assembly election demonstrated once again the Social Conservatives' weakness. Even counting the dissident Gómez Hurtado (whose National Salvation Movement came in second with 16 percent of the vote), the party won only a fourth of the seats.

The results of these elections indicate that Colombia's traditional two-party system is in crisis. Widespread voter abstention, disaffection with the major parties and their failed promises, political polarization represented by the rise of alternative movements of the left and right, all point to a serious national malaise. It remains to be seen if the Social Conservatives can find the unity and programmatic appeal to survive as a major contender in the country's turbulent political arena.

UNIÓN PATRIÓTICA. *See* PATRIOTIC UNION.

Political Parties—Historical

ALIANZA NACIONAL POPULAR. *See* NATIONAL POPULAR ALLIANCE.

CHRISTIAN SOCIAL DEMOCRATIC PARTY (PARTIDO SOCIAL DE-MÓCRATA CRISTIANO—PSDC). A small party led by intellectuals and professionals with links to the international Christian Democratic movement, the PSDC was active in the 1960s and early 1970s. It advocated a third way between capitalism and socialism.

COLOMBIAN POPULAR SOCIALIST PARTY (PARTIDO POPULAR SOCIALISTA COLOMBIANO—PPSC). Formed in the 1950s, the PPSC offered an alternative to Colombia's Liberal and Communist parties with a program similar to that of Jorge Eliécer Gaitán. It dissolved in the early 1960s over tactical disagreements.

COMMUNIST PARTY OF COLOMBIA—MARXIST-LENINIST (PARTIDO COMUNISTA DE COLOMBIA—MARXISTA-LENINISTA). This pro-Chinese splinter group broke with the Communist Party and formed a guerrilla organization in the mid-1960s.

NATIONAL PARTY (PARTIDO NACIONAL). A short-lived party of the late nineteenth century, it was led by Rafael Núñez.

NATIONAL POPULAR ALLIANCE (ALIANZA NACIONAL POPULAR—ANAPO). The political vehicle of the movement led by the former dictator, General Gustavo Rojas Pinilla, ANAPO challenged the National Front with a populist platform in the 1970s.

PARTIDO COMUNISTA DE COLOMBIA—MARXISTA-LENINISTA. See COMMUNIST PARTY OF COLOMBIA—MARXIST-LENINIST.

PARTIDO NACIONAL. See NATIONAL PARTY.

PARTIDO POPULAR SOCIALISTA COLOMBIANO. See COLOMBIAN POPULAR SOCIALIST PARTY.

PARTIDO SOCIAL DEMÓCRATA CRISTIANO. See CHRISTIAN SOCIAL DEMOCRATIC PARTY.

PARTIDO SOCIALISTA REVOLUCIONARIO. See REVOLUTIONARY SOCIALIST PARTY.

REPUBLICAN UNION (UNIÓN REPUBLICANA). Middle-of-the-road Liberals and Conservatives formed the union for several years in the early twentieth century to oppose the strongman rule of Rafael Reyes.

REVOLUTIONARY LEFTIST NATIONAL UNION (UNIÓN NACIONAL IZQUIERDISTA REVOLUCIONARIA—UNIR). Organized by Jorge Eliécer Gaitán in 1933, UNIR briefly challenged the ruling Liberal Party with a reformist program.

REVOLUTIONARY SOCIALIST PARTY (PARTIDO SOCIALISTA RE-VOLUCIONARIO—PSR). The 1920s forerunner of the Colombian Communist Party, the PSR provided political training and experience for an entire generation of Colombian reformist politicians and trade unionists.

UNIÓN REPUBLICANA. *See* REPUBLICAN UNION.

UNIÓN NACIONAL IZQUIERDISTA REVOLUCIONARIA. *See* REVOLUTIONARY LEFTIST NATIONAL UNION.

Richard E. Sharpless

COSTA RICA

Costa Rica is a small Central American republic much admired for its democracy. Its total area comprises 19,725 square miles, about the size of the state of West Virginia, and it has a population (July 1990) of 3,032,795. Costa Rica's size, however, is no measure of its reputation for sane behavior. About the only controversy surrounding it is the argument among scholars over the reasons for its exceptionalism and for the depth of its democratic order. Few would dispute the observation of the late President José Figueres that Costa Rica produces good coffee and decent people.

Clearly, the lack of a military establishment has contributed to Costa Rica's success. Civilians, not soldiers, achieved Costa Rica's independence and no external threat or internal division supported the maintenance of an armed force. Cultural homogeneity and the existence of a significant, small freeholder class promoted an egalitarian and independent spirit. Moreover, the old families who had governed Costa Rica since its founding adopted a laissez-faire economic outlook, laced with strong anticlericalism—quite distinct from the descendants of the conquistadors in other parts of Latin America. Well before the commercial cultivation of coffee altered Costa Rica's economic order, the republic was accustomed to a government that provided essential services and favored no particular class. This was especially evident in the commitment to public education.

Under these circumstances, political parties were slow to develop. In fact, for a long time, parties were considered bad form in a society that prided itself on harmony. Nonetheless, rivalries among certain families produced contention and even led to the establishment of a dictatorship under Tomás Guardia (1870–1882). Sobered by this experience, the so-called Generation of 1888 governed for almost the next fifty years, providing honest and efficient government and nurturing the electoral process, which became progressively popular with growing literacy and the introduction of the secret ballot. The era was dominated by the five presidential terms of two remarkable men: Cleto González Víquez (1906–1910 and 1928–1932) and Ricardo Jiménez Oreamuno (1910–1914, 1924–1928, and 1932–1936). In an essentially one-party system, they represented the Republican Party, but personality reigned over issues and programs. These fair-minded "Olympians" actually facilitated change, although they failed to keep up with it themselves.

The failure of the mainstream leadership to acknowledge new economic and social issues brought on by the coffee and banana trade and by a population increase (the population expanded from 360,000 in 1910 to 660,000 by 1940) created a restlessness if not an unrest. In the 1920s, Jorge Volio, a former cleric, organized the short-lived Reformist Party, which called for an income tax and better working conditions and wages for labor. In 1931 Manuel Mora Valverde founded the Communist Party, which became strong in the banana zones of Limón on the Atlantic coast. But the man who really introduced partisan politics to Costa Rica was Rafael Angel Calderón Guardia.

Elected president as a Republican in 1940, Calderón became "a traitor to his class" by proposing a Social Security program, amending the constitution to include "social guarantees," and enacting a comprehensive Labor Code. During his domination of Costa Rican affairs for eight years, he fashioned the Victory Bloc, a coalition made up of his own National Republican Party (founded in 1941), the Catholic Church, and the Communist Party (renamed the Popular Vanguard Party in 1943). Ineligible by law to succeed himself in the presidency, he sponsored the election of Teodoro Picado Michalski in 1944 and then tried to impose his own reelection in 1948, which led to one of the bloodiest conflicts to ever occur in Costa Rican history.

The opposition to Calderón consisted of political conservatives, who wanted to restore the benign rule of former times; the coffee barons, who had been the silent force behind the old order and who had benefitted from it; and youthful social democrats, who applauded Calderón's social programs but deplored his clericalism and his alliance with the Communists. These elements were combined by the catalyst José Figueres, who told them that they would have to fight to get rid of Calderón. When Calderón tried to steal the election of 1948, Figueres led a six-week War of National Liberation that cost 2,000 lives and sent Calderón, Mora, and Picado into exile.

From May 1948 to November 1949, Figueres headed the Founding Junta of the Second Republic, which initiated a new stage of Costa Rican history. He retained the social programs of Calderón but virtually overhauled the economy by nationalizing banking and insurance and by enlarging the public sector to provide services directly in electrical energy, telecommunications, and transportation. He oversaw the drafting of the Constitution of 1949, which abolished the army and created the Supreme Electoral Tribunal, a virtual fourth branch of government, with absolute power to guarantee the integrity of elections. Figueres turned over the presidency to Otilio Ulate, the legitimate winner in 1948, but he was back in four years after being elected president in his own right.

In the meantime, Figueres helped found the National Liberation Party (PLN) in 1951. For over thirty years afterward, the PLN was the most consistent force in Costa Rican politics. Following Figueres's tenure (1953–1958), PLN candidates won four-year presidential terms in 1962 (Francisco Orlich), 1970 (Figueres), 1974 (Daniel Oduber Quirós), 1982 (Luis Alberto Monge Alvarez), and 1986 (Oscar Arias Sánchez), and it enjoyed a majority most of these years in the unicameral national congress (Legislative Assembly).

The only times that the PLN lost an election occurred when it experienced internal divisions, or opposition groups and personalities managed to unite in coalition, or there was a combination of the two. This happened in 1958, when Mario Echandi took advantage of a split within the PLN to win the presidency; in 1966, when ex-Presidents Ulate and Calderón (back from exile) organized the National Unification coalition to support the candidacy of José Joaquín Trejos; and in 1978, when Rodrigo Carazo Odio, a PLN maverick, formed his own party and joined with three other parties to produce the Unity coalition. Participating in the Unity coalition was the Calderonist Republican Party (PRC), headed by Rafael Angel Calderón Fournier, the son of Calderón Guardia, who had died in 1970. Clearly, with Costa Rica almost equally divided between Liberation and anti-Liberation, a de facto two-party system was in operation during these years. In the 1980s, this situation evolved into something more definite.

In 1982 the PLN's Monge regained the presidency against Unity's Calderón Fournier. Monge won a spectacular victory, with 58.7 percent of the vote, but the Unity coalition, under the youthful Calderón (who was only thirty-two at the time), was not shattered. Calderón could shift much of the blame for his defeat on the failed presidency of Carazo, who had been plagued by debt and inflation (brought on by declining coffee prices and rising energy costs) and scandal (Carazo profitted from contraband arms sales to Sandinista rebels in Nicaragua). While Monge was grappling with these problems as president, complicated by the conflict between the United States and Nicaragua, Calderón strengthened his position as the most prominent leader outside the PLN and took steps to convert Unity from a coalition into a permanent party.

The coalition—comprising the PRC; Carazo's Democratic Renovation Party (PRD); the Christian Democratic Party (PDC), small and embryonic; and the Popular Union Party (PUP), a nonparty representing the coffee barons—was broad enough to attract most of the elements that were in opposition to the PLN but was also moderate and remained in the mainstream. Only the left, fragmented and ineffective, had nowhere to go in this evolving situation. Junior Calderón, who exploited his father's populist reputation, was strongly influenced by his father's progressive Catholic philosophy. He reorganized Unity as the Social Christian Unity Party (PUSC) in 1985 and ran again for president in 1986; this time there was no identification on the ballot of PUSC as a coalition or a listing of participating parties, as had been the case with Unity in 1982. But Calderón did not win the election of 1986; Oscar Arias did.

For only the second time in its history, the PLN succeeded itself in the presidency. Calderón had been expected to win, but his strong anti-Sandinista stance alarmed many Costa Ricans, who feared that he might involve them in a war. Opinion polls showed that most Costa Ricans opposed the Sandinistas but supported Monge's policy of military neutrality. Monge had not, however, remained neutral; he secretly yielded to U.S. pressure to cooperate in the anti-Sandinista (Contra) operation, with economic assistance as the carrot. Monge received U.S. aid, brought inflation under control, and achieved a renewed economic growth, but all this was accomplished at the cost of agreeing to deep budget cuts that took the heart out of the PLN's mixed economy concept and put blinders on its social vision. As Costa Rica moved toward a two-party system in 1986, the two parties were converging on the center, and Calderón's hard-line stand on Nicaragua may have made the difference.

The Arias presidency marked a further erosion of the PLN's commitment to social democracy, influenced additionally by the worldwide decline of socialism, and Arias, who was forty-four, represented a new, more pragmatic generation that was breaking free of the party's old guard. Though Arias received U.S. balance-of-payments assistance, with its insistence upon austerity, and even caught the privatization bug, he resisted further attempts by the Reagan administration (even bullying by Lt. Col. Oliver North) to involve Costa Rica in the Contra war. Instead, he took the initiative in proposing a Central American peace plan calling for direct negotiations among conflicting elements, linked to progress toward democratization and demilitarization. Arias understood that the restoration of peace was essential for Costa Rica's economic recovery and for solving the problem of refugees, though many Costa Ricans did not make the connection and complained that he spent too much time on foreign policy. Despite winning the Nobel Peace Prize in 1987, Arias's coattails were not long enough to enable the PLN to win the presidency and retain control of the Legislative Assembly in the elections of 1990.

On his third try, Calderón Fournier won the presidency, defeating the PLN's Carlos Manuel Castillo Morales. In a close election (Calderón won 51.4 percent of the vote, while Castillo received 47.2 percent), Calderón's ability to mold the Unity coalition into a single unit, the Social Christian Unity Party, was critical. Despite Arias's popularity, Calderón exploited the concern of Costa Ricans over what would be an unprecedented third consecutive term for the PLN. Moreover, Costa Rica's debt problems and inflation persisted (reinforcing the perception that Arias had neglected domestic affairs), and a drug-trafficking scandal touched certain leaders of the PLN. In the aftermath of the election of 1990, there was more concern over the holding together of the PLN than the PUSC.

With four ex-presidents and a defeated candidate in the wings, the contest for leadership of the PLN began within hours of its defeat. Figueres died in June, which ended an era, but his daughter Muni (a candidate for second vice president in 1990) seemed ready to claim his mantle; Oduber was disadvantaged by a corruption scandal; and Monge and Arias were strong rivals and each had his own favorite for the position of PLN secretary general and for the party's presidential candidate in 1994 (each was ineligible for reelection under the constitution as amended in 1969). The list of precandidates for 1994 appeared early: Castillo, of course, wanted a second chance; Monge favored his nephew, Rolando Araya Monge; Arias backed his wife, Margarita; and there were at least four other contenders. If personal rivalries and fading ideology do not fracture the PLN, it is possible that Costa Rica could elect a woman as president in 1994. As for the PUSC, its future will depend on making good its claim that it is not solely an anti-Liberation coalition, but a party with goals and programs. The test will be to survive now that its dominant personality, Calderón Fournier, has satisfied his ambition to be president.

The reality of Costa Rica's two-party system, which seemed to be in place in the election of 1990, may be measured by the frustration of the left. In the election of 1990, a common theme among the numerous parties of the left was the criticism that the PLN and PUSC were indistinguishable ("bipartisanism") and that only they themselves offered any true alternative. But Costa Rica's left was too fragmented for this strategy to be effective. In the elections of 1978 and 1982, the Costa Rican Socialist Party (PSC) and the Popular Vanguard Party (PVP) had some success operating as an electoral coalition, the United People. But in 1984, the PVP removed Manuel Mora (its leader since 1931) in a dispute over his electoralist policy. Mora then formed the Costa Rican People's Party (PPC).

As a result, two coalitions of leftist parties contested the 1986 election: the United People, representing the PSC, the PPC, the Workers' Party, and the New Republic Movement (MNR); and the Popular Alliance, representing the PVP and the Broad Democratic Front (itself a conglomerate of splinter groups). Rodrigo Gutiérrez Sáenz, the presidential candidate of the Popular Alliance, had been the standard-bearer for United People in 1982. In 1990, the Popular Alliance had disappeared, and Gutiérrez was back again with United People as a candidate for deputy, but a new rival leftist coalition, the Progressive Party (PP), composed of the Humanist Party, the PSC, and the MNR, presented the candidacy of Isaac Felipe Azofeifa Bolaños, one of the founders of the PLN, as the "true alternative." During the 1980s, Costa Rica's left was clearly in disarray, and its total vote in the presidential and congressional elections of the decade declined progressively.

Entering the last decade of the twentieth century, a two-party system appeared to be functioning in Costa Rica. Costa Ricans complained that the campaign of 1990 was dull but that did not dampen the spirit of their banner-waving, auto-horn-honking *fiesta cívica*, nor did it deter 80 percent of the electorate from voting. Despite a degree of uncertainty about the stability of the two mainstream parties, given their blandness and Costa Rica's personalist tradition, if each governs honestly (which is the sine qua non of Costa Rican politics) and each retains the ability to reward its faithful, the PLN and PUSC will probably continue to dominate politics for many years to come.

Bibliography

Charles D. Ameringer. *Democracy in Costa Rica*. Praeger, New York, 1982.

————. *Don Pepe. A Political Biography of José Figueres of Costa Rica*. University of New Mexico Press, Albuquerque, 1979.

Tom Barry. *Costa Rica. A Country Guide*. The Inter-Hemispheric Education Resource Center, Albuquerque, N.M., 1989.

John A. Booth and Mitchell A. Seligson, eds. *Elections and Democracy in Central America*. University of North Carolina Press, Chapel Hill, N.C., 1989.

John A. Booth and Thomas W. Walker, eds. *Understanding Central America*. Westview Press, Boulder, Colo., 1989.

Marc Edelman and Joanne Kenen, eds. *The Costa Rica Reader*. Grove Weidenfeld, New York, 1989.

Frank McNeil. *War and Peace in Central America*. Charles Scribner's Sons, New York, 1988.

Harold Nelson, ed. *Costa Rica. A Country Study*. American University, Washington, D.C., 1983.

Myron Weiner and Ergun Ozbudun, eds. *Competitive Elections in Developing Countries*. Duke University Press, Durham, N.C., 1987.

Political Parties—Active

ALIANZA NACIONAL CRISTIANA. *See* NATIONAL CHRISTIAN ALLIANCE.

ALIANZA POPULAR. *See* POPULAR ALLIANCE.

BROAD DEMOCRATIC FRONT (FRENTE AMPLIO DEMOCRÁTICO). The Broad Democratic Front is not an organized political party, but rather an amalgam of dissident and protest groups (mainly on the left) which participated in the election of 1986 as part of the Popular Alliance coalition.

CALDERONIST REPUBLICAN PARTY (PARTIDO REPUBLICANO CALDERONISTA—PRC). Founded in 1970 after the death of Rafael Angel Calderón Guardia, the PRC may be traced to the Republican Party of the first four decades of the twentieth century and the breakaway National Republican Party founded by Calderón Guardia in 1942. It is essentially linked to the populist and progressive Catholic ideals of Calderón, who served as president (1940–1944), and became the political vehicle of his son, Rafael Angel Calderón Fournier. The younger Calderón used the party to participate in the Unity coalition in 1978 and eventually to form the Social Christian Unity Party in 1985, which enabled him to win the presidency in 1990. *See* SOCIAL CHRISTIAN UNITY PARTY.

CHRISTIAN DEMOCRATIC PARTY (PARTIDO DEMÓCRATA CRISTIANO—PDC). Formally organized in 1967 by a group of Catholic intellectuals with the support of the Confederation of Christian Workers and Peasants, the Christian Democratic Party did not fare well on its own in the elections of 1970 and 1974. Under the leadership of Rafael Grillo Rivera, it has had more success participating as a member of the Unity coalition, in 1978, and, since 1985, as a part of the Social Christian Unity Party, although possibly at the cost of its separate identity. *See* SOCIAL CHRISTIAN UNITY PARTY.

CIVIL PEOPLE'S PARTY (PARTIDO DEL PUEBLO CIVILISTA). The Civil People's Party is one of several left-wing splinter parties. It formed part of the United People coalition in the election of 1990. *See* UNITED PEOPLE.

COMMUNIST PARTY (PARTIDO COMUNISTA). Formally organized as a party by Manuel Mora Valverde in 1931, the Communist Party has had little success in Costa Rica, except for the "eight years"—the period of Rafael Angel Calderón Guardia's rule from 1940 to 1948. For tactical reasons and because it was outlawed from 1948 to 1974, it has used a variety of labels. Originally known as the Workers and Peasants Bloc (Bloque de Obreros y Campesinos), it changed its name to the Popular Vanguard Party (Vanguardia Popular—PVP) in 1943, as a concession to Catholics participating in the Victory Bloc, the wartime coalition of the Communist Party and Calderón Guardia's National Republican Party. As part of the Victory Bloc, the Popular Vanguard Party shared in the electoral triumph of 1944, but the coming of the cold war and consequent opposition to any Communist influence in the government contributed to the outbreak of the 1948 civil war and the eventual outlawing of the party. The PVP has still not recovered from this setback.

The Popular Vanguard label continues in use today, but, in order to participate in national elections during the time that it was banned, it adopted different names, such as the Popular Democratic Action Party (Partido Acción Demócrata Popular) in 1962 and the Socialist Action Party (Partido Acción Socialista) in 1970 and 1974. These names should not be confused with the numerous dissident groups that have appeared beginning in the 1960s espousing a more militant brand of Marxism or socialism, nor with the fact that, since 1978, the Popular Vanguard Party has not participated in national elections independently, but rather under the label of some electoral coalition.

Given the collapse of communism in Eastern Europe and the Soviet Union, coalition politics may be the only way for the PVP to remain viable. Having ousted the venerable Manuel Mora as leader in 1983, the PVP may have achieved some renewal, but it lost whatever it gained by denouncing Mora's nonthreatening electoralist thesis as bourgeois and revisionist. Even in the banana regions and within the trade union movement, where the PVP has been relatively strong, such rhetoric and internecine wrangles have sapped its energy and rendered it ineffective. Humberto Vargas Carbonell has led the PVP since 1984.

COSTA RICAN PEOPLE'S PARTY (PARTIDO DEL PUEBLO COSTAR-RICENSE—PPC). The PPC was founded by Manuel Mora Valverde, after his ouster as head of the Popular Vanguard Party in 1983, to provide himself with some leverage in Costa Rica's fragmented left. The PPC participated in the United People coalition for the 1986 elections.

COSTA RICAN SOCIALIST PARTY (PARTIDO SOCIALISTA COSTAR-RICENSE—PSC). Founded in 1962, the Costa Rica Socialist Party was one of the first of the more militant Marxist groups to break with the Moscow-line of the Popular Vanguard Party (PVP). Led by a former deputy of the National Liberation Party, Marcial Aquilúz, a Caribbean Legionnaire (member of the exile group that aided José Figueres in 1948), the pro-Castro PSC acted as a link with the Cuban Revolution, even though it was outlawed during the 1960s and until 1975. In 1978, it was reconciled with the PVP and organized the United People coalition for the elections of 1978 and 1982. In 1986, it remained with United People, but the PVP (because of the Manuel Mora Valverde flap) formed a rival coalition. Four years later, it did not even appear on the ballot; its fortunes are declining with those of Fidel Castro.

DEMOCRATIC PARTY (PARTIDO DEMÓCRATA). The Democratic Party label has experienced several reincarnations. León Cortés (a former Republican president, 1936 to 1940) adopted it for his unsuccessful presidential race in 1944, and Fernando Castro Cervantes used it again in 1953, as the party showed some vitality. The candidates who used it in 1974, 1978, and 1982 had nothing in common and did not represent a permanent organization.

DEMOCRATIC RENOVATION PARTY (PARTIDO RENOVACIÓN DE-MÓCRATA—PRD). The Democratic Renovation Party was organized by Rodrigo Carazo Odio in 1974 to support his presidential candidacy. Carazo had been virtually driven from the National Liberation Party because he dared challenge José Figueres for the party's nomination in 1970. Though unsuccessful in 1974, Carazo used the PRD to form the Unity coalition and win the presidency in 1978. With Unity transformed into the Social Christian Unity Party in 1985, which elected Rafael Angel Calderón Fournier as president in 1990, the Democratic Renovation Party may be totally absorbed and disappear, especially since Carazo is without influence. See SOCIAL CHRISTIAN UNITY PARTY.

FRENTE AMPLIO DEMOCRÁTICO. See BROAD DEMOCRATIC FRONT.

INDEPENDENT PARTY (PARTIDO INDEPENDIENTE). There is no Independent Party as such. It is another of those labels that is used every four years by a particular personality with the time and inclination to run for president. Its most serious use was probably its first use when, in 1958, National Liberation Party (PLN) leader Jorge Rossi used the label when he was unable to get his own party's nomination. His running independently may have cost the PLN the election that year. In 1978 the label reappeared to identify the candidacy of Geraldo W. (G.W.) Villalobos, who won few votes but attracted a great deal of attention by riding a white horse and firing shots at the home of Robert Vesco. When Eugenio Jiménez Sancho used the label in 1986, he admitted that he did not have a party or organization and that his candidacy was simply a protest against the lack of programs on the part of the major parties.

MILITANT WORKERS' REVOLUTIONARY PARTY (PARTIDO REVOL-UCIONARIO DE LOS TRABAJADORES EN LUCHA—PRT). The PRT is a self-described Trotskyist miniparty which supported the presidential candidacy of Edwin Badilla Agüero in 1990. Taking a completely independent stand as "a revolutionary socialist," Badilla refused to participate with other Marxist parties in an electoral coalition.

MOVIMIENTO DE LA NUEVA REPUBLICA. See NEW REPUBLIC MOVEMENT.

MOVIMIENTO REVOLUCIONARIO DEL PUEBLO. See REVOLUTION-ARY MOVEMENT OF THE PEOPLE.

NATIONAL CHRISTIAN ALLIANCE (ALIANZA NACIONAL CRIS-TIANA). The National Christian Alliance, a new party, presented presidential candidates in 1986 and 1990. It is not a Christian Democratic or Socialist party—its program does not include economic or social goals—but rather it criticizes the alleged moral decay of Costa Rican government and politics. Its candidates have called for a spiritual uplifting and a return to the "values" of the past. Alejandro Madrigal Benavides, the candidate in 1986, condemned the election as a "carnival" and a waste of money in the midst of hunger. In 1990, candidate Fernando Ramírez Muñoz prescribed Christian love as a cure for the ills of Costa Rica. Each candidate received less than 1 percent of the vote in the respective elections.

NATIONAL LIBERATION PARTY (PARTIDO LIBERACION NA-CIONAL—PLN). The National Liberation Party has been Costa Rica's dom-inant political party since its founding in 1951. Its roots may be found in the Center for the Study of National Problems, organized in 1940 by a group of young men interested in the economic and social reform of Costa Rica, and Democratic Action, a liberal wing of León Cortés's Democratic Party of the mid-1940s, led by José Figueres and Francisco Orlich. These two groups merged in 1945 to form the Social Democratic Party. But the PLN's strength originated in Figueres's military victory in 1948 and the consequent eighteen-month gov-ernment of the Founding Junta of the Second Republic (May 1948–November 1949) and the Constitution of 1949. It is ironic that a fiercely democratic party, which is identified with the abolition of the army, sprang from what amounted to a seizure of power by a force of arms.

During its first twenty-five years, the period in which Figueres was the dominant leader, the PLN developed an unswerving social democratic character. While strengthening Costa Rica's democratic institutions, it transformed the economy, establishing the principles of government planning and regulation and enlarging the public sector through the creation of autonomous agencies to provide services and to promote growth and development. A very successful party at the polls, the PLN has elected presidents in six of ten elections from 1953 to 1990 and has controlled the unicameral congress (Legislative Assembly) for most of the same period.

Since the mid-1970s, the party has been undergoing a great deal of change. This change is being caused by the greying of the leadership; criticism of an overblown state bureaucracy that jeopardizes the very programs it was created to administer and promote; serious instances of various types of corrupt practices, including arms smuggling and narcotrafficking; and the deterioration of the Costa Rican economy, brought on principally by external factors (the energy crunch and the Central American war), for which the solutions involve pressures to abandon the social democratic order.

Luis Alberto Monge and Oscar Arias Sánchez, both younger leaders, seem to have successfully challenged the primacy of the old guard, but each has been troubled by corruption and each has made fundamental changes in the state's role in the economy and the provision of social services. In order to obtain assistance from the International Monetary Fund and the U.S. Agency for International Development (AID), both leaders were obliged to sacrifice the PLN's ideological base. Certain reforms were probably beneficial and necessary, but the party will be more difficult to maintain in the future without its particular mystique, making it vulnerable to cynicism and personalism, which may not be new but is more threatening under the circumstances.

NATIONAL MOVEMENT PARTY (PARTIDO MOVIMIENTO NA-CIONAL). The National Movement Party is a meaningless label used by former President Mario Echandi (1958–1962) in his presidential bid in 1982. It was Echandi's personal vehicle and has not been heard from since.

NEW REPUBLIC MOVEMENT (MOVIMIENTO DE LA NUEVA REPÚB-LICA—MNR). The MNR is a minor leftist party led by Sergio Erick Ardón Ramírez. Ardón formerly led the Revolutionary Movement of the People, which helped organize the United People coalition in 1978. Renouncing Marxism-Leninism, the MNR joined the eclectic Progressive Party coalition for the 1990 elections.

PARTIDO COMUNISTA. See COMMUNIST PARTY.

PARTIDO DE LOS TRABAJADORES. *See* WORKERS' PARTY.

PARTIDO DEL PROGRESO. *See* PROGRESSIVE PARTY.

PARTIDO DEL PUEBLO CIVILISTA. *See* CIVIL PEOPLE'S PARTY.

PARTIDO DEL PUEBLO COSTARRICENSE. *See* COSTA RICAN PEO-PLE'S PARTY.

PARTIDO DEMÓCRATA. *See* DEMOCRATIC PARTY.

PARTIDO DEMÓCRATA CRISTIANO. *See* CHRISTIAN DEMOCRATIC PARTY.

PARTIDO DEMOCRÁTICO POPULAR. *See* UNITED PEOPLE.

PARTIDO INDEPENDIENTE. *See* INDEPENDENT PARTY.

PARTIDO LIBERACION NACIONAL. *See* NATIONAL LIBERATION PARTY.

PARTIDO MOVIMIENTO NACIONAL. *See* NATIONAL MOVEMENT PARTY.

PARTIDO RENOVACION DEMÓCRATA. *See* DEMOCRATIC RENO-VATION PARTY.

PARTIDO REPUBLICANO CALDERONISTA. *See* CALDERONIST RE-PUBLICAN PARTY.

PARTIDO REVOLUCIONARIO DE LOS TRABAJADORES EN LUCHA. *See* MILITANT WORKERS' REVOLUTIONARY PARTY.

PARTIDO SOCIALISTA COSTARRICENSE. *See* COSTA RICAN SO-CIALIST PARTY.

PARTIDO UNIDAD SOCIAL CRISTIANA. *See* SOCIAL CHRISTIAN UN-ITY PARTY.

PARTIDO UNIÓN POPULAR. *See* POPULAR UNION PARTY.

PARTIDO VANGUARDIA POPULAR. *See* COMMUNIST PARTY.

POPULAR ALLIANCE (ALIANZA POPULAR—AP). The AP was a coalition composed of the Broad Democratic Front and the Popular Vanguard Party (PVP), which supported the candidacy of Rodrigo Gutiérrez Sáenz for president in 1986. It sprang from the ousting of Manuel Mora Valverde as head of the PVP and the consequent splintering of the United People coalition. The Popular Alliance folded after the election.

POPULAR DEMOCRATIC PARTY (PARTIDO DEMOCRÁTICO POPU-LAR). See UNITED PEOPLE.

POPULAR UNION PARTY (PARTIDO UNIÓN POPULAR—PUP). Popular Union is a small party representing old moneyed interests in Costa Rica (Union Club/"coffee barons"). Founded in 1974 and led by Cristian Tattenbach Iglesias, it is more a pressure group (anti-Liberation) than a political party. Being content to play coalition politics, it has never presented a separate candidate for president or a slate of candidates for the Legislative Assembly. It supported National Unification in 1974 and participated in the Unity coalition in 1978 and 1982. Although it may have been absorbed into the Social Christian Unity Party in 1985, Tattenbach's strategy paid off handsomely when Rafael Angel Calderón Fournier was elected in 1990. See SOCIAL CHRISTIAN UNITY PARTY.

POPULAR VANGUARD PARTY (PARTIDO VANGUARDIA POPU-LAR—PVP). See COMMUNIST PARTY.

PROGRESSIVE PARTY (PARTIDO DEL PROGRESO—PP). Organized in 1989, the Progressive Party is the most recent attempt of the Costa Rican left to create a united front. Rejecting old-style Communist orthodoxy, the PP seeks to be a "true alternative to bipartisanism" (the sameness of the major parties) and a "voice of protest." The PP incorporates a variety of elements from erstwhile Marxist parties (the New Republic Movement, the Humanist Party, and the Costa Rican Socialist Party) to environmentalists. Under the leadership of Javier Solís, the Progressive Party participated in the 1990 presidential election, presenting the candidacy of Isaac Felipe Azofeifa Bolaños, a founding member of the National Liberation Party. Professor Azofeifa's son was the student involved in the Figueres slapping incident in 1971.

PUEBLO UNIDO. See UNITED PEOPLE.

REVOLUTIONARY MOVEMENT OF THE PEOPLE (MOVIMIENTO RE-VOLUCIONARIO DEL PUEBLO). This small Marxist party helped organize the United People coalition for the 1978 elections. Organized in sympathy to Sandinista elements in Nicaragua, the party eventually rejected the orthodox Communist position of its coalition partner, the Popular Vanguard Party, and left United People altogether after the 1982 elections. Its leader, Sergio Erick

Ardón Ramírez, subsequently formed the New Republic Movement and participated in the Progressive Party coalition in the election of 1990.

SOCIAL CHRISTIAN UNITY PARTY (PARTIDO UNIDAD SOCIAL CRISTIANA—PUSC). Organized in 1985 by Rafael Angel Calderón Fournier (Junior Calderón), the Social Christian Unity Party represented the culmination of a twenty-year effort to create a viable party in opposition to the National Liberation Party. The search began with the organization of the National Unification coalition in 1965 by ex-Presidents Rafael Angel Calderón Guardia and Otilio Ulate, which elected José Joaquín Trejos in 1966, and gained steam with Rodrigo Carazo Odio's Unity coalition in 1978, which enabled him to win the presidency. Calderón Fournier kept up the momentum with a good showing in the 1982 elections, and he moved to convert Unity (made up of the Calderonist Republican, Christian Democratic, Democratic Renovation, and Popular Union parties) into a permanent political party. Having yet to prove that the PUSC stands for something more than anti-Liberation, the election of Calderón Fournier as president in 1990, nonetheless, is a strong indication that a two-party system has evolved in Costa Rica.

UNITED PEOPLE (PUEBLO UNIDO). United People, a coalition of Marxist parties, was first organized in 1978 by the Costa Rican Socialist (PSC), Popular Vanguard (PVP), and Revolutionary Movement of the People parties. Ever since the fragmentation of the Costa Rican left in the 1960s (reflecting worldwide developments), there has been a search for some means of reuniting the left, at least in an election year, but with little success.

The United People coalition held together fairly well for the election of 1982, winning four seats in the Legislative Assembly and achieving 3.3 percent of the vote for its presidential candidate, Rodrigo Gutiérrez Sáenz. Since then, particularly in view of the PVP split in 1983, United People has been in disarray. The coalition was made up of the PSC, the Revolutionary Movement of the People, the Workers' Party, and the New Republic Movement in the 1986 election, being challenged by a new leftist coalition, the Popular Alliance. In 1990 more fragmentation occurred, with the appearance of the Popular Democratic and Civil People's miniparties along with yet another leftist umbrella organization, the Progressive Party. The future of United People is bleak.

UNITY (UNIDAD). Rodrigo Carazo Odio organized the Unity coalition for his successful presidential campaign in 1978. Composed of the Calderonist Republican, Christian Democratic, Democratic Renovation, and Popular Union parties, the coalition was converted into the Christian Socialist Unity Party in 1985, after its defeat in the 1982 election. See CHRISTIAN SOCIALIST UNITY PARTY.

WORKERS' PARTY (PARTIDO DE LOS TRABAJADORES). See UNITED PEOPLE.

Political Parties—Historical

ACCIÓN DEMÓCRATA. *See* NATIONAL LIBERATION PARTY.

BLOQUE DE OBREROS Y CAMPESINOS. *See* COMMUNIST PARTY.

COSTA RICAN POPULAR FRONT PARTY (PARTIDO FRENTE POPU-LAR COSTARRICENSE). The Popular Front Party was a small Marxist party active in the 1970s.

DEMOCRATIC ACTION (ACCIÓN DEMÓCRATA—AD). *See* NA-TIONAL LIBERATION PARTY.

FRENTE NACIONAL. *See* NATIONAL FRONT.

INDEPENDENT NATIONAL PARTY (PARTIDO NACIONAL INDEPEN-DIENTE). The Independent National Party was organized by conservative busi-nessman Jorge González Martén to promote his presidential candidacy in 1974. González Marten won a surprising 11 percent of the vote in the 1974 election, but his refusal to join the Unity coalition in 1978, if he could not be its candidate, led to a humiliating defeat and indebtedness that accelerated the party's demise.

NATIONAL FRONT (FRENTE NACIONAL). The National Front, also known as the Third Front, supported the candidacy of Virgilio Calvo Sánchez in 1970. An anti-Liberation party, it actually aided the election of José Figueres in 1970 by siphoning votes from the opposition National Unification coalition.

NATIONAL REPUBLICAN PARTY (PARTIDO REPUBLICANO NA-CIONAL—PRN). The PRN was founded by President Rafael Angel Calderón Guardia in 1941, when he lost the support of the traditional Republican Party. The PRN and the Popular Vanguard Party formed the Victory Bloc in 1943, extending Calderón's dominance until 1948, when both parties were banned in the aftermath of the civil war that year. The National Republican Party was reborn as the Calderonist Republican Party in 1970 and eventually (1985) was absorbed into the Social Christian Unity Party.

NATIONAL UNIFICATION (UNIFICACIÓN NACIONAL—UN). Na-tional Unification was a coalition formed in 1965 by ex-Presidents Rafael Angel Calderón Guardia and Otilio Ulate. Though it elected José Joaquín Trejos to the presidency in 1966, its leaders were old and battle scarred, and the coalition disappeared with the emergence of the more positive, more vital Unity coalition.

NATIONAL UNION PARTY (PARTIDO UNIÓN NACIONAL—PUN). The PUN was the personal electoral vehicle of Otilio Ulate, who won the disputed election of 1948 and served as president from 1949 to 1953. A conservative party, adhering to "traditional values," it successfully backed Mario Echandi in 1958. It formed part of the winning National Unification coalition in 1966, but it disappeared as an active party after Ulate's death in 1973.

PARTIDO ACCIÓN DEMÓCRATA POPULAR. See COMMUNIST PARTY.

PARTIDO ACCIÓN SOCIALISTA. See COMMUNIST PARTY.

PARTIDO FRENTE POPULAR COSTARRICENSE. See COSTA RICAN POPULAR FRONT PARTY.

PARTIDO NACIONAL INDEPENDIENTE. See INDEPENDENT NATIONAL PARTY.

PARTIDO REFORMISTA. See REFORMIST PARTY.

PARTIDO REPUBLICANO. See REPUBLICAN PARTY.

PARTIDO REPUBLICANO NACIONAL. See NATIONAL REPUBLICAN PARTY.

PARTIDO SOCIAL DEMÓCRATA. See SOCIAL DEMOCRATIC PARTY.

PARTIDO UNIÓN CÍVICA REVOLUCIONARIA. See REVOLUTIONARY CIVIC UNION PARTY.

PARTIDO UNIÓN NACIONAL. See NATIONAL UNION PARTY.

POPULAR DEMOCRATIC ACTION PARTY (PARTIDO ACCIÓN DEMÓCRATA POPULAR). See COMMUNIST PARTY.

REFORMIST PARTY (PARTIDO REFORMISTA). A short-lived party of the 1920s, the Reformist Party, although closely identified with the political career of Jorge Volio, was the first Costa Rican political party to advocate social reform.

REPUBLICAN PARTY (PARTIDO REPUBLICANO). The Republican Party was Costa Rica's dominant political party from the end of the nineteenth century to 1940. It was, in turn, dominated by the "Olympians" Cleto González Víquez and Ricardo Jiménez Oreamuno, who, together, served as president for twenty of the thirty years between 1906 and 1936. Although the party provided efficient and honest government, its failure to keep up with the times, particularly economic and social change, led to its disappearance in 1940. Its spirit lingers on, as the party that nurtured Costa Rican democracy and built schools, bridges, and roads.

REVOLUTIONARY CIVIC UNION PARTY (PARTIDO UNIÓN CÍVICA REVOLUCIONARIA—PUCR). The PUCR, the ultimate in personalist parties, was used by its founder, Frank Marshall Jiménez, to win a seat in the Legislative Assembly in 1958. Marshall, a combat hero of the 1948 civil war, represented the gun-toting segment of Costa Rican society, and his miniparty was a forerunner, in a way, of the right-wing, paramilitary organization, the Free Costa Rica Movement (Movimiento Costa Rica Libre—MCRL).

SOCIAL DEMOCRATIC PARTY (PARTIDO SOCIAL DEMÓCRATA— PSD). Founded in 1945 through the merger of Democratic Action and the Center for the Study of National Problems, the PSD is the parent organization of the National Liberation Party. See NATIONAL LIBERATION PARTY.

SOCIALIST ACTION PARTY. See COMMUNIST PARTY.

TERCER FRENTE. See NATIONAL FRONT.

THIRD FRONT (TERCER FRENTE). See NATIONAL FRONT.

UNIFICACIÓN NACIONAL. See NATIONAL UNIFICATION.

WORKERS AND PEASANTS BLOC (BLOQUE DE OBREROS Y CAMPESINOS). See COMMUNIST PARTY.

Charles D. Ameringer

CUBA

The Republic of Cuba encompasses the major island of Cuba, the Isle of Youth (formerly the Isle of Pines), and some 1,600 islets and keys, covering a total area of about 45,000 square miles, roughly equivalent in size to the state of Pennsylvania. When Christopher Columbus landed in 1492, three different Indian groups coexisted, but the Spanish conquest quickly decimated their members. In consequence, Cuba's cultural values and ethnic roots are to be found in a mixture of Spanish, African, and criollo elements.

During the last half of the eighteenth century, the development of the sugar industry became the major force shaping Cuba's economy and society, which it has remained to the present time. The economic relationship virtually preordained by proximity to the United States would cast a long shadow over future developments in the island.

The Cuban wars of independence from Spain spanned a period of thirty years in the last third of the nineteenth century. The first military struggle dragged on for ten years (1868–1878) with inconclusive results. The War of Independence (1895–1898), organized under the political and intellectual genius of José Martí and the military leadership of Máximo Gómez and Antonio Maceo, quickly gained widespread support among the Cuban people. But within two years, Martí and Maceo perished on the field of battle and the war effort became stalemated. At this point, the United States interposed its might in the Cuban struggle for independence, and in a few months the Spanish-American War produced the collapse of Madrid's long domination over the island. Cuba entered republican life under the tutelage of the United States, conditioned by the military occupation (1898–1902) and constrained by the Platt Amendment to the Cuban Constitution (which granted Washington, D.C., the right of intervention). To most Cubans, the latter was a bitter imposition.

The Republican Era

In May 1902, the first Cuban president was inaugurated and the Republic of Cuba started its history. However, large sugarcane landholdings, urban-rural inequalities, commercial dependence on the United States, and the *Plattista* mentality, among other factors, conspired against the development of a responsible, stable self-government. *Personalismo*, the allegiance to the leader, became the staple of Cuban politics. Small wars and rebellions were constant threats to social stability. In sum, the first twenty-five years of republican existence were characterized by corruption, violence, electoral fraud, dependence, and cynicism.

The accumulated pressures on the socioeconomic fabric joined with the political breakdown generated by the Gerardo Machado dictatorship of the late 1920s to usher in the revolution of August 1933. The revolutionary government, in power for only five months, implemented remarkable political and economic changes in Cuba under a populist-nationalist platform. However, Fulgencio Batista, then an army sergeant with the backing of the United States, assumed control in Havana and ruled the country, directly and through puppet regimes, until 1944. A brief democratic interlude ensued under two administrations, which flew the banner of the Authentic Party (Partido Auténtico—PA). But the *Auténticos*, Ramón Grau San Martín and Carlos Prío Socarrás, succeeded only partially in containing civil disorder while corruption escalated to unprecedented levels.

In March 1952, Batista staged another military coup and built a coalition with business and labor groups. It was on 26 July 1953 that Fidel Castro directed a group of young students and workers in an attack on the Moncada army garrison in Santiago. Later, guerrilla warfare in the mountains and terrorist tactics in the cities brought down Batista's dictatorship. The first day of January 1959 started a new era in Cuban history.

The Socialist Experiment

From the start, the Cuban Revolution manifested strong nationalist and antiimperialist tendencies and pursued populist economic policies. After some hesitation, all pre-1959 political parties except the Communists were banned under the new regime. Political power was concentrated in Castro; it flowed from him through a small cadre of trusted veterans of Moncada and the Sierra Maestra. When a formal political structure was created, the old Communists provided the organizational expertise, but the Castro loyalists retained control over policymaking. Many times during the 1960s, the relationship between old Communists and Fidelistas was severely strained. After the failure of the utopian economic goals and policies of the later 1960s (which emphasized a new society achieved through socialization, centralization, and moral incentives), and propelled by the debacle of the 1970 ten-million-ton sugar harvest, Castro turned toward the Soviet model of political and economic organization.

During the 1970s and early 1980s, the process of institutionalization produced significant changes in party structure, government decision making, legal statutes, and even politico-administrative boundaries (there are now fourteen rather than six provinces). In terms of the economic model, the System of Economic Planning and Management (Sistema de Dirección y Planificación de la Economia—SDPE) sought to introduce rudimentary elements of the market to Cuban practice. The basic aim of the institutionalization process was to reduce charismatic leadership and to increase institutional policy-making. Although some progress was registered along these lines, especially compared to the record of the 1960s, the character of the political system continued to be defined by the commanding presence of the *líder máximo*. Moreover, by the late 1980s, Cuban political culture had turned once more toward the unquestioned exercise of charismatic leadership. There was also a marked change in the locus of interest and action of the top decision makers.

For ten years starting in 1975, Castro focused his attention on world affairs, positioning Cuba at the forefront of international solidarity with the Third World across multiple issues. Cuban soldiers fought in Angola and Ethiopia to bolster socialist regimes. Doctors and teachers rendered valuable assistance to social programs in Nicaragua and several African countries. Castro served a term as president of the Non-Aligned Nations Movement. Numerous conferences and meetings held in Havana, to deal with the foreign debt crisis of the less-developed countries, featured Castro's call for debt relief and the protection of social equity under economic adjustment programs. With Castro otherwise occupied, institutional development registered healthy gains and the economy performed moderately well.

By the mid-1980s, however, the international situation had changed in the direction of limiting Cuban targets of opportunity and reducing Moscow's interest in collaborating to exploit them. Further prompted by clear signs of internal unease (the 1980 Mariel boat exodus and youth disaffection in 1982), domestic concerns became predominant in the leadership's agenda. In addition, policy decisions turned against the pragmatism of the recent past and veered toward an ideological rigidity reminiscent of the late 1960s.

The Rectification Process, firmly in place since mid-1986, is characterized by politics over economics, bureaucrats over technocrats, party over government, vision over reality. Its economic praxis is centralist, personalist, antimarket, and anti-incentives, with heavy emphasis on ideological and political values. Elite consensus, under a supreme and unchallenged leader, remains the currency of Cuban politics. The implementation of the Rectification Process entailed broad elite agreement on political conformity and social discipline as exalted goals. Apparently, acquiescence was not universal. To enforce the objectives, the regime tried and executed General Arnaldo Ochoa, a highly decorated hero of the Angolan campaign, and three other military officers in the summer of

1989. The Ochoa affair, which led to a massive restructuring of the internal security organs, constituted the most serious threat ever to the supremacy of Castro.

In December 1986, Castro declared that "now we are really going to build socialism." It is incontrovertible that Castro made the revolution, but he may be incapable of building socialism. His forceful leadership and his strict discipline were decisive factors in the insurrectional victory. His visionary projections and ideological intransigence were critical elements in the socialist transformation. These personal attributes and individual traits may also explain the institutional weakness and policy instability in the Cuban process of socialist construction.

The changed socialist world, which emerged from the momentous year of 1989, represents a major challenge to the building of Cuban socialism. With the subsequent collapse of socialism in Eastern Europe and the epochal changes occurring in the economics and the politics of the former Soviet Union, what is Cuba to do? Castro's answer is to circle the wagons and defend the revolution to the last drop of blood. In fact, the Cuban people are being told that it is their historical privilege and responsibility to be thrust in a position to become the only true socialist state on earth. In late 1990, Cuba implemented what is termed "a special period in time of peace," a period of draconian policy measures (increased food and energy rationing and tightened internal security) designed to ensure the survival of the socialist state under hostile conditions.

But the crucial question remains: What is the future of the Cuban Revolution as it confronts the failure and collapse of the socialist community worldwide? At least some Cuban leaders and officials must be asking themselves that question in Havana these days.

Bibliography

Luis Aguilar. *Cuba 1933: Prologue to Revolution.* Norton, New York, 1974.

Robert J. Alexander, ed. *Political Parties of the Americas: Canada, Latin America, and the West Indies.* Vol. 1, *Anguilla–Grenada*, pp. 325–44. Greenwood Press, Westport, Conn., 1982.

Juan M. del Aguila. *Cuba, Dilemmas of a Revolution.* Westview Press, Boulder, Colo., 1988.

Jorge I. Dominguez. *To Make A World Safe for Revolution.* Harvard University Press, Cambridge, Mass., 1989.

Morris H. Morley. *Imperial State and Revolution—The United States and Cuba 1952–1986.* Cambridge University Press, Cambridge, 1987.

Louis A. Perez, Jr. *Cuba—Between Reform and Revolution.* Oxford University Press, New York, 1988.

Sergio G. Roca. *Socialist Cuba—Past Interpretations and Future Challenges.* Westview Press, Boulder, Colo., 1988.

Hugh Thomas. *Cuba: The Pursuit of Freedom.* Harper and Row, New York, 1971.

Political Parties—Active

Since 1959 Cuba has been a one-party state, with Castro and his loyalists exercising power through several organizational schemes culminating with the formation of the Communist Party in 1965. Thus, all other political parties in Cuba are classified under the rubric of historical parties and are listed as such in the next section. For a full discussion of their ideological development and historical impact in prerevolutionary Cuba, see Robert J. Alexander, ed., *Political Parties of the Americas*, vol. 1.

CUBAN COMMUNIST PARTY (PARTIDO COMUNISTA DE CUBA—PCC). The establishment of the Cuban Communist Party as the official party of the Castro regime went through three phases. The first of these was the establishment in the latter part of 1961 of the Integrated Revolutionary Organizations (Organizaciones Revolucionarias Integradas—ORI). This transitional arrangement attempted to bridge the gap between the collection of several anti-Batista revolutionary groups and the formation of the definitive party of the Cuban Revolution. The ORI was an umbrella-type organization under which the twenty-sixth of July Movement (Movimiento 26 de Julio—M-26–7), the Revolutionary Student Directorate (Directorio Estudiantil Revolucionario—DER), and the Popular Socialist Party (Partido Socialista Popular—PSP) were assembled starting in the summer of 1961.

The ORI never attained significant membership and never acquired operational importance. At best, it was an informal vehicle for general discussion among the top revolutionary leadership; it lacked policy-making powers. In 1963 the ORI was transformed, without much substantive change, into the United Party of the Socialist Revolution (Partido Unido de la Revolución Socialista—PURS). The main function of the PURS, of which Fidel Castro was secretary-general, was to build up party membership among rank-and-file workers and peasants in order to proceed to the founding of the PCC.

The process of party-building culminated in October 1965 when the creation of the Cuban Communist Party was announced by the revolutionary leadership. In view of its antecedents, the initial membership of the PCC was derived mostly from the M-26–7, the DER, and the PSP.

Under the firm control of Fidel Castro and his loyalists, the PCC came to life without the holding of a founding congress and without any public debate about its goals and functions. The executive organs of the party (the politburo with eight members and the secretariat with six members) and its deliberative body (the central committee with one hundred members) seldom met during the 1960s. The central committee included sixty-seven military officers. Party membership in 1969 was estimated at 55,000 militants and candidates. During the late 1960s, many former PSP members were removed from leadership positions in the party and the government. At the same time, the PCC became increasingly involved with detailed administrative matters related to the economy, foreign policy, and labor unions.

The First Congress of the PCC was held in December 1975, with 3,116 delegates in attendance. The politburo was enlarged to thirteen members to include three former PSP leaders (Arnaldo Milián, Blas Roca, and Carlos Rafael Rodríguez), a symbolic move which, after many years in purgatory, formalized the restitution of the old Communists to revolutionary legitimacy. Total party enrollment, including the youth section and candidates, stood at 212,000 members in 1975. The First Congress approved the draft of the new Socialist constitution, the first five-year economic plan, the new system of economic management, the politico-administrative division of the country into fourteen provinces, and the temporary party platforms. In the late 1970s, despite attempts to clearly separate the functions of the party and the government, the PCC remained involved in operational details. Likewise, despite the introduction of decentralization in party policy-making, Castro and his inner circle retained overwhelming control over the conduct of PCC affairs.

The Second Congress, held in December 1980, discussed and approved the definitive party program outlining the objectives and strategies for the construction of communism in Cuba. This party gathering took place at a time when the regime basked in the glow of favorable circumstances. In the international domain, Cuban armies were victorious in Africa, the Sandinistas held power in Nicaragua, Castro was leading the nonaligned nations, and Soviet economic assistance and political support were dependable realities. In the domestic realm, the process of institutionalization was proceeding apace, and the economy benefitted from high world-market sugar prices.

The 1980 politburo, with its sixteen full members and eleven alternates, represented an incorporation of major institutional players in the Cuban system without venturing outside the inner circle of trusted comrades. All three of the new full members were veterans of the M-26-7. Many of the new alternates were leaders of significant institutions: armed forces, mass organizations, government bureaucracy, and provincial party structure. Party membership doubled to about 450,000 cadres.

When the Third Congress of the PCC met in February 1986 (followed by a deferred session in December), Castro's assessment of the economic and political accomplishments of the preceding period was strongly critical. The foreign debt crisis (which surfaced in 1984) and the corruption and materialism associated with the economic reform model (SDPE) would presage the advent of the Rectification Process in the interval between the two sessions of the congress.

For the first time in the history of the revolution, there was substantial turnover in the composition of the politburo and the central committee. In the top party organ, four full members were removed and four alternates were demoted; three women, one black, and four provincial party secretaries joined the body. In the central committee, about 40 percent of the 1980 members still alive were dropped in 1986. While the share of women and young people (under thirty-five years old) in the central committee remained unchanged, the pattern of representation for blacks increased substantially for the first time.

In sum, the Third Congress introduced significant changes in both dimensions of the exercise of party power. External control over society increased as centralization and discipline displaced market socialism and internal clout shifted to the provincial secretaries who replaced military and civilian technocrats. The party, being in charge of *trabajo político*, solidified its key role in Cuban society.

In 1989, as the socialist world collapsed, it became apparent that the Fourth Congress of the PCC would not be routine. To start, the setting of the meeting date was postponed repeatedly. Above all, the Cuban regime seeks to retain power, and the Cuban party wants to maintain its uniqueness. Whereas the Soviet party renounced its political monopoly, the PCC reasserted its total control. While others embrace capitalism, Havana insists upon command-economy methods. At a time when socialist bloc nations prepare to enter the world economy, Cuba makes plans to subsist in near autarky. When cooperation flourishes among major and minor powers alike and regional conflicts recede, Castro keeps high the flag of class struggle and the banner of international solidarity.

As 1990 unfolded, several indications pointed to disarray in the conduct of party affairs. In the spring, a morose and formalistic discussion of the Fourth Congress agenda among party rank and file prompted a lengthy editorial in the party paper encouraging more lively and open debate, but also reasserting the tight limits of dissension. In October, the Fourth Congress organizing committee, appropriating functions delegated to the central committee or in the domain of the party congress itself, acted upon several important issues related to the structure and work of the PCC. Among these measures were the elimination of two positions from the secretariat, the reduction in the number of central committee departments and personnel by 50 percent, the transfer of party control over the military directly to the politburo, and the cutting in half of the staff of provincial party organizations.

It is clear that the top party leadership is extending its tight control over the minutiae of party life and government affairs. Indeed, the new guiding principle is for the party "to exercise its advisory and control roles in an even more encompassing and comprehensive manner," adjusting party work to concrete priorities instead of formal requirements. It remains to be seen whether the Cuban party, in its audacious defiance of the historical fate of its counterparts elsewhere, can survive as currently constituted and led.

Political Parties—Historical

ABC PARTY (PARTIDO ABC). The *abecedarios*, like many political parties in Cuba, entered public life as a revolutionary movement. The ABC group was organized in October 1931 to combat the dictatorship of President Gerardo Machado, who had illegally extended his term of office.

ALA IZQUIERDA ESTUDIANTIL. *See* STUDENT LEFT WING.

AUTHENTIC PARTY (PARTIDO REVOLUCIONARIO CUBANO (AU-TÉNTICO) or PARTIDO AUTÉNTICO—PA). The *Auténticos* were organized by Ramón Grau San Martín shortly after his removal as president and the collapse of the revolutionary government in January 1934.

AUTONOMIST PARTY (PARTIDO AUTÓNOMISTA). After the failure to achieve independence through the Ten Years' War (1968–1978), many Cubans turned to *autonomismo*, seeking some measure of self-governance under the Spanish flag.

COMMUNIST PARTY (PARTIDO COMUNISTA). *See* POPULAR SO-CIALIST PARTY.

COMMUNIST REVOLUTIONARY UNION PARTY (PARTIDO UNIÓN REVOLUCIONARIA COMUNISTA. *See* POPULAR SOCIALIST PARTY.

CONSERVATIVE PARTY (PARTIDO CONSERVADOR or PARTIDO MODERADO). After independence was achieved, the Conservative Party took shape around the remnants of assorted small colonial parties, and included several prominent *Autonomistas*.

CONSTITUTIONAL UNION PARTY (PARTIDO UNIÓN CONSTITU-CIONAL). The Constitutional Union Party was organized in the summer of 1878 as the "Spanish party," in reaction against the gathering of so many criollos into the Autonomist Party.

CUBAN PEOPLE'S PARTY (PARTIDO DEL PUEBLO CUBANO-ORTODOXO—PPC). In protest against the wave of corruption and gangsterism engulfing the Grau administration of the 1940s, Eduardo Chibás led a large group of disaffected *Auténticos* to found the PPC in May 1947.

CUBAN REVOLUTIONARY PARTY (PARTIDO REVOLUCIONARIO CUBANO—PRC). The Cuban Revolutionary Party was organized by José Martí in 1892 while he was in exile in the United States. It drew its support from Cuban tobacco workers in Tampa, Florida, and Latin American intellectuals in New York.

DIRECTORIO ESTUDIANTIL. *See* STUDENT DIRECTORATE.

DIRECTORIO ESTUDIANTIL REVOLUCIONARIO. *See* REVOLUTION- ARY STUDENT DIRECTORATE.

INDEPENDENT PARTY OF COLORED PEOPLE (PARTIDO INDEPEN- DIENTE DE COLOR). In 1908, during the second United States occupation, Evaristo Estenóz, a Dominican and a veteran of the War of Independence, founded the Independent Party of Colored People for black Cubans.

LIBERAL PARTY (PARTIDO LIBERAL—PL). The Liberals broke into Cuban politics in classic fashion befitting that genre: They abstained from running candidates in the 1905 election due to allegations of fraud, and the next year they revolted against the Conservatives, precipitating the second United States occupation.

MOVIMIENTO 26 DE JULIO. *See* TWENTY-SIXTH OF JULY MOVEMENT.

NATIONAL DEMOCRATIC UNION (UNIÓN NACIONAL DEMOCRÁ- TICA—UND). The National Democratic Union was organized in 1936 by Mario García Menocal, the former Conservative president.

NATIONALIST UNION PARTY (UNIÓN NACIONALISTA). The Na- tionalist Union Party was founded in 1927 by Carlos Mendieta, a former Liberal, in an effort to join all anti-Machado politicians into a common front.

ORGANIZACIÓN AUTÉNTICA. *See* AUTHENTIC PARTY.

ORGANIZACIONES REVOLUCIONARIAS INTEGRADAS. *See* CUBAN COMMUNIST PARTY.

PARTIDO ABC. *See* ABC PARTY.

PARTIDO ACCIÓN UNITARIA. *See* UNITED ACTION PARTY.

PARTIDO AUTÉNTICO. *See* AUTHENTIC PARTY.

PARTIDO AUTÓNOMISTA. *See* AUTONOMIST PARTY.

PARTIDO COMUNISTA. *See* POPULAR SOCIALIST PARTY.

PARTIDO COMUNISTA DE CUBA. *See* CUBAN COMMUNIST PARTY.

PARTIDO CONSERVADOR. *See* CONSERVATIVE PARTY.

PARTIDO DE ACCIÓN PROGRESISTA. *See* PROGRESSIVE ACTION PARTY.

PARTIDO DEL PUEBLO CUBANO-ORTODOXO. *See* CUBAN PEOPLE'S PARTY.

PARTIDO INCONDICIONAL ESPAÑOL. *See* SPANISH UNCONDITIONAL PARTY.

PARTIDO INDEPENDIENTE DE COLOR. *See* INDEPENDENT PARTY OF COLORED PEOPLE.

PARTIDO LIBERAL. *See* LIBERAL PARTY.

PARTIDO MODERADO. *See* CONSERVATIVE PARTY.

PARTIDO NACIONAL CUBANO. *See* REPUBLICAN PARTY.

PARTIDO POPULAR. *See* POPULAR PARTY.

PARTIDO REPUBLICANO. *See* REPUBLICAN PARTY.

PARTIDO REVOLUCIONARIO CUBANO. *See* CUBAN REVOLUTIONARY PARTY.

PARTIDO REVOLUCIONARIO CUBANO (AUTÉNTICO). *See* AUTHENTIC PARTY.

PARTIDO SOCIALISTA POPULAR. *See* POPULAR SOCIALIST PARTY.

PARTIDO UNIÓN CONSTITUCIONAL. *See* CONSTITUTIONAL UNION PARTY.

PARTIDO UNIÓN REVOLUCIONARIA. *See* POPULAR SOCIALIST PARTY.

PARTIDO UNIÓN REVOLUCIONARIA COMUNISTA. *See* POPULAR SOCIALIST PARTY.

POPULAR PARTY (PARTIDO POPULAR). In 1919 Alfredo Zayas left the Liberal Party because José Miguel Gómez had wrested for himself its presidential candidacy. Afterward, Zayas founded the Popular Party, which, in conjunction with Mario García Menocal and the Conservatives, carried Zayas to the presidency in 1920.

POPULAR SOCIALIST PARTY (PARTIDO SOCIALISTA POPULAR— PSP). The Popular Socialist Party was the last name to be used by Cuba's orthodox Stalinist Communist Party. The Communist Party was first organized in Havana in 1925 by student leader Julio Antonio Mella, former Martí collaborator Carlos Baliño, and Polish-born Fabio Grobart.

PROGRESSIVE ACTION PARTY (PARTIDO DE ACCIÓN PROGRESISTA—PAP). For the 1954 elections, held to attempt to legitimize his regime, Fulgencio Batista built a coalition around the newly formed Progressive Action Party, in fact a reorganization of the old United Action Party (Partido de Acción Unitaria).

REFORMIST PARTY (PARTIDO REFORMISTA). The Reformist Party, in fact a loose coalition of diverse forces, was organized in 1865 to channel existing reformist aspirations.

REPUBLICAN PARTY (PARTIDO REPUBLICANO) (1930s). The Republican Party was founded in the mid-1930s by Miguel Mariano Gómez, former Liberal mayor of Havana and the son of José Miguel Gómez.

REPUBLICAN PARTY (PARTIDO REPUBLICANO) (1940s). In the same year that the first Republican Party was dissolved, a new Republican Party was organized by Gustavo Guervo Rubio, who had split with the National Democratic Union, taking many party adherents with him.

REVOLUTIONARY STUDENT DIRECTORATE (DIRECTORIO ESTUDIANTIL REVOLUCIONARIO—DER). In the pattern of the anti-Machado groups of the 1920s and 1930s, the DER was formed in December 1956 to fight against the Batista dictatorship.

SPANISH UNCONDITIONAL PARTY (PARTIDO INCONDICIONAL ESPAÑOL). The Spanish Unconditional Party was hastily organized in 1865 to respond to the perceived threat to Spanish sovereignty over Cuba represented by the demands of the criollo-led Reformist Party.

STUDENT DIRECTORATE (DIRECTORIO ESTUDIANTIL—DE). It was students from the University of Havana who, banded together in the DE of 1927, first protested against Machado's usurpation of power.

STUDENT LEFT WING (ALA IZQUIERDA ESTUDIANTIL—AIE). This radical student group was organized in the spring of 1931 by splinter elements of the 1930 Directorio Estudiantil (DE), together with some former members of the 1927 and 1929 DE groups.

TWENTY-SIXTH OF JULY MOVEMENT (MOVIMIENTO 26 DE JULIO—M-26–7). The attack on the Moncada garrison in Santiago by Fidel Castro and his group on 26 July 1953 started the armed struggle against Fulgencio Batista's second dictatorship. Brutal repression by the army cost the lives of dozens of Castro's followers after they surrendered. Castro and some of his close associates were captured, tried, and given long prison sentences. After his release under a general amnesty and before leaving for Mexico, Castro organized the M-26–7 at a Havana meeting in July 1955.

UNIÓN NACIONAL DEMOCRÁTICA. *See* NATIONAL DEMOCRATIC UNION.

UNIÓN NACIONALISTA. *See* NATIONALIST UNION PARTY.

UNITED ACTION PARTY (PARTIDO DE ACCIÓN UNITARIA—PAU). *See* PROGRESSIVE ACTION PARTY.

Sergio G. Roca

DOMINICA

Dominica is a heavily forested, very mountainous island state, just 29 miles by 16 miles (290 square miles) in size. Although approximately half of its 80,000 population is under the age of sixteen, its 1989 per capita gross domestic product of U.S.$1,848 is in the middle strata among the member nations of the Organization of Eastern Caribbean States (OECS), trailing only Antigua, Saint Kitts-Nevis, and still-colonial Montserrat. Dominica, part of the Windward group of islands, is sandwiched between two French Overseas Departments, Martinique and Guadeloupe. Prior to the establishment of permanent British colonial control during the nineteenth century, Dominica experienced considerable French influence. The resultant French cultural "coloration" directly impacts eight of ten Dominicans today, according to Vera Green (1982), but includes the entire Dominican society if one considers such phenomena as dialect, legal practice, and tenant-landlord relations. Afro–West Indians dominate the Dominican population although the island also has scattered Europeans and Asians as well as one of the very few settlements of so-called black Caribs in the region.

Some Political History

As a sustained British colony for more than 150 years, Dominica experienced much the same colonization pattern established in other Commonwealth West Indian societies: elitist Crown governance in 1871; five elected council members after 1936; universal adult suffrage by 1951; home rule and Associate State status in 1967 (after two efforts to effect a federation had failed); and, finally, singular independence in 1978. All during this time, numerous efforts were made to confederate Dominica with other British colonies: in 1940, with the Leeward group of colonies; in 1956, with the Windward group. Compared with other Commonwealth Caribbean countries, Dominica was slow to develop political parties.

Personalities, Conflict, and Party Development

Three names and two parties have dominated the political development of Dominica in the modern era. The names are Edward Oliver LeBlanc, Patrick R. John, and Mary Eugenia Charles and the parties are those led by this trio: the Dominica Labour Party (DLP), under the leadership of LeBlanc and John, and the Dominica Freedom Party (DFP), founded and led by Charles. Conflict surrounds both the personalities and their parties. No other West Indian country in the post–World War II period, in fact, has experienced as much popular protest, shoot-outs between citizens and government, threatened coups, and even invasion threats made by U.S. klansmen, as has Dominica. Ironically, a relatively stable government has emerged from the dissonance, a government led by Eugenia Charles and her DFP.

As noted, political parties were slow to develop in Dominica. This island state was the last independent member of the insular Commonwealth Caribbean to have political parties control its government. There is no clear agreement among researchers as to specific dates of party development or data relating to early (prefederation) elections in Dominica. Vera Green, Charles Kunsman, and Patrick Emmanuel disagree on the founding date of the DLP, which they place between 1952 and 1955. Gary and Rosemary Brana-Shute place the date at 1984, but this obviously refers to the postinsurrection restructuring of the DLP. Most of the credit for organizing the DLP, however, goes to Phyllis Shand Allfrey, a Dominican-born white creole of Fabian socialist persuasion. Like many other party builders in the Commonwealth territories, Allfrey was recruited to Trinidad to hold a cabinet post in the federal government headed by Grantley Adams.

In the 1956 general election, just prior to the federal experiment, authors Vera Green and Charles Kunsman attribute three local parliamentary seats to the DLP, albeit the DLP still lost to the old-line independents. In 1961, the DLP secured its first majority, winning seven seats to four in the now-defunct Dominica United People's Party (DUPP). The party chairmanship went to Edward LeBlanc, under whose guidance the DLP also won the general election of 1966 (10 to 1). The following year LeBlanc became the island's first premier. The DLP's victorious pattern altered in 1970 when the party divided into two factions. LeBlanc's renegade faction, called the LeBlanc Labour Party, won eight seats to but one for the DLP and two for a new actor on the block, the DFP founded two years earlier by Eugenia Charles. After the election the LeBlanc faction and the DLP reunited.

In 1974 the increasingly hard-pressed LeBlanc resigned from parliament and resigned as chair of the DLP. His party post went to Patrick R. John, who led the DLP to a smashing comeback in the 1975 general election, winning sixteen seats to just two for independent candidates. John, thus, became Dominica's first prime minister. The John–DLP years in government would be turbulent.

Protest had already swept Dominica in the late 1960s. Charles was then in the forefront of organized protest against the Seditious and Undersirable Publication Act of Premier LeBlanc, which severely restricted civil liberties. Her opposition DFP, which won two seats in 1970, emerged out of this conflict. In 1974, as black power swept the Caribbean, harsh legislation, passed to forbid dreadlocks and to restrict civil liberties, contributed to rising protests.

Although more conservative than the typical West Indian leader, by June 1977 Charles had led her party into the Committee of National Salvation (CNS), a loose amalgam of opposition groups formed to defy the government of John, a government that was perceived to be both antilabor and antidemocratic. The DFP also led the opposition to the pending 1978 independence, fearing that John would capture the leadership reins of Dominica. Following independence in October 1978, the crisis intensified. The Dominican military opened fire on a CNS demonstration, killing three and producing major casualties. This led to a massive national strike and to loss of support for the ruling DLP and for John. An interim coalition government was established on 21 June 1979, following the displacement of Prime Minister John's government.

The Dominican electorate had now had enough. First a repressive LeBlanc, then an authoritarian John: The DLP must go. And go it did in the election of July 1980, which saw Charles's DFL capture seventeen of twenty-one seats. Charles's rule has not been without reaction. In 1983, as Chair of the OECS, she elicited considerable wrath from antimilitary youth for her stance as point person for the Reagan administration's military policy in the region, and for being the key legitimizer for Reagan's intervention in Grenada. But the worst negative has been the depressed economy. As *The Economist* notes, Dominica is still poor, and Dominicans gaze enviously at neighboring Antigua, Barbados, Martinique, and Guadeloupe. Many also consider Charles's DFP to be overly authoritarian. In the words of one Grenadian executive, "Why bug telephones in a country as open and gossip-ridden as Dominica?"

As it did throughout the OECS, the Grenada action benefited Charles overall. Her party won the 1985 election with sixteen seats to four for the DLP and one for the United Dominica Labour Party (UDLP). Although rising unemployment and growing unpopularity among youth drained away votes in the general election of 1990, Charles and the DFP once again were victorious, winning eleven seats to six for the United Workers Party and four for the reformed DLP. With the economy still lagging, and Charles not expected to remain in office for her full five-year term, there may be a better opportunity for opposition gains before the next election than there has been for more than a decade.

Bibliography

Gary Brana-Shute and Rosemary Brana-Shute. "The Organization of Eastern Caribbean States," in James M. Malloy and Eduardo A. Gamarra, ed., *Latin America and Caribbean Contemporary Record*, vol. 7, 1987–1988, B504–6. Holmes and Meier, New York, 1990.

————. "The Anglophone Eastern Caribbean and British Dependencies," in Abraham Lowenthal, ed., *Latin America and Caribbean Contemporary Record*, vol. 6, 1986–1987, B424–27. Holmes and Meier, New York, 1989.

"Dominica." *South America, Central America, and the Caribbean 1991*, 241. Europa Publications, Ltd., London, 1990.

Patrick A. M. Emmanuel. *General Elections in the Eastern Caribbean*. Letchworth Press, Ltd., for Institute of Social and Economic Research, University of the West Indies, Barbados, 1979.

Vera Green. "Dominica," in Robert J. Alexander, ed., *Political Parties of the Americas*, vol. 1, 345–51. Greenwood Press, Westport, Conn., 1982.

Percy C. Hintzen and W. Marvin Will. Biographies of Dominican political leaders in Robert J. Alexander, ed., *Biographical Dictionary of Latin American and Caribbean Political Leaders*, Greenwood Press, Westport, Conn., 1988.

Charles H. Kunsman, Jr. "The Orgins and Development of Political Parties in the British West Indies." Ph.D. diss., University of California, Berkeley, 1963.

"The Lady Goes on Ruling." *The Economist* 315, 2 June 1990, p. 42.

Political Parties—Active

DOMINICA FREEDOM PARTY (DFP). Mary Eugenia Charles formed the (DFP) in 1968 as a reaction against the anti–civil libertarian Seditious and Undesirable Publication Act of Premier Edward Oliver LeBlanc. The DFP won two seats in the 1970 general election, although Charles lost her bid for a seat. Charles, the party leader, did capture a seat in 1975 when the DFP won three seats and became the official opposition party. In June 1977, Charles led her party into the Committee of National Salvation (CNS), a loose amalgam of opposition groups that formed against the government of Patrick R. John, a regime that was perceived to be both antilabor and antidemocratic. The DFP also opposed the 1978 independence move. Charles kept the DFP out of the interim coalition government established on 21 June 1979, following the removal of Prime Minister John's government. This proved to be good strategy; the DFP won seventeen of twenty-one seats in the July 1980 election.

As chair of the Organization of Eastern Caribbean States, Charles became the prime legitimizer in the region for Reagan's intervention in Grenada in 1983. Charles and her party won the 1985 election, sixteen seats to four for the Dominica Labour Party and one seat for the United Dominica Labour Party. Although rising unemployment and growing unpopularity among the youth cost the DFP votes and five seats in the July 1990 general election, Charles and the DFP captured a five-seat plurality over the United Workers Party and a one-seat majority over the combined opposition.

Heading the government of a small, poor state in the shadow of the lone superpower presents inherent problems. As Charles once commented, when you are poor and small you have to learn to beg carefully. Her skills will be tested in the years ahead as the United States reduces its interest in the Caribbean and directs its gaze toward Eastern Europe and the Middle East.

DOMINICA LABOUR PARTY (DLP). The DLP was formed in 1955 through the efforts of Phyllis Shand Allfrey, a white creole Dominican whose clever use of patois helped her gain a large labor following. In the 1956 general election, according to Vera Green and Charles Kunsman, the DLP won three of the seven races it contested. Patrick Emmanuel doubts the accuracy of this account, however, and suggests the first DLP electoral contest may have been as late as 1961, by which time Edward Oliver LeBlanc had been selected party leader. Gary and Rosemary Brana-Shute (1989 and 1990) contend the DLP was founded in 1984, but obviously they are referring to the restructuring of the party subsequent to the excesses of Patrick R. John.

After weathering a split in the DLP in 1970 (see LeBlanc Labour Party), LeBlanc became premier of Dominica. He resigned that post in 1974 amd was succeeded by John. Conflict returned to the DLP during John's semiauthoritarian rule. Although he became the country's first prime minister following Dominican independence in 1978, John and his government were forced out of power in June 1979 when most of his DLP parliamentarians and ministers withdrew in the face of national protest. Following his ouster as prime minister, John was charged with a coup attempt, and he was implicated in the March 1981 attempted invasion of Dominica by lawless elements from the United States, including klansmen. John has only recently been released from prison.

John's government was replaced by an interim coalition led by Oliver Seraphine. The DLP was restructured in 1984 in an attempt to rekindle the reformist elements following the excesses and debacle of John's government. This restructuring took place under the leadership of Michael Douglas; Oliver Seraphine; Henry Dyer, a former Dominica Freedom Party (DFP) cabinet member; and, after 1988, Roosevelt "Rosie" Douglas. With four seats in parliament, the DLP was the official opposition party to the Charles–DFP government in the late 1980s. The DLP again took four seats in the July 1990 election but was displaced as the official opposition party by the United Workers Party, which captured six seats. The DLP, reformed or not, must act reformed and, most difficult of all, if it is to outlive the negative legacies of the Patrick John era, the voters must perceive that it has changed.

DOMINICA LIBERATION MOVEMENT ALLIANCE (DLMA). Founded in 1979 from the federation of four small leftist groups, the DLMA is led by Atherton Martin.

LABOUR PARTY OF DOMINICA (LPD). The LPD is led by former Prime Minister Patrick R. John, who was forced to resign as prime minister in 1979. (See Dominica Labour Party.)

UNITED WORKERS PARTY (UWP). The United Workers Party was formed in 1988. Edison James, who was a primary contributor to the founding of the UWP, is the current party leader. In the 28 May 1990 general election, the

UWP won six seats to become the official opposition party to the Eugenia Charles government. The UWP appears to have a good chance at closing the electoral gap by 1995.

Political Parties—Historical

ALL ISLAND INDUSTRIAL AND FARMERS PARTY (AIFP). The AIFP banner was put forth only in the 1961 general election, according to Patrick Emmanuel. Robert Douglas is listed as the AIFP leader.

CARIBBEAN FEDERAL LABOUR PARTY (CFLP). The CFLP fielded six candidates in the 1975 election and then faded from the scene.

DEMOCRATIC LABOUR PARTY (DLP). The DLP was founded in 1979 by former Dominica Labour Party members opposed to Patrick John. Its leader was former Prime Minister Oliver Seraphine. Since the restructuring of the Dominica Labour Party, many Democratic Labour Party members have returned to the fold. (*See* Dominica Labour Party.)

DOMINICA DEMOCRATIC PARTY (DDP). The DDP fielded candidates in only one electoral contest, the general election of 1961.

DOMINICA UNITED PEOPLE'S PARTY (DUPP). The DUPP, according to Patrick Emmanuel, was formed in 1958. Its leaders were R. H. Lockhart and Franklin Baron. The DUPP dissolved following the 1966 election.

LEBLANC LABOUR PARTY (LLP). According to Patrick Emmanuel, the LLP was really the LeBlanc faction of the Dominica Labour Party (DLP) that con-tested the general election of 1970. The DLP faction opposing Edward Oliver LeBlanc, led by W. S. Stevens and Nicholson Ducreay, was successful in winning control of the DLP but was unsuccessful electorally as the LLP captured eight seats. Following its sizeable electoral victory, the LLP team reassumed the DLP party label. (*See* Democratic Labour Party.)

PEASANT AND WORKERS MOVEMENT (PWM). The PWM is sometimes listed as a small electoral group that was formed to contest four constituencies in the 1961 general election. The PWM leader was Stafford Estrade.

PEOPLE'S DEMOCRATIC PARTY (PDP). The PDP, led by William Reviere, was a small but viable opposition party in 1979.

PROGRESSIVE LABOUR PARTY (PLP). The PLP was founded in 1975 and contested the election only in that year.

UNITED DOMINICA LABOUR PARTY (UDLP). The UDLP was apparently formed in 1984 as an attempt to rekindle the reformist elements of the Dominica Labour Party (DLP) following Patrick R. John's debacle. The original leaders were Michael Douglas and Oliver Seraphine. Gary and Rosemary Brana-Shute (in their 1989 and 1990 essays on Dominica) refer to this party simply as the Dominica Labour Party. (*See* Dominica Labour Party, especially portions relating to its history before 1978–1979.)

W. Marvin Will

DOMINICAN REPUBLIC

The Dominican Republic occupies the eastern two-thirds of the island of Hispaniola in the Caribbean Sea. Four major mountain ranges, running northwest to southeast, traverse the country, impairing communication but also forming the rims of several fertile valleys, chief of which is the Cibao in the north. The 1989 population estimates of the Dominican Republic yield the following information: total population, 7.1 million; population density, 146 per square kilometer (the country's area is 48,442 square kilometers or slightly more than 18,698 square miles); and population of Santo Domingo, the capital, 1.5 million. The country is overwhelmingly mulatto (between 60 and 73 percent); Spanish is the national language; and the estimated per capita income in 1985 was U.S. $1,809.

Hispaniola was discovered by Christopher Columbus on his first voyage to the New World and was kept under the rule of Spain until the French forced Spain to cede the western third of the island in the Treaty of Ryswick in 1697. This duality, resulting in the island being split into units representing different languages, cultures, and racial configurations, has persisted to this day. The French imported slaves into their third of the island (then called Saint-Dominique) and enjoyed notable commercial success, but their treatment of the slaves resulted in a slave revolt in 1791 which eventually drove the French out of Saint-Dominique. The new black-dominated nation, formed in 1804 and then called Haiti, eventually controlled the Spanish part of the island to the east and ruled from 1822 to 1844, at which time the Dominican Republic was formed by virtue of a successful revolt led, initially, by Juan Pablo Duarte, popularly known as the Father of the Dominican Republic.

The Dominican Republic has the unique tradition of having fought for its independence and sovereignty against a neighboring country (Haiti) on the same island. This fact is extremely important because it was the danger of Haitian reconquest that motivated the first Dominican presidents (Pedro Santana, Buenaventura Báez) to make overtures to major foreign powers for protection. As a result, the country reentered colonial status with Spain in 1861 (only to be overturned by the Dominicans' second independence struggle in 1865) and President Báez nearly succeeded in getting the Dominican Republic annexed to the United States, between 1869 and 1871.

The last third of the nineteenth century was a period of *el ciclo de colores* (the cycle of colors), in which the Reds (led by Báez and his supporters) and the Blues (nominally liberals led by Gregorio Luperón and his allies) alternated in the presidency. The last eighteen years of the century were dominated by dictator General Ulises Heureaux, whose corruption and repression would eventually be surpassed by those of Rafael Trujillo in the twentieth century. Opposition to Heureaux existed, but it was chiefly distilled down to two main factions: the Jimenista party of Juan Isidro Jiménez and the Horacista party of Horacio Vásquez. Heureaux's assassination in 1899 by Ramón Cáceres did not alleviate the problems of Dominican government, which descended to such a low point that U.S. President Theodore Roosevelt initiated a customs receivership in 1905, controlled by the United States. A short period of calm (1906–1911) under Cáceres as president was cut short by his assassination; once again, the United States sought to maintain order, this time with an occupation from 1916 to 1924. U.S. forces built roads, improved sanitation, extended America's already substantial financial control, and, significantly, created a Dominican-staffed constabulary to maintain order.

When the last U.S. forces left in 1924, a young Dominican officer, Rafael Trujillo, who had been quietly building a power base, eventually challenged Horacio Vásquez, who served as president until 1930. Trujillo's "election" as Dominican president in 1930 was a culmination of a sustained campaign of duplicity, fraud, and murder. From 1930 to 1961, Trujillo succeeded in establishing a government as nearly totalitarian as the country's technology, resources, and location would permit. To do this, he created several layers of secret police, more efficient forms of taxation, puppet presidents, effective lobbying to court U.S. support, nationalization (really "Trujilloization") of essential industries, and generous support of the military. Trujillo's 1961 assassination ushered in the "modern era" of Dominican politics. Many of the same figures politically active then are active today—men such as Joaquín Balaguer and Juan Bosch. The return of Bosch from exile eventually resulted in his election to the presidency in 1962. Bosch's democratic election did not, however, result in a long administration; a right-wing military coup removed him from office within seven months.

Agitation to reinstall Bosch, coupled with dissatisfaction with the triumvirate, headed by Donald Reid Cabral, which replaced him, led to open revolt in April 1965. Right-wing opposition to the rebellion was later buttressed by the United States, which eventually sent 20,000 troops to "maintain order." Bosch's return from his second exile was aborted at this time, although he was later a candidate for president, running against Joaquín Balaguer, a former puppet president under Trujillo and the recipient of a great deal of support from business and other conservative sectors. Balaguer was elected in 1966 and served three consecutive terms as president, ending in 1978, when Antonio Guzmán, representing the Dominican Revolutionary Party (PRD)—Bosch's party until he split from it in the early 1970s—won the presidency.

Guzmán's election marked a philosophical shift in policy toward more openness in the press, more respect for human rights, more professionalism in the military, and more tolerance of different political parties and stances. Unfortunately for Guzmán, increasing oil prices, falling sugar prices, heavier debt burdens, and difficulty in creating social reform programs spelled an economic crisis which alienated his supporters and provided political ammunition for his critics. Dismayed by evident corruption, budget inefficiency, an increase in the government bureaucracy from 80,839 employees in 1980 to 125,232 in 1981, ineptness in public affairs, and decreases in sugar production, many Dominican voters lost their enchantment with Guzmán's moderate approach and started to long for the prosperity of Balaguer's "Dominican Miracle" of 1966–1978, which had been largely fueled by rising sugar prices and massive U.S. aid. The election of 1982 (in which Guzmán promised not to run for reelection) pitted the new PRD candidate Salvador Jorge Blanco, a moderate-left lawyer, against the familiar Dominican veterans Balaguer, representing the Reformist Party (PR), and Bosch, then head of the Dominican Liberation Party (PLD).

Jorge's victory provided optimism for Dominicans who hoped that, finally, a way could be found to attain economic progress without the repression evident in Balaguer's previous administrations. In July 1982, one month before Jorge's inauguration, Guzmán, depressed over charges of corruption involving his government and members of his own family, committed suicide in the bathroom of his office in the National Palace. Perhaps influenced by this sobering event, new president Jorge Blanco, in his inaugural address, combined promises of more social reform and better efforts to help the unemployed with calls for austerity measures such as tax increases, pay freezes, oil conservation measures, and, significantly, appeals to the International Monetary Fund (IMF).

A 1983 agreement between the Dominican government and the IMF for a $599 million Extended Fund Facility, which would provide for a series of loans over a three-year period, called for a variety of austerity measures, chief of which were tax hikes, import restrictions, and peso devaluation. Disenchantment of the urban masses with the implementation of these actions erupted into street violence, the worst the country had seen since 1965 (the official death toll was 37, with 157 wounded and 4,358 arrested). Although the primary causes for the violence were economic, political reactions quickly occurred in the wake of the government's harsh suppression of the unrest. Opposing factions within Jorge's own PRD, as well as those of other parties, found more cause for criticism of the government.

Stung by this criticism, as well as by the downward spiral of an economy buffeted by falling sugar prices and a worsening balance of payments, the Dominican government was forced to reevaluate the IMF agreement. Its delay in completing the IMF guidelines brought the country to the point where it was on the verge of defaulting on a number of government loans. Only an emergency loan of $50 million by the United States aborted these defaults. On 23 January 1985, the government was also forced to abolish the artificial rate of exchange between the peso and the dollar.

Up to this point, the 1980s had seen the Dominican Republic dominated politically by the PRD, whose main figures were Guzmán, Jorge Blanco, José Francisco Peña Gómez, and Jacobo Majluta. The Reformist Party (which eventually came to be combined with the Social Christian Revolutionary Party to form the Social Christian Reformist Party), led by Balaguer, was second, and the PLD, led by Bosch, was a distant third. Although the PLD had not managed to attract a huge following in presidential elections, it was starting to make inroads in the municipal and congressional arenas.

The worsening Dominican economy, however, had changed the political scene. In 1978 the PRD itself, once seen as a beacon of hope by the Dominican masses, splintered into factions and, as the 1986 elections approached, the party, although managing to nominate Majluta, was not able to stave off the appearance of disunity. Opposing Majluta were Balaguer and Bosch, making the 1986 election one in which three ex-presidents were running against each other. Each candidate had his own calling card. Majluta was the standard-bearer of the established PRD, which had been in power for over eight years. Balaguer evoked days of prosperity, which coincided with his previous administrations. Bosch presented himself as a champion of the masses and a major opponent of excessive U.S. influence as well as IMF restrictions.

Again, although many other political parties participated in the 1986 elections, the contest came down to a battle among these three. The election was very close, and Majluta declared himself the winner in the early going. In the end, Balaguer's eventual victory was acknowledged by Majluta only when he was persuaded that Balaguer had more votes and that continued protest would not only be futile but damaging to the nation's image. Bosch received less than 20 percent of the total vote. His party, the PLD, was able to place two persons in the Senate (6.7 percent) and sixteen persons (13.3 percent) in the House of Representatives (Cámara de Diputados). Seventy percent of the Senate consisted of Reformist Party members (now called the Partido Reformista Social Cristiano—PRSC); 23.3 percent of the 30-person Senate consisted of PRD members. In the 120-person Cámara de Diputados, there was a more even split: 40 percent PRD and 46.66 percent PRSC. Clearly, Bosch's PLD had come up in electoral popularity, having gained only seven Diputado seats in 1982. Bosch had also gained less than 10 percent of the presidential vote in 1982. The PLD's progress as a party would be a harbinger of things to come.

When Balaguer returned to power in 1986, conditions in the Dominican Republic were markedly different than they had been in 1966, the year of Balaguer's first truly elected presidency. Gone were the days of abundant oil and high sugar prices. Moreover, knowledgeable insiders on the Dominican scene were aware that the portion of the electorate voting for Bosch took away votes primarily from Majluta's camp. This would mean, of course, that Balaguer's mandate was less than it would appear. True to form, Balaguer returned to the personal style of government that had marked his previous administrations. One difference between this administration and the one operating in the early 1970s was a reduction in politically inspired terrorism. Aside from that, Balaguer's leadership style seemed to be quite the same as before. One became accustomed to seeing public works projects advertised as *his* projects, new roads as *his* roads, new schools as *his* schools.

Thus Balaguer continued to rule and continued to confound those who had predicted his demise or retirement. One of those waiting for Balaguer's exit from the political scene was Fernando Alvarez Bogaert, a Reformist Party member who had been quietly building a power base from which to contend for the presidency. One of Balaguer's first acts in office was to have former Dominican president Jorge Blanco jailed for "crimes" committed as president (corruption). This provided a modicum of entertainment in the newspapers, but it did little to divert attention from pressing economic problems. In late 1987 and early 1988, the rate of exchange of the peso to the dollar was roughly five pesos to one dollar. By the summer of 1989, that rate rose to 6.35 pesos to the dollar, and, by early 1990, it approached ten pesos to the dollar.

To be sure, this situation was exacerbated by financial speculators, but this did little to console Dominican consumers buffeted by the high cost of living. This resulted in a number of strikes and projected strikes throughout the late 1980s, and the cry of *huelga* was never far from newspaper headlines. Ironically, the deteriorating economic situation did not strengthen the political parties opposed to Balaguer, but, instead, increased fragmentation occurred. The PRD became even more factionalized; Majluta eventually formed his own party.

As the 1990 election approached, all signs pointed to a more complicated political picture. Jorge Blanco was removed from the political scene, but Bosch, Balaguer, Majluta and Peña Gómez emerged as the main contenders for the Dominican presidency. Alvarez Bogaert, a younger PRSC leader, was derailed in his bid for the 1990 presidency by Balaguer's refusal to retire from Dominican politics.

In terms of political parties, Balaguer, as always, was the standard-bearer of the PRSC; Bosch represented the PLD. The once dominant PRD split into factions, and Majluta eventually left the PRD to form his own party, the Independent Revolutionary Party (PRI). Peña Gómez, meanwhile, remained in the PRD. The election eventually came down to a political test of strength between two veterans of Dominican politics, Bosch and Balaguer, who had, in one way or another, dominated the Dominican political scene for the previous thirty years.

As the final months and weeks counted down, each major candidate came out with various "polls" that announced his popularity—while the Dominican economy plummeted to new lows. None of the candidates seemed to offer viable solutions for the pressing economic problems affecting the Dominican Republic, although the upper classes and the U.S. Embassy seemed to prefer a continuation of the Balaguer regime. According to the Central Electoral Commission, Balaguer won the 1990 presidential election.

As in 1978, charges of vote fraud were leveled against Balaguer. Foreign news sources pointed to evidence of blatant miscounting of votes at various locations. The difference between 1990 and 1978 was the shift in attitude by the United States. Balaguer received little reprimand from the Republican administration of George Bush. Balaguer took office on 16 August 1990, and the economic situation continued to decline, with more numerous power shortages and higher prices on food. At the start of the 1990s, the Dominican political situation is far less promising than it was at the start of the 1980s. The population has increased such that the margin of error for Dominican politicians is much less. Moreover, there is substantial evidence of increased voter apathy in comparison to previous elections.

Nevertheless, no new political leaders capable of infusing new ideas and new approaches have been able to shoulder aside the veterans who were already old hands at Dominican politics when Rafael Trujillo was alive thirty years ago.

Bibliography

Jan Knippers Black. *The Dominican Republic: Politics and Development in an Unsovereign State*. Allen and Unwin, Boston, 1986.

Juan Bosch. *El partido: Concepción, organización y desarrollo*. 3d ed. Editora Alpha y Omega, Santo Domingo, 1988.

———. *The Unfinished Experiment: Democracy in the Dominican Republic*. Praeger, New York, 1964.

Julio G. Campillo Pérez. *Historia electoral dominicana 1848–1986* (El Grillo y el Ruiseñor; 4th ed.). Junta Central Electoral, Santo Domingo, 1986.

Robert D. Crassweller. *Trujillo: The Life and Times of a Caribbean Dictator*. Macmillan Co., New York, 1966.

Theodore Draper. *The Dominican Revolt: A Case Study in American Policy*. Commentary, New York, 1968.

César A. Franco. Director del Archivo Histórico de Santiago. Interviews, 25–29 June 1990 and 22 October 1990, in Santiago, Dominican Republic.

Franklin J. Franco. *Historia de las ideas políticas en la República Dominicana*. Editora Nacional, Santo Domingo, 1981.

Carlos María Gutiérrez. *The Dominican Republic: Rebellion and Repression*. Monthly Review Press, New York, 1972.

James R. Hodges. Investigative political reporter. Interview, 25–29 June 1990, in Santiago, Dominican Republic.

Hoy (daily newspaper), 14 July 1990.

La Información (daily newspaper), 16 May 1990.

Michael J. Kryzanek and Howard J. Wiarda. *The Politics of External Influence in the Dominican Republic*. Praeger, New York, 1988.

El Nacional (daily newspaper), 20 May 1990.

Table 1
Elected Presidents by Party, 1963 to the Present

President and Party	Term	Votes Won
Juan Bosch, PRD	27 February 1963- 25 September 1963	619,491 out of 1,027,220 cast
Joaquín Balaguer, PR	1 July 1966- 16 August 1970	759,887 out of 1,315,124 cast
Joaquín Balaguer, PR	16 August 1970- 16 August 1974	653,565 out of 1,238,205 cast
Joaquín Balaguer, PR	16 August 1974- 16 August 1978	942,726 out of 1,113,419 cast
Antonio Guzmán, PRD	16 August 1978- 4 July 1982	856,084 out of 1,655,807 cast
Jorge Blanco, PRD	16 August 1982- 16 August 1986	854,868 out of 1,922,367 cast
Joaquín Balaguer, PR	16 August 1986- 16 August 1990	855,563 out of 2,189,515 cast
Joaquín Balaguer, PR	16 August 1990- present	678,065 out of 1,933,921 cast

William Javier Nelson. *Almost a Territory: America's Attempt to Annex the Dominican Republic.* University of Delaware Press, Newark, 1990.

Pan American General Secretary, Organization of American States, Department of Public Instruction, Pan American Union, Washington, D.C. 21 vols. *The Dominican Republic* (vol. 8), 1964.

Valentina Peguero and Danilo de los Santos. *Visión general de la historia dominicana.* Editora Taller, Santo Domingo, 1981.

El Siglo (daily newspaper), 12 May 1990.

Howard J. Wiarda and Michael J. Kryzanek. *The Dominican Republic: A Caribbean Crucible.* Westview Press, Boulder, Colo., 1982.

Political Parties—Active

CHRISTIAN POPULAR PARTY (PARTIDO POPULAR CRISTIANO—PPC). The PPC was formed in early September 1981 in response to the differences within the Social Christian Revolutionary Party (PRSC). It was recognized by the Junta Central Electoral (JCE) on 16 March 1982. In 1986, it supported

Table 2
Congressional Control by Party, 1962 to the Present (The Domination of Three Parties)

	1962	1966	1970	1974	1978	1982	1986	1990
PRD								
Senators:	22	5	- -	- -	11	17	7	2
Deputies:	49	26	- -	- -	48	62	48	33
PR/PRSC								
Senators:	- -	22	21	23	16	10	21	16
Deputies:	- -	48	45	75	43	50	56	41
PLD								
Senators:	- -	- -	- -	- -	- -	- -	2	12
Deputies:	- -	- -	- -	- -	- -	7	16	44
TOTALS								
Senators:	22	27	21	23	27	27	30	30
Deputies:	49	74	45	75	91	119	120	118
TOTAL # SEATS								
Senate:	27	27	27	27	27	27	30	30
Chamber:	74	74	74	91	91	120	120	120
3-PARTY DOMINATION BY PERCENTAGE								
Senate:	81	100	78	85	100	100	100	100
Chamber:	62	100	60	82	100	99	100	98

Jacobo Majluta, of the Dominican Revolutionary Party, contributing 5,055 votes. It is one of the parties that formed a consortium—Group of Emerging Parties [Grupo de Partidos Emergentes (GPE)]—which supported the presidential candidacy of Roberto Saladín, former head of the Central Bank (Banco Central de la República Dominicana), in the 1990 election. Saladín finished with 4,338 votes.

COMMUNIST PARTY OF THE DOMINICAN REPUBLIC (PARTIDO COMUNISTA DE LA REPÚBLICA DOMINICANA—PACOREDO). The PACOREDO was formed in 1966 by Luis Adolfo ("Pin") Montás, who was director of the young student branch of the Fourteenth of June Movement. In its sixty-page declaration of principles, fifty-seven pages are devoted to expounding the Communist thesis of Mao Tse-Tung and attacking "Soviet Revisionists," as well as explaining motives for the organization's founding. The declaration laid down the guidelines for Communist struggle and castigated the Dominican Communist Party as a tool of the bourgeoisie and North American imperialism.

In the 1990 elections, its founder, Pin Montás, ran for president, gaining 1,886 votes.

CONSTITUTIONAL ACTION PARTY (PARTIDO ACCIÓN CONSTITUCIONAL—PAC). The PAC was founded in the first weeks of April 1965 by Dr. Angel Severo Cabral, with some former members of the National Civic Union. After a long period of absence from participating in presidential elections, the PAC supported Jacobo Majluta in 1986 and offered its own candidate, José Rafael Abinader, in 1990, who obtained 4,926 votes.

DEMOCRATIC INTEGRATION MOVEMENT (MOVIMIENTO DE INTEGRACIÓN DEMOCRÁTICA—MIDA). The MIDA was founded in the last months of 1969 by Francisco Augusto Lora, who had been vice president of the republic in the Balaguer administration commencing in 1966 and was becoming a principal government casualty. The party, recognized on 13 January 1970, nominated Lora as a presidential candidate for the 1970 elections. The ballot color is red and white with a yellow stripe on the left side. In 1978, the MIDA once again offered Lora as a presidential candidate; he gained 13,400 votes. In 1982 Lora ran again; this time he gained fewer votes (7,066), less than the 5 percent required for the MIDA to continue as a political party.

DEMOCRATIC QUISQUEYAN PARTY (PARTIDO QUISQUEYANO DEMÓCRATA—PQD). Founded in 1967 by General Elías Wessin y Wessin, the PQD was recognized by the Junta Central Electoral on 19 January 1968. It made its first appearance in the 1970 general elections with Wessin y Wessin as its presidential candidate, who received 168,751 votes. Its symbol consists of outstretched hands over a map of the Domincan Republic; the color of the ballot is yellow with gray borders. Although its influence has been marginal over the years, its conservative stance provided some support for Joaquín Balaguer's election in 1990. The party leaders are Elías Wessin Chávez, Pedro Bergés Vargas, and Lorenzo Valdéz Carrasco.

DOMINICAN COMMUNIST PARTY (PARTIDO COMUNISTA DOMINICANO—PCD). The defeat of the democratic forces in the Spanish Civil War led to a large immigration of Republican Spaniards to Santo Domingo, which commenced during the last months of 1939, at the height of Rafael Trujillo's dictatorship. This flow continued in subsequent years and formed the important nucleus of intellectuals and Communist functionaries. This nucleus, with unique experience and orientation, breathed life into the moribund sector of Dominican Marxists and forged, in 1942, the first entity of Dominican Marxist philosophy: the Dominican Democratic Revolutionary Party, from which later appeared the Popular Socialist Party (PSP), in 1946, which, in turn, gave birth to the Dominican Communist Party in the last months of 1964.

The PSP defined as their central objective the construction of a socialist society in the Dominican context. The axis of their propaganda revolved around the struggle for liberty and democracy—against the Trujillo regime. This last fact, together with the reality that the Socialists had the only organization opposed to Trujillo, greatly helped their popularity, especially among the youth of the middle class and among university intellectuals. As a result, the Democratic Youth (Juventud Democrática) organization was formed.

As this sentiment grew, the Trujillo regime was forced to take the Socialists seriously (as a threat), and a strategy was formed which included, first, a legalization of their organization on 15 March 1946. This decree had the effect of luring the leaders from the underground into the public eye and from there it was relatively simple to order their elimination.

The PSP accepted the challenge and, on 1 July 1946, published in the newspaper La Opinion a declaration of its purposes. This game lasted a short while; some public acts and some written releases were made against a backdrop of repression that worsened day by day. This situation was exacerbated by the development of the cold war between the United States and the Soviet Union. Finally, on 4 June 1947, Trujillo promulgated a law that prohibited any Communist activities.

Many Socialists were either driven into exile or killed in the ensuing months and years. Many Socialist leaders did not return to the Dominican Republic until after the death of Trujillo.

Between 1961 and 1965, Socialist influence was weak and its growth was scant. Confined to a small sector of the population, it never really penetrated the ranks of the masses. As a result, Socialists devoted much of their efforts to infiltrating various political, cultural, and student organizations.

During the 1962 elections, of the three Marxist groups, only the PSP adopted a realistic position; ironically, due to sparse membership, it was not allowed to compete in the elections.

Although the United States sent troops to the Dominican Republic in 1965, partly out of a fear of Communism, the PCD has been only a negligible force in Dominican national elections. It abstained from participating in the 1966, 1970, and 1974 presidential elections, but it surfaced again as a political party in the 1978, 1982, and 1986 presidential elections, each time with Narciso Isa Conde as the presidential candidate. In 1990, Isa Conde called for abstention of the PCD from the presidential elections.

DOMINICAN DEMOCRATIC REVOLUTIONARY PARTY (PARTIDO DEMOCRÁTICO REVOLUCIONARIO DOMINICANO—PDRD). See DOMINICAN COMMUNIST PARTY.

DOMINICAN LIBERATION PARTY (PARTIDO DE LA LIBERACIÓN DOMINICANA—PLD). Founded on 15 December 1973 by Juan Bosch, the party, which possesses an organization which highly corresponds to the philosophies of Bosch, is an outgrowth of Bosch's new political direction after his return to the Dominican Republic in 1970. Bosch, convinced that the integrity of the Dominican Revolutionary Party (PRD) was compromised in the wake of the upsurge in right-wing terrorism in the Dominican Republic in the early 1970s, decided to modify the political stance of the PRD (which he had also founded in 1939).

After the guerilla landing of Colonel Francisco Alberto Caamaño Deñó in February 1973, the differences between Juan Bosch and José Francisco Peña Gómez publically heightened and soon became irreconcilable. Thus, the struggle against the authoritarian Balaguer administration experienced a notable split.

Bosch accused the PRD of betraying the masses and, in December 1973, renounced the PRD. His departure was quickly followed by almost all the members of the party's permanent commission (Comisión Permanente). Twenty-seven days later, Bosch announced the formation of the PLD, which he used as a vehicle for his new political and organizational ideas.

Choosing as its theme national liberation, the new party abstained from participating in the 1974 elections. For the PLD, the 1974 elections were an "electoral slaughterhouse" which had no social, political, or economic relevance for the Dominican people. Four years later, the PLD decided, nevertheless, to take part in the elections, nominating as presidential and vice presidential candidates Bosch and Rafaél Albuquerque, respectively. The party tried to mobilize the voting public around the theme of the party.

The PLD growth has been steady. From 17,000 votes in 1978, the party gained more than 387,000 votes in 1986. In the elections of 1990, the PLD, with Bosch as a presidential candidate, lost a close election to Joaquín Balaguer, who was running as a member of the Social Christian Reformist Party. Bosch gained 653,595 votes to Balaguer's 678,065 votes.

DOMINICAN REVOLUTIONARY PARTY (PARTIDO REVOLUCIONA-RIO DOMINICANO—PRD). The PRD was founded in 1939 by Juan Bosch, who was at that time in exile from the Dominican Republic. From the first, it was a party of national democracy and liberation. The PRD, with the arrival in the Dominican Republic of leaders Juan Bosch, Angel Miolán, Ramón A. Castillo, and Nicolás Silfa, after the assassination of Rafael Trujillo in 1961, took upon itself the task of reeducating Dominicans for democratic participation in government.

The PRD, upon return from exile, was recognized on 22 March 1962. Its leader at that time was Bosch. In the 20 December 1962 general elections, Bosch ran for president of the republic on the PRD ticket with Dr. Segundo Armando González Tamayo as his running mate (the ballot color is white).

The PRD won the presidency. Bosch garnered over 600,000 votes; his opponent, Dr. Viriato Fiallo of the National Civic Union, won 317,327 votes (60 percent to 30 percent of the total votes cast). The Junta Central Electoral declared Bosch the winner on 22 January 1963. The PRD also picked up twenty-two of twenty-seven seats in the Senate and forty-nine of seventy-four representative seats in Congress.

On 25 September 1963, Bosch was removed from office in a military coup; however, his supporters called for his return in 1965, which resulted in the civil war of April 1965.

In the general elections held in June 1966, Bosch was once again the candidate for president. Although he lost to Joaquín Balaguer, he nevertheless gained almost 40 percent of the vote while waging a campaign in which he rarely left his house.

Throughout the years, the PRD has undergone fragmentation due to the different orientations of its leaders. After the civil war of 1965, the PRD became divided between the followers of Bosch (who himself had become more radical in the years after the civil war) and Bosch's opponents. Bosch, postulating the theme "dictatorship with popular backing" fell out of step with other PRD leaders, although many of Bosch's ideas were fairly progressive for that time. Receiving little support for his thesis from the PRD, Bosch abandoned the PRD and eventually formed the Dominican Liberation Party (PLD) in 1973.

Upon Bosch's departure, José Francisco Peña Gómez, who assumed the mantle of PRD leadership, purged the PRD of most vestiges of Bosch's philosophies. To this end, Peña Gómez postulated his aims of a "national democratic revolution," with the necessity of a class alliance, in a pamphlet published by the PRD Department of Education, presumably in 1975.

Peña Gómez's participation in the International Socialist Congress, held in Geneva, Switzerland, in 1976, oriented the PRD more to ideologies held by organizations in attendance—these included working toward societies in which all people could develop their economic, cultural, and political potential in an atmosphere of liberty.

The acceptance of the social democratic philosophy (deeply rooted in the Christian ethic) by the PRD led to some shifts in political strategy, which included such things as advocating restructuring of relationships with foreign-based companies in the Dominican Republic as opposed to nationalization. Nevertheless, so as not to lose sight of the economic and social problems (unemployment, standard of living, and so on) affecting the country, the PRD decided to maintain emphasis on the idea of "revolution," a significant part of the PRD's standard.

Although the PRD was successful in capturing the presidency in 1978 and 1982, with Antonio Guzmán and Salvador Jorge Blanco, respectively, the rosy Dominican future envisioned by Peña Gómez failed to materialize, as the country was racked by plummeting sugar prices, high energy costs, and an uncertain global order. As a result, the PRD has become increasingly factionalized in recent years. It lost the 1986 elections after major intraparty squabbles and, finally, splintered so much that it finished behind both the Social Christian

Reformist Party and the PLD in the 1990 general elections. Its candidate, Peña Gómez, gained 449,399 votes.

FUERZA NACIONAL PROGRESISTA. *See* PROGRESSIVE NATIONAL FORCE.

INDEPENDENT REVOLUTIONARY PARTY (PARTIDO REVOLUCION-ARIO INDEPENDIENTE—PRI). The PRI was founded by Jacobo Majluta in 1989 after an intraparty dispute with a fellow member of the Dominican Revolutionary Party, José Francisco Peña Gómez; its followers are chiefly supporters of Majluta. The PRI participated in the 1990 presidential elections, with Majluta as its presidential candidate, who obtained 135,649 votes. It also offered candidates for congressional and regional offices, placing one representative in the House.

MOVIMIENTO DE INTEGRACIÓN DEMOCRÁTICA. *See* DEMOCRATIC INTEGRATION MOVEMENT.

NATIONAL ACTION PARTY (PARTIDO ACCIÓN NACIONAL—PAN). Founded in 1980 by General Neit Rafael Nivar Seijas, it participated in the 1982 presidential elections but garnered only 3,702 votes and thereby lost its eligibility. It declined after its founder's death a few years later.

PARTIDO ACCIÓN CONSTITUCIONAL. *See* CONSTITUTIONAL ACTION PARTY.

PARTIDO ACCIÓN NACIONAL. *See* NATIONAL ACTION PARTY.

PARTIDO ALIANZA SOCIAL DEMÓCRATA. *See* SOCIAL DEMOCRATIC ALLIANCE PARTY.

PARTIDO COMUNISTA DE LA REPÚBLICA DOMINICANA. *See* COMMUNIST PARTY OF THE DOMINICAN REPUBLIC.

PARTIDO COMUNISTA DOMINICANO. *See* DOMINICAN COMMUNIST PARTY.

PARTIDO DE LA LIBERACIÓN DOMINICANA. *See* DOMINICAN LIBERATION PARTY.

PARTIDO DEMOCRÁTICO REVOLUCIONARIO DOMINICANO. *See* DOMINICAN COMMUNIST PARTY.

PARTIDO POPULAR CRISTIANO (PPC). *See* CHRISTIAN POPULAR PARTY.

PARTIDO QUISQUEYANO DEMÓCRATA. *See* DEMOCRATIC QUIS-QUEYAN PARTY.

PARTIDO REFORMISTA. *See* SOCIAL CHRISTIAN REFORMIST PARTY.

PARTIDO REFORMISTA SOCIAL CRISTIANO. *See* SOCIAL CHRISTIAN REFORMIST PARTY.

PARTIDO REVOLUCIONARIO DOMINICANO. *See* DOMINICAN REV-OLUTIONARY PARTY.

PARTIDO REVOLUCIONARIO INDEPENDIENTE. *See* INDEPENDENT REVOLUTIONARY PARTY.

PARTIDO REVOLUCIONARIO SOCIAL CRISTIANO. *See* SOCIAL CHRISTIAN REVOLUTIONARY PARTY.

PARTIDO SOCIALISTA POPULAR. *See* DOMINICAN COMMUNIST PARTY.

POPULAR SOCIALIST PARTY. *See* DOMINICAN COMMUNIST PARTY.

PROGRESSIVE NATIONAL FORCE (FUERZA NACIONAL PROGRES-ISTA—FNP). The founding of the FNP, on 6 July 1980, with the motto "Peace, Justice, Liberty," by Marino Vinicio Castillo (Vincho), was regarded by many as Castillo's declaration of independence from Joaquín Balaguer. The party participated in general elections for the first time in 1982, with Castillo as a presidential candidate. Nevertheless, since the FNP had been recognized by the Junta Central Electoral only two months before, its impact was negligible. In 1986, with Castillo running as a presidential candidate for the second time, the FNP gained 6,684 votes, equivalent to 0.32 percent of those registered. In the 16 May 1990 election, Castillo again ran, this time seeking backing from the poor, the peasants, and all Dominicans "who hoped for a decent future." To this end, Castillo promised a more even distribution of wealth by way of agri-cultural reform. For Castillo, this constituted a basic, fundamental structural change. The FNP proposed to more fully integrate the various sectors of Do-minican society, to stimulate production, to combat narcotics traffickers, to fight against corruption, and to improve sanitation. These perspectives were not enough to significantly improve the FNP's performance over 1986.

REFORMIST PARTY (PARTIDO REFORMISTA—PR). *See* SOCIAL CHRISTIAN REFORMIST PARTY.

SOCIAL CHRISTIAN REFORMIST PARTY (PARTIDO REFORMISTA SO-CIAL CRISTIANO—PRSC). Formed in 1964 by Dr. Joaquín Balaguer in San Juan, Puerto Rico, it was recognized as the Reformist Party (PR) by the Junta Central Electoral on 20 April 1964. From its inception, the Reformist Party was the beneficiary of political and social forces affected in various degress by Trujilloism. The leadership of Balaguer established a political vehicle for those elements of Dominican society which had benefited from the dictatorship, as well as newer conservative groups.

The Reformist Party, which has been relatively vague in terms of its ideology or doctrine, conformed mostly to the dictates of Balaguer during his long political life. In 1966, with U.S. troops occupying Dominican territory, Balaguer and the Reformist Party won the presidential elections over Juan Bosch and the Dominican Revolutionary Party (PRD).

Presenting himself as a standard-bearer of a "revolution without blood," Balaguer had garnered the majority of the votes of women and peasants, important sectors in a society primarily rural. The Reformist Party experienced success in the 1968 municipal elections and returned to power in the presidential elections of 1970 and 1974, both times with Balaguer as its presidential candidate. The PRD beat the Reformist Party in the 1978 presidential elections, after twelve years of Reformist administration.

Balaguer's "revolution without blood" resulted in presidential administrations which witnessed the disappearance and deaths of more than 2,000 persons as well as hundreds of deportations and countless other outrages and violations of human rights. These abuses would not be forgotten by the Dominican people in the 1978 elections.

In 1979, Balaguer unveiled his intentions of fusing the Reformist Party with the Social Christian philosophy. To this end, he undertook discussions with the heads of the Venezuelan Social Christian Party (COPEI).

Six years later, in 1985, the Reformists fused with the Social Christian Revolutionary Party (PRSC), changed its name to the Social Christian Reformist Party (also PRSC), and adopted more of the Social Christian ideology.

The degree of adoption of this ideology is to be considered relative, however. Dominated by the personality of its leader, Balaguer, the new PRSC has been notably lacking in a stable, political philosophy, other than to say that Balaguer possesses a certain conservatism.

Although members of the old Social Christian Revolutionary Party have occupied positions in the new PRSC after the fusion, their influence has not been comparable to that which they had exercised in the old organization.

Balaguer, nominated by the new PRSC, ran for president of the republic in 1986 and won over Jacobo Majluta of the PRD. The new PRSC also dominated both houses of Congress. In 1990, after a steady rise in popularity, the Dominican Liberation Party, with Juan Bosch as its presidential candidate, lost to Balaguer and the PRSC in a close election.

SOCIAL CHRISTIAN REVOLUTIONARY PARTY (PARTIDO REVOLU-CIONARIO SOCIAL CRISTIANO—PRSC). The PRSC was founded in 1962 by a group of exiles who had been in contact with progressive ideas and phi-losophies of countries more advanced than the Dominican Republic. These men were able to become acquainted with new ideas that had been circulating around the world, especially ideas that touched on economic and social reform, with special attention to the dispossessed classes.

The party was recognized on 15 June 1962 at the request of Mario Read Vittini, Victor Hidalgo Justo, Alfonso Moreno Martínez, Luis E. Martínez, and Caonabo Javier Castillo. The PRSC took part in the 1962 elections and gained a total of 56,794 votes. Its presidential and vice presidential candidates were Alfonso Moreno Martínez and Josefina Padilla Viuda Sánchez, respectively. The ballot color was green and the party's symbol was the machete.

In the 1966 elections, the PRSC supported Juan Bosch and Antonio Guzmán of the Dominican Revolutionary Party and contributed 30,660 votes.

The PRSC participated in the 1970 and 1978 presidential elections. Its can-didate in 1970, Moreno Martínez, obtained 63,697 votes. Its candidate in 1978, Jorge Alfonso Lockward Pérez, gained only 7,981 votes, thereby losing party elegibility for electoral participation. In 1985 the party merged with the Re-formist Party (Partido Reformista) and took the name of the Social Christian Reformist Party (Partido Reformista Social Cristiano).

SOCIAL DEMOCRATIC ALLIANCE PARTY (PARTIDO ALIANZA SO-CIAL DEMÓCRATA—ASD). Founded by Dr. Juan Isidro Jiménez Grullón upon his return to the Dominican Republic from exile in 1961, the party was recognized on 19 September 1962. Its leader was Jiménez Grullón; its ballot color was yellow-gold; and its candidate for president of the republic was Jiménez Grullón, who was an eloquent orator and a favorite of intellectuals. Jiménez Grullón was the author of the phrase "lend me your vote, my brother" (prestame tu voto, hermano). The party gained 17,898 votes. Its influence waned after-ward, and it swung its support in favor of the Dominican Revolutionary Party in the 1978 elections. In 1982, it participated in the national elections and gained 9,208 votes.

Political Parties—Historical

ACCIÓN DOMINICANA INDEPENDIENTE. See INDEPENDENT DOMIN-ICAN ACTION.

AGRUPACIÓN POLÍTICA 14 DE JUNIO. See FOURTEENTH OF JUNE MOVEMENT.

AUTHENTIC DOMINICAN REVOLUTIONARY PARTY (PARTIDO RE-VOLUCIONARIO DOMINICANO AUTÉNTICO—PRDA). Founded by Nicolás Silfa as president and Dr. Rafael E. Ruíz Mejía as secretary, the PRDA gained 5,306 votes in the 20 December 1962 election but did not offer presidential or vice presidential candidates. As in the case of the Christian Democratic Progressive Party, it was founded by dissident leaders of the Dominican Revolutionary Party. It was recognized by the Junta Central Electoral on 7 July 1962 (provisional). Its president was listed as Silfa; its ballot color was white with a yellow border. The party offered only congressional candidates in some provinces.

CHRISTIAN DEMOCRATIC PROGRESSIVE PARTY (PARTIDO PRO-GRESISTA DEMÓCRATA CRISTIANO—PPDC). As in the case of the Authentic Dominican Revolutionary Party, the PPDC was founded by Dominican Revolutionary Party dissidents in 1962. It was provisionally recognized by decree on 8 April 1966, but it did not offer a candidate for that election; instead, the PPDC supported Joaquín Balaguer. In the Dominican Republic, candidates may be supported by more than one party. The color of the ballot was green and white with yellow borders.

DEMOCRATIC FRONT PARTY (PARTIDO FRENTE DEMOCRÁTICO—PFD). Formed in 1962, the party had a short life. It took the philosophy of Julio F. Peynado, son of Francisco J. Peynado, presidential candidate in 1924. Julio F. Peynado originally accepted the mantle of leadership, but he was later dissuaded as a result of political opposition, which very much influenced him to keep political activity at a distance.

DEMOCRATIC REVOLUTIONARY NATIONALISTIC PARTY (PARTIDO NACIONALISTA REVOLUCIONARIO DEMOCRÁTICO—PNRD). Founded by General Miguel Angel Ramírez Alcántara, the party supported Virgilio Mainardi Reyna, who obtained 36,764 votes, in the elections held on 20 December 1962.

The PNRD was recognized by the Junta Central Electoral on 15 June 1962. The party's president was Ramírez Alcántara; its ballot color was rose; its presidential candidate was, of course, Mainardi Reyna. The PNRD elected one senator and four representatives in that election.

In the June 1966 elections, the party offered Rafael F. Bonnelly (who was also a candidate for other political parties) as a presidential candidate, but it failed to gain enough votes (5 percent) for continued recognition as a political party. It also failed to place anyone in either legislative house.

DOMINICAN PARTY (PARTIDO DOMINICANO—PD). The impetus for the PD, founded on 16 August 1931, came from a group of Trujilloists, including Mario Fermín Cabral, Augusto Chotin, Rafael Vidal, Teófilo Piña Chevalier, and Manuel de Jesús Castillo. The movement began with a proclamation from the Main Committee of the Provisional Directorate, organizer of Rafael Trujillo's party, which plainly stated the type of party to be formed. On 11 May 1932, the party was registered officially with the Junta Central Electoral. The director of the PD was Rafael Trujillo, and the executive director was Fermín Cabral. From 1932 until 1961, the Dominican Party was the only party recognized in the Dominican Republic. The PD altered the entire Dominican political scene.

The mandate of the Dominican Party was to suppress all forms of political opposition to Trujillo. It was also the civil mechanism by which Trujillo ran for "election." In addition, the party served as a spy network, ferreting out various enemies of Trujillo. Cited in the constitution as the "agent of civilization for the Dominican people," the party also served as a backdrop for a series of "cultural acts," "conferences," "tributes," "patriotic celebrations," "recitals," and so on, designed to eulogize (often to the point of nausea) the virtues of Trujillo and those of his ancestors and relatives. Intellectuals and other public figures were forced to concur with these activities. The party thus provided an excellent vehicle by which various sycophants were able to ingratiate themselves with Trujillo. Curiously, the initials of the party's motto—Rectitude, Liberty, Work (trabajo), and Morality—were also the initials of Trujillo: Rafael Leónidas Trujillo Molina.

The Dominican Party was intricately connected with all phases of Dominican government. It was the instrument of maintenance of Trujillo's regime. As such, the party had no real political philosophy, no doctrine, and no set of predetermined principles. All depended on the whim of Trujillo. Nevertheless, Trujillo cleverly exploited past prejudices and ideologies to serve his purposes. In this way, Trujillo could also pose as a deliverer of the Dominican people. In the restricted world of Dominican politics, the Dominican Party used anti-Communism as a pretext to present Trujillo as a defender of democracy.

The military nature of the Dominican Party was reflected by its composition of active military personnel and various forms of Trujilloists. Its funding was provided by a tax levied on all public employees, as well as by other levies. Its organization consisted of a central seat and various branches in all parts of the country.

The most potent symbol of the Dominican Party was the identification card (containing a design of a small palm), which had more political and military value than any other.

The Dominican Party was not a typical and traditional party of the liberal gentry; rather, it was a manifestation of a fascist dictatorship which negated any form of democracy. Ultimately, the party was simply one of the bulwarks of Trujillo's regime. Both legislative chambers were composed of members of the Dominican Party only, and their function was to provide a rubber stamp for Trujillo's policies.

Upon Trujillo's death, the Dominican Party was dismantled, as a result of public pressure. At first, Trujilloists tried to maintain the party, but strong anti-

Trujillo public sentiment, as well as weakness on the part of those who would continue Trujillo's policies, spelled the end of the Dominican Party. Under the weight of this reality, the DP was dissolved on 28 December 1961, in an extraordinary national assembly.

DOMINICAN POPULAR MOVEMENT (MOVIMIENTO POPULAR DOM-INICANO—MPD). The MPD was founded in the first months of 1956 in Havana, Cuba, by Pablo Antonio Martínez, Andrés Ramos Paguero, Máximo López Molina, Julio César Martínez, and other associates.

Pablo Martínez and López Molina had been militants in exile with the Popular Socialist Party (PSP) (see Political Parties—Active) and, in those days of general demoralization during exile, were expelled from the PSP after questioning the orientation and apparent indecisiveness of the PSP against Trujillo.

An article published by Pablo Martínez a few months after the founding of the MPD, "Lucha Interna o Trujillo Siempre" (internal struggle or Trujillo always), crystallized the difference between those expelled Marxists and the direction of the PSP.

In line with the ideas expressed in the article, the leaders of the MPD decided to return to Santo Domingo in 1960 to organize against Trujillo. The results were the same as the results in 1946–1947 with the PSP: Trujillo permitted the MPD to exist legally for several months; lured its leaders out of hiding; and then imprisoned, tortured, or assassinated them, just when they were beginning to make inroads into the masses.

After Trujillo's death, remaining MPD members, who had entered the country in 1960, combined with certain middle-class intellectuals. The party gained support among poor students, unemployed urban dwellers, and marginal communities. Their influence among the working class was very small, although it was better than that of the PSP, inasmuch as they portrayed themselves in Communist circles as the party of the working class.

The MPD was greatly strengthened in December 1966 when a substantial group of leaders from the Fourteenth of June Movement—including Rafael (Fafa) Taveras, Guido Gil, Moisés Blanco Genao, Manuel ("Lucky") Pozo, Pedro Bonilla, and Amín Abel Hasbún—entered the fold.

The party's influence had largely disappeared in the 1970s, however, even though it sought, unsuccessfully, to gain legal recognition for the 1978 elections. Its role in the 1980s has been mostly confined to agitation and infiltration of other organizations.

DOMINICAN REVOLUTIONARY VANGUARD PARTY (PARTIDO VANGUARDIA REVOLUCIONARIA DOMINICANA—PVRD). The PVRD was founded by Horacio Julio Ornes Coiscou. Although he at first declined to be a presidential candidate, he changed his stance when the PVRD slated candidates for certain provincial offices. The party was recognized on 15 June 1962; its ballot color was white with green and red borders; and its presidential candidate was Ornes Coiscou, who gained 6,886 votes. It eventually swung its support in favor of the Dominican Revolutionary Party.

EVOLUTIONARY LIBERAL PARTY (PARTIDO LIBERAL EVOLUCIONISTA—PLE). The party was formed on 21 November 1963 by Luis Amiama Tió. On 10 April 1966, the party proclaimed as its presidential candidate Rafael F. Bonnelly, who had been heading a group called the National Integration Movement, in which he had had aspirations as a presidential candidate. In the party assembly, Dr. Tabaré Alvarez Pereyra was chosen to be Bonnelly's running mate. Eventually, Alvarez Pereyra declined the place on the ticket, and the party took another direction as it swung its support in favor of the Reformist Party ticket of Joaquín Balaguer and Francisco Augusto Lora.

FOURTEENTH OF JUNE MOVEMENT (AGRUPACIÓN POLÍTICA 14 DE JUNIO—1J4). The principal anti-Trujillo movement, the 1J4 took its name from the romantic example of the guerilla movement, when a small but potentially dangerous group of guerillas, supported by Fidel Castro, invaded the Dominican Republic on 14 June 1959. Many Dominican youths were influenced not only by simplistic, stereotypical images but also by the profound psychological and social impact of the actual invasion from Cuba.

Strictly speaking, the ideology of the 14th of June Movement, stated and reiterated many times by its leader, Dr. Manuel Tavárez Justo, could be placed within the confines of urban, middle-class principles of democracy. Nevertheless, certain radical sectors of the 1J4 made notable efforts to impel the political orientation along a road other than the one intended by the founders. At times, the 1J4 seemed to model itself after the post-1959 Cuban example.

Numerous Dominicans, especially the young, were predisposed to sympathize with a clandestine, anti-Trujillo organization, and they soon extended its influence over many areas of the country. After being discovered by Trujillo's secret police in January 1960, the majority of 1J4 leaders were condemned to prison or tortured and executed.

In August 1961, the 1J4 elected to alter its clandestine status, and the party announced publicly the formation of the 14th of June Movement, under the leadership of its president Tavárez Justo, who had just been released from prison.

The 14th of June Movement, consisting mostly of young university intellectuals, who had been in the vanguard of anti-Trujillo resistance, earned a great deal of popular respect. As a result, the 1J4 became one of the most important political groups during this time. Its leader, Tavárez Justo, occupied an important place in the hearts and minds of the young, as well as in the hearts and minds of a significant portion of the working class and farmers. In accord with the general policy in the Dominican Republic, which at that time was dominated by the United States, the Council of State called for general elections for the constituency, to take place in December 1962. The 1J4, which was the principal force on the left, decided to abstain from the election. It can be said that the absence of the 1J4 assured the Dominican Revolutionary Party (PRD) of their victory, as the majority of 1J4 sympathizers voted for the PRD.

After the military coup of 25 September 1963, which toppled Juan Bosch, a triumvirate was formed which took power a day later. Bosch had been accused of altering the national destiny, of allowing or tolerating Communists in the Dominican Republic, and of creating disturbances with foreign powers.

One of the original triumvirate members, Emilio de los Santos, eventually resigned his office in protest against the death of Tavárez Justo, the 1J4 leader who had formed a group of guerillas in the mountains to topple the Triumvirate. Tavárez Justo's death, in December 1963, had followed a decree making the 1J4 illegal in the Dominican Republic.

During the elections set for 14 June 1966, the 1J4 supported Bosch and Antonio Guzmán as candidates (although they had their own candidates for lesser offices); Bosch rejected this support. The 1J4 does not appear anymore in the annals of the Junta Central Electoral.

INDEPENDENT DOMINICAN ACTION (ACCIÓN DOMINICANA INDEPENDIENTE—ADI). This organization, created on 13 March 1963, labeled itself as an "apolitical organization of men and women with democratic convictions." It took the lead in opposition to the Bosch government, issued strong censures, and held demonstrations.

MOVIMIENTO DE INTEGRACIÓN NACIONAL. See NATIONAL INTEGRATION MOVEMENT.

MOVIMIENTO POPULAR DOMINICANO. See DOMINICAN POPULAR MOVEMENT.

NATIONAL CIVIC UNION (UNIÓN CÍVICA NACIONAL—UCN). The UCN was founded as an apolitical action group of citizens on 11 July 1961 by notable people in the professional, commercial, and entrepreneurial worlds who had declined to collaborate with Trujillo and thus had broken with him prior to his May 1961 death. The head of this group was a physician, Viriato A. Fiallo. The group's original purpose was to crystallize and galvanize public support against the remaining relatives of Trujillo who still aspired to the deceased dictator's legacy.

Those aligned with the UCN came principally from the conservative elements of Dominican society who opposed Trujillo and his policies, including substantial businessmen, who had suffered under the Trujillo regime and well-to-do ranchers in the Cibao, a region in which the UCN's popularity increased rapidly and which became a solid UCN base. On 11 July 1961, a growing number of Dominicans residing in Santo Domingo wrote to the executive director of the Dominican Party, renouncing its power and hegemony over Dominican society. On the same date, the same group wrote to President Joaquín Balaguer, who had assumed power after Trujillo's death, to proclaim that a patriotic association, called the National Civic Union, had been formed.

Successful in helping eliminate the vestiges of Trujilloism, the UCN, originally an apolitical group, decided to evolve into a political party. A national assembly was held in February 1962, and a declaration of the principles of the new party was issued, under the motto of "Integral Revolution." The symbol chosen was that of a little cane hat, which stood for the head of the peasant. In this manner, the UCN portrayed itself as a revolutionary and democratic party.

The UCN was recognized by the Junta Central Electoral on 26 June 1962. The party president continued to be Fiallo; its ballot color was light blue; eventually, the party's presidential candidate for the general election to be held on 20 December 1962 was Fiallo himself. In that election, Fiallo lost to Juan Bosch by a two-to-one margin; nevertheless, Fiallo himself gained 317,327 votes, and the UCN picked up four senate seats as well as twenty representatives.

After the 1962 election, the UCN's power and influence declined rapidly. In the 1966 elections, the UCN nominated, as presidential candidate, Rafael F. Bonnelly, who obtained 16,152 votes. After this election, the UCN confined itself to supporting more powerful candidates of other parties.

NATIONAL INTEGRATION MOVEMENT (MOVIMIENTO DE INTE-GRACIÓN NACIONAL—MIN). This political group, originally known as the Movement of National Unity (Movimiento de Unidad Nacional), was headed by Rafael F. Bonnelly, who assumed that position in the first weeks of April 1965.

NATIONAL PARTY (PARTIDO NACIONAL—PN). This party was a weak resurrection of the old Horacista faction. It was recognized by the Junta Central Electoral on 19 December 1961. Its president was Virgilio Vilomar; its ballot color was white with a red border; its candidate for the president of the country was Raúl Carbuccia Abreu, who got 1,667 votes. Eventually, it swung its support in favor of the Dominican Revolutionary Party.

NATIONALIST PARTY (PARTIDO NACIONALISTA—PN). The PN was founded on 26 December 1924 by a group of intellectuals and political leaders headed by Américo Lugo, Federico Henríquez y Carvajal, Viriato A. Fiallo, Enriquillo Hernández, Enrique A. Henríquez, Pedro M. Archambault, Germán Ornes, Miguel Peregrin, Luis C. del Castillo, and other men who had distinguished themselves in opposition to the 1916–1924 North American occupation of the Dominican Republic. In that same era, these men had opposed the Hughes-Peynado Plan, which had called for a withdrawal of U.S. troops, but which had also enormously limited Dominican sovereignty—this Lugo had called a "crime" against the Dominican Republic.

The political platform of the Nationalist Party could be defined as the highest political expression organized by the radical Dominican petite bourgeoisie against U.S. hegemony in those days. The views of the Nationalist Party touched on economic and social philosophies which could be labeled as renovative, within the context of political expression at that time. In fact, only the later exiles of the 1940s and 1950s surpassed the Nationalists in this regard.

In its initial declaration, the Nationalist Party called for the "restoration of the Dominican Republic in its condition as an absolutely sovereign state," and in consequence proclaimed the "annulment of the validity of the military legislation brought about by North American occupation and of the laws that would so bind . . . with the goal of obtaining reparations for damage done."

In purely political and administrative aspects, the Nationalist Party platform postulated "the constitutional organization of electoral power without reelection; at the same time the decentralization together with more autonomy for the provinces, municipalities and the universities." It also called for "constitutional organization of judicial power as an independent entity." In the social aspects, it supported "the recognition and respect of all the rights of the working class."

With regard to education, the party proclaimed "the Nationalist Party believes that it is vital to eradicate illiteracy completely in the Republic as a significant step toward the possibility of public education and of equality of opportunity among citizens."

This last proclamation, intimately connected to party articles numbers 8 and 9, conformed to the party philosophy of caring, paternal government in the Latin American tradition. The ultimate downfall of the Nationalist Party, which crumbled after only a short period of influence, was typical of other short-lived Dominican political organizations existing between 1924 and 1930, giving evidence of the lack of Dominican political development, as well as of the deep economic divisions within Dominican society.

NATIONALIST REVOLUTIONARY PARTY (PARTIDO NACIONALISTA REVOLUCIONARIO—PNR). Upon return from exile in 1961, the party's leadership consisted of Dr. Pedro A. Pérez Cabral (Corpito) and Prof. Dato Pagán Perdomo. The party decided to abstain from the 1962 elections, but their members by and large voted for the Dominican Revolutionary Party.

PARTIDO DOMINICANO. See DOMINICAN PARTY.

PARTIDO FRENTE DEMOCRÁTICO. See DEMOCRATIC FRONT PARTY.

PARTIDO LIBERAL EVOLUCIONISTA. See EVOLUTIONARY LIBERAL PARTY.

PARTIDO NACIONAL. See NATIONAL PARTY.

PARTIDO NACIONALISTA. See NATIONALIST PARTY.

PARTIDO NACIONALISTA REVOLUCIONARIO. *See* NATIONALIST REVOLUTIONARY PARTY.

PARTIDO NACIONALISTA REVOLUCIONARIO DEMOCRÁTICO. *See* DEMOCRATIC REVOLUTIONARY NATIONALISTIC PARTY.

PARTIDO PROGRESISTA DEMÓCRATA CRISTIANO. *See* CHRISTIAN DEMOCRATIC PROGRESSIVE PARTY.

PARTIDO REVOLUCIONARIO DOMINICANO AUTÉNTICO. *See* AUTHENTIC DOMINICAN REVOLUTIONARY PARTY.

PARTIDO VANGUARDIA REVOLUCIONARIA DOMINICANA. *See* DOMINICAN REVOLUTIONARY VANGUARD PARTY.

UNIÓN CÍVICA NACIONAL. *See* NATIONAL CIVIC UNION.

William Javier Nelson
Diómedes Pérez

ECUADOR

A nation deeply penetrated by Spanish values of authoritarianism and personalism, Ecuador has been characterized historically by the regional bifurcation
between the coast (*costa*) and the Andean highlands (*sierra*). While the population of some 10 million is evenly divided between the two, inhabitants of
the coast reflect an ethnic and racial mixture that includes a sizeable African
component. The port city of Guayaquil, Ecuador's largest, is the center of
freewheeling business, commerce, social values, and political behavior. Populism
and personalistic demagoguery have long been hallmarks of electoral and party-
based activity, with the mayor of Guayaquil second only to the president of the
republic in terms of political power and influence.

In contrast, the highlanders enjoy a heritage of a stratified society in which
mestizos and particularly the Indian masses are dominated by a small socioeconomic elite. The national capital of Quito is quiet, subdued, and broadly conservative in style and outlook. Its rivalry with Guayaquil has roots dating back
to the sixteenth century and remains conflictual to this day. In more recent
years, the competition has often centered over economic and political control
of the oil reserves located in the Amazon jungle area (*oriente*)—the largely
unpopulated eastern half of the nation. Since the beginning of its short-lived
oil boom in the 1970s, Ecuador has been largely dependent on petroleum earnings to finance its modernization. The result has been a distorted economy,
uneven development, and a drawing down of limited subsoil deposits. In the
meantime, the agricultural tradition has endured, with the spread of industry
slower than in most other South American states.

Traditional political patterns, in which personality was far more important
than party or program, prevailed until the 1970s. The classic Conservative-
Liberal competition saw the hegemony of the former shattered by the civil war
of 1895 when the Liberals under Eloy Alfaro gained control. This lasted until
1944, when the political scene became dominated by a stereotypical caudillo,
José María Velasco Ibarra. Reaching the presidency five times between 1934
and 1968, Velasco was a flambouyant orator whose policies fluctuated widely

through the years. Yet his basic posture customarily served vested economic and business elites. At the same time, his maladroit administrative skills spurred the turmoil which caused all but one of his presidencies to end in a nonconstitutional intervention by the military. An outspoken critic of political parties, Velasco was instrumental in discouraging the emergence of well-organized, doctrinally oriented, mass-based political organizations.

The final intervention to terminate a Velasco presidency came in 1972, and the armed forces remained in power for seven years before they returned to the barracks. It was during this period that the traditional Conservative and Liberal parties began to recede. The retirement and subsequent death of Velasco brought an end to the *velasquista* movement as well, and a set of younger, more programmatically oriented parties began to appear. The elections of 1978–1979, which marked the return of formal democracy, included the Democratic Left (ID) and the Popular Democracy (DP), representatives respectively of social democracy and Christian democracy. The Marxist left consisted as usual of several competing groups but, as with the ID and DP, it was now directed by a younger generation of leaders. Populism was still very much alive, especially on the coast; this ideology was epitomized by the Concentration of Popular Forces (CFP) and Assad Bucaram, a controversial figure of impoverished background who had become the single most popular mass leader since the heyday of Velasco.

The outgoing military, determined to control the electoral outcome, disqualified both Bucaram and all former presidents as well as the candidates of four political parties, ranging from Maoists to Christian Democrats. Much to its consternation, the armed forces saw the CFP replacement for Bucaram win a solid victory in the first round, followed by a decisive triumph over the Conservative Sixto Durán Ballén by a margin of better than two to one in the April 1979 runoff. Jaime Roldós Aguilera thereby entered office as a modernizing reformer. He was accompanied by his DP running mate Osvaldo Hurtado Larrea; both men were in their thirties. However, the CFP's reigning caudillo was still Bucaram, who was embittered by the unwarranted denial of his certain presidential victory and determined to rule the country from his position at the head of a large CFP delegation to the unicameral National Chamber of Representatives (Cámara Nacional de Representantes—CNR).

The CFP was nearing a definitive split between *roldosistas* and Bucaram loyalists when the president and his wife died in a plane crash in May 1981 and Bucaram died of natural causes six months later. In the confused aftermath, a drastically reduced CFP was eventually captured by Assad's son Averroes, while his nephew (and brother of Roldós's wife) Abdalá Bucaram put together the Ecuadorean Roldosist Party (PRE). Abdalá's sister Elsa was subsequently elected mayor of Guayaquil, and throughout the decade of the 1980s the heritage of CFP populism was contested interminably by members and friends of the extended Bucaram clan. At the same time, politics on the coast was also shaken by the outspoken vigor of León Febres Cordero, a well-connected businessman who became the chief congressional critic of the Roldós-Hurtado administration.

Although he was a member of the small and weak Social Christian Party (PSC), Febres became an articulate spokesman for traditional and modernizing business interests. As such, he was vociferous in his attacks on the halting reformism of the government, and by 1984 he was the candidate for a reunited right which coalesced as the Front for National Reconstruction (FRN). With the CFP fragmented and Hurtado's small DP tainted by the unpopularity of his tough austerity measures, the reformist banner fell naturally to the ID and its founder, Rodrigo Borja Cevallos.

Borja had gained national visibility through his symbolic candidacy in 1978, when the ID was easily the best-organized party in the country. Moreover, its social democratic message was the clearest non-Marxist expression of ideas and policies before the electorate. When Borja won the first round of presidential elections and entered the runoff against Febres Cordero, it was commonly accepted that his victory was assured. However, the conservative candidate mounted a powerful campaign studded with expansive promises and commitments. While this was contrary to his avowed belief in the Chicago school of economics, it enabled Febres to win a clear if narrow victory over Borja. Upon entering office in August 1984, the new president faced a situation in which his supporters were only loosely organized, while the ID was girding itself for concerted opposition.

During the Febres years, the party system was tortuously strained by the clash between traditionalist and modernizing forces. During the first two years, the president contemptuously rode roughshod over his opposition, perilously stretched his constitutional powers, and secured enough would be opposition congressmen through intimidation or bribery to gain a majority. As his policies failed to revive the economy, however, Febres suffered a resounding defeat in 1986 off-year elections. He also lost a concurrent plebiscite which would have reformed the laws regulating political parties. This cost him control of the legislature, and a subsequent kidnapping by disaffected officers—albeit short lived—left Febres personally and politically shaken. In the final phase of his administration, the president concentrated his attention solely on surviving his constitutional term, and the Conservatives were in retreat by the time of the 1988 presidential elections.

The ID, after a brief flurry of internal opposition to its founder, agreed upon a third Borja candidacy. The party entered the campaign with the best-organized national party and prepared a major effort for Guayaquil and the coast, where it had always been weak. The DP, which had been slowly building up its ranks in the highlands, ran the youthful protégé of Hurtado, Jamil Mahauad. For the right, never fully organized in party terms and demoralized by the public rejection of Febres, the respected Durán Ballén again took up the banner. Conservative forces hoped that he might reach the runoff against Borja. At the same time, little credence was given to the populist potential, represented in 1988 by the PRE and Abdalá Bucaram. As expected, Borja won the first round with 24.1 percent of the valid vote against nine rivals. Bucaram ran second with 17.6 percent; Durán followed at 15.2 percent; next was General Frank Vargas Pazzos for a leftist coalition with 13.4 percent; and Mahauad finished fifth with 11.6 percent; all of the others were in single digits. The runoff between Borja and Bucaram proved to be the nastiest in national history; Bucaram engaged in personal attacks to which Borja responded. Bucaram and the PRE ran a surprisingly respectable race in the highlands, but Borja was unable to crack his party's coastal difficulties. Borja's victory was far from the landslide some had predicted, although he entered power with the ID holding thirty of the seventy-one seats in the CNR. It was an easy task to put together a congresional majority, one which held until the ID defeat in the 1990 off-year elections.

Despite his social democratic proclivities, Borja's attention necessarily focused on the economic crisis, one more profound than that which had faced Febres Cordero in 1984. He therefore introduced new austerity measures while promising a gradualist approach to reforms. The next two years proved disappointing to most citizens, and the ID was duly chastised in the 1990 off-year elections. This left the president without a congressional majority while the opposition, although swollen by a doubling of the PSC delegation, was far from cohesive. The prospects for effective and productive government were not encouraging, and the disorderly party system constituted an enduring problem.

Conservative forces continued to operate with a number of separate parties and, although the PSC was numerically the strongest, its established organizational strength was occasional and episodic. On the left, where the Socialists had forged ahead of other Marxist parties, characteristic doctrinal and tactical differences weakened the party's general effectiveness. The ID remained the best articulated, best structured party, although the fate of the Borja administration was not helpful in the short run. The other reformist party, the DP, had not yet built anything approaching a true natural constituency and was overshadowed on the so-called center-left by the ID. Adding to this the ideologically incoherent but electorally persuasive populism of the PRE and Abdalá Bucaram, it was clear that Ecuador in the 1990s would retain a fragmented, highly partisan, and frequently opportunistic party system which stubbornly resisted true modernization. The process of maturation still had a long distance to cover. In the meantime, personalistic and traditionalistic manifestations of party leadership remained characteristics certain to endure into the twenty-first century.

Bibliography

George I. Blanksten. *Ecuador: Constitutions and Caudillos.* University of California Press, Berkeley, 1951.

Catherine M. Conaghan. *Restructuring Domination: Industrialists and the State in Ecuador.* University of Pittsburgh Press, Pittsburgh, Pa., 1988.

David Corkill and David Cubitt. *Ecuador: Fragile Democracy.* Latin American Bureau, London, 1988.

Agustín Cueva. *The Process of Political Domination in Ecuador.* Trans. Danielle Salti. Transaction, New Brunswick, N.J., 1982.

John Samuel Fitch. *The Military Coup d'Etat as a Political Process: Ecuador, 1948–1966.* Johns Hopkins University Press, Baltimore, Md., 1977.

Howard Handelman and Thomas G. Sanders. *Military Government and the Movement Toward Democracy in South America.* Indiana University Press, Bloomington, 1981.

Osvaldo Hurtado. *Political Power in Ecuador.* Trans. Nick D. Mills, Jr. University of New Mexico Press, Albuquerque, 1980.

John D. Martz. *The Military in Ecuador: The Policy and Politics of Authoritarian Rule.* Latin American Institute, University of New Mexico Press, Albuquerque, 1988.

———. *Politics and Petroleum in Ecuador.* Transaction, New Brunswick, N.J., 1987.

———. *Ecuador: Conflicting Political Culture and the Quest for Progress.* Allyn and Bacon, Boston, 1972.

Martin C. Needler. *Anatomy of a Coup d'Etat: Ecuador 1963.* Institute for the Comparative Study of Political Systems, Washington, D.C., 1964.

Linda Alexander Rodriguez. *The Search for Public Policy: Regional Politics and Government Finances in Ecuador, 1830–1940.* University of California Press, Berkeley, 1985.

David W. Schodt. *Ecuador: An Andean Enigma.* Westview Press, Boulder, Colo., 1987.

Political Parties

ACCIÓN POPULAR REVOLUCIONARIA ECUATORIANA. *See* ECUADOREAN REVOLUTIONARY POPULAR ACTION.

ALFARIST RADICAL FRONT (FRENTE RADICAL ALFARISTA—FRA). Former Liberal Abdón Calderón Muñoz founded the FRA in 1972 and finished fifth in the 1978 presidential race. When he was assassinated in Guayaquil several months later, he was succeeded by his daughter Cecilia Calderón de Castro. In the 1980 municipal elections, the FRA drew upon a sympathy vote and polled nearly 20 percent of the vote. Four years later, with Calderón de Castro too young to be eligible, the FRA ran Jaime Aspiazu Seminario for president. He finished in fifth place with 5.6 percent of the vote; the FRA placed six candidates in congress.

With the sympathy vote dissipated and the FRA lacking any clear doctrine or ideology, it turned in 1985 from opposition to support of President León Febres Cordero. Rewarded by the election of Cecilia's husband Iván Castro as vice president of the congress, the FRA then saw its delegation cut in half by the 1986 off-year elections. In 1988 the total was cut to two, a figure that was maintained in the 1990 elections. For the FRA, with its popularity limited to a few coastal regions, the future is not bright.

BROAD LEFTIST FRONT (FRENTE AMPLIO DE IZQUIERDA—FADI). The FADI was created in 1978 as an electoral alliance in which the Partido Comunista was the principal member. In 1984 the FADI supported the presidential candidacy of Communist Rene Maugé Mosquera. Maugé ran a distant eighth with 3.5 percent of the vote. The FADI won two congressional seats and added a third. The FADI renewed efforts to produce a leftist coalition united behind a single presidential candidate in 1988, but without success.

The FADI, accompanied by the Democratic Popular Movement (MPD) and eight tiny leftist groups, instead organized the United Leftist Front (Frente de Izquierda Unida—FIU), which backed the candidacy of the MPD's Jaime Hurtado González, who finished seventh with 4.6 percent of the valid vote. The FADI and the MPD soon split; the FADI backed Rodrigo Borja Cevallos in the runoff. Two FADI members were returned to congress. The FADI supported the Borja government during its first two years and became identified with unpopular policies. It retained two seats in the 1990 off-year elections but failed to achieve primacy among the Marxist organizations. Under the influence of Maugé and the Conservative Party, the electoral coalition has customarily pursued pragmatic tactics and strategy. The commitment to construction of a united Marxist coalition—at least for electoral purposes—remains a strong if difficult goal.

COALICIÓN INSTITUCIONALISTA DEMÓCRATA. See DEMOCRATIC INSTITUTIONALIST COALITION.

COMMUNIST PARTY OF ECUADOR (PARTIDO COMUNISTA DEL ECUADOR). See BROAD LEFTIST FRONT.

CONCENTRACIÓN DE FUERZAS POPULARES. See CONCENTRATION OF POPULAR FORCES.

CONCENTRATION OF POPULAR FORCES (CONCENTRACIÓN DE FUERZAS POPULARES—CFP). Founded by Guayaquil caudillo Carlos Guevara Moreno as the Unión Popular Republicana, this coastal party was christened the CFP in 1949. For a decade it was a populist force based on the urban proletariat of the coast. With Guevara Moreno gradually withdrawing from politics, the CFP entered a new era under another charismatic personalistic boss, Assad Bucaram. Elected mayor of Guayaquil in 1962, Bucaram remained the unchallenged party chief while rising from regional to national prominence.

Strongly mistrusted, as well as feared by José María Velasco Ibarra, the armed forces, and the nation's socioeconomic elite, Bucaram drew obsessive opposition. His anticipated electoral victory in the 1972 elections was among the reasons for the military's seizure of power. When the armed forces eventually decided upon a return to the barracks, they employed a host of specious grounds to rule out a Bucaram candidacy. The CFP, however, formed a coalition with the

Popular Democracy, and Jaime Roldós Aguilera, the husband of Bucaram's niece, was nominated in his place. With the slogan, "Roldós to the Presidency, Bucaram to Power," the CFP swept to victory. With twenty-nine CFP seats ensuring Bucaram his election as president of congress, Bucaram challenged Roldós for national leadership.

As the Bucaram–Roldós rift became irreparable, the CFP itself was torn apart. By the time of the 1984 elections, Roldós had been killed in a plane crash, Bucaram had died of a heart attack, and the erstwhile followers of the two men were seeking to repair the damage. In the 1984 elections, however, the CFP's presidential candidate Angel Duarte placed a distant third, and the party's congressional representation plummeted to seven. Under Bucaram's youthful son Averroes, the CFP moved from opposition to support for the Febres government. Among the rewards was the presidency of congress for Averroes as well as government appointments. In 1988 the party again presented Duarte as its standard-bearer, but he could do no better than sixth with 7.4 percent of the vote. The CFP, with much of its support drained away to the Ecuadorean Roldosist Party, captured six seats in congress. In the 1990 congressional elections, it dropped to three, although the party again displayed its skill at opportunistic maneuvering by negotiating the 1990–1992 congressional presidency for Averroes Bucaram. By this time, the once powerful party had become but one more of the ideologically incoherent, vaguely populistic organizations competing for votes on a predominantly regional basis.

CONSERVATIVE PARTY (PARTIDO CONSERVADOR ECUATORIANO—PCE). One of Ecuador's two oldest and most traditional parties, the Conservatives were officially established in 1883 and remained a major political actor into the 1970s. Camilo Ponce Enríquez, a former party member who had founded his own Social Christian Party in 1951, effectively represented conservative interests during his presidency (1956–1960). Traditionally the defender of highland landowners, the Conservatives remained powerful until universal adult suffrage was introduced by the 1978 constitution. The party had also been weakened by the departure of its progressive wing, headed by Julio César Trujillo Vásquez, to form the Popular Democracy.

In 1979 the Conservatives backed Sixto Durán Ballén of the Social Christians. They suffered the lowest percentage of the vote in party history while electing ten congressmen. The party again backed the Social Christian presidential candidate in 1984, for a time held a cabinet position, but saw its congressional delegation reduced to two. By 1990 both seats had been lost, and those generally sympathetic to conservative views shunned the party in favor of the Social Christians or some other rightist grouping.

DEMOCRACIA POPULAR. See POPULAR DEMOCRACY.

DEMOCRATIC INSTITUTIONALIST COALITION (COALICIÓN INSTI-TUCIONALISTA DEMÓCRATA—CID). Guayaquil businessman and former Liberal Otto Arosemena Gómez formed the CID in 1965 and maneuvered himself into the provisional presidency of the nation in 1966. The party never achieved significant power after he left office in 1968, although Arosemena served as a deputy. The CID won three seats in the 1979 congressional elections, and in 1984, the party backed León Febres Cordero for president. The CID dissolved after the death of Arosemena.

DEMOCRATIC LEFT (IZQUIERDA DEMOCRÁTICA—ID). A group of young Liberals led by Rodrigo Borja Cevallos broke with the Liberal Party in 1968 and participated in the 1970 elections as the ID. In 1978, following the withdrawal of the military government, Borja established his image and that of his party while running fourth in the elections. The ID won fifteen congressional seats and continued to build its national organization. While maintaining a moderate opposition to the Roldós and Hurtado governments, the ID sought to avoid parliamentary crises or unchecked partisanship.

In 1984 Borja won the ten-candidate vote with 23.9 percent, followed by 22.7 percent for León Febres Cordero. While his triumph in the runoff was widely assumed, the energetic populism of Febres allowed him to squeeze out a victory: 51.5 to 48.5 percent. Despite this disappointment, the ID stood as the main opposition party. It held twenty-four seats and led the opposition to the Febres government for the next four years. Although losing seven seats in 1986 elections, the party anticipated a victory in 1988. After putting down a rebellion inside the party, Borja won on his third try, capturing the first round and then defeating Abdalá Bucaram in the runoff.

Although the ID has been consistently weak along the coast, elsewhere its organization is the best of all Ecuador's parties. Doctrinal concerns have also been important to the party, which is a member of the Socialist International. Borja's inauguration attracted a number of chiefs of state, including several others from Social Democratic political parties. Faced with the chaos left by his predecessor, the new government adopted austerity measures which provided little opportunity to develop social programs. In 1990 the ID was subsequently punished by the voters; it dropped from 22.7 to 13.0 percent, and its contingent of deputies fell from twenty-nine to fourteen. Barring unexpected success for the latter half of the Borja period, the ID faced difficulties in the short run. Yet it remained well organized and committed to a reformist program which, in the long run, was attractive to many Ecuadoreans.

DEMOCRATIC PARTY (PARTIDO DEMÓCRATA—PD). The PD was founded by Francisco Huerta Montalvo in 1978 after he broke away from the Liberal Party. A mildly reformist group which initially drew middle-class support, the PD backed Huerta's unsuccessful presidential bid in 1984, when it secured five seats in the congress. Internal factionalism soon led to the defection of all five deputies to other parties, and the PD faded away.

DEMOCRATIC POPULAR MOVEMENT (MOVIMIENTO POPULAR DE-MOCRÁTICO—MPD). The origins of the MPD lie in the 1963 departure of the Maoists from the Communist Party of Ecuador (PCE) to form the Marxist-Leninist Communist Party of Ecuador (PCMLE). The PCMLE created the MPD as an electoral vehicle, and in 1979 it elected Jaime Hurtado González to congress. It refused to cooperate with the PCE and stood outside any form of leftist coalition.

In 1984 Hurtado was named presidential candidate and finished fourth with 6.1 percent of the vote; the party secured three seats, which rose to four after the 1986 congressional elections. A strong critic of the Febres administration, the MPD finally agreed to work with the Broad Leftist Front (FADI) in the 1988 electoral coalition United Leftist Front (Frente de Izquierda Unida—FIU). Hurtado was the candidate, but won only 4.6 percent of the vote and finished seventh. The MPD saw its congressional delegation fall to three, and it broke with the FADI and joined the anti-Borja opposition. In 1990, when the party gained but a single seat, it appeared to be more opportunistic than ideological in its political behavior.

ECUADOREAN REVOLUTIONARY POPULAR ACTION (ACCIÓN POP-ULAR REVOLUCIONARIA ECUATORIANA—APRE). First created by Carlos Guevara Moreno in the 1960s after he split from the Concentration of Popular Forces, the APRE became moribund when Guevara retired from politics. Reorganized in 1970 as the Guevarista National Party (Partido Nacional Guevarista) and then renamed the APRE once again, the party lost legal status in 1978 when it failed to win 5 percent of the vote in two consecutive elections. The party was later reconstituted under the leadership of José Hanna Musse.

In 1988 the APRE joined with the Ecuadorean Socialist Party to form a coalition supporting the presidential candidacy of General Frank Vargas Pazzos. This so-called People's Patriotic Union (Unión Patriótica del Pueblo—UPP) finished fourth with 13.4 percent of the vote, but the APRE failed to elect any congressmen.

ECUADOREAN ROLDOSIST PARTY (PARTIDO ROLDOSISTA ECUA-TORIANO—PRE). With the shakeup of parties following the deaths of Jaime Roldós Aguilera and Assad Bucaram in 1981, supporters of the former wrestled with the effort to shape a new party in the image of the departed president. The Concentration of Popular Forces had already fragmented, and the *roldosista* People, Change, and Democracy (PCD) was also rent by internal conflict. Out of this came the movement headed by Abdalá Bucaram, the nephew of Assad and the brother-in-law of Roldós. Legally registered as the PRE in 1982, it first won three congressional seats in 1984 and two years later won five. Abdalá, a fiery and controversially outspoken leader from Guayas, became a bitterly un-compromising critic of President León Febres Cordero.

Accused of misappropriating funds while mayor of Guayaquil and charged with disrespect toward the armed forces for inflammatory public statements, Bucaram went into exile. Subsequently permitted to return by Febres, he launched his party's presidential campaign for 1988. Bucaram unexpectedly finished second with 17.6 percent of the vote before he lost the subsequent runoff to Rodrigo Borja Cevallos. The PRE gained eight congressional seats and raised that number to thirteen in the 1990 race. The party continues to fight for Bucaram's exoneration in the courts while it prepares for his next presidential candidacy. The party, which has remained ideologically incoherent while shift-ing back and forth from right to left of center, has enjoyed the populistic appeal of Abdalá Bucaram much as did the CFP in earlier years with his uncle Assad.

ECUADOREAN SOCIALIST PARTY (PARTIDO SOCIALISTA ECUATO-RIANO—PSE). Originally founded in 1926, the Socialists have divided and reunited several times through the years. The party periodically has supported progressive governments, and its attitude toward the Communists has also varied through the years. It was slow to reorganize and win legal status following the departure of the armed forces from power in 1979. In 1984 the Socialists, the weakest of the Marxist groups, won only a single seat, but the delegation in-creased to six in 1986. In 1988 the PSE regained some prominence by spear-heading the People's Patriotic Union coalition which backed the candidacy of Frank Vargas Pazzos; the PSE's Enrique Ayala was named as Vargas's running mate. Vargas's strong fourth-place finish further boosted the party and, after two years of strong opposition to the Borja government, helped augment the PSE's congressional representation in 1990 to eight. Their percentage increased from 4.4 to 4.9, and the PSE entered the final two Borja years with a much enhanced image.

FRENTE AMPLIO DE IZQUIERDA. See BROAD LEFTIST FRONT.

FRENTE DE IZQUIERDA UNIDA. See BROAD LEFTIST FRONT.

FRENTE DE RECONSTRUCCIÓN NACIONAL. See SOCIAL CHRISTIAN PARTY.

FRENTE RADICAL ALFARISTA. See ALFARIST RADICAL FRONT.

FRONT FOR NATIONAL RECONSTRUCTION (FRENTE DE RECON-STRUCCIÓN NACIONAL—FRN). See SOCIAL CHRISTIAN PARTY.

IZQUIERDA DEMOCRÁTICA. See DEMOCRATIC LEFT.

LIBERAL PARTY (PARTIDO LIBERAL RADICAL—PLR). *See* RADICAL LIBERAL PARTY.

MARXIST-LENINIST COMMUNIST PARTY OF ECUADOR (PARTIDO COMUNISTA MARXISTA-LENINISTA DEL ECUADOR—PCMLE). *See* DEMOCRATIC POPULAR MOVEMENT.

MOVIMIENTO POPULAR DEMOCRÁTICO. *See* DEMOCRATIC POPULAR MOVEMENT.

PARTIDO COMUNISTA DEL ECUADOR. *See* BROAD LEFTIST FRONT.

PARTIDO COMUNISTA MARXISTA-LENINISTA DEL ECUADOR. *See* DEMOCRATIC POPULAR MOVEMENT.

PARTIDO CONSERVADOR ECUATORIANO. *See* CONSERVATIVE PARTY.

PARTIDO DEMÓCRATA. *See* DEMOCRATIC PARTY.

PARTIDO DEMÓCRATA CRISTIANO. *See* POPULAR DEMOCRACY.

PARTIDO LIBERAL RADICAL. *See* RADICAL LIBERAL PARTY.

PARTIDO NACIONAL VELASQUISTA. *See* VELASQUIST NATIONAL PARTY.

PARTIDO NACIONALISTA REVOLUCIONARIO. *See* REVOLUTIONARY NATIONALIST PARTY.

PARTIDO PUEBLO, CAMBIO Y DEMOCRACIA. *See* PEOPLE, CHANGE, AND DEMOCRACY.

PARTIDO REPUBLICANO. *See* REPUBLICAN PARTY.

PARTIDO ROLDOSISTA ECUATORIANO. *See* ECUADOREAN ROLDOSIST PARTY.

PARTIDO SOCIAL CRISTIANO. *See* SOCIAL CHRISTIAN PARTY.

PARTIDO SOCIALISTA ECUATORIANO. *See* ECUADOREAN SOCIALIST PARTY.

PEOPLE, CHANGE, AND DEMOCRACY (PARTIDO PUEBLO, CAMBIO Y DEMOCRACIA—PCD). When President Jaime Roldós Aguilera and the Concentration of Popular Forces broke apart in 1980, *roldosistas* guided by the president's wife Martha founded the PCD. Following the May 1981 plane crash which took the lives of the presidential couple, the PCD was headed by Jaime's brother León. It briefly supported Osvaldo Hurtado Larrea before going into opposition and supported the candidacy of Rodrigo Borja Cevallos in 1984. The party's claim on *roldosistas* was severely damaged by the emergence of the Ecuadorean Roldosist Party, and the PCD won less than 2 percent of the congressional vote. In June 1986 the party won a single seat, and the resignation of León Roldós marked the PCD's death knell.

PEOPLE'S PATRIOTIC UNION (UNIÓN PATRIÓTICA DEL PUEBLO—UPP). *See* ECUADOREAN REVOLUTIONARY POPULAR ACTION.

POPULAR DEMOCRACY (DEMOCRACIA POPULAR—DP). The origins of the DP, customarily treated as a Christian Democratic party, date from 1964 and the original Partido Demócrata Cristiano (PDC). Its ideological heritage was the work of a small group of Catholic university professors and students, most notably Osvaldo Hurtado Larrea. In preparation for the post-dictatorial elections scheduled for 1978, the PDC was fused with the progressive wing of the Conservative Party (PCE) which Julio César Trujillo Vásquez had led from the PCE in 1976. Withstanding strong pressures from the departing military regime, the DP allied with the Concentration of Popular Forces, and Hurtado became the running mate of Jaime Roldós Aguilera. When Roldós died in 1981, Hurtado succeeded to the presidency and completed the final three years of the constitutional term.

Economic pressures forced Hurtado to adopt austerity policies, to renegotiate the foreign loan, and to curtail social programs and reforms. Hampered by the resultant unpopularity of the DP government, the party's 1984 candidate Trujillo was doomed to a seventh-place finish, and the party won only four congressional seats. Opposition to the Febres administration aided the DP in doubling its congressional representation in June 1986. Two years later, its candidate Jamil Mahuad received some 240,000 votes, 11.6 percent of the valid vote.

The DP then underwent a severe and protracted internal struggle over the issue of a possible collaboration with the incoming Borja administration. Over the protests of Hurtado, the party agreed to back the government. As Hurtado had predicted, two years later the DP was associated with unpopular government policies. After an arduous campaign, the party retained its 11-percent share of the legislative vote, which translated into seven seats. The DP hoped to polish its doctrinal image as a center-leftist party and to move toward greater national power in the decade of the 1990s.

RADICAL LIBERAL PARTY (PARTIDO LIBERAL RADICAL—PLR). Customarily termed simply the Liberal Party, the PLR, founded in 1878, is the nation's oldest party. First seizing power under its famed leader Eloy Alfaro after the 1895 civil war, the PLR dominated national politics until its last president, Carlos Arroyo del Rio, was ousted in 1944. In the 1950s the PLR became subject to factionalism and saw its position slowly decline. This movement was hastened with the schisms that led to the creation of the Democratic Left and the Alfarist Revolutionary Front. In 1978 younger party members, headed by Francisco Huerta Montalvo, were rebuffed in their bid for leadership, and they left the PLR to form the Democratic Party and to prepare for the 1984 elections. The old guard then turned to a former candidate, the uncle of Huerta Montalvo, Raúl Clemente Huerta.

Clemente Huerta only narrowly missed the runoff between the two leading presidential vote getters, although there were only four Liberals in congress. By 1984 the PLR was even more fragmented, and León Febres Cordero chose the Liberal Blasco Peñaherrera as his vice presidential running mate. The remnants of the historic party, which stood clearly to the right of center politically, won barely 3 percent of the congressional vote that year. In 1988 the situation was even grimmer: Miguel Albornez, a little-known presidential candidate, ran ninth in the field of ten. The PLR won only three seats in congress, and the number was unchanged by the 1990 vote. Once the dominant spokesman of coastal business interests, the PLR by 1990 had been totally eclipsed by a host of newer parties with greater relevance for the electorate.

REPUBLICAN PARTY (PARTIDO REPUBLICANO—PR). Newly formed for the January 1988 presidential elections by a small group of businessmen, the PR supported Guillermo Sotomayor, who finished last in the field of ten with 1.1 percent of the vote.

REVOLUTIONARY NATIONALIST PARTY (PARTIDO NACIONAL-ISTA REVOLUCIONARIO—PNR). Supporters of former *velasquista* Carlos Julio Arosemena Monroy created this original movement in opposition to the military dictatorship that ousted him in 1963. In 1966 the party took the name PNR and became increasingly personalistic in character. When the democratic system was reestablished in 1978, the PNR won two legislative seats, falling to one in 1984. Since 1986 it has been without congressional representation.

SOCIAL CHRISTIAN PARTY (PARTIDO SOCIAL CRISTIANO—PSC). For nearly three decades following its 1951 founding by former Conservative Camilo Ponce Enríquez as the Movimiento Social Cristiano (MSC), the PSC was long a minor player among the nation's parties. It was the influence of Ponce—the elected president from 1956 to 1960—which ensured its survival. Essentially a personalistic vehicle for Ponce, the PSC put forward his final presidential bid in 1968. By the time of Ponce's death in the 1970's, however, the PSC had abandoned its confessional organization and was taking shape as an organization representative of the modernizing business sector. As such, the PSC joined other rightist elements to back the 1978 presidential candidacy of former Quito mayor Sixto Durán Ballén.

Durán ran second to Jaime Roldós Aguilera, but he was then overwhelmed by a vote of more than two to one in the April 1979 runoff. Among those supporting his candidacy, the PSC secured three congressional seats. It was one of these three Congressmen, León Febres Cordero, who became the champion of business and conservative interests in the congress and emerged as the obvious candidate for 1984. Febres's coalition, the so-called Front for National Reconstruction (Frente de Reconstrucción Nacional—FRN), included members of the growing PSC. Nine were elected to congress that year, and in two years the ranks had grown to fifteen. With the virtual disintegration of the Febres administration in its final months, the 1988 PSC candidacy of Durán was ill-starred from the outset. Durán missed the runoff by finishing third with 15.2 percent of the valid vote, and eight congressional seats were won.

By 1990, with the Borja government itself increasingly unpopular in the face of unyielding economic and social problems, the PSC bounced back with a resounding victory, capturing nearly 25 percent of the vote. With its congressional delegation doubled to sixteen, the PSC was the largest party. PSC collaboration with the Concentration of Popular Forces and other smaller parties ensured it a leading opposition voice, and the prospects for recapturing the presidency in 1992 were favorable. While the PSC does not give high priority to ideological statements, its fundamental probusiness outlook has been clear, and policy positions have been generally consistent with the party view of Ecuador and the world around it.

UNIÓN PATRIÓTICA DEL PUEBLO. See ECUADOREAN REVOLUTIONARY POPULAR ACTION.

UNITED LEFTIST FRONT (FRENTE DE IZQUIERDA UNIDA—FIU). See BROAD LEFTIST FRONT.

VELASQUIST NATIONAL PARTY (PARTIDO NACIONAL VELASQUISTA—PNV). Prior to winning his fifth nonconsecutive presidential term in the 1968 elections, José María Velasco Ibarra permitted his followers to organize a *velasquista* federation on his behalf. It disintegrated after his ouster in 1972 but was reconstituted as the PNV before the 1978–1979 elections. Velasco himself returned from exile but died shortly thereafter. The PNV won a single seat between 1979 and 1984, received less than 1 percent of the vote in 1984, and disappeared from the political scene.

John D. Martz

EL SALVADOR

With a population approaching 5 million, the smallest country (8,081 square miles) on the Western Hemisphere's landmass has the highest population density. With Guatemala on the west, Honduras to the north, and no Atlantic coast, El Salvador's geographic location has shaped its history and ethnic composition; unlike most of Central America, it has no African-American population and few indigenous peoples. Social, economic, and political conditions are rooted in the colonial and early national periods. Lacking natural resources, El Salvador's wealth lay in the rich volcanic soil that supported a mono-crop export economy after the conquest. Cacao, which was under cultivation when the Spanish arrived in 1524, was followed by indigo and then, in the nineteenth century, coffee. After World War II, there was some effort to diversify export crops and to industrialize. Still, coffee continued to dominate, accounting for 61 percent of exports in the 1980s even as civil war reduced production 18 percent between 1980 and 1987.

The agro-economic pattern led to a growing concentration of land and wealth, a decreasing number of landowners (the "oligarchy"), and the extreme deprivation and political repression of the peasant majority. The members of the oligarchy, who were overwhelmingly Liberal, opted for a laissez-faire economic philosophy and a classical liberal belief in the sanctity of private property and the purpose of government—to maintain order. It created an army, the National Guard, and its own private forces to keep a periodically rebellious peasantry in line. The country never experienced the Conservative-Liberal conflicts that plagued its neighbors; the last Conservative president was Francisco Dueñas (1863–1871) whose primary conservative credentials were respect for the Catholic church and for indigenous institutions—for which he was rewarded with Indian support and national stability. When Dueñas was toppled in 1871, however, the Liberals began to usurp communal lands, and the Indian revolts began again. Thereafter all presidents were Liberal oligarchs, until a coup d'état in December 1931 created a division of labor: The army took control of the state, and the oligarchy continued to run the economy. This arrangement, punctuated by occasional coups and periodic elections, continued until an October 1979 coup, led by young, progressive officers, ended the symbiotic relationship.

The 1931 coup toppled the nine-month-old regime of Arturo Araujo, a progressive oligarch who had run under the banner of the Salvadorean Labor Party and who had made promises to the working class that frightened his peers. When, a month later, local elections occurred in which the Communist Party of El Salvador (PCS) won some mayoral races, the new government, headed by former vice president and general Maximiliano Hernández Martínez, refused to certify the elections. Following a Communist-led uprising in late January 1932 and a subsequent massacre by the army a few days later, the party was proscribed. For the next thirteen years, the only party, the Pro-Fatherland National Party, was a personalist, official party created by Martínez.

Despite the establishment of a military academy in the nineteenth century and a certain level of institutionalization, the army officer corps was impeded in its pretensions to professionalization by the development of a *tanda* system in which each academy graduating class was promoted in lockstep regardless of competence or rectitude. As a result, the only way to effect change in the armed forces or in the society was through a coup, which was usually carried out by younger, more progressive officers. Such coups, or attempted coups, occurred five times between 1944 and 1979. Even when elections were held regularly after 1944, the official party tenaciously held on to power. The reality of this situation was demonstrated in 1972 when a civilian coalition, the National Opposition Union (UNO), composed of the Christian Democrat Party (PDC), the Revolutionary National Movement (MNR), and the Nationalist Democratic Union (UDN), was denied its electoral victory by the army.

This event was preceded by a decade of political party development. Several parties that would have an impact into the 1990s were founded, including the PDC in 1960; the third (and last) incarnation of the official party, the Party of National Conciliation (PCN) in 1961; the MNR in 1964; and the UDN in 1969. The PDC, MNR, and UDN, along with the Renovating Action Party (PAR), which had been around since 1944, mounted a growing challenge to the PCN through the decade; but, as Stephen Webre has observed, the logical flaw in this opening of political space was that it "encouraged an active opposition but, by definition, forbade that opposition to come to power" (Webre 1979, 181).

Recognition of this reality led growing numbers of Salvadoreans to opt for a revolutionary alternative which included political (mass, grass-roots organizing) and military (armed struggle) dimensions. Thus, five revolutionary organizations, which had their roots in nineteenth-century peasant uprisings, in labor organizations of the 1920s, and in the PCS, began working among peasants and urban laborers in 1970. Divided over ideology and strategy for a decade, the five took a major step toward unity with the creation of the Farabundo Martí Front for National Liberation (FMLN) in October 1980. Three months later, the FMLN began military operations which, until 1984, threatened to defeat the army. Thereafter, the U.S.–supplied air power of the armed forces halted the guerrillas' advances and forced them to alter their strategy. Still, the FMLN expanded its operations from five provinces (of fourteen) in 1981 to thirteen in 1988.

A coup in October 1979 sought to remove military conservatives, derail the revolutionary movement, and institute long-overdue socioeconomic reforms. A number of prominent political party leaders, many of whom had been in exile for several years, returned to accept high positions in the new government. Among them were Guillermo Manuel Ungo (MNR), a member of the junta; Rubén Zamora (PDC), secretary of the presidency; and Héctor Dada Hirezi (PDC), foreign minister. Within two months, however, it became clear that a group of extremely conservative officers had successfully displaced the progressive coup leaders. In late December, the civilians in government resigned; the United States encouraged the Christian Democrats to join the military in a new government; and Dada became a member of the junta, while many other party members refused to participate. In early March 1980, after Zamora's brother, Mario, was assassinated in his own home, Dada resigned, went into exile, and was replaced by José Napoleón Duarte. The PDC split. The departing faction, led by Rubén Zamora, who had gone into exile, founded the Popular Social Christian Movement (MPSC) in May.

The United States, fearing a second revolution on the heels of Nicaragua's, increased its involvement through a Janus-headed policy: Politically, reforms and elections were emphasized; and militarily, the Salvadorean armed forces were trained in counterinsurgency. In March 1980, an agrarian reform was promulgated, and the banks and external commerce—the major export crops of coffee, cotton, and sugar cane—were nationalized. After January 1981, the Reagan administration considered the agrarian and other reforms socialistic, but while congressional pressure prevented their rollback, the pace of implementation slowed markedly. The political emphasis shifted to sponsoring elections, which would ostensibly put El Salvador on the road to democracy and rob the revolutionary movement of any remaining raison d'être. Elections for a Constituent Assembly were held in 1982, for president in 1984 and 1989, and for the Legislative Assembly in 1985, 1988, and 1991. These elections gave El Salvador a "democratic government" that rarely exhibited the conditions of a functioning democracy: freedom of speech, the media, and party organization; freedom for interest groups; the absence of state-sponsored terror; and the absence of fear and coercion among the population. Nor was the military subordinated to civilian rule. The armed forces increased from 11,000 to 56,000 between 1980 and 1987 and this, plus training the military to fight guerrillas, ensured that, although the armed forces no longer occupied political office, they continued to wield considerable political power.

While the war continued, other developments changed the internal dynamics of El Salvador. One was the emergence of an extreme right-wing political party, the Nationalist Republican Alliance (ARENA) in 1981, whose shadowy origins and direct ties to death squads are well documented. Another was unanticipated: The electoral process opened political space that repression had closed in the early 1980s. New political parties emerged, split, and faded; and grass-roots organizations and existing labor unions began to organize and demand better wages and working conditions, economic reforms, and peace. ARENA and the PDC tried to organize or coopt parts of this movement; those that resisted were labeled FMLN "fronts" and suffered renewed repression. The MPSC and MNR, in 1985, began returning party activists to test the political waters. These men and women maintained a low profile for two years; then, in November 1987 Zamora and Ungo returned to stay. The MPSC applied for and received legal standing, and both parties began to operate more openly. Shortly thereafter, the MPSC, MNR, and the newly founded Social Democrat Party (PSD) joined in forming the Democratic Convergence (CD), under whose banner they would participate in subsequent elections.

El Salvador's first civilian president in fifty-three years, Christian Democrat José Napoleón Duarte, was elected in 1984 on a platform promising economic reforms and peace negotiations with the FMLN. In March 1989, having delivered on neither while presiding over one of the most corrupt governments in Salvadorean history, his party, which had split once again, in 1988, lost to ARENA. The most interesting moment in the campaign came, not from the participating parties, but from the FMLN, who reversed its long-standing policy of disparaging the elections as an instrument in the counterinsurgency war and offered to participate if the elections were postponed for six months and the military was confined to barracks for the duration. After several rounds of talks among all the parties, the proposal was vetoed by ARENA, who correctly saw victory within its grasp.

The new president, Alfredo Cristiani, promised to seek peace and responded positively to an FMLN initiative to begin peace talks, the first of which was held in September. After Cristiani's inauguration in June, however, repression against the unions and other mass organizations escalated. In late October, the bombing of the headquarters of El Salvador's largest union federation convinced the FMLN that the government was not serious about negotiations. Two weeks later, the FMLN opened a countrywide offensive and brought the war to the capital. In 1990 government and the FMLN returned to the negotiating table. The major stumbling block was the future of the armed forces which, the rebels insisted, had to be significantly reduced and purged of any officers associated with human rights abuses. Late in the year, the talks bogged down once again, and the FMLN responded with a series of coordinated military actions around the country that it declined to call an offensive. Despite official charges that the FMLN was not really interested in peace, the net effect was an increase in the frequency and intensity of negotiations and a narrowing of differences between the two sides.

Meanwhile, the campaign for the 1991 assembly and mayoral elections got under way. For the first time since 1982, the FMLN did not attempt in any way to impede the electoral process. Five parties plus the Democratic Convergence participated. The campaign was marred by violence; a week before the election, the CD issued a nine-page list of documented cases that ranged from assassination to destruction of property to intimidation. The offices of El Salvador's only opposition newspaper, *El Diario Latino*, were destroyed in an arson fire in early February. On election day, there was evidence that the computerized voting lists had been tampered with; in areas where the CD was expected to do well, hundreds of voters found that, although they had registered and held voting cards, they were not on the list and were not allowed to vote. On election eve, in a number of these same areas, the polling station had been arbitrarily and inexplicably moved without public notice.

As election day approached, it became clear that the big question was how well the CD, which had won only 3.8 percent of the vote in 1989, would do. Indeed, by election day, the question was whether the CD or the PCN would come in third, after ARENA and the PDC. In the end, despite various other irregularities in the vote count, the CD gained 12 percent and nine seats in the assembly. The PCN, which won only 9 percent of the vote, also won nine seats, thanks to a byzantine system of proportional representation. ARENA lost its majority, winning thirty-nine of eighty-four seats in a newly expanded assembly. While its alliance with the PCN ensured continued control, it would have to deal with an articulate and politically astute democratic left who had made it clear that it would both inform and consult with the people on a regular basis. In a symbolic gesture of this commitment, the nine CD deputies and one UDN deputy took their oaths of office before a 1 May gathering of 10,000 people in San Salvador; thousands more were prevented from entering the city by army roadblocks set up on all major highways.

Following the election, President Cristiani's deputy chief of staff, Ernesto Altschul, commented that ARENA was not looking at "one or two more terms but a longer period of domination for a center-right party" (Norton 1991). While Altschul denied in a subsequent interview that this statement implied intent to control the electoral process, the attitude, to the extent that it is shared by other Arenistas, does not bode well for the future of democracy in El Salvador. Further, the possibility of even greater polarization and conflict in the electoral process was, ironically, exacerbated by the peace accords, signed in Mexico City on January 16, 1992, and the formal recognition on May 1 of the FMLN as a legal political party.

Democracy means, among other things, losing elections as well as winning them. The outpouring of popular support for the FMLN in the wake of the accords and the cease fire on February 1 stunned ARENA and the army, and suggested the real possibility of a political battle in the 1994 elections whose outcome could not be predicted. If, as the 1991 elections suggest, ARENA employs a variety of sordid tactics to prevent the left from eventually winning an election (whether in 1994 or later), then conditions for opposition parties will not have changed appreciably from the late 1960s and Stephen Webre's "logical flaw" will have reappeared. For the third time in Salvadorean history (1929–1931 and 1961–1972), increased political space for the opposition, opened in the 1990s by the peace talks and the accords, would not be large enough to allow the left to win an election.

Bibliography

Thomas P. Anderson, *Matanza, El Salvador's Communist Revolt of 1932*. University of Nebraska Press, Lincoln, 1971.

Ricardo Córdova Macías. "El Salvador: Análisis de las elecciones presidenciales de Marzo de 1989." *Presencia* (San Salvador), 2, 50, April–June, 1989, pp. 87–103.

"El Salvador's 1985 Elections: Legislative Assembly and Municipal Councils." Resource Book. U.S. Department of State, Washington, D.C., February 1985.

"El Salvador's Presidential Elections." Resource Book. U.S. Department of State, Washington, D.C., March 1984.

Estudios Centroamericanos (ECA). (Monthly journal published by Universidad Centroamericana José Simeón Cañas, San Salvador).

Edgar Jiménez C., et al. *El Salvador: Guerra, política y paz (1979–1988)*. CINAS/CRIES, San Salvador, 1988.

Hector Lindo-Fuentes. *Weak Foundations: The Economy of El Salvador in the Nineteenth Century 1821–1898*. University of California Press, Berkeley, 1990.

Italo López Vallecillos. "El proceso militar-reformista en El Salvador." *ECA* 403–4, May–June 1982, pp. 369–420.

Mario Lungo Uclés. *El Salvador en los 80: Contrainsurgencia y revolución*. EDUCA, San José, Costa Rica, 1990.

Tommie Sue Montgomery. *Revolution in El Salvador: Origins and Evolution*. Westview Press, Boulder, Colo., 1982, 1991.

Chris Norton. "Rightist Intimidation Wins in El Salvador." *In These Times*. 3–9 April 1991, p. 9.

Patricia Parkman. *Nonviolent Insurrection in El Salvador: The Fall of Maximiliano Hernández Martínez*. University of Arizona Press, Tucson, 1988.

Proceso. Centro Universitario de Documentación e Información, Universidad Centroamericana José Simeón Cañas, San Salvador. (News and analysis published weekly.)

"A Step Toward Peace? The March 1991 Elections in El Salvador." WOLA Elections Brief, Washington Office on Latin America, 1 March 1991.

Stephen Webre. *José Napoleón Duarte and the Christian Democratic Party in Salvadoran Politics 1960–1972*. Louisiana State University Press, Baton Rouge, 1979.

Alastair White. *El Salvador*. Praeger, New York, 1973.

Political Parties—Active

ALIANZA REPUBLICANA NACIONALISTA. *See* NATIONALIST REPUBLICAN ALLIANCE.

AUTHENTIC CHRISTIAN DEMOCRAT MOVEMENT (MOVIMIENTO AUTÉNTICO DEMÓCRATA CRISTIANO—MADC). *See* AUTHENTIC CHRISTIAN MOVEMENT.

AUTHENTIC CHRISTIAN MOVEMENT (MOVIMIENTO AUTÉNTICO CRISTIANO—MAC). The MAC was created in 1988 after the Christian Democrat Party (PDC) nominated Fidel Chávez Mena as its presidential candidate. After waging a losing battle during the summer, dissident Christian Democrats, who saw Julio Adolfo Rey Prendes as the logical successor to José Napoleón Duarte, left the PDC in September, founded the Authentic Christian Democrat Movement (MADC), and then fused with the Centrist Republican Stable Movement (MERECEN) to form the MAC. The party chose Rey Prendes as presidential candidate. The MAC exodus included twelve of the twenty-two PDC National Assembly delegates and a majority of the seventy-nine PDC mayors, all of whom had been elected in March 1988. In the 1989 presidential elections, the MAC received 0.99 percent of the vote; in 1991, the party won only one seat in the assembly.

CENTRIST REPUBLICAN STABLE MOVEMENT (MOVIMIENTO ESTABLE REPUBLICANO CENTRISTA—MERECEN). Founded in March 1983 by Juan Ramón Rosales, as a personalist vehicle for his ideals, MERECEN won 0.52 percent of the vote in 1984 and 0.15 percent in coalition with the Party of Popular Orientation in 1985. On 2 October 1988, it fused with the Authentic Christian Democrat Movement to form the Authentic Christian Movement (MAC). It is still legally inscribed as a party because the MAC won more than 0.5 percent of the vote in 1989.

CHRISTIAN DEMOCRAT PARTY (PARTIDO DEMÓCRATA CRISTIANO—PDC). The PDC was founded in 1960 and, like other Christian Democratic parties in Latin America, promised a "third way" to a "revolution in liberty" via social and economic reforms using the developmental model and an end to military rule. In El Salvador the PDC encompassed three ideological positions which would ultimately cause profound schisms. While all three came from Catholic thought, one strain was reactionary, and its partisans soon left to help found the Party of National Conciliation (PCN). Of the remaining two, one was inspired by progressive Catholic social doctrine and programmatically shared much in common with the international social democratic movement. The other, although reformist, was influenced by a streak of anticommunism.

The PDC's first electoral participation came in 1964 when it won fourteen (of fifty-two) assembly seats, thirty-seven mayoralties, and 26 percent of the vote. It increased that percentage through the 1960s, and in 1968 the PDC won the mayoralties of El Salvador's three largest cities. In 1972 the PDC joined in the National Opposition Union (UNO) coalition with the Revolutionary National Movement (MNR) and the Nationalist Democratic Union (UDN) and ran José Napoleón Duarte for president, with Guillermo Manuel Ungo (MNR) for vice president. By all objective accounts, the UNO ticket won the election, but when Duarte carried San Salvador by a two-to-one margin, the army prohibited further announcement of the returns. Twenty-four hours later, the Election Council announced that the PCN's Colonel Armando Molina had won by 22,000 votes. A coup attempt in support of Duarte failed. He was arrested for publicly supporting the coup and sent into exile; he returned only after the October 1979 coup.

A handful of Christian Democrats, all from the progressive wing, participated in the new government, but they all resigned, along with the rest of the cabinet (minus the minister of defense) and the civilians on the junta, in late December 1979. The Duarte faction, encouraged by the U. S. Embassy, joined with the military to form a new government in mid-January 1980. This "second junta" lasted until Mario Zamora, the PDC attorney general, was assassinated in his home in late February. In early March, the entire left wing of the PDC left the party, Duarte got himself elected to a "third junta," and in December he was named president of the junta in yet another executive reorganization, a post in which he served until the 1982 elections. In that election, the PDC won 36 percent of the vote and twenty-four of sixty seats in the Constituent Assembly, making it the largest single party. It was stymied in pushing its political program, however, because the other parties, all of which were to the PDC's right, formed a working coalition.

In the 1984 presidential election, Duarte ran on a platform of peace and economic reform. He came in first but did not gain a majority of the votes; in the runoff with Roberto D'Aubuisson, of the Nationalist Republican Alliance (ARENA), Duarte won 54 percent of the valid votes cast. A year later, the PDC captured a clear majority in the National Assembly, winning thirty-three of sixty seats, and 153 of 262 mayoralties. The party, however, largely because of opposition from the military and the U. S. Embassy, was unable to deliver on either plank of the 1984 platform and, during the three years that the Christian Democrats controlled the executive and legislative branches of government, the party became increasingly implicated in petty and massive corruption.

In March 1988, a disillusioned electorate gave the PDC only twenty-two seats in the assembly and seventy-nine mayoralties. On the heels of the election, an internal struggle erupted in the PDC over who would be the standard-bearer in the 1989 presidential election. The fight between Fidel Chávez Mena and Julio Adolfo Rey Prendes split the party; Rey Prendes left and formed the Authentic Christian Movement (MAC). Chávez Mena garnered 36 percent of the vote in losing to ARENA. In the 1991 assembly and municipal elections, the PDC took 26 percent of the vote and placed twenty-six deputies.

COMMUNIST PARTY OF EL SALVADOR (PARTIDO COMUNISTA DE EL SALVADOR—PCS). The oldest political party—and the first revolutionary organization—in El Salvador was founded during a period of political liberalization in the late 1920s by Augustín Farabundo Martí, the educated son of a mestizo landowner. The party focused its early organizing in the southwestern part of the country and participated in assembly and municipal elections in

January 1932. In some areas, where the PCS was strong, elections were suspended; in others, the party claimed victory but the government refused to certify the elections. The PCS concluded that the regime was unwilling to let it participate or hold office through legal means; it decided to revolt, but the uprising was put down and followed by a massacre of 30,000 people. Martí and other leaders were shot; the party was proscribed and went underground for the next half century. Nevertheless, every significant period of popular protest against a succession of military governments from 1944 on included PCS militants.

In 1969 an intraparty debate over whether the time had once again come for armed struggle split the PCS. Its secretary-general, Salvador Cayetano Carpio, left and founded the first of the contemporary revolutionary organizations, the Popular Forces of Liberation (FPL). The remaining members decided the time had once again come to participate in elections, and they organized a legal front, the Nationalist Democratic Union (UDN). In 1977 the PCS reversed its earlier decision and began to create a revolutionary armed force. In October 1981, it joined with four other revolutionary organizations in founding the Farabundo Martí Front for National Liberation (FMLN).

CONVERGENCIA DEMOCRÁTICA. *See* DEMOCRATIC CONVERGENCE.

DEMOCRATIC ACTION PARTY (PARTIDO ACCIÓN DEMOCRÁTICA—AD). The AD, created in November 1981, soon became known as the "Rotary Club" of the oligarchy's lawyers, although its political base was broader than that, including owners of medium-sized farms and businesses, midlevel business managers, and professional people. Ideologically, the AD was originally closer to the Christian Democrats than other parties inasmuch as it supported the first phase of the agrarian reform, which had been promulgated in March 1980, although it advocated return of the banks and external commerce to their original owners, the oligarchy. In the 1982 Constituent Assembly elections, the AD won two seats; in 1985, one seat; in 1988, no seats. In the 1991 assembly and municipal elections, the AD garnered 0.64 percent of the vote, which automatically eliminated it as a recognized party.

DEMOCRATIC CONVERGENCE (CONVERGENCIA DEMOCRÁTICA—CD). The CD was founded on 7 November 1987 by three democratic left parties: the Popular Social Christian Movement (MPSC); the Revolutionary National Movement (MNR), and the Social Democrat Party (PSD). The CD, led by Guillermo Manuel Ungo (MNR) and Rubén Zamora (MPSC), put forward a "programmatic platform" in September 1988, in which it defined the "four great problems" facing El Salvador: civil war, loss of national sovereignty, absence of real democracy, and the extreme poverty of the Salvadorean people. Ungo and Zamora, the CD candidates for president and vice president, respectively, ran on this platform in the 1989 elections, in which the CD garnered 3.8 percent of the vote. Dismissed by the Nationalist Republican Alliance (ARENA) and the U. S. Embassy as a blip on the political screen, the CD continued its organizing efforts around the country, especially in urban areas. In the 1991 assembly and municipal elections, the CD won 12 percent of the vote, which made it the third largest political force in the country after ARENA and the Christian Democrat Party, and nine seats in the assembly.

DEMOCRATIC REVOLUTIONARY FRONT (FRENTE DEMOCRÁTICO REVOLUCIONARIO—FDR). See POPULAR SOCIAL CHRISTIAN MOVE- MENT and REVOLUTIONARY NATIONAL MOVEMENT.

FARABUNDO MARTÍ NATIONAL LIBERATION FRONT (FRENTE "FARABUNDO MARTÍ" PARA LA LIBERACIÓN NACIONAL—FMLN). The FMLN was founded on October 11, 1980 by five political-military orga- nizations that, except for the Communist Party, had all been founded in the early 1970s. The FMLN's original objective was to achieve a military victory over the Salvadorean Armed Forces, eliminate the oligarchy as the controlling economic elite, and establish a leftist-dominated socialist state, not unlike that of Sandinista Nicaragua.

That the FMLN and its constituent groups considered themselves "political- military organizations" is not insignificant; they had clearly defined political programs that, during the 1970s, reflected profound political and sectarian di- visions. Beginning in 1980, however, as the five groups moved toward unity, they began to speak with one voice and a unified political program emerged, even before the FMLN's founding. This program evolved and changed through- out the decade, becoming increasingly more pragmatic and flexible, less dogmatic and Marxist-Leninist. The increasing pragmatism was no doubt helped by the FMLN's successes on the battlefield; by 1983 the guerrillas had fought the Armed Forces into a situation that one analyst called a "dynamic equilibrium"; neither side could defeat the other but the character of the civil war kept changing as the U.S.-directed army kept trying new strategies.

In January 1989, as the country prepared for presidential elections, the FMLN, to the shock and chagrin of the Christian Democratic Party (PDC), National Republican Alliance (ARENA), and the United States, suddenly issued a dra- matic proposal in which it offered to participate in the elections and honor the outcome if they were postponed for six months—from March to September— and the military confined to its barracks, to give the rebels time to organize politically. Dr. Miguel Saenz, a top FMLN analyst and spokesman, said at the time that the FMLN had spent the previous fall analyzing the "correlations of forces" in El Salvador and had concluded that they were the "number one" political force in the country. Thus they did not fear trusting their political fate to elections. But the FMLN's participation was not to be: after several meetings among the political parties and FMLN in Mexico (with some support from the new Bush Administration), ARENA, smelling victory, nixed the plan.

Peace talks between the new ARENA government and FMLN took place in the late summer and early fall of 1989 but, in the wake of a growing number of human rights violations, culminating in the noon-time bombing of the headquarters of El Salvador's most powerful union federation, and an increasingly intransigent government, the FMLN launched the biggest offensive of the war and brought the battle to the streets of San Salvador. The offensive had the intended effect: it brought a more flexible government back to the negotiating table. Meanwhile, the democratic left made significant gains in the 1991 election; even the Salvadoran Communist Party's (PCS) legal front, the Nationalist Democratic Union (UDN), won one seat in the Legislative Assembly.

Twenty months after peace talks began, just minutes before 1992 arrived, the FMLN and Salvadorean government signed the last in a series of accords that had been reached over the previous eighteen months. The accords reflected a number of FMLN successes as well as significant concessions. With regard to the electoral arena, the FMLN won the right to become a legally inscribed political party and thereby participate in the 1994 elections. It demanded and got a series of electoral reforms that make the process more democratic and reduce the control that the party in power exercised over it. Finally, the accords removed the traditional, constitutional role of the military as guarantor of the constitutional order, and insure that the army will be in its barracks during the campaign and on election day for the first time in decades.

The FMLN began transforming itself from a political-military organization into a purely political organization even before the final peace accords were signed. It began sending political activists back to El Salvador eighteen months earlier and while their work was largely clandestine, it was explicitly political, laying the groundwork for the moment when the FMLN would be legal, which it did, on May 1, 1992.

FRENTE DEMOCRÁTICO REVOLUCIONARIO. See POPULAR SOCIAL CHRISTIAN MOVEMENT and REVOLUTIONARY NATIONAL MOVEMENT.

FRENTE "FARABUNDO MARTÍ" PARA LA LIBERACIÓN NACIONAL. See FARABUNDO MARTÍ NATIONAL LIBERATION FRONT.

LIBERATION PARTY (PARTIDO LIBERACIÓN). After the Nationalist Republican Alliance lost the 1985 legislative elections, a fight erupted within the party and a small minority of its deputies, led by Hugo Barrera and Vicente Amado Platero, left and formed the "Patria Libre" party. The Central Election Council disallowed the chosen name, whereupon the party renamed itself "Liberación," and participated in the 1988 legislative elections where it won 3.8 percent of the vote. In March 1989, Liberación joined with the Salvadorean

Institutional Authentic Party and the Salvadorean Popular Party to form the Unión Popular coalition, but it won only 0.49 percent of the vote, 0.01 percent less than it needed to stay alive. As a result, both the coalition and its constituent parties disappeared.

MOVEMENT OF NATIONAL SOLIDARITY (MOVIMIENTO DE SOLIDARIDAD NACIONAL—MSN). In mid-November 1991, the leaders of this new party presented petitions with the required 3,000 signatures to the Central Election Council, requested inscription as a legal party, and announced its intent to participate in the 1994 elections. The leadership is fundamentalist Protestant and has received substantial funds from unidentified sources, a fact that became apparent when the MSN threw a lavish party at an expensive hotel to celebrate its inscription in early 1992. Politically, however, the MSN has virtually no political relevance.

MOVIMIENTO AUTÉNTICO CRISTIANO. See AUTHENTIC CHRISTIAN MOVEMENT.

MOVIMIENTO AUTÉNTICO DEMÓCRATA CRISTIANO. See AUTHENTIC CHRISTIAN MOVEMENT.

MOVIMIENTO DE SOLIDARIDAD NACIONAL. See MOVEMENT OF NATIONAL SOLIDAIRTY.

MOVIMIENTO ESTABLE REPUBLICANO CENTRISTA. See CENTRIST REPUBLICAN STABLE MOVEMENT.

MOVIMIENTO NACIONAL REVOLUCIONARIO. See REVOLUTIONARY NATIONAL MOVEMENT.

MOVIMIENTO POPULAR SOCIAL CRISTIANO. See POPULAR SOCIAL CHRISTIAN MOVEMENT.

NATIONALIST DEMOCRATIC UNION (UNIÓN DEMOCRÁTICA NACIONALISTA—UDN). The UDN made its first appearance with a political statement in October 1969, ran in the 1970 assembly and municipal elections, and won only one mayoralty, the city of Usulután. In 1972 it joined the Christian Democrat Party and the Revolutionary National Movement in an electoral coalition, the National Opposition Union (UNO), which was cheated of victory by the military (see Christian Democrat Party). The UDN participated with the UNO in the 1974 elections, but the coalition abstained in 1976 in protest over certain fraud. In the 1977 presidential election, the UDN once again participated with the UNO, and once again the election was stolen by the army.

After that, the UDN concentrated its efforts on mass organizing and reappeared in late 1979 as one of five mass organizations that would, in January 1980, form the Revolutionary Coordination of the Masses. Until the late 1980s, the UDN functioned as part of the Democratic Revolutionary Front (FDR), the negotiating arm of the FMLN, but in 1990 it decided once again to join the electoral process. It ran several candidates for deputies and mayors in March 1991, but won only one seat in the assembly.

NATIONALIST REPUBLICAN ALLIANCE (ALIANZA REPUBLICANA NACIONALISTA—ARENA). The antecedents of this extreme right-wing party were sown in the fall of 1979 with the creation of the Broad Nationalist Front (FAN) and related organizations of women and youth. Meanwhile, the founders were also engaged in another activity: the formation, in cooperation with the army, of paramilitary death squads. Thus, from its inception, ARENA had both a public face and a clandestine side, both of which were manipulated from the beginning by National Guard Major Roberto D'Aubuisson, who used information he had collected as an intelligence officer to publicly attack and threaten prominent individuals whom he accused of being Communists. Often, in 1980 and 1981, these individuals were soon after assassinated.

The founders of ARENA were given advice and support by the Nationalist Liberation Movement (MLN) in Guatemala; the formal founding of ARENA took place in Guatemala on 22 May 1981 with thirty-five charter members in attendance. The "Republican" in ARENA was chosen in honor of the U.S. Republican Party, some of whose members and staffers gave ARENA advice about lobbying on Capitol Hill and running a political campaign. ARENA's creed was a mixture of the 1980 Republican Platform and neo-Nazi principles: laissez-faire, free-market economics, a Hobbesian definition of the state that emphasized maintaining order, an all-out war against the insurgents, and removing human rights constraints from the armed forces in their prosecution of the war.

D'Aubuisson became the party standard-bearer. A charismatic and indefatigable campaigner, he crisscrossed the country rallying large groups of peasants and urbanites with red, white, and blue banners, T-shirts, and balloons and haranguing them with themes such as, "El Salvador will be the tomb of the Communists." ARENA stunned everyone by capturing 26 percent of the vote and nineteen seats in the 1982 Constituent Assembly elections. Together with other rightist parties, ARENA held majority control, and D'Aubuisson had visions of getting himself elected provisional president of the country. He did not consider, however, the extent to which the Reagan administration was prepared to go to prevent this, so he had to settle for president of the assembly, a position he held until he resigned to run for president in 1984. In that election, D'Aubuisson forced José Napoleón Duarte into a runoff, which Duarte won.

In 1985 ARENA suffered a further setback when the Christian Democrat Party (PDC) swept the assembly elections, leaving ARENA and its coalition partner, the National Conciliation Party, with twenty-five deputies and 108 mayoralties. During the next three years, the presence of D'Aubuisson as the party's standard-bearer became an increasing liability in the United States, especially in the U.S. Congress. Nonetheless, as the PDC frittered away its electoral mandates of 1984 and 1985, ARENA mounted yet another effective campaign, using the floor of the assembly, to begin to question growing corruption in the Duarte administration. As a result, in 1988, ARENA won thirty seats and control of the assembly.

With this victory, ARENA began to look toward the 1989 presidential elections and decided it needed a more moderate image. In June 1988, therefore, the party chose political unknown Alfredo Cristiani, a young, U.S.–educated member of the oligarchy, to be its candidate. D'Aubuisson handpicked the candidate for vice president: Francisco Merino. While ARENA ran another effective, U.S.–style campaign in 1989, the PDC's woes virtually guaranteed Cristiani a victory, which he won in the first round with 54 percent of the vote. From the beginning, Cristiani adopted a more moderate line than D'Aubuisson; he pledged a government, as he stated, "based on the principles of liberty, honesty, legality and security"; he promised to get the economy moving; and he called for negotiations with the Farabundo Martí Front for National Liberation (FMLN).

By 1991, with negotiations between government and rebels under way, and despite a 3.6-percent growth in gross national product, the vast majority of Salvadoreans did not benefit, and ARENA experienced the same fate as the PDC in 1988: Its percent of the vote dropped ten points, and it won only thirty-nine seats in an assembly that had been expanded to eighty-four deputies.

PARTIDO ACCIÓN DEMOCRÁTICA. See DEMOCRATIC ACTION PARTY.

PARTIDO ACCIÓN RENOVADORA. See RENOVATING ACTION PARTY.

PARTIDO AUTÉNTICO INSTITUCIONAL SALVADOREÑA. See SALVADOREAN INSTITUTIONAL AUTHENTIC PARTY.

PARTIDO COMUNISTA DE EL SALVADOR. See COMMUNIST PARTY OF EL SALVADOR.

PARTIDO DE CONCILIACIÓN NACIONAL. See PARTY OF NATIONAL CONCILIATION.

PARTIDO DE ORIENTACIÓN POPULAR. See PARTY OF POPULAR ORIENTATION.

PARTIDO DEMÓCRATA CRISTIANO. See CHRISTIAN DEMOCRAT PARTY.

PARTIDO LIBERACIÓN. See LIBERATION PARTY.

PARTIDO POPULAR SALVADOREÑO. See SALVADOREAN POPULAR PARTY.

PARTIDO SOCIAL DEMÓCRATA. See SOCIAL DEMOCRAT PARTY.

PARTY OF NATIONAL CONCILIATION (PARTIDO DE CONCILIA-CIÓN NACIONAL—PCN). The PCN was the third and last official party established in El Salvador, after the Revolutionary Party of Democratic Unification and the Pro-Fatherland National Party. Founded in August 1961, the PCN served as the instrument for guaranteeing the army's control of the executive and legislative branches through 1977. Its leaders came from the small professional bourgeoisie in concert with the landed oligarchy and, by the late 1970s, the industrial and financial oligarchy as well. A few months after the October 1979 coup, the PCN began to publish extended analyses of the situation in the country and sought to define for itself a position that called for social transformation.

In the 1982 Constituent Assembly elections, the PCN came in third with 19.8 percent of the vote and fourteen delegates. In the assembly it often joined the Nationalist Republican Alliance to promote a conservative agenda. In February 1983, a split in the PCN produced a new party, the Salvadorean Institutional Authentic Party. In 1984 the PCN presidential candidate, José Francisco (Chachi) Guerrero, came in third with 19.3 percent of the vote. A year later, the PCN's share of the vote dropped to 8.4 percent, and in 1988 it remained the same, with the party winning seven seats in the assembly. In the 1989 presidential election, the PCN's share of the vote was halved, to 4.1 percent, but in 1991, amid charges of electoral fraud, the party received 9 percent of the vote and nine assembly seats.

PARTY OF POPULAR ORIENTATION (PARTIDO DE ORIENTACIÓN POPULAR—POP). The POP was created in the late 1970s in opposition to President Humberto Romero by individuals with coffee, cattle, and sugarcane interests. Its leader was René Segovia, but General José Alberto Medrano emerged as its principal figure before the 1982 election, in which the POP earned 0.92 percent of the vote. In 1984, it won 0.37 percent of the vote and, in 1985, it formed a coalition with the Centrist Republican Stable Movement, which together won 0.15 percent of the vote. The party remained on the scene until 1988, in which year its portion of the vote was 0.19 percent, and it lost its legal standing.

POPULAR SOCIAL CHRISTIAN MOVEMENT (MOVIMIENTO POPU-LAR SOCIAL CRISTIANO—MPSC). The MPSC was founded on 10 May 1980 by Rubén Zamora and other former leaders of the Christian Democrat

Party who had left the party two months earlier. It subsequently joined the Democratic Revolutionary Front (FDR) and held one seat, until 1987, on the Political-Diplomatic Commission of the FDR–Farabundo Martí Front for National Liberation. Between 1982 and 1987, the MPSC refused to participate in elections, arguing that they were part of the U.S. counterinsurgency project to hang a democratic mask on a repressive state body. It did participate with the FDR–FMLN in peace talks with the government in the fall of 1984. In 1985 the MPSC, whose political program was closer to that of the social democrats than to that of the Marxist FMLN, began quietly sending some of its leaders back to El Salvador, from which they had been exiled for five years, to test the waters. Finally, in November 1987, Zamora returned permanently to El Salvador and founded, together with the Revolutionary National Movement and the Social Democrat Party, the Democratic Convergence (CD). By 1988 the MPSC and CD had reevaluated their posture toward elections and decided to participate in the 1989 presidential campaign. In the meantime, MPSC members were actively and aggressively building the party at the grass roots in major cities, working with limited resources and in a climate of fear. This work returned dividends in 1991, when six MPSC candidates were elected to the assembly. Zamora won a "national" seat and was subsequently elected a vice president of the assembly.

RENOVATING ACTION PARTY (PARTIDO ACCIÓN RENOVADORA— PAR). Organized in the wake of the 1944 revolt against Maximiliano Hernández Martínez, the PAR, for twenty years, provided virtually the only opposition to the official army candidates and did so from a progressive position. After the 1961 coup, Fabio Castillo, who had been a member of the short-lived junta between October 1960 and January 1961, emerged as the PAR's new standard-bearer. The party swung well to the left of the Christian Democrats and stayed there through the 1960s. For its efforts, it was labeled "Communist" but, despite this, garnered 14.4 percent of the vote in the 1967 presidential election and was immediately thereafter proscribed. The PAR reappeared in 1982, a shadow of its former self. It ran candidates in 1985, 1988, and 1989, winning less than 1 percent of the vote each time. In 1989 its poor showing (0.34 percent) caused it to be eliminated as a legally inscribed party.

REVOLUTIONARY NATIONAL MOVEMENT (MOVIMIENTO NACIONAL REVOLUCIONARIO—MNR). The MNR, which began as a discussion group among friends in 1964, initiated public activities a year later. It affiliated with the Socialist International (SI) and ultimately its secretary-general, after 1969, Guillermo Manuel Ungo, became an international vice president of the SI. The MNR remained a small party, largely of intellectuals, but it established and maintained a presence in Salvadorean electoral politics from the late 1960s into the 1990s. In 1968 it won two seats in the assembly;

in 1972 it was a member of the National Opposition Union (UNO) coalition, and Ungo was José Napoleón Duarte's vice-presidential candidate.

After the 1979 coup, Ungo became a member of the civilian-military junta, but he resigned two-and-a-half months later along with his other civilian colleagues and the cabinet. In the spring of 1980, the MNR helped found the Democratic Revolutionary Front (FDR), and Ungo became its president at the end of the year. He was a member, until 1987, of the Political-Diplomatic Commission of the FDR–Farabundo Martí Front for National Liberation (FMLN), and he participated in FDR–FMLN peace talks with the Duarte government in October and November 1984.

Like the Popular Social Christian Movement, the MNR decided to reenter traditional party politics in 1987 and they, together with the Social Democrat Party, formed the Democratic Convergence (CD) in November. Ungo ran for president in the 1989 elections, but the CD won only 3.8 percent of the vote. In January 1990, the party suffered the first of two major blows when its under secretary-general, Hector Oquelí Colindres, was kidnapped and murdered on his way to the airport in Guatemala City. Eleven months later, Ungo, who was a candidate for the National Assembly on the CD ticket, died after surgery in Mexico City.

SALVADOREAN INSTITUTIONAL AUTHENTIC PARTY (PARTIDO AUTÉNTICO INSTITUCIONAL SALVADOREÑO—PAISA). The PAISA was founded on 17 February 1983 when nine delegates in the Constituent Assembly broke with the Party of National Conciliation (PCN) and declared that they would support other parties only in what "coincided with the interests of the people." The PAISA would see the next two years as the high point of its relatively short existence. Its ideology was, in fact, to the right of the PCN. Its candidate for president in 1984 was retired Colonel Roberto Escobar García, who attracted only 1.2 percent of the vote. In the 1985 assembly elections, the PAISA increased its margin to 3.4 percent, then dropped to 2.1 percent in 1988. In the 1989 presidential elections, the PAISA joined with the Liberation Party and the Salvadorean Popular Party in a coalition called the Unión Popular, which garnered only 0.49 percent of the valid votes and thereby put both the coalition and its three constituent parties out of business.

SALVADOREAN POPULAR PARTY (PARTIDO POPULAR SALVADOR-EÑO—PPS). The PPS, founded in 1966, was composed of dissident members of the Renovating Action Party and the Party of National Conciliation, who cast themselves as the right-wing opposition to the government. The PPS participated in the 1967 presidential election and came in fourth; in 1970, it tried to broaden its appeal to what it called the "silent majority"; in 1972, it nominated a laissez-faire liberal, José Antonio Rodríguez Porth, who ran a distant fourth; in 1974, it won four seats in the assembly.

The PPS stayed around and reappeared in 1981, but its thunder was stolen by the Nationalist Republican Alliance. In 1982, it garnered 2.9 percent of the vote and one seat in the Constituent Assembly; in 1984, 1.9 percent; and in 1985, 1.7 percent. In 1989, it helped form a coalition of three parties called the Unión Popular, which gained 0.49 percent of the vote in the presidential election. By 0.01 percent (approximately ninety-four votes), both the coalition and its constituent parties failed to remain legally inscribed.

SOCIAL DEMOCRAT PARTY (PARTIDO SOCIAL DEMÓCRATA— PSD). According to Patricia Parkman, a Social Democrat Party existed in 1944 and apparently played a role in the events leading to the removal of Maximiliano Hernández Martínez. In 1960 a Social Democratic Party, with a progressive agenda, was founded by former members of the Revolutionary Party of Democratic Unification and supporters of former president Oscar Osorio, but it disappeared after 1962. A new PSD was founded in March 1987, and the following November it joined the Revolutionary National Movement and the Popular Social Christian Movement in forming the Democratic Convergence (CD). The PSD's secretary-general, Mario Reni Roldán, joined Guillermo Manuel Ungo on the CD ticket as the vice-presidential candidate in 1989. In 1991 the PSD continued to be the smallest member of the CD.

UNIÓN DEMOCRÁTICA NACIONALISTA. See NATIONALIST DEMOCRATIC UNION.

Political Parties—Historical

APRIL AND MAY REVOLUTIONARY PARTY (PARTIDO REVOLUCIONARIO ABRIL Y MAYO—PRAM). Founded in 1959, and named for the months in 1944 when Maximiliano Hernández Martínez was overthrown, the clearly left-wing PRAM included Communists. After the October 1960 coup, when the junta, which many military officers considered too radical, let it be known that the PRAM would be legalized, a countercoup removed the junta and outlawed the party.

CENTRAL AMERICAN UNION PARTY (PARTIDO UNIONISTA CENTROAMERICANO—PUCA). The PUCA appeared and disappeared in the 1960s, but during its short life, it advocated nineteenth-century dreams of Central American unity.

CONSTITUTIONAL DEMOCRATIC PARTY (PARTIDO DEMOCRÁTICO CONSTITUCIONAL—PDC). The PDC was a small army faction which supported the presidential candidacy of Colonel Rafael Carranza Amaya in the 1956 elections; the party disappeared thereafter.

DEMOCRATIC INSTITUTIONAL PARTY (PARTIDO INSTITUCIONAL DEMOCRÁTICO—PID). Founded in 1930 and based in Santa Ana, the PID nominated José Alberto Funes in the 1956 presidential election. The party was supported by a small faction of disenchanted army officers, and it was declared illegal after 1956.

FRENTE UNIDO DEMOCRÁTICO INDEPENDIENTE. See INDEPENDENT DEMOCRATIC UNITED FRONT.

INDEPENDENT DEMOCRATIC UNITED FRONT (FRENTE UNIDO DE-MOCRÁTICO INDEPENDIENTE—FUDI). An adhoc right-wing group rooted in the landed oligarchy and reportedly funded by the Salaverría family of Ahu-achapán, the FUDI organized to promote the candidacy of General José Alberto Medrano in the 1972 presidential election and polled 10 percent of the vote. Medrano, who had been commander of the National Guard in the 1960s and was on the CIA payroll, was fired in December 1970 when he became too closely identified, even for the military government, with a series of political assassi-nations. The FUDI vanished in 1977.

MAY 9TH REVOLUTIONARY PARTY (PARTIDO REVOLUCIONARIO 9 DE MAYO—PR-9M). The political successor to the April and May Revo-lutionary Party, the PR-9M operated openly in the early 1970s but was su-perceded in the electoral process by the Nationalist Democratic Union.

NATIONAL ACTION PARTY (PARTIDO DE ACCIÓN NACIONAL—PAN). Organized in 1956 to oppose the candidacy of Colonel José María Lemus, the official nominee, it found support among younger army officers and civilians unhappy with the military domination of the political process.

NATIONAL REFORMER PARTY (PARTIDO REFORMADOR NA-CIONAL—PRN). Founded in 1961 as the successor to the banned April and May Revolutionary Party, the PRN was supported by students and Marxists. It was proscribed in 1963 when its leftist political orientation became known.

NATIONALIST DEMOCRAT PARTY (PARTIDO DEMÓCRATA NA-CIONALISTA—PDN). The PDN was created by Major José Alvaro Díaz in 1956 to oppose President Oscar Osorio's effort to handpick his successor, José María Lemus. The party disappeared during Lemus's administration.

PARTIDO DE ACCIÓN NATIONAL. See NATIONAL ACTION PARTY.

PARTIDO DEMÓCRATA NACIONALISTA. See NATIONALIST DEM-OCRAT PARTY.

PARTIDO DEMOCRÁTICO CONSTITUCIONAL. See CONSTITU-TIONAL DEMOCRATIC PARTY.

PARTIDO INSTITUCIONAL DEMOCRÁTICO. See DEMOCRATIC IN-STITUTIONAL PARTY.

PARTIDO LABORISTA SALVADOREÑO. See SALVADOREAN LABOR PARTY.

PARTIDO NACIONAL PRO-PATRIA. See PRO-FATHERLAND NA-TIONAL PARTY.

PARTIDO RADICAL DEMOCRÁTICO. See RADICAL DEMOCRATIC PARTY.

PARTIDO REFORMADOR NACIONAL. See NATIONAL REFORMER PARTY.

PARTIDO REPUBLICANO DE EVOLUCIÓN NACIONAL. See REPUBLI-CAN PARTY OF NATIONAL EVOLUTION.

PARTIDO REVOLUCIONARIO ABRIL Y MAYO. See APRIL AND MAY REVOLUTIONARY PARTY.

PARTIDO REVOLUCIONARIO DE UNIFICACIÓN DEMÓCRATA. See REVOLUTIONARY PARTY OF DEMOCRATIC UNIFICATION.

PARTIDO REVOLUTIONARIO DE UNIFICACIÓN DEMOCRÁTICA AU-TÉNTICO. See REVOLUTIONARY PARTY OF AUTHENTIC DEMO-CRATIC UNIFICATION.

PARTIDO REVOLUCIONARIO 9 DE MAYO. See MAY 9TH REVOLU-TIONARY PARTY.

PARTIDO UNIONISTA CENTROÁMERICANO. See CENTRAL AMERI-CAN UNION PARTY.

PRO-FATHERLAND NATIONAL PARTY (PARTIDO NACIONAL PRO-PATRIA). The first in a succession of official parties, Pro-Patria was founded by General Maximiliano Hernández Martínez in the early 1930s and functioned as his personalist vehicle until his overthrow in 1944.

RADICAL DEMOCRATIC PARTY (PARTIDO RADICAL DEMOCRÁ-TICO—PRD). Founded in 1959, the party called for a return to civilian government and land reform—both of which led to government proscription.

REPUBLICAN PARTY OF NATIONAL EVOLUTION (PARTIDO REPUB-LICANO DE EVOLUCIÓN NACIONAL—PREN). Primarily a personalist vehicle for Colonel Luis Roberto Flores, with substantial funding from wealthy members of the Salvadorean Palestinian community, the PREN participated in the 1964 and 1966 legislative elections, then dissolved.

REVOLUTIONARY PARTY OF AUTHENTIC DEMOCRATIC UNIFICA-TION (PARTIDO REVOLUCIONARIO DE UNIFICACIÓN DEMOCRÁ-TICA AUTÉNTICO—PRUDA). Founded in 1959 by former president Oscar Osorio after he broke with President José María Lemus. The party disappeared after the October 1961 coup.

REVOLUTIONARY PARTY OF DEMOCRATIC UNIFICATION (PAR-TIDO REVOLUCIONARIO DE UNIFICACIÓN DEMÓCRATA—PRUD). Founded as the newest official party in the fall of 1949 by Major Oscar Osorio, a leader of the 1948 coup, the PRUD became his vehicle for election as president in 1950. Early promises to remove the army from politics soon proved empty, and the PRUD squelched most of the opposition in the 1954 and 1955 elections. Osorio's handpicked successor, Lieutenant Colonel José María Lemus, won the 1955 election, and the PRUD became so identified with Lemus that, after two coups in 1960 and 1961, the party was dissolved and replaced by a third official party, the Party of National Conciliation.

SALVADOREAN LABOR PARTY (PARTIDO LABORISTA SALVADOR-EÑO). Organized in the late 1920s, this was the first Salvadorean party to appeal to and attract a mass following, even though it was a personalist party whose sole objective was to promote the successful presidential candidacy of Arturo Araujo in 1931. Following Araujo's overthrow in December 1931, however, the party was repressed, then disappeared.

Tommie Sue Montgomery

FALKLAND ISLANDS

The Falkland Islands (called the Islas Malvinas by Argentines) consist of some 200 islands located 480 miles northeast of Cape Horn in the South Atlantic. Most of the 1,915 residents (1989 official estimate) live on the two largest islands, East Falkland and West Falkland; 1,329 live in Stanley, which is the capital. Almost all the population is of British descent, but the French, British, Spanish, and Argentines have all had settlements on the islands. Argentine settlers were forced to leave by a British expedition in 1832, and the Falklands became a British Crown Colony in 1833. Argentina has continued to claim sovereignty ever since.

Sheep raising has traditionally been the major economic activity. The economy has been dominated by the Falkland Islands Company, established in 1851. The company owns about half the total land and most of the almost 750,000 sheep. Workers live in company houses and shop in company stores.

Great Britain and Argentina began negotiations over the sovereignty issue in 1966 but achieved little progress. On 2 April 1982, Argentine forces invaded the islands, expelled the governor, and established military rule. Ten weeks later, on 14 June, a British task force defeated the Argentines and regained control of the islands. A defense force of 4,000 British military men (later reduced to 1,600 troops) has remained after the war, staying in the Falklands to repair war damage and to create new services. This short 1982 Falklands War dramatically changed life on the islands.

The Falkland Islands Development Corporation was founded in 1983 and began operations in 1984. Its task was to foster development and diversify the economy. To that end, it helped start a number of new businesses such as dairying, lumber, seafood, tourism, and fisheries. The British government committed extensive financial resources to the Falklands after the war, constructing an airport capable of handling wide-body jets and greatly expanding the road system and port facilities.

A major economic change in the late 1980s came from the revenue generated from the sale of fishing rights to foreign commercial fisherman. This revenue soon exceeded that from sheep. An even more dramatic growth in revenue is expected from the sale of oil exploration rights.

Although a Legislative Council had existed since 1845, the first election of members by universal adult suffrage occurred in 1949. In 1985 a new constitution was approved. This constitution provides for eight elected members of a Legislative Council. As a British Crown Colony, the Falklands are administered by an appointed governor. He is assisted by an Executive Council composed of two ex-officio members and three members elected by the Legislative Council, which, in turn, is composed of two ex-officio members and eight elected members. In the elections held on 11 October 1989, all eight elected seats on the Legislative Council were won by independent candidates. The main thrust of the campaigns of all those elected was that there should be "no links with Argentina." Since the 1985 constitution specifically guarantees the islanders the right to self-determination, their adamant feelings are certain to present difficulties in all future discussions between Argentina and Great Britain aimed at resolving the sovereignty of the Falklands.

Bibliography

Edward Fursdon. *The Falklands Aftermath: Picking up the Pieces.* Leo Cooper, London, 1988.
Kessing's Record of World Events. New York, 1989.
South America, Central America, and the Caribbean. 3d. ed. Europa Publishers, London, 1991.

Political Party

DESIRE FOR THE RIGHT PARTY. The Desire for the Right Party is the only political party in the Falkland Islands. No political parties existed before its formation in late 1988. The party's candidates were defeated by independents for every Legislative Council seat contested in the 1989 election.

John T. Deiner

FRENCH GUIANA

French Guiana has been an Overseas Department of France since shortly after World War II. Located on the northeast coast of South America, east of Suriname and north of Brazil, it has a population of only about 60,000 people, the vast majority of whom live on a narrow coastal plain. Almost half the people live in the only major city, Cayenne, and a disproportionately large part of the population works for the government. Since the 1960s, France has had its principal satellite launching site there, at the town of Kourou.

In the early 1980s, the government of French President François Mitterand substantially increased local autonomy to the Overseas Departments and increased the number of Guianese deputies in the French National Assembly from one to two. The department also has one member in the French Senate. French Guiana has popularly elected municipal governments; an elected General Council which, until 1982, administered the expenditure of funds from local sources and some French government contributions; and a regional council, which handles money from the French government's Fund for Investment in the Overseas Departments. In 1982 the executive power of the prefect, named by the French government, was transferred to the General Council.

Traditionally, the parties of French Guiana have been those of France. It is still true that the French right-wing parties represent the right in French Guiana. However, since the middle of the 1950s, the Guianese Socialist Party has been separate from the French Socialist Party, although its members in the French parliament sit as part of the Socialist bloc in that body. In recent years, parties seeking either greater autonomy for French Guiana or complete independence have begun to show some strength.

In the 1980s, elections were generally characterized by a confrontation of alliances of the left-wing and right-wing parties. Overall, the left-wing coalition has been somewhat more successful than its rival.

In the Regional Council elections of 1983, the left coalition got a majority of the votes, but not a majority of the seats in the council. The balance of power was held by the Union of Guianese Workers, a separatist group which, in November 1985, was renamed the National Popular Party.

In the 1986 French National Assembly election, in which French Guiana elected two deputies instead of one, the left and right coalitions each got one seat. On the same day, in Regional Council elections, the left was victorious, and Georges Othely of the Guianese Socialist Party was reelected president of that body.

President Mitterand received 52 percent and 60 percent of the total vote in French Guiana in the first and second rounds (in April and May) of the 1988 presidential election. In the parliamentary election of June of the same year, the left and right again each won one seat in the National Assembly. Subsequently, in elections for the General Council, in September and October, the left coalition was victorious, winning fourteen of the nineteen seats contested.

Municipal elections were held in March 1989. The left parties carried thirteen municipalities, including Cayenne, where they won thirty-five of thirty-nine seats. The right parties won control of seven municipalities.

In June 1989, Georges Othely was expelled from the Guianese Socialist Party, and, in September, he ran as the right's successful candidate for the department's one seat in the French Senate, defeating a Socialist.

Two terrorist or insurrectionist groups advocating independence showed some activity in French Guiana during the 1980s: the Fo Nou Liberé la Guyane, which threw several bombs in 1980, and the Caribbean Revolutionary Alliance (Alliance Révolutionnaire Caraibe), a group based in Guadeloupe, which engaged in bombings in May 1983.

Bibliography

The Europa World Year Book 1990. Europa Publications, Ltd., London, 1990.
Facts on File. Facts on File, New York.
Keesings Record of World Events. New York.

Political Parties

ACTION DÉMOCRATIQUE GUYANAISE. *See* GUIANESE DEMO-CRATIC ACTION.

FRONT NATIONALE. *See* NATIONAL FRONT.

GUIANESE DEMOCRATIC ACTION (ACTION DÉMOCRATIQUE GUY-ANAISE). André Lecante leads this relatively new party, which is generally aligned with the left in French Guianese politics. The party won four seats in the Regional Council election of 1986.

GUIANESE SOCIALIST PARTY (PARTI SOCIALISTE GUYANAIS—PSG). This party broke away from the Guianese Federation of the French

Socialist Party in 1956. It emerged as the single strongest party in the department and the major element in the left-wing coalition.

In the 1986 French National Assembly election, Elie Castor of the PSG received the highest vote, with 48.1 percent in a proportional representation poll. He was reelected in the June 1988 National Assembly election.

In the Regional Council election of 1986, the Guianese Socialist Party won 42.1 percent of the vote and seated fifteen (instead of the previous fourteen) members on the thirty-one member council. In September and October 1988, in a two-round election for seats in the General Council, with the triumph of the leftist coalition, deputy Elie Castor was elected president of the council.

However, in 1989, the Socialists lost the department's seat in the French Senate. A few months before the election, Georges Othely was expelled from the party, and he ran for the senate seat as the candidate of the right and defeated the Socialist nominee, Raymond Tarcy.

MOUVEMENT POUR LE PROGRÈS GUYANAIS. See MOVEMENT FOR GUIANESE PROGRESS.

MOVEMENT FOR GUIANESE PROGRESS (MOUVEMENT POUR LE PROGRÈS GUYANAIS). This small, right-wing party, which favors greater autonomy in economic affairs for the department, is usually aligned with the right-wing coalition. In 1978, however, it ran its leader, Claude Ho A. Chuck, as an independent candidate for the French National Assembly.

NATIONAL FRONT (FRONT NATIONALE). The Guianese branch of the extreme rightist National Front of France, led in French Guiana by Guy Malon; it is a very small group.

NATIONAL POPULAR PARTY (PARTI NATIONALE POPULAIRE— PNP). The PNP originated with the French Guianese affiliate of the French Conféderation Génerale du Travail (CGT), the Communist-controlled trade union organization. In 1964 it separated from the CGT as the Union of Guianese Workers (Union des Travailleurs Guyanais—ITG) and functioned as both a trade union and a political organization. After the 1983 Regional Council election, it held the balance of power in that body, between the leftist and rightist coalitions.

Led by Claude Robo, the PNP, which was generally aligned with the leftist coalition during most of the 1980s, favors independence for French Guiana. It assumed its present name in November 1985.

PARTI NATIONALE POPULAIRE. See NATIONAL POPULAR PARTY.

PARTI SOCIALISTE GUYANAIS. See GUIANESE SOCIALIST PARTY.

RALLY FOR THE REPUBLIC (RASSEMBLEMENT POUR LA RÉPUB-LIQUE—RPR). The French Guianese affiliate of the neo-Gaullist party led in France by Jacques Chirac, it is one of the two major parties in the department's rightist coalition.

In 1986, the RPR candidate Paulin Bruné won one of the department's two seats in the French National Assembly. In elections for the Regional Council on the same day, the party elected nine members, the second largest represen-tation. In 1988 it again captured one of the seats in the French National Assembly.

RASSEMBLEMENT POUR LA RÉPUBLIQUE. *See* RALLY FOR THE REPUBLIC.

UNION DES TRAVAILLEURS GUYANAIS. *See* NATIONAL POPULAR PARTY.

UNION FOR POPULAR DEMOCRACY (UNION POUR LA DÉMOCRA-TIE POPULAIRE—UDP). The French Guianese affiliate of the party of former French president Valery Giscard d'Estaing, it is one of the two major parties in the rightist coalition in the department. In 1986 it elected three members to the Regional Council.

UNION OF GUIANESE WORKERS. *See* NATIONAL POPULAR PARTY.

UNION POUR LA DÉMOCRATIE POPULAIRE. *See* UNION FOR POP-ULAR DEMOCRACY.

Robert J. Alexander

GRENADA

Grenada, the southernmost and the most densely populated state in the Windward Island chain (between ninety and one hundred miles from Trinidad and Tobago, Barbados, and Saint Vincent), has one of the highest per capita ratios of political parties in the Americas. In this nation, with an eligible electorate of approximately half its population of 103,000, four major parties and as many as four minor parties competed in the 1989–1990 election campaign. The four major Grenadian parties are the National Democratic Congress (NDC), led by Nicholas Brathwaite (currently in power); the Grenada United Labour Party (GULP), the highly personalist "loyal" opposition party led by the aged Sir Eric Matthew Gairy; the New National Party (NNP), under the leadership of Dr. Keith Mitchell; and The National Party (TNP), a splinter group of the NNP formed by the late prime minister Herbert Blaize in July 1989 following his displacement as NNP head, which campaigned for the 1990 election led by the acting prime minister Ben Jones. Minor parties include the Maurice Bishop Patriotic Movement (MBPM), now led by Dr. Terrence Marryshow, and a variety of other, largely ephemeral groups including the Grenada People's Movement (GPM) which, before it dropped out of 1989–1990 electoral activities, perceived national leadership needs as a cross between a New England town meeting and Moammar Gaddafi's *jamahiriyat*; the one-candidate Good Ole Democracy, with a religious miracle theme and GOD as its acronym; and another group, headed by Davidson Budhoo, that withdrew from the 1989–1990 campaign prior to the election, with a focus on alleged conspiracies of the International Monetary Fund and World Bank.

Grenada's modern political awakening dates to efforts made by T. A. Marryshow, as early as World War I. Marryshow's political message was by necessity focused on the literate, largely brown-skinned, middle sectors of Afro-Grenadians. While Marryshow was fond of saying it is better to light a candle than to curse the darkness, by the 1940s the "stage arrive[d]," writes Gordon Lewis, "when the darkness must be cursed, [and] the entire system engaged".

The individual destined to curse and engage Grenada's political system was Gairy.

Gairy, GULP, and the Birth of Mass Parties in Grenada

Despite important party and union building activity in the Caribbean during the 1930s, this movement did not establish itself in Grenada for more than another decade. Too many of Grenada's potential labor leaders had left the Spice Island in search of employment—leaders such as Uriah Butler, who became a labor and political organizer and the precursor of the 1935–1937 dislocations in Trinidad. By the late 1940s another potential leader emerged, a "blue black Grenadian"—as he describes himself—who, despite minimal formal education, learned powerful leadership lessons during his sojourn as an organizer of West Indian workers engaged in oil refinery employment in Aruba. This man was Eric Gairy.

Deported by the Dutch authorities at the end of 1949 on charges of labor agitation, Gairy's return to Grenada was the stimulus that at last engaged the Grenadian masses. Blending heavy doses of God, Marx, and class and racial frustration with his own genuine charisma, Gairy initiated a movement to stimulate pride and increase economic rights among Grenadian workers, beginning with the workers on a large plantation where the new non-Grenadian owner had initiated sweeping eviction activities. Gairy rushed to the defense, becoming in the process "the Galahad of workers and peasants," according to M. G. Smith (1965). By July 1950, Gairy had formed and, in 1951, registered his 27,000-member Grenada Manual and Metal Workers Union (GMMWU) and named himself president-general. When his demand for a 50-percent wage increase for sugar workers was rejected, Gairy immediately called a strike and presented a demand to the employers' society for a 20-percent raise for all workers on cocoa and nutmeg estates, two of the island's principal export crops. He then called a massive national strike in early 1951. Mass participation was under way. Gairy's subsequent arrest and incarceration almost guaranteed mass support for his labor politics movement.

Gairy's martyr-like status was parlayed into ballot strength for GMMWU candidates in 1951 and 1954—and later for the evolving GULP, the island's first mass party. In the 1951 general election, the only non-Gairyite to win an elected seat was the aged—but still popular—Marryshow. This electoral success was ongoing with Gairy's candidates winning majorities in six of eight general elections between 1951 and 1976. The charismatic Gairy institutionalized little of his personal magic and accepted few legal or moral limits, however. By 1962 the British had suspended the Grenadian constitution and removed Gairy from office, charging him with deliberate and systematic violations of financial regulations, alleged browbeating of public servants, destruction of civil service morale, and illegal use of public monies. During the Gairy regime, repressive public laws and edicts were implemented, which harassed opposition parties and the media. There was also degradation of legislative, judicial, and executive institutions, and the nation's socioeconomic and educational needs were neglected—even though public education was made mandatory.

After Grenadian independence in 1974, Gairy accepted still fewer limits, as noted by the Duffus Report of 1975, which charged Gairy with such serious breaches as victimization of public servants; making selective concessions to favored business supporters; harassment of workers and the civil service; imprisonment of persons without bail or trial; brutality by the police force and, after 1967, by his personally recruited "Mongoose Gang"; and transforming police and magistrates into his partisan agents. These activities produced a regime of terror, including the killing of Maurice Bishop's father, Rupert Bishop, in 1974. As has occurred in too many charismatically led regimes, Gairy began as an agent for positive change but became an authoritarian figure whose actions laid the groundwork for the Commonwealth Caribbean's first successful coup (1979), which ushered in its first sociopolitcal revolution.

Despite his shortcomings, Gairy played an important role in raising the political consciousness of the Grenadian masses. Those who were first "raised" remain loyal to Gairy and GULP. This party, which still attracted over one-third of the electoral vote in the 1984 general election, was to provide the major challenge to the NDC in the 1990 general election.

The Grenada National Party

Another major party to contest the 1990 general election was the NNP, which was initiated as an amalgamation of three centrist parties just prior to the 1984 election. Since the Grenada National Party (GNP) dominated this alignment and was the principal party alternative to Gairyism prior to the late 1970s, it deserves special attention.

Formed in 1956 by Dr. John Watts with assistance from Herbert Blaize, the GNP contested every election from that year through 1976, at which time it entered a People's Coalition (PC) with the New Jewel Movement (NJM) in an unsuccessful last-gasp effort to counter electorally the abuses of Gairyism. Blaize, a planter and barrister from Carriacou, Grenada's largest Grenadine dependency twenty-four miles to the north, campaigned unsuccessfully for the Carriacou/ Petit Martinique seat as an independent in 1954, but he consistently won the seat from 1957 to 1976 as a member of the GNP.

The island's first real coalition government was formed following the 1957 general election, the first election in which there was significant party competition in Grenada. GULP captured only two seats, although it outpolled the GNP nearly two to one; two seats went to the GNP; two seats went to the no-longer active People's Democratic Movement (PDM); and two seats went to independent candidates, which permitted the formation of an anti-Gairy government. By the 1961 general election, parliamentary constituencies in Grenada had been increased from eight to ten. GNP fragmentation had again occurred, and GULP won all eight of Grenada's rural seats and control of the government.

The only time the GNP was able to defeat GULP in a straight party vote occurred in the general election of 1962, but even this victory required external assistance in the form of Britain's suspension of the Grenadian constitution and the removal of Gairy from office three months prior to the balloting. Even with this unusual circumstance, plus help from a second issue—possible Grenadian integration with Trinidad—the GNP captured only a bare popular majority, with a six-to-four majority in parliament. Blaize, who had served as chief minister of Grenada in 1960, regained this position.

There was little to differentiate the prerevolutionary governments in the area of public policy. The Gairy government extended suffrage to eighteen-year-olds and distributed small parcels of land to the landless faithful. The Blaize administrations were able to enact limited reforms in agriculture, education, and health to expand the distribution of potable water, and to create an agriculture bank, but these measures were no match for Gairy's often race- and class-tinged populism in which he presented himself as a black messiah against the brown-skinned professionals. In reality, neither party put forth many working-class candidates or offered a legislative threat to the island's dependent capitalistic structure.

The Revolutionary Option

The GNP functioned primarily as an opposition party which countered GULP's sometimes authoritarian rule; GULP's appeal centered on identity with working-class voters and charismatic leadership qualities. GULP continually scored high in both of these categories, even in the preindependence election of 1972, which drew 83.5 percent of the electorate. GULP's victory pattern was repeated in 1976 when it defeated the People's Alliance (also known as the Popular Coalition), which joined GNP forces with candidates from the three-year-old NJM, including founder Maurice Bishop, and the United People's Party (UPP). Although three of four NJM candidates won parliamentary seats in 1976, the overall electoral failure of the coalition appears to have convinced the NJM of the impotence and ultimate institutional bankruptcy of party politics as a vehicle for defeating Gairy and, by implication, of the incongruence of the Westminster model with local needs. This became a rationale for displacement of Gairy by force, which led to the formation of the People's Revolutionary Government (PRG) in 1979.

Although many in Washington, D.C., disagree, Grenada appears to have experienced sufficient levels of overturning change of institutions, values, and policies (1979–1983) to produce a genuine social revolution. Such overturning was demonstrated most obviously in the shift from parliamentary governance—albeit inefficient and often corrupt—to a Marxist-Leninist model of "guided" democracy. With this formal shift in structure came external policy change toward nonalignment, which was more supportive of Cuba and Moscow than even Daniel Ortega's Nicaragua. The failure to schedule elections also became a primary point of contention between the PRG and neighboring Caribbean governments.

Most Grenadians polled in 1984 felt that positive domestic changes occurred under the PRG, especially changes involving improved housing and public utilities, elevated women's rights and mass education, increased employment, and agricultural development. The "rev" also fired the imagination and the will to participate on the part of many youth and women. As a result, Maurice Bishop and his Grenadian revolution continue to be positively supported by the bulk of the Grenadian electorate, with more than 75 percent indicating continuous support for the revolution and more than 80 percent indicating continued admiration of Bishop. The PRG's socioeconomic and educational changes were so popular, in fact, that there has come to be perceptive denial that some of the negative attributes of the regime occurred. Only freedom of speech and openness of the electoral process are officially perceived to have deteriorated during the PRG tenure. Nonetheless, an equally high percentage of Grenadians welcomed the intervention force in 1983.

Amalgamating the New National Party

External Intervention by Other Means

To forestall a victory by either Gairy or the remaining revolutionaries led by the MBPM in the 1984 general election, formation of a party amalgamation seemed requisite. Herbert Blaize, who had maintained a GNP presence for more than two decades, was promoted as the best choice to head the proposed coalition. Thus, in a meeting on Saint Vincent's Union Island in August 1984, which included prime ministers from four neighboring islands, a partisan amalgamation was arranged involving the GNP of Herbert Blaize, the National Democratic Party (NDP) of George Brizan, and the Grenada Democratic Movement (GDM) led by Francis Alexis. An accord was signed creating a single political party to be known as the New National Party, and Blaize was appointed leader and chairman of the new party.

A fourth party leader, Winston Whyte of the Christian Democratic Labour Party (CDLP), also signed the accord. Whyte, however, withdrew almost immediately over allegations that Blaize was tampering with the candidate selection process to favor his GNP. When the list of fifteen candidates for the 1984 campaign finally was presented, more than half (eight) came from the GNP, four from the NDP, and three from the GDM. By 1990 the CDLP had ceased to exist, but in 1984 the CDLP, with five candidates, and another no longer existing party, the one-candidate Grenada Federated Labour Party (GFLP), contested the election as noncoalition parties.

Party institutionalization is, of course, of continuing vital concern, as Blaize noted in the *Grenadian Voice* on the eve of the Union Island talks:

What I am concerned about is the effectiveness of the team. . . . Not merely to put a team together and say Hooray, but a team that [is capable of governing] the day after election. . . . The leader must be assured of the support and loyalty of all the members. Pledges are one thing . . . , but th[ey are] not enough. . . . You need a sort of in-depth feeling of loyalty.

In-depth feelings of party identity were not to grow within the NNP, despite initial electoral assistance from Caribbean prime ministers and party leaders and, later, significant help from the Jamaica Labour Party and from various U.S. groups. Despite some evidence of intra–NNP tension, which became a factor in the later dissolution of the party, the amalgamation paid off electorally in 1984 as the NNP swept fourteen seats to one for GULP.

A Return to Fragmentation

By 1987, however, the principals of the smaller parties who had joined with the GNP to form the NNP had left the coalition to organize the NDC. Even the nine remaining NNP representatives were less than united: leadership and policy differences between Mitchell and Blaize resulted in the replacement of Blaize by Mitchell as NNP leader in January 1989. Major points of contention between these two leaders included personal ambition as well as policy differences centering on means of reducing the double-digit unemployment in Grenada and on government restrictions of civil liberties and rights. The party institutionalization and internal political integration Blaize had sought had not transpired. Nonetheless, the Blaize government had contributed some needed legitimacy.

Blaize's refusal to let go or compromise on policy was struck head on by Mitchell's impatience. Mitchell wrested party leadership from Blaize at an NNP convention in January 1989. Although ill and increasingly ineffective, Blaize retained the office of prime minister until his death in December 1989. During this period, the 1984 coalition eroded almost in tandem with Blaize's failing health and energy. The government faced near paralysis and an empty treasury, which was devastating to Grenada's economic health, as well as an increasingly reduced sympathy in Washington, D.C.

Mitchell, a former mathematics professor at Howard University and a liberal-moderate in socioeconomic areas, is probably the most charismatic of all current party leaders in Grenada. He maintains solid links with the black working class and frequently receives praise from Gairy. Mitchell, in fact, sustains solid support from and seems "at home" with the many GULP supporters in his Saint George N.W. constituency. During mid-1989, as Mitchell encouraged rumors that he would soon undertake drastic steps to force Blaize to relinquish the prime ministership, Blaize dismissed Mitchell from the cabinet—together with Mitchell allies. At the same time, Blaize took his faction of the NNP into a new party called The National Party.

Upon the death of Blaize on 20 December 1989, the former deputy prime minister Ben Jones assumed leadership of both the Grenadian government and the newly formed TNP. These activities, which led to a splintering of the NNP, predictably limited the potential for electoral success by both Mitchell and Jones in the 1990 election.

The National Democratic Congress

By 1987 the NNP's fourteen-to-one parliamentary majority had been reduced to a nine-to-six majority by cabinet and party defections resulting from dissatisfaction with NNP leadership and policies. This led directly to the formation of the National Democratic Congress now led by Nicholas Brathwaite, an educator from Carriacou. Although lacking charismatic appeal for maintenance of popular support, Brathwaite anchored the NDC to business interests and older voters. He also offered qualities of integrity and stability and proof that he could work with the United States, all seemingly positive contributions to the NDC's need for accelerated legitimization and leadership institutionalization as well as external economic support. These traits were probably key factors when acting leader George Brizan recruited Brathwaite to head the new party.

The NDC leadership triumvirate includes two co-deputy leaders, Brizan and Francis Alexis. Brizan, also an educator, is a representative from Saint George N.E. who polled 84 percent of the votes in that constituency in 1984. He played a significant role in the 1990 election. Alexis, a leading barrister who was a senior lecturer in law at the University of the West Indies, maintained national "leadership" exposure throughout the 1989–1990 campaign as a weekly newspaper columnist.

The NDC team stressed pragmatic over messianic themes in the 1989–1990 campaign. In terms of policy issues, they agreed that the Blaize government had not been sufficiently progressive, economically inclusive, or adequately supportive of regional integration. This leadership triumvirate felt Grenada should renew its membership in the nonaligned movement while maintaining close ties with the West. Although many Grenadians felt the diffuse leadership of the NDC could prove problematic, this author projected the congress as the electoral victor in 1990.

Maurice Bishop Patriotic Movement—
and Other Minor Parties

Although as many as four minor parties initially gave indications of contesting the 1990 general election, by election day, only one minor party really contested the election; a second party, the Good Ole Democracy, was a one-candidate—if not a one-person—party.

The MBPM, representing the Bishop wing of the fallen PRG, remained a national party although its lack of electoral support was puzzling to many. While the revolution maintains a high approval rating among Grenadians, and Bishop's memory retains very high support, the party that bears his name is not well supported at the polls. Receiving only 5 percent of the popular vote in 1984, the MBPM was expected to do even worse in 1990 under its less charismatic new leader, Marryshow. Could the MBPM substantially improve on its 1984 showing in the upcoming election? Most observers felt not.

The 1990 Party Face-Off

The 1989–1990 campaign ended as it had informally begun months earlier, with high spirit and emotion. Stakes were high: the right to rule and implement public policy alternatives; a rewarding and prestigious job versus economic uncertainty; and, in the case of some, including the timeless but now nearly blind Sir Eric, a chance, perhaps a last chance, to hold national office. All parties campaigned until the last possible moment. The major parties concluded the campaign with motor caravans and major rallies.

Last minute heroics would be conducted in the "must win" districts. In Grenada, on 13 March 1990, those electoral districts included suburban Saint George South, a vital swing district where Gairy was pitted against Phinsley St. Louis for the NDC, Cephas Pilgrim for the MBPM, and Winston Whyte for the NNP. The major rallies scheduled for the final night of the campaign were conducted in this district—and the audio systems of two rallies, the NDC and NNP, were within easy range of each other.

Each rally offered some drink and food, an abundance of enthusiastic partisans, and the most informative and entertaining orators the parties could deliver: Mitchell for the NNP, Alexis and Brizan for the NDC, and Gairy for GULP. The mood projected both seriousness and light-hearted fun. It was an orientation North Americans are forgetting—that it takes a party to have a Party! Grenadians demonstrated both of these attributes as they projected as much enthusiasm as observed in any Caribbean election campaign, from the Bahamas to Trinidad. Yet, despite the local equivalent of what neighboring Trinidadians call the "three Rs of Politics—Rum, Roti, and Rantin," and a decidedly greater partisan atmosphere, there was little room for violence—only two or three minor skirmishes. Grenada, like the commonwealth Caribbean as a whole, is orderly on election day.

Finally it was 13 March 1990, a banner day for Grenadians for, on that same day in 1979, Gairy had been toppled and the New Jewel Revolution had begun. It is certain this date was not selected randomly. Still the government was financially insolvent, and unemployment was rampant (approximately 30 percent). Voter response was uncertain.

It would take extra effort from the electorate on this election day. No morning sun appeared, just sullen clouds and steady rain. Still the lines in front of each polling place were long and orderly. The weather induced some decline in voter turnout, to be sure, and numbers were also reduced by a degree of disgust with the negative thrust evidenced in the final days of the campaign. Despite these factors, it was refreshing to find three-fourths of the Grenadian electorate participating in the election and to witness no exit polls and no telecasts announcing the victorious candidates prior to the closing of the polls. The only electoral speculation came via the radio airwaves and old-fashioned argumentation.

Firm results of the election were not available for hours after the polls closed. Even on the following day, the only public announcement regarding the electoral outcome was that the NDC, with seven seats, had indeed won a plurality, missing a majority by one; GULP, by securing up to five seats, would be the "loyal opposition," although Gairy himself had been defeated; the NNP would have two seats, including that of Mitchell; and the TNP had been victorious in only one race, that of Jones, but would eventually gain the final too-close-to-call parliamentary seat (by a mere thirteen votes) to give it two seats.

Each of the leadership triumvirate in the NDC had won his constituency handily; Brathwaite and Brizan each secured over 60 percent, and Alexis and Mitchell received clear majorities. Since the NDC remained one vote short of a majority, however, it was conceivable that a coalition government could be formed by other parties and individuals in the electoral contest. Two factors discouraged this outcome: Brathwaite's offer to coalesce with either Jones and his TNP or with any individual parliamentarian(s) willing to serve the NDC government, and Edzel Thomas's decision to give the NDC a bare majority by crossing the aisle from GULP to NDC. Acting Prime Minister Jones was finally induced to relinquish the prime ministership on Friday, 16 March, three days following the election. On the same day, Brathwaite was sworn in as prime minister. A new, relatively progressive governing team now seemed to be in place. At this point, Jones brought his two TNP seats to form a coalition with the NDC government, but, by mid-1991, Jones and the TNP had left the coalition, allegedly over budgetary disagreements. This action leaves the government with a most fragile one-seat majority and declining public support.

The 1990 election was an important test for Grenadian democracy, however, and for U.S. policy in the region. As this author projected (Will 1991), the new NDC–led government would place a renewed emphasis on education and civil liberties, plus much greater emphasis on regional integration. In July 1991, as noted in the chapter on Saint Vincent and the Grenadines, Grenada is scheduled to join Saint Vincent, Saint Lucia, and Dominica in a series of plebiscites to measure support for a planned merger. Should this integration effort prove successful, the result could be positive for economic development in Grenada and in the subregion. As Deputy Prime Minister George Brizan stated to this author during the 1990 election campaign, "Due to the market and resource limitations of our small states, and to the integration patterns occurring in Europe and North America, we in the eastern Caribbean must further integrate to survive." A positive role by the United States would be beneficial in promoting such integration as well as this latest effort at the democratization of Grenada.

Bibliography

Timothy Ashby. "The Reagan Years," in Scott B. MacDonald, Harald M. Sandstrom, and Paul B. Goodwin, Jr., eds., *The Caribbean after Grenada: Revolution, Conflict, and Democracy*. Praeger, New York, 1988.

Patrick A. M. Emmanuel. *General Elections in the Eastern Caribbean: A Handbook*. Institute of Social and Economic Studies, University of the West Indies, Cave Hill, Barbados, 1979.

Patrick Emmanuel, Farley Brathwaite, and Eudine Barriteau. *Political Change and Public Opinion in Grenada, 1979–1984*. Institute of Social and Economic Studies, University of the West Indies, Cave Hill, Barbados, 1986.

EPICA Task Force. *Grenada: The Peaceful Revolution*. Ecumenical Program for Interamerican Communication and Action, Washington, D.C., 1982.

Government of Grenada. *Report of the Commission of Enquiry on Grenada*, under the chair of Sir Herbert Duffus [of Jamaica]. Government Printery, St. George's, Grenada, 1975.

Government of Grenada. *Report of the Commission of Enquiry into the Control of Public Expenditure in Grenada during 1961 and Subsequently*. Government Printery, St. George's, Grenada, 8 May 1962.

Percy Hintzen and W. Marvin Will. Biographies on Herbert Blaize, Maurice Bishop, and T. A. Marryshow in Robert J. Alexander, ed., *Biographical Dictionary of Latin America and the Caribbean Political Leaders*, Greenwood Press, Westport, Conn., 1988.

Gordon K. Lewis. *The Growth of the Modern West Indies*. Monthly Review Press, New York, 1968.

Bonham C. Richardson. "Grenada," in Robert J. Alexander, ed., *Political Parties of the Americas*, vol 1. Greenwood Press, Westport, Conn., 1982.

M. G. Smith. "Structure and Crisis in Grenada, 1950–1954," M. G. Smith, ed., *The Plural Society in the British West Indies, 1950–1954*. University of California Press, Berkeley, 1965.

Tony Thorndike. *Grenada: Politics, Economics and Society*. Frances Pinter (Publishers), London, 1985.

West India Royal Commission Report, 1938–39. Colonial Office, Cmd. 6697, H.M.S.O., London, 1945.

W. Marvin Will, "From Authoritarianism to Democracy in Grenada." *Studies in Comparative International Development*, 26, Summer, 1991. (A portion of this essay is abstracted from this article.)

———. Election observations and personal interviews with most party leaders, 1973–1990.

Newspaper references utilized for this essay include *Barbados Advocate*, 1 August 1984; *Caribbean Contact*, February, September, and October 1990; *Miami Herald*, 8 July 1985; *E[astern] C[aribbean] News*, 28–29 July 1989; *Grenadian Voice*, 1 September and 25 August 1984.

Political Parties—Active

GRENADA PEOPLE'S MOVEMENT (GPM). Founded in the 1980s and led by Dr. Raphael Fletcher, the GPM is more of a "good government" interest group than an electoral party. The GPM did not field candidates in the 1990 election, although it expressed an early intent to do so. It is patterned after Lloyd Best's Tapia House program in Trinidad. The GPM is accused of receiving funds from Libya and is considered leftist by Washington, D.C.

GRENADA UNITED LABOUR PARTY (GULP). GULP evolved to party status from the Grenada Manual and Metal Workers Union (1950–1951) and became the first mass party in the country. It was the ruling party in Grenada in all but two governments from the 1950s to 1979. In the late 1980s, it was the "loyal" opposition party. In the 1990 election, GULP again earned that position despite the defection of one member elected under the GULP banner to the plurality-winning National Democratic Congress. Led by Sir Eric Gairy since its founding, GULP has a loyal but aging following. It is not likely to reach majority status again until its controversial leader is replaced.

MAURICE BISHOP PATRIOTIC MOVEMENT (MBPM). Led by Dr. Terrence Marryshow, the MBPM was founded in 1983–1984. The lack of voting appeal by the MBPM may be explained by at least four factors: (1) although supportive of Bishop, three-fourths of the Grenadian electorate actually express negative feelings toward the MBPM; (2) since some of the strongest opposition to the People's Revolutionary Government comes from the business community, the possibility of subtle blackmail exists; (3) Grenadians, along with most Caribbean Basin peoples, are basically conservative and the MBPM remains dogmatically committed to socialism; and (4) a real effort is being made by both the New National Party and the National Democratic Congress to recruit and reach out to the former revolutionaries, stealing voters and workers, if not issue planks. Due to the Blaize administration's refusal to accept his Cuban medical credentials, the new president of the MBPM, the grandson of the late Grenadian hero T. A. Marryshow, remained an unlicensed and unemployed medical doctor on election eve in 1990. This status of Terrence Marryshow has been rectified since the election.

NATIONAL DEMOCRATIC CONGRESS (NDC). The NDC, the current majority party in Grenada, was founded in 1987 by a merger of the George Brizan and Francis Alexis factions of the New National Party (NNP) amalgamation, the National Democratic Party and the Grenada Democratic Movement, respectively. Brizan recruited Nicholas Brathwaite, former interim prime minister of Grenada (1983–1985), to lead the NDC and, under his leadership, the NDC won a plurality in the 1990 general election. This plurality became a bare one-seat majority when parliamentarian Edzel Thomas crossed the aisle from

GULP to the NDC. The NDC was bolstered briefly during 1990 and early 1991, however, by coalition support from The National Party.

The present one-seat majority of the NDC is most fragile as Grenada faces rising unemployment, an increasing debt burden, and only a modest economic forecast. Should the upcoming integration discussions with neighboring Saint Vincent, Saint Lucia, and Dominica flounder, discussions that are not likely to receive support from the opposition parties in Grenada, the NDC government could face an early demise. Support from the United States would seem crucial in this critical phase of democratization in Grenada.

NEW NATIONAL PARTY (NNP). Under the leadership of Keith Mitchell, the NNP was founded in 1984 as an amalgamation of the Grenada National Party and up to five minor parties. The NNP, under the leadership of Herbert Blaize, easily won the 1984 election, stopping both Eric Gairy (of the Grenada United Labour Party—GULP) and the revolutionaries (the Maurice Bishop Patriotic Movement and its allies). Within three years, however, the NNP had suffered the defection of most of its new followers, and in 1989 the party convention replaced Blaize with Mitchell as party leader. In 1990 the NNP won just two seats. Due to good relations between Mitchell and most GULP leaders, plus a degree of support from The National Party, it is conceivable the New National Party will be a force to be reckoned with in the next election, whether that election transpires in the normal five-year cycle or occurs a good deal sooner as the result of the break-up of the narrow National Democratic Congress majority.

THE NATIONAL PARTY (TNP). The National Party was the last of the splinter groups to defect from the then-governing New National Party (NNP). The new party was formed in 1989 by the late prime minister Herbert Blaize following his displacement from leadership of the New National Party by Keith Mitchell. Due to the death of Herbert Blaize in December 1989, TNP was led by Acting Prime Minister Ben Jones in the 1990 election.

The dominant group in TNP is the segment of the Grenada National Party (GNP), 1956–1984, most loyal to Blaize, and later to Jones. Although both Jones and Alleyne Walker walked out of the National Democratic Congress coalition in 1991, the future of TNP remains clouded since Jones accepted a cabinet post in that government and Walker, the second candidate elected under the TNP label in 1990, displayed support for the Brathwaite–NDC government. Potential TNP voters in the next election, depending on the eventual outcome of the NDC government and the state of the Grenadian economy, may decide this much movement was not in the interest of the TNP—or the obverse. The TNP appears too personalist a party to endure long separately. It is most likely to seek an alignment, either with Mitchell's NNP or Eric Gairy's Grenada United Labor Party, prior to the next election.

Political Parties—Historical

CHRISTIAN DEMOCRATIC LABOUR PARTY (CDLP). The CDLP, led by Winston Whyte, was organized to compete in the postrevolutionary election of 1984. It initially joined the New National Party (NNP) amalgamation but almost immediately withdrew over perceived election maneuvering by Herbert Blaize. The CDLP was unsuccessful in 1984 and ceased to exist prior to the 1990 election, at which time Whyte was an unsuccessful candidate for the NNP.

GRENADA DEMOCRATIC MOVEMENT (GDM). The GDM was organized by Francis Alexis following the 1983 military intervention. In 1984 Alexis moved his base from Barbados, where he had been serving as a lecturer at the University of the West Indies, back to Grenada. Prior to the 1984 election, the GDM was induced to confederate with the Grenada National Party and several minor parties to form the New National Party (NNP). The GDM broke ties with the NNP in 1987, as did the National Democratic Party, to form the currently governing National Democratic Congress. (*See* National Democratic Congress.)

GRENADA FEDERATED LABOUR PARTY (GFLP). The GFLP was organized to compete in the election of 1984. Its one candidate in the election was unsuccessful, and the party ceased to exist shortly thereafter.

GRENADA NATIONAL PARTY (GNP). The GNP, the second oldest of the modern parties in Grenada, was founded in 1956, primarily by John Watts. Herbert Blaize was its leader of long standing. The GNP twice managed to replace the Gairy government: once as part of a coalition effort and once, in 1962, with a majority. In 1976 the GNP joined with the New Jewel Movement and the United People's Party to form the People's Alliance (also known as the Popular Coalition) in an unsuccessful attempt to defeat the Gairy regime. In 1984, the GNP was coalesced (with external assistance) into the New National Party (NNP), an amalgamation of the GNP and as many as five minor parties. The NNP, under Blaize's leadership, won the 1984 general election but by 1987 had lost most of its amalgamated units. Left largely with the GNP core, the NNP divided still further in 1989 when Blaize was disposed as leader by Keith Mitchell. Blaize renamed the remnants of the NNP that remained under his control The National Party (TNP). The new party was led by Ben Jones in the 1990 election due to the death of Blaize in December 1989. (*See* New National Party and The National Party.)

NATIONAL DEMOCRATIC PARTY (NDP). The NDP was founded in February 1984 by historian George Brizan, a member of the New Jewel Movement in its pre-Marxist period. The NDP affiliated with the Grenada National Party and several minor parties in 1984 to form the New National Party (NNP). The

Brizan faction left the NNP in 1987 to form the National Democratic Congress. (*See* National Democratic Congress.)

NEW JEWEL MOVEMENT (NJM). Upon return from his legal studies in England in 1970, the highly charismatic Maurice Bishop formed a legal partnership with Kendrick Radix. These two Grenadian attorneys quickly became most active in attempting to form mass organizations in Grenada. A group called FORUM, founded by Bishop in 1972, lasted less than a year. The Committee of Concerned Citizens (CCC), made up of commercial elites, also short lived, soon merged with the Movement for the Advancement of Community Effort (MACE). In 1972, the Joint Endeavor for Welfare, Education and Liberation (JEWEL) was founded by a discouraged former Grenada National Party (GNP) candidate and educator, Unison Whiteman. All of these groups contributed to what would evolve into the New Jewel Movement by early 1973 as a response to frustrations following the failure to unseat Gairyism, as well as out of sensed political impotence and the growing belief that the Gairy-controlled Westminster model was unreformable, especially as an option for coming independence.

In 1976 the NJM coalesced with the GNP and the United People's Party (UPP) to form the People's Alliance (also known as the Popular Coalition) in an unsuccessful last-ditch attempt to defeat Eric Gairy electorally. This was the only time the NJM faced the electorate in a general election. The party's statement of principles committed it to a "people's democracy," full employment, health care based on need, cooperatives, and civil liberties. Although its origins were more socialist than Leninist, as Tony Thorndike writes, radicalization emerged rapidly under the leadership of such committed Marxists-Leninists as Bernard Coard. The growth of the NJM was no doubt hastened by the arrest and murder of several of the movement's members, plus the torching of some members' homes by Gairy's Mongoose Gang. After its coup-turned revolution in 1979, the NJM formed the nucleus of the People's Revolutionary Government (PRG). The NJM died, along with many PRG and NJM leaders, including Bishop, Jacqueline Creft, and Whiteman, in the intrarevolution killings that took place prior to the military intervention of October 1983. Many in the Maurice Bishop Patriotic Movement today perceive that they are carrying on the JEWEL's more moderate socialist tradition.

PEOPLE'S DEMOCRATIC MOVEMENT (PDM). The PDM was formed in 1957 to contest the elections that year. It ceased to exist following this election.

PEOPLE'S PROGRESSIVE MOVEMENT (PPM). The PPM, led by Derek Knight, was a short-lived party which contested the 1961 election.

UNITED PEOPLE'S PARTY (UPP). The UPP faced its only election as part of the abortive 1976 People's Alliance (also known as the Popular Coalition) to unseat the Gairy regime.

WEST INDIAN FEDERAL LABOUR PARTY (WIFLP). The WIFLP was the political banner under which David and Joseph Felix contested the 1957 general election. The party name was no doubt chosen to further its linkage with the federal coalition of labor parties of that year.

W. Marvin Will

GUADELOUPE

Political parties in Guadeloupe, the French Overseas Department in the Leeward Islands, have until recent years been almost exclusively branches of the parties of France. However, although the two principal right-wing parties are still affiliates of continental French parties, both the Socialist and Communist parties have become to a greater or lesser degree independent of their French counterparts. Also, in the 1980s there was some modest growth of indigenous parties favoring independence for the department.

Although, in the 1970s, the Guadeloupean Federation of the Socialist Party refused to be part of the Union of the Left, as was its counterpart in France, and thus to join forces with the local Communist party, that policy changed substantially in the 1980s. The two parties joined forces in some local and parliamentary elections, with considerable success, against an alliance of the right-wing parties.

Until the 1980s, there existed a popularly elected General Council of the department, which administered funds gathered from local sources and some provided by the French government. In 1982, executive powers formerly held by the Paris-appointed prefect were transferred to the General Council. An appointed Regional Council (established in 1974) administered money from the French government's Fund for Investment in Overseas Departments. As the result of changes brought about by the Socialist government of President François Mitterand of France, direct popular elections were instituted for the Regional Council. There are forty-one members in the Regional Council and forty-two in the General Council.

In the first elections held for the Regional Council in February 1983, the right-wing coalition won a majority; however, in the March 1985 elections for the General Council, the Socialist/Communist alliance was successful, and Socialist party leader Dominique Larifla was chosen as president of the General Council.

In the French parliamentary elections of March 1986, the number of Guadeloupean deputies was increased from three to four. The two sitting Socialist and Communist deputies were reelected, and the candidates supported by the right-wing Rally for the Republic won the other two seats. In concurrent elections for the Regional Council, the left-wing coalition received 52.4 percent of the vote, compared with 43.1 percent three years before, and increased their representation from twenty to twenty-two members (twelve Socialists and ten Communists). Socialist Félix Proto was chosen as president of the Regional Council. In September of the same year, Communist Henri Bagou and Socialist François Louisy were elected members of the French Senate.

In the April–May 1988 French presidential election, the Socialist candidate François Mitterand received 55 percent and 69 percent of the vote in Guadeloupe in the two rounds. In the following French parliamentary election, the Socialist/Communist alliance won three of the department's four seats.

In September and October 1986, the leftist parties won twenty-six of the forty-two seats in the General Council of the department. In March 1989, in municipal elections, the left-wing parties carried twenty cities and towns, including the two biggest, Basse-Terr and Point-à-Pitre; the right won only thirteen.

During the 1980s, although the parties organized around the demand for independence rarely won over 5 percent of the popular vote, several pro-independence terrorist or insurrectionist groups were active. In 1980 and 1981, an organization calling itself the Armed Liberation Group (Groupe Liberation Armée) made bomb attacks on several hotels and government offices. In 1984 the Caribbean Revolutionary Alliance (Alliance Revolutionnaire Caraibe—ARS), which operated at the same time in Martinique and French Guiana, engaged in several bombings. In November 1986, there were further bombings, responsibility for which was claimed by a group named the Armed Revolutionary Organization (Organisation Revolutionnaire Armée). In April and May 1989, separatists demonstrated in the town of Port Louis and demanded the release of "political prisoners," that is, those arrested for terrorist activities. In June of that same year, the French National Assembly approved an amnesty for all crimes committed before July 1988 that were motivated by the desire to undermine French authority in the Overseas Departments.

Bibliography

The Europa World Year Book 1990. Europa Publications, Ltd., London, 1990.
Keesings Record of World Events. London.
Personal contacts of the writer.

Political Parties

ALLIANCE REVOLUTIONNAIRE CARAIBE. See CARIBBEAN REVOLUTIONARY ALLIANCE.

ANTILLES TROTSKYIST GROUP (GROUPE TROTSKYISTE ANTILLAIS). See TROTSKYISTS.

CARIBBEAN REVOLUTIONARY ALLIANCE (ALLIANCE REVOLUTIONNAIRE CARAIBE). This party, which began as a terrorist or insurrectionist group, operated in Guadeloupe, Martinique, and French Guiana. After the party carried out several bombings in Guadeloupe in 1984, it was outlawed. Its principal leader, Luc Reinette, was twice arrested. He escaped from prison both times, but, the second time he was caught, in Saint Vincent in July 1987, he was taken to Paris for trial, along with four other people. He was amnestied in July 1989. In October 1986, the group had announced that it was suspending further bombings pending the approaching elections. The party subsequently announced that it was dissolving and joining the Popular Movement for an Independent Guadeloupe.

COMBAT OUVRIER (WORKERS COMBAT). See TROTSKYISTS.

FÉDERATION GUADELOUPÉEN DU PARTI SOCIALISTE (GUADELOU-PEAN FEDERATION OF THE SOCIALIST PARTY). See SOCIALIST PARTY.

GROUPE RÉVOLUTIONNAIRE SOCIALISTE (REVOLUTIONARY SO-CIALIST GROUP). See TROTSKYISTS.

GROUPE TROTSKYISTE ANTILLAIS. See TROTSKYISTS.

GUADELOUPE DEPARTMENTALIST SOCIALIST MOVEMENT (MOUVEMENT SOCIALISTE DÉPARTMENTALISTE GUADELOU-PÉEN). Formed in 1974 by a group within the Guadeloupean Federation of the Socialist Party, led by Lucien Bernier, the party opposed reconciliation of the federation with the French Socialist Party, after a period of estrangement. This small group tends to align itself with the Union for French Democracy of the former French president Valery Giscard d'Estaing. Although, in the late 1970s, its popular following equalled that of the Socialist Party, it declined sharply in the subsequent decade.

GUADELOUPEAN COMMUNIST PARTY (PARTI COMMUNISTE GUADELOUPÉEN). Established following World War II as the Guadeloupe Federation of the Communist Party of France, but, because it supported a program of Guadeloupean autonomy from France, it decided in 1952 to declare its independence of the French party and to take its present name.

Although the Guadeloupean Communists supported greater autonomy for the department, they did not seek complete independence—explaining that this would run counter to the general opinion of the Guadeloupean citizenry—until February 1988, when they declared themselves in favor of the independence of Guadeloupe.

During the 1980s, the Guadeloupean Communist Party formed an electoral bloc with the Socialist Party. As a consequence, the Communists did well in the elections held during this decade. In March 1986, the party's principal leader, Ernest Moutoussany, was reelected to the French Chamber of Deputies, and he was reelected in June 1988. In September 1986, Henri Bagou, the long-time Communist mayor of Pointe-à-Pitre, the largest city, was elected to the French Senate by the Socialist/Communist coalition, along with a Socialist.

In March 1986, also, the Communists elected ten members of the Regional Council, as part of the victorious left-wing slate. The party also elected several mayors and a substantial number of municipal councilmen.

The Communists control the largest single trade union group in the department, the Conféderation Génerale du Travail de Guadeloupe (CGTG). The union was part of the French CGT until 1962, when it separated from that group. Overall, the trade union movement of Guadeloupe is not particularly strong.

GUADELOUPEAN FEDERATION OF THE SOCIALIST PARTY (FÉDERATION GUADELOUPÉEN DU PARTI SOCIALISTE). See SOCIALIST PARTY.

GUADELOUPEAN PROGRESSIVE MOVEMENT (MOUVEMENT PROGRESSISTE GUADELOUPÉEN). This small party was established in 1976 by Marcel Esdras, the mayor of Pointe Noire. Starting as an advocate of independence, it subsequently modified that position. It appears to have been a member of the leftist coalition during the 1980s.

LE PARTI DE GUADELOUPE. See THE PARTY OF GUADELOUPE.

MOUVEMENT POPULAIRE POUR UNE GUADELOUPE INDÉPENDANTE. See POPULAR MOVEMENT FOR AN INDEPENDENT GUADELOUPE.

MOUVEMENT PROGRESSISTE GUADELOUPÉEN. See GUADELOUPEAN PROGRESSIVE MOVEMENT.

MOUVEMENT SOCIALISTE DÉPARTAMENTALISTE GUADELOUPÉEN. See GUADELOUPE DEPARTMENTALIST SOCIALIST MOVEMENT.

PARTI COMMUNISTE GUADELOUPÉEN. See GUADELOUPEAN COMMUNIST PARTY.

POPULAR MOVEMENT FOR AN INDEPENDENT GUADELOUPE (MOUVEMENT POPULAIRE POUR UNE GUADELOUPE INDÉPENDANTE—MPGI). Led by Simone Faisans-Renac, the MPGI is one of the smaller groups that advocates the independence of the territory. One of its leaders, Georges Faisans, was jailed by the authorities in 1985, which provoked several protest demonstrations. It does not appear that the MPGI has been successful in electing any public officials during the 1980s. In 1986, when the Caribbean Revolutionary Alliance, which had been a terrorist group, announced its dissolution, it announced that its members were joining the MPGI.

POPULAR UNION FOR THE LIBERATION OF GUADELOUPE (UNION POPULAIRE POUR LA LIBÉRATION DE GUADELOUPE—UPLG). The largest party advocating Guadeloupean independence, the UPLG is led by Claude Makouke. The party boycotted the elections for the French president and parliament, on the grounds that they were irrelevant to Guadeloupe. However, the UPLG did participate in at least some municipal and departmental elections in the 1980s, but, until 1988, it seldom received more than 5 percent of the vote. In the 1988 elections for the General Council, the UPLG received about 10 percent of the vote, although in subsequent municipal elections, held in March 1989, it placed only a handful of municipal council members.

RALLY FOR THE REPUBLIC (RASSEMBLEMENT POUR LA RÉPUBLIQUE—RPR). The largest right-wing party in Guadeloupe, the RPR is a departmental federation of the French party of the same name led by Jacques Chirac, the neo-Gaullist. Although in 1979 the RPR succeeded in electing all three of its candidates for the French Chamber of Deputies, and although in February 1983 the right-wing alliance of which it was the larger part had won control of the Regional Council in the first popular election for that body, the party's fortunes declined substantially thereafter, in the face of a generally leftward move of the electorate.

In the 1981 parliamentary election, the RPR lost two of its seats in the French National Assembly, one to the Socialists and one to the Communists. Nevertheless, the third seat was won by a candidate of the other right-wing party, the Union for French Democracy (UDF), with RPR support.

In February 1986, the RPR president of the Regional Council resigned to join the UDF. As a consequence, the two parties, which had been coalition partners in earlier elections, ran separate candidates in the March 1986 French parliamentary election, in which Guadeloupe's representation was increased from three to four. In this election, the Socialist and Communist were reelected; the UDF deputy was defeated; and the two nominees supported by the RPR, Lucette Michaux-Chévry and Henri Beaujon, won the other two seats. In the June 1988 parliamentary election, a Socialist defeated Beaujon; however, Michaux-Chévry was reelected with RPR support.

In the March 1986 elections for the Regional Council, the RPR won the most seats of any party, fifteen; however, the rightists suffered an overall defeat in that poll, partly, at least, because of the split between the RPR and the UDF.

RASSEMBLEMENT POUR LA RÉPUBLIQUE. *See* RALLY FOR THE REPUBLIC.

REVOLUTIONARY SOCIALIST GROUP (GROUPE RÉVOLUTION-NAIRE SOCIALISTE). *See* TROTSKYISTS.

SOCIALIST PARTY (PARTI SOCIALISTE—PS). The oldest party in Guadeloupe, the PS was founded at the turn of the century. It soon became the Guadeloupe Federation of the French Socialist Party, a status it still officially holds. During World War II, headed by Admiral Robert, the Socialists took a leading role in the resistance to the Vichy regime in the territory. As a consequence, the party emerged from the war as the strongest political group in Guadeloupe, and it maintained its position until the 1960s.

When the Union of the Left alliance was formed between the Socialists and Communists in France in the early 1970s, the Guadeloupean Socialists refused to form a coalition with local Communists. As a result of several splits, in the 1960s and 1970s, the party's fortunes fell considerably. In the 1980s the Socialists followed a different policy. They agreed to cooperate with the Communists and some other smaller groups. Also, the Socialists were the biggest beneficiaries of a general move to the left in Guadeloupean public opinion.

Although Socialist Party deputy Frédéric Jalton had been defeated in the 1978 election for the French National Assembly, he was returned in 1981, and elected again in 1986 and 1988. In the 1988 poll, the Socialist Dominique Larifla defeated the sitting RPR deputy Henri Beaujon and joined Jalton in the assembly. In 1986 another Socialist, François Louisy, had been elected (along with a Communist) as one of the Guadeloupean members of the French Senate.

The Socialists also did well in departmental and municipal elections. When the leftist alliance won the elections for General Council in 1985, Socialist Larifla was chosen president of the council. In September 1988, the Socialists, who seated fourteen members in that body, had the largest representation. When the leftists increased their margin of control of the Regional Council in the March 1986 elections, Socialist Félix Proto became president of that body, replacing a rightist.

The Socialists control the Force Ouvrière and the CFDT labor groups in the department.

THE PARTY OF GUADELOUPE (LE PARTI DE GUADELOUPE). This small center-rightist party was established in January 1984 by Lucette Michaux-Chévry, who was then president of the General Council of Guadeloupe. In subsequent elections, the party allied itself with the Rassemblement pour le République (RPR), and Michaux-Chévry was elected to the French Chamber of Deputies in March 1986 with RPR support, and was reelected in 1988.

TROTSKYISTS. Each of the three small Trotskyist parties in Guadeloupe is associated with a different faction of International Trotskyism. The oldest group,

Workers Combat (Combat Ouvrier), was established in the 1960s as a group seeking independence for the department. Subsequently, it became part of the International Trotskyist currently headed by the Lutte Ouvrière party of France.

The second Trotskyist party, the Revolutionary Socialist Group (Groupe Révolutionnaire Socialiste—GRS), was formed by elements thrown out of the Communist Party because they were found guilty of "Guevarism." The GRS joined the United Secretariat of the Fourth International in December 1973. In 1974 it supported the candidate of the French Trotskyist party, Ligue Communiste Révolutionnaire, Alain Krivine, in the first round of the French presidential election, and François Mitterand in the second. In 1981 it urged abstention in both rounds.

The newest Trotskyist group, the Antilles Trotskyist Group (Groupe Trotskyiste Antillais), held its first congress in June 1984. The party supports independence for Guadeloupe, Martinique, and French Guiana. Its relations with the GRS have sometimes been tense.

All three Trotskyist groups have branches in both Guadeloupe and Martinique. None has, insofar as is known, participated in any elections held in Guadeloupe.

UNION FOR FRENCH DEMOCRACY (UNION POUR LA DÉMOCRATIE FRANÇAISE—UDF). The UDF is the Guadeloupean federation of the party of the same name in France, headed by former French president Valery Giscard d'Estaing. In the 1970s and until 1985, the party was in coalition with the Rally for the Republic (RPR); however, when the RPR president of the National Council resigned from his party to join the UDF, there was a break between the two parties. As a result, they ran separate tickets in the March 1986 parliamentary elections, and Marcel Esdras, the UDF member of the French National Assembly, was defeated, and the UDF won only four seats in the concurrent Regional Council election. Although the electoral alliance was subsequently renewed, the UDF remained the junior partner in the coalition, and the party did not regain its seat in the National Assembly.

UNION POPULAIRE POUR LA LIBÉRATION DE GUADELOUPE. See POPULAR UNION FOR THE LIBERATION OF GUADELOUPE.

UNION POUR LA DÉMOCRATIE FRANÇAISE. See UNION FOR FRENCH DEMOCRACY.

WORKERS COMBAT. See TROTSKYISTS.

Robert J. Alexander

GUATEMALA

Guatemala, the northernmost, most populous country of Central America, borders on the Caribbean Sea and Belize on the northeast, Honduras and El Salvador on the east and southeast, the Pacific Ocean on the south, and Mexico on the west and north. Approximately 60 percent of the population of 9 million people are Indians, who speak one or more of twenty-two Mayan languages still in existence in Guatemala. Although Guatemala City has grown dramatically in the past three decades, becoming a city of over 2 million people, Guatemala remains one of the more rural nations of Latin America.

Guatemala is generally mountainous, with a broad fertile plain on the Pacific coast, and tropical rain forests on the northerly and easterly slopes of its main mountain chains. Most of the people live in highland valleys, where the skyline is dominated by a chain of volcanoes, many of which are active. This area, with its scenic beauty and pleasant climate, has been the destination for most of Guatemala's tourism and has inspired the slogan by which Guatemala is often described: "the land of eternal spring." By contrast, much of eastern Guatemala is dry and desert-like.

The Petén region, Guatemala's northern area, is a recently developed frontier, in which tropical forests are being turned into large cattle ranches and plantations aimed at export markets. Guatemala also has oil and nickel reserves in the north. Population pressures in the highlands have led to the migration of people into the region, but these migrants have often found themselves in conflict with landed interests, including military officers, seeking to exploit the region for their own profit. As a result, the Petén has been a conflictive area since at least the mid-1970s. In the 1990s, a guerrilla insurgency has been operating in the area, with some impunity, and the Petén has become heavily militarized.

Socially and economically, the roots of Guatemala's current situation are best found in the Liberal Reforms of the 1870s, a series of laws which accomplished two principal goals. First, the government transformed the communal lands of Indian communities into private property which could be used for coffee production, and coffee has remained Guatemala's leading source of foreign exchange to the present day. Second, the Liberal Reforms established legal controls over workers, especially Indians, ensuring an adequate supply of extremely cheap labor for landowners producing coffee for export. The major issues in Guatemala's current political processes can be traced to the inequalities and social injustices perpetuated by these laws.

Guatemala's modern political history, which begins with the October Revolution of 1944, can be divided into four stages. The Decade of Spring (1944–1954) marked Guatemala's first steps towards democratization of its political system and modernization of its economic system, along with social reforms which improved the lot of the poor, especially the Indians. Two political parties emerged from this era: the Revolutionary Party (Partido Revolucionario—PR) and the Guatemalan Workers Party (Partido Guatemalteco de Trabajo—PGT). President Juan José Arévalo (1945–1951) initiated several social reform programs, but none of his was as controversial as President (and Colonel) Jacobo Arbenz Guzmán's agrarian reform decree of 1952, which took land from, among others, the United Fruit Company, then closely connected with the U.S. Department of State and the Central Intelligence Agency (CIA).

This brief respite from the constant injustice and degradation imposed on Guatemala by the Spanish Conquest ended in 1954, with a counterrevolution led by a CIA–trained invasion force. The invasion led directly to the formation of the National Liberation Movement (Movimiento de Liberación Nacional—MLN), which continues to be one of Guatemala's political parties of the extreme right. The new government of Colonel Carlos Castillo Armas (1954–1957) reversed social and political reforms, and enforced the new order with massive repression. The economic reforms that had made Guatemala a more efficient producer of export commodities were left intact, but the profits flowed to a small elite rather than into the social programs developed in the previous decade.

The system imposed by the counterrevolution of 1954 was unable to resolve the social and political tensions it generated. During this second stage, the Alliance for Progress, announced in Washington, D.C., in 1961, held out the prospect of massive military and economic aid from the United States. But because of the ineffective government of General Miguel Ydígoras Fuentes and factionalization among the elite and within the military—which included the development of a guerrilla insurgency led by dissident military officers after a failed military coup—Guatemala initially was unable to profit from this assistance.

With the state showing these signs of weakness and decline, Colonel Enrique Peralta Azurdia led a military coup d'état in 1963, which moved Guatemala into the third stage of its modern political history. In 1965 the Guatemalan military decreed a new constitution for the nation, and Peralta Azurdia, with U.S. assistance, modernized the Guatemalan military. These factors set the stage for a new round of elections in 1966. These, partly because of U.S. pressure, resulted in victory for a civilian, Julio César Méndez Montenegro. Méndez, the candidate of the Revolutionary Party, initially described his presidency as the third government of the October Revolution of 1944, but he implemented no social reforms, exhibited little civilian control over the military, and indeed was forced to watch as the Guatemalan army systematically killed thousands of people in eastern Guatemala in the late 1960s, in order to defeat an insurgency made up of a relative handful of guerrilla fighters. The architect of that repression, Colonel Carlos Arana Osorio, was rewarded with the presidency in the 1970 elections.

The 1970s were characterized by increasing levels of repression (though with some moments of relief), increasing dominance of the Guatemalan economy by military officers, and a pattern of fraudulent elections "won" by military officers, including General Kjell Laugerud García (1974–1978) and General Fernando Romeo Lucas García (1978–1982). After 1976 systematic repression of rural leaders became the characteristic military and conservative response to organized pressures for social reform. In 1979 two of Guatemala's leading democratic and progressive political leaders, Manuel Colom Argueta, of the United Front of the Revolution (Frente Unido de la Revolución—FUR), and Alberto Fuentes Mohr, of the Democratic Socialist Party (Partido Socialista Democrático—PSD), were assassinated, shortly after their movements had been granted legal status as political parties.

Massive repression had become the order of the day by 1980: In the rural highlands, the Guatemalan army carried out dozens of village massacres in order to combat an increasingly popular guerrilla movement; in the cities, hundreds of labor leaders and other popular activists disappeared or were murdered or driven into exile. In spite of these incredible levels of state terrorism, the ruling faction of the Guatemalan military was unable to sustain its position; its system broke down with the fraudulent election of 1982. The resulting wave of protests by political parties—all of the center or the right of the political spectrum—revealed massive fissures within the ruling elite and widespread elite dissatisfaction with the Lucas García clique. As in 1963, the tensions were resolved by a military coup, which, though led by a group of junior officers, installed the messianic, retired General Efraín Ríos Montt as chief of state. The coup ushered in the fourth stage of Guatemala's modern political history.

The Ríos Montt government, as well as the government of General Oscar Mejía Víctores that replaced it after another military coup in 1983, adopted a new counterinsurgency strategy. As in earlier periods, the U.S. government was involved in planning and supporting this strategy, whose stated goal was to eliminate the Guatemalan guerrilla movement. The actual goal of the strategy, however, was to secure the Guatemalan army's continued control over the nation's economic resources by neutralizing organized opponents throughout the social and economic spectrum. Part of this strategy involved continuing the massive repression against rural villages suspected of supporting insurgents. Another part of the strategy involved creating a new constitution, new procedures for the registration of political parties, and new elections.

As this scenario of repression was escalating, the formal political system saw changes as well. To General Ríos Montt, preparing Guatemala for new elections meant purging the system. Along with the rural repression, Ríos proclaimed several changes, resulting in new conditions that effectively reduced the formal level of democratic participation in the Guatemalan system. The traditional political parties had initially welcomed the Ríos Montt coup, since it had overturned a patently fraudulent election that had robbed them of direct electoral participation in government, but the honeymoon between the political parties and the new military rulers ended quickly, not over rural repression but over electoral politics.

Among Ríos Montt's reforms was a new law of political parties, which sought to weaken the established political parties; Ríos used the half-true rationales that the party system had to be opened up to all political persuasions and that the traditional party leaders were corrupt. All parties were officially disbanded. Any group could form a new political party by meeting new organizational and signature provisions, according to a set timetable. A group could become registered as a "party in formation" or as a civic committee, for example, with only 500 signatures. The new provisions reduced the number of signatures needed for final legalization from 50,000 to 4,000. The resulting proliferation of registered groups came as no surprise, much to the chagrin of the established parties.

Although it has become easier to register new political parties, it has become harder for smaller parties to maintain their legal identity. Any party that does not participate in presidential elections or does not gain more than 4 percent of the valid votes—or does not win at least one seat in the congress—has its registration canceled. Conversely, the parties that do survive receive government funds, 2 quetzales per valid vote, payable in four annual installments after the election (in 1991, the quetzal converted at about four to the U.S. dollar).

The army portrayed this process of party reorganization as part of a return to democracy, even though the new law weakened the organized sectors that could mobilize public opinion within the electoral process. In terms of maintaining the appearance of democracy, however, the reforms were a resounding success. Only one new major party came into existence during this transition period: the Union of the National Center (Unión del Centro Nacional—UCN). Most of the traditional parties survived. Guatemalan voters were able to participate in the Constituent Assembly election of 1984, as well as the national elections of November 1985, which culminated in the inauguration of the civilian government of Vinicio Cerezo Arévalo, the candidate of the Guatemalan Christian Democratic Party (Democracia Cristiana Guatemalteca—DCG).

None of the parties that participated in these elections campaigned on platforms suggesting social or progressive reforms, and none challenged the dominant role of the military officer corps in the political process. Reformist parties, such as the DCG and the PSD, abandoned their ideologies in favor of personalistic, media-oriented campaigns. In short, the counterinsurgency plan was successful in demobilizing political parties as vehicles for social change, while retaining political parties as functioning, cooperative components of a procedural democracy that posed little threat to the social dominance of the army.

The five years of the DCG government, under the leadership of President Cerezo, did little to alter the basic thrust of this model. Although reformist in its official ideological statements, the DCG proposed only minor reforms itself. From 1985 to 1990, most social reform was the result of organized, sometimes disruptive mobilizations led by popular organizations representing rural and urban workers and human rights activists. Reflecting Guatemala's historic pattern of elite response to organized demands for social progress, these mobilizations were met by increasing levels of selective repression, including dozens of assassinations and the disappearances of leaders and activists. Meanwhile, social and economic conditions worsened, poverty became more widespread, and environmental degradation emerged as a key problem, a symptom of both continuing poverty and of elite (including military) impunity as the nation's resources were plundered.

Guatemala's 1990 national elections were honest in terms of legal provisions and ballot counting, but they reflected the continuing counterinsurgency process, which is designed to help protect the dominant position of the army in society. None of the candidates offered solutions for social problems, other than neoliberal economics, and violence aimed at popular sectors was a characteristic of the campaign atmosphere. The combination of violence and the lack of a campaign based on progressive solutions to important social and economic problems produced widespread disgust with the traditional parties and even with electoral processes.

As a result, apathy was high, and Guatemalans who did participate voted to sweep out the traditional parties to the extent possible and elected the presidential candidate least involved with a conventional party, Jorge Serrano Elías. Although Serrano had finished third in the 1985 presidential elections, the Solidarity Action Movement (MAS) was a minor factor in the 1990 electoral process, up to the eve of the 1990 elections. When General Ríos Montt was declared ineligible as a candidate, Serrano inherited Ríos's widespread support, and he became an overnight front-runner in the 1990 election. Up to that point, Ríos Montt, whose campaign promised a reprise of the anticorruption program he had aimed at the traditional parties in 1982 and 1983, was the leading candidate in preelection polls.

Serrano finished second in the first round of elections in 1990, but his party, the MAS, finished a distant third in congressional balloting. The MAS won only 18 of 116 seats, although Serrano himself swept to the National Palace with 67 percent of the vote in the runoff election held against Jorge Carpio Nicolle, the candidate of the UCN. The Christian Democrats finished third in the first round of elections, with only 17.5 percent of the vote, and were eliminated from further contention.

In sum, Guatemala entered the 1990s with exacerbated levels of social and political injustice, but with fewer institutions for resolving the resulting tensions.

Political parties continued to appear unable to lead society toward progressive policies. Moreover, the parties seemed to be abandoning the task to popular organizations—such as labor and rural groups—who remain the only major actors within the political process pushing Guatemala toward social progress and toward political democracy. Because these groups have resisted coming under the sway of the political parties, and hence have remained more restive and effective, popular organizations have borne the brunt of systematic repression.

The long-range prospects for social stability in Guatemala are poor. Political parties, though participating at one level in an apparently pluralistic political process, have abdicated their potential leadership position in the more fundamental struggle for justice and democracy. Armed struggle and weak political institutions continue to characterize Guatemalan politics.

Bibliography

Tom Barry. *Guatemala: A Country Guide*, 2d. ed. The Resource Center, Albuquerque, N.M., 1990.

Peter Calvert. *Guatemala: A Nation in Turmoil*. Westview Press, Boulder, Colo., 1985.

Robert M. Carmack, ed. *Harvest of Violence: The Maya Indians and the Guatemalan Crisis*. University of Oklahoma Press, Norman, 1988.

Georges Fauriol and Eva Loser. *Guatemala's Political Puzzle*. Transaction Books, New Brunswick, N.J., 1988.

James Goldston. *Shattered Hope: Guatemalan Workers and the Promise of Democracy*. Westview Press, Boulder, Colo., 1989.

Jim Handy. *Gift of the Devil: A History of Guatemala*. South End Press, Boston, 1984.

INCEP. "Guatemala: Elecciones generales 1990." *Panorama Centroamericano: Reporte Político*, vol. 21, Special Issue, November 1990.

Inforpress Centroamericana. *Guatemala: Elections 1985*. Inforpress Centroamericana, Guatemala City, 1985.

NISGUA. *Election Information Packet*. Network in Solidarity with Guatemala—NISGUA, Washington, D.C., 1990.

Robert H. Trudeau. "The Guatemalan Election of 1985: Prospects for Democracy," in John A. Booth and Mitchell A. Seligson, eds., *Elections and Democracy in Central America*. University of North Carolina Press, Chapel Hill, 1989.

Political Parties—Active

ALIANZA POPULAR CINCO. *See* SOCIAL CHRISTIAN POPULAR ALLIANCE PARTY.

ANTI-COMMUNIST UNIFICATION PARTY (PARTIDO DE UNIFICACIÓN ANTI-COMUNISTA—PUA). The PUA is a recent (post-Ríos Montt's coup) reincarnation of the PUA of the 1950s, which had opposed Colonel Jacobo Arbenz Guzmán in the election of 1951. The PUA is an extreme right-wing group, founded by an original member of the 1954 counterrevolution,

Leonel Sisniega Otero, a participant in the military coups of both 1982 and 1983 (Inforpress 1985, 30–31). In spite of its ideologically conservative origins, however, the PUA reflects pragmatic power struggles and internecine factional conflicts more than any other form of right-wing politics. The group, which is more concerned with acquiring power than with any commitment to electoral processes or democratic institutions, has participated in both elections and military coups with regularity.

AUTHENTIC NATIONALIST CENTER PARTY (CENTRAL AUTÉNTICO NACIONALISTA—CAN). Originally called the Aranista Nationalist Center, after its founder General Carlos Arana Osorio, who was elected president in 1970, the CAN has remained a party of the extreme right. Throughout the 1970s, the CAN often participated in elections in coalition with other parties representing the military elite, such as the Democratic Institutional Party and, by 1978, the Revolutionary Party and the National Unity Front. In 1982 the CAN nominated its own candidate for president, indicating its unwillingness to go along with the ruling Fernando Romeo Lucas García faction of the army. The CAN did not participate as a party in the 1990 elections.

CENTRAL AUTÉNTICO NACIONALISTA. See AUTHENTIC NATION-ALIST CENTER PARTY.

DEMOCRACIA CRISTIANA GUATEMALTECA. See GUATEMALAN CHRISTIAN DEMOCRATIC PARTY.

DEMOCRATIC INSTITUTIONAL PARTY (PARTIDO INSTITUCIONAL DEMOCRÁTICO—PID). The PID was originally formed to act as the political party of the ruling military clique after the Peralta Azurdia coup in 1963, and it continued to represent dominant military factions through the 1970s. A party of the extreme right, it has been associated with the death squad activities of the late 1970s and early 1980s. The PID was a prominent coalition partner in the Lucas García government, but it was not a major force in the 1985 elections, when it won only one seat in the congress. Although the PID was part of the ruling coalition that was expelled by General Efraín Ríos Montt in 1982, the party supported the Ríos candidacy in 1990 as part of the Alianza No-Venta coalition. When Ríos was ruled ineligible, the PID, like its coalition partners, the National Unity Front and the Guatemalan Republican Front, was left to compete only at the parliamentary and municipal levels.

DEMOCRATIC PARTY (PARTIDO DEMOCRÁTICO—PD). A minor party of the conservative right, the PD is less extreme in its pronouncements than the National Liberation Movement and other extreme right-wing groups. The PD's presidential candidate in 1990, Jorge Reyna Castillo, a deputy in the national congress during the Cerezo administration, finished last of twelve, with 0.41 percent of the vote.

DEMOCRATIC PARTY OF NATIONAL COOPERATION (PARTIDO DEMOCRÁTICO DE COOPERACIÓN NACIONAL—PDCN). A party of the neoliberal right, this minor party won just over 2 percent of the presidential votes in 1990. The party has often participated in electoral coalitions since the late 1970s, sometimes with the Guatemalan Christian Democratic Party. In 1985, the PDCN's candidate (in a coalition with the Revolutionary Party) was Jorge Serrano Elías, who later founded the Solidarity Action Movement and won the presidential election in 1990.

DEMOCRATIC SOCIALIST PARTY (PARTIDO SOCIALISTA DEMOCRÁTICO—PSD). Registered as a legal party in the late 1970s, the PSD "paid the price" in the assassination of its founding leader Alberto Fuentes Mohr in 1978. By 1980 repression had driven most PSD leaders into exile. The party returned to participate in the 1985 elections, but it was more effective in gaining international legitimacy for the electoral system decreed by the military than it was in gaining votes. In 1990, the PSD's presidential candidate was a dissident member of the Guatemalan Christian Democratic Party, and one of its own major leaders, Luis Zurita, supported the Christian Democratic candidate, not the PSD's slate. Although technically a party of the left, and although the party took the unusual stance of nominating a woman as its vice-presidential candidate in 1990, the PSD has not proposed progressive reforms in its campaigns. The party has enjoyed little support from organized labor as a result. In 1990 the coalition of the PSD and the Social Christian Popular Alliance Party won one seat in the congress and only 3.59 percent of the presidential vote.

EMERGING MOVEMENT OF HARMONY (MOVIMIENTO EMERGENTE DE CONCORDANCIA—MEC). The MEC, which emerged after the Ríos Montt coup, was led by retired Colonel Luis Gordillo, one of the three members in the Ríos Montt junta. The party is right of center, but it has no clear ideological position. The MEC is perceived as the personal vehicle of Colonel Gordillo, not as a force in electoral politics. Although Gordillo had participated in the coup that removed the Lucas García faction from power, the MEC nominated General Benedicto Lucas García, the brother of former president Fernando Romeo Lucas García, as its candidate in 1990. Lucas received barely 1 percent of the votes cast, and the MEC won no races at either the parliamentary level or the municipal level.

FRENTE DE AVANCE NACIONAL. See NATIONAL ADVANCEMENT FRONT.

FRENTE DEMOCRÁTICO POPULAR. See POPULAR DEMOCRATIC FRONT.

FRENTE REPUBLICANO GUATEMALTECO. See GUATEMALAN RE-PUBLICAN FRONT.

FRENTE UNIDO DE LA REVOLUCIÓN. See UNITED FRONT OF THE REVOLUTION.

FRENTE UNIDO NACIONAL. See NATIONAL UNITY FRONT.

GUATEMALAN CHRISTIAN DEMOCRATIC PARTY (DEMOCRACIA CRISTIANA GUATEMALTECA—DCG). The DCG is the only major party in Guatemala with a clear ideological tradition and stance, a body of doctrine that places it squarely in the reformist center of the political spectrum. Given the lack of practical reformist alternatives, the ideological stance of the DCG lets the party be perceived as the only party that proposes progressive changes in Guatemala. Yet, in practice, the party has been ineffective in office and has become perceived as a corrupt organization rather than as a reformist party. The party's performance during the administration of President Vinicio Cerezo Arévalo has largely discredited it with most of its earlier supporters. The DCG has retained voting support only in the rural areas most heavily populated by Indians, where the party's organization has remained strong, in spite of the overall atmosphere of repression, perhaps because of the party's cooperation with the military during the Cerezo administration. In 1990, the DCG candidate, Alfonso Cabrera Hidalgo, finished third, with 17.5 percent of the vote; the party won 27 of 116 seats in the congress and 86 of 300 mayoralty races.

GUATEMALAN REFORMIST PARTY (PARTIDO REFORMADOR GUA-TEMALTECO—PREG). A minor party of the extreme right, the PREG did not participate in the 1990 elections because it became a registered party after the deadline for filing candidacies had passed.

GUATEMALAN REPUBLICAN FRONT (FRENTE REPUBLICANO GUA-TEMALTECO—FRG). The FRG was created as an electoral vehicle for the 1990 national elections, to support the candidacy of the former chief of state Efraín Ríos Montt. The party joined with the Democratic Institutional Party and the National Unity Front in a coalition called the No-Venta Alliance. In Spanish, the name translates as a play on words meaning "1990," as well as "not for sale," an allusion to Ríos Montt's continued stance that civilian political leaders are corrupt.

GUATEMALAN WORKERS PARTY (PARTIDO GUATEMALTECO DE TRABAJO—PGT). The PGT was the Guatemalan Communist Party during the 1940s and 1950s. As such, it is one of the oldest political parties in Guatemala, although it has been an illegal party since 1954. Operating underground, the PGT has split into factions over the years, and some groups participated as part of the guerrilla insurgency in the 1980s. Some elements of this party, and of other left organizations, such as the Revolutionary October Party, remain open to forming coalitions on the left both as an electoral vehicle—should a genuine left position become possible in the Guatemalan context—and as a negotiating vehicle in national dialogue processes between the guerrillas and the army.

MOVIMIENTO DE ACCIÓN SOLIDARIA. See SOLIDARITY ACTION MOVEMENT.

MOVIMIENTO DE LIBERACIÓN NACIONAL. See NATIONAL LIBER-ATION MOVEMENT.

MOVIMIENTO EMERGENTE DE CONCORDANCIA. See EMERGING MOVEMENT OF HARMONY.

NATIONAL ADVANCEMENT FRONT (FRENTE DE AVANCE NA-CIONAL—FAN). The new FAN, a small faction of the extreme right wing, participated in the 1990 elections as part of a coalition with the National Liberation Movement.

NATIONAL LIBERATION MOVEMENT (MOVIMIENTO DE LIBERA-CIÓN NACIONAL—MLN). The MLN derives its ideology and its early membership from the CIA–led 1954 counterrevolution invasion. Founded as a party in 1958, the MLN has been extremely vociferous, and actively violent, in its extreme right-wing politics since that time. Perhaps because of its intransigence in the face of changing political realities, the MLN has become increasingly isolated at the extreme right of the spectrum, and it has often publicly opposed what it has portrayed as the communistic or socialistic tendencies of some factions of the Guatemalan army. Elements of the party have broken away from the original leader, Mario Sandoval Alarcón, and have formed new parties that are alleged to have participated in several military coup attempts in the past decade. In 1990, the MLN, in coalition with the National Advancement Front, won 4.81 percent of the presidential vote and four seats in the national congress.

NATIONAL OPPOSITION UNION (UNIÓN DE OPOSICIÓN NA-CIONAL). This coalition, created for the 1982 presidential elections, was made up of moderate elements of the Revolutionary Party, the Party of National Renewal, and the Guatemalan Christian Democratic Party. The alliance finished third in the fraudulent voting, and its leaders and candidates participated in the demonstrations that followed the elections and helped precipitate the Ríos Montt coup of March 1982.

NATIONAL UNITY FRONT (FRENTE UNIDO NACIONAL—FUN). The FUN, a minor party, has consistently surfaced during electoral events as a coalition partner with political parties of the right. It has usually allied itself with the ruling military faction, and it has been successful at maintaining this tack even as the pattern of military rule changed from the late 1970s to the 1990s. Participating as a member of the Alianza No-Venta in 1990, the FUN, like its coalition partners the Democratic Institutional Party and the Guatemalan Republican Front, was left to compete at the parliamentary and municipal levels when the coalition's candidate, Efraín Ríos Montt, was ruled ineligible.

ORGANIZED NATIONALIST UNION (UNIDAD NACIONALISTA ORGANIZADA—UNO). Registered in 1987, the UNO describes itself as a party of the conservative right. It did not participate as a party in the 1990 elections.

PARTIDO DE AVANZADA NACIONAL. See PARTY OF NATIONAL ADVANCEMENT.

PARTIDO DE UNIFICACIÓN ANTI-COMUNISTA. See ANTI-COMMUNIST UNIFICATION PARTY.

PARTIDO DEMOCRÁTICO. See DEMOCRATIC PARTY.

PARTIDO DEMOCRÁTICO DE COOPERACIÓN NACIONAL. See DEMOCRATIC PARTY OF NATIONAL COOPERATION.

PARTIDO GUATEMALTECO DE TRABAJO. See GUATEMALAN WORKERS PARTY.

PARTIDO INSTITUCIONAL DEMOCRÁTICO. See DEMOCRATIC INSTITUTIONAL PARTY.

PARTIDO NACIONAL RENOVADOR. See PARTY OF NATIONAL RENEWAL.

PARTIDO REFORMADOR GUATEMALTECO. See GUATEMALAN REFORMIST PARTY.

PARTIDO REVOLUCIONARIO. See REVOLUTIONARY PARTY.

PARTIDO SOCIALISTA DEMOCRÁTICO. See DEMOCRATIC SOCIALIST PARTY.

PARTY OF NATIONAL ADVANCEMENT (PARTIDO DE AVANZADA NACIONAL—PAN). A party of the neoliberal right, the PAN identifies itself as a party of technocrats concerned with efficiency and good government, rather than with ideology and posturing, but is connected to agro-exporters of the

344 / POLITICAL PARTIES OF THE AMERICAS

conservative side of the spectrum. In an atmosphere characterized by widespread disgust with both the traditional political parties and the violence and corruption of the military alternatives, the PAN has emerged as a major electoral player in spite of its lack of organization at the national level. In 1985 its candidate, Alvaro Arzú, won the mayoralty race in Guatemala City but he never took office because of the Ríos Montt coup.

In 1990 Arzú campaigned for president and garnered 17.3 percent of the vote, only a fraction less than the Guatemalan Christian Democratic Party (DCG). In spite of this level of popularity, the party won only twelve seats in the congress, compared to twenty-seven for the DCG, which reflects the PAN's lack of a national organization. Nonetheless, by winning municipal-level races in major urban areas, the PAN controlled the municipal governments of over 25 percent of the Guatemalan population.

PARTY OF NATIONAL RENEWAL (PARTIDO NACIONAL RENOVA-DOR—PNR). Originally registered in 1978, the PNR, a party of the conservative right, includes remnants of the Revolutionary Party (PR). By itself, the PNR has never been a major force in electoral politics, and it earned less than 1 percent of the vote in 1990. Nevertheless, the party has been involved in coalitions with various parties throughout the past two decades, including Jorge Carpio Nicolle's Union of the National Center, the PR, and, earlier, the Guatemalan Christian Democratic Party. The PNR's leading figure from 1978 through the 1985 election was Alejandro Maldonado Aguirre, who originally helped organize the National Liberation Movement but broke with that group to pursue a less extremist style of politics.

POPULAR DEMOCRATIC FRONT (FRENTE DEMOCRÁTICO POPU-LAR—FDP). The FDP, the electoral alliance created for the military's candidate in the 1982 elections, General Aníbal Guevara, included the Democratic Institutional Party, the Revolutionary Party, and the National Unity Front, all consistent political allies of the military during the 1970s. Guevara was declared the victor in the 1982 elections, but amidst widespread allegations of fraud, the election became moot when the Lucas García government was overthrown, by a junta led by General Efraín Ríos Montt, within weeks of the election.

REVOLUTIONARY PARTY (PARTIDO REVOLUCIONARIO—PR). The PR was originally founded in the late 1950s in an attempt to build a political movement around the democratic reforms of the administration of President Juan José Arévalo (1945–1951). When the party's leader and candidate, Mario Méndez Montenegro, was assassinated before the 1966 elections, the party's reins, and candidacy, were taken up by his brother Julio César Méndez Montenegro. Julio Méndez won the election but enjoyed little political power. The party drifted to the right, away from its original intentions, and by 1978, the PR was in open coalition with the extremely repressive and corrupt government of General Fernando Romeo Lucas García. Nevertheless, suggesting a lack of ideological consistency, the party nominated Carlos Gallardo Flores, exiled during the Lucas regime because of his opposition to the government, as its vice-presidential candidate in 1990.

SOCIAL CHRISTIAN POPULAR ALLIANCE PARTY (ALIANZA POPULAR CINCO—AP-5). The AP-5, an alliance of several small groups that reflect a social Christian program, includes factions that have broken away from the Guatemalan Christian Democratic Party (DCG) and from progressive movements to the left of the DCG. The party has usually participated in elections as part of larger coalitions. Most of its components supported the Christian Democrats in 1985, and the alliance supported the Democratic Socialist Party (PSD) slate in 1990. In 1990 the AP-5/PSD coalition was able to elect only one representative to the congress.

SOLIDARITY ACTION MOVEMENT (MOVIMIENTO DE ACCIÓN SOLIDARIA—MAS). The MAS was founded in the aftermath of the Ríos Montt coup by one of Efraín Ríos Montt's civilian associates in government, Jorge Serrano Elías. The MAS, a party of the right, has offered little by way of a program for leading Guatemala out of its social and economic morass. Instead, when functioning, the party has been a personal vehicle for Serrano and has reflected his evangelical Christian stance on social issues, including attempts to initiate dialogue between the insurgent guerrilla leadership and the government (and military). Once a member of the Guatemalan Christian Democratic Party, Serrano has also been a member of the Party of National Renewal and the Democratic Party of National Cooperation.

UNIDAD NACIONALISTA ORGANIZADA. See ORGANIZED NATIONALIST UNION.

UNIÓN DE OPOSICIÓN NACIONAL. See NATIONAL OPPOSITION UNION.

UNIÓN DEL CENTRO NACIONAL. See UNION OF THE NATIONAL CENTER.

UNION OF THE NATIONAL CENTER (UNIÓN DEL CENTRO NACIONAL—UCN). The UCN is the only major party that has emerged since the 1982 Ríos Montt coup. Founded by Jorge Carpio Nicolle, owner and publisher of a leading Guatemala daily newspaper, the UCN has portrayed itself as a business-oriented, centrist party committed to economic reforms within a market model. Although centrist in self-portrayal, the UCN's positions are decidedly right of center, especially on economic questions.

Carpio finished second in the 1985 elections, losing to Vinicio Cerezo Arévalo and the Guatemalan Christian Democrats, whose vice-presidential candidate was Carpio's brother Roberto. The UCN emerged as a major force in the national congress, in effect making the party the "loyal opposition" during the Cerezo presidency, although it was consistently a strident and not particularly loyal voice. Carpio ran again in 1990; this time he barely finished first in the initial round of elections, with 25.7 percent of the vote, but he lost badly to Jorge Serrano Elías in the runoff. Although Carpio lost, the UCN won the largest bloc of seats in the national congress—41 of the 116 seats—and 132 of the 300 mayoralty races that were contested.

UNITED FRONT OF THE REVOLUTION (FRENTE UNIDO DE LA REVOLUCIÓN—FUR). Organized as an attempt to carry on the Arevalist tradition interrupted in 1954, by the CIA's counterrevolution, and in the mid-1960s, by the Revolutionary Party's drift to the right, the FUR became a registered political party in the late 1970s. Like the Democratic Socialist Party, the FUR suffered assassinations, and most of its surviving leaders—including the sitting vice president, Francisco Villagrán Kramer—had gone into exile by 1980. Some factions of the FUR, however, continued to participate in elections during the regime of General Fernando Romeo Lucas García, which led to the discrediting, perhaps intentional, of the party. By 1990 the FUR was a minor party representing no clear ideological position on the spectrum. Its candidate, Leonel Hernández, was identified as a social democrat, but he had served as a government minister during the military dictatorship before the 1985 election. The FUR won less than 1 percent of the vote in 1990.

Political Parties—Historical

CONSERVATIVE PARTY (PARTIDO CONSERVADOR). The Conservatives, one of Guatemala's two traditional parties in the nineteenth century, opposed the Liberal Party's attempts to modernize Guatemalan capitalism and to weaken the position of the Catholic Church. The only major Conservative president during the period was Rafael Carrera. As an ideological movement, the Conservative Party essentially disappeared after the 1870s, when party members began to support the liberal reforms of the period.

FRENTE POPULAR LIBERTADOR. See POPULAR LIBERATION FRONT.

LIBERAL PARTY (PARTIDO LIBERAL). The Liberals, formed as a coherent party at the time of Guatemala's independence, led Guatemala's movement toward a modern style of economic development with their reforms in the 1870s. Led by Justino Rufino Barrios and later by Manuel Estrada Cabrera, the Liberals were dominant well into the twentieth century but disappeared as a coherent party when their ideological program became the consensus position for Guatemalan elites, who began to divide, and form, parties over other issues.

MOVIMIENTO DEMOCRÁTICO NACIONAL. *See* NATIONAL DEMO-CRATIC MOVEMENT.

NATIONAL DEMOCRATIC MOVEMENT (MOVIMIENTO DEMOCRÁ-TICO NACIONAL—MDN). This right wing organization served as the political party of Carlos Castillo Armas, a military officer selected by the Central Intelligence Agency to lead an armed invasion of Guatemala in 1954. Castillo emerged as president of Guatemala after that successful coup, but after his assassination in 1957, and after its apparent electoral victory was overturned in 1958, the MDN split. One faction, the National Liberation Movement (MLN), remained a major party of the right wing well into the 1980s. The other faction, the National Reformist Movement, never became a major factor in electoral politics.

PARTIDO CONSERVADOR. *See* CONSERVATIVE PARTY.

PARTIDO DE ACCIÓN REVOLUCIONARIA. *See* REVOLUTIONARY AC-TION PARTY.

PARTIDO DE LA REVOLUCIÓN GUATEMALTECA. *See* PARTY OF THE GUATEMALAN REVOLUTION.

PARTIDO DEL PUEBLO. *See* PEOPLE'S PARTY.

PARTIDO LIBERAL. *See* LIBERAL PARTY.

PARTIDO SOCIALISTA. *See* SOCIALIST PARTY.

PARTIDO UNIONISTA. *See* UNIONIST PARTY.

PARTY OF THE GUATEMALAN REVOLUTION (PARTIDO DE LA REV-OLUCIÓN GUATEMALTECA). Created as a non-Communist alliance during the Arbenz administration in the 1950s, the party disappeared with the demise of Jacobo Arbenz Guzmán's government after the CIA–led coup of 1954.

PEOPLE'S PARTY (PARTIDO DEL PUEBLO). This party was the personal vehicle of Jorge García Granados, a leader of the October Revolution of 1944 who opposed the progressive governments that followed that event. The party was García's personal vehicle in the early 1950s, but it disappeared after 1954.

POPULAR LIBERATION FRONT (FRENTE POPULAR LIBERTADOR—FPL). This middle-class group participated in the October Revolution of 1944 and in Juan José Arévalo's 1945 election as part of the United Front of Arevalist Parties, but it distanced itself from the Arévalo government that followed. The

FPL joined the Party of the Guatemalan Revolution coalition in support of President Jacobo Arbenz Guzmán in 1952, but the party disappeared after 1954.

REVOLUTIONARY ACTION PARTY (PARTIDO DE ACCIÓN REVOLUCIONARIA—PAR). This party was the mainstay of President Juan José Arévalo's coalition during his 1945 election campaign and in the government that followed. The PAR became part of the Party of the Guatemalan Revolution coalition in 1952, but it reemerged as an independent party shortly thereafter. It disappeared after the 1954 coup that overthrew the Arbenz government.

REVOLUTIONARY DEMOCRATIC UNITY (UNIDAD REVOLUCIONARIA DEMOCRÁTICA—URD). The URD was formed originally as a faction of the Revolutionary Party, which had itself been formed in the early 1960s in an attempt to reorient Guatemalan public policy toward some of the socially progressive goals of the presidency of Juan José Arévalo in the 1940s. The URD functioned throughout the 1960s and into the 1970s, but it never participated in an electoral campaign on its own.

SOCIALIST PARTY (PARTIDO SOCIALISTA). The Socialist Party emerged during the Arbenz administration in the early 1950s, as an alternative to the Communist Party's influence. It merged with other groups to form the Party of the Guatemalan Revolution coalition in 1952.

UNIDAD REVOLUCIONARIA DEMOCRÁTICA. See REVOLUTIONARY DEMOCRATIC UNITY.

UNIONIST PARTY (PARTIDO UNIONISTA). Essentially nonideological, the Unionist Party emerged as an opposition movement during the Estrada Cabrera regime of the early twentieth century, and it supported the reunification of Central America. The party was the vehicle used by General Jorge Ubico in his rise to power in the early 1930s, but the party disappeared during Ubico's personalist dictatorship.

Robert H. Trudeau

GUYANA

Guyana lies between Venezuela, Brazil, and Suriname on the northeast coast of the South American continent. Although it has a relatively large territory (83,000 square miles), its population is only 755,800 (mid-1988), most of which is concentrated along the coastal area. A beleaguered economy has contributed to heavy outmigration over the past few decades. Guyana has the potential to be a wealthy country, endowed as it is with abundant natural resources—forests; rivers, for hydroelectricity; a variety of minerals, including bauxite, gold, and diamonds; fertile agricultural soils; and marine resources. However, political and economic mismanagement have reduced Guyana to the status of one of the poorest countries in the hemisphere. Bauxite, sugar, and rice are Guyana's main exports.

Guyana was disputed by Spain, Holland, and Britain for three centuries until the British gained control by the Treaty of London (1814). The British introduced Crown Colony government with limited popular participation. As happened elsewhere in the West Indies, social and political discontent beginning in the late 1930s led to some changes, culminating in the introduction of universal suffrage and responsible parliamentary government in 1953. It was not until 1966, however, that Guyana gained its independence from Britain. Independence was delayed by internal disturbances, including racial conflict, and by the refusal of Venezuela to relinquish a historical claim to five-eighths of Guyana's territory. (The claim was frozen in 1970 for a period of twelve years, which allowed Guyana to proceed to independence.) In 1970 Guyana was declared to be a Cooperative Socialist Republic.

Guyana's population is composed mainly of the descendants of African slaves (43 percent) and the descendants of indentured laborers from India brought in after emancipation (51 percent). The rest of the people are native Amerindians, who live primarily in the interior, and the descendants of Chinese and Portuguese contract workers. Race has been a persistent factor in Guyanese politics, especially in view of the absence of crosscutting cleavages that might foster a more heterogeneous political environment. Whereas the African population has been predominantly urban, Christian, and involved in the mining sectors and the bureaucracy, the East Indian population has remained primarily rural, Hindu, and engaged in agriculture. The cleavages have been reflected in trade union as well as party representation.

The country's first modern political party was the People's Progressive Party (PPP), which was formed in 1950 by Cheddi Jagan, a Marxist, and Linden Forbes Burnham, who professed socialism. The party, led in this way by an Indian and an African, attempted to transcend racial conflict and, for a time, race played a secondary role to ideology. The PPP won the 1953 general elections, but the government it formed lasted only 133 days before it was forcibly removed by the British colonial office on the grounds that it was attempting to set up a "Communist-dominated" state. Not long after, Burnham, professing to disagree with Jagan's adherence to orthodox pro-Soviet socialism, broke with Jagan on ideological grounds. Two PPPs contested the 1957 elections: the East Indian, Jagan-led PPP and the Burnham-led PPP, supported mainly by Afro-Guyanese. The Burnham-led PPP, which lost the election, later became the People's National Congress (PNC). The PPP won the election again in 1961, winning 42.6 percent of the vote (the PNC won 40.9 percent), but between 1962 and 1964 the country was torn by violence stemming from economic problems and racial hostilities.

In 1964, Jagan and Burnham, participating in constitutional talks as a prelude to independence, agreed to leave the issue of an appropriate constitution to the British. The resulting proposal called for elections under a single system of proportional representation. All elections since have been held under this system, which allowed Burnham to come to power in 1964 with the help of a small Portuguese-supported conservative party, the United Force (UF). (The PPP won 45.8 percent of the vote; the PNC, 40.59 percent; the UF, the rest.) The UF left the governing coalition in 1968 in opposition to a new bill that allowed overseas voting. One-fifth of the total electorate, a suspiciously high number, was deemed eligible to vote as overseas residents. The PNC went on to win the 1968 elections, capturing thirty of fifty-three parliamentary seats, a figure that was increased by seven in the 1973 elections. In that election, the UF joined with a small Indian-based party, the Liberator Party (LP), to win two seats, and the PPP captured the remaining fourteen. However, Jagan alleged electoral fraud and led a boycott of parliament that did not end until 1975. The UF–LP coalition split as a result of the UF's decision not to follow Jagan's boycott.

In 1974, Burnham issued the Declaration of Sophia in which the PNC was declared to be paramount and socialist. In 1978 a referendum was held to gain approval for a new socialist constitution. Although opposition figures estimated the voting turnout at just over 14 percent, the PNC reported a 71.45-percent turnout and a 97.7-percent approval. As a consequence, elections were postponed until 1979, in order to facilitate the drawing up of the new constitution. In 1979 Burnham postponed the elections for another year. Meanwhile, a constituent assembly, which was boycotted by the opposition parties, drew up a new constitution which created an executive president with broad powers that included the right to veto acts of parliament, immunity from civil and criminal prosecution, and provisions that made it almost impossible to remove the president from power.

In 1979 a new party, the Working People's Alliance (WPA), was formed. The party, which grew out of the 1975 alliance of several cultural, intellectual, and revolutionary organizations, sought to overcome racial divisions and to offer a revolutionary alternative to the traditional parties. The year 1979 was turbulent for Guyana, with widespread industrial unrest and opposition demonstrations triggered by the arrest of WPA leaders after the firebombing of a government building. In June 1980, one of the WPA's leaders, Walter Rodney, a historian respected throughout the Third World, was killed by a bomb blast in suspicious circumstances. The incident brought negative international publicity to a government just recovering from the world attention that had focused in late 1978 on the suicide of 914 members of a religious sect (led by the North American Jim Jones) at a settlement sanctioned by the government in the interior of Guyana. Questions were raised at the time about PNC involvement with religious sects, one of which, the House of Israel, was implicated in the murder of a Roman Catholic priest during antigovernment demonstrations in 1979. Moreover, the Rodney murder raised questions about the government's human rights record and cooled Guyana's ties with its nonaligned and socialist allies.

In 1980 general elections were held under the new constitution which had been duly ratified. That the elections were fraudulent was the conclusion reached not only by the Guyanese opposition but also by a team of independent observers led by a British peer, Lord Avebury. Burnham was duly inaugurated as the country's first executive president. Official statistics reported a 91-percent voting turnout in the elections: The PNC received 77.66 percent of the vote (forty-one seats, four more than in the election of 1973); the PPP, 19.46 percent (ten seats, four less than in 1973); and the UF, 2.88 percent (two seats). The PNC also won most of the regional democratic councils created by the new constitution, and it was elected to all twelve of the local government seats (which are based on nominations from the regional democratic councils and local democratic organs) in the National Assembly. In all, the party gained more than a four-fifths majority in the National Assembly (fifty-three out of sixty-five seats).

Between 1980 and 1985, Guyana continued to stagnate politically and economically under its rigid authoritarian and statist system. In August 1985, President Burnham died and was succeeded by his vice president and prime minister, Desmond Hoyte. Hoyte was not the favorite of the rank and file of the party, who preferred another deputy, Hamilton Green, but Green cooperated in the election of Hoyte and was made prime minister. Hoyte has sought to liberalize the economy, and he made some changes in the electoral system prior to the general elections held in 1985. Specifically, he restricted overseas voting to diplomats; he limited proxy voting to the blind and other incapacitated persons; and he abolished postal voting. However, he refused opposition demands for a preliminary ballot count at polling places (as a way to forestall ballot stuffing) on the grounds that it would be logistically impractical. As a result, the opposition charged that irregularities took place in the 1985 polling, not only ballot stuffing but also multiple voting by PNC supporters. Opposition polling agents were allegedly prevented from monitoring the vote at some polling stations. The official results were: PNC, forty-two seats; PPP, eight; UF, two; and WPA, 1. The voting turnout was an estimated 73.83 percent; the PNC captured 77.58 percent of the vote; the PPP, 15.57 percent.

In the wake of the 1985 election, the PPP, WPA, and three smaller parties—the Democratic Labour Movement (DLM), the People's Democratic Movement (PDM), and the National Democratic Front (NDF)—formed an umbrella organization, the Patriotic Coalition for Democracy (PCD), to work toward free and fair elections in Guyana. New elections constitutionally are due in Guyana by March 1991, although it appears that they will be postponed to later in the year in order to accommodate work on electoral changes. The PNC has been experiencing sharp intraparty differences between the supporters of Hoyte and those of Green (the Burnhamite faction). However, the only opposition party that appears to be a challenge to the PNC at the present time is the PPP, which has begun to downplay its ideological rigidity, in view of the reforms that have taken place in much of the socialist world. The elections of 1991 also promise to be freer and fairer than in the past: President Hoyte has agreed, at the urging not only of the opposition but also of the former U.S. president Jimmy Carter, who heads an eighteen-member Council of Freely Elected Heads of Government, to the compilation of a new electoral roll and a preliminary count of ballots at places of polling.

Bibliography

Colin Baber and Henry Jeffrey. *Guyana: Politics, Economics and Society.* Lynne Rienner, Boulder, Colo., 1986.

Festus Brotherson, Jr. "The Politics of Permanent Fear: Guyana's Authoritarianism in the Anglophone Caribbean." *Caribbean Affairs* 1, 3, 1988, pp. 57–76.

Cheddi Jagan. *The West on Trial: My Fight for Guyana's Freedom.* Michael Joseph, London, 1966.

Gordon K. Lewis. *The Growth of the Modern West Indies.* McGibbon and Kee, London, 1968.

Robert H. Manley. *Guyana Emergent: The Post-Independence Struggle for Non-Dependent Development.* G. K. Hall, Boston, and Schenkman, Cambridge, Mass., 1979.

Local and regional newspaper sources.

Personal contacts of author.

Political Parties—Active

BERBICE PROGRESSIVE PARTY (BPP). This small party, launched in 1987, is dependent on East Indian support. A strongly regionalist party, it appears to be dormant in 1990.

CONSERVATIVE PARTY OF GUYANA (CPG). The CPG, a minor right-wing party, was formed in Canada in the early 1980s. It is known primarily for the fact that a member was charged with plotting to assassinate Prime Minister Linden Forbes Burnham and other officials in 1983. It appears to be dormant in 1990.

DEMOCRATIC LABOUR MOVEMENT (DLM). The DLM grew out of the Right to Work Association, founded in 1982 by Paul Nehru Tennassee, an author, historian, lecturer, and trade unionist. It is a centrist party with a social democratic orientation, international ties, and a base that has expanded to include some working-class support. The party contested the 1985 election and won 0.73 percent of the vote.

LIBERATOR PARTY (LP). This small, right-wing party was formed in 1972 with a base in the East Indian community. The party allied with the United Force (UF) in 1973 and won two seats in the National Assembly. The party broke with the UF after the UF decided not to cooperate in an opposition boycott of parliament, and its two seats were reassigned to the UF. In 1980 the LP joined with the Working People's Vanguard Party and the People's Democratic Movement to form the Vanguard for Liberation and Democracy.

NATIONAL DEMOCRATIC FRONT (NDF). This minor party, led by Joseph Bacchus, was formed to contest the 1985 election, in which the party received 156 votes.

NATIONAL REPUBLICAN PARTY (NRP). A conservative party, the NRP was formed in 1990 by Robert Gangadeen, the ousted leader of the United Republican Party.

PATRIOTIC COALITION FOR DEMOCRACY (PCD). The PCD is a loose alliance of five opposition parties organized after the 1985 general elections, which, the opposition claimed, were conducted unfairly. The five parties involved are the People's Progressive Party, the Working People's Alliance, the Democratic Labour Movement, the People's Democratic Movement, and the National Democratic Front. The PCD is committed to the restoration of elective democracy in Guyana.

PEOPLE'S DEMOCRATIC MOVEMENT (PDM). This small party was formed in 1973 by Llewellyn John, a former executive member of the People's National Congress. It has received only a few hundred votes in elections. It appears to be centrist, but its program and membership are ill-defined.

PEOPLE'S NATIONAL CONGRESS (PNC). The PNC emerged after a leadership dispute between Cheddi Jagan and Linden Forbes Burnham led to a split in the People's Progressive Party (PPP) in 1955. Burnham's faction of the PPP, which later became the PNC, drew its support primarily from Afro-Guyanese, particularly urban residents and those involved in the mining industry. After the Burnham-led PPP was defeated in the 1957 general elections, the faction merged with the United Democratic Party under the name of the People's National Congress. The PNC lost again to the PPP in 1961, but, in 1964, after a system of proportional representation was introduced, at the suggestion of the British as a prelude to independence, the PNC was finally able to form a government with the support of a minor party, the United Force (UF). The PNC has been in power since that time, and its leader, Burnham, was the head of government until his death in 1985. PNC longevity has been attributable in no small measure to electoral and political manipulation, for example, by the introduction of overseas voting (in 1973); by postponement of elections while constitutional reform was under way, a process that led to the promulgation in 1980 of a constitution giving the executive president very broad powers; and by the holding of elections which were widely viewed as marred by irregularities, including a referendum on the constitution in 1978 and elections in 1980 and 1985 that gave the PNC forty-one and forty-two of fifty-three seats, respectively.

The PNC began with a moderate socialist platform, but in 1970 it introduced "cooperative socialism," an experiment that was to include self-reliance and collectivization but was operationalized, instead, as rigid state control of the economy. In 1974 the party was declared to be paramount and socialist. Between 1970 and 1985, Guyana stagnated as excessive bureaucratization was accompanied by increasing authoritarianism and militarization and a deepening economic crisis. Burnham was succeeded in 1985 by Desmond Hoyte, who has purged the PNC of some Burnhamite stalwarts, halted some overt authoritarian practices, liberalized the economy, and introduced some electoral reforms, while maintaining the dominance of the PNC.

PEOPLE'S PROGRESSIVE PARTY (PPP). The PPP, Guyana's first modern political party, was established in 1950 by Cheddi Jagan, a pro-Soviet Marxist. Linden Forbes Burnham became the party's chairman, and the party sought to rise above racial politics. It was instrumental in achieving some gains for labor and in persuading the British to introduce some political reforms. In 1953 the PPP handily won the first elections held under universal suffrage. In government, the party attempted to introduce social legislation that was construed as communistic by the British, given the global cold war environment. Britain sent troops into Guyana and removed the government after it had been in power only 133 days. The PPP later split, and Burnham went on to form the People's National Congress (PNC).

A new constitution was introduced in 1957, and the PPP won the elections held under this system both in 1957 and in 1961. While in power, the PPP tried to improve the country's agriculture and infrastructure, but its efforts were hindered in its second term by racial and labor unrest in which the U.S. Central

Intelligence Agency was implicated. Meanwhile, efforts were under way to gain independence from Britain, and in 1964 PPP leader Jagan agreed to give British Secretary of State Duncan Sandys carte blanche in creating a constitution for elections and independence. The Sandys proposal called for early elections under a system of proportional representation. Elections were held in 1964, and, although the party won 45.8 percent of the vote to the PNC's 40.59 percent, the PPP was replaced by a government coalition of the PNC and the United Force.

The PPP has been the major opposition party since 1964: it won fourteen parliamentary seats in 1973, ten in 1980, and eight in 1985. The PPP boycotted parliament in 1973, citing irregularities in the conduct of the elections, and Jagan called for a campaign of civil resistance and noncooperation. The PPP returned to parliament in 1975, offering its "critical support" for the PNC government, which had declared at that time its committment to socialism. The PPP also boycotted the Constituent Assembly that formulated a new constitution in 1980. After the 1985 elections, it joined the Patriotic Coalition for Democracy, a loose coalition of parties that oppose the PNC.

The PPP's support base is primarily the East Indian and rural community; Jagan is also the head of the Guyana Agricultural Workers' Union, a large sugar union. The PPP, which has articulated a pro-Soviet Marxist ideology, has often been perceived as lacking a program that addresses the practical realities. However, its orthodoxy has recently been moderated to take into account the Soviet Union's own turn toward more liberal policies.

UNITED FORCE (UF). This party has been the consistent third force in Guyanese politics, but it has a limited base of support. Formed in 1961 by Portuguese industrialist Peter D'Aguiar, it has espoused a conservative, pro-West, free enterprise approach, and it has been strongly supported by the business community. Its ethnic base has traditionally been the Portuguese and Amerindian community and other minority groups. The UF allied with the People's National Congress to form the government in 1964, but it left the coalition in 1968 in protest over the introduction of overseas voting. In 1973, under the leadership of Marcellus Felden Singh, it contested the elections in alliance with the Liberator Party (LP). When the LP left the coalition because the UF rejected an opposition call to boycott parliament, the UF took over the two seats originally assigned to the LP. The UF won two seats in 1980 and retained them in 1985.

UNITED REPUBLICAN PARTY (URP). The URP was launched in the United States in 1987 and entered the political arena in Guyana in 1988. It has a conservative platform. Internal wrangling in 1990 led to the removal of URP leader Robert Gangadeen and to his replacement by Dr. Leslie Ramsammy. Gangadeen formed a rival party, the National Republican Party, which has the same platform as the URP.

VANGUARD FOR LIBERATION AND DEMOCRACY (VLD). Composed of the Liberator Party (LP), the Working People's Vanguard Party (WPVP), and the People's Democratic Movement (PDM), this odd alliance put together in 1980 advocated civil disobedience against the People's National Congress. Despite the inclusion of the WPVP, the VLD platform was ideologically moderate, advocating foreign investment and a freeze on nationalizations. The PDM appears to be the only party of the alliance that survived to contest the 1985 elections.

WORKING PEOPLE'S ALLIANCE (WPA). The WPA began in the mid-1970s as an alliance of left-wing groups that were disenchanted with the conduct of the elections of 1973. These groups included the African Society for Cultural Relations with Independent Africa (ASCRIA), led by former People's National Congress member Eusi Kwayana; the Indian Progressive Revolutionary Associates (IPRA), led by former People's Progressive Party member Moses Bhagwan; the intellectual RATOON group; and the Working People's Vanguard Party (WPVP), which withdrew in 1977. When the alliance became a political party in 1979, its platform emphasized multiracialism and revolutionary socialism. In that year, three of its leaders—Walter Rodney, Rupert Roopnarine, and Omawale—were arrested on arson charges, which sparked major demonstrations in the capital. In June 1980, Rodney was killed in a bomb blast under suspicious circumstances.

The WPA did not contest the 1980 elections on the grounds that the elections were fraudulent. In 1985, the party won 1.39 percent of the vote and one seat in parliament. The WPA announced in 1985 that Guyana was not ready for socialism, but it has not clarified its ideology since then. The party has made some inroads into the labor movement.

WORKING PEOPLE'S VANGUARD PARTY (WPVP). This small left-wing party, sometimes described as Maoist, was established in 1969 as a result of a split in the People's Progressive Party and was led by Brindley Benn, a former deputy premier in the Jagan administration. In 1980 it joined with the Liberator Party and the People's Democratic Movement to form the Vanguard for Liberation and Democracy.

Political Parties—Historical

GUIANA NATIONAL PARTY (GNP). The GNP was organized in the early 1950s to contest the 1953 general election.

LABOUR PARTY. Organized in 1947, the Labour Party dissolved with the rise of the People's Progressive Party.

NATIONAL DEMOCRATIC PARTY (NDP). Organized in the early 1950s, the NDP merged in 1955 with other factions to form the United Democratic Party.

POPULAR PARTY. The first formally organized political party in Guyana, it was active in the late 1920s and early 1930s.

UNITED DEMOCRATIC PARTY (UDP). Formed in the mid-1950s by the National Democratic Party and other factions, the UDP became part of the People's National Congress.

Jacqueline Anne Braveboy-Wagner

HAITI

The Martinican Frantz Fanon (1968) said that "political parties start from living reality and it is in the name of this reality . . . that they fix their line of action." In few instances is this assessment accurate with reference to Haiti. Fanon's statement and Haiti's constitutions are idealized positions that bear little resemblance to reality. When they exist at all, parties may tend to isolate and specify certain interests, and their role tends to enhance the status quo and the political system in which they have a stake. The role of such a Western institution in what is essentially a borrowed political system is difficult and fits, with difficulty, a non-Western political culture.

The Republic of Haiti, which occupies the western third of the island of Haiti (or Hispaniola) which it shares with the Dominican Republic, was the first independent state in Latin America, declaring its independence in 1804. With many other Latin American countries, it shares a "bifurcated" population in which small elites of whites, mulattos, or mestizos, Western in their orientation, control the economic and political life of all others who are of African, indigenous, or mixed descent and often culturally distinct. Because the top 1 percent of the Haitian population owns approximately 48 percent of the national wealth, Haitian political life has been one in which political repression and tyranny have substituted for governmental legitimacy with a continuing cycle of repression as each government sensed its vulnerability. The crisis of the system came early, with the Piquet revolt of 1844 and with the lengthy Caco uprisings.

The U.S. military takeover, which occurred between 1915 and 1934, led to reprisals against the peasant insurgency in which as many as 50,000 may have died and as many as 300,000 peasants may have gone abroad in involuntary economic and political exile—out of a population of 2 million. The United States founded the new Haitian army and consolidated all powers in Port-au-Prince, to the detriment of provincial centers. The culmination of these measures and policies, as well as the result of class antagonisms masked as the "color question," was the Duvalier dictatorship from 1957 until 1986.

The Haitian Revolution of 1791—at which time more than half of the slaves were African born—was betrayed in 1806, when a mostly *mulâtre* oligarchy of former *affranchis* consolidated itself in power and became Haiti's answer to the Spanish American criollos. When, in 1946, the middle classes achieved political power, the peasantry—90 percent of the population—was excluded from power and was still disenfranchised. The peasantry and the urban working class, largely through their autonomous organizations, such as the *vodun* (voodoo) religion and the *Ti Legliz* (grass-root Roman Catholic organizations), led the revolt against Duvalierism, influenced the writing of the Constitution of 1987, and elected President Jean-Bertrand Aristide in December 1990. These social groups have made it clear that without them the country would be ungovernable. As in 1946, the country is entering a revolutionary phase. Between 1801 (with Toussaint Louverture) and 1991 (with Aristide), Haiti has had forty chiefs of state—not counting provisional presidencies—and twenty-five constitutions.

The many chiefs of state, the various governments they headed, and the numerous constitutions used all shared many features. They represented about 10 percent of the population and its interests. And whether upper class or middle class, *mulâtre* or *noiriste*, brown or black, or even a combination of all of these, the governments represented an ideological spectrum situated between liberalism at one end and conservatism and fascism at the other. Indeed, if res publica (the public thing) was the "thing" of an elite with a narrow ideological spectrum, then political parties were neither necessary nor desired. The Cacos were crushed permanently by U.S. forces in 1929. Furthermore, the creation of the Haitian army by the United States "may have ended forever the possibility of an agrarian revolt against the central authority," according to U.S. anthropologist Sidney W. Mintz, who added that these circumstances "turned the army into the major focus of non-electoral, president-making power."

Outside the contemporary era, two parties flourished in the late nineteenth century, when the Liberal and then the Conservative parties held sway. Both espoused positivism, and both were patterned after European and Latin American parties and ideology, as is the case in Haitian parties today. Mere variations on a theme, they represented tendencies within the elites, between free trade and protectionism (as elsewhere), between *mulâtres* and elite blacks, and never engaged the hearts and minds of average Haitians, except perhaps their fortunes as foot soldiers in the bloody battles that engulfed both camps.

The first experiment with middle-class rule, that of President Dumarsais Estimé (1946–1950), saw the rise of left-wing alternatives. The urban working class formed unions, while the government experimented with a minimum wage and an income tax and repaid the foreign debt owed the United States, which power strongly disapproved of the policies and politics of Estimé. The Haitian Communist party organized in the 1930s from various socialist parties partially influenced these developments. They made some efforts, never realized, toward a mass-based party in contradistinction to other *partis de cadre* whose platforms are indistinguishable one from the other. More often than not, Haitian political parties reflect the ambitions of one man, rather than popular aspirations, and serve as a vehicle for political power for one man's clients. Even in the very unusual times of the contemporary period, in which the peasantry has been truly mobilized, political parties have followed, largely, a pre-1957 "politics-as-usual" approach, which is partly the result of the segmented nature of Haitian society, the division between elites and mass. Except perhaps for the Unified Party of Haitian Communists (PUCH), the Rally of Progressive National Democrats (RDNP), or the Movement for the Organization of the Country (MOP), parties have either failed to institutionalize, or have not had the time or the finances to do so. Few will survive their founders, if history serves as a guide.

The study of Haitian political parties is thus problematic, and it may prove a futile exercise until the dust settles, or perhaps it may prove to be as much an academic exercise as the study of Haitian constitutional law. The formal structure of the state has been at odds with the national culture and the political culture. Ultimately, the distinction and the antagonism are between the social classes and their differing worldviews.

Because of the change in political consciousness today, the study of political *movements* rather than political parties might seem more realistic. Defining broad popular tendencies in the context of a historical moment, political movements possibly are a more "precise" instrument. An analysis of the hundreds of organizations that crisscross Haiti remains to be done. One may want to compare these movements to what occurred in the United States with the civil rights and black power movements in the 1960s and 1970s, and the difficulty encountered in institutionalizing them into operational organizations that would survive the test of time in the face of habitual repression.

In a text by Sabine Manigat, two Haitian scholars suggested that the interregnum between 1986 and 1991 was caused by the difficulty of "meshing" movement into party: "The story of this long transition is due largely to [the problem] of political parties struggling desperately to conquer popular legitimacy, and a suspicious mass movement with a parallel evolution." The erstwhile leaders did not understand the people, and the people showed no enthusiasm for the twenty-five candidates who represented almost as many parties—all *interlocuteurs valables*—until Aristide entered the race, party-less for all practical purposes. Indeed, voting leaders in and out of office according to a timetable does not represent democracy, and this procedure will not be able to resolve the fundamental crisis of the system.

In a sense, the Haitian people are redefining democracy away from its traditional Western moorings, from narrow concerns about civil and political rights, toward the broad human rights captured in the Constitution of 1987; and away from party and electoral politics, which can easily be subverted by antagonistic social groups who may appropriate for themselves the symbols of democracy, toward newer (and at once, ancient) forms of consentaneous democracy reminiscent of the Haitian countryside and the African past, in which the chief ruled autocratically with safeguards and constraints. In its ideal form, this approach represents a triumph of content over form; at its worst, abject dictatorship. The idea of competing ideological paradigms seems alien in such contexts. If the political culture of the Afro-Haitian masses clash with the vision and the interests of the westernized elites, this is due to their differing worldviews and class interests, not necessarily to a healthy political pluralism. Neither the army, which destines itself to be the power behind weak presidencies in reasserting its role as national arbiter in politics, nor the United States as the paramount power in a unipolar world, nor again the political culture of Haiti will, each for its own reasons, favor ideological pluralism in the long run. Educated Haitians are learning to speak anew and will need to convince all others that party politics can and will guarantee a newly emerging *Haitian* democracy.

If the lengthy Duvalier dictatorship has proven disastrous to the evolution of political parties, it has simultaneously seen, not so paradoxically, the development of a political consciousness not experienced since the end of the eighteenth century. A steadily declining standard of living and an awareness of blatant governmental corruption and the absence of all pretense and safety valves over thirty-three years proved sufficient. The parties, created almost weekly it seemed, some of which disappeared almost as quickly, combined and recombined in alliances and fronts with other political formations that were almost identical. These combinations are impossible to record short of a massive day-by-day study.

The Duvalier era also created situations in which some sectors benefited in terms of wealth and power at the expense of the nation at large. Perhaps as many as 20,000 Haitians died at the hands of government officials, and the fortune of the former president alone is estimated at $600 million. The men, and the few women, who participated in the dictatorship and are now forbidden to compete as candidates until 1997, according to article 291 of the constitution, have taken extralegal and illegal measures to reassert their power to impose Duvalierism *sans* Duvalier. Besides resorting to terrorism in the form of death squads, massacres, bureaucratic sabotage, and the like, they have at the same time created numerous amorphous but well funded parties in an effort to position themselves politically to reclaim power in the not so distant future. The Haitian population so far has rejected all such parties, although many continue to exist as vehicles for the ambitions of one man or as standard-bearers for Duvalierism, Estimism, or simply the middle class. Though no one is confused by the game, the very efforts at establishing the rule of law so precisely destroyed by Duvalierism are now undermined by the appeals of the Duvalierists to fair play and their constitutional arguments. Haiti is not unique—Eastern European states faced a similar dilemma recently, and fascism survived its World War II defeat in Germany and Italy—but the societal structures and the overall organization of these states were sturdier than those of the Haitian state and polity.

Bibliography

Jean-Bertrand Aristide. *In the Parish of the Poor: Writings from Haiti*. Orbis Books, New York, 1990.

Patrick Bellegarde-Smith. *Haiti: The Breached Citadel*. Westview Press, Boulder, Colo., 1990.

Patrick Bellegarde-Smith. *In the Shadow of Powers: Dantès Bellegarde in Haitian Social Thought*. Humanities Press, Atlantic Highlands, N.J., 1985.

Suzy Castor. *La Ocupación norteamericana de Haití y sus consecuencias, 1915–1934*. Ediciones siglo veintiuno, Mexico D.F., 1971.

Wade Davis. *Passage of Darkness: The Ethnobiology of the Haitian Zombie*. University of North Carolina Press, Chapel Hill, 1988.

Maya Deren. *Divine Horsemen: The Living Gods of Haiti*. McPherson and Company, New Paltz, N.Y., 1983.

Alex Dupuy. *Haiti in the World Economy: Class, Race and Underdevelopment since 1700*. Westview Press, Boulder, Colo., 1988.

Frantz Fanon. *The Wretched of the Earth*. Grove Press, New York, 1968.

Charles R. Foster and Albert Valdman, eds. *Haiti Today and Tomorrow: An Interdisciplinary Study*. University Press of America, Washington, D.C., 1984.

C.L.R. James. *The Black Jacobins: Toussaint Louverture and the San Domingo Revolution*. Vintage Books, New York, 1963.

James G. Leyburn. *The Haitian People*. Yale University Press, New Haven, Conn., 1966.

Rayford W. Logan. *The Diplomatic Relations of the United States with Haiti, 1776–1891*. University of North Carolina Press, Chapel Hill, 1941.

Mats Lundhal. *The Haitian Economy: Man, Land, and Markets*. Crown Helm, London, 1983.

Sabine Manigat. *Les partis politiques*. Dossier 3. CRESDIP, Port-au-Prince, 1990.

Sidney W. Mintz. *Sweetness and Power*. Viking, New York, 1985.

Lyonel Paquin. *The Haitians: Class and Color Politics*. Multi-Tyler, New York, 1983.

Brenda G. Plummer, *Haiti and the Great Powers*. Louisiana State University Press, Baton Rouge, 1988.

Hans Schmidt. *The United States Occupation of Haiti, 1915–1934*. Rutgers University Press, New Brunswick, N.J., 1971.

Clive Y. Thomas. *The Rise of the Authoritarian State in Peripheral Societies*. Monthly Review Press, New York, 1984.

Michel-Rolph Trouillot. *State against Nation: The Origin and Legacy of Duvalierism*. Monthly Review Press, New York, 1988.

Political Parties—Active

ALLIANCE NATIONALE POUR LA DÉMOCRATIE ET LE PROGRÈS. *See* NATIONAL ALLIANCE FOR DEMOCRACY AND PROGRESS.

CONFEDERATION FOR DEMOCRATIC UNITY (KONFEDERASYON INITE DEMOCRATIK-KID). *See* NATIONAL CONGRESS OF DEMOCRATIC FORCES and NATIONAL FRONT FOR CHANGE AND DEMOCRACY.

CONGRÈS NATIONAL DES FORCES DÉMOCRATIQUES. *See* NATIONAL CONGRESS OF DEMOCRATIC FORCES.

DEMOCRATIC MOVEMENT FOR THE LIBERATION OF HAITI/REVO-LUTIONARY DEMOCRATIC PARTY OF HAITI (MOUVEMENT DÉ-MOCRATIQUE DE LIBÉRATION D'HAÏTI/PARTI RÉVOLUTIONNAIRE D'HAÏTI—MODELH/PRDH). Founded in 1969, earlier than most parties, this center-right party, created in the Dominican Republic, established a strong base to fight for the rights of sugarcane workers. The party adopted a strong anti-Communist stance and adopted a course for national reconciliation rather than one about "justice" against Duvalierists. Its founder, Louis-Eugène Athis, was murdered in August 1987 by a group that accused him of being a Communist. The standard-bearer then became François Latortue, a former justice minister and long-term exile, who gained less than 1 percent of the vote in the run for president in December 1990. The MODELH/PRDH elected two deputies in the 1991 round.

FRONT NATIONAL DE CONCERTATION (FNC). See NATIONAL CON-GRESS OF DEMOCRATIC FORCES.

FRONT NATIONAL POUR LE CHANGEMENT ET LA DÉMOCRATIE. See NATIONAL FRONT FOR CHANGE AND DEMOCRACY.

HAITIAN CHRISTIAN DEMOCRATIC PARTY (PARTI DÉMOCRATE CHRÉTIEN HAÏTIEN—PDCH). Protestant minister Sylvio Claude, who was arrested eight times and tortured over five years under the Duvalier regime, became a martyr in the struggle against Duvalierism. His personal courage helped his party acquire some prominence in the slum areas of Port-au-Prince. He was acknowledged to be among the four top contenders, les présidentiables, until the arrival of Jean-Bertrand Aristide in the race. Specific positions of the party on any given national question tend to be sketchy or unavailable. Claude received 3 percent of the presidential vote, and the PDCH elected one senator and seven deputies in 1990–1991.

HAITIAN NATIONALIST PROGRESSIVE AND REVOLUTIONARY PARTY (PARTI NATIONALISTE PROGRESSISTE RÉVOLUTIONNAIRE HAÏTIEN—PANPRA). This party is one incarnation of an earlier political formation, the Union of Patriotic and Democratic Haitian Forces (IFOPADA), formed in 1980. A member of the International Socialist Movement, it has forged strong ties with the French Socialist Party. Although the trajectory of IFOPADA led it into the Marxist camp, PANPRA's connection to the world-wide socialist movement helped it adopt some centrist positions and even to develop some strategic alliances with parties of the center right. These positions were elaborated partly because of party leader Serge Gilles. PANPRA's program favors agrarian reform, socialized medicine, and government regulation of key economic sectors.

HAITIAN SOCIAL CHRISTIAN PARTY (PARTI SOCIAL CHRÉTIEN HAÏTIEN—PSCH). The PSCH challenged the Duvalier government while it advocated a continuing dialogue with it. Though persecuted by the government, the party took a neo-Duvalierist, *noiriste*, and conservative approach on major national issues. The party, which seems to be one man, Gregoire Eugène, a constitutional lawyer, has neither much of a discernable structure nor much of an elaborated platform.

KONFEDERASYON INITE DEMOCRATIK. See CONFEDERATION FOR DEMOCRATIC UNITY.

MOBILIZATION FOR NATIONAL DEVELOPMENT (MOBILISATION POUR LE DEVELOPPEMENT NATIONAL—MDN). As with most other parties, the MDN is submerged by the personality of its leader, Professor Hubert de Ronceray who, after a stint as a cabinet minister in the Duvalier fils government, shifted increasingly to the opposition after 1980. He is seen as a neo-Duvalierist by many, and the creation of the MDN seems to have been an afterthought. The center-right party gathered 3 percent of the votes for the presidency and five seats in the lower house in 1990.

MOUVEMENT DÉMOCRATIQUE DE LIBÉRATION D'HAÏTI/PARTI RÉVOLUTIONAIRE D'HAÏTI. See DEMOCRATIC MOVEMENT FOR THE LIBERATION OF HAITI/REVOLUTIONARY DEMOCRATIC PARTY OF HAITI.

MOUVEMENT D'ORGANIZATION DU PAYS. See MOVEMENT FOR THE ORGANIZATION OF THE COUNTRY.

MOUVEMENT POUR L'INSTAURATION DE LA DÉMOCRATIE EN HAITI. See MOVEMENT FOR INSTALLING DEMOCRACY IN HAITI.

MOVEMENT FOR INSTALLING DEMOCRACY IN HAITI (MOUVEMENT POUR L'INSTAURATION DE LA DÉMOCRATIE EN HAITI—MIDH). Marc Bazin's image as "Mr. Clean" came about after his efforts to lessen the corruption in Jean-Claude Duvalier's government failed. Finance minister, at the urging of Haiti's aid donors, he became known quickly as the United States' man in Haiti. He entered the presidential race as the leader of a center-right party devised for his political ambitions. The strongly technocratic MIDH emphasizes a rightist program of development. Bazin's competence as a World Bank economist made him an appealing candidate to some, but he failed to engage the peasantry and enlist it to his electoral project when he spoke of national reconciliation with the Duvalierists rather than justice. He came in second in the presidential race in December 1990 with 14 percent of the vote.

MOVEMENT FOR THE ORGANIZATION OF THE COUNTRY (MOUVE-MENT D'ORGANIZATION DU PAYS—MOP). First called the Workers and Peasant Movement, the MOP accorded strong support to the Estimé government. Its base has been the Port-au-Prince working class, and its efforts have been in the direction of leading an alliance between peasants and workers. The party is populist, though ideologically somewhat confused, à la Juan Peron of Argentina or Mustafa Kemal (Ataturk) of Turkey. In 1957, the party's founder, Daniel Fignolé, served for nineteen days as provisional president. At his death in 1986, the MOP started a slide toward a moderate wing and a more radical wing, which was completed by 1989.

NATIONAL AGRARIAN INDUSTRIAL PARTY (PARTI AGRICOLE IN-DUSTRIEL NATIONAL—PAIN). Founded more than thirty years ago by Louis Déjoie *père*, who ran against François Duvalier in 1957, the party retained its center-right position until 1987. After the electoral massacre of 29 November 1987, it adopted a more center-left stance and became more critical of the military dictatorship and more populist. Louis Déjoie II became more respected and popular as a result of that change. He amassed 5 percent in the presidential balloting in 1990, and the PAIN elected two senators and six deputies.

NATIONAL ALLIANCE FOR DEMOCRACY AND PROGRESS (ALLI-ANCE NATIONALE POUR LA DÉMOCRATIE ET LE PROGRÉS—ANDP). The center-right party of Marc Bazin (Movement for Installing Democracy in Haiti) and the center-left party of Serge Gilles (Haitian Nationalist Progressive and Revolutionary Party), together with the smaller National Patriotic Movement of 28 July of Déjean Bélizaire, joined for the 1990 election in a conservative bloc, in which the constituting parties were not to lose their profile. The coalition elected the second largest bloc of senators and deputies in the National Assembly: six senators and seventeen deputies.

NATIONAL ALLIANCE FRONT (FRONT NATIONAL DE CONCERTA-TION—FNC). See NATIONAL CONGRESS OF DEMOCRATIC FORCES.

NATIONAL CONGRESS OF DEMOCRATIC FORCES (CONGRÉS NA-TIONAL DES FORCES DÉMOCRATIQUES—KONAKOM). The party, which resulted from the amalgamation of numerous and diverse groups, such as professional groups and associations, peasant groups, human rights groups, and women's groups, emerged as a political party three and a half years after its founding in 1986. A populist and democratic party with socialist leanings, KONAKOM supported the presidential candidacy of Gerard Gourque of the National Alliance Front (FNC) in the aborted 1987 election. Together with the National Democratic Progressive Party of Haiti, the Confederation for Democratic Unity, and the Alliance for Haitian Migrants, it formed the National Front for Change and Democracy in June 1990 and supported the candidacy of

President Jean-Bertrand Aristide, who was elected with nearly 68 percent of the vote in the first balloting.

NATIONAL DEMOCRATIC PROGRESSIVE PARTY OF HAITI (PARTI NATIONAL DÉMOCRATIQUE PROGRESSISTE D'HAITI—PNDPH). *See* NATIONAL CONGRESS OF DEMOCRATIC FORCES and NATIONAL FRONT FOR CHANGE AND DEMOCRACY.

NATIONAL FRONT FOR CHANGE AND DEMOCRACY (FRONT NATIONAL POUR LE CHANGEMENT ET LA DÉMOCRATIE—FNCD). The FNCD is an electoral alliance that served as the vehicle for the candidacy of the populist Roman Catholic priest Jean-Bertrand Aristide, who was subsequently elected by almost 68 percent of the vote. The alliance consists of a number of political parties and mass organizations at the national, regional, and local levels. Among them are the National Congress of Democratic Forces; the National Democratic Progressive Party of Haiti, the party of Turneb Delpé; and the Confederation for Democratic Unity, the party of Evans Paul, the elected mayor of Port-au-Prince. Although the FNCD elected the largest bloc in the National Assembly, thirteen senators and twenty-seven deputies, it was far short of a majority (twenty-seven senators and eighty-three deputies), not having fielded enough candidates for these positions. The FNCD represents a left-wing alliance, juxtaposed to the National Alliance for Democracy and Progress.

NATIONAL PATRIOTIC MOVEMENT OF 28 JULY (MNP-28). *See* NATIONAL ALLIANCE FOR DEMOCRACY AND PROGRESS.

PARTI AGRICOLE INDUSTRIEL NATIONAL. *See* NATIONAL AGRARIAN INDUSTRIAL PARTY.

PARTI DÉMOCRATE CHRÉTIEN HAÏTIEN. *See* HAITIAN CHRISTIAN DEMOCRATIC PARTY.

PARTI NATIONAL DEMOCRATIQUE PROGRESSISTE D'HAITI. *See* NATIONAL DEMOCRATIC PROGRESSIVE PARTY OF HAITI.

PARTI NATIONALISTE PROGRESSISTE RÉVOLUTIONNAIRE HAÏTIEN. *See* HAITIAN NATIONALIST PROGRESSIVE AND REVOLUTIONARY PARTY.

PARTI SOCIAL CHRÉTIEN HAÏTIEN. *See* HAITIAN SOCIAL CHRISTIAN PARTY.

PARTI UNIFIÉ DES COMMUNISTES HAÏTIENS. *See* UNIFIED PARTY OF HAITIAN COMMUNISTS.

RALLY OF PROGRESSIVE NATIONAL DEMOCRATS (RASSEMBLE-MENT DES DÉMOCRATES NATIONAUX PROGRESSISTES—RDNP). The RDNP, founded in Venezuela, is a well-organized, highly centralized party, but it has failed to stir a response from the population. The party, which balances economic liberalism and nationalism with a large governmental role, is technocratic and modernizing in its approach to national development. After the election day massacre of 29 November 1987, the RDNP's leader, Leslie Manigat, became one of the few candidates who maintained his candidacy in the army-sponsored elections held in January 1988, and he was selected in a fraudulent election in which approximately 5 percent of the electorate voted. After serving less than five months in office, Manigat was removed by the same army that had placed him there. The RDNP elected one senator and six deputies in the 1990–1991 elections.

RASSEMBLEMENT DES DÉMOCRATES NATIONAUX PROGRESS-ISTES. See RALLY OF PROGRESSIVE NATIONAL DEMOCRATS.

UNIFIED PARTY OF HAITIAN COMMUNISTS (PARTI UNIFIÉ DES COMMUNISTES HAÏTIENS—PUCH). The PUCH succeeded the much earlier political formations that had begun in the 1930s, for example, the Democratic Reaction Party (1934), the Popular Socialist Party, and the Haitian Communist Party. The most immediate antecedents were the Party of Popular Accord and the Popular Party of National Liberation, both of which were formed in the 1950s and were restructured into the PUCH. All these parties were efforts to transcend the cult of personality in traditional Haitian political life and to expand the discourse. The PUCH is a relatively moderate party of the left, not far from some others in its nationalistic vision and its approach to societal reforms and social change. It suffered many casualties under Duvalierism. René Théodore, its presidential candidate, garnered 1.8 percent of the vote in the December 1990 election.

UNION OF PATRIOTIC AND DEMOCRATIC HAITIAN FORCES (IFO-PADA). See HAITIAN NATIONALIST PROGRESSIVE AND REVOLU-TIONARY PARTY.

Political Parties—Historical

In keeping with the argument that political parties have not been very significant in Haiti, even in terms of elite politics, these notes have been kept to a minimum. The author is indebted to Leslie Péan, and others, who have preceded me in this task.

COMMUNIST PARTY OF HAITI (PARTI COMMUNISTE D'HAÏTI—PCH). Created early in 1946, the PCH is one of the many Communist groups and subgroups that have been founded since the 1930s. Because this particular party was a proponent of *noirisme* (black consciousness), it was seen as the black Marxist party as distinct from the Popular Socialist Party, which was regarded as the *mulâtre* Marxist party. Its platform was a blend of progressive and reformist policies. It disbanded in fifteen months so as not to impede Haiti–United States relations. Among its leaders may be cited Dorléan Juste Constant, Edriss St. Amand, Odnell David, Gérard Montas, Gérald Bloncourt, Gérald Chenet, and Fréda Seïde.

DEMOCRATIC REACTION PARTY (PARTI DE LA RÉACTION DÉMO-CRATIQUE). Founded in 1934 by Max Hudicourt, Marcel Hérard, Jean F. Brierre, Lys Dartiguenave, Georges Rigaud, and several others, the party promulgated a platform for far-reaching political reforms based on racial awareness and included woman's rights. It was persecuted by President Sténio Vincent, and many of the party leaders were jailed.

HAITIAN COMMUNIST PARTY (PARTI COMMUNISTE HAÏTIEN—PCH). The first organized Communist party in Haiti, the PCH was formed in 1932 by the famed novelist Jacques Roumain, Christian Beaulien, Étienne Charlier, Anthony Lespès, and Dorléan Juste Constant. A *parti de cadres*, the PCH consisted largely of upper-class individuals who had suffered persecution at the hands of the government. The anti-Communist law of 1936, as well as disarray in the leadership, sent the party underground. Roumain's death in Mexico in 1944 really ended the party, although it limped along until 1946. The successors of the PCH were the Popular Socialist Party and the Communist Party of Haiti.

HAITIAN PATRIOTIC UNION (UNION PATRIOTIQUE HAÏTIENNE). This movement was formed in 1920 by Georges Sylvain, Perceval Thoby, Jean Price-Mars, and Sténio Vincent in token opposition to the U.S. invasion of 1915–1934. It soon acquired as many as 35,000 members, although its leadership was derived largely from the elite. It declined abruptly in 1930 with the rise of one of its members, Vincent, to the presidency.

HAITIAN WORKERS PARTY (PARTI DES TRAVAILLEURS HAITIENS—PTH). *See* POPULAR PARTY OF NATIONAL LIBERATION.

LIBERAL PARTY (PARTI LIBÉRAL). The Liberal Party, Haiti's first political party, was founded in 1870. A list of the party's founders reads like a who's who of Haitian elite society: Edmond Paul, Boyer Bazélais, Armand Thoby, Nemours Auguste, Louis Audain, and Boisrond Canal. The founders fought for a bourgeois democracy which included checks on the executive and checks against militarism, and they argued for industrialization. Perceived as a *mulâtre* party, its slogan was "power to the most competent." Successful in legislative elections, the party suffered setbacks starting in 1874, even after the rise to power of one of its members, Canal, to the presidency in 1876–1879. The party came to an end in a disastrous military campaign in 1883.

NATIONAL PARTY (PARTI NATIONAL). The National Party, the nemesis of the Liberal Party, was regarded as representing the black segment of the Haitian upper class. Among its founders were Lysius Félicité Salomon, Septimus Rameau, J. Audain, Demesvar Delorme, Frédéric Marcelin, Louis-Joseph Janvier, and Denis Légitime. Though in tone it was more nationalist and less progressive than the Liberal Party, both parties were essentially positivist and both represented mostly divisions within elite groups. The genesis of the National Party occurred early under President (and then emperor) Faustin Soulouque (1847–1859). Though the National Party divided into several quarreling groups, one of its members, Lysius F. Salomon, reached the presidency, between 1879 and 1888. The party, in a sense, announced the Haitian *indigéniste* movement (negritude) of the 1930s.

NATIONAL PROGRESSIVE PARTY (PARTI NATIONAL PROGRESSISTE). Founded by President Louis Borno in 1925, the National Progressive Party opposed the "nationalist" position adopted by the Haitian Patriotic Union by advocating Haiti–United States cooperation during the military occupation. It disappeared after the end of Borno's presidency in 1930.

NATIONAL UNITY PARTY (PARTI UNITÉ NATIONALE—PUN). The party coalesced from diverse political groups in existence since the mid–1930s; it was formally established seven months before François Duvalier reached the presidency in September 1957. Its leaders included Lamartinière Honorat, Michel Aubourg, Frédéric Desvarieux, Léonce Viaud, Jean Montès Lefranc, Paul Blanchet, Joseph Baguidy, Victor Nevers Constant, and François Duvalier. All the leaders were to play significant roles in Duvalierism. Middle class in origin, the party fought for its version of black power. It collapsed in 1961, four years after one of its members, Duvalier, had become president.

PARTI COMMUNISTE D'HAÏTI. *See* COMMUNIST PARTY OF HAITI.

PARTI COMMUNISTE HAÏTIEN. *See* HAITIAN COMMUNIST PARTY.

PARTI DE LA RÉACTION DÉMOCRATIQUE. *See* DEMOCRATIC REACTION PARTY.

PARTI DES TRAVAILLEURS HAITIENS. *See* POPULAR PARTY OF NATIONAL LIBERATION.

PARTI DÉMOCRATIQUE POPULAIRE DE LA JEUNESSE HAÏTIENNE. *See* POPULAR DEMOCRATIC PARTY OF HAITIAN YOUTH.

PARTI D'ENTENTE POPULAIRE. *See* PARTY OF POPULAR ACCORD.

PARTI LIBÉRAL. *See* LIBERAL PARTY.

PARTI NATIONAL. *See* NATIONAL PARTY.

PARTI NATIONAL PROGRESSISTE. *See* NATIONAL PROGRESSIVE PARTY.

PARTI POPULAIRE DE LIBÉRATION NATIONALE. *See* POPULAR PARTY OF NATIONAL LIBERATION.

PARTI POPULAIRE SOCIAL CHRÉTIEN. *See* POPULAR SOCIAL CHRISTIAN PARTY.

PARTI SOCIALISTE POPULAIRE. *See* POPULAR SOCIALIST PARTY.

PARTI UNITÉ NATIONALE. *See* NATIONAL UNITY PARTY.

PARTY OF POPULAR ACCORD (PARTI D'ENTENTE POPULAIRE— PEP). This Communist party was founded in 1959 by celebrated novelist Jacques Stephen Alexis, Joseph Roney, Gérald Brisson, Alix Lamauthe, Rony Lescouflair, and Gérard Pierre-Charles. Alexis was murdered in April 1961. An early strategy of the party was to ally with other organizations to overthrow the Duvalier dictatorship. This strategy had turned to armed struggle by 1967. Together with the Party of the Union of Haitian Democrats it is the forerunner of the Unified Party of Haitian Communists, which was formed in 1969.

PARTY OF THE UNION OF HAITIAN DEMOCRATS (PUDA). *See* POPULAR PARTY OF NATIONAL LIBERATION.

POPULAR DEMOCRATIC PARTY OF HAITIAN YOUTH (PARTI DÉMOCRATIQUE POPULAIRE DE LA JEUNESSE HAÏTIENNE—PDPJH). Formed in early January 1946, the PDPJH disappeared less than nine months later. Its impact, however, was lasting partly because of its leadership and partly because of its platform. It included in its membership Jacques Stephen Alexis, René Depestre, Théodore Baker, Rodolphe Moïse, Gérald Bloncourt, and Gérald Chenet. Its newspaper, *La Ruche* (the beehive), played a significant role in the overthrow of the Lescot government. Its position was decidedly nationalist and pro-black. After its dissolution, members joined primarily the Popular Socialist Party and the Communist Party of Haiti.

POPULAR PARTY OF NATIONAL LIBERATION (PARTI POPULAIRE DE LIBÉRATION NATIONALE—PPLN). Formed under a different name in

1954 during the presidency of Paul-Eugène Magloire, the PPLN consisted of individuals previously active in other Communist parties. The party acquired its final name in 1960. Two prominent members were poet and novelist René Depestre and historian Roger Gaillard. Their most ardent antagonist was another Communist, the celebrated novelist Jacques Stephen Alexis, a founder of the Party of Popular Accord. After some initial success in its activities, the PPLN divided in 1964 on the issue of armed struggle, and the party disbanded shortly afterward. Two years later, some of its members, who had not been murdered or exiled by the Duvalier regime, resurfaced in the Haitian Workers Party and the Party of the Union of Haitian Democrats. The PPLN is a forerunner of the Unified Party of Haitian Communists.

POPULAR SOCIAL CHRISTIAN PARTY (PARTI POPULAIRE SOCIAL CHRÉTIEN—PPSC). Created in 1946 by Paul Cassagnol, Edouard Tardieu, Jacques Désinor, Emmanuel Lajoie, and René Déjean, the PPSC was anti-Communist and pro–private property. A liberal elite party, it took liberal to progressive positions on a number of socioeconomic and political issues, notably on the protection of Haitian merchant interests against foreign monopolies. It finally dissolved in 1950.

POPULAR SOCIALIST PARTY (PARTI SOCIALISTE POPULAIRE—PSP). The PSP was created in early 1946 by Max Hudicourt, Étienne Charlier, Anthony Lespès, Jules Blanchet, and others. Later, Rossini Pierre-Louis, a member of the Chamber of Deputies, joined the party. It lasted four years. The PSP united the remnants of the Haitian Communist Party and the Democratic Reaction Party. The party entertained excellent relations with other Latin American Communist parties and followed the line suggested by Moscow at the time. Hudicourt was elected senator, but he was assassinated in April 1947. The PSP championed the development of a national bourgeoisie from which had come most of its members, and individual party members occupied high diplomatic posts under the regime the party decried. The party was banned by the Magloire regime in 1950.

UNION PATRIOTIQUE HAÏTIENNE. See HAITIAN PATRIOTIC UNION.

Patrick Bellegarde-Smith

HONDURAS

Honduras is a poor, mountainous country that lies at the center of the politically troubled Central American isthmus. In spite of recent urban migration to Tegucigalpa, its capital, and to San Pedro Sula, its chief industrial center, well over 50 percent of the nation's 4.8 million people still live in rural areas. Limited by an economy based principally on the export of bananas and coffee, Honduras's gross domestic product per capita equaled only U.S.$917 in 1988. Although economic growth has been slow in recent years, population growth exceeds 3 percent annually. Illiteracy is widespread.

No organized, national political parties existed in Honduras until very late in the nineteenth century. By the 1870s, most of the Honduran political elite had embraced liberal, positivist ideas, but factional conflict and chronic political instability delayed the establishment of a formal Liberal Party structure until 1890. From the time of its founding by Policarpo Bonilla, the Liberal Party of Honduras (PLH) was divided by competing personal ambitions. In 1916 a dissident group led by Manuel Bonilla organized the National Party of Honduras (PNH), which became the Liberals' major rival. Prominent rural landowners dominated both of these loosely organized, nonideological parties. Over time, strong partisan attachments also developed among the peasantry.

The traditional Liberals and Nationals are the only two political parties to figure significantly in twentieth-century Honduran politics. One or another of the various competing Liberal factions controlled the Honduran government until the critical 1932 election when National Party caudillo Tiburcio Carías Andino captured the presidency after several failed attempts. Carías soon banned his Liberal competitors and imposed a personalist dictatorship which endured for seventeen years. As the official party in a one-party regime, the Nationals monopolized all political offices. After Carías's retirement in 1949, his successor Juan Manuel Gálvez embarked on a program of economic modernization and political liberalization. The PLH revived in this more tolerant atmosphere under the direction of reformist physician Ramón Villeda Morales, and it began to attract newly emerging urban middle-class and working-class elements.

President Gálvez's democratization policy displeased ex-president Carías and divided the PNH. When free elections were restored in 1954, Villeda Morales won a 48-percent plurality in a three-way race with the aged former dictator and a dissident National Reformist Movement (MNR) candidate. However, after the election, the two PNH factions cooperated in congress to block confirmation of the Liberal triumph. In these confused circumstances, Gálvez's vice president Julio Lozano Díaz seized power and organized the National Unity Party (PUN) to support himself until he was ousted by the small Honduran army in 1956. In 1957 the military supervised new constituent assembly elections, which were won handily by the Liberals.

Villeda Morales ruled as a moderate reformer during his term from 1957 to 1963. He created a social security system, a pilot agrarian reform, and a civil guard to counter the increasingly powerful army. The next Liberal candidate for the presidency, Modesto Rodas Alvarado, was more conservative than his party rival Villeda, but, nonetheless, he also campaigned on a reformist platform. Shortly before the 1963 election, however, the military intervened to keep Rodas out of office. The commander of the armed forces, Oswaldo López Arellano, then ruled for eight years in close collaboration with right-wing PNH boss Ricardo Zúñiga Augustinius. The authoritarian civil-military government blatantly rigged the electoral machinery to ensure PLH hegemony and repressed most popular organizations.

After El Salvador's defeat of Honduras in a 1969 border war, the López–Zúñiga regime weakened. Under considerable popular pressure, López agreed to step down and be replaced by a bipartisan National Unity Pact civilian government in 1971. While this bipartisan experiment floundered in partisan wrangling, however, General López found new political allies. In 1972 he returned to power by military coup at the head of a reformist coalition encompassing labor unions, peasant groups, and progressive businessmen. López's new administration maintained a distinctively populist and nationalist orientation until he was deposed in 1975 after allegedly accepting a bribe from North American banana interests. Military conservatives gradually reasserted control, and, by the late 1970s, the armed forces again were aligned with the PNH.

The collapse of the Somoza family dictatorship in Nicaragua in 1979 and promises of increased U.S. foreign aid enabled the Carter administration to convince the Honduran armed forces that a democratic transition would be in the military's long-term interest. Barriers to opposition political activity were removed, and elections for a new constituent assembly took place in 1980. Strong antimilitary sentiment gave the Liberals an unanticipated victory in these elections with 49 percent of the vote and thirty-five of the seventy-one assembly seats. The Nationals obtained 42 percent of the vote and thirty-three seats; the Innovation and Unity Party (PINU), a small new centrist party organized by dissident Liberals, drew 3.5 percent and three seats. Nevertheless, while the 1981 constitution was being debated in the new assembly, the military under

Colonel Policarpo Paz García retained the executive branch, and National Party politicians continued to direct many government ministries.

Capitalizing on the continued strength of reformist and antimilitary feelings in the country, rural physician Roberto Suazo Córdoba, a longtime ally of Rodas, campaigned very misleadingly as a progressive in 1981. His efforts were successful, and the Liberals took the presidency with an enlarged share of the vote (54 percent) defeating PNH standard-bearer Zúñiga (42 percent). The PINU and the tiny, left-of-center Christian Democratic Party of Honduras (PDCH) accounted for the remainder of the votes cast. Suazo entered office with a clear Liberal congressional majority of forty-four seats to the Nationals' thirty-four.

Although the Liberal victory raised hopes for civilian democratic rule in Honduras, the army remained the country's most influential political actor throughout the 1980s. Even before he took the oath of office, President Suazo allied himself with right-wing military chief General Gustavo Alvarez Martínez, who became the country's acknowledged political strongman until he was overthrown in an internal military coup in 1984. While the unsavory Alvarez–Suazo coalition held sway, political pluralism declined, human rights abuses mounted, and the armed forces became more powerful than ever. Both Suazo and the military prospered while the United States poured unprecedented amounts of money into the country to ensure continued support for the basing of the Nicaraguan Contras in Honduras.

After Alvarez's fall, President Suazo continued to show little regard for democratic institutions, and he even resorted to bribery and other illegal measures in a failed effort to perpetuate himself in power. The corrupt Liberal chief executive used his control over the National Electoral Tribunal and the Supreme Court to manipulate both the Liberals' and the Nationals' presidential nomination processes. Suazo's actions had a divisive effect on both traditional parties, and they precipitated a constitutional crisis in 1985 when his congressional opponents attempted to oust pro-Suazo Supreme Court justices. Ultimately, it became necessary for the military, with support from the private sector and organized labor, to intervene to resolve the crisis. After a great deal of negotiation, the army persuaded all of the warring political factions to agree to an electoral formula that allowed each of them to offer a separate slate of candidates in the 1985 elections.

For the 1985 contest alone, all factions in both major parties accepted a modified electoral system similar to Uruguay's, under which the presidency would be awarded to the leading vote getter from the party whose several factional candidates together amassed the greatest combined vote. Nine presidential candidates and their accompanying congressional lists competed in this contest, representing four PLH factions, three PNH factions, the PINU, and the Christian Democrats.

The three most important contestants for the presidency in 1985 were José Azcona del Hoyo, a center-right Liberal and former Suazo ally now at odds with the president; Oscar Mejía Arellano, a Liberal stalwart loyal to Suazo; and the Nationals' young Rafael Leonardo Callejas, an agricultural economist from a wealthy landowning family. Callejas had served as minister of natural resources in pre–1982 military governments and had been a close associate of General Alvarez. During the 1985 campaign, the three principal presidential candidates devoted most of their time to slandering one another and said very little about pressing national problems, such as the growing role of the United States in Honduras, the presence of the Contras, and the deteriorating economic conditions of the Honduran peasantry. Increasing use of sophisticated mass media advertising, especially by Callejas, raised the cost of the campaign without clarifying its issues.

The four Liberal candidates together collected 51 percent of the vote in 1985, hence, under the terms of the electoral pact, the Liberal front-runner Azcona, with a mere 27.5 percent of the ballots was elected president. Callejas, with 43 percent of the vote, was the most popular presidential candidate, but he lost the race because the other two PNH contestants attracted less than 3 percent of the vote. The two minor political parties won only 3.4 percent of the vote between them.

When Azcona took office in 1986, he faced a stagnating economy, civil wars on two borders, and the legacy of four years of presidential power abuse. During his term, Azcona clearly helped to strengthen Honduras's fragile democratic institutions by respecting the constitutional limits on his office much more faithfully than his predecessor, but, otherwise, he accomplished little. Azcona never managed to construct a strong following within his factionalized PLH, and his temporary (1986–1987) governing coalition with PNH elements failed to agree on a common legislative program. Although the Liberal president thus lacked the backing needed to take action on major issues, most observers doubted that he actually had any coherent policy design of his own. Criticized as a passive president with no capacity for leadership, Azcona responded ineffectually to the worst financial crisis in the nation's modern history and to the additional problem of rising crime. Partly as a consequence of the president's weakness, the political influence of the armed forces and the U.S. Embassy remained unchecked. Not surprisingly, Azcona's poor record posed a handicap for the PLH as the 1989 elections drew near.

Callejas won the 1989 PNH presidential nomination without serious opposition, and he successfully united his party and much of the business community behind him. Compared to the old National political bosses of the past, the energetic Callejas represented a modern and dynamic brand of conservative leadership. The more divided Liberals chose as his opponent industrial engineer Carlos Flores Facussé, an Arab-Honduran scion of a newspaper publishing family with links to important industrial interests. Although regarded as a conservative like Callejas and backed by ex-president Suazo, Flores also had found enough progressive allies within the PLH to win a close primary contest for the nomination.

Just as in 1985, the 1989 campaign was full of personal invective but empty of serious policy debate. Since the two major candidates held nearly identical pro–US and economically conservative views, the campaign soon degenerated into endless rounds of insults and inflammatory accusations. Some Hondurans may have been disgusted by the extremely negative tone of the campaign because voter turnout fell to about 76 percent of those registered in 1989 compared to 84 percent in 1985 and to 81 percent in 1981 and 1980.

Despite the PLH's supposed advantage in mass party identification, Callejas won the 1989 race by 51 percent to 43 percent, and the Nationals obtained a solid congressional majority (seventy-one PNH, fifty-five PLH, and two PINU). The Nationals also emerged victorious in 230 of Honduras's 289 municipal races. Most political analysts suggested that these elections were won by the Nationals because Callejas projected a much more attractive candidate image than Flores and because the unusually high inflation rate and atmosphere of financial crisis discredited the governing Liberals.

The inauguration of PNH leader Callejas in January 1990 marked Honduras's first democratic transfer of power between competing political parties in nearly sixty years. Nevertheless, in spite of this apparent milestone and a full decade of free elections, the nation's democratic transition appeared very incomplete at the beginning of the 1990s. Military officers and U.S. Embassy officials still wielded more influence than elected officials in many policy areas. Furthermore, in the absence of any real tradition of public interest or policy-oriented parties, most Liberal and National politicians continued to concentrate exclusively on the battle for patronage and personal gain while largely ignoring the nation's deepening social and economic problems.

Honduras's grave economic situation posed an additional obstacle to democratic consolidation in the 1990s. Indeed, President Callejas took office in the midst of the country's worst economic circumstances since the Great Depression. In 1989 Honduras's inability to service its external debt caused a boycott by foreign lenders which forced Callejas to impose a harsh economic austerity program despite growing social unrest. Moreover, Honduran officials could no longer count on generous U.S. financial aid to ease the economic pain now that the United States had no need of Honduran territory for the disbanded Contras. This combination of political and economic difficulties indicated that Honduras's still embryonic democratic system and its two traditional political parties would be severely tested in the 1990s.

Bibliography

Ronald H. McDonald and J. Mark Ruhl. *Party Politics and Elections in Latin America.* Boulder, Colo., Westview Press, 1989.

James A. Morris. *Honduras: Caudillo Politics and Military Rulers.* Boulder, Colo., Westview Press, 1984.

Mario Posas and Rafael del Cid. *La construcción del sector público y del estado nacional de Honduras, 1876–1979*. EDUCA, San José, Costa Rica, 1979.

Mark B. Rosenberg. "Can Democracy Survive the Democrats?: From Transition to Consolidation in Honduras," in John A. Booth and Mitchell A. Seligson, eds., *Elections and Democracy in Central America*, 40–59. University of North Carolina, Chapel Hill, 1989.

Mark B. Rosenberg and Philip L. Shepherd, eds. *Honduras Confronts Its Future*. Lynne Rienner, Boulder, Colo., 1986.

James D. Rudolph, ed. *Honduras: A Country Study*. U.S. Government Printing Office, Washington, D.C., 1984.

Leticia Salomón, ed. *Honduras: Panorama y perspectivas*. Centro de Documentación de Honduras, Tegucigalpa, 1989.

William S. Stokes. *Honduras: An Area Study in Government*. University of Wisconsin Press, Madison, 1950.

Political Parties—Active

CHRISTIAN DEMOCRATIC PARTY OF HONDURAS (PARTIDO DEMÓCRATA CRISTIANO DE HONDURAS—PDCH). The origins of the PDCH lie in the Catholic Church's rural community development programs of the 1950s. Individuals involved in these initiatives became active in the creation of peasant leagues, labor unions, and ultimately a Christian Democratic Movement (Movimiento Demócrata Cristiano de Honduras—MDCH) in the late 1960s. In 1975 two Christian Democrats entered General Melgar Castro's military government and, in 1978, the Christian Democratic Movement submitted the documentation required for inscription as a regular, legal political party. Fearing a loss of votes to the new group, National Party members of the National Electoral Tribunal at first blocked recognition of the Christian Democrats and prevented their participation in the 1980 elections, but the PDCH was legalized in time to compete in 1981.

The Christian Democratic Party is a reformist party which draws its inspiration from progressive Catholic social doctrines. Influenced by liberation theology, the PDCH has evolved into the most left-of-center of the Central American Christian Democratic parties. The party is highly critical of the Honduran traditional parties' disinterest in social reforms and human rights issues and of their subservience to the United States.

Christian Democratic leaders are drawn mostly from the urban middle class, but the party's greatest electoral support is usually found in economically backward, rural areas of the country. In the face of strong traditional party identification, the PDCH has had little electoral success, garnering only 1.9 percent of the presidential vote for longtime leader Hernán Corrales Padilla in 1985 and 1.4 percent for respected economist Efraín Díaz Arrivillaga in 1989. The Christian Democrats held two seats in the congress after the 1985 race but lost them both in 1989. In recent years, the PDCH has become increasingly divided by internal disputes, and it appears to have little future as a force in Honduran party politics.

COMMUNIST PARTY OF HONDURAS (PARTIDO COMUNISTA DE HONDURAS—PCH). The PCH was founded over sixty years ago in 1927, but it has been banned from normal political activity for most of its history. The traditionally pro-Moscow PCH is a tiny but disciplined party organized under the Leninist principle of democratic centralism. Nonetheless, the party has frequently been troubled by personalist and ideological divisions. In 1971 a minority Maoist faction seceded from the PCH to create the Marxist-Leninist Communist Party of Honduras (PCH-ML). The PCH is influential in some student groups and in unions such as the United Federation of Honduran Workers (FUTH), but the party has little electoral support. Independent leftist candidates associated with the Honduran Patriotic Front (including some Communists) who ran in the 1980 and 1981 elections were harassed by government authorities and won very few votes. In 1985 the PCH boycotted the election while its PCH-ML rival urged its adherents to vote for the reformist Christian Democrats or for the Innovation and Unity Party. Communist candidates also did not run for office in 1989. The four small Marxist guerrilla groups operating in the country condemned the electoral process throughout the 1980s.

INNOVATION AND UNITY PARTY (PARTIDO DE INOVACIÓN Y UNIDAD—PINU). The PINU was first organized in 1970 by businessman Miguel Andonie Fernández, but the party did not receive legal recognition until 1979. A moderately reformist party of the political center, the PINU favors private property but also urges government action to create new economic opportunities for Honduras's impoverished majority. Party leaders argue that the nation's deep social inequalities are an obstacle to economic development.

The modest electoral support the PINU has won thus far has been concentrated among the more urban, educated sectors of the population. Physician Enrique Aguilar Cerrato, who once served in the populist government of General Oswaldo López Arellano, has been the PINU's presidential candidate in the last two elections but he captured just 1.5 percent of the vote in 1985 and 1.9 percent in 1989. The party held only two seats in the Honduran congress after the 1985 and 1989 elections; it does not figure very significantly in national politics at this time.

LIBERAL PARTY OF HONDURAS (PARTIDO LIBERAL DE HONDURAS—PLH). The Liberal Party is the oldest of the two Honduran traditional parties. Its origins lie in the principles of separation of church and state, representative government, and economic liberalism associated with Honduran politicians Célio Arias and Marco Aurelio Soto in the late nineteenth century. Formally organized by Policarpo Bonilla in 1890, the Liberal Party once was considered the more reformist and antimilitary of the two traditional parties, particularly after Ramón Villeda Morales became its leader during the 1950s. The right-wing, military-linked administration of Liberal Roberto Suazo Córdoba (1982–1986) largely erased that progressive image, although the Liberals, unlike the Nationals, do contain a reformist, social democratic faction. Today, Liberal politicians still talk about the need for change, but they offer few coherent social programs and largely accept the socioeconomic status quo. In any case, for PLH bosses, and for their National Party (PNH) counterparts, policy issues have never been of great concern compared to the all-consuming scramble for patronage and personal power.

The PLH is a classic patron-client party which integrates a large number of locally based personalist networks. These networks are responsible for an extensive Liberal grass-roots organization over which a semblance of central control is exercised by a party president and a central executive committee. The PLH has been plagued by in-fighting among its personalist factions ever since its foundation, and it has tended to have more problems maintaining party unity than the Nationals. In the early 1980s, the Liberals were split into two formally organized factions: the conservative Rodista Liberal Movement (MLR), led by Suazo Córdoba, and the smaller, progressive Popular Liberal Alliance (ALIPO), associated with Carlos Roberto Reina and Jorge Arturo Reina. By 1985, however, President Suazo's drive to stay in power had splintered the party into five factions, of which all but ALIPO (which backed José Azcona del Hoyo) ran separate presidential candidates in the election held that year. Azcona and Efraín Bu Girón, formerly allies of Suazo in the MLR, created their own factions, and the most reformist element of ALIPO, under the Reina brothers, left that group to form the Liberal Democratic Revolutionary Movement (M-LIDER). Competing presidential ambitions again factionalized the Liberals in 1989 and resulted in a hard-fought December 1988 primary contest won by conservative Carlos Flores Facussé who rather surprisingly enjoyed the support of party progressive Jorge Arturo Reina. Carlos Roberto Reina and congress president Carlos Orbin Montoya finished in a virtual tie for second place.

The PLH is a multiclass party which traditionally is strongest in urban areas and in the economically more developed north coast departments. In addition, the Liberals can count on a number of rural strongholds where traditional Liberal party identification remains a powerful factor. The Liberals defeated their PNH adversaries in all of the elections held in the 1980s except the last. In 1989, the PLH was swept from power when its vote plummeted to 43 percent from 51 percent in 1985.

MARXIST-LENINIST COMMUNIST PARTY OF HONDURAS (PARTIDO COMUNISTA DE HONDURAS MARXISTA-LENINISTA—PCH-ML). See COMMUNIST PARTY OF HONDURAS.

MOVIMIENTO NACIONAL REFORMISTA (NATIONAL REFORMIST MOVEMENT). See NATIONAL PARTY OF HONDURAS.

NATIONAL PARTY OF HONDURAS (PARTIDO NACIONAL DE HON-DURAS—PNH). The PNH was created by former Liberal Manuel Bonilla in 1916. For the next thirty years, the party was dominated by Tiburcio Carías Andino who used it as the principal organizational structure of his dictatorship (1932–1949). The PNH became divided in the mid–1950s when Carías quarreled with his more tolerant successor Juan Manuel Gálvez. Carías's former vice president Abraham Williams Calderón headed the National Reformist Movement (Movimiento Nacional Reformista—MNR) from 1953 to 1957. From 1954 to 1956, de facto President Julio Lozano Díaz tried to construct his own National Unity Party (Partido de Unidad Nacional—PUN).

From the 1950s through 1982, the PNH was regarded as the more conservative of the two traditional parties and was usually viewed as allied to the Honduran military. However, today, policy differences between the Liberals and the Nationals are few. To a great extent, their conflict is simply over the spoils of office.

The National Party, a patron-client party, is made up of many personalist networks and is organized much like the Liberal Party. Historically, factionalization has been less of a problem for the Nationals. Although three formal PNH factions contested the 1985 election, Rafael Leonardo Callejas's Nationalist Rafael Callejas Movement (MONARCA) won almost all of the PNH votes. Although the party suffered serious divisions in 1988 during the Tegucigalpa mayoral primary, the Nationals again unified around Callejas in 1989. Under Callejas, the PNH appears to be beginning the process of transforming itself into a more modern and programmatic political party. The Nationals are ahead of the Liberals in this respect.

The PNH is a multiclass party whose greatest electoral strength traditionally is found in rural Honduras. However, the Nationals also have acquired a sizeable urban following, especially in Tegucigalpa. Although thought to have become the minority party among traditional party-identified voters during the 1980s, the Nationals won the presidency and control of the congress by a comfortable margin in 1989.

NATIONAL REFORMIST MOVEMENT (MOVIMIENTO NACIONAL RE-FORMISTA—MNR). See NATIONAL PARTY OF HONDURAS.

NATIONAL UNITY PARTY (PARTIDO DE UNIDAD NACIONAL—PUN). See NATIONAL PARTY OF HONDURAS.

PARTIDO COMUNISTA DE HONDURAS. See COMMUNIST PARTY OF HONDURAS.

PARTIDO COMUNISTA DE HONDURAS MARXISTA-LENINISTA. See COMMUNIST PARTY OF HONDURAS.

PARTIDO DE INOVACIÓN Y UNIDAD. *See* INNOVATION AND UNITY PARTY.

PARTIDO DE UNIDAD NACIONAL (NATIONAL UNITY PARTY). *See* NATIONAL PARTY OF HONDURAS.

PARTIDO DEMÓCRATA CRISTIANO DE HONDURAS. *See* CHRISTIAN DEMOCRATIC PARTY OF HONDURAS.

PARTIDO LIBERAL DE HONDURAS. *See* LIBERAL PARTY OF HONDURAS.

PARTIDO NACIONAL DE HONDURAS. *See* NATIONAL PARTY OF HONDURAS.

PARTIDO REVOLUCIONARIO HONDUREÑO. *See* HONDURAN REVOLUTIONARY PARTY.

Political Parties—Historical

HONDURAN REVOLUTIONARY PARTY (PARTIDO REVOLUCIONARIO HONDUREÑO—PRH). The PRH was a small, reformist party linked to the Confederation of Honduran Workers (Confederación de Trabajadores Hondureños—CTH), which was most active in the late 1970s and early 1980s.

PARTIDO REVOLUCIONARIO HONDUREÑO. *See* HONDURAN REVOLUTIONARY PARTY.

J. Mark Ruhl

JAMAICA

Jamaica is the largest of the English-speaking Caribbean islands and the third largest Caribbean island, although, as a nation, it is superseded in land area by the 700-island Bahamas. Its population of 2.4 million (1988) is smaller than Puerto Rico's, but it is substantially larger than the population of other English-speaking Caribbean states. For this reason, and because of its proximity to the United States (it is ninety miles south of Cuba which is itself about the same distance from Florida), Jamaica has been the most internationally visible of the independent Commonwealth Caribbean countries. Jamaica's economy is heavily dependent on the export of bauxite, sugar, and other agricultural products. It also depends on tourism, and its proximity to the United States has made it a favored vacation spot for North American tourists.

Three-quarters of Jamaica's population is of African descent. The remainder is made up of people of mixed European-African descent and small percentages of people of European, Indian, Chinese, and Arab ancestry. Traditionally, the non-African groups have been overrepresented among the elite, but there has been a degree of social transformation in the postindependence era.

Jamaica was colonized by Spain between 1509 and 1655, when it was captured by Britain. After a period of restrictive (white planter) representative government, the Crown Colony system was introduced. The catalyst for the removal of planter autonomy was the Morant Bay Rebellion, a postemancipation rebellion of plantation workers. Under the Crown Colony system, various reforms were introduced, but it was not until the 1930s, when social unrest swept the region, that more substantial political and social reforms were instituted. Universal suffrage was introduced in 1944, and the island's first general elections were held that December.

In 1938 the island's first mass party, the People's National Party (PNP), and the first island-wide trade union, the Bustamante Industrial Trade Union (BITU), were established. The BITU had been formed by labor activist William Alexander Bustamante, who had played a leading role in earlier riots. The PNP, led by lawyer Norman Washington Manley, a cousin of Bustamante, was a merger of three progressive groups: the National Reform Association, the Federation of Citizens' Association, and the Jamaican Progressive League. The BITU and the PNP were allied for a time, but policy differences led Bustamante to form another political party, the Jamaica Labour Party (JLP), while the PNP formed its own trade union, the Trade Union Congress (TUC). In the 1950s, the PNP disassociated itself from the TUC, accusing one of the TUC's leading lights, Ken Hill, a PNP member, of espousing communism. The PNP expelled Hill and went on to found a new union, the National Workers Union (NWU).

The JLP, focusing on improving working conditions, easily won the 1944 general elections and went on to govern until 1955. The democratic socialist PNP won its first general election then and again in 1960. Full internal self-government had been attained in 1959. By this time, the West Indies Federation had been formed, at British urging, as a halfway house between colonial status and independence for the small states of the English-speaking Caribbean. The ongoing federal negotiations broke down in 1961, primarily because of disagreements between the two larger islands—Jamaica and Trinidad—over such issues as taxation, parliamentary representation and voting rights, and the location of the federal capital site. The PNP was supportive of the federation, but the voters were not. In a referendum held in 1961, Jamaicans opted to leave the federation and seek independence. New elections were called, which the PNP lost. Jamaica became independent in 1962 under a JLP government, again led by Bustamante.

Bustamante retired in 1967 and was succeeded by Donald Sangster, who died shortly after. Hugh L. Shearer led the party into the elections in 1972, which were won by the PNP, now led by Michael Manley, son of the founder. Manley was prime minister for two terms before losing to Edward Seaga's JLP in 1980. In turn, Seaga relinquished the leadership to Manley in 1989.

What many analysts find remarkable is that the two main Jamaican political parties have alternated in power every eight years or so in what almost seems to be a cyclical inevitability. But this orderly change can also be viewed in terms of the failure of successive regimes to "earn" longevity by dealing effectively with the socioeconomic problems of the island. In such a situation, barring any perceived barriers to change (such as ethnic polarization, as is the case in Guyana and in Trinidad and Tobago, or constitutional breakdown), the highly politicized Jamaican masses have tended to give each party a two-term "chance."

Analysts note that twin forces were at work in the politicization of the Jamaican masses between 1938 and 1962: the growth of class awareness and nationalism. The PNP centered its program on the constitutional struggle, which was of concern, in the beginning, only to the educated middle class. In time, the PNP organized the lower classes, especially through its trade union links. The PNP's platform of "democratic socialism" included a fundamental interest in social and economic reform. Meanwhile, Bustamante's focus on bread-and-butter issues earned the JLP strong support from the proletariat and peasants, but, in time, this support base was broadened to include the middle class. As the parties became more indistinguishable, the working class became politically polarized, and, as constitutional change was achieved, the ideological elements of positive nationalism and racial pride were jettisoned. Instead, the competition between the two Jamaican parties degenerated into a zero-sum game, based essentially on competition for patronage. This competition was aggravated in the 1970s by the reinjection (this time more deeply) of ideology into the political sphere.

By the early 1970s, it was clear that the Jamaican economic strategies—pursued by both parties in power, although the PNP was somewhat more nationalistic—were not producing desirable results. The gap between rich and poor was vast and growing, and unemployment was high. The strategies that had been pursued combined openness to foreign investment with import substitution industrialization. Throughout the region, however, there was an intellectual push, influenced by Third World currents of thought, for greater control of national resources, more nationalistic economic policies, and greater attention to social needs. The international environment of the Vietnam war, the struggle for civil rights in the United States, and the rise of Third World concerns also fostered a climate of political and economic experimentation. In 1968 riots occurred in Jamaica after a university protest was made over the government's expulsion of Walter Rodney, a respected Guyanese lecturer who had been lecturing on Third World, neo-Marxist themes. In 1970 there was widespread unrest in nearby Trinidad (see chapter on Trinidad and Tobago). The Jamaican elections of 1972 were therefore contested in a climate of regional social agitation.

The PNP won thirty-seven seats to the JLP's fifteen in 1972. (One seat was held by an independent, Robert Lightbourne, the former minister of trade and industry who had defected from the JLP after the election.) For the next few years, Manley sought to make Jamaica more self-reliant in agriculture, to bring in more revenue from bauxite production through taxes on the multinational companies, to improve the social infrastructure, and to decrease unemployment. His programs met with only limited success owing to severe balance-of-payment difficulties resulting from the unexpected increases in oil prices and to the resistance he encountered from the bauxite companies and from some national sectors. In 1976 the PNP was returned to power with 56.8 percent of the vote and forty-seven seats. Both the voting turnout (85 percent) and the margin of victory were described as unprecedented in Jamaican history, and the PNP appeared to have made considerable inroads into the traditional rural JLP constituencies. Nevertheless, the voting took place under a state of emergency imposed in June to stem social and political unrest.

During Manley's second term, the problems of the first term were compounded. The PNP intensified its socialist program. Capital flight, balance-of-payments deterioration, the denial of aid by the United States and harsh conditions imposed by multilateral lending agencies, and the decline of tourism because of fear of the island's instability—these were just some of the problems that plagued the government and country. Society and polity became polarized as economic hardships were experienced, and the JLP took on the role of conservative alternative. In June 1980, a dozen members of the Jamaica Defense Force and a few civilians were arrested and charged with conspiracy. (Two soldiers were later found guilty, but the others were released before trial or acquitted.)

Prime Minister Manley had negotiated an agreement with the International Monetary Fund (IMF) in 1976, shortly after the election. However, in renegotiations with the IMF, Manley refused the demand that public expenditures be further reduced by $300 million and 11,000 workers be laid off. A crisis ensued as the IMF suspended its aid. Manley then chose to call an early election, which was essentially a referendum on Jamaica's negotiations with the IMF. The election was marred by violence—more than 700 persons were killed during the year. Nevertheless, the electoral turnout was high, 80 percent, and the JLP, which won overwhelmingly (fifty-one seats to the PNP's nine) won 57.4 percent of the vote.

The new government of Edward Seaga represented a sharp swing to the right. A program of privatization and divestment of state enterprises formed an important part of a structural adjustment program advocated by international agencies. Jamaica received large amounts of external financial aid, and its debt burden increased considerably, but local and foreign capital returned and the tourist industry was revived. Still, the JLP was unable to show major economic gains, and unemployment, the plight of the poor, and deteriorating health and educational services became issues in the general election of 1989.

In 1983 Prime Minister Seaga called an early election in reponse to opposition calls for him to resign as finance minister following a major devaluation of the dollar. This was the first time in Jamaican electoral history that an election had been called so early. At the time, the JLP had increased its popularity as a result of the leading role played by Seaga in assisting the United States and the Eastern Caribbean in resolving the Grenada crisis. A still-disorganized PNP chose to boycott the elections, citing a 1980 agreement with the JLP precluding an election until the electoral lists had been revised. The JLP won all the parliamentary seats, fifty-four of which were not contested. Three independent candidates and four from minor parties contested the elections unsuccessfully.

In February 1989, Jamaicans again went to the polls. Although elections were constitutionally due in December 1988, they were postponed because of the devastation wreaked by Hurricane Gilbert in September 1988. This time, an electorate, disillusioned by economic hardships under the JLP, gave the PNP forty-five seats (55.8 percent of the vote) to the JLP's fifteen (44.1 percent). The PNP had succeeded in getting the electoral lists revised and had overwhelmingly won local elections in 1986, so that a PNP win was not unexpected. Voting turnout was relatively light by Jamaican standards (about 70 percent), reflecting uncertainty about the capacity of both parties to solve the island's problems.

Throughout the election campaign, the PNP had stressed a new centrism: a continued commitment to participatory democracy and the revitalization of the economy and social services but, at the same time, a conciliatory attitude toward foreign investment and aid. (In the 1980s, Manley had dissociated himself from the left wing of his party and had repudiated any alliance with the Marxist Workers Party which had supported him since 1978.) In power, Michael Manley used "continuity" as a watchword, and he continued the JLP's policy of highly centralized government, privatization, and divestment, in keeping with the terms of the structural adjustment loans extended by the IMF, and muted his previously strong commitment to socialism. Some referred to the "new Manley" 's moderated politics as the politics of expediency; others saw it more charitably as "facing the reality." The year 1989 therefore marked the return to ideological similarity between Jamaica's two parties.

In March 1990, the PNP won a sweeping victory in local elections, but voting turnout was very low (47–49 percent). News reports noted that the election underscored the public's mood of ambivalence, lukewarm sentiments of loyalty, and deep doubts as to the ability of both political parties to solve Jamaica's critical social and economic problems.

Both parties currently are confronting a number of internal problems. Manley has alienated some members both by his new centrism and by his perceived authoritarianism. The issue of leadership is also surfacing. Illness has kept Manley away from the job several times in recent years, and there has been talk of his resigning in favor of his deputy P. J. Patterson. (In March 1992, Manley, citing poor health, did indeed resign. The PNP named Patterson to replace him.) Meanwhile, the JLP has more serious leadership and intraparty differences. Leader Edward Seaga has long been accused of autocratic behavior and arrogance, and his leadership style became a public issue when five dissidents were expelled from Seaga's shadow cabinet and barred from running in any elections on a JLP ticket. The so-called Gang of Five claimed that they did not want to oust Seaga as leader but wanted him to change his dictatorial style and institute greater internal democracy. Seaga, however, accused them of breaching party discipline and attempting to sabotage his leadership. The issue remained unsettled into 1991.

Bibliography

Darrell E. Levi. Michael Manley. The Making of a Leader. University of Georgia Press, Athens, 1990.

Gordon K. Lewis. The Growth of the Modern West Indies. McGibbon and Kee, London, 1968.

Michael Manley. Jamaica, Struggle in the Periphery. Third World Media Limited in association with Writers and Readers Publishing Cooperative Society Limited, London, 1982.

Evelyne Huber Stephens and John D. Stephens. Democratic Socialism in Jamaica: The

Political Movement and Social Transformation in Dependent Capitalism. Princeton University Press, Princeton, N.J. 1986.

Carl Stone. *Democracy and Clientalism in Jamaica*. Transaction Books, New Brunswick, N.J., 1980.

Local, regional, and international newspaper sources and anthologies.

Political Parties—Active

CHRISTIAN CONSCIENCE. This conservative party fielded one candidate unsuccessfully in the 1983 general elections.

JAMAICA COMMUNIST PARTY (JCP). This party, formed in 1975, is led by Chris Lawrence. It is affiliated with the small Independent Trade Union Action Council. It supported the PNP in the late 1970s and early 1980s.

JAMAICA LABOUR PARTY (JLP). The JLP was founded by William Alexander Bustamante, then head of the Bustamante Industrial Trade Union, a union formed after the worker riots of 1938. Bustamante initially supported the People's National Party (PNP), but he differed with his cousin Norman Washington Manley on policy issues during World War II. Bustamante formed the JLP in 1942 to contest the country's first general elections of 1944. He led the party until his retirement in 1967, and he became the nation's first prime minister at independence in 1962. Bustamante's successor Donald Sangster died accidentally shortly after taking office. He was succeeded by Hugh L. Shearer, who retired after the party lost to the PNP in 1972. The party has since been led by Edward Seaga.

The JLP's support base initially lay in the proletarian and rural classes, but in time the party also acquired a middle-class and business-elite following. Bustamante focused on improving the working conditions of the masses, and the JLP also emphasized the "open economy" model of development, encouraging multinational exploitation of the country's bauxite resources. At the same time, a manufacturing base was established through an import substitution industrialization policy.

Under Bustamante's leadership, the JLP won general elections in 1944 and 1949, lost to the PNP in 1955 and 1960, but recaptured power in early elections in 1962, called after the ruling PNP's defeat in a referendum to determine whether Jamaica should continue to participate in the West Indies Federation. The JLP, which in 1944 had opposed self-government on the ground that it would bring "brown-man rule," was in 1961 closer than the PNP to the pulse of the nation in opposing Jamaica's participation in the federation. After serving two terms, the JLP lost power to the PNP in 1972. During the next few years in opposition, its pro-capitalist economic program and pro-West foreign policy served as a counterpoint to the PNP's socialist platform, opening the party to accusations of collaboration with external elements in the destabilization of the country. In 1980, the party swept back into power. Once at the helm, Prime Minister Seaga cemented ties with the United States and other Western powers and embarked on an economic management program that gave a primary role to private industry and enterprise. Nevertheless, the party is more centrist than right wing, and it maintains a strong identification with Third World and nonaligned concerns. However, despite Seaga's active role in the Grenada invasion of 1983, the JLP was as opposed to regional political integration in the 1980s as it had been in the 1960s.

The JLP ruled with no parliamentary opposition after the PNP boycotted early elections called by Seaga in 1983. A semblance of parliamentary democracy was maintained by Seaga's decision to widen the (appointed) senate to include non–JLP members. He also announced that nonmembers would be able to address the House of Representatives. In 1984 Seaga postponed local elections until a new electoral list, demanded by the PNP, was completed. In 1989 general elections were postponed past the constitutional term after Hurricane Gilbert devastated Jamaica.

The JLP lost the 1989 elections and has since been plagued by internal problems. Objections to Seaga's "dictatorial" leadership style have led to calls by some party members for restructuring the party. So far, Seaga has responded by removing dissident members from their party positions.

JAMAICA UNITED FRONT. This right-wing party contested one constituency in the 1983 general elections. The party leader, Charles Johnson, was arrested in 1980 on a charge of conspiracy to overthrow the government, but he was acquitted in 1981 after a witness was judged to be unreliable.

PEOPLE'S NATIONAL PARTY (PNP). The first mass party established in Jamaica, the PNP was formed in 1938 by a merger of three groups: the National Reform Association, a pressure group that worked for economic and political reform; the Federation of Citizens' Association, committed to legislative integrity and quality; and the Jamaican Progressive League, based in New York and an advocate of nationalism. The PNP was led by Norman Washington Manley, a prominent lawyer. Although the party had a middle-class and intellectual base, it was informally allied with a union, the Bustamante Industrial Trade Union, until policy differences led to the formation of the rival Jamaica Labour Party (JLP) by William Alexander Bustamante. In turn, the PNP formed a new union group, the Trade Union Congress, and garnered urban working-class support. The PNP made inroads into the traditionally JLP rural areas in the 1976 election.

The PNP's essentially nationalist platform focused on achieving self-government for Jamaica. The PNP also considered itself socialist (in the tradition of the British Labour Party), a democratic socialism that became more defined in the 1970s. The party's early focus was on improving social conditions, but by 1965 it was advocating land reform, economic nationalism, and redistributive socialism. In reality, however, the party was pro-West and only mildly nationalistic, and in 1952 several key members of the party were expelled for espousing Communist doctrines. The PNP joined the Socialist International after World War II.

The PNP won elections in 1955 and 1960, but its advocacy of Jamaican participation in the West Indies federation led to its defeat at the polls in 1962. In 1961, after federal negotiations were stalemated, primarily by differences between Jamaica and Trinidad, the PNP government called a referendum to decide Jamaica's continued participation in the regional arrangement. Defeat in the referendum led to new elections which the PNP lost.

The PNP returned to power in 1972 under Michael Manley, son of the founder. Manley's government stressed improved social development, employment generation, agricultural reform, economic nationalism, regionalism, and Third World and socialist solidarity (especially with Cuba). In its second term (1976–1980), the PNP was supported by the Jamaica Communist Party and the Marxist Workers' Party of Jamaica. International hostility to Manley's socialist experimentation, coupled with the increases in oil prices and the flight of capital from Jamaica, created serious economic hardships for Jamaicans. Political polarization between the two parties aggravated the situation, and in 1980 Manley called early elections after the breakdown of negotiations with the International Monetary Fund. After a resounding loss in the elections, Manley spent the next few years reorienting the PNP toward a more moderate platform.

In 1983 the PNP boycotted general elections called after Manley had criticized the prime minister's economic program. The PNP maintained that the electoral list included about 100,000 people who had died or emigrated and excluded 150,000 others who were eligible to vote. The boycott led to the PNP's loss of its parliamentary seats, but the party held public forums and rallies when necessary to achieve its goals. In 1986 the party won local elections (held on the basis of revised voter lists) on a platform that was careful not to mention "socialism." In 1989 it won the general elections and has since pursued a pragmatic and centrist program that includes elements that are very distinct from the program of the 1970s: continuity, deregulation, and good relations with the United States and multilateral economic organizations.

REPUBLICAN PARTY. This conservative party unsuccessfully fielded two candidates in the 1983 general elections.

WORKERS' PARTY OF JAMAICA (WPJ). This party, formed in 1978 from the Workers' Liberation League, is led by Trevor Munroe, a university lecturer. A Communist party, the WPJ is committed to anti-imperialism and socioeconomic transformation. The party gave "critical support" to the PNP in the late 1970s and supported the PNP slate in the 1989 elections, but Michael Manley broke completely with the WPJ in 1983, rejecting any chance of a future electoral alliance between the two parties. The WPJ entered the electoral arena in the 1981 parish elections and fielded two candidates who trailed behind those of the established parties. It boycotted the 1983 general elections but contested the 1986 local elections, capturing no seats in the thirteen constituencies it contested.

Political Parties—Historical

FARMERS PARTY. This planter-based party was formed to compete in the general elections of 1944 and was dissolved soon after the elections.

JAMAICA DEMOCRATIC PARTY. Based in planter and mercantile classes, the party unsuccessfully contested the 1944 elections. It was dissolved soon afterward.

JAMAICA PEOPLE'S PARTY. Established by Jamaican national hero Marcus Garvey in 1928, the party disappeared shortly after its founding.

NATIONAL LABOUR PARTY (NLP). The NLP was formed by Ken Hill after his 1952 expulsion from the People's National Party on the grounds of advocating communism. The party disappeared in the 1960s.

PEOPLE'S FREEDOM MOVEMENT (PFM). The PFM was formed by Richard Hart after his 1952 expulsion from the People's National Party on the grounds of advocating communism. The party disappeared after the 1955 general elections.

Jacqueline Anne Braveboy-Wagner

MARTINIQUE

Since World War II, the politics of Martinique, the Leeward Islands territory which since 1946 has been an Overseas Department of France, has been notable particularly for the importance of the Martinican Progressive Party (PPM). Led by the distinguished poet and historian Aimé Césaire, this party, committed to autonomy for the island, has been the largest element on the left since the mid-1950s.

During the 1980s, there was a considerable movement to the left in Martinican politics. This was stimulated by the united electoral front established among the three principal left-wing parties of the island: the PPM, the Martinican Communist Party, and the Socialist Federation of Martinique.

Most of the parties of Martinique have traditionally been local branches of French parties. This is still true of the two principal right-wing groups and of the principal Socialist organization. However, in 1957, the Martinican Communists severed their direct ties with their French counterpart, and, of course, the PPM never had any direct connection with a French party.

Support for complete independence of Martinique from France, so far very limited, finds electoral expression principally through the Martinique Independence Movement.

There are thirty-four municipalities on the island, each with elected mayors and councils. Two political and administrative bodies cover the whole island: the General Council and the Regional Council. The General Council directs the spending of locally raised revenues and some funds from the French government, and, following the reforms made by the regime of French President François Mitterand in the early 1980s, it performs the administrative responsibilities that were formerly in the hands of a Paris-appointed prefect. The Regional Council, which administers funds from the French government's Fund for Development, is now, as a result of the Mitterand reforms, an elected body rather than an appointed body.

For forty years after World War II, the General Council was controlled by right-wing parties. However, in the first popular election for the Regional Council held in February 1983, the left-wing parties won a small majority and Césaire became president of the Regional Council. In the March 1986 elections for the Regional Council, the three-party Union of the Left again won twenty-one of the forty-one seats. Césaire continued as president until June 1988, when he resigned and was succeeded by another member of his party, Camille Darsières.

Meanwhile, in the elections held for the General Council in March 1985, the left-wing parties increased their representation, but the right continued to have a majority. It was not until the General Council elections of September-October 1988, that the left-wing parties, for the first time in forty years, achieved a majority of twenty-three members out of the Council's forty-four. However, when there was a tie vote for president of the General Council, a member of the right-wing Rally for the Republic, Émile Maurice, continued in that post on the grounds of having the longest seniority in the council.

In the municipal elections of March 1989, the right won control of eighteen and lost three to parties of the left and one to an independent. The left won sixteen municipalities, including the capital, Fort-de-France, which has about one-third of the total population of the department.

In the French parliamentary elections of March 1986, Césaire and a Socialist candidate won two of the island's posts in the National Assembly, gaining 51.2 percent of the vote. The right-wing parties took the other two posts and received 42.4 percent of the ballots cast. In the June 1988 parliamentary election, however, all four seats in the National Assembly were won by members of the left coalition: two by the PPM, one by the Socialist Party, and one by an independent apparently backed by the three-party left coalition. In June 1986, for the first time, a member of the PPM was elected to the French Senate; the other senatorial post went to a member of the Union for French Democracy, who was reelected.

Some political violence was carried out during the 1980s by terrorist and insurrectionist groups favoring independence. In 1984 and 1985, several bombs were placed by the Caribbean Revolutionary Alliance (Alliance Révolutionnaire Caraibe), a group with its base in Guadeloupe. In August 1987, after the alliance had announced its abandonment of such activity, a bomb went off outside the main post office in Fort-de-France; the perpetrators were never identified.

Bibliography

The Europa World Year Book 1990. Europa Publications, Ltd., London, 1990.
Facts on File. Facts on File, New York.
Keesings Record of World Events.
Personal contacts of the writer.

Political Parties

ANTILLES TROTSKYIST GROUP (GROUPE TROTSKYISTE ANTILLAIS). *See* TROTSKYISTS.

COMBAT OUVRIER (WORKERS COMBAT). *See* TROTSKYISTS.

FÉDERATION SOCIALISTE DE LA MARTINIQUE (SOCIALIST FEDER-ATION OF MARTINIQUE). *See* SOCIALIST PARTY.

GROUPE RÉVOLUTIONNAIRE SOCIALISTE (REVOLUTIONARY SO-CIALIST GROUP). *See* TROTSKYISTS.

GROUPE TROTSKYISTE ANTILLAIS (ANTILLES TROTSKYIST GROUP). *See* TROTSKYISTS.

INDEPENDENCE MOVEMENT OF MARTINIQUE (MOUVEMENT IN-DEPENDANTISTE DE MARTINIQUE—MIM). The only group dedicated principally to advocating the independence of the island and organized formally as a political party, the MIM is led by Alfred Marie-Jeanne. The party has had only modest success at the polls. As early as 1976, Marie-Jeanne was elected to the General Council, although he was not reelected. In the first direct election for the Regional Council held in February 1983, the MIM received only about 3 percent of the votes. In March 1989, the MIM received only a handful of seats on municipal councils and lost one of their two mayors.

MARTINICAN COMMUNIST PARTY (PARTI COMMUNISTE MARTI-NIQUAIS). Established in the early 1920s as a local group separate from the French Communist Party, it was not until 1944 that it officially became a federation of the French party, a status which it maintained until 1957, when it formally separated from the French Communists and assumed its current name. The party still maintains relations with its French counterpart.

For a decade following World War II, the Martinican Communist Party, which dominated the capital city of Fort-de-France and some interior towns, usually elected two of the island's three deputies in the French National As-sembly. However, the influence of the party has declined drastically since Aimé Césaire, mayor of Fort-de-France and a National Assembly deputy, defected in 1956. Now the smallest of the country's three principal left-wing parties, it nevertheless continues to control Martinique's principal labor organization, the Confédération Génerale du Travail de Martinique (CGTM).

During the 1980s, the Communist Party was part of the left-wing coalition. Although it had a leading position in some of the municipalities controlled by the left and held seats in the Regional Council and General Council, none of its members was elected to the French National Assembly or Senate. The principal leader of the party, which favors autonomy for Martinique, is currently Armand Nicolas.

MARTINICAN PROGRESSIVE PARTY (PARTI PROGRESSISTE MAR-TINIQUAIS—PPM). Aimé Césaire, mayor of Fort-de-France and a member of the French National Assembly, established this party after he broke with the Martinican Communist Party in 1956 over the Soviet invasion of Hungary. Césaire, one of the leading French poets of his generation as well as a noted historian, took with him virtually the whole Communist membership in Fort-de-France, and his new party became the largest in the island.

The PPM has been principally characterized by its advocacy of autonomy for the island. It has sought more local control both over the funds raised in the island and those contributed by France, and it has emphasized the need for France to recognize the existence of a Martinican nation as the basis for a continued relationship between the island and France.

During the 1980s, the PPM was the largest party in the left-wing coalition, which gained strength consistently during the decade. With the popular election of the Regional Council for the first time in February 1983, and a left-wing victory, Césaire became president of that body, a post he held until 1988, when he resigned and was succeeded by another member of his party, Camille Darsières.

On the parliamentary level, too, the PPM did well. In March 1986, Césaire was, as usual, reelected a deputy in the National Assembly. In June 1988, when the left coalition took all four Martinican seats, Césaire was joined by his fellow party member, Claude Lise. Three months later, in September 1988, for the first time, a member of the PPM, Rodolph Désire, was elected to the French Senate.

Finally, in the March 1989 municipal elections, the PPM, the strength of which had traditionally been concentrated in Fort-de-France, won control of four other municipalities while it maintained its hold on the capital.

In the French parliament, the PPM deputies and senator sit with the bloc of the French Socialist Party.

MARTINICAN SOCIALIST PARTY (PARTI SOCIALISTE MARTINIQUAIS). See SOCIALIST PARTY.

MOUVEMENT INDEPENDANTISTE DE MARTINIQUE. See INDEPENDENCE MOVEMENT OF MARTINIQUE.

PARTI COMMUNISTE MARTINIQUAIS. See MARTINICAN COMMUNIST PARTY.

PARTI PROGRESSISTE MARTINIQUAIS. See MARTINICAN PROGRESSIVE PARTY.

PARTI RÉPUBLICAINE. See REPUBLICAN PARTY.

PARTI SOCIALISTE (SOCIALIST PARTY). See SOCIALIST PARTY.

45155575555655

PARTI SOCIALISTE MARTINIQUAIS (MARTINICAN SOCIALIST PARTY). *See* SOCIALIST PARTY.

RALLY FOR THE REPUBLIC (RASSEMBLEMENT POUR LA RÉPUBLIQUE—RPR). The Martinican branch of the French Neo-Gaullist party of the same name led by Jacques Chirac, the RPR is led by Stephen Bagée. The RPR won one of the three Martinican seats in the French National Assembly in 1981 and repeated this performance in March 1986. However, two years later, in June 1988, when the left swept the parliamentary election, the party lost its seat in the assembly.

Throughout the 1980s, the RPR engaged in electoral coalitions with the other principal right-wing party—the Union for French Democracy—but there is little information concerning the distribution of seats, according to party, in the Regional Council, the General Council, and the municipalities. However, throughout the period, a member of the RPR, Émile Maurice, continued to serve as president of the General Council. Throughout the decade, the two right parties and their allies consistently lost ground to the parties of the left.

RASSEMBLEMENT POUR LA RÉPUBLIQUE. *See* RALLY FOR THE REPUBLIC.

REPUBLICAN PARTY (PARTI RÉPUBLICAINE). The Martinican branch of the French party of the same name, this party is an organization of the moderate right. Headed by Jean Bailly, it was, during the 1980s, a partner of the Rally for the Republic and the Union for French Democracy.

REVOLUTIONARY SOCIALIST GROUP (GROUPE RÉVOLUTIONNAIRE SOCIALISTE). *See* TROTSKYISTS.

SOCIALIST FEDERATION OF MARTINIQUE (FÉDERATION SOCIALISTE DE LA MARTINIQUE). *See* SOCIALIST PARTY.

SOCIALIST PARTY (PARTI SOCIALISTE). The oldest existing party in Martinique, the Socialist Party was established before World War I as a branch of the French Socialist Party. For a short while after World War II, the Socialists competed with the Communists for leadership of the left, but the Socialist Party subsequently declined.

When Aimé Césaire founded the Martinican Progressive Party (PPM) in the late 1950s, the Socialists split. One faction, which formed the Martinican Socialist Party (PSM), allied itself with the PPM. The strength of the PSM lay principally in Fort-de-France. The other faction, known formally as the Socialist Federation of Martinique (Féderation Socialiste de la Martinique—FSM), found its strength in the interior. At that time, the PSM favored autonomy for the island, and the FSM supported continuing a close association with France.

During the 1980s, the PSM did not play a major role; however, the FSM, headed by Michel Yoyo, formed part of the left coalition with the PPM and the Communist Party. As a result of this alliance, the FSM did well. In March 1986, a member of the party, Joseph Dogue, was elected to the French National Assembly, and he was reelected in 1988. In the June 1989 European parliament election, the FSM was the only left party to participate, and it received 35 percent of the votes cast in a poll in which there was an 83.9 percent abstention rate.

There is no breakdown of the share of the Socialists in representation in the Regional and General Councils—except for the election of five members to the General Council in 1986—or in the municipalities. In all of these, the left made substantial gains during the 1980s. The left controls both councils and has made major advances on the local level.

TROTSKYISTS. Three parties espousing international Trotskyism are found in Martinique. In all three cases, the organizations involve both Martinique and neighboring Guadeloupe. The oldest of these groups is Workers Combat (Combat Ouvrier), which is associated with the French party Lutte Ouvrière. The largest group would seem to be the Revolutionary Socialist Group (Groupe Révolutionnaire Socialiste—GRS), which is affiliated with the United Secretariat of the Fourth International, led by Gilbert Pago. As long ago as 1976 the GRS won a seat in the island's General Council, but it is not known whether it continued to hold that position. The third Trotskyist element is the Antilles Trotskyist Group (Groupe Trotskyiste Antillais), which was formed in June 1984. All three Trotskyist parties favor independence for Martinique.

UNION FOR FRENCH DEMOCRACY (UNION POUR LA DÉMOCRATIE FRANÇAISE—UDF). The UDF is the Martinican branch of the French party of the same name, which is led by former president of France Valery Giscard d'Estaing. The party was organized originally around his first campaign for the presidency in 1974. In the 1980s, it formed part of a right-wing coalition which included the Rally for the Republic and other, smaller groups. Led by Jean Maran, the UDF succeeded in holding its seat in the French National Assembly in the March 1986 election, although it lost that post in the left sweep that occurred in the June 1988 parliamentary election. Three months later, Roger Lise of the UDF was elected to the French Senate. There is no specific information concerning the proportion of seats held by the UDF among the right candidates who were elected to the Regional Council, the General Council, and the municipalities during the 1980s.

UNION OF THE LEFT. An electoral coalition, formed in the 1980s, of the three principal left-wing parties: the Martinican Communist Party, the Martinican Progressive Party, and the Socialist Federation of Martinique.

UNION POUR LA DÉMOCRATIE FRANÇAISE. *See* UNION FOR FRENCH DEMOCRACY.

WORKERS COMBAT (COMBAT OUVRIER). *See* TROTSKYISTS.

Robert J. Alexander

MEXICO

Mexico is characterized by marked regional variation in geography, economic development, social stratification, ethnic composition, and politics. Geographically, Mexico is the third largest of the Latin American countries covering over 756,000 square miles. The territory is broken by high mountain ranges along the east, west, and south, which separate the coastal plains from the high central plateau. To the north, the land is arid or semiarid desert; tropical highlands and lowlands characterize the coastal plains and intermountain valleys. There is substantial variability in annual rainfall throughout the territory, which creates an enormous diversity in agricultural productivity, employment, and rural poverty. Mexico City, the largest metropolitan area in the world with an estimated population of 18.5 million in 1990, is located in the high central plateau.

Mexico's population, officially stated to be 81.1 million by the 1990 census but estimated by demographers to be closer to 84.9 million, has become highly urbanized. More than two-thirds of the population lives in communities of over 2,500 inhabitants concentrated especially in the three largest cities: the Mexico City metropolitan area, Monterrey, and Guadalajara. Culturally, the population is mestizo: mixed Spanish or European and Indian ancestry. About 8.5 percent of the population, concentrated in the south, is either monolingual or bilingual in an Indian dialect. This segment of society is also among the poorest, has the least access to public services, and has experienced limited benefits from any economic or political reforms that have taken place since the revolution.

Postindependence History

Before the arrival of the Spanish conquerors in 1520, Mexico was the home of various complex Indian civilizations, including the Olmec, Toltec, Maya, and Aztec, some of whom had expansive empires. The Spanish colonial period lasted for 300 years until a series of insurrections led by Mexican-born Spaniards, beginning in 1810, led to Mexico's independence from Spain in 1821.

After independence, much of Mexico's political history of the nineteenth century was absorbed in a series of conflicts among regional political figures, between liberals and conservatives, and in struggles against incursions by foreign powers. Half of Mexico's territory was lost to the United States with the annexation of Texas in 1845 and the peace treaty concluding the Mexican-American War in 1848. Mexican political parties of the nineteenth century divided primarily between anticlerical, federalist Liberals and proclerical, centralist Conservatives. These were parties of elites and regional or national strongmen. President Benito Juárez's efforts to abolish special privileges associated with colonial rule and to restrain the power of the Catholic Church through the adoption of the 1857 constitutional reforms led to three years of civil war between the Liberals who supported him and the Conservatives who opposed him. The Conservatives' attempt to ally with the French to establish a monarchy in Mexico failed in 1867, and Juárez's reforms were adopted as the formal law of the land.

Between 1876 and 1910, Mexico was ruled by General Porfirio Díaz who established a strong, authoritarian central government by working closely with large landholders (including foreign investors), mining corporations, and the Catholic Church. Many of Juárez's reforms were reversed. As poverty and hardship increased for peasants and the small working class, some middle-class groups and landowners excluded from the ruling coalition also began to demand political reform. Led by Francisco I. Madero, they called for political changes: "effective suffrage, no reelection."

Díaz fled Mexico, and Madero, who became president in 1910, was assassinated in 1911. His death opened up a period of civil war and a succession of coups which lasted nearly a decade, during which nearly one million were killed and the economic infrastructure was substantially damaged. The victory of the armies of the northern states under Venustiano Carranza led to the adoption of the 1917 constitution and the defeat or pacification of residual insurrections by peasant armies under Emiliano Zapata and Francisco Villa.

Postrevolutionary History

Immediately after the revolution, political parties became vehicles for promoting the careers of particular individuals, military leaders, or regional alliances. They entailed informal coalition building, typically top-down. This would be true of the Constitutionalist Party, which Carranza formed in 1917, as well as the Liberal Constitutionalist Party which backed Alvaro Obregón in 1920. Parties with an ideological agenda as well included the National Agrarian Party (PNA), the National Labor Party (PNL), and the Socialist Party of the Southeast (PPS).

This pattern of regional parties was broken in 1929 when President Plutarco Elías Calles established the National Revolutionary Party (Partido Nacional Revolucionario, PNR). After gradually establishing its authority, the PNR became the dominant party in Mexico, aggregating most regional and sectoral interest groups within its inclusive organizational structure, or politically marginalizing those groups it could not attract. The PNR was subsequently renamed and reorganized as the Party of the Mexican Revolution (Partido Revolucionario Mexicano, PRM) in 1938 and as the Institutional Revolutionary Party (Partido Revolucionario Institucional, PRI) in 1946. Party members have monopolized elected public offices at all levels as well as appointive offices within the state and federal bureaucracies.

The government instituted a range of reforms from the late 1920s through the 1940s. These included the adoption of legislation allowing labor unionization and government policies which sporadically encouraged PRI–affiliated trade unions, an extensive program of land reform, and a system of free and compulsory lay public education. Seeking to enforce constitutional provisions limiting the power of the Catholic Church, they provoked three years of armed insurrection by militant Catholics (1926–1929) before a peace accord was reached with the Church. Reforms established the basis for a mixed capitalist economy, based on state ownership of utilities and corporations to develop key natural resources such as petroleum, state regulation of foreign investment, and high levels of state investment in key infrastructure projects.

Resistance to these reforms led to the formation of the opposition National Action Party (Partido de Acción Nacional, PAN) in 1939. The PAN remains the best organized of the opposition political parties in Mexico, and it has posed strong electoral challenges to the PRI within some regions. Conversely, when government reformism declined, some political parties were established by dissidents from the official party. Among these still extant parties are the Authentic Party of the Mexican Revolution (Partido Auténtico de Revolución Mexicana, PARM) and the Popular Socialist Party (Partido Popular Socialista, PPS).

Beginning in the late 1940s under President Miguel Alemán (1946–1952), state economic policy shifted sharply to favor the expansion of industrial capacity, the modernization of agriculture, and the expansion of tourism. Mexico entered a period of economic expansion led by government-financed infrastructural investments and exceptional currency stability between 1953 and 1976. The economy grew at an annual rate of from 5 to 6 percent with an average annual rate of inflation of about 5 percent.

By the late 1960s, however, there were signs of political and economic strain. Organized resistance by teachers, physicians, and railroad workers in the late 1950s had been repressed. The violent attack on student demonstrators in 1968 under President Gustavo Díaz Ordaz led to the formation of new political associations, many of them in provincial cities and rural communities. These new organizations led in turn to the development of popular movements and opposition political parties during the late 1970s. However, with the exception of Luis Echeverría Alvarez's support for independent trade unionist currents, formal political reforms were modest and did not begin until 1977.

In the economy, inflation began to increase, and the unequal distribution of the benefits of economic growth became more apparent. Still, structural reforms in the economy were not adopted. Díaz Ordaz's successor, Echeverría Alvarez

(1970–1976), failed to address some of the structural problems of the Mexican economy, for example, strong reliance on public investment and spending to promote economic growth, a steadily declining rate of growth in agriculture as investments concentrated on urban and industrial projects, or the low rate of taxation as a source of government revenues. Moreover, Echeverría's populist rhetoric had a negative impact on tourism and on domestic and foreign investment. The combination of politics and economics led to higher inflation (about 15 percent average annual rate during his term) and capital flight to which the administration finally responded in 1976 with a devaluation of the peso (from $12.50 to $23 to the dollar) and tighter restraints on credit.

The discovery of massive oil and natural gas resources in the state-owned energy sector in the latter half of the decade allowed José López Portillo (1976–1982) to finance economic expansion while continuing to avoid structural reform. The economic expansion of the late 1970s was based on deficit spending, financed by loans granted on the promise of oil reserves and the rising price of oil on the world market. Mexico's foreign debt was $30.5 billion dollars in 1976, but it rose to $82 billion by 1982, requiring annual debt service payments of nearly $16 billion. Private foreign investment began gradually to increase again after the 1976 stabilization program. The dollar revenues from oil sales, and easy bank credits, were used to finance a wide range of government projects and an expansion of government services and subsidies as well as capital and consumer goods imports. Government spending and rising consumer demand fueled inflation to average annual rates of 36 percent, until the crisis became unmanageable in August 1982.

The oil boom collapsed in 1982 due to falling oil prices; at the same time, interests rose on Mexico's foreign debt and the U.S. economy suffered a recession. Real wages and the standard of living plummeted in Mexico. Before leaving office, López Portillo nationalized the banking system and initiated a massive devaluation in the peso to ease the problem of capital flight which may have involved as much as US$50 billion dollars in transferred assets. At the end of 1982, the Mexican government announced temporary suspension in the payments on debt principal and opened renegotiation with creditors. This was the first in a series of difficult debt negotiations; the most recent was completed in 1990.

President Miguel de la Madrid Hurtado (1982–1988) began his administration by negotiating an economic stabilization program with the International Monetary Fund which brought two years of severe recession (1982–1983) before beginning a gradual recovery in 1984. De la Madrid's economic program was based on promoting non-oil exports, opening the Mexican economy to foreign investment and competitive trade, reducing state ownership by beginning privatization of publicly owned corporations, severely cutting government subsidies and expenditures on social programs, and emphasizing the role of the state as "regent" of the economy. Reductions in the rate of inflation and a gradual recovery in growth were undermined in the second half of 1985 by a second oil price drop and by a devastating earthquake in Mexico City in September of the same year. The average annual rate of inflation under de la Madrid was 91 percent, with a high of 159 percent in 1987.

Beginning in 1987, organized labor, business, and the government have signed a series of economic solidarity pacts, renewed every twelve to eighteen months, designed to control inflation by limiting wage and price increases. The pacts have been more effective at severely restricting wage increases than at controlling prices. Between 1980 and 1990, minimum real wages in Mexico declined by 66 percent. By 1987, according to the government's own statistics, more than half of the population fell below the official poverty line, and more than 20 percent were living in extreme poverty.

Early in de la Madrid's administration, municipal and congressional elections in the north (in Durango and Chihuahua) provided a forum for the opposition PAN and raised the opposition's expectations for electoral contestation. In Chihuahua, the opposition (principally the PAN) was so strong that they defeated the PRI in eleven of sixty-seven municipal elections. But in Oaxaca and the next year in Coahuila, there were violent conflicts between the ruling party and the electoral opposition. Concern about electoral fraud and political corruption increased in 1986 in the elections held in Chihuahua, provoking public threats from the Catholic archbishop in the state to suspend church services in protest over the fraud.

Responding to the political and economic crises, a number of popular movements developed in Mexico between 1968 and 1988, asserting their independence from the Mexican state and political parties. These included such political organizations as the Organization of the Revolutionary Left, Mass Line (Organización de Izquierda Revolucionaria, Linea de Masas) and such groups as the Urban Popular Movement (Movimiento Urbano Popular—MUP) and its national coordinating organization (CONAMUP), as well as the dissident teachers' union, the National Coordinating Committee of Workers in Education (Coordinadora Nacional de Trabajadores de la Educación—CNTE), and the Coalition of Workers, Peasants and Students of the Isthmus (Coordinadora de Obreros, Campesinos y Estudiantes del Istmo—COCEI). In Mexico City, in the wake of the devastating earthquake in September 1985, many popular organizations emerged to help rescue victims, build replacement housing, and assist with urban planning and environmental problems. At the National University in 1986, conflicts over university governance led to the establishment of the University Student Council (Consejo Estudiantil Universitario—CEU).

Until the mid-1980s, most of these independent popular movements rejected collaboration with political parties and generally declined to engage in electoral competition, despite the incentives to form political parties established by the 1977 electoral reform. In Mexico City, however, growing demands for self-government in the Federal District and its territorial subdivisions led to the formation by popular movements of the unofficial Neighborhood Assembly (Asamblea de Barrios). On the official side, the 1986 electoral reforms created the capital city's Representative Assembly (Asamblea de Representantes del Distrito Federal), a popularly elected board of sixty-six representatives who advise the appointed government of Mexico City.

Between 1985 and 1988, some popular movements adopted an electoral strategy, running their own candidates especially in local elections. Although movement leaders were persuaded to negotiate with progressive political parties, rank-and-file members were less inclined to vote. Candidates supported by popular movements seldom won.

In August 1986, a number of nationally prominent PRI leaders, all members of the party's left wing, formed a dissident movement which they called the Corriente Democrática (CD). Two prominent CD members are Cuauhtémoc Cárdenas, son of former president Lázaro Cárdenas and himself former governor of Michoacán, and Porfirio Muñoz Ledo, a former minister of labor, former head of the PRI, and unsuccessful precandidate for a presidential nomination in 1976. The CD criticized the economic restructuring program of the de la Madrid administration and urged a democratization of the PRI's candidate selection process, especially the selection of presidential candidates. They particularly sought to avoid the nomination of another technocrat, especially Carlos Salinas de Gortari, as the party's presidential candidate for the 1988–1994 sexenio. The CD's demands for internal reform were resoundingly rejected, and they withdrew from the PRI in October 1987. Shortly thereafter, Cárdenas accepted the presidential nomination of the PARM and began to build the National Democratic Front (FDN). Salinas de Gortari, secretary of programming and budget under Miguel de la Madrid, became the ruling party's nominee for the July 1988 elections for the presidency.

Like the campaign, the official voting returns for the 6 July elections took the ruling party by surprise. Official returns gave Salinas 50.75 percent of all ballots cast. Based on their own projections, the FDN and Cárdenas claimed a victory and charged a "technical coup" on the part of the PRI. For the first time, a PRI presidential candidate lost the plurality vote in five states. Four opposition senators were elected from the FDN. The PRI lost 66 out of 300 single-member districts. Although the PRI retained a simple majority in the Chamber of Deputies, only coalition with other parties would give it the two-thirds vote needed to pass constitutional amendments.

The 1988 presidential elections appeared to reconfigure the political geography of Mexico, marking the opening of a new era of party politics. The electoral campaign, the tabulation of results, and the postelection charges of fraud came toward the end of a decade of intense, dispersed social movement activity, increasingly fractious and partisan political conflict, and economic crisis. The day following the election, Salinas announced on national television that "the era of a virtual one-party system [in Mexico] has ended," giving way to "intense political competition."

After the election, Cárdenas and others from the FDN established a new political party, the Party of the Democratic Revolution (PRD). The PRD has continued to deny the legitimacy of the Salinas government (based on the claim of electoral fraud in the presidential election), and many members refuse to negotiate with the government.

Since 1988 the most spectacular elections for the opposition were held in 1989 in Baja California where Ernesto Ruffo Appel, the first opposition governor since 1929, was elected on the PAN ticket. In 1991 the gubernatorial elections in Guanajuato and San Luis Potosí were hard-fought contests. In both cases, preliminary returns showed a victory for the official party's candidate, but protests of electoral fraud and threats of civil disobedience led to the cancellation of electoral results in Guanajuato, and to the resignation of the newly elected PRI governor in San Luis Potosí. Both states will hold new gubernatorial elections within eighteen months of August 1991. For the 1991–1994 congress, the PRI will hold 61 of 64 Senate seats; two are held by the PRD and one by the PAN. In the Chamber of Deputies, the PRI holds 320 seats; the PAN, 89; the PRD, 41; the Cardenista Front Party for National Reconstruction (PFCRN), 23; the PARM, 15; and the PPS, 12.

At the time of the 1988 elections, many commentators regarded this as a shift toward the institutionalized, electoral expression of popular demands; however, the results of subsequent state and local elections suggest that electoral participation may have been a conjuncturally appealing strategy. Voters in the same regions that supported Cárdenas's bid for the presidency must now negotiate with the government agencies that make credit available, facilitate marketing of agricultural products, legalize urban land titles, and distribute public services. While the PRD hopes to retain the popular movements' support, it is the PRI government apparatus that controls the resources to satisfy these claims.

To address immediate and highly localized demand making, the Salinas government has created a new, nationwide mechanism for delivery of small-scale material benefits to low-income Mexicans: the National Solidarity Program (the Programa Nacional de Solidaridad—PRONASOL). This highly visible program coordinates most of the national investment in community infrastructure: piped water, electricity, sewage systems, paved streets, medical clinics, housing, and school repairs. Beneficiaries are expected to make material or labor contributions to projects. Although they are administratively separated, PRI operatives eagerly take credit for the material rewards dispensed through the PRONASOL program. This program, and the president's own approval rating, partly explain the PRI's electoral comeback in some parts of the country, especially in the 1991 midterm elections.

As the former secretary of programming and budget under de la Madrid and therefore the architect of the de la Madrid economic reforms, Salinas has expanded and intensified the program of economic restructuring in Mexico. He has accelerated the program of privatization, selling off publicly owned corporations including the banks, some major industries, and public services such as Teléfonos de México. He has reduced annual inflation to a projected rate of 20 percent for 1991. Beginning in 1990, President Salinas proposed extending the economic restructuring program to include the creation of a North American free-trade agreement to cover Mexico, the United States, and Canada. His government is relying on this strategy to help sustain economic growth, to generate some of the 1 million new jobs required each year to meet the needs of a growing labor force, and to secure the revenue required to make debt payments.

The Political System

The Mexican Constitution of 1917 outlined a presidential system of government characterized on paper by three autonomous branches of government: the executive, a bicameral federal legislature, and a judiciary—each with the capacity to check and balance the others, and each with considerable autonomy at the local level (el municipio libre). In practice, however, Mexico has developed a highly centralized state with a strong presidency which dominates the system at all levels. One party, the PRI, has dominated national politics since 1946. As organized political parties, the PAN and the PRD were distant second and third political forces in the national elections held in late 1991. These are followed by a range of very small parties, most of which are arrayed to the left of the political spectrum.

Elected officials are voted into office by plurality vote in direct popular elections, with no reelection for executive positions (governors and presidents) and no immediate reelection for seats in the state and federal legislatures. The 1917 constitution specified universal male suffrage for all married men eighteen years and older and all unmarried men twenty-one years and older. In 1947, women were given the right to vote and be elected in municipal elections; in 1953, women were granted the right to run in federal elections; in 1969, the age limit to vote was lowered for all persons to eighteen years and older. The president serves a six-year term as do senators. Beginning in 1991, one senator from each federal entity is elected in the midterm elections; the other's term runs concurrently with the president's. Diputados (representatives in the Chamber of Deputies) serve three-year terms. Three hundred diputados are elected in an equal number of single-member electoral districts on a first-past-the-post rule; another 200 are chosen in five national multimember districts on the basis of the party's proportional share of the vote.

The initial postrevolutionary electoral law, enacted in 1918, placed control over elections entirely at the municipal and state levels, including registering candidates, compiling voter registration lists, distributing voter credentials and ballots, and selecting polling place observers. By the terms of the 1946 reforms in the electoral law, the registration of political parties and the preparation, conduct, and certification of federal election results came entirely under federal control. (Comparable laws granting authority to state governments were subsequently passed by most states for local elections.) One of the most important provisions of the reforms, still in force, specified that only registered parties may nominate candidates for public office and appear on the ballot. Unregistered parties may form, but they cannot directly compete in elections.

The conditions to be met in order to become a registered party have varied (the "Active Parties" section includes parties that have won and lost their registrations). In general, however, parties are required to present a party platform, to issue regularly a party publication, to be governed by a national executive committee, to hold a national assembly meeting, and to demonstrate support in two-thirds of the federal "entities" (states, territories, and the Federal District). The parties' support in these areas has been measured by a variety of mechanisms ranging from a minimum number of names on petitions to register the party through the proportion of votes cast for the party's candidates in federal elections. Currently, parties may become nationally registered by demonstrating that they have polled 1.5 percent of the national vote in federal elections; or held at least 16 state assembly meetings, each of which was attended by 3,000 participants; or held at least 150 district assembly meetings, each of which was attended by 300 people. Alternatively, parties may also show evidence of having 3,000 affiliates in each of one half of the 32 federal entities or 300 affiliates per district in at least one half of the 300 federal electoral districts. Following the August 1991 midterm congressional elections, and based on the official voting returns from that election, there are currently six registered parties: the PRI, the PAN, the PRD, the PFCRN, the PARM, and the PPS. All the other parties, which continue to participate in political debate and organization, have failed to secure permanent registration and must continue to compete electorally on a "conditional registration" pending voting returns.

Since 1977, and especially since 1985, opposition political parties have intensified their challenge to the PRI's hegemony. Always critical of electoral fraud, they have resorted to confrontation and civil disobedience to draw attention to their complaints. They have organized against policies such as the 1982 nationalization of the banks as an instance of flagrant abuse of state power, and against high debt service payments because of the social cost entailed in this use of public resources. The left's criticisms have focused on the government's lack of concern for social problems of the poor and loss of sovereignty over the economy; the right's, on the corruption, inefficiency and invasiveness of an overweening state. In an important shift in strategy, both the left and right tried during the 1980s to secure international media publicity and support from international organizations for their claims against the government and the ruling party.

Such changes appear to signal an increased importance of opposition parties in Mexican politics. However, while more opposition party candidates may now be considered serious contenders for public office, opposition parties are still weakly linked to organized interest groups, internally divided over party leadership and strategy, and less programmatically or ideologically coherent than they were during the electoral struggles of 1988. A plurality of Mexicans appear to have no party preference, and polls show that the best predictors of voters' candidate preferences are the perceived personal qualities of the candidate, not the party's platform. Political leaders like Cárdenas and Salinas are more popular than the parties they lead.

The 1977 electoral reform (Ley Federal de Organizaciones Políticas y Procesos Electorales—LOPPE) relaxed requirements under which parties could qualify to register, allowing the formation of parties with a smaller number of supporters or a reduced share of the vote. The new law also created a new channel for minority party representation in the congress. This reform involved a significant change in the Chamber of Deputies, the lower house of the federal legislature, adding 100 *diputados plurinominales* to the existing 300 first-past-the-post single-member districts. The *diputados plurinominales* were to be selected from a closed list of party candidates running at large in five multimember districts. Any party polling at least 1.5 percent of the national vote would be entitled to at least one *diputado plurinominal* for each district, for a total of a minimum of five, with the balance of seats to be distributed among minority parties on the basis of relative vote share in each district. Finally, the LOPPE guaranteed access to the mass media for all registered parties and provided modest government subsidies for their campaigns.

In 1986 further changes in electoral laws increased the number of deputies from multimember districts (*plurinominales*) to 200 and added complexity to the formulas for winning representation in these districts. Now, the PRI is eligible to secure proportional representation seats. The 1986 reforms introduced a "governability clause" assuring that, in the event a winning party obtained less than 51 percent of the national vote and fewer than 251 seats (out of 500) in the Chamber of Deputies, the winning party would nonetheless still be assigned 251 seats.

The most recent electoral reforms (Código Federal de Instituciones y Procedimientos Electorales—COFIPE) were approved by the congress in July 1990. The COFIPE replaced the institutional mechanism for overseeing elections and adjudicating disputed returns (the Comisión Federal Electoral—CFE) with a new entity, the Instituto Federal Electoral (IFE). Unlike its predecessor, the IFE's composition ensures that no party will have majority control, although, if the parastatal parties retain representation in the IFE, the PRI may yet control a majority. Several provisions are directed at the procedures leading up to elections, including the preparation of a new list of registered voters, to reduce the opportunities for fraud. The new electoral law also restricts "joint candidacies" (such as the Cárdenas–FDN candidacy in 1988) by prohibiting individual parties from nominating the same candidate unless they form strictly regulated coalitions.

The revised electoral code still includes a "governability clause," which gives the party winning a plurality of votes (higher than 35 percent and less than 51 percent) an automatic majority in the Chamber of Deputies, although the formula for calculating the distribution of proportional representation seats was changed again. This provision virtually guarantees continued control of the congress by the PRI and, through it, the president. The PRI regarded the governability clause as a guarantee should its position further erode in the 1991 midterm elections. As it turned out, 320 PRI candidates won in the election, so the governability clause has not yet been invoked to secure a PRI majority.

Bibliography

Hector Aguilar Camín. *Después del milagro*. Cal y Arena, Mexico City, 1988.

Arturo Alvarado, ed. *Electoral Patterns and Perspectives in Mexico*. Center for U.S.– Mexican Studies, University of California, San Diego, Monograph no. 22, La Jolla, Calif., 1987.

John Bailey. *Governing Mexico: The Statecraft of Crisis Management*. St. Martin's Press, New York, 1988.

Miguel Basañez. *El pulso de los sexenios: 20 años de crisis en México*. Siglo Veintiuno, Mexico City, 1990.

Edgar Butler and Jorge Bustamante, eds. *Sucesión presidencial: The 1988 Mexican Presidential Election*. Westview Press, Boulder, Colo., 1991.

Cuauhtémoc Cárdenas, et al. *Radiografía de un fraude electoral*. Editorial Nuestro Tiempo, Mexico City, 1989.

Centro de Estudios Sociológicos. *México en el umbral del milenio*. El Colegio de México, Mexico City, 1990.

Kenneth Coleman and Charles L. Davis. *Politics and Culture in Mexico*. Institute for Social Research, University of Michigan, Ann Arbor, 1988.

Rolando Cordera, Raúl Trejo Delarbe, and Juan Enrique Vega, eds. *México: El reclamo democrático*. Siglo Veintiuno, Mexico City, 1988.

Wayne A. Cornelius, Judith Gentleman, and Peter H. Smith, eds. *Mexico's Alternative Political Futures*. Center for U.S. Mexican Studies, University of California, San Diego, La Jolla, Calif., 1989.

Joe Foweraker and Ann L. Craig, eds. *Popular Movements and Political Change in Mexico*. Lynne Rienner, Boulder, Colo., 1990.

Luis Javier Garrido. *El partido de la revolución institucionalizada: La formación del nuevo estado en México, 1928–1945*. Siglo Veintiuno, Mexico City, 1982.

Judith Gentleman, ed. *Mexican Politics in Transition*. Westview Press, Boulder, Colo., 1987.

Adolfo Gilly. "El perfil del PRD." *Nexos* 152, August 1990, pp. 61–71.

Friedrich Katz, ed. *Riot, Rebellion and Revolution: Rural Social Conflict in Mexico*. Princeton University Press, Princeton, N.J., 1988.

Alan Knight. *The Mexican Revolution*. Cambridge University Press, Cambridge, 1986.

Daniel Levy and Gabriel Szekely. *Mexico: Paradoxes of Stability and Change*, 2d ed. Westview Press, Boulder, Colo., 1987.

Soledad Loaeza and Rafael Segovia, eds. *La vida política mexicana en la crisis*. El Colegio de México, Mexico City, 1987.

Soledad Loaeza and Claudio Stern, eds. *Las clases medias en la coyuntura actual*. El Colegio de México, Cuadernos del CES, no. 33, Mexico City, 1990.

Arnaldo Martínez Verdugo, ed. *Historia del comunismo en México*. Grijalbo, Mexico City, 1983.

Juan Molinar Horcasitas. *El tiempo de la legitimidad: Elecciones, autoritarismo, y democracia en México*. Cal y Arena, Mexico City, 1991.

Carlos Monsivais. *Entrada libre: Crónicas de la sociedad que se organiza*. Ediciones Era, Mexico City, 1987.

Abrahám Nuncio, ed. *La sucesión presidencial en 1988*. Grijalbo, Mexico City, 1988.

José Luis Reyna and Richard W. Weinert, eds. *Authoritarianism in Mexico*. Institute for the Study of Human Issues, Philadelphia, Pa., 1977.

Peter H. Smith. *The Labyrinths of Power: Political Recruitment in Twentieth Century Mexico*. Princeton University Press, Princeton, N.J., 1979.

Political Parties—Active

For additional historical background on all parties established before 1980 (i.e., all but the Labor Party, the National Democratic Front, the Party of the Democratic Revolution, and the Mexican Ecologist Party), see Robert J. Alexander, ed., "Mexico," in *Political Parties of the Americas*, vol. 2, 501–28 (Greenwood Press, 1982). The parties that secured their registration, based on their ability to poll at least 1.5 percent of the national vote in the official returns for the 1991 congressional elections, are marked by an asterisk.

*AUTHENTIC PARTY OF THE MEXICAN REVOLUTION (PARTIDO AUTÉNTICO DE LA REVOLUCIÓN MEXICANA—PARM). The PARM was established in 1954 by dissidents of the Institutional Revolutionary Party (PRI) who were dissatisfied with the PRI's candidates and policies. Most prominent among the founders were General Jacinto B. Treviño, a presidential candidate in 1929, and General Juan Barragán. The PARM, which first obtained its registration in 1957, has been regarded as a parastatal party, which usually supports the PRI and its national candidates but periodically provides institutional support for candidacies by dissident PRI*istas*. It has advocated protection of private property but also expansion of land reform and social programs consistent with the principles of the revolution. Its greatest strength has been in Tamaulipas, but it has also been active in Nuevo León, Jalisco, and the Federal District.

The PARM ran its own candidates for *diputado* and won several seats beginning in 1958, most often through proportional representation after 1963. Failing to win enough votes to retain its registration, the PARM lost its official status in 1982 and barely recovered it in 1985. In 1988, for the first time, the PARM nominated its own candidate for the presidency, Cuauhtémoc Cárdenas, hoping that he would capture enough votes to retain the party's registration. Indeed, the PARM won thirty *diputado* seats, five of them in single-member district elections. In the 1991 congressional elections, the PARM's support declined to 2.2 percent of the vote for the Chamber of Deputies elections, reducing its congressional delegation to fifteen deputies through proportional representation.

*CARDENISTA FRONT PARTY FOR NATIONAL RECONSTRUCTION (PARTIDO DEL FRENTE CARDENISTA DE RECONSTRUCCIÓN NACIONAL—PFCRN). The Socialist Workers' Party (PST) was founded in 1973 by Rafael Aguilar Talamantes as a Marxist party, calling for the expropriation of financial institutions and most industries and for worker and peasant management of state enterprises. Talamantes and other leaders had formed part of the Comité Nacional de Auscultación y Organización, which was founded in 1971–1972 by individuals who had been imprisoned for their involvement in the 1968 student movement. The students, intellectuals, and some peasants and urban squatters who compose the social base of the party continue to be led by Talamantes. The PST secured its registration in 1978 and won proportional representation seats in the Chamber of Deputies in 1979, 1982, and 1985 when they won eleven, nine, and twelve seats, respectively.

The PST was renamed in 1988 and supported Cárdenas in that year's presidential election as the PFCRN. The party's share of the congressional votes more than tripled between 1985 and 1988 when the party secured a total of forty-one seats, seven in single-member district contests. However, the party's support slipped considerably in 1991 to 4.4 percent of the votes for the Chamber of Deputies, for a total of twenty-three deputies, all won on proportional representation.

The PFCRN still sometimes votes with the Party of the Democratic Revolution in the congress, but it has reverted to its prior status as a parastatal party, successfully negotiating with President Carlos Salinas de Gortari and the Institutional Revolutionary Party and voting with the government on various laws, including the electoral reform law.

FRENTE DEMOCRÁTICO NACIONAL (FDN). See NATIONAL DEMOCRATIC FRONT.

*INSTITUTIONAL REVOLUTIONARY PARTY (PARTIDO REVOLUCIONARIO INSTITUCIONAL—PRI). When the ruling party was established as the National Revolutionary Party (PNR) in 1929 by General Plutarco Elías Calles, its main function was to resolve conflicts among independent special-interest parties, local political machines, regional military leaders, and some mass organizations (such as the Confederación Regional Obrera Mexicana). In addition to these groups, party membership was based on government employees, all of whom were required to join the party. The party was a loose, individual membership, territorially based coalition composed of most of the organized political groups in Mexico at the time. The party has retained this catch all character, embracing a variety of social groups often with sharply conflicting interests. While this varied composition reflects the party's co-optative skill and adaptability, it has also been the source of party factionalism and occasional major electoral defections.

President Lázaro Cárdenas reorganized the ruling party in 1938 as the Party of the Mexican Revolution (PRM), giving it features of a mass party and establishing the simultaneously sectoral and territorial organization which the party still retains. The PRM was organized into four sectors, each dominated by one highly centralized mass organization: the campesino sector, dominated by the Confederación Nacional Campesina (CNC), consisting of beneficiaries of the land reform program; the organized labor sector, composed most prominently of the Confederación de Trabajadores de México (CTM); the popular sector, with the Confederación Nacional de Organizaciones Populares (CNOP), as the peak organization after its creation in 1943 by President Manuel Avila Camacho, which represented most government employees, other middle-class professionals, small merchants, private rural landowners, and low-income urban neighborhood groups; and finally, the military sector. By the end of the Cárdenas era, political activity by high-ranking military men had been further restricted within a set of civilian-dominated institutions. The military sector was eliminated as a separate entity in 1940, and most of its members were folded into the CNOP by President Miguel Alemán, who reorganized and renamed the party the Institutional Revolutionary Party in 1946.

The party is governed by the National Executive Committee (Comité Ejecutivo Nacional—CEN); the National Council (Consejo Nacional), which monitors the work of state and municipal assemblies; and the National Assembly, which consists of 1,500 representatives chosen in municipal and state assemblies who meet infrequently to ratify the work of the CEN. The National Assembly has met also in November before presidential elections to ratify the CEN's nominee for the party's presidential nomination. Luis Donaldo Colossio has been president of the party since 1988.

Although the revolution did not produce a formal ideology, it did yield a loose set of symbols, myths, or principles that have come to be known as the "ideology of the Mexican revolution." Among the most important of these principles are social justice (including agrarian reform and labor's right to organize), economic nationalism (at least in terms of state ownership of subsoil resources), limitations on the wealth and influence of the Catholic Church, and freedom from self-perpetuating dictatorship, symbolized by the slogan "effective suffrage, no reelection" (*sufragio efectivó, no reelección*). The PRI has formally adopted this ideology of the revolution as its own, even though the PRI government's policies are not consistent with this set of principles. Presidents Miguel de la Madrid (1982–1988) and Carlos Salinas de Gortari (1988–1994) have modified the government's stand on some of these issues. Both have opened up the economy to more foreign investment and to increased international trade. Salinas has moved toward rapprochement with the Catholic Church and, in November 1991, he proposed legislation that would lead to substantial changes in the legal status and organization of the *ejidos* (community lands).

Despite Calles's design, the PRI has not always been able to contain elite conflict within its institutional boundaries. The PRI has experienced several serious ruptures within the party elite which have led to electoral defections and to the formation of new political parties, for example, the opposition candidacies of General Jacinto B. Treviño in 1929, General Juan Andreu Almazán in 1940, Ezekiel Padilla in 1946, and Miguel Henríquez Guzmán in 1952. The most spectacular, most recent schism within the PRI was provoked by the prospect of the 1988 presidential elections.

In August 1986, several nationally prominent PRI*istas*, led by Cuauhtémoc Cárdenas and Porfirio Muñoz Ledo, formed the Democratic Current (Corriente Democrática—CD) within the PRI. The CD drew from the nationalist wing of the party (critical of the recent economic policy) and from a group of reformists who called for broader participation in the party's candidate selection process. The CD's proposals, which focused particularly on presidential succession, were rejected, and many of the members withdrew from the party in October 1987 to form the National Democratic Front (FDN).

The departure of the leadership of the CD from the PRI and their unexpectedly strong electoral showing in 1988, supporting Cárdenas for the presidency, further polarized the PRI, already deeply divided over economic policy and political reform. At a minimum, the party now includes a traditional, nationalist-populist wing, and a more internationalist, technocratic wing committed to neoliberal economic policies. This division over economic policy is further crosscut by one faction, which resists conceding power to opposition political parties or to reformists within the PRI, and another, which would support more open political competition. These conflicts have greatly complicated the task of party reform.

The decline in voter support for the PRI, which began in the congressional elections in 1964, did not threaten the party's grasp on state governorships or a majority of the congressional single-member districts until the mid-1980s. However, a series of highly charged municipal and gubernatorial elections in 1983, 1985, and 1986 posed serious challenges from the National Action Party (PAN).

In 1988 opposition parties officially defeated the PRI in 66 of the country's 300 single-member district electoral contests, leaving the PRI in a position of a bare majority in the Chamber of Deputies with 260 seats. This was not enough to pass a constitutional amendment by the two-thirds margin constitutionally required without forming alliances with other parties. This figure represented nearly as many defeats in one year as the party had conceded to the opposition between 1946 and 1985. In the official returns for the presidential election, the PRI's candidate, Salinas, tabulated a bare majority of 50.7 percent if annulled and null ballots are excluded from the tally. For the first time, the PRI candidate lost a majority of the presidential vote in five states to the candidate of the FDN (Baja California Norte, Distrito Federal, Michoacán, Morelos, and the state of México).

In 1991 the party recovered considerable support, winning 61.5 percent of the votes for the Chamber of Deputies, 290 single-member districts, and 30 proportional representation seats for a total of 320. In the Senate, the party won thirty-one of thirty-two elections, reducing opposition representation in the Senate to three (two for the Party of the Democratic Revolution, or PRD, and one for the PAN).

Based on analyses of public opinion surveys and electoral returns, support for the PRI has been declining for some time. Between 1961 and 1991, the PRI's share of the vote for elections in the Chamber of Deputies declined from 90.2 percent to 61.5 percent. Support waned particularly among the better educated and younger members of the electorate, among urban voters, and among middle-class voters. Salinas polled his highest vote totals in the poorest, rural states of Chiapas, Tabasco, and Campeche, although he also ran strong in Puebla and Nuevo León.

A key element in the PRI's decline, especially during the 1980s, has been the collapse of support from the middle class and the demise of the so-called sectoral vote, that is, the votes of major population segments that fall within the purview of the party's sectoral organizations. Each of the party's sectors has ceased to defend the interests of rank-and-file members. Campesinos have formed dissident movements outside of the CNC to advance their claims against the state when the CNC has been unwilling to articulate or satisfy their demands for land reform, higher crop prices and better access to markets, protection of the rural ecology, and more jobs in rural areas. In fact, in November 1991, President Salinas proposed constitutional reforms which would lead to dramatic changes in land ownership, access to credit, and the organization of production in the *ejidos*. At the same time, the labor sector has been unable to resist the government's economic austerity and restructuring policies of the 1980s which led to real wage declines and soaring underemployment before showing an improvement at the end of the decade.

Meanwhile, the Salinas government has supported a number of new-generation labor union leaders, such as Francisco Hernández Suárez, leader of the union at Teléfonos de México, forcibly deposing the old-line leaders of the petroleum workers' union (Joaquín Hernández Galicia, "La Quina") and of the National Union of Workers in Education (SNTE) (Carlos Jonguitud Barrios). He has also supported small rural producers' organizations and urban popular movements, via the National Solidarity Program, or PRONASOL. This support reduces the influence of old-guard PRI*ista* sectoral leaders and, emphasizing territorial political activity, further undermines the sectoral organizations.

Of the three sectors of the PRI, only the popular sector has been restructured to reflect the changes in Mexican society. Until quite recently, the CNOP's active membership has consisted mainly of government bureaucrats, teachers, and workers in the public marketplaces of urban centers. As a result, the popular sector has not been very effective in structuring the political participation of the growing middle classes in the private sector, or the low-income, nonunionized urban labor force, who constitute the majority of the economically active population in most cities. In 1990 the CNOP was renamed the Unión Nacional Electoral (UNE) and restructured into five movements to make it more attractive to urban social movements and other previously organized population segments.

Nonetheless, in late 1991, the government employees unions, especially the Federation of Unions of State Workers (FSTSE) and the SNTE, were still the organized core of the UNE.

Reformists within the party have periodically called for open primary elections for the party's nominations. Abortive experiments with open primaries were conducted in a few states by party presidents Alfonso Corona del Rosal in the mid-1960s, Jesús Reyes Heroles in the mid-1970s, and again in the mid-1980s by Jorge de la Vega Domínguez, but the primaries were suspended each time amid much confusion and anger among the disappointed contenders and their followers. In 1989 President Salinas again began selectively to authorize municipal and gubernatorial PRI primaries with very mixed results. In the state of Chihuahua, open municipal primaries were used successfully to revive and rebuild popular support for a PRI apparatus that had lost much ground to the PAN during the 1980s. In March 1991, two open gubernatorial primaries were held in Nuevo León and Colima, but these experiments were marred by the use of standard vote fraud tactics. However much open primaries, or more open nominating conventions, might change the party's rank and file, its candidates, and its image, they are not likely to be adopted without a significant restructuring of the party's sectors. The leaders of the sectoral organizations have zealously guarded the power associated with the ability to nominate candidates.

The party's last three presidential candidates (José López Portillo, de la Madrid, and Salinas) have all been chosen from the national political leadership with considerable political skills but very limited party experience and no experience in elective office. Their cabinets have also been composed in large measure of individuals whose careers have been made in the bureaucracy, in part based on their technical expertise earned in advanced university studies at home and abroad. This has fueled debates to open up the process of selecting party candidates. The closest the party has come to open competition for the nomination was in 1987 when President de la Madrid for the first time publicly identified six precandidates for the nomination before finally making his decision among them in the time-honored, behind-closed-doors tradition.

The most recent reforms of the PRI's internal governance statutes were approved at the party's fourteenth National Assembly, held in September 1990. The PRI's sectoral structure was retained, but opportunities were created for individuals and groups not affiliated with any sectoral organization (such as PRONASOL affiliates) to join the party. The representation of local and state committees in the PRI's decision-making bodies was increased to give them parity with the sectoral organizations. The assembly also resolved that all PRI candidates for elective office, except the presidency, must demonstrate the support of a specific percentage of the "directive committees" of PRI-affiliated organizations or of the registered voters in a given district. This expression of support should lead to the final selection of PRI candidates at party conventions, to which delegates will be "elected democratically." However, under a "unanimity rule," also approved by the assembly, action by a party nominating convention can be waived in the event that only one candidate comes forward for a given office. There was little evidence of the implementation of the new selection rules in the nominations for the 1991 midterm congressional elections.

Another reform approved by the assembly involves a change in the procedure for selecting the PRI's presidential nominee, beginning in 1993. To prevent another schism, similar to that of 1987–1988, when the closed, secretive nature of the presidential selection process was the dissidents' principal complaint, the new PRI statutes call for the party's presidential candidate to be selected by a National Political Council composed of 150 prominent party members, who will vote by secret ballot. However, the president retains the power to nominate party leaders personally loyal to him as members of the National Political Council, and their votes are likely to reflect his preference.

LABOR PARTY (PARTIDO DEL TRABAJO—PT). The Labor Party emerged out of the radical left which formed around the 1968 student movement and followed a "mass line" in organizational strategy. The most important of these groups was the Organization of the Revolutionary Left, Mass Line (Organización de Izquierda Revolucionaria, Linea de Masas—OIR/LM). Cadre from this group participated in the formation of urban popular movements in squatter settlements including the Popular Front Land and Liberty (Frente Popular Tierra y Libertad—FPTyL), in Monterrey; the Committees for Popular Defense (Comités de Defensa Popular), in Durango and Chihuahua; the Movement of the Revolutionary Left (Movimiento de Izquierda Revolucionaria), in León; and the Popular Organization of Street Venders (Unión Popular de Vendedores Ambulantes de 18 de Octubre), in Puebla. All of these popular movements followed a Maoist strategy of popular organization.

By the time the PT was formed in 1990, the OIR/LM group was joined by smaller groups from the Proletarian Line (Linea Proletaria), the Popular Transition (Transición Popular), the Union Alternative (Alternative Sindical), and the Committee for Popular Defense in Chihuahua. Until 1990 most of these organizations had stridently disavowed electoral competition.

The distinctive feature of the party in 1991 was that it represented the first case of popular movements expanding their strategy to include the adoption of partisan, electoral politics but by forming their own political party rather than by adhering to an already existing one.

The PT has been led by Alberto Anaya, a leader of the FPTyL, and Luis Hernández Navarro, a former leader of the dissident teachers' union, the National Coordinating Committee of Workers in Education (Coordinadora Nacional de Trabajadores en la Educación—CNTE). Most leaders of the party are simultaneously leaders of popular organizations and of the party.

The party's electoral platform called for reforms in the electoral law, in the judiciary, and in the mass media and its ties to the state; an end to corporatist political organization (sectors of the Institutional Revolutionary Party—PRI); statehood for the Valley of Mexico; the defense of human rights; and consideration of environmental issues. In the 1991 midterm elections, the party polled only 1.14 percent of the national vote; its support was concentrated in Durango, Nayarit, Chihuahua, Zacatecas, and Nuevo León.

MEXICAN COMMUNIST PARTY (PARTIDO COMUNISTA MEXICANO—PCM), MEXICAN SOCIALIST PARTY (PARTIDO MEXICANO SOCIALISTA—PMS), and UNIFIED SOCIALIST PARTY OF MEXICO (PARTIDO SOCIALISTA UNIFICADO DE MÉXICO—PSUM). The most disciplined core of the Mexican left is composed of remnants of the oldest political party in Mexico, the Mexican Communist Party (PCM), which was established as a vanguard party in 1919 by M. N. Roy, Francisco Cervantes López, and Charles F. Phillips. Early prominent activists also included Ursulo Galván and muralists David Alfaro Siqueiros and Diego Rivera. Throughout the 1920s, the PCM cadre was influential in local and regional politics, particularly in issues involving public schools, labor organization, and, on occasion, agrarian concerns. The party published several newspapers and journals, including El Machete.

At its peak in the late 1930s, the PCM had only 35,000 to 40,000 members and thus has never been a mass party. While frequently internally divided, the party has been coherent and disciplined in its relations with other parties and the government. Until it was influenced by the Eurocommunism of the 1970s, the PCM was closely linked to the Soviet Communist Party, and it would have been characterized as Stalinist at least in its national organization.

Despite its early establishment, the PCM was not legally registered as a party until the presidency of Lázaro Cárdenas, the period of its largest membership and its maximum influence within the state apparatus. Before 1934, PCM members had been active mostly in labor organizations (the CGT and the CROM) and intermittently in the establishment of peasant organizations (especially the Liga Nacional Campesina Ursulo Galván). Under Cárdenas, the PCM supported government policies of agrarian reform, expropriation of foreign-owned oil companies, and the nationalization of the railroads. Some party cadres were also active in the CTM and influential in shaping the policy of "socialist education."

The PCM suffered serious blows from the Hitler-Stalin pact, the outbreak of World War II, and the assassination of Leon Trotsky in Mexico in 1940. When the party failed to meet the minimum membership requirements of the new electoral code of 1946, it lost its legal registration. PCM cadres returned to a strategy of political consciousness raising and mobilization within some labor unions, but they encountered strong anti-Communist resistance and repression. The party lost some members to the Worker and Peasant Party of Mexico (POCM), established in 1940, and to the Popular Party (PP), which gained its registration in 1949.

From 1946 through the 1960s, the PCM's core base of support remained urban (intellectuals, a few teachers, students, and some pockets within industrial unions), and, territorially, it was concentrated in Mexico City, Oaxaca, among some peasant organizations in the Laguna, and the mountainous parts of Guerrero state. Depending on their relations with the Comintern, the PCM was led off and on in the 1940s by Dionisio Encina, Valentín Campa, and Hernán Laborde. During the 1960s and 1970s, the PCM, maintaining a strict position against armed struggle, led the party to expel the guerrilla leader, Lucio Cabañas, and his followers in the early 1970s.

Arnaldo Martínez Verdugo was secretary general of the party after 1964. Valentín Campa was the party's candidate for the presidency in 1976, but he could not appear on the ballot because the party was not registered.

Reregistered in 1978 as a legal party under the terms of the 1977 electoral reform, the PCM managed to win 5 percent of the national vote (and eighteen deputies) in the 1979 congressional elections with the support of the unregistered Revolutionary Socialist Party (PSR) and the Mexican Popular Party (PPM). During the 1980s, the PCM participated in a series of party mergers intended to broaden its social base of support and to unify the leftist opposition. Despite the mergers, the coalition's share of the vote was never again as high as it was in 1979. In each of these mergers, the PCM faction remained the most coherent, disciplined, and organized of the elements in the coalition. In 1982, to bolster the left's prospects in the elections of 1982 and 1985, the PCM ceded its legal registration to the newly formed Unified Socialist Party of Mexico (PSUM).

The PSUM involved a merger between the PCM and four small, unregistered parties established out of the 1968 student movement and the independent trade union movement: the Movement for Popular Action (Movimiento de Acción Popular—MAP), which was founded in 1980 by intellectuals and independent trade unionists, especially electrical workers; the Movement for Socialist Action and Unity (Movimiento de Acción y Unidad Socialista—MAUS); the Revolutionary Socialist Party (Partido Revolucionario Socialista—PRS); and the Socialist Revolutionary Party (Partido Socialista Revolucionario—PSR), which emerged from the Socialist Workers' Party (PST). The PRS initially had been established as the Party of the Mexican People (Partido del Pueblo Mexicano—PPM) in 1976 by dissidents from the Popular Socialist Party (PPS). It briefly joined the PSUM between 1981 and 1985 before it established its own independence.

The new PSUM garnered 4.4 percent of the congressional vote in 1982 and 3.2 percent in 1985, retaining its legal registration in both instances. The party's candidate for the presidency in 1982 was Martínez Verdugo.

In 1987, anticipating the upcoming presidential elections, four small, unregistered parties of the left and the PMT joined forces with the PSUM to form the Mexican Socialist Party (PMS). The four small parties were the Revolutionary Movement of the People (Movimiento Revolucionario del Pueblo), the Patriotic Revolutionary Party (Partido Patriótico Revolucionario), dissidents from the PST, and the Left Unity (Unidad de Izquierda). Heberto Castillo Martínez (of the PMT) won the party's presidential nomination through open regional primary elections conducted by the party. However, as Cuauhtémoc

Cárdenas's popularity grew, the PMS leadership compared public opinion polls on the prospects of Castillo and the National Democratic Front's Cárdenas. Castillo reluctantly surrendered his position as PMS candidate for the presidency to Cárdenas, who replaced him on the party ballot. PMS candidates won nineteen proportional representation seats in the congressional vote in 1988 (compared with eighteen seats in 1979, sixteen in 1982, and twelve in 1985).

In 1989 the PMS ceded its registration to the newly formed Party of the Democratic Revolution (PRD). *See also* National Democratic Front.

MEXICAN DEMOCRAT PARTY (PARTIDO DEMÓCRATA MEXICANO—PDM). The PDM defines the extreme right of the political spectrum in Mexico. Its origins are in the National Sinarquista Union (UNS), which was established in León, Guanajuato, in 1937. The UNS drew support from conservative Catholics, including campesinos who had been involved during the previous decade in the armed insurrection against the state and in defense of the Catholic Church (*la Cristiada*) and who were disturbed as well by the statist and socialist policies of the Cárdenas administration. Divided by World War II, the Sinarquistas regrouped and moderated their position after the war, briefly establishing a political party which ultimately lost its registration.

Later, remnants of the UNS, led by Juan Aguilera Azpeitia, established the PDM in 1971–1972 again in the state of Guanajuato. The PDM also took up the cause of the Catholic Church, defending the clergy, parochial education, and closer ties between church and state. The party took a strong stand against communism and government corruption. Within four years, it had expanded its platform to include a spirited defense of privatization, including the *ejidos*.

The PDM, which secured legal registration in 1978, was successful in appealing to conservative peasants, small landowners, and middle- and lower-middle-class groups in the country's central plateau region (Guanajuato, northeastern Jalisco, San Luis Potosí, and Michoacán) and won municipal presidencies and several proportional representation congressional seats in 1979 (nineteen seats), 1982 (nine seats), and 1985 (twelve seats). In 1982 the party's presidential candidate, Ignacio González Gollaz, polled 2.28 percent of the vote. However, the party's popularity slipped in 1988 when its presidential candidate was Gumersindo Magaña, and it lost its registration which it was unable to recover in 1991 when PDM candidates won only 1.08 percent of the congressional vote. It does not have any representation in the Chamber of Deputies for the 1991–1994 legislative session.

MEXICAN ECOLOGIST PARTY (PARTIDO ECOLOGISTA MEXICANO—PEM). This party, which arose out of the Mexican Ecologist Movement (Movimiento Ecologista Mexicano) early in the 1980s, was led by Alfonso Ciprés Villareal and Jorge González Torres. The two leaders later split; González Torres formed the National Ecologist Alliance (Alianza Ecologista Nacional) and in 1985 the Mexican Green Ecologist Party (Partido Verde Ecologista

Mexicano), which dropped the "green" to gain its registration as the PEM in 1985.

The PEM began by opposing the nuclear power plant in Laguna Verde and the airport expansion in Mexico City, but it has addressed a wide range of environmental and ecological issues in Mexico. González Torres continues to lead the party with a nearly mystical personal style, organizing to promote awareness of ecological issues and problems and to secure respect for the environment. The PEM has a diffuse organizational base.

In 1991 its strongest base of support was in the Mexico City metropolitan area where it won enough votes in the midterm elections to secure registration as a local party and to win representation on the Assembly of Representatives (Asamblea de Representantes) of the Distrito Federal. Elsewhere, it also had support in Jalisco, Morelos, and Michoacán. Nationally, however, its votes totaled only 1.46 percent of the national vote, hundredths of a point shy of the 1.5 percent required for registration as a national political party.

MEXICAN POPULAR PARTY (PARTIDO POPULAR MEXICANO). *See* MEXICAN COMMUNIST PARTY.

MEXICAN SOCIALIST PARTY (PARTIDO MEXICANO SOCIALISTA. *See* MEXICAN COMMUNIST PARTY.

MEXICAN WORKERS' PARTY (PARTIDO MEXICANO DE LOS TRA-BAJADORES—PMT). The PMT was founded in 1974 by Heberto Castillo Martínez, a civil engineer from Veracruz, and Demetrio Vallejo, once a member of the Mexican Communist Party (PCM) and a veteran of the bitter railroad workers' strikes in 1958 and 1959. Both men also had been members of the Comité Nacional de Auscultación y Coordinación, an organization developed in 1971 and 1972 by individuals who had been active in a range of political activities on the left between 1958 and 1968 and who had been imprisoned for their participation in the student movement in 1968.

The PMT has favored economic nationalism, a strong role for the state in the economy, and a strong defense of the rights of workers. It has been most closely associated with the independent railroad and electrical workers.

The party declined to participate in elections in 1978 and 1982, arguing that the process was too much controlled by the Institutional Revolutionary Party; however, the PMT applied to register and to run in the 1985 congressional elections. Clinging precariously in 1985 to a small share of the vote in congressional elections (1.6 percent) that barely allowed the party to register, in 1987 the PMT joined with the Unified Socialist Party of Mexico to establish the Mexican Socialist Party, which itself later joined the Party of the Democratic Revolution in 1989. (*See also* Party of the Democratic Revolution.)

•NATIONAL ACTION PARTY (PARTIDO DE ACCIÓN NACIONAL—PAN). For more than fifty years, Mexico's best organized national opposition party has been the PAN, founded in 1939 by Manuel Gómez Morín who remained the party's president through 1949. The PAN was established largely as a reaction to the political and economic reforms initiated under President Lázaro Cárdenas, and in defense of Catholic social principles. Its founders were Catholic professionals supported initially by some businessmen. Throughout its history, the party has maintained its opposition to the anticlerical provisions of the 1917 constitution, especially the government's monopoly over public education and prohibitions on the clergy's right to participate in politics and to vote. The PAN has focused programmatically on the Institutional Revolutionary Party (PRI) and on the government's abuse of power and resources. Harkening to the revolutionary promise of "effective suffrage," the PAN has been strident in its criticism of electoral fraud. It has criticized federal incursions on municipal autonomy and state government, and it has harshly condemned corruption among public officials. During the 1950s and 1960s, under the guidance of Adolfo Christlieb, Manuel González Hinojosa, and Efraín González Morfín, the PAN adopted party platforms emphasizing Christian humanism. However, the expansionary and interventionist economic policies of presidents Luis Echeverría Alvarez (1970–1976) and José López Portillo (1976–1982), together with highly publicized cases of official corruption in high places, led the PAN to reassert its commitment to a lean state and the guaranteed sanctity of private property. This strengthened the more conservative, free-market-oriented wing of the PAN, led by José Angel Conchello and Pablo Emilio Madero.

Most particularly, President López Portillo's decision to nationalize the banking system in September 1982 was viewed by elements of the business community as a flagrant abuse of state power which severely threatened private property and the carefully negotiated economic spaces reserved to the private sector. Some businessmen, who had until that time withheld their financial support from the PAN, began to channel money into the opposition party; a few opted to run for elective office on the PAN ticket. One of the most prominent of these new candidates was Manuel Clouthier, the party's presidential candidate in 1988 and gubernatorial candidate in Sinaloa in 1985. Other leaders of business organizations who became active in the PAN include Fernando Canales Clariond, Emilio Goicochea Luna, José Luis Coindreau, and José María Basagoiti.

These broad shifts in PAN*ista* ideology and tactics were not accomplished without internal conflict. Indeed, since the mid-1970s, the PAN has been divided into moderate-progressive and militant-conservative (*neopanista, doctrinario*) factions, which have jockeyed for control of the party machinery and have carried out purges of opposing faction members when they were in power within the party. Since the late 1980s, with the government's shift to neoliberal economic policies, the most divisive issues within the PAN have been strategic rather than ideological. The conflict centers on whether the PAN should negotiate with the state and ruling party in order to gradually gain electoral and institutional concessions (the position of the pragmatists), or whether it should preserve an uncompromising opposition and doctrinal purity to shape and educate the voting public (the position of *doctrinarios* and *neopanistas*).

Since 1988 the divisions within the PAN have been widened by the willingness of the moderate leadership under Luis H. Alvarez to make tactical alliances with the Salinas government, a strategy opposed by the party's Foro Doctrinario y Democrático and its principal spokesman, Conchello. This collaboration has included a congressional alliance between PAN*istas* and PRI*istas* to secure passage of constitutional amendments to the electoral laws and reprivatization of the banks, in exchange for the promise of cleaner elections and greater opposition representation on the federal commission to certify electoral results.

Among Mexico's opposition parties, the PAN has by far the most extensive national organization. Its most committed electoral constituency has been the urban middle and lower-middle classes, particularly in northern border states and the Mexico City metropolitan area. However, it has also been able to attract some support among socially conservative peasants in several states and among the working class in urban areas. Women have also been very important in the party's local committees and have been crucial to its efforts to defend the PAN vote against PRI–government fraud. Territorially, the PAN has developed its strongest organizational base in the northern border states, Jalisco, Guanajuato, Yucatán, and Mexico City.

The PAN has concentrated its resources in contesting local and federal elections in its regional strongholds. However, since 1946, the party has developed a nominal presence throughout the country, and it regularly fields candidates for a wide range of elected positions. The PAN has been strongly represented in gubernatorial, legislative, and municipal elections in the states of Chihuahua, Sonora, and Baja California Norte. PAN candidates have won elections for the Chamber of Deputies since 1946. (PAN*istas* won their first municipal elections the same year in Michoacán and Oaxaca.) In the 1988 elections, official returns gave the PAN the second largest contingent of deputies (after the PRI) with 101 *diputados*, 38 in single-member districts and 63 by proportional representation. The party repeated this feat, but with a declining number of deputies, in 1991, with ten single-member district victories and seventy-nine proportional representation seats, won by polling 17.7 percent of the votes for the Chamber of Deputies. It also won its first Senate seat.

The PAN has also won more than a score of municipal presidencies, including such major cities as Hermosillo, Ciudad Juárez, Chihuahua, Tijuana, and Mérida. It is widely assumed to have won, or come close to winning, the gubernatorial elections in Sonora (1985) and Chihuahua (1986) and to have been the victim of serious irregularities in Nuevo León in 1985 and Guanajuato in 1991. However, the first gubernatorial candidate of any opposition party to have his victory officially recognized since 1929 was PAN*ista* Ernesto Ruffo Appel, a businessman with no prior experience in elective office, who became the governor of the state of Baja California Norte in 1989.

Although the PAN nominated its first presidential candidate (Efraín González Luna) in 1952, it did not employ open party nominating conventions until 1958. For the party to name a presidential candidate, the party rules require 80 percent of the convention delegates to support the nominee. In the 1958 presidential election, the PAN*ista* candidate (Luis H. Alvarez) won 9.42 percent of the vote and with it placed second in the national vote totals. The party's nominee has retained second place in each subsequent election except 1976 (when the PAN failed to nominate a presidential candidate) and 1988 (when the PAN's Clouthier surrendered second place to Cuauhtémoc Cárdenas of the National Democratic Front). In each presidential election until 1988, the PAN's candidates (Christlieb in 1964, with 11.1 percent; González Morfín in 1970, with 13.9 percent; and Madero in 1982, with 15.7 percent) gained a rising share of the presidential vote. The 16.8 percent share of the votes accorded to the PAN's presidential candidate Clouthier in 1988 and the 17.3 percent share of the congressional vote won by the party's candidates probably represents the core of the PAN's *national* share of the electorate. Clouthier won his largest share of the vote in Sinaloa, Guanajuato, Chihuahua, and Jalisco, states in which he polled between 30 and 38 percent of the total vote. (In some regions, for local elections, the support for the PAN has been much higher.)

Currently the PAN does not have many leaders of national stature and broad appeal, especially after Clouthier died in an automobile accident in October 1989. Ruffo (governor of Baja California, 1989–1995), Alvarez (party president, former presidential candidate, and former mayor of Chihuahua City), Abel Vicencio Tovar (head of the party's congressional delegation in 1988–1991), Conchello, and Madero (both past presidents of the party) do not have the personal following and magnetism that would pose a strong challenge to the PRI's presidential nominee in future elections. Furthermore, especially since 1982, the PAN has found it difficult to define a national project or set of policies that constitutes a clear alternative to the PRI government's own policies of privatization, deregulation, integration with the U.S. and world economies, and rapprochement with the Catholic Church. These issues, which had been banners of the PAN, once helped differentiate it from the PRI. Government corruption and electoral fraud are the two distinctive issues that remain on the PAN's agenda, but these do not add up to a positive, alternative program, and since 1988 the leftist Party of the Democratic Revolution has more effectively exploited the fraud issue.

NATIONAL DEMOCRATIC FRONT (FRENTE DEMOCRÁTICO NACIONAL—FDN). In August 1986, a group of national leaders formed the Democratic Current (Corriente Democrática—CD) within the Institutional Revolutionary Party (PRI). Led by Cuauhtémoc Cárdenas, Porfirio Muñoz Ledo, and others, they argued for change in the party's candidate selection process and for a change in the policy of economic restructuring. When their position was rejected by the PRI, many left the party.

After he left the PRI in October 1987, Cárdenas accepted the presidential nomination of the Authentic Party of the Mexican Revolution (PARM). Later, the Socialist Workers' Party, the Cardenista Front Party for National Reconstruction, dissidents from the PRI, and—just one month before the July elections—the Mexican Socialist Party (PMS) joined the PARM to form an electoral coalition, the National Democratic Front (FDN). In 1988 the FDN thus became the second most popular political force in Mexico, although it was not really a political party. The FDN worked to support Cárdenas's campaign for the presidency and to present a unified, nationalist challenge to the PRI. Each party or political organization within the coalition retained its own identity. In some cases, the FDN supported a single candidate for the 1988 elections, but in others the parties in the coalition ran their own candidates. For the 1988–1991 legislative session, the FDN won four senatorships and thirteen single-member district seats in the Chamber of Deputies. Proportional representation seats were distributed among the parties in the coalition since only they could claim the right of proportional representation.

Cárdenas campaigned for a moratorium on debt payments, for a more aggressive policy to deal with poverty in the countryside, and for a limit on oil exports. Like his father before him, he gathered large crowds, which were drawn to the man and what he symbolized.

According to official returns for the 1988 elections, the FDN's candidate, Cárdenas, was the second most popular candidate, winning 31.1 percent of the official returns in the presidential vote. Cárdenas accused the government of fraudulently depriving him of victory by a "technical coup." For the first time, the PRI's presidential candidate was defeated (by Cárdenas) in the Federal District and in Morelos, Michoacán, Baja California Norte, and the state of Mexico. In these states, the FDN's candidate polled between 49 and 64 percent of the vote.

Following the election, Cárdenas and other leaders of the FDN urged the formation of a new party, the Party of the Democratic Revolution, to which the PMS gave its registration in 1989. (See also Party of the Democratic Revolution.)

PARTIDO AUTÉNTICO DE LA REVOLUCIÓN MEXICANA. See AUTHENTIC PARTY OF THE MEXICAN REVOLUTION.

PARTIDO DE ACCIÓN NACIONAL. See NATIONAL ACTION PARTY.

PARTIDO COMUNISTA MEXICANO. See MEXICAN COMMUNIST PARTY.

PARTIDO DE LA REVOLUCIÓN DEMOCRÁTICA. See PARTY OF THE DEMOCRATIC REVOLUTION.

PARTIDO DEL FRENTE CARDENISTA DE RECONSTRUCCIÓN NA-CIONAL. *See* CARDENISTA FRONT PARTY FOR NATIONAL RECONSTRUCTION.

PARTIDO DEL TRABAJO. *See* LABOR PARTY.

PARTIDO DEMÓCRATA MEXICANO. *See* MEXICAN DEMOCRAT PARTY.

PARTIDO ECOLOGISTA MEXICANO. *See* MEXICAN ECOLOGIST PARTY.

PARTIDO MEXICANO DE LOS TRABAJADORES. *See* MEXICAN WORKERS' PARTY.

PARTIDO MEXICANO SOCIALISTA (MEXICAN SOCIALIST PARTY). *See* MEXICAN COMMUNIST PARTY.

PARTIDO POPULAR (POPULAR PARTY). *See* POPULAR SOCIALIST PARTY.

PARTIDO POPULAR MEXICANO (MEXICAN POPULAR PARTY). *See* MEXICAN COMMUNIST PARTY.

PARTIDO POPULAR SOCIALISTA. *See* POPULAR SOCIALIST PARTY.

PARTIDO REVOLUCIONARIO DE LOS TRABAJADORES. *See* REVOLUTIONARY WORKERS' PARTY.

PARTIDO REVOLUCIONARIO INSTITUCIONAL. *See* INSTITUTIONAL REVOLUTIONARY PARTY.

PARTIDO SOCIALISTA DE LOS TRABAJADORES (SOCIALIST WORKERS' PARTY). *See* CARDENISTA FRONT PARTY FOR NATIONAL RECONSTRUCTION.

PARTIDO SOCIALISTA UNIFICADO DE MEXICO (UNIFIED SOCIALIST PARTY OF MEXICO). *See* MEXICAN COMMUNIST PARTY.

*PARTY OF THE DEMOCRATIC REVOLUTION (PARTIDO DE LA REVOLUCIÓN DEMOCRÁTICA—PRD). Finding no satisfaction within the ruling Institutional Revolutionary Party (PRI), leaders of the Democratic Current within the PRI left the party. Together with the Authentic Party of the Mexican Revolution (PARM), the Cardenista Front Party for National Reconstruction

(PFCRN), the Socialist Workers' Party (PST), and the Mexican Socialist Party (PMS), they formed the National Democratic Front (FDN) as an electoral coalition in 1988.

In November 1988, Cuauhtémoc Cárdenas and some other leaders of the FDN coalition (Porfirio Muñoz Ledo, Ifigenia Martínez, Adolfo Gilly, Gilberto Rincón Gallardo, Arnaldo Córdova, and Jorge Alcócer, among others) called for the formation of a new party, which was formally founded in May 1989 as the Party of the Democratic Revolution. The PMS conceded its party registration to the new PRD. The PRD brought together a disparate group of partisan and quasi-partisan groups on the left: the PMS, the Movement toward Socialism (Movimiento al Socialismo—MAS), the National Revolutionary Civic Association (Asociación Cívica Nacional Revolucionaria—ACNR), Punto Crítico, dissident defectors from the PRI, and citizens without prior party affiliation.

The PRD's program has been characterized as nationalist, popular, and democratic. Its nationalism derives from the ardent defense of principles of national sovereignty over economic policy, political reform, and foreign policy. It is "popular" in its social base of support, its concern about the social costs of economic restructuring, and its defense of rights won through the revolution by workers and peasants. Finally, it is "democratic" in its call for an end to parties of the state, respect for the vote, alternation in power, broad discussion of national policy (versus centralized imposition of policy decisions), and protection of human rights.

The PRD has been deeply divided over issues of party organization, political strategy, and leadership. Governed by a National Council (Consejo Nacional) of 300 people and a 32-member National Executive Committee (Comité Ejecutivo Nacional), it remains a heterogeneous front. Its first fractious party congress was held in November 1990. It is still composed of remnants of earlier parties and movements and the strong personalities who led them, masking numerous ideological and strategic differences. PRD leaders struggle to balance the need for representation of these differences within the party against the need to construct a strong, coherent electoral vehicle capable of effectively challenging the PRI. Current divisions within the PRD center on questions of democracy in party governance and on strategies for dealing with the PRI–government apparatus (negotiation versus permanent confrontation).

In party governance, divisions have arisen within the PRD over the process for nominating party candidates to compete in elections, selecting lists of candidates for multimember districts, and choosing members of the party's national executive committee. One faction, identified with PRD leader Cárdenas, seems to favor a strong central direction; other party activists press for broad participation in party governance.

As far as political strategy is concerned, the most important debates within the PRD, and the Mexican left as a whole, revolve around two sets of choices: whether to negotiate with the state for gradual reform or to engage in antisystem behavior and whether to emphasize electoral competition or political education and support for social movements and class-based organizations in civil society.

Since the 1988 election, the parties of the loyal opposition, for example, the PFCRN, the PARM, and the PPS, have been willing to negotiate with the PRI, especially in the congress. One wing of the PRD has also argued for a strategy of selectively negotiating with the state. This strategy is opposed by Cárdenas and other members of the PRD's national leadership, who refuse to negotiate with a government that they consider illegitimate because of its fraudulent accession to power and its failure to defend the principles and programs of the Mexican revolution. This faction has been unwilling to collaborate with government initiatives, such as the 1990 electoral reform law, and has been much more inclined to advocate public demonstrations, confrontations in the congress, and other forms of resistance. The intransigence of one wing has been fueled by the violence targeted at FDN and PRD candidates and supporters during the 1988 campaign and in subsequent elections, especially in Michoacán, Morelos, and Guanajuato in 1990.

Reference to these divisions should not obscure the consensus that *does* exist within the PRD on issues of public policy. There is general agreement about the need to retain an independent foreign policy which protects national sovereignty. There is general opposition to neoliberal economic policies, especially because of the high social costs of such policies, the implied abdication of national control over the economy, and the way in which these policies have been imposed from above without public debate. There is acceptance of the idea that Mexico will become more integrated into the world economy, but this is qualified by arguments that such integration should be carefully negotiated, based upon broad social consultation, and with careful consideration of the distribution of the social costs.

Like the National Action Party (PAN), the PRD is stronger in some regions than in others. Its principal bases of voter support are in the Mexico City metropolitan area and in the states of Michoacán and Guerrero. In addition, the PRD has developed a core of party activists in Veracruz, Tabasco, and Oaxaca. It has retained the urban voters who traditionally supported the independent parties of the left, but it has also begun to attract support away from the PRI in rural areas.

The PRD's fortunes in electoral contests since 1988 have been highly variable. For example, in 1989, its candidates won nearly half of the municipal presidencies in Michoacán, sixteen each in Guerrero and Oaxaca, and six in Puebla; however, in 1990, the PRD won none of the municipal elections it contested. In the 1991 midterm elections, the PRD won 8.3 percent of the votes for the Chamber of Deputies, winning forty-one seats by proportional representation but not one victory in single-member districts. Muñoz Ledo came in a distant third in the gubernatorial elections in Guanajuato, which were nullified by President Carlos Salinas de Gortari in the wake of strong protests about fraud from all three parties (PRD, PAN, and PRI).

POPULAR PARTY (PARTIDO POPULAR). *See* POPULAR SOCIALIST PARTY.

*POPULAR SOCIALIST PARTY (PARTIDO POPULAR SOCIALISTA—
PPS). The first of the so-called parastatal parties to emerge in the postwar era,
the PPS drew some members away from the Mexican Communist Party (PCM)
and also from the progressive wing of the PRI. Vicente Lombardo Toledano,
once head of the Mexican Workers' Confederation (CTM) and close labor
adviser to Lázaro Cárdenas, split from the Institutional Revolutionary Party
(PRI) to establish the Popular Party (PP) in 1948. Lombardo Toledano differentiated his new party from the PRI by calling for a larger state-owned sector
of the economy, a deepening of land reform, and a "peoples' democracy." It
was distinguished from the PCM chiefly by the PP's willingness to identify
progressive sectors of the PRI with which it was willing to collaborate. The PP
created as its mass base the General Union of Workers and Peasants of Mexico
(Unión General de Obreros y Campesinos de México—UGOCM), which has
had regional pockets of strength (Veracruz, Oaxaca, Nayarit) and has captured
small groups that dissented from the CTM line.

The Lombardista party was reconstituted as the Popular Socialist Party in
1964 when it was joined by the Worker and Peasant Party of Mexico (POCM).
The POCM had been established as a splinter party by Hernán Laborde in 1940
when he was expelled from the Communist Party. The new PPS advocated
socialism as a goal. The PPS is widely believed to have won the 1975 gubernatorial election in Nayarit, but federal authorities refused to recognize the
victory. In compensation, PPS candidate Jorge Cruickshank won an uncontested
election as senator from Oaxaca in 1976. He was the first and only opposition
party senator until 1988 when the National Democratic Front (FDN) took four
senate seats. In 1952 Lombardo Toledano ran for president on the PP ticket.
Since then, the PP or PPS always endorsed the official party's presidential
candidate, until 1988 when it supported Cuauhtémoc Cárdenas and a range of
candidates supported by the FDN. The party won its first four victories in single-
member districts in 1988 to bring its total delegation to thirty-six (compared
with twelve seats in 1979, ten in 1982, and eleven in 1985, all by proportional
representation).

The party remains a small party of urban intellectuals and trade unionists.
Alejandro Gazcón Mercado and Jorge Cruickshank are the principal party
leaders.

REVOLUTIONARY WORKERS' PARTY (PARTIDO REVOLUCIONARIO
DE LOS TRABAJADORES—PRT). The PRT, established in 1976, was the
first of the new leftist parties to be spawned by the 1968 movement. It brought
together two Trotskyist groups and the Liga Obrera Marxista. Trotskyist in its
ideology, the PRT favored a class-based party anchored in grass-roots organization, and it has been less oriented toward electoral politics. Its members were
active in some urban, popular movements during the 1970s and 1980s. It has
gained visibility by its defense of human rights, including feminism, gay rights,

the "disappeared" (political victims of the state), and the environment. In national elections, the PRT has been unable to retain its official registration.

The PRT gained national visibility by running Rosario Ibarra de Piedra as its presidential candidate in 1982 (the first woman to run for the presidency) and again in 1988, largely on a platform demanding an end to human rights violations. The first year, the PRT won 1.76 percent of the presidential vote. Only in 1985 did the party win enough votes to gain five proportional representation seats. The PRT vote fell below the registration threshold in 1988 and 1991, when it won only 0.6 percent of the vote. In 1988 the party refused to form an electoral alliance with either the Mexican Socialist Party or later with the National Democratic Front. This refusal provoked a major split in the party leadership, and some leaders left the party to support Cuauhtémoc Cárdenas.

SOCIALIST WORKERS' PARTY (PARTIDO SOCIALISTA DE LOS TRABAJADORES). See CARDENISTA FRONT PARTY FOR NATIONAL RECONSTRUCTION.

UNIFIED SOCIALIST PARTY OF MEXICO (PARTIDO SOCIALISTA UNIFICADO DE MÉXICO). See MEXICAN COMMUNIST PARTY.

Political Parties—Historical

ANTIREELECTIONIST PARTY (PARTIDO ANTI-REELECCIONISTA). See INSTITUTIONAL REVOLUTIONARY PARTY.

CONSERVATIVE PARTY (PARTIDO CONSERVADOR—PC). This proclerical party, founded by Servando Mier in 1823, advocated centralism and drew its support from the landed aristocracy, the military, the clergy, and Scottish Rite Masons. Periodically in and out of power, the party reorganized after the Juárez reforms of 1857 and supported Porfirio Díaz's dictatorship. It dissolved in 1911.

CONSTITUTIONALIST PARTY (PARTIDO CONSTITUCIONALISTA) (1857). The party of Benito Juárez in defense of the Constitution of 1857.

CONSTITUTIONALIST PARTY (PARTIDO CONSTITUCIONALISTA) (1951). Established in 1951 by General Francisco Múgica to serve as the core of the Federation of People's Parties of Mexico (Federación de los Partidos del Pueblo de México—FPPM), the Constitutionalist Party ran General Miguel Henríquez Guzmán for the presidency in 1952 (against the candidate of the Institutional Revolutionary Party—PRI, Adolfo Ruiz Cortines). Henríquez Guzmán, a dissident expelled from the PRI, posed one of the most important presidential election challenges to the PRI, winning 15.9 percent of the votes (to Ruiz Cortines's 74 percent) according to official voting returns.

CONSTITUTIONALIST PROGRESSIVE PARTY (PARTIDO CONSTI-TUCIONALISTA PROGRESISTA—PCP). Formed by Francisco I. Madero in 1910, the PCP supported him and later General Venustiano Carranza. The party was absorbed into the National Revolutionary Party in 1929.

FUERZA POPULAR (POPULAR FORCE). See NATIONAL SINARQUISTA UNION.

NATIONAL REVOLUTIONARY PARTY (PARTIDO NACIONAL RE-VOLUCIONARIO). See INSTITUTIONAL REVOLUTIONARY PARTY.

NATIONAL SINARQUISTA UNION (UNIÓN NACIONAL SINAR-QUISTA—UNS). A fascist group established in 1937, the UNS based its program on strong defense of traditional Spanish values, authoritarian govern-ment, and the Catholic Church. The UNS briefly established a political party, the Popular Force, after World War II with some success. Popular Force dis-banded in 1948, and the remnants of the UNS were absorbed into the Mexican Democrat Party in 1971.

PARTIDO ANTI-REELECCIONISTA (ANTIREELECTIONIST PARTY). See INSTITUTIONAL REVOLUTIONARY PARTY.

PARTIDO CATÓLICO NACIONAL. See NATIONAL CATHOLIC PARTY.

PARTIDO CONSERVADOR. See CONSERVATIVE PARTY.

PARTIDO CONSTITUCIONALISTA. See CONSTITUTIONALIST PARTY (1857).

PARTIDO CONSTITUCIONALISTA. See CONSTITUTIONALIST PARTY (1951).

PARTIDO CONSTITUCIONALISTA PROGRESISTA. See CONSTITU-TIONALIST PROGRESSIVE PARTY.

PARTIDO DE LA REVOLUCIÓN MEXICANA (MEXICAN REVOLU-TIONARY PARTY). See INSTITUTIONAL REVOLUTIONARY PARTY.

PARTIDO DEMOCRÁTICO MEXICANO. See MEXICAN DEMOCRATIC PARTY.

PARTIDO LIBERAL. See LIBERAL PARTY.

PARTIDO NACIONAL AGRARISTA. *See* NATIONAL AGRARIAN PARTY.

PARTIDO NACIONAL LABORISTA. *See* NATIONAL LABOR PARTY.

PARTIDO NACIONAL REVOLUCIONARIO (NATIONAL REVOLUTIONARY PARTY). *See* INSTITUTIONAL REVOLUTIONARY PARTY.

LIBERAL PARTY (PARTIDO LIBERAL). Founded in 1823 by Miguel Ramos Arizpe, the anticlerical party strongly favored a federalist government. Under President Benito Juárez, the Liberals helped separate church and state and to nationalize church property. Out of power under the French rule and suppressed under Porfirio Díaz, the party was revived in 1908 under the leadership of the brothers Enrique, Ricardo, and Jesús Florés Magón. It was absorbed into the National Revolutionary Party.

MEXICAN DEMOCRATIC PARTY (PARTIDO DEMOCRÁTICO MEXICANO—PDM). The PDM was established in 1945 as the personal vehicle for Ezekiel Padilla, a dissident member of the Institutional Revolutionary Party, who ran against Miguel Alemán in the 1946 presidential election. Padilla polled 19.3 percent of the vote.

MEXICAN REVOLUTIONARY PARTY (PARTIDO DE LA REVOLUCIÓN MEXICANA). *See* INSTITUTIONAL REVOLUTIONARY PARTY.

NATIONAL AGRARIAN PARTY (PARTIDO NACIONAL AGRARISTA—PNA). Organized by followers of Emiliano Zapata in 1919, the PNA joined the National Revolutionary Party in 1929.

NATIONAL CATHOLIC PARTY (PARTIDO CATÓLICO NACIONAL). Founded in 1911, hoping to influence Francisco I. Madero's policy toward the Catholic Church, this party was subsequently suppressed by Victoriano Huerta.

NATIONAL LABOR PARTY (PARTIDO NACIONAL LABORISTA—PNL). Organized by Luis Morones in 1920 as a political arm of the principal national labor confederation, the Regional Confederation of Mexican Workers (Confederación Regional Obrera Mexicana—CROM), the PNL supported Presidents Alvaro Obregón and Plutarco Elías Calles, but it declined after 1928.

PARTIDO OBRERO Y CAMPESINO DE MEXICO (WORKER AND PEASANT PARTY OF MEXICO). *See* MEXICAN COMMUNIST PARTY.

PARTIDO REVOLUCIONARIO DE UNIFICACION NACIONAL. *See* REVOLUTIONARY PARTY OF NATIONAL UNIFICATION.

PARTIDO SOCIALISTA DEL SURESTE. *See* SOCIALIST PARTY OF THE SOUTHEAST.

PARTIDO SOCIALISTA REVOLUCIONARIO (REVOLUTIONARY SOCIALIST PARTY). *See* MEXICAN COMMUNIST PARTY.

POPULAR FORCE (FUERZA POPULAR). *See* NATIONAL SINARQUISTA UNION.

REVOLUTIONARY PARTY OF NATIONAL UNIFICATION (PARTIDO REVOLUCIONARIO DE UNIFICACION NACIONAL—PRUN). The PRUN was established in 1939 as a vehicle for the candidacy of General Juan Andreu Almazán, who ran a strong opposition to the Mexican Revolutionary Party candidate, General Manuel Avila Camacho, in 1940. Almazán won 5.7 percent of the vote.

REVOLUTIONARY SOCIALIST PARTY (PARTIDO SOCIALISTA REVOLUCIONARIO). *See* MEXICAN COMMUNIST PARTY.

SOCIALIST PARTY OF THE SOUTHEAST (PARTIDO SOCIALISTA DEL SURESTE—PSS). Established in 1920 in Yucatán, Quintana Roo, and Campeche by General Salvador Alvarado and Felipe Carrillo Puerto, the Socialist Party of the Southeast later supported Presidents Alvaro Obregón and Plutarco Elías Calles. It was absorbed into the National Revolutionary Party in 1929.

UNIÓN NACIONAL SINARQUISTA. *See* NATIONAL SINARQUISTA UNION.

WORKER AND PEASANT PARTY OF MEXICO (PARTIDO OBRERO Y CAMPESINO DE MÉXICO). *See* MEXICAN COMMUNIST PARTY.

Ann L. Craig

MONTSERRAT

Montserrat is an island of about 39 square miles, with about 13,000 people, who derive their livelihood from tourist-related activities, agriculture, and some assembly industry. The generally impoverished population is characterized by a high degree of emigration to the United States and Canada. The territory is governed by a British-appointed governor and, as with other British colonies, an Executive Council and a Legislative Council. The latter consists of seven members who are elected by universal adult suffrage. The leader of the winning party or coalition is elected chief minister from within the ranks of the Legislative Council. Queen Elizabeth II, the head of state, has been represented locally by Governor Christopher J. Turner, who has served in that post since 1987. The head of government is Chief Minister John A. Osbourne, the leader of the People's Liberation Movement (PLM), who has held this elected position since 1978.

In 1978 Osbourne and the PLM captured all seven seats in the Legislative Council, and Osbourne became chief minister, a post which he secured again after the 1983 elections, when the PLM won five seats, and yet again after the 1987 elections, even though the PLM's seats shrank to four. During the 1987 elections, the National Development Party (NDP) appeared for the first time and succeeded in garnering two seats.

Osbourne has gone on record during the 1980s as favoring political independence. The first occasion followed the unwillingness of the British-appointed governor to allow Osbourne to send a peace-keeping force to Grenada in 1983 in conjunction with several sovereign Eastern Caribbean states. In the late 1980s, Chief Minister Osbourne and Governor Turner disagreed over the governor's constitutional right to assume the portfolio of the secretary of finance in the wake of allegations of misconduct in that ministry. The governor prevailed, despite Osbourne's criticisms that the governor was initiating a new period of colonialism on the island. Osbourne has tempered his talk of independence, as voter enthusiasm for the issue has waned. Osbourne's main rival (and cousin), Bertrand Osbourne of the NDP, is decidely against independence.

Although not yet independent, Montserrat is a member of the Organization of Eastern Caribbean States (OECS), along with the independent English-speaking states of Saint Kitts–Nevis, Antigua and Barbuda, Dominica, Saint Vincent and the Grenadines, Saint Lucia, and Grenada. Limitations on Montserrat's full participation in the OECS, in such matters as defense and foreign policy, are defined through the governor's office.

Bibliography

Robert J. Alexander. "Montserrat," in Robert J. Alexander, ed., *Political Parties of the Americas*. Greenwood Press, Westport, Conn., 1982.
Central Intelligence Agency. *The World Factbook, 1990*. Central Intelligence Agency, Washington, D.C., 1990.
Sandra Meditz and Dennis Hanratty, eds. *Islands of the Commonwealth Caribbean: A Regional Study*. Area Handbook Program, U.S. Government Printing Office, Washington, D.C., 1989.
Stuart Philpott. *West Indian Migration: The Montserrat Case*. Athlone, London, 1973.

Political Parties

NATIONAL DEVELOPMENT PARTY (NDP). A new party under the leadership of Bertrand Osbourne, the NDP contested elections for the first time in 1987, when it won two seats out of seven in the Legislative Council. When independence became a political issue in the early to mid-1980s, the NDP emerged to take a strong stand in opposition to independence.

PEOPLE'S LIBERATION MOVEMENT (PLM). The PLM, formed in 1976 by John A. Osbourne, has been the governing party ever since it won the 1978 elections, and Osbourne has held the post of chief minister concurrently. During the 1980s, the PLM's majority in the Legislative Council has been declining, possibly reflecting waning public support for the PLM's pro-independence stand.

PROGRESSIVE DEMOCRATIC PARTY (PDP). Founded in 1970 by Austin Bramble, the PDP is Montserrat's oldest active political party. It was the governing party until the 1978 election, when it was shut out by the People's Liberation Movement. Currently, it has one seat in the Legislative Council, and it is led by Howell Bramble, the latest of this politically active family to participate in public life.

UNITED NATIONAL FRONT (UNF). The UNF, a small party founded in the 1980s by George Irish, reflects the generally personalist nature of Montserrat politics. It has no representatives in the Legislative Council.

Gary Brana-Shute
Rosemary Brana-Shute

NETHERLANDS ANTILLES

Since 1 January 1986, when the island of Aruba broke away as a separate part of the Kingdom of the Netherlands, the Netherlands Antilles has consisted of five islands in the Caribbean Sea. Two of these, known locally as the Leeward Islands—Curaçao and Bonaire—lie off the coast of Venezuela; the other three, the Windwards—Sint Maarten, Saba, and Saint Eustatius—are 500 miles to the northeast.

With, in sum, a population of considerably less than 250,000 people, the great disproportion between Curaçao, with nearly eight-ninths of the total, and the smaller islands has been a major cause of political difficulty since the entire Netherlands Antilles group moved toward self-government after World War II. Not only did it lead to the withdrawal of Aruba, but it is blocking the achievement of full independence by the remaining five areas of the Netherlands Antilles.

For two decades following the granting of universal adult suffrage and some degree of self-government by the Netherlands in 1948, the politics of the Netherlands Antilles was dominated by the Democratic Party of Curaçao. However, after serious riots occurred in Curaçao in 1969, new parties began to emerge. The result was that, in the 1970s and 1980s, the politics and government of the region were marked by a considerable degree of instability, complicated by a growing economic crisis resulting from the closure, or threatened closure, of Curaçao and Aruba's oil refineries, which provided a major part of the territory's income and foreign exchange.

As the Democratic Party of Curaçao began to splinter, elections in 1973 brought to power a coalition government headed by Juancho M. G. Evertz, the leader of the National United People's Party of Curaçao (NVP). That coalition also contained members of the Electoral Movement of the People (MEP) of Aruba, the Workers' Liberation Front (FOL) and the Democratic Party of Bonaire.

The Evertz government lasted until the 1977 election, after which a new government was established. Headed by Silvio Rozendal of the Democratic Party of Curaçao, the NVP also participated in this government. For several months that year, the MEP and the FOL boycotted the Staten, the legislature.

New elections in July 1979 brought still another coalition government, this time headed by Domenico (Don) F. Martina of the New Antilles Movement (MAN) with representatives of his party, as well as the MEP and the Bonaire Patriotic Union. The Democratic Party of Curaçao joined the coalition in December 1979.

In September 1981, the MEP left the government, but the cabinet's majority was restored by inclusion of the Democratic Party of Sint Maarten. New elections were held in June 1982, but it was October before a new coalition government could be formed, with Martina still as minister president. That cabinet resigned in June 1984, and it was three months before a new government, including five parties and headed by Maria Liberia-Peters of the NVP, was formed. When elections were held again in November 1985, the NVP was still the largest party in the Staten, but Liberia-Peters could not form a cabinet and Martina again became head of a coalition administration.

This Martina coalition resigned in March 1988, after it lost the support of the Democratic Party of Sint Maarten and the FOL. In May, Liberia-Peters returned as minister president and head of a coalition of all parties, except the MAN and the Democratic Party of Curaçao, with a majority of thirteen in a twenty-two-member Staten. Remaining in power, however, depended upon the Democratic Party of Sint Maarten and the FOL, which had brought down the previous cabinet.

Meanwhile, in 1986, Claude Wathey, head of the Democratic Party of Sint Maarten, had come out in favor of independence or separate status for Sint Maarten, but the Netherlands refused to entertain the idea. In January 1989, Don Martina of the MAN expressed support for a much looser federation of the five islands. In early 1990, the government of the Netherlands announced that it would not insist on independence for the Netherlands Antilles if the people of the territory did not want it.

In the general election of March 1990, Liberia-Peters of the NVP returned to the prime ministership as head of still another coalition. Her party had won seven Curaçao seats in the Staten, but one of her coalition partners, the Democratic Party of Sint Maarten, had lost one of its seats in the Staten to a competing local party.

The legislature of the Netherlands Antilles, the Staten, has twenty-two members. After the secession of Aruba, there were fourteen members from Curaçao, three each from Bonaire and from Sint Maarten, and one each from Saba and Saint Eustatius.

Three languages are used in the names of the various parties. In Curaçao and Bonaire they are referred to by their Dutch or Papamiento (the local language) names; in the three northern islands, English is predominant. The parties are presented in the language used locally in the following section. The parties from

Aruba are not included here in view of the separation of that island from the Netherlands Antilles. (See the chapter on Aruba.)

Bibliography

The Europa World Year Book 1990. Europa Publications, Ltd., London, 1990.
Facts on File. Facts on File, New York, London.
Keesings Record of World Events.
Personal contacts of the writer.

Political Parties

BONAIRE PATRIOTIC UNION (UNIÓN PATRIÓTICO BONAIRIANO). This party, which first achieved some prominence in the 1970s, is led by L. R. (Rudi) Ellis and C. V. Winklaar. The party participated in most of the coalition governments during the late 1970s and 1980s. In the 1990 election, it won all three of Bonaire's seats in the Staten.

BONAIRE WORKERS PARTY (PARTIDO OBRERO DI BONAIRE). A breakaway party from the Democratic Party of Bonaire, it participated in some of the coalition governments of the 1980s.

DEMOCRATIC PARTY OF BONAIRE (DEMOCRATISCHE PARTIJ VAN BONAIRE). The Democratic Party of Bonaire was established in 1954 as an ally of the Democratic Party of Curaçao. When the Curaçao counterpart declined in the 1970s and afterward, the Democratic Party of Bonaire, led by Jopie Abraham, participated in some of the coalition governments in opposition to the Curaçao party. It did not elect any member of the Staten in the election held in 1990.

DEMOCRATIC PARTY OF CURAÇAO (DEMOCRATISCHE PARTIJ VAN CURAÇAO). The oldest still existing party in the Netherlands Antilles, the Democratic Party of Curaçao was established in 1944 and, for the next twenty-five years, it dominated politics in the territory. However, following serious riots that occurred in Curaçao in the summer of 1969 (under a regime controlled by the party), it suffered splits and a decline in its general influence in the Netherlands Antilles.

Defeated in the 1973 elections, it went into the opposition. In 1977, after new elections, the last government under the leadership of the Democratic Party of Curaçao was formed, headed by the party's leader Silvio Rozendal. Although the party lost the leadership of the government after the elections of 1979, it continued to participate for three years in the administration headed by Domenico (Don) F. Martina of the New Antilles Movement. During the rest of the 1980s, the party was in the opposition. In the election of 1990, the party's representation in the Staten was reduced to one deputy, an all-time low. The current leader of the party is Augustin Díaz.

Traditionally, the Democratic Party of Curaçao has had fraternal relations with the Netherlands Labor Party, as well as contacts with the Socialist International. The party played a major role in the establishment of an organized labor movement, and its loss of control of the trade unions was a major factor in its decline.

DEMOCRATIC PARTY OF SAINT EUSTATIUS (DEMOCRATISCHE PARTIJ STATIA). Originally organized as an ally of the Democratic Party of Curaçao, it is the principal party of Saint Eustatius. It is led by Kenneth van Patten. In the election of 1990, the party continued to hold the island's one seat in the Staten.

DEMOCRATIC PARTY OF SINT MAARTEN. Originally established as an ally of the Democratic Party of Curaçao, it supported the Curaçao party's governments in the 1960s and early 1970s. When the Curaçao party declined, it took a more independent course. The party participated in most of the coalition governments of the 1980s. Until the election of 1990, this party controlled all of Sint Maarten's representation in the Staten; in 1990, it lost one of the three seats.

In 1986 the longtime leader of the Democratic Party of Sint Maarten, Claude Wathey, came out in support of separation of the island from the Netherlands Antilles, but the government of the Netherlands vetoed that proposal.

DEMOCRATISCHE PARTIJ STATIA. See DEMOCRATIC PARTY OF SAINT EUSTATIUS.

DEMOCRATISCHE PARTIJ VAN BONAIRE. See DEMOCRATIC PARTY OF BONAIRE.

DEMOCRATISCHE PARTIJ VAN CURAÇAO. See DEMOCRATIC PARTY OF CURAÇAO.

FRENTE OBRERO IN LIBERASHON 30 DI MEI. See WORKERS LIBERATION FRONT OF MAY 30.

MOVIMENTU ANTIJAS NOBO. See NEW ANTILLES MOVEMENT.

NATIONAL UNITED PEOPLE'S PARTY OF CURAÇAO (NATIONALE VOLKSPARTIJ UNIE VAN CURAÇAO—NVP). Also known as the Partido Nashional di Pueblo—PNP), the NVP, a party of Social Christian orientation, is generally considered the most conservative of the major parties. Appearing in the 1960s, it first led the government after the 1973 election, when its leader Juancho M. G. Evertz became minister president. In 1977, when the Evertz government fell, the party entered a new coalition headed by Silvio Rozendal of the Democratic Party of Curaçao.

After the election of 1979, the NVP remained in the opposition until September 1984, when its new leader, Maria Liberia-Peters, became minister president at the head of a five-party coalition. However, although the party received the largest representation in the Staten in the general election of November 1985, six out of twenty-two deputies, Liberia-Peters was unable to form a new coalition. It was not until May 1988 that she returned as minister president as the head of a new coalition of all but two of the parties in the Staten.

In the general election of March 1990, the NVP won seven Curaçao seats in the Staten, and Liberia-Peters returned to office as minister president.

NATIONALE VOLKSPARTIJ UNIE VAN CURAÇAO. See NATIONAL UNITED PEOPLE'S PARTY OF CURAÇAO.

NEW ANTILLES MOVEMENT (MOVIMENTU ANTIJAS NOBO—MAN). Described as a socialist party, the MAN first appeared in Curaçao in the 1970s as a strong supporter of the continued unity of the Netherlands Antilles. The party first contested elections in July 1979, when it won seven seats of the twenty-two in the Staten, most of them in Curaçao. The MAN's leader, Domenico (Don) F. Martina, formed a coalition government with his own party, the Movimentu Electoral di Pueblo of Aruba, and the Bonaire Patriotic Union; a few months later, these parties were joined by the Democratic Party of Curaçao.

After the election of June 1982, Martina again headed a coalition government, although it took him four months to form his cabinet. The government stayed in office until June 1984. After the general election of November 1985, Martina formed yet another coalition administration, but it was forced to resign in March 1988, in the face of serious economic difficulties after it lost the support of the Democratic Party of Sint Maarten and the Workers' Liberation Front. When a new cabinet was formed by the leader of the National United People's Party of Curaçao, Maria Liberia-Peters, the MAN remained in the opposition, along with the Democratic Party of Curaçao. In the 1990 election, the party's representation in the Staten fell from four to two.

In spite of the early support of the MAN for the continued unity of the Netherlands Antilles, in January 1989, Martina came out in favor of the reorganization of the territory as a looser federation of the five remaining islands.

NOS PATRIA CURAÇAO. See OUR CURAÇAO FATHERLAND.

OUR CURAÇAO FATHERLAND (NOS PATRIA CURAÇAO). A relatively new party, led by Chin Behlia, it attained some following in the late 1980s. It won its first representation in the Staten in 1990, when it won one seat from Curaçao.

PARTIDO NASHIONAL DI PUEBLO. *See* NATIONAL UNITED PEOPLE'S PARTY OF CURAÇAO.

PARTIDO OBRERO DI BONAIRE. *See* BONAIRE WORKERS PARTY.

SINT MAARTEN PEOPLE'S MOVEMENT. This new party in Sint Maarten is led by Fance James. In the general election of March 1990, when it captured one of Sint Maarten's three seats in the Staten, it broke what had hitherto been the monopoly of the Democratic Party of Sint Maarten in representation in the Netherlands Antilles legislature.

SOCIAL INDEPENDIENTE. *See* SOCIALIST INDEPENDENT.

SOCIALIST INDEPENDENT (SOCIAL INDEPENDIENTE—SI). This party was founded in Curaçao in 1986 by four members of the National United People's Party of Curaçao in the Staten. In the 1990 election, the party formed a coalition with the Workers' Liberation Front.

UNIÓN PATRIÓTICO BONAIRIANO. *See* BONAIRE PATRIOTIC UNION.

WINDWARD ISLANDS PEOPLE'S MOVEMENT. This party, led by Will Johnston and Dave Lovenstone, emerged in Saba in the 1980s. It won Saba's one seat in the Staten in the 1990 election.

WORKERS LIBERATION FRONT OF MAY 30 (FRENTE OBRERO IN LIB-ERASHON 30 DI MEI—FOL). The FOL was formed after a split occurred in the Democratic Party of Curaçao after the labor riots in 1969. Its leader is W. Godett. Although in 1979 it did not win any seats in the Staten, it did acquire representation in 1985. In the election of March 1990, its representation rose from one to three. It participated in several of the coalition governments of the 1970s and 1980s.

Robert J. Alexander

NICARAGUA

The Republic of Nicaragua—largest and most thinly populated nation in Central America—is a roughly triangularly shaped country of 3.7 million people who live in a land area of 57,143 square miles, about the size of Alabama. Two large inland lakes—Managua and Nicaragua—plus the San Juan River have contributed to the country's being a traditional crossing route over the Central American Isthmus; this location has made Nicaragua subject to more than its share of outside meddling in its internal affairs, as well as its own politicians seeking to influence events in neighboring nations.

Throughout most of its colonial period and after independence was achieved from Spain, Mexico, and the Central American Federation, the tropical lowlands of the eastern Mosquito coast remained an autonomous "kingdom" under British protection until 1860, when Nicaragua acquired legal sovereignty over the region. The region's English-speaking, Protestant population has often been at odds with the more populous Spanish-speaking, Roman Catholic highlands and Pacific Coast lowlands. In the 1980s, the government—dominated by the Sandinista National Liberation Front—sought both to integrate the mosquito coast into the national society through a variety of governmental services and improved transportation facilities and to carry out one of the hemisphere's most thoroughgoing social revolutions. Ultimately, this program, and the accompanying censorship of the media—especially of *La Prensa* newspaper—led to covert support by the United States, under the Reagan administration, of the guerrilla fighters known as Contras and support of the civilian opposition forces who won a surprising victory in the February 1990 elections.

Shortly after the five provinces of Central America proclaimed their independence from Spain on 15 September 1821, Nicaragua became part of the Mexican Empire under Agustín Iturbide. When his regime collapsed in 1823, Nicaragua helped form the United Provinces of Central America. In addition to disputes among the provinces, which led Nicaragua to secede from the union in 1838, an intense rivalry developed between Granada, which aligned itself with Conservative factions favoring close church-state relations, and León, whose Liberals favored separation of church and state. Although meaningful ideological differences had disappeared by the end of the nineteenth century, the struggle between the two cities, and between the Liberals and Conservatives, continued into the contemporary era.

Perhaps the most important consequence of these differences between Conservatives and Liberals was their calling upon private U.S. soldiers of fortune, such as William Walker, and railroad magnate Cornelius Vanderbilt, for help in their disputes over who would dominate the country and its important isthmian position. Finally, the United States sent small groups of U.S. Marines and soldiers to occupy the country and to operate the customs service between 1909 and 1933. On one of these occasions, Augusto César Sandino, leader of one of the several Liberal factions, refused to abide by the truce arrangements worked out in 1927 by Henry L. Stimson between other Liberal leaders and Conservatives. Subsequently, Sandino defied efforts of both the Marines and a newly established National Guard to lay down his arms. On 21 February 1934, Sandino was assassinated under a flag of truce by soldiers loyal to Anastasio Somoza García, another Liberal leader, who had risen to the command of the National Guard. In 1936 Somoza, generally known as "Tacho," ousted Juan Bautista Sacasa—his uncle—from the presidency and set up a system of family rule that lasted until 19 July 1979.

Tacho Somoza governed directly or indirectly until his assassination on 21 September 1956, during the middle of a reelection campaign, by a dissident member of his own Liberal Party. On his death, Luis Somoza Debayle, his thirty-three-year-old son and the president of the Nicaraguan Congress, became president. In 1966, another Somoza son, Anastasio "Tachito" Somoza Debayle, head of the National Guard, took over following President René Schick's sudden fatal heart attack. Tachito Somoza won 70.8 percent of the 249,312 votes cast in the February 1967 elections; 27.2 percent of the votes went to Fernando Agüero Rocha, a dissident Conservative who was heading up a coalition of the Traditionalist Conservative Party (PCT), the Independent Liberal Party (PLI), and the Social Christian Party (PSC).

Following Luis Somoza's death by heart attack in April 1967, Tachito Somoza dominated the country as much as his father had through the use of patronage, favors, and sometimes force. Three important events dominated Somoza's rule to July 1979, when he went into exile. First, Somoza used the government and foreign funds collected in the aftermath of the December 1972 earthquake that devastated downtown Managua to benefit himself and his close associates. Second, Carlos Fonseca Amador and other disenchanted individuals founded the Sandinista National Liberation Front (FSLN) in 1961. Subsequently, they undertook guerrilla operations in the countryside near the Honduran and Costa Rican borders, after receiving financial and military support from the government of Fidel Castro after Fonseca Amador went into exile in Cuba in 1970. Third, on 10 January 1978, Pedro Joaquín Chamorro Cardenal, a Conservative who had become editor of the family newspaper, La Prensa, was assassinated.

Chamorro may have been killed because of La Prensa articles about the

Nicaraguan operations of a firm owned by an anti-Castro Cuban exile, in which Somoza had stock, which collected 38,000 pints of human blood and plasma per month and shipped it all to the United States. Chamorro's death provoked two days of street protests and a seventeen-day general strike. More important, in April, sixteen opposition groups joined together to form the Broad Opposition Front (Frente Amplio de Oposición—FAO) under the leadership of Rafael Córdova Rivas, an attorney and Nicaraguan Conservative Party (PCN) leader, and Alfonso Robelo Callejas, an industrialist. The FAO, which called for Somoza's resignation, developed a minimum program for a future government, including organization of a "national democratic and pluralistic government," reorganization of the National Guard, and agrarian reform.

Further violence and strikes continued through 1978. After various guerrilla groups, operating under loose FSLN control, took over several cities in September, Somoza refused to negotiate seriously with the FAO, despite efforts made by the Organization of American States (OAS) and the government of Jimmy Carter to mediate the political crisis. By November, although the National Guard—now under the command of Anastasio Somoza Portocarrero, Tachito's son—had regained nominal control of the cities and countryside, FSLN forces had increased to at least 2,000 men and women who staged hit-and-run attacks on National Guard positions and then retreated to sanctuary behind the Honduran and Costa Rican borders—a tactic followed by the Contra guerrillas in the 1980s.

In February 1979, the United States ended military and economic assistance to Nicaragua. In June, the FSLN established a government-in-exile in Costa Rica headed by a five-member junta made up of three Sandinista leaders—thirty-three-year-old Daniel Ortega Saavedra; Moisés Hassan Morales, a leftist engineer heading the People's United Movement (MPU), made up of anti-Somoza government workers and trade unionists; and Sergio Ramírez Mercado, a lawyer-writer—and two non-Sandinistas—Robelo Callejas, the businessman who helped organize the FAO, and Violeta Barrios de Chamorro, the fifty-year-old widow of Pedro Joaquín Chamorro, the editor of *La Prensa* whose death had played a major role in igniting popular opposition against Somoza. When Somoza finally fled the country on 19 July 1979, to exile in the United States and Paraguay, this Junta of National Reconstruction took over the day-to-day operations of the government, although a nine-member Directorate of the FSLN was really the ultimate government authority.

About 50,000 people were killed during the eighteen months of civil war that continued from January 1978 until July 1979; another 150,000 were wounded. The country had less than $3 million in foreign reserves and was encumbered with a foreign debt of $1.6 billion; Somoza had sacked the country's banks before he left.

The Immediate Post-Somoza Regime (1979–1980)

In the first two months after assuming power, the junta implemented various reforms and issued a temporary fourteen-page constitution, which established

equality under the law, abolished the death penalty, guaranteed free and obligatory primary and secondary education, and granted various procedural rights.
Some 1,250 farms and ranches, covering approximately 1.7 million acres which
belonged to Somoza and his closest allies, were expropriated and put under the
jurisdiction of a new National Agrarian Reform Institute (INRA).

The FSLN took over the presses of *Novedades*, the Somoza newspaper, and
began to publish *Barricada*, under the direction of Carlos Fernando Chamorro
Barrios, one of the sons of the deceased Pedro Joaquín Chamorro. *La Prensa*
continued its previous independent and conservative political stance under Jaime
Chamorro Cardenal, a brother of Pedro Joaquín Chamorro. In addition, as a
consequence of a family dispute, Xavier Chamorro Cardenal, another brother
of Pedro Joaquín, and a group of *La Prensa* employees left in early 1980 to begin
publishing a third newspaper, *El Nuevo Diario*, which, although sympathetic to
many aspects of the FSLN program, also carried news about opposition political
parties and trade union groups that *Barricada* would not publish. *La Prensa*
continued its strong support for freedom of expression and the role of private
enterprise in a mixed economy. All three newspapers have followed a policy of
sensationalism and yellow journalism—part of the Nicaraguan tradition.

On 19 April 1980, Violeta Barrios de Chamorro resigned from the junta.
Three days later, Robelo Callejas also resigned, saying that he feared Nicaragua
was moving toward a totalitarian regime like Cuba and that the Sandinista junta
members had disregarded the wishes of Violeta Chamorro and himself. After
intense negotiations between FSLN leaders and groups in the private sector,
Códova Rivas, president of the Democratic Conservative Party of Nicaragua
(PCDN), and Dr. Arturo Cruz, president of the Central Bank and a member
of the reformist Los Doce (the Group of Twelve, an organization that linked
businessmen and the FSLN before July 1979), were appointed to represent the
private sector on the junta.

The Council of State, the provisional legislative body of the new government,
was a corporatist-type legislative body—different from those normally found in
the United States and Latin America—although the concept of functional
representation by mass organizations was similar to the National Advisory Council (CONASE) that General Juan Alberto Melgar Castro established in neighboring Honduras from 1975 to 1978. Among these organizations were the
Association of Nicaraguan Women Confronting the National Problem
(APRONAC), the neighborhood Sandinista Defense Committees (CDS), the
Sandinista Workers Central (Central Sandinista de Trabajadores—CST), the
Association of Rural Workers (ATC), and the Sandinista army.

As it became clear that the FSLN was serious about its efforts to effect
fundamental economic and political changes, a new set of political groupings
began to develop between 1982 and 1983. On the right were individuals who
had fled to Miami, Costa Rica, and Honduras and who ultimately formed the
leadership of the different Contra guerrilla groups in Nicaragua. A second bloc
comprised forces ranging from the extreme left to the center-right who sought

to advance their positions "within the Revolution" and opposed many of the FSLN's specific policies and its efforts to co-opt Sandinismo and the popular organizations. These forces were generally known as the "patriotic opposition." To the left of the Sandinistas were the Communist Party of Nicaragua (PCdeN), a Trotskyite party; the Marxist-Leninist Movement of Popular Action (MAP-ML); and the Revolutionary Party of the Workers (PRT), all of whom argued for radicalizing the revolution by expanding land reform, expropriating the remaining businesses and farms as part of a guided economy, and creating a "dictatorship of the proletariat."

To the immediate right of the FSLN were three parties which entered into a formal alliance known as the Patriotic Front (Frente Patriótica—FP): the Popular Social Christian Party (PPSC), the Nicaraguan Socialist Party (PSN), and the PLI. In addition, the Conservative Democratic Party of Nicaragua (PCDN) shared the general FP political perspective, although it was never formally a participant. Although FP members and the PCDN had program differences with the FSLN, they generally supported the FSLN political program and strongly opposed U.S. intervention. They supplied several government ministers, ambassadors, and Supreme Court justices as part of the Sandinistas' efforts to build a larger coalition or consensus within Nicaraguan society through co-optation of groups on both the left and the right.

During the fighting to oust Somoza, the Sandinistas vowed to promote a pluralistic political system in which all sectors of Nicaragua's society would be able to participate freely. Shortly before Somoza fled to Miami, the FSLN told the OAS that it would hold free elections for representatives to municipal councils and to a constituent assembly. This commitment was codified in the Interim Constitution for the New Government of National Reconstruction. When the first anniversary of the revolution passed with no mention of an electoral timetable, many opposition leaders reminded the Sandinistas of their oft-repeated pledge to hold early elections. Defense Minister Humberto Ortega Saavedra, one of the nine *comandantes* in the FSLN's National Directorate, declared in August 1980 that elections would not be held until 1985 and that no electoral activity of any type would be allowed until 1984. This declaration— along with other policy actions such as the confiscation of peasant produce by government officials at barricades along the highways in 1980 and 1981 in order to maintain an urban food supply—was ultimately responsible for several thousand peasants and others taking up arms to overthrow the Sandinista regime.

In March 1982, the government declared a state of emergency and severely curtailed the civil and political rights of the citizenry, including censorship of the press and restrictions on the activities of opposition political parties. In October, the Sandinistas unveiled a six-point program to institutionalize the revolution, including plans for a Political Parties Law and an Electoral Law. The Political Parties Law, enacted in September 1983, created two bodies— the National Assembly of Political Parties and the National Council of Political Parties—to oversee party activities. It required all parties to be anti-imperialist and to support the revolution in order to obtain legal standing. During the debate in the quasi-legislative Council of State, opposition parties walked out in protest. In February 1984, the FSLN introduced the Electoral Law to the Council of State. While the law was being debated, the fundamental statute was amended to provide for the election of a president, a vice president, and ninety members of a National Assembly. The Electoral Law, decreed in March and amended in July, then defined the process by which these officials would be elected. Once again, the opposition walked out of the Council of State, protesting the bias of the Electoral Law in favor of the FSLN's dominance of the Supreme Electoral Tribunal, the lowering of the voting age to sixteen, the enfranchising of more than 100,000 youths who had been "indoctrinated" by the Sandinista-controlled education system, and the strict limits set on the length of the electoral campaign and media exposure. While the Electoral Law was before the Council of State, junta coordinator Daniel Ortega—prompted by mounting pressure for elections from West European and Latin American governments—proclaimed on 21 February that the date of the elections was being advanced from 1985 to 4 November 1984; officials elected on that date would take office on 10 January 1985.

During June and July, political parties held conventions and meetings to select their candidates. All the non-FSLN parties delayed registering their candidates, awaiting the 19 July celebration of the anniversary of the revolution, when the state of emergency was to elapse. To their disappointment, junta coordinator Ortega announced that the state of emergency was being extended.

On 23 July, the FSLN submitted its list of candidates with the Supreme Electoral Council; six opposition parties filed their lists on the 25 July deadline day: the PSN, which was allied with the FSLN in the Patriotic Front; the PCdeN; the MAP-ML, so small it could not name candidates for all ninety seats in the National Assembly; the PPSC; the PLI, one of whose leaders, Virgilio Godoy Reyes, had served as minister of labor in the Government of National Reconstruction (GNR) from 1979 to 1980; and the PCDN, whose leaders were involved in a factional fight for control that resulted in over a dozen of the party's candidates for the National Assembly asking that their names be removed from the PCDN slate, a request that was not granted by the Supreme Electoral Council.

The Democratic Coordinating Board (Coordinadora Democrática—CDN)—formed in 1981 by the PSC, the Social Democratic Party (PSD), and the Liberal Constitutionalist Party (PLC); two independent labor confederations, the Trade Union Confederation of Unity (Confederación de Unidad Sindical—CUS) and the Council of Trade Union Action and Unity (Consejo de Acción y Unidad Sindical—CAUS); and various private sector and professional organizations under the leadership of the Superior Council of Business Enterprise (COSEP)—refused to register. As its prospective but never formally declared presidential candidate, the CDN chose Arturo Cruz, who had been director of the Central Bank in the first year after Somoza's flight and then served as Nicaraguan ambasssador to the United States in 1980 and 1981. The CDN pursued what Eric Weaver and William Barnes have called a "brinksmanship electoral strategy, coupling ever-escalating demands for concessions from the FSLN with threats to abstain from the elections" (1991, 125), which ultimately they did.

The FSLN gradually agreed to demands to modify the state of emergency to restore the freedom to travel, freedom to organize, freedom of the press, the right to strike, and guarantees of at least four and one-half minutes of free air time per day. Although some public funding was available to the opposition parties, they often found it difficult to purchase paper, ink, and paint for campaign materials. In addition, the GRN's gasoline rationing, which allocated 20 gallons per vehicle per month, inhibited the ability of the opposition to campaign in many areas outside of the capital; the FSLN had access to government trucks and supplies. The FSLN, however, refused to agree to August proposals of the CDN to negotiate with the Contras as a final essential precondition to CDN participation in the election.

While the U.S. government dismissed the 4 November elections as not fulfilling "the promise of a free election which the Sandinistas made to the Nicaraguan people and the world," the Contadora Group (Mexico, Panama, Colombia, and Venezuela) seeking to mediate Central American conflicts since January 1983, the Socialist International, and many independent observers characterized the election process as free, honest, and contributing to the democratic institutionalizing of the revolution. Of the 1,551,597 persons registered to vote, 1,170,142 voters cast their ballots (75.4 percent) at 3,876 polling stations throughout the country, 16 of which could not be opened because they were located in war zones with very little security. When the ballots were counted, the FSLN—with Daniel Ortega and Sergio Ramírez heading the ticket—emerged as the dominant force in the country with 67 percent of the vote for the National Assembly (see Table 1).

The results led to a considerable debate—both inside and outside of Nicaragua—as to their meaning. The Sandinistas continued to enjoy strong popular support, but analysts observed that many traditional political affiliations also remained strong, despite five years of political mobilization by FSLN organizations and a reorganized education system.

Despite the strong showing of popular support for the FSLN at the polls, the Reagan administration and its rightist allies in the United States and Central America continued their efforts to overthrow the Sandinista regime. In October 1984, the Contras launched the first of a new series of offensives emphasizing civilian rather than military targets, and the war escalated sharply. While newly trained and equipped counter insurgency battalions reduced the Contra's ability to threaten the revolution by late 1985, the war continued to devastate the countryside, to impair Nicaragua's relations with its neighbors, and to disrupt the economy. By April 1986, for example, while the official exchange rate for the cordoba was still sixty-three to the U.S. dollar, the exchange rate on the Honduran border ranged from 1,800 to 2,100 to the dollar, and simple staples,

Table 1
Voting for Political Parties and Assembly Seats Won, 1984

Party	Votes	Percent	Seats
FSLN	735,967	66.7%	61
PCDN	154,327	14.0%	14
PLI	105,560	9.6%	9
PPSC	61,199	5.6%	6
PCdeN	16,034	1.5%	2
PSN	14,494	1.3%	2
MAP-ML	11,352	1.0%	2
Valid Votes	1,098,933		
Null Votes	71,209		
Total	1,170,142	~100.0%	96

such as beer, inner tubes for tires, soft drinks, milk, and bread, were unavailable in Managua and other cities.

While the Contadora nations had tried in vain to mediate not only the dispute between the Sandinista regime and the Contras but also other disputes in El Salvador and Guatemala, it was not until August 1987—when Nicaragua signed a peace agreement with its neighbors at Esquipulas, Guatemala, following a proposal by Costa Rica's Oscar Arias, who won a Nobel Peace Prize for his efforts—that a real end to the civil war seemed possible. Before Esquipulas, Ortega's government rejected all political negotiations with the Contra forces and denied Contra leaders participation in the electoral process.

In addition, a series of events had been taking place within Nicaragua that led to the adoption of a new constitution in January 1987 which—with several additional Central American agreements—led to the holding of elections on 25 February 1990. On the eve of the November 1984 elections, the FSLN had held a long series of talks with the "patriotic opposition." The opposition parties had committed themselves to defending the revolution and national sovereignty and had agreed to define the Contra war as outside intervention rather than civil war. In exchange, the FSLN publicly committed itself once again to political pluralism within the revolution, continued democratization, broad civil liberties, and the depolitization of the Sandinista Defense Committees. When the FSLN reimposed the state of emergency in October 1985 during intense fighting, many opposition politicians of both left and right condemned the decree and temporarily withdrew from the National Assembly. After the Supreme Court, including FSLN–allied justices, unanimously condemned the decree, the FSLN softened its terms or never enforced the harshest provisions. Ultimately, most politicians—with the notable exception of the PLI's Virgilio Godoy—returned to the constitutional debate that had started in the Council of State.

While the FSLN had originally supported the idea of participatory democracy through the election of representatives from mass organizations directly to government bodies, rather than electing political leaders who sought to balance the interests of different sectors—including the middle class and elites—it ultimately accepted a more traditional Western-style representative structure with legislative, judicial, and executive branches. The FSLN favored a strong executive; the opposition favored a strong legislature, with checks on other government branches, as well as control of the budget, the army, and limits on presidential power to declare a state of emergency. Ultimately, a compromise was worked out whereby the legislature was given the authority to approve or reject a budget prepared by the president except in time of war. The FSLN insisted on presidential reelection and the power to declare a state of emergency. The new constitution was finally adopted in January 1987 and was signed by eighty-three of the National Assembly's ninety regular members.

Over the next two years, opposition political leaders began to reorganize their parties, and President Ortega agreed to negotiate the demobilization of the Contras by requesting the presence of United Nations and OAS forces. In February 1989, President Ortega agreed with the other Central American presidents to move the national elections scheduled by the constitution for November 1990 to February and to enter into a dialogue with the opposition on additional reforms to the 1988 electoral law. On 3–4 August 1989, President Ortega conducted a televised national dialogue with representatives of nearly all of the functioning political parties to seek agreements to be submitted to the National Assembly and the Supreme Electoral Council. After a televised twenty-eight-hour marathon negotiating session, at which international observers were present, all the parties agreed to participate in future national elections and called on the Contras to demobilize by 5 December, the first day of the formal campaign period.

The 1990 Campaign

Twenty-four political parties contested the 25 February 1990 elections, excluding the ethnic-political organizations of the Atlantic Coast. Of the twenty-four, three did not have legal status. The abundance of parties was surprising in relation to the population of approximately 3.7 million people and in comparison with the number of parties represented in the 1984 election. The distinctions between the three blocs of parties involved in the 1984 election "blurred to the point of disappearing," especially with respect to ideological coherence, to use the words of Weaver and Barnes (1991, 136). Fourteen parties to the left and right of the FSLN in the patriotic opposition and the CDN joined with counterrevolutionary rightists to form the National Opposition Union (Unión Nacional de Oposición—UNO) which selected Violeta Barrios de Chamorro as its presidential candidate and Virgilio Godoy, longtime PLI leader, as its vice-presidential nominee. The PLC and the PSD, which had joined the CDN and abstained in 1984, now joined the UNO coalition.

The PSC, another CDN participant and 1984 abstainer, was joined by a faction of the PPSC, led by Mauricio Díaz, to form a Social Christian Alliance, which was also joined by the Atlantic Coast Yatama Organization, led by Brooklyn Rivera and Steadman Fagoth, to oppose both the UNO and the FSLN. Moisés Hassan—former FSLN guerilla leader, government junta member, minister of construction, and Mayor of Managua—split with the FSLN in 1988 and formed the United Revolutionary Movement (MUR) to run for the presidency with vice-presidential candidate Francisco Samper. Six other minor parties on the left and right also nominated candidates for the presidency, the ninety-six seats in the National Assembly, the 131 municipal councils, and the two forty-five-member regional councils for the two Autonomous Atlantic Coast Regions. Most of these parties did not develop over ideological or program differences. The historical reasons were tactical differences, fights over leadership, and opposition to a party's internal organization.

The leadership of nearly every Nicaraguan party comes from professional elements within the middle class, especially lawyers, physicians, university professors, and university students; several have leaders who are businessmen. The FSLN and Marxist groups are exceptions to this pattern. Nearly every party has a trade union sector; several have peasant groups that increase the size of their "popular" bases.

Three groups, including the FSLN, claim to be democratic socialist parties and have sent representatives to Socialist International meetings. It is difficult to tell which of them is closest to the European-style social democracy seen in the formerly West German or Scandinavian parties or in the Aprista-type parties of Latin America, such as Peru's APRA or Costa Rica's National Liberation Party. Four Christian democratic parties exist as a consequence of splits in the PSC, founded in 1957. Four parties carried the Conservative label; four more claimed to be the true Liberal Party. There were also three Marxist parties on the far left: the MAP-ML, the PCdeN, and the PRT, which is affiliated with the Trotskyite International.

While the 1990 campaign featured more parties and more candidates than any previous Nicaraguan election, the race quickly boiled down to a contest between the UNO, led by Violeta Chamorro, and the FSLN, led by Daniel Ortega. Three major issues confronted the contenders: the war, the economy, and national reconciliation. Economic deterioration since the 1984 election, as measured by falling urban wages, continued scarcities of basic commodities, unemployment, reduced government services, and a steady fall in the value of the cordoba, undoubtedly hurt FSLN reelection chances, despite FSLN claims that the war was largely to blame. Income per capita fell virtually every year between 1984 and 1990; inflation topped 30,000 percent in 1988, but fell to 1,689 percent in 1989. While the standard of living of many increased dramatically in the first four years of the revolution, through programs of agrarian reform, universal free health care, subsidized foodstuffs for urban workers, and expanded literacy and education programs, the austerity programs imposed in

1985 and 1986 eliminated most of the subsidies for basic necessities and forced a reduction in health services and agrarian reform efforts.

The UNO promised dramatic improvements, extensive U.S. financial support, an end to U.S. blocking of multilateral loans, and cessation of the U.S. trade embargo. President George Bush pledged an end to the embargo if Chamorro won, implying that, if the FSLN won—even fairly—the United States would maintain hostile economic policies. The UNO's platform was sometimes vague in telling whether—if victorious—it would reverse the revolution or merely modify it. While the platform did not call for outright counterrevolution, it did call for reviewing the confiscation of non-Somoza family land, even if the previous owners had collaborated with the Somocistas. The UNO planned to restructure the Sandinista Popular Army to deprive it of its "partisan" character, with the implicit goal of converting it into a force willing to enforce whatever policies the UNO might mandate. The UNO also planned to end the draft immediately. Owing to its extraordinary ideological mix, some Nicaraguans questioned the ability of a UNO government to create coherent economic policies and to maintain political order under continued austerity in the face of a well-organized and determined FSLN opposition.

The Election Results

The 25 February 1990 election was one of the most intensely observed in history. A broad array of international organizations, such as the United Nations, the OAS, and European parliamentary delegations, and private groups, such as the Council of Freely Elected Heads of Government, led by former president of the United States Jimmy Carter, and the Latin American Studies Association observed the campaign.

As results trickled in to the Supreme Electoral Council, it became apparent that the UNO was going to score a stunning upset victory at all levels. After Carter, Elliot Richardson (the personal representative of United Nations Secretary General Pérez de Cuellar), and João Baena Soares (the secretary general of the OAS) met with Ortega and Chamorro, the two candidates announced the projected victory of the UNO coalition and called for calm and reconciliation. Of the 1,752,088 registered voters, 1,510,838 persons voted (86 percent), 339,696 more than in 1984 (75 percent). While 1,420,584 votes were considered valid, only 90,294 votes (6 percent) were nullified—about the same as in 1984. The national totals are shown in Table 2.

The UNO won the presidential race with 54.7 percent of the vote to 40.8 percent for the FSLN. Hassan Morales of the MUR was the only minor party presidential candidate to receive as much as 1 percent of the valid votes. The most important change from the 1984 voting was 150,401 fewer votes for Daniel Ortega, while the UNO coalition gained approximately 350,000 more votes

Table 2
Presidential Voting and Assembly Representation, February 1990

Party	Votes	Percent	Assembly	Seats and Votes
UNO	777,552	54.7%	51	764,748
PSOC	5,798	0.4%	0	6,226
PLIUN	3,151	0.2%	0	3,515
PRT	8,500	0.5%	0	10,586
FSLN	579,566	40.8%	39	591,196
MAP-ML	8,115	0.6%	0	8,174
PSC	11,136	0.7%	1	12,738
PUCA	5,065	0.3%	0	5,426
PCDN	4,500	0.3%	0	4,683
MUR	16,751	1.1%	1	14,013
Total	1,420,134	~100.0%	92	1,421,305

than the opposition parties running in 1984—excluding the PSC, the MUR, and the PRT.

The UNO victory was reflected nationwide: the FSLN won a plurality only in Estelí and in Rio San Juan on the Atlantic coast. The FSLN fared poorly even in the capital city of Managua where it won 188,071 (42.9 percent) of the 301,418 valid votes cast to 209,572 votes for the Chamorro–Godoy slate (53.4 percent). The UNO coalition also did well in the voting for assembly candidates, winning in every region except Estelí and Rio San Juan—gaining 53.9 percent of the valid votes—while the FSLN did slightly better than in the presidential race with 40.9 percent of the votes cast. The UNO captured fifty-one of the seats; the FSLN won thirty-nine. The minor parties gained only two seats: the PSC, allied with the Yatama Indian Organization, won one in the North Atlantic Autonomous Region; the MUR won one seat for its defeated presidential candidate Hassan.

The ability of the UNO to build attractive slates for the system of proportional representation by region is shown in terms of the seats won in the assembly by each of its parties:

PNC	5	PLC	3
MDN	3	PAPC	5
PSD	5	PLI	5
PALI	2	PLC	3
PAN	4	PCdeN	5
PSN	3	PPSC	2

The UNO won majorities in 99 of the 131 municipal council races, including Managua, Granada, and Matagalpa. In Managua, the UNO won 52 percent of the vote, and—because the electoral formula used in municipal races awards additional seats to the victor—controls sixteen of the twenty council seats. The UNO won control of councils in twenty-eight of the other cities with a population of over 20,000; the FSLN controls the councils in ten. Of the smaller, more rural municipalities, the UNO candidates won a majority in seventy-one; the FSLN won twenty. By these measures, the UNO's victory was slightly more pronounced in the more rural areas than in the urban areas, but it was sweeping in both categories. The only major cities captured by the FSLN were León and Estelí. On the other hand, León voted for the UNO at the presidential and assembly levels and for the FSLN at the local level. The FSLN majority of eight to two on the León municipal council can probably be attributed to the popularity of its mayoral candidate and to the fact that four of the five top FSLN candidates were not members of the FSLN prior to the campaign. As further evidence of the weakness of the third parties, no third party gained a municipal seat in any of the cities with a population of over 20,000.

Nicaragua under the Chamorro Regime (1990–1991)

The government of Violeta Barrios de Chamorro has shown a remarkable resiliency in dealing with the nation's economic and political problems since assuming office in April 1990. Although the Contra guerrillas have been demilitarized and brought back into civilian life, the UNO–controlled government still faces severe problems of finding land for the former guerrillas who expected to receive land as one of the conditions for their laying down of arms—a condition incidentally demanded by Sandino in the 1927–1934 period. The inflation problems that contributed to the FSLN defeat do not appear to have been solved: The December 1989–November 1990 inflation rate of 8,500 percent was nearly five times the rate in the last year of the Ortega government. Chamorro has been able to solve at least two severe general strikes, which were mounted by the FSLN trade union affiliates, without having to use the army. In addition, her government weathered the dismissal in early August 1990 of Colonel Manuel Pichado as chief of the Sandinista Air Force who reportedly had "policy differences" with army commander Humberto Ortega.

Bibliography

Avance (weekly newspaper of the Partido Comunista de Nicaragua).
Barricada (daily newspaper of the Frente Sandinista de Liberación Nacional, Managua).
Barricada Internacional, Managua, 28 Julio 1990.
Pedro Camejo and Fred Murphy, eds. The Nicaraguan Revolution. Pathfinder Press, New York, 1979.
Jaime Chamorro. The Republic of Paper. Freedom House and University Press of America, New York, 1988.
Arturo J. Cruz Sequeira and José Luis Velázquez, Nicaragua: Regresión en la revolución. Asociación Libro Libre, San José, Costa Rica, 1986.

El Nuevo Diario (independent daily newspaper, Managua).

Electoral Democracy under International Pressure. Report of the Latin American Studies Association Commission to Observe the 1990 Nicaraguan Election, 15 March 1990. Latin American Studies Association, University of Pittsburgh, Pittsburgh, Pa., 1990.

Envío. Central American Historical Institute, Georgetown University, Washington, D.C., 1989–1990.

Foreign Broadcast Information Service. *Daily Report*, Latin America.

Elia Maria Kuant and Trish O'Kane. *Nicaragua: Political Parties and Elections 1990.* Coordinadora Regional de Investigaciones Económicas y Sociales, Managua, 1989.

La Prensa (daily newspaper, Managua).

Ronald H. McDonald and J. Mark Ruhl. *Party Politics and Elections in Latin America.* Westview Press, Boulder, Colo., 1989.

Mimeographed publications of the Movimiento Democrático Nicaragüense, Partido Comunista de Nicaragua, Partido Social Cristiano, Partido Revolucionario de los Trabajadores.

Nicaragua, Documentos sobre la revolución, desde antes del triunfo hasta la derrota electoral. Correo Internacional, Partido Revolucionario de los Trabajadores, Managua, April 1990.

Richard Millett. *Guardians of the Dynasty: A History of the U.S. Created Guardia Nacional de Nicaragua and the Somoza Family.* Orbis Books, Maryknoll, New York, 1977.

Neale J. Pearson. "Nicaragua," in Robert J. Alexander, ed., *Political Parties of the Americas*, vol. 2. Greenwood Press, Westport, Conn., 1982.

Angela Saballos. *Elecciones 90, mil preguntas.* Centro de Investigaciones de la Realidad de America Latina (CIRA), Managua, 1990.

United States Department of State. *Resource Book, Sandinista Elections in Nicaragua*, Washington, D.C., 1990.

Thomas W. Walker. "Nicaragua," in Howard J. Wiarda and Harvey F. Kline, eds., *Latin American Politics and Development*, 2d ed. Houghton Mifflin, Boston, 1985.

———. *Nicaragua, The Land of Sandino.* Westview Press, Boulder, Colo., 1981.

———. *The Christian Democratic Movement in Nicaragua.* Institute of Government Research, Comparative Government Studies no. 3, University of Arizona Press, Tucson, 1970.

Eric Weaver and William Barnes. "Opposition Parties and Coalitions," in Thomas W. Walker, ed., *Revolution and Counter-Revolution in Nicaragua.* Westview Press, Boulder, Colo., 1991.

Xavier Zavala. *1984, Nicaragua.* Asociación Libro Libre, San José, Costa Rica, 1985.

Interviews by the writer in Managua in July 1980 and July–August 1990.

Political Parties

ACCIÓN DEMOCRÁTICA. *See* DEMOCRÁTIC ACTION.

ACCIÓN NACIONAL CONSERVADORA (CONSERVATIVE NATIONAL ACTION). *See* CONSERVATIVE PARTY.

ALIANZA POPULAR CONSERVADORA. See CONSERVATIVE POPU-LAR ALLIANCE.

AUTHENTIC CONSERVATIVE PARTY (PARTIDO CONSERVADOR AUTÉNTICO). See CONSERVATIVE PARTY.

CENTRAL AMERICAN PARTY OF INTEGRATION (PARTIDO DE IN-TEGRACIÓN DE AMÉRICA CENTRAL—PIAC). Founded in 1989, this very small party has not been able to meet the requirements of the Supreme Electoral Council to be registered. Its principal officers are Alejandro Pérez Arévalo, president, and Francisco Gutiérrez Soto, secretary general. Its program centers on one issue: a United Federation of a Democratic Central America.

CENTRAL AMERICAN UNIONIST PARTY (PARTIDO UNIONISTA CENTROAMERICANO—PUCA). The PUCA was originally founded in 1904 as a cultural group which promoted "Central Americanization." Renamed the Committee of State in 1944, it developed ties to many social circles. With the victory of the Sandinistas in 1979, it began to act as a political party whose slogan "Central Americanization" was seen as a solution to all national problems. Its presidential ticket of Blanca Rojas and Daniel Urcuyo won only 5,065 votes (0.3 percent) in the 25 February 1990 elections but did slightly better in the voting for the National Assembly with 5,565 or 0.4 percent of the votes. Most of its strength is found in Managua, Matagalpa, and Jinotega. Rojas—a lawyer who was imprisoned and exiled several times during the rule of Tachito Somoza—gained a lot of attention and respect during the campaign for her strong arguments on behalf of woman's rights and greater male responsibility for household chores and child care and for her criticism of men who were able to walk away from legal or common law marriages without legal liability. She told one interviewer that "unilateral divorce" should be abolished. She was also an articulate exponent of the view that senior military commanders ought to be rotated periodically in order to avoid the creation of a military establishment (poder militar) which could oust elected civilian regimes. She was critical of the two-year period of military service for conscripts (six months of service is sufficient) and of the forced recruiting of so many individuals.

COALICIÓN DEL CENTRO DEMOCRÁTICO. See COALITION OF THE DEMOCRATIC CENTER.

COALITION OF THE DEMOCRATIC CENTER (COALICIÓN DEL CEN-TRO DEMOCRÁTICO—CD). The CD, a coalition of the Nicaraguan Conservative Party, the Social Christian Party, the Social Democratic Party, and the Nicaraguan Democratic Movement, was committed to seeking a political solution to the conflict between the Sandinista government and the Contras.

Presided over by Alfredo César Aguirre, the CD dissolved itself after the Sapoa Agreement and the calling of the February 1990 elections.

COMMUNIST PARTY OF NICARAGUA (PARTIDO COMUNISTA NI-CARAGÜENSE—PCdeN). The PCdeN was formed in 1967 as a result of an internal division in the Nicaraguan Socialist Party (PSN). The PCdeN is an orthodox Marxist party which once defended Leonid Brezhnev but now, with the same fervor, supports perestroika. On the other hand—like the PSN— Secretary General Elí Altamirano Pérez considers Stalinism a distortion (tergiversación) of Marxism-Leninism. Its principal organizational base is the Central of Action and Labor Unity (Central de Acción y Unidad Sindical—CAUS), which was formed in 1963. The PCdeN had serious problems with the Sandinista-dominated government in March 1980 when it launched a political offensive that included the strike of 2,000 Managua factory workers for higher pay as a means of forcing the process toward a "more Socialist" revolution. Due to these tactics, the Ortega government—which was trying to maintain social consensus at the time—arrested fifty-five PCdeN–CAUS leaders and charged Altamirano and Allan Zambrano Salmerón with involvement in a CIA destabilization campaign and counterrevolutionary activity. The party's attitude changed when Contras began military activity against the Ortega government and the party said that it would "defend the revolution's achievements against [U.S.] imperialism." Nevertheless, the PCN continued to call the Sandinista National Liberation Front (FSLN) government a "Bonapartist dictatorship," and it joined the National Opposition Union (UNO) coalition because it believed that the FSLN had "abandoned democratic government in the first years of the revolution."

A small party of from 200 to 1,000 members in late 1979, the PCdeN's support grew to 16,034 votes in the 1984 elections, and it won two seats in the National Assembly. Its strength in 1991 is difficult to gauge because it ran as part of the UNO coalition. Altamirano won a seat in the National Assembly, with Zambrano as his *suplente* (alternate). In the 1990 Managua City Council elections, Yamileth Bonilla Madrigal won a spot with her fourth place ranking on the UNO slate. Ariel Bravo, Roberto Moreno, and Manuel Pérez Estrada are other important leaders.

Although the PCdeN is organized, theoretically, under the principles of "democratic centralism," in which the maximum decision-making body is the National Assembly of Militants, Altamirano has been accused of developing a personality cult and of dominating the decision-making process.

The PCdeN weekly newspaper *Avance* was critical of various aspects of the Chamorro regime in mid-1990 and has been carrying articles about different Managua neighborhoods seeking potable water, electricity, health clinics, paved streets, and other municipal services. *Avance* has also carried stories on local trade unions, in different parts of the country, which have broken away from the Sandinista Labor Central (CST) and have joined the CAUS.

CONSERVATIVE DEMOCRATIC PARTY (PARTIDO CONSERVADOR DEMÓCRATA). See CONSERVATIVE PARTY.

CONSERVATIVE NATIONAL ACTION (ACCÍON NACIONAL CONSERVADORA). See CONSERVATIVE PARTY.

CONSERVATIVE PARTY (PARTIDO CONSERVADOR—PC). One of the two traditional Nicaraguan parties with origins in the nineteenth century, the PC was first known as the Legitimists (Legitimistas). Assuming the name Conservative only after 1893, the party at first represented the interests of the ruling families in and around the city of Granada, in opposition to those of the city of León. Only after 1893 can it be said to have become a really national party.

In 1950 Emiliano Chamorro, the principal leader of the Conservatives, concluded a "Pact of the Generals" with Anastasio "Tacho" Somoza García, which assured the Conservatives representation in the congress in return for Somoza's continuation in power. However, in 1954, Chamorro and other leaders were exiled after an unsuccessful revolt against Somoza, after which the party assumed a new name, the Traditionalist Conservative Party (PCT), and reorganized to participate in the 1956 elections. Following the assassination of Tacho Somoza during the election campaign, Luis Somoza Debayle, his son and the president of the congress, became president until new elections were held in 1957. While some PCT leaders were in exile, others—who favored working with the Somozas—organized the Nicaraguan Conservative Party (PCN). In 1963 the PCN won about 10 percent of the vote in elections held to choose a successor to Luis Somoza. In the meanwhile, Fernando Agüero Rocha and a group of younger Conservatives had assumed leadership of the PCT.

By the early 1970s, the Conservatives were divided into at least four rival parties: the PCT, the PCN, the Conservative National Action (ANC), and the Authentic Conservative Party (PCA). All four differed in how to deal with the Somoza regime. Thus, Agüero served as a Conservative member of a triumvirate to whom Anastasio "Tachito" Somoza Debayle turned over power in 1971 while a new constitution was being drafted in order to permit his reelection as president. Agüero was ousted—along with the other two triumvirate members—when Somoza reassumed personal control of the government following the 1972 earthquake.

The Conservatives remained divided until 18 March 1979, when representatives of the principal factions met in Managua to join forces as the Democratic Conservative Party of Nicaragua (PCDN) under the leadership of Rafael Córdova Rivas.

During the leadership of the Government of Reconstruction, in 1979 and 1980, Córdova Rivas was a member of the Council of State and later a member of the Junta of the Government of Reconstruction with Arturo Cruz, when Violeta Barrios de Chamorro and Alfonso Robelo Callejas resigned in April 1979. When Adolfo Portocarrero, the political secretary, and other prominant

PCDN leaders left the country in March 1982 to join the Contra guerrillas of the National Democratic Front (FDN) in Honduras, other important leaders, such as Mario Rappaccioli, Jaime Chamorro Cardenal, and Dr. Silviano Matamoros Montalvan, left the PCDN to form the National Conservative Party (PNC) over the issue of the party's participation in the 1984 elections. Another group, led by Miriam Argüello Morales, also split away to form the Conservative Popular Alliance (PAPC). In the 1984 elections, the PCDN won 14.04 percent of the vote and fourteen of the ninety-six seats in the National Assembly. The PCDN refused to sign the new constitution but decided later to participate in the February 1990 elections with a presidential ticket headed by Dr. Eduardo Molina Palacios and Hugo Torrez Cruz. This small remnant of the Conservatives won only 4,500 votes (0.3 percent) in the presidential race and only 4,683 votes for its National Assembly candidates. The PAPC joined the Nation Opposition Union alliance, and Doctora Argüello became president of the National Assembly for its 1991 session.

CONSERVATIVE POPULAR ALLIANCE (ALIANZA POPULAR CONSERVADORA—PAPC). In 1984 some members of the Democratic Conservative Party of Nicaragua (PCDN), led by Miriam Argüello Morales, left the party over the issue of whether to participate in the national elections to be held that year. Argüello, an operator of a set of flower shops in Managua, had moved up in the ranks of the traditional Conservative Party earlier when Fernando Agüero Rocha was the leader. She served as deputy Nicaraguan ambassador to the United Nations from 1971 to 1972 when Agüero was a member of the triumvirate that governed Nicaragua while a new constitution was being written. She began to study law in 1975, and she returned to prominence in opposition politics when she spent six months in jail for participating in an opposition protest march in Nandaime in July 1988.

The PAPC won five assembly seats in the February 1990 elections, and Argüello became president of the assembly for the legislative session beginning in April 1990. She lost that position in early 1991, principally because she was perceived as a closer ally to strongly conservative Vice President Virgilio Godoy Reyes, of the PLI, rather than to President Violeta Barrios de Chamorro. Francisco Anzoátegui Lacayo, who won a seat in the National Assembly in the February 1990 elections as the second-ranked member of the National Opposition Union slate for Region IV (Granada, Masaya, and Rivas), and Alfredo Mendieta are two other important leaders of the PAPC.

COORDINADORA DEMOCRÁTICA NICARAGÜENSE. See NICARAGUAN DEMOCRATIC COORDINATING BOARD.

DEMOCRATIC ACTION (ACCIÓN DEMOCRÁTICA—AD). Manuel Elvir leads this party, which was formed in 1989. The party was unable to meet the requirements of the Electoral Law to operate legally during the election campaign of 1990.

DEMOCRATIC CONSERVATIVE PARTY OF NICARAGUA (PARTIDO CONSERVADOR DEMÓCRATA DE NICARAGUA). See CONSERVATIVE PARTY.

FRENTE DEMOCRÁTICO NACIONAL (NATIONAL DEMOCRATIC FRONT). See CONSERVATIVE PARTY.

FRENTE SANDINISTA DE LIBERACIÓN NACIONAL. See SANDINISTA LIBERATION FRONT.

INDEPENDENT LIBERAL PARTY (PARTIDO LIBERAL INDEPEN-DIENTE—PLI). The PLI was formed in 1944 by Liberals who were opposed to Anastasio Somoza García's domination of the traditional Liberal Party. Until that year, many individual Liberals had opposed Somoza but had not been able to unite into a single organization.

The PLI remained small for many years. Occasionally, the party was able to elect a few members to congress, and occasionally the PLI joined forces with the Conservatives in opposition to the Somozas, but such efforts usually proved fruitless. One of its long-term members, Virgilio Godoy Reyes, served as minister of labor in the Government of National Reconstruction until 1984. Godoy quit the Patriotic Revolutionary Front then to run for president; however, in a surprising turn of events, Godoy quit the race two days after meeting the U.S. ambassador, which led many to speculate that he had succumbed to pressure from the U.S. government. This move led to a split within the party between those who wished to participate in the election and the Godoy faction who did not. The PLI forces who remained in the race won 9.6 percent of the vote and nine seats in the National Assembly. Despite the split and despite the partic-ipation of this group in the drafting of the 1987 constitution, Godoy maintained himself at the head of the party, which has become one of the most anti-Sandinista goups in Nicaragua on the political right.

The ideology of the PLI is generally couched in vague terms similar to those of nineteenth-century liberalism, such as "the effectiveness of the state's orga-nization lies in human rights, social justice, and the egalitarian and harmonic coexistence of the components of society." Godoy and the PLI were in favor of an amnesty for the Contras, and Godoy has said on numerous occasions that Nicaragua "did not need an army nor did El Salvador or Guatemala."

Godoy, one of the most active proponents of a rightist bent in government policy, is nearly always engaged in a power struggle with Antonio Lacayo Or-anguyen, Violeta Barrios de Chamorro's principal campaign adviser and the minister of presidency in the new government. During the election campaign, Godoy rarely appeared alongside Chamorro. Some supporters of the National

Opposition Union (UNO) do not trust Godoy because of his stint as minister of labor from 1979 to 1984; on the other hand, leaders of the CAUS, the CUS, and the Communist Party of Nicaragua do not like him because he put down the strike for higher wages engineered by the CAUS and the PCdeN in 1980.

Wilfredo Navarro Moreira, the previous secretary general of the PLI, was a candidate for the party presidency, to replace Godoy in mid-1990. The vice president of the PLI, Jaime Bonilla López, won election to the National Assembly in 1990 with his number three position on the UNO slate of fourteen persons from Region III (Managua). Julia de la Cruz Mena Pinera was the party's principal leader in Granada as well as the PLI representative to the UNO council with Bonilla.

LIBERAL CONSTITUTIONALIST PARTY (PARTIDO LIBERAL CON-STITUCIONALISTA—PLC). The PLC is essentially an anti-Communist party that developed in 1968 when Ramiro Sacasa Guerrero split with Anastasio "Tachito" Somoza Debayle. The party's principal leaders in 1989 and 1990 were Ernesto Somarriba, who had been a magistrate of the Supreme Court, and Jaime Cuadra S. Somarriba illustrates the personality differences that mark the Liberal factions by noting that Dr. José Luís Tijerino was the "real" leader of the Neo-Liberal Party (PALI), a group formed in 1985, and not Dr. Andrés Zúñiga, although Somarriba was holding conversations with Zúñiga about reuniting the Liberal Party factions. Both Somarriba and Cuadra were critical of Virgilio Godoy Reyes's collaboration with the Sandinista regime as minister of labor from 1979 to 1984.

The PLC won three places in the National Opposition Union (UNO) delegation to the National Assembly in 1990 with deputies from Estelí, Managua, and Region VI. Somewhat surprisingly, Arnaldo Alemana Lacayo of the PLC won the mayorship of Managua over candidates of other UNO parties when the elections were held in April 1990.

LIBERAL PARTY OF NATIONAL UNITY (PARTIDO LIBERAL DE UNI-DAD NACIONAL—PLIUN). Sometimes called the Independent Liberal Party of National Unity, the PLIUN was created by a group led by Dr. Rodolfo Robelo Herrera and Dr. Eduardo Conrado, who felt that the Liberals ought to participate in the 1984 elections in opposition to the Godoy faction which withdrew. The Robelo–Conrado faction claimed the nine seats won by the Independent Liberal Party and signed the 1987 constitution. The PLIUN participated in the formation of the National Opposition Union in 1989 but was expelled for proposing individual party lists to the Supreme Electoral Council. The PLIUN then ran its own ticket in 1990 composed of Robelo for president and Lombardo Martínez Cabezas for vice president as well as slates for each electoral region. This strategy did not prosper because the PLIUN received only 3,151 votes for its presidential ticket and only 3,515 for its assembly slate, and it came in ninth or tenth in every electoral region. Its worst showing came in Rio San Juan, where its candidates won only 2 votes out of 11,641 votes cast, and the South Atlantic Autonomous Region, where its candidates did not receive a single vote.

The PLIUN places the responsibility for the country's economic crisis in the 1980s on U.S. aggression and has criticized the Sandinista government's violation of the principles of "political pluralism, non-alignment and a mixed economy."

LIGA MARXISTA REVOLUCIONARIA (MARXIST REVOLUTIONARY LEAGUE). *See* REVOLUTIONARY PARTY OF THE WORKERS.

MARXIST-LENINIST MOVEMENT OF POPULAR ACTION (MOVIMIENTO DE ACCIÓN POPULAR MARXISTA-LENINISTA—MAP-ML). This radical leftist party has its origins in a 1967 split of the Nicaraguan Socialist Party, which led to the creation of the Popular Action Movement (MAP), and another split in 1972 of the Sandinista National Liberation Front (FSLN), which led to the creation of the MAP-ML. From the beginning, the MAP-ML closely identified itself with Maoism and called itself a "party of the proletariat for the proletariat."

During the 1970s, the party remained small although it organized a Workers Front (Frente Obrero—FO) trade union group in 1974 and published a newspaper *El Pueblo*, which appealed to factory workers and university students. The MAP-ML was also the only party, other than the FSLN, to organize itself into a military group to fight Anastasio "Tachito" Somoza Debayle by organizing its members into the People's (or Popular) Anti-Somoza Militia (MILPA), which was dissolved in 1979 after Somoza went into exile. *El Pueblo* was closed briefly in 1979, and its presses were confiscated in January 1980. The newspaper had published an article stating that there was a "need to abolish the Nicaraguan bourgeoisie, that the Sandinista Revolution was not a workers' revolution but a bourgeois revolution." The newspaper was also in conflict with the Junta of National Reconstruction over its support of Workers Front demands for higher wages and the right to strike.

In 1984 the party won 11,352 votes, or 1.0 percent of the total, and two seats in the National Assembly. While the party signed agreements with other leftist parties during the National Dialogue of 1989, it made no alliance with them or with the National Opposition Union coalition that developed. Its decision to run a separate presidential ticket, with Secretary General Isidro Téllez Toruno and Carlos Cuadra Cuadra, resulted in the collection of only 8,115 votes, and 8,174 votes for its assembly candidates—not enough to elect a single deputy. Most of its voting support came from the city of Managua and the northwestern departments of Chinandega-León and Matagalpa-Jinotega. *El Pueblo* resumed thrice-weekly publication in 1989, but it has not been generally available at newsstands or bookstores.

MARXIST REVOLUTIONARY LEAGUE (LIGA MARXISTA REVOLU-CIONARIA). See REVOLUTIONARY PARTY OF THE WORKERS.

MOVIMIENTO DE ACCIÓN POPULAR MARXISTA-LENINISTA. See MARXIST-LENINIST MOVEMENT OF POPULAR ACTION.

MOVIMIENTO DE UNIDAD REVOLUCIONARIA. See UNITED REVO-LUTIONARY MOVEMENT.

MOVIMIENTO DEMOCRÁTICO NICARAGÜENSE. See NICARAGUAN DEMOCRATIC MOVEMENT.

NATIONAL CONSERVATIVE PARTY (PARTIDO NACIONAL CONSER-VADOR). See CONSERVATIVE PARTY.

NATIONAL DEMOCRATIC FRONT (FRENTE DEMOCRÁTICO NA-CIONAL). See CONSERVATIVE PARTY.

NEO-LIBERAL PARTY (PARTIDO NEO-LIBERAL—PALI). The Neo-Liberal Party, founded in 1985, has the ignominious distinction of being considered by many as the heir to Anastasio "Tacho" Somoza García's Liberal Party because many of its members were magistrates or functionaries of the Somoza regime. Before the PALI was formed, many of these persons solicited membership in the Liberal Constitutionalist Party but were rejected because of their former Somoza connections. Many PALI members claim that they collaborated with the Sandinista National Liberation Front before its 1979 triumph.

The PALI, a member of the Nicaraguan Democratic Coordinating Board, played a key role in promoting Violeta Barrios de Chamorro's candidacy by casting a last-minute vote for a National Opposition Union slate of Chamorro and Virgilio Godoy Reyes rather than for a ticket headed by Enrique Bolaños of the Superior Council of Business Enterprise. That vote caused a crisis within the PALI. Two factions developed, each of which claimed to be the legitimate heir of the party label. One faction was led by José Luis Tijerino, a dentist educated in Chile, and the other by Dr. Andrés Zúniga. When the Supreme Electoral Council ruled that the party label and the archives belonged to the Tijerino faction, Zúniga went to the Nicaraguan Supreme Court for a favorable decision. In the 1990 election, two members of the Zúniga faction—Adolfo García Esquivel, from León-Chinandega, and Ivan Madriz Aguilar, from Granada-Rivas—won seats in the National Assembly.

Tijerino says that the Neo-Liberals accept many of the ideas of Montesquieu and Rousseau on liberty and justice but do not accept the idea of "labor being sold like merchandise." Tijerino notes that his party has tried to keep as many Somocistas as possible out of the party, but he also says that it is impossible to keep out of the party anyone who ever had a government position at the local level or anyone who ever engaged in business relations with the Somozas. He further states, "Somocismo was never liberalism but a doctrine that was nearly medieval, an autarchy, a centralization of power and an economic liberty that was relative."

Although Zúniga has felt that a reunification of the two factions was not possible, a Liberal alliance might be achieved in 1996.

NICARAGUAN CONSERVATIVE PARTY (PARTIDO CONSERVADOR NICARAGÜENSE). See CONSERVATIVE PARTY.

NICARAGUAN DEMOCRATIC COORDINATING BOARD (COORDI-NADORA DEMOCRÁTICA NICARAGÜENSE—CDN).

The CDN, founded in 1981 by the Higher Council of Private Enterprise (Consejo Superior de Empresa Privada—COSEP), was a coalition of parties opposed to the Sandinista National Liberation Front (FSLN). The coalition included the Liberal Constitutionalist Party (PLC), the Social Christian Party (PSC), the Social Democratic Party (PSD), three trade union groups, and the COSEP. Ramiro Gurdian served as president and Roger Guevara Mena as secretary-general. The CDN was the principal center-right civilian political group, operating openly in Nicaragua, that was supported by the Reagan administration, at least until the late 1980s.

The CDN followed a "brinksmanship electoral strategy" in the events that led to the 1984 national elections. When the 1990 elections were on the horizon in mid-1988, the CDN dissolved. Several of its political parties and trade unions joined the National Opposition Union coalition; the PSC and selected individuals ran independently of both the UNO and the FSLN groupings.

NICARAGUAN DEMOCRATIC MOVEMENT (MOVIMIENTO DEMO-CRÁTICO NICARAGÜENSE—MDN).

The MDN was founded in March 1978 by Alfonso Robelo Callejas, a chemical engineer and industrialist educated in the United States, and several businessmen and young professionals not previously active in partisan politics. Like many of the other parties that have developed since the 1960s, the MDN revolves around a personality, that of Robelo, who was a cofounder, with Pedro Joaquín Chamorro, of the anti-Somoza Democratic Liberation Union (UDEL) coalition in 1977 and the Broad Opposition Front (Frente Amplio de Oposición—FAO), which succeeded it in April 1978 after the death of Chamorro. With the triumph of the revolution in July 1979, Robelo became a member of the junta that guided the government for nine months until March-April 1980 when differences over the Marxist-Leninist content of the government's literacy campaign—or those carrying it out—and a concern that Nicaragua was falling into a Cuban or Soviet sphere of influence led to his resignation.

In March 1982—after threats, arrests, and jailings of various party members, as well as the destruction of party headquarters by Sandinista mobs (*turbas divinas*)—Robelo and the party's Political Council decided that the "political space in which they could operate was very closed and that it was necessary to seek help in the international community, working from abroad." The leaders left Nicaragua to join the Democratic Revolutionary Alliance and Contra groups in Costa Rica and Honduras. The party went dormant inside Nicaragua until 1988, when Robelo and other leaders returned after the Esquípulas and Sapoa agreements.

In both the pre-1982 and post-1988 stages, the MDN has been a strong defender of private property, freedom of expression and religion, trade unions, and political pluralism. In its early years, its application for admission to the Socialist International was rejected, as were the applications of the Sandinista National Liberation Front and the Social Democratic Party (PSD). The MDN program adopted in 1989 continued the thrust of "socialism in freedom"; Nicaragua "must push forward its own authentic solutions, free from the injustices of capitalism as well as totalitarian and transpersonalist solutions."

Although the MDN did not have a distinct trade union sector, many leaders of the Confederation of Labor Unity (Confederación de Unidad Sindical—CUS) collaborated with the MDN in the early 1980s and again after the top party leaders returned in 1988. The party claimed 12,000 members in 1980. In late 1989, Secretary-General Roberto José Urroz Castillo said that the party had been able to rebuild its structure in twelve of Nicaragua's departments, in twenty-five *municipios*, and had 5,000 members.

In a significant trade union election, Zacarías Hernández Bustamante—a CUS member who returned from exile in 1988—led a slate that regained the leadership of the Corinto Dockworkers Union in early 1990. In addition, Hernández won a seat in the National Assembly on the National Opposition Union slate for León-Chinandega, as did Urroz in Managua and Daniel Blandon Gadea in Matagalpa-Jinotega.

There are ideological and program similarities in the MDN and the PSD; however, so far, efforts at creating a unified Social Democratic Party have failed. Urroz thinks that unification might be possible by 1996.

NICARAGUAN SOCIALIST PARTY (PARTIDO SOCIALISTA NICARAGÜENSE—PSN). The PSN has been the pro-Moscow "grandfather" of the Nicaraguan left since its founding in 1937. Declared illegal one year later by Anastasio "Tacho" Somoza García, the party reemerged from the underground and formed an informal alliance with President Somoza, who legalized the party in 1944 and tolerated its penetration of the labor movement. Shortly after the end of World War II, Somoza outlawed the PSN and virtually destroyed its labor confederation.

The party then operated clandestinely with about 250 members until Anastasio "Tachito" Somoza Debayle was overthrown in 1979. Many of these members were lawyers, university students, and manual workers who belonged to the General Confederation of Workers; some of them had fought as Sandinista guerrillas against Somoza.

The PSN took part in the Patriotic Revolutionary Front until July 1984 when it decided to run its own candidates for the congress. PSN leaders protested in August 1984 that party members had had their ration cards revoked by the neighborhood Sandinista Defense Committees because of their involvement in the political campaign and that four PSN activists had been arrested for distributing campaign materials. PSN leaders joined the leaders of the Nicaraguan Conservative Party, the Democratic Conservative Party of Nicaragua, and the Popular Social Christian Party in a joint letter sent to the Sandinista National Liberation Front insisting that the minimal conditions for free elections did not exist and appealing for the lifting of the state of emergency—extended by President Daniel Ortega Saavedra on 19 July—that restricted the press and the conduct of public meetings.

Running independently in 1984, the PSN received 14,494 votes and two seats in the assembly. In February 1990, the PSN was a member of the National Opposition Union slate, and three top leaders, including Secretary-General Luis Sánchez Sancho, were elected to the National Assembly.

PARTIDO COMUNISTA NICARAGÜENSE. See COMMUNIST PARTY OF NICARAGUA.

PARTIDO CONSERVADOR. See CONSERVATIVE PARTY.

PARTIDO CONSERVADOR AUTÉNTICO (AUTHENTIC CONSERVATIVE PARTY). See CONSERVATIVE PARTY.

PARTIDO CONSERVADOR DEMÓCRATA DE NICARAGUA (CONSERVATIVE DEMOCRATIC PARTY). See CONSERVATIVE PARTY.

PARTIDO CONSERVADOR NICARAGÜENSE (NICARAGUAN CONSERVATIVE PARTY). See CONSERVATIVE PARTY.

PARTIDO CONSERVADOR TRADICIONALISTA (TRADITIONALIST CONSERVATIVE PARTY). See CONSERVATIVE PARTY.

PARTIDO DE INTEGRACION DE AMÉRICA CENTRAL. See CENTRAL AMERICAN PARTY OF INTEGRATION.

PARTIDO LIBERAL CONSTITUCIONALISTA. See LIBERAL CONSTITUTIONALIST PARTY.

PARTIDO LIBERAL DE UNIDAD NACIONAL. See LIBERAL PARTY OF NATIONAL UNITY.

PARTIDO LIBERAL INDEPENDIENTE. See INDEPENDENT LIBERAL PARTY.

PARTIDO NACIONAL CONSERVADOR (NATIONAL CONSERVATIVE PARTY). See CONSERVATIVE PARTY.

PARTIDO NEO-LIBERAL. See NEO-LIBERAL PARTY.

PARTIDO POPULAR SOCIAL CRISTIANO. See POPULAR SOCIAL CHRISTIAN PARTY.

PARTIDO REVOLUCIONARIO DE LOS TRABAJADORES. See REVO-LUTIONARY PARTY OF THE WORKERS.

PARTIDO SOCIAL CRISTIANO. See SOCIAL CHRISTIAN PARTY.

PARTIDO SOCIAL DEMÓCRATA. See SOCIAL DEMOCRATIC PARTY.

PARTIDO SOCIALISTA NICARAGÜENSE. See NICARAGUAN SO-CIALIST PARTY.

PARTIDO UNIONISTA CENTROAMERICANO. See CENTRAL AMERI-CAN UNIONIST PARTY.

POPULAR SOCIAL CHRISTIAN PARTY (PARTIDO POPULAR SOCIAL CRISTIANO—PPSC). The PPSC was formed in 1976 by a group of young intellectuals, professionals, and workers, led by Dr. Manolo Morales, who broke away from the Social Christian Party (PSC) over the nature of the PSC's opposition to the Somoza regime. They also objected to the efforts of PSC leader Reynaldo Antonio Téfel to focus PSC energies on agrarian reform and rural change even though they were interested in a better distribution of the wealth of society and in overcoming social inequalities.

The PPSC participated in the Patriotic Revolutionary Front but broke away from the Sandinista National Liberation Front (FSLN) under the leadership of Mauricio Díaz, a lawyer, over the government's "militarization of society." The PPSC was much more supportive of a mixed economy than the FSLN, and it also supported obligatory religious education. Díaz and the PPSC won 61,199 votes (5.6 percent) in the 1984 elections.

Although the PPSC was a part of the National Opposition Union (UNO), Díaz led a faction out of the coalition, reportedly over the "unjust distribution" of places on the UNO National Assembly slate, and joined the PSC in a Social Christian Alliance with Erick Ramírez Benavente as its candidate. Other PPSC leaders, such as Luis Humberto Guzmán Arenas—editor of La Cronica, a new newspaper which began publishing in 1988—and two lawyers, Luisa del Carmen

Larios and José Moya, remained with the UNO coalition. In the February 1990 elections, Guzmán and Larios won election to the National Assembly on the UNO slate; the Social Christian Alliance failed to win a single assembly seat.

The bulk of the PPSC membership comes from Catholic progressives in the Nicaraguan Workers Central (Central de Trabajadores de Nicaragua—CTN), which was created in September 1977 out of the reorganization of the Nicaraguan Autonomous Trade Union Movement (Movimiento Sindical Autónomo Nicaragüense—MOSAN), which was originally organized in 1961.

REVOLUTIONARY PARTY OF THE WORKERS (PARTIDO REVOLUCIONARIO DE LOS TRABAJADORES—PRT). This Trotskyite party was formed in 1972 by university students who gave themselves the title, Towards the Popular Revolution (HLRP), in a split of military tactics to be taken against the Somoza government. The HLRP later reorganized itself into the Marxist Revolutionary League (Liga Marxista Revolucionaria—LMR) in 1975, defined itself as Trotskyite, and joined the United Secretariat of the Fourth International. Trotskyite parties from several Latin American countries collaborated with the LMR to organize an international Simón Bolívar Brigade, numbering 250 members, who fought alongside the Sandinista National Liberation Front in Managua and Bluefields, on the Atlantic coast, in the closing phases of the struggle against Anastasio "Tachito" Somoza Debayle. Some forty Colombians and other Latin Americans were then expelled from Nicaragua in 1979 by the Government of National Reconstruction. Interior Minister Tomás Borge Martínez said that the brigade had been dissolved because it "adopted ultra-leftist and undisciplined positions that were creating problems for the Sandinista Revolution." Comandante Bayardo Arce added that the brigade members had undertaken the task of organizing more than seventy worker syndicates in Managua and of organizing popular militias in Bluefields "outside of the directives of the FSLN and the statutes of the Government Junta."

In early 1980, Bonifacio Miranda Bengochea and other leaders were arrested and jailed for continuing to criticize the FSLN as a "petit bourgeois party"; Miranda also criticized the Sandinistas for allowing "patriotic producers" to continue the ownership of their land and for not breaking up the largest privately owned sugar plantations and refineries into separate plots of land for those peasants without access to parcels of land.

The party reorganized itself into the PRT in 1984, but it was unable to meet the legal requirements necessary to run candidates in that year's elections. The party established a newspaper, Correo Internacional, in 1984, which was not printed from 1985 to 1989, and continued recruiting activities among factory workers, hotel and hospital workers, and secondary and university students. The PRT, however, lost status in the 1989 university elections after achieving some success in 1987. The party was legalized to run candidates in the February 1990 elections, but it declined to enter into an alliance with either the Marxist-Leninist Movement of Popular Action or the United Revolutionary Movement, with whom its leaders have an ideological affinity. Its presidential ticket of Bonifacio Miranda and Dr. Juan Carlos Leiton, a gastroenterologist, won 8,500 votes; its assembly slate won 10,586 votes, mostly in the national capital and the electoral region of León-Chinandega.

SANDINISTA NATIONAL LIBERATION FRONT (FRENTE SANDI-NISTA DE LIBERACIÓN NACIONAL—FSLN). The FSLN was founded in July 1961 by Carlos Fonseca Amador, Silvio Mayorga, Tomás Borge Martínez, and a small group of opponents of the Somoza regime, who felt that armed struggle was the only way to take power. In 1972, various members broke off to form what later became the Marxist-Leninist Movement of Popular Action and the Marxist Revolutionary League, now the Revolutionary Party of the Workers. The FSLN was also divided internally into three factions over how best to defeat the Somoza regime: the Prolonged Popular War faction (GPP), the Proletarian Tendency (TP), and the *Terceristas*, who promoted a strategy of combining military strikes in the cities with organizing a broad anti-Somoza movement that included support from progressive business groups.

Since 1979 the top leadership of the FSLN has remained the same. With the exception of Borge, the top leaders of the FSLN are still relatively young guerrilla intellectuals who come from professional or small business families, although several come from working-class families. Although most Sandinistas, including the National Directorate, use a great amount of Marxist-Leninist rhetoric and analysis, most do not call themselves Marxists.

Following the 1990 elections, Humberto Ortega Saavedra, a brother of President Daniel Ortega (1984–1990) and minister of defense since 1979, resigned his position on the directorate as a result of criticism from Sandinista opponents that the army and the Ministry of Defense should not be a party organization but a professional organization subject to the control of the president and the National Assembly.

The Sandinistas perceived themselves as the vanguard of the people in an irreversible process of social transformation and insisted that they had a historical right to rule. From this ideological perspective, elections were superfluous to Bayardo Arce and Borge, since it would be impossible "logically" for the people (often described as those whose political consciousness had been raised by revolutionary education) to choose any leadership other than that of their own vanguard, the FSLN. Sandinista leaders espoused the concept of "participatory democracy," in which citizens become involved at the local level in making decisions on issues that directly affect their lives and their neighborhood. Hence, the Sandinistas put a lot of time and effort into organizing Sandinista Neighborhood Defense Committees (CDS), which played an important role in consolidating the revolution in 1979 and 1980 and which organized a variety of neighborhood improvement projects in many parts of the country. However, the work of the committees was strongly criticized in 1985 and 1986 because of the arbitrary way in which many CDS leaders denied food rationing coupons and gasoline coupons, even though there were surpluses in government stores and gas stations, as well as for their efforts at promoting ideological conformity in a nation where ideological conformity has never been strong. The Sandinistas also organized groups for women, children, teachers, health workers, and professionals, as well as the Sandinista Workers Confederation (CST), perhaps the largest trade union group in the country. Formally founded on 26 July 1979, the CST had over 500 member unions and 100,000 members in 1988.

In mid-1990 and early 1991, various FSLN leaders, such as Luis Carrión Cruz and Carlos Tunnerman, a former university rector, minister of education, and leader of the 1979–1980 literacy campaign, called on the National Directorate and the National Assembly to reorganize the party's leadership structure and program since it was no longer the governing party and had been rejected by so many voters, especially in rural areas. As of May 1991, a National Congress still had not met to discuss these questions despite various schedulings and postponements since April 1990.

SOCIAL CHRISTIAN PARTY (PARTIDO SOCIAL CRISTIANO—PSC). The PSC was founded in 1957 by individuals who had been active in the National Popular Alliance Union (Unión Nacional Alianza Popular), a group which lasted from 1949 to 1955 but which never developed into a real political party. The PSC was then joined in the early 1960s by disenchanted elements of the Traditionalist Conservative Party, which helped it build enough strength to win a few seats in the national congress. In 1967 the PSC joined the PCT and the Independent Liberal Party to form the National Opposition Union (UNO) to oppose the presidential bid of Anastasio Somoza Debayle. Thereafter, the PSC was a significant element in the forces opposing the Somoza dictatorship.

It suffered a split in 1975–1976 when a group, led by Manolo Morales, left to form the Popular Social Christian Party (PPSC). After the fall of Somoza, the PSC reorganized itself at a September 1979 congress and elected Adán Fletes Calle, a lawyer, as its president.

Fletes, a member of the Nicaraguan Permanent Commission of Human Rights, became one of the nation's most outspoken critics of the Sandinista National Liberation Front (FSLN) and of government violation of criminal procedures and of the freedom of expression. The party, a strong supporter of educational and ideological pluralism, argues that "there is a role for Catholic schools and the PSC is opposed to any uniformity of education, be it humanistic, Marxist or Catholic, at either the private or public levels." The PSC also criticized the FSLN's close linking of the state, the party, and the army, and it has called for their separation. The PSC called for respect for the Catholic hierarchy and defended private property "within the concept of the community's well-being." In this respect, the PSC thought the government's role in agrarian reform cooperatives should be reduced: [T]hey have only served to convert the peasant into an instrument of a policy destined to serve one party." The party also supported the right of conscientious objection to military service. Both the PSC and its trade union affiliate, the Federation of Social Christian Workers (FE-TRAL-SC), criticized Sandinista efforts to create a unified labor movement under the direction of the FSLN.

The PSC was a founding member of the Nicaraguan Democratic Coordinating Board and abstained from participating in the 1984 elections. In 1989 PSC leaders participated in the initial stages leading to the formation of the National Opposition Union, but they were expelled in September for presenting their own slate of candidates to the Supreme Electoral Council.

Erick Ramírez Benavente, a new PSC leader coming out of university student political activity in the 1960s, opted to run a separate presidential race in alliance with a PPSC faction led by Mauricio Díaz and the Yamata Atlantic Coast Organization, led by former Contra leaders Steadman Fagoth and Brooklyn Rivera. Ramírez and his vice-presidential running mate, Rina Córdoba de Taboada, won only 11,136 votes (0.8 percent of the total). The National Assembly slate did not do much better, except that the Yatama legislative candidates won 13,201 votes in the North Atlantic Autonomous Region, compared to 3,365 votes for the Ramírez–Taboada ticket. The overall assembly totals of 22,218 votes enabled the unusual slate to gain one National Assembly seat.

SOCIAL DEMOCRATIC PARTY (PARTIDO SOCIAL DEMÓCRATA—PSD). The PSD is made up primarily of former Conservative dissidents who were not able to find a home in the Democratic Conservative Party of Nicaragua (PCDN) when it was formed in March 1979. Strong conflicts with the Sandinista National Liberation Front (FSLN) began when founders Wilfredo Montalvan, a lawyer, and Dr. Luis Rivas Leiva tried to use the adjective "Sandinista" in the party's name: the Partido Sandinista Social Demócrata-(PSSD). The junta issued a decree prohibiting them and other groups from calling themselves Sandinistas.

The PSD was the first group openly to criticize the FSLN and the junta for not complying with the Sandinista program. Montalvan and Rivas criticized the Sandinistas for their efforts at creating a single unified political party and a single trade union movement, their violations of the criminal judicial process, and their efforts to force government employees to attend government-sponsored demonstrations.

Although the PSD participated in the first Council of State, it left in protest over the approval of several laws. Some of the leaders of the PSD joined with the Social Christian Party, the Liberal Constitutionalist Party, and the Nicaraguan Conservative Party in the work of the Nicaraguan Democratic Coordinating Board, but they abstained from participating in the 1984 elections. Others, such as Fernando Chamorro Rappacioli and Alfredo César Aguirre, went to Honduras to join the Contra guerrillas in 1982. With the return of various exiles to Nicaragua in 1988 and 1989, César Aguirre became an important adviser to Violeta Barrios de Chamorro, and he headed the list of the

National Opposition Union candidates for the assembly, guaranteeing him and four other PSD members seats after the February 1990 elections. The PSD has maintained links to the Confederation of Labor Unity, headed by Alvin Guthrie Rivez, an Atlantic Coast worker and trade union leader.

TRADITIONALIST CONSERVATIVE PARTY (PARTIDO CONSERVA-DOR TRADICIONALISTA). *See* CONSERVATIVE PARTY.

UNITED REVOLUTIONARY MOVEMENT (MOVIMIENTO DE UNIDAD REVOLUCIONARIA—MUR). The MUR was formed in July 1988 by dissidents from several leftist parties—the Sandinista National Liberation Front, the Popular Action Movement (MAR), the Revolutionary Party of the Workers (PRT), and the Communist Party of Nicaragua—who disagreed with the internal workings of their parties. Its principal leader has been Moisés Hassan Morales, a leading FSLN militant who occupied the positions of minister of construction, vice minister of the interior, and mayor of Managua until he split with the FSLN in 1988 over the issue of corruption within the party and the government, as well as the party's efforts "to put a tentacle into every corner of the country, to control trade union and professional organizations, to control neighborhood organizations, to put a political commissar over government officials." Hassan also criticized the opportunism of many individuals who said they were "Sandinistas and Revolutionaries but were not."

The MUR has been one of the few opposition parties to defend military service, saying it is necessary "to protect the revolution from U.S. aggression." The MUR also supports the nationalization of the private banks and the state monopoly on foreign trade.

When conversations with the MAP and the PRT to run a single ticket failed, Hassan and Francisco Samper ran as a solo ticket. They did much better than any other minor party, winning 16,751 votes for the presidential ticket and 14,013 for assembly candidates—sufficient to win Hassan a seat in the assembly under the proportional representation aspects of the Electoral Code.

Neale J. Pearson

PANAMA

The isthmus of Panama, which connects Central and South America, measures 480 miles long and from 37 to 110 miles wide, encompassing 28,753 square miles. The least populated Latin American nation, Panama contains approximately 2.3 million people, of whom 70 percent are mestizos (of mixed European-Indian ancestry), 14 percent are black, and 10 percent are from a predominantly white group, which controlled the country's politics until 1968 and again after 20 December 1989. Indians and orientals make up the other 6 percent of the population. Also, Panama has the highest percentage of foreign investment and the highest per capita debt in Latin America.

When the movement for independence began in Spanish America in 1810, the Panamanians defeated the Spanish troops on the isthmus. Panama then became part of the Republic of Gran Colombia. After independence was secured in 1821, Panama continued as part of Colombia, but it developed unique economic interests, which it resented sharing with the rest of the country. Efforts to build a canal across Panama, a topic of discussion since the sixteenth century, moved closer to reality toward the end of the nineteenth century when a French company undertook the project but failed. The U.S. government then bid for the job.

A revolt broke out in Panama, and it proclaimed its independence on 3 November 1903. The United States, which had warships present to prevent the landing of Colombian troops when the Panamanian revolt began, recognized the new nation within a few days. The United States and Panama agreed to the Hay-Bunau Varilla Treaty, which gave the United States the right to build the canal and to have control "as if it were sovereign" over a ten-mile-wide strip bisecting the republic: the Panama Canal Zone. The Panama Canal, which opened in 1914, became the economic lifeline of the country; however, the 1903 treaty, and problems associated with it, dominated Panamanian politics until the 1970s.

Panama's sections of Colombia's traditional Liberal and Conservative parties functioned independently, but ineffectively, until the 1920s, while irresponsible oligarchs and U.S. officials held power on the isthmus. The United States, under powers granted by the 1903 treaty, supervised elections in 1904, 1908, 1912, and 1920. Throughout the 1930s, members of Panama City's white-dominated Union Club controlled politics in the nation. New political parties, centered around personalist leaders representing elite groups, emerged. A Communist party formed in 1925, and a Socialist party was established in 1933. Unlike the elitist parties, the leftists espoused specific programs. In 1936 the United States formally relinquished its power to intervene in Panama's internal affairs, but it retained considerable influence in the nation.

Profascist Arnulfo Arias broke the oligarchical tradition by opposing the United States and advocating *Panameñismo*, or government by Panamanians for the benefit of Panamanians. With the support of a small, often racist, middle class, he captured the presidency in 1940. During World War II, Panama's military (the National Guard) became the arbiter of the country's politics, and it ousted President Arias in 1941. In 1948 Arias was reelected but prevented from taking office by the National Guard. The following year, the Guard placed Arias, who it was believed had changed his totalitarian views, in the presidency. After he engaged in corrupt practices, ignored the constitution, and tried to destroy the Supreme Court, Arias was again deposed.

An official government party, the National Patriotic Coalition (CPN), formed under the guidance of National Guard leader José Remón in 1952, dominated politics until 1960. During Remón's presidency (1952–1955), the CPN initiated Panama's first significant economic and social development programs. In 1960 the National Opposition Union (UNO), led by the National Liberal Party (PLN), became the official government coalition. By 1964 nineteen political parties existed at the national level, and UNO chief Marcos A. Robles was president of Panama. A new coalition, the National Union, headed by Arnulfo Arias's Panamanian Party (PP), secured the presidency in 1968.

A junta, led by National Guard commander Omar Torrijos, ousted Arias in October 1968 and abolished all political parties. Torrijos strove to build political support among urban and rural workers, advocated a "new politics," and adopted a strong anti-imperialist position. He dedicated his efforts to negotiating a new Panama Canal treaty with the United States, one that would ensure ultimate Panamanian control of the waterway and its environs. After the enactment in 1978 of new treaties with the United States, which transferred control over the canal to Panama in the year 2000 and provided for the immediate end of the Canal Zone, Torrijos partially withdrew from politics in favor of civilian president Aristides Royo.

Political parties were legalized, and Torrijos established the Democratic Revolutionary Party (PRD), a nationalistic, multiclass, reform-oriented organization. The PRD's membership ran the political spectrum from left to slightly right of center. By 1980 the reform program of the PRD had deteriorated, and the party was opposed by the National Opposition Front (FRENO), a coalition of parties, centered around Arias, representing a wide political range from the old oligarchical interests on the right to left-of-center social democrats. Royo encouraged the formation of other political parties, and he set 1984 as the date to initiate political democracy via a direct presidential election.

When Torrijos died in a plane crash in July 1981, a dozen years of what he had called the "dictatorship with a heart" ended. He had recovered the canal, but he had not fostered political cohesion and he had not eliminated U.S. economic and political influence in Panama. His populist pronouncements, some reforms, and his nationalist stance on the canal had built a large mass following, but the banking and industrial sectors, not the masses, were the ones who had primarily benefited from Torrijos's programs.

Torrijos left no plans for institutionalizing or transferring political power. In reality, no individual could become president without the endorsement of the National Guard and its commander. Three Guard officers—Rubén Darío Paredes, whom Torrijos had prepared for political office; Manuel Antonio Noriega; and Roberto Díaz Herrera—vied for political and military leadership. Paredes assumed command of the Guard in March 1982, and he began to campaign against Royo whom he blamed for Panama's faltering economy and public corruption. In July 1982, the Guard replaced Royo with a civilian vice president, Ricardo de la Espriella, a U.S.–educated banker who approved of sharing power with the military. In 1983 Panama created a new sixty-seven-member Legislative Assembly to be elected every five years by popular ballot according to proportional representation, changed the name of the National Guard to the Panama Defense Forces (FDP), and approved a referendum banning the participation in elections by active members of the military.

Guard commander Paredes retired and received, at first, the PRD nomination for the presidency in the September 1984 elections. In a ploy for personal power, Noriega, the new FDP commander, forced Paredes out of the nomination and supported civilian, middle-of-the-road, U.S.–educated Nicolás Ardito Barletta for the presidency in the 1984 elections. Also, prior to the 1984 elections, Noriega replaced De la Espriella, who approved of the military's intention to manipulate the voting, elevating Vice-President Jorge Illueca to the presidency.

Ardito Barletta ran under the auspices of the National Democratic Union (UNADE), a six-party coalition consisting of the PRD, the Panama Labor and Agrarian Party (PALA), the Republican Party (PR), the PP, the PLN, and a group of professionals and bureaucrats—the Broad Popular Front (FRAMPO). He was opposed by the aged Arias and the Democratic Opposition Alliance (ADO), composed of the Authentic Panamanian Party (PPA), the Christian Democratic Party (PDC), and the National Liberal Republican Movement (MOLIRENA). Five small independent parties also ran candidates in the 1984 election. Arias, who had campaigned against the corruption of the military rulers, apparently won at the polls, but the Noriega-led FDP rigged the final tally and announced Ardito Barletta as the winner. The United States initially declared neutrality in the election, then supported the Ardito Barletta campaign financially, and finally recognized Ardito Barletta's presidency. Paredes ran a distant third on the Popular Nationalist Party (PNP) ticket, and candidates from the Communist Party (PdeP), the Socialist Workers Party, and the Revolutionary Workers Party (PRT) received a small fraction of the vote. Despite a general lack of public confidence in the integrity of the electoral process, 75 percent of Panama's eligible voters participated in the 1984 election.

Ardito Barletta's attempts to initiate an International Monetary Fund–sponsored austerity program elicited negative responses from trade unions, students, and professionals. Some of his military and political supporters resented his refusal to continue spending government funds to satisfy the poor, the political left, and the FDP. When, in 1985, he moved to investigate the murder of Hugo Spadafora, a critic of the FDP who had accused Noriega of drug and arms dealing, Noriega forced him to resign and replaced him with Eric Delvalle, a wealthy sugar planter and leader of the moderately conservative PR. Delvalle, one of the most detested public figures in Panama, then served as a figurehead president.

Panamanian politics continued under the façade of civilian leadership, but Noriega determined the policies. The greedy general, formerly head of military intelligence and a paid CIA informant since the 1960s, functioned as a double agent in Latin America, cooperating with both sides in the conflicts between the United States and its ideological opponents Cuba and Nicaragua. He embarrassed the United States by ousting Ardito Barletta whom Washington had supported. In 1987, when Noriega resisted cooperating with the United States–directed and financed Contra war against Nicaragua, Washington no longer had any use for him.

The comic opera continued in February 1988, when President Delvalle, with U.S. support, tried to dismiss Noriega as head of the FDP. Noriega forced out Delvalle and replaced him with Manuel Solís Palma. Washington, in a futile gesture, continued to recognize Delvalle. To reduce Noriega's power, the United States imposed economic sanctions against Panama, which resulted in a 30-percent decline in the nation's gross national product and doubled its unemployment rate to over 25 percent. The economic moves created greater public hostility toward Noriega, whom Washington accused of drug running and money laundering. The United States indicted Noriega on criminal charges and sought to extradite him, as Panama prepared for the 1989 presidential elections. A loose coalition of 150 business, civic, and professional groups had formed the National Civic Crusade (CCN) in 1987 to oppose Noriega. Associated with the Civic Crusade were the PDC, the Popular Action Party (PAPO), and the PPA. The CCN's members initially supported the U.S. economic sanctions against Panama.

The perennial presidential candidate and opponent of Noriega, Arnulfo Arias, died in 1988. That year saw the formation of the Democratic Opposition Civic Alliance (ADOC), which included members of the CCN and the other participants in the ADO who had opposed Barletta and had supported Arias in 1984. The ADOC, with additional backing from Panama's strong financial sector and several small parties, nominated for the presidency Guillermo Endara, a

U.S.–educated lawyer and political protégé of Arias. Endara, who promised, if elected, to remove Noriega as head of the FDP, had broken from the PPA and represented the newly formed Authentic Liberal Party (PLA). The ADOC selected Christian Democrat Ricardo Arias Calderón for first vice president and Guillermo Ford of MOLIRENA for second vice president. The only common goal of the ADOC members was opposition to Noriega.

The PPA nominated its secretary-general Hildebrando Nicosia Pérez for president in 1989. For that election, the progovernment (Noriega) National Liberation Coalition (COLINA) consisted of seven parties: the PRD, the PALA, the PLN, the PR, the PdeP, the Revolutionary Workers Party, and the Socialist Workers Party. COLINA chose businessman Carlos Duque as its presidential candidate. He and his cohorts promised a return to the anti-imperialistic, antioligarchical, mass-oriented politics of Torrijos.

Prior to the election, President George Bush of the United States announced publicly that his government had given $9 million to support the ADOC slate. Although the ADOC apparently won the May 1989 election, Endara and his running mates did not assume office. Noriega nullified the election results on the grounds that the votes had been bought by U.S. dollars and that the voters had been influenced by implied threats that the United States would continue its oppressive economic sanctions and completely ruin Panama's economy if Endara was not elected.

After Noriega nullified the vote, he installed Francisco Rodríguez in the presidency; Washington clung to the myth that Delvalle still held that position. When the 1984–1989 presidential term expired in September 1989, the United States claimed that Endara was the legitimate president. In Panama, no political consensus existed. Noriega's supporters, primarily those dependent on government patronage for a living and those who associated the PRD with the economic and social promises of the Torrijos regime, believed that the May 1989 election was properly invalidated because of CIA interference. ADOC supporters recognized Endara as the rightful president. Most other Panamanians wanted to hold a new election, free from foreign interference, a stand backed by many other Latin American governments.

The United States invaded Panama on 20 December 1989, ostensibly to remove Noriega from the country and to protect the canal and the lives of "endangered" U.S. citizens. U.S. troops destroyed the FDP and captured Panama City, utilizing sophisticated weaponry, including Stealth fighter bombers. Endara was taken to a U.S. military base and installed as president, while Panama was occupied by U.S. military personnel. The pro–United States, oligarchical politics that had prevailed before 1968 returned as a result of the eleventh U.S. invasion of Panama in the twentieth century. A U.S.–controlled "Public Force," composed primarily of former FDP troops and officers, replaced the FDP. U.S. officials exercised authority in every Panamanian government ministry, including the presidential office. Under a U.S. Defense Department program, codenamed Project Liberty, a purge of all nationalist and anti–U.S. forces took place, and Washington began to exert pressure on Panama to permit the fourteen U.S. military bases in the country, scheduled to close at the end of 1999, to remain under U.S. control for at least two more decades. To protest these incursions by the United States, four organizations—Vanguardia Torrijista, the left wing of the PRD; the PRT; the Socialist Workers Party; and the People's Party—joined in 1990 to form the United Patriotic Front.

An institutionalized and effective political party system has never existed in Panama. In eleven of the nation's seventeen pre-1989 presidential elections, a broad coalition has won. The National Liberal Party, directed by a strong political boss, won the other six elections. Historically, the coalitions have been temporary alliances, often bringing together parties with vastly different philosophies, based on immediate electoral needs rather than on specific programs. Except for the Christian Democrats and the Marxist organizations, parties are still primarily organized according to private interests rather than programs. Aside from the Marxists, the parties tend to have demagogic, oligarchical leaders who base their control on charisma and authority and impose political values from the top down. The Panamanian people have developed a cynical attitude toward, and a sense of alienation from, their political system, which traditionally has been corrupt, pervaded by the self-interests of its leaders, and controlled by foreign businesses and governments, which frequently do not operate in Panama's best national interests.

Bibliography

Tom Barry. *Panama: A Country Guide*. Inter-Hemispheric Education Resource Center, Albuquerque, N.M., 1990.

John Dinges. *Our Man in Panama: How General Noriega Used the United States and Made Millions in Drugs and Arms*. Random House, New York, 1990.

Independent Commission of Inquiry on the U.S. Invasion of Panama. *The U.S. Invasion of Panama: The Truth behind Operation 'Just Cause.'* South End Press, Boston, 1991.

Frederick Kempe. *Divorcing the Dictator: America's Bungled Affair with Noriega*. G. P. Putnam's Sons, New York, 1990.

Walter LaFeber. *The Panama Canal: The Crisis in Historical Perspective*. Oxford University Press, New York, 1989.

Raúl Leis. "The Cousins' Republic." *NACLA Report on the Americas*, vol. 22, no. 4, July/August 1988, pp. 23–26; and "Panama: The Other Side of Midnight." *NACLA Report on the Americas*, vol. 23, no. 6, April 1990, pp. 4–6.

Sheldon B. Liss. "Panama," in Robert J. Alexander, ed., *Political Parties of the Americas*. Greenwood Press, Westport, Conn., 1982.

Ronald H. McDonald and J. Mark Ruhl. *Party Politics and Elections in Latin America*. Westview Press, Boulder, Colo., 1989.

Sandra W. Meditz and Dennis M. Hanratty, eds. *Panama: A Country Study*. U.S. Government Printing Office, Washington, D.C., 1989.

George Priestly. *Military Government and Popular Participation in Panama: The Torrijos Regime, 1968–1975*. Westview Press, Boulder, Colo., 1986.

John Weeks and Phil Gunson. *Panama: Made in the U.S.A.* Latin American Bureau, London, 1991.
John Weeks and Andrew Zimbalist. *Panama at the Crossroads.* University of California Press, Berkeley, 1991.

Political Parties—Active

AUTHENTIC LIBERAL PARTY (PARTIDO LIBERAL AUTÉNTICO— PLA). This Guillermo Endara–led organization broke from the Authentic Pan-amanian Party, following the death of Arnulfo Arias in April 1988. The PLA, which contains many of Arias's staunch adherents, supported the Democratic Opposition Civic Alliance in the 1989 elections. It worked with the United States to oust Manuel Antonio Noriega from power. Despite the fact that its leader is the president of Panama, it does not wield a great deal of political power.

AUTHENTIC PANAMANIAN PARTY (PARTIDO PANAMEÑISTA AU-TÉNTICO—PPA). The majority of those who split off from the Panamanian Party for the 1984 election formed this new organization. Led by Arnulfo Arias, it supported his candidacy for president in 1984 under the auspices of the Democratic Opposition Alliance coalition. After Arias's death, the PPA broke into two factions, one of which became the Authentic Liberal Party. Hilde-brando Nicosia Pérez ran for the presidency under the PPA banner in 1989.

MOVIMIENTO LIBERAL REPUBLICANO NACIONAL. *See* NATIONAL LIBERAL REPUBLICAN MOVEMENT.

NATIONAL LIBERAL REPUBLICAN MOVEMENT (MOVIMIENTO LIB-ERAL REPUBLICANO NACIONAL—MOLIRENA). This party evolved in 1984 as an alliance of traditional, oligarchy-controlled, primarily conservative organizations, in particular, the Republican, National Liberal, and National parties which opposed the government. Led by Guillermo Ford, MOLIRENA joined the Democratic Opposition Alliance in 1984, which supported the can-didacy of Arnulfo Arias. In 1989 it backed the Democratic Opposition Civic Alliance and the candidacy of Guillermo Endara. It advocates private control of all property, and, in the Endara government, it has responsibility for the ministries of Planning and Economy, Social Welfare, Treasury, Health, and Foreign Relations.

PANAMA LABOR AND AGRARIAN PARTY (PARTIDO LABORISTA AGRARIO—PALA). The PALA was conceived in 1982 by military and busi-ness interests to support the presidential candidacy of General Rubén Darío Paredes. The PALA eventually dropped him as a candidate and backed the National Democratic Union and its candidate Nicolás Ardito Barletta in the

1984 election. In 1989 it allied with the National Liberation Coalition and its candidate Carlos Duque.

PARTIDO DE ACCIÓN POPULAR. See POPULAR ACTION PARTY.

PARTIDO LABORISTA AGRARIO. See PANAMA LABOR AND AGRARIAN PARTY.

PARTIDO LIBERAL AUTÉNTICO. See AUTHENTIC LIBERAL PARTY.

PARTIDO NACIONALISTA POPULAR. See POPULAR NATIONALIST PARTY.

PARTIDO PANAMEÑISTA AUTÉNTICO. See AUTHENTIC PANAMANIAN PARTY.

PARTIDO REVOLUCIONARIO DE TRABAJADORES. See REVOLUTIONARY WORKERS PARTY.

PARTIDO SOCIALISTA DE LOS TRABAJADORES. See SOCIALIST WORKERS PARTY.

POPULAR ACTION PARTY (PARTIDO DE ACCIÓN POPULAR— PAPO). Established by urban, middle-class social democrats in 1982, the PAPO vehemently opposed the Noriega-led National Democratic Union coalition in 1984 and ran its own candidate, Carlos Iván Zúñiga, for president. In 1987 it joined the National Civic Crusade.

POPULAR NATIONALIST PARTY (PARTIDO NACIONALISTA POPULAR—PNP). The PNP was created in 1983 to back the presidential candidacy of Rubén Darío Paredes, who ran a distant third in the 1984 election.

REVOLUTIONARY WORKERS PARTY (PARTIDO REVOLUCIONARIO DE TRABAJADORES—PRT). This Trotskyist organization criticized but supported the Noriega regime and urged it to follow the nationalist policies of the Torrijos government, especially the building of popular democracy. Led by Graciela Dixon, in 1988 the PRT encouraged the government to strengthen the role of the masses in the political process.

SOCIALIST WORKERS PARTY (PARTIDO SOCIALISTA DE LOS TRABAJADORES—PST). A small Trotskyist group that ran dead last in the 1984 elections. In 1990, after the overthrow and arrest of Manuel Noriega, the PST joined the United Patriotic Front to protest the U.S. intervention.

Political Parties—Historical

COALICIÓN PATRIÓTICA NACIONAL. *See* NATIONAL PATRIOTIC COALITION.

CHRISTIAN DEMOCRATIC PARTY (PARTIDO DEMÓCRATA CRISTIANO—PDC). One of Latin America's most conservative Christian Democratic parties, this anti-Communist organization participated in the 1984 presidential election as part of the antimilitary Democratic Opposition Alliance coalition, and in the 1989 election as part of the Democratic Opposition Civic Alliance. Still led by Ricardo Arias Calderón, the party supports a U.S.-directed private sector approach to economic development and the progressive social doctrine of the Catholic Church. It is the most cohesive, most powerful party in the Endara government coalition.

COMMUNIST PARTY (PARTIDO COMUNISTA) or PEOPLE'S PARTY (PARTIDO DEL PUEBLO—PdeP). Factions within this party cooperated with the Torrijos regime. In 1984 it broke away from the progovernment National Democratic Union (UNADE) coalition because UNADE no longer followed the reformist ideas of Torrijos. The PdeP ran its own presidential candidate in 1984; in 1989, the party supported the progovernment National Liberation Coalition.

DEMOCRATIC REVOLUTIONARY PARTY. (PARTIDO REVOLUCIONARIO DEMOCRÁTICO—PRD). The PRD endorsed the National Democratic Union in 1984 and the National Liberal Coalition in 1989. The party affiliated with the Socialist International as a "consulting member" in 1986, thereby co-opting some of the strength of Panama's leftist parties.

NATIONAL LIBERAL PARTY (PARTIDO LIBERAL NACIONAL—PLN). This conservative party backed the broad-spectrum National Democratic Union in 1984 and the National Liberation Coalition in 1989. Some of its leaders defected and supported the Democratic Opposition Civic Alliance in 1989. Weakened by internal splits, it no longer stands as one of Panama's premier political organizations.

NATIONAL PATRIOTIC COALITION (COALICIÓN PATRIÓTICA NACIONAL—CPN). Formed in 1952 to support the presidential candidacy of Colonel José Antonio Remón, the CPN, a coalition of several small parties, was eventually reorganized as a single party. It was the government party during Remón's presidency and remained a strong force until its collapse in the late 1960s.

PANAMANIAN PARTY (PARTIDO PANAMEÑISTA—PP). For the 1984 election, a small faction of this party broke from the majority and, continuing under the Panamanian Party name, supported the National Democratic Union.

PARTIDO COMUNISTA. *See* COMMUNIST PARTY.

PARTIDO DEL PUEBLO. *See* COMMUNIST PARTY.

PARTIDO DEMÓCRATA CRISTIANO. *See* CHRISTIAN DEMOCRATIC PARTY.

PARTIDO LIBERAL NACIONAL. *See* NATIONAL LIBERAL PARTY.

PARTIDO PANAMEÑISTA. *See* PANAMANIAN PARTY.

PARTIDO REPUBLICANO. *See* REPUBLICAN PARTY.

PARTIDO REVOLUCIONARO DEMOCRÁTICO. *See* DEMOCRATIC REVOLUTIONARY PARTY.

PARTIDO SOCIALISTA. *See* SOCIALIST PARTY.

PEOPLE'S PARTY (PARTIDO DEL PUEBLO). *See* COMMUNIST PARTY.

REPUBLICAN PARTY (PARTIDO REPUBLICANO—PR). This moderate to conservative party, founded in 1960, has generally had a multiracial membership. Led by members of the aristocratic Bazan and Delvalle families, in 1984 it supported the National Democratic Union (UNADE), and its leader Eric Delvalle was elected to a vice presidency on the UNADE ticket. In 1989 the PR backed the National Liberation Coalition's candidate, Carlos Duque.

SOCIALIST PARTY (PARTIDO SOCIALISTA). The Socialist Party re-emerged in the 1984 election in opposition to the military and Manuel Antonio Noriega. The party subsequently worked against the implementation of the International Monetary Fund's economic austerity measures, which generally prove detrimental to the interests of the working class.

Sheldon B. Liss

PARAGUAY

Paraguay, a landlocked country the size of California, is located in the geographical center of South America. Most of its 4.2 million citizens are mestizos. Paraguay's history has been dominated by a series of military caudillos.

José Gaspar Rodríguez de Francia ("El Supremo") ruled from 1814 until his death in 1840. A dictator who allowed no political opposition, he isolated Paraguay from world events. Although his policy of isolation kept the nation free of the violence and turmoil that was sweeping much of the rest of Latin America, it also prevented Paraguay from experiencing development and modernization.

After El Supremo's death, Carlos Antonio López and his son, Francisco Solano López, emerged as Paraguay's new strongmen. The father opened the country up to foreign trade and amassed a personal fortune in the process. He also created a large army and got involved in quarrels with neighboring countries.

Francisco Solano López, who succeeded his father in 1862, soon led Paraguay into the disastrous War of the Triple Alliance. Fought almost entirely on Paraguayan soil, the war against Argentina, Brazil, and Uruguay lasted from 1865 to 1870. Nearly 300,000 Paraguayan lives (out of an 1865 population of 525,000) were lost, and the country was left with a male population of less than 30,000. Despite Paraguay's tremendous losses, Solano López emerged as a national hero, and Paraguayans took pride in their five-year struggle against overwhelming odds.

Paraguay had to rebuild after the war. National politics, which excluded the rural masses, consisted of struggles for power among rivals from the upper class. The Colorados and the Liberals, the nation's two dominant political parties, were created in these postwar years, but their existence merely masked the personalism at the heart of the elite's struggles for power. The Liberal Party gained control from the previously dominant Colorados in 1904, and it ruled the country until 1936. The occasional violence and disputes that occurred reflected personal struggles, not different opinions about national policy.

From 1932 to 1936, Paraguay again was at war. Military heroes and new political ideas emerged from this Chaco War, fought against Bolivia. A coup in February 1936, which ousted the Liberal government, led to the creation of the Febrerista Party, the first Paraguayan political party to call for broad social reforms. Febrerista proposals for land reform and state intervention in the economy were too radical for the time, however, and the Febreristas themselves were ousted in a 1937 coup.

Three years of instability ended when General José Felix Estigarribia, the hero of the Chaco War, became president. His presidency was cut short by his death in an aircraft accident, and he was succeeded by General Higinio Morínigo, who ruled from 1940 to 1948. Morínigo's rule was based on support from the Colorado Party and the military. He was unable to assert complete control of the two, however, and he was overthrown in a coup in 1948, which was supported by factions of the Colorados and the military. The six following years of confusion and instability were ended in 1954 when General Alfredo Stroessner took power in a coup. Stroessner ruled for the next thirty-five years.

Although Stroessner had had little contact with the Colorado Party before he took power, he soon gained control of the party by purging his opponents and by imposing his own followers as party leaders. He made the Colorado Party the government party, and he used it as a façade for his own personalist dictatorship. The party could not oppose the wishes of the general.

Stroessner's control was exerted under extended states of siege, which were lifted only for one-day periods to allow the holding of patently fraudulent elections. Opposition trade union and political party leaders were jailed or exiled. Students were beaten and jailed. The government did not hesitate to use force against its critics, but it strove to reduce the visibility of these tactics. As a result of such governmental tactics, opposition parties were fragmented and ineffective. It was not until 1979 that these groups were able to form the National Accord, a loosely unified front, opposed to the government, which lasted through the 1980s. In the absence of effective political party opposition, the Catholic Church became the most visible opponent of the Stroessner government. After 1987, conflicts with the Church became increasingly bitter. Church leaders and organizations were attacked, and Church publications were closed. In return, some government leaders were virtually excommunicated.

The economic boom of the 1970s slowed dramatically in the early 1980s, when the hydroelectric projects with Brazil were completed and international commodity prices dropped. Brazil replaced Argentina as Paraguay's most important, most powerful neighbor. By 1989 Paraguay had resumed steady economic growth. The Stroessner government received international criticism because of human rights violations, charges of extensive involvement in the international drug trade, and corruption and smuggling among governmental and military leaders.

A split in the Colorado Party became public in 1987, when a faction called the militants purged the traditionalist faction from the party. That split was paralleled by a rift in the military. The military was aware that authoritarian military governments in neighboring Brazil, Argentina, and Uruguay had been replaced by elected civilian governments. These events contributed to military concern over a successor to the aging Stroessner. Army leaders feared that Stroessner might name his son Alfredo, an air force officer, as his successor, possibly lessening the dominance of the army. Further worries were caused by army officer ties to traditionalists in the Colorado Party, while the dominant militant faction of the party favored Stroessner's son as his successor. Consequently, General Andrés Rodríguez staged his 3 February 1989 coup after the president began to remove and reassign possible military rivals at the end of January 1989.

Coup leader Rodríguez easily won the presidency in a May 1989 election. General Rodríguez, the Colorado nominee, polled 74 percent of the vote; Domingo Laíno, the leading opposition party candidate, gained 18 percent. Although there were irregularities in the election, all observers agreed that Rodríguez had won by a very large majority. All opposition parties except the Communists were allowed to participate.

During his first two years in office, President Rodríguez began democratization processes. He legalized opposition political parties, allowed freedom of assembly, initiated trials of former government officials for corruption, and authorized a 1991 convention to reform the constitution. He also took steps to privatize inefficient state-run companies and to attract foreign investment. Paralleling these measures, the military retained a strong political role, the government harshly opposed peasant demands for land reform, and the charges of governmental corruption continued.

Historical Overview of Paraguayan Political Parties

On the surface, there is a strong two-party tradition in Paraguay. Since their founding, the Colorado and Liberal parties have dominated national politics. These two, along with their various offshoots, are still the leading national parties; however, others, such as Febreristas and Christian Democrats, have also become part of the political scene. In reality, however, political parties have served as a façade behind which personalist leaders, such as General Stroessner, have dominated and controlled the political system. Personalist leaders and the military, not political parties, have been the nation's major power contenders. Whether or not this situation will change with the removal of General Stroessner in 1989 remains to be seen.

Despite their historical lack of autonomy, the Liberal and Colorado parties and traditions cannot be completely dismissed. The Colorado Party has benefited from its many years as the government party. It has local organizations and ancillary structures such as youth and trade union affiliates throughout the country. Party membership has been a requisite for employment in many occupations, and the party claims to have almost one-third of Paraguay's citizens as members. For many, party loyalty may be emotional, or it may be rooted in family history and tradition.

During the second half of the twentieth century, national politics revolved around General Stroessner. Stroessner also dominated all political parties. The major decision that opposition party politicians made was how to oppose Stroessner. For many, opposition meant imprisonment, exile, or worse. The opposition parties were weakened, fragmented, and made impotent by Stroessner's policies. Stroessner also dominated and controlled his own Colorado party. That party, even with its countrywide organization and its monopoly on the distribution of patronage, had virtually no autonomy as long as the general ruled.

The May 1989 elections, which followed the February coup, demonstrated the continuing problematic situation facing Paraguay's political parties. The Colorados gained over 70 percent of the presidential vote. The leading opposition party, the Authentic Radical Liberals, gained 18 percent of the vote; no other party gained more than 2 percent of the vote. The government party was controlled by the president, and the opposition parties had no possibility of offering an effective alternative.

It has been a paradox of Paraguay's political and party history in the twentieth century that parties have been allowed to flourish only when they posed no threat to the government. When the parties became a threat, the government typically outlawed them and exiled their leaders. This situation may change now that President Stroessner is gone, but Paraguay's past provides little basis for hope that its parties or party system can become the basis for democracy in the nation.

Bibliography

Efraím Cardozo. *Breve historia del Paraguay*. Editorial Universitaria de Buenos Aires, Buenos Aires, 1965.

J. Eliseo da Rosa. "Paraguay," in Abraham F. Lowenthal, ed., *Latin America and Caribbean Contemporary Record*, 1985–1986, 143–67. Holmes and Meier, New York, 1988.

John T. Deiner. "Paraguay," in Robert J. Alexander, ed., *Political Parties of the Americas*, vol. 2, 569–85. Greenwood Press, Westport, Conn., 1982.

Juan Natalicio González. *Proceso y formación de la cultura paraguaya*. Editorial Guarania, Asunción, 1948.

Dennis M. Hanratty and Sandra W. Meditz, eds. *Paraguay: A Country Study*. U.S. Government Printing Office, Washington, D.C., 1990.

Paul Lewis. *Socialism, Liberalism, and Dictatorship in Paraguay*. Politics in Latin America Series. Praeger, New York, 1982.

———. *Paraguay under Stroessner*. University of North Carolina Press, Chapel Hill, 1980.

———. *The Politics of Exile: Paraguay's Febrerista Party*. University of North Carolina Press, Chapel Hill, 1972.

Leo B. Lott. *Venezuela and Paraguay: Political Modernity and Tradition in Conflict*. Rinehart and Winston, New York, 1972.

Ronald H. McDonald and J. Mark Ruhl. *Party Politics and Elections in Latin America.* Westview Press, Boulder, Colo., 1989.

George Pendle. *Paraguay, A Riverside Nation.* Royal Institute of International Affairs, London, 1954.

Phillip Raine. *Paraguay.* Scarecrow Press, New Brunswick, N.J., 1956.

Harris Gaylord Warren. *Paraguay, An Informal History.* University of Oklahoma Press, Norman, 1949.

John Hoyt Williams. "Paraguay's Stroessner: Losing Control?" *Current History* 86, 516, January 1987, pp. 25–28.

World Bank. *World Development Report.* Oxford University Press, New York, 1988.

Political Parties

ACUERDO NACIONAL. *See* NATIONAL ACCORD.

ASOCIACIÓN NACIONAL REPUBLICANA—PARTIDO COLORADO. *See* COLORADO PARTY.

AUTHENTIC RADICAL LIBERAL PARTY (PARTIDO LIBERAL RADICAL AUTÉNTICO—PLRA). The PLRA, which represents the largest faction of the extremely fragmented Liberals, is the continuer of the Liberal tradition in Paraguay.

The PLRA emerged from a tangled series of events following a split among Liberal leaders over whether to oppose President Alfredo Stroessner in the 1963 elections. In 1970 a majority faction of the movement formed the Radical Liberal Party (PLR). In 1977 a majority faction of the PLR tried to bring all factions of the Liberals together, but was prevented from doing so by legal maneuvers of a minority faction. Following this legal action, the PLR majority faction, led by Domingo Laíno, created the Authentic Radical Liberal Party. The PLRA had a center-left political orientation.

The PLRA was barred from the 1978 election. Its leader, Laíno, was arrested, tortured, and exiled numerous times during the 1970s and 1980s because of his criticism of the Stroessner regime. The government also harassed and arrested other PLRA leaders and supporters who actively opposed governmental policies.

The PLRA and Laíno were at the center of the negotiations that led to the creation of a coalition of anti-Stroessner parties, the National Accord (AN), in 1979. Laíno remained one of the most visible opponents of the Stroessner regime throughout the 1980s, often while in exile. He was also the acknowledged leader of the AN. His active opposition helped focus international attention on the Stroessner regime's abuse of human rights.

Laíno was once again the PLRA candidate in the May 1989 presidential elections. Placing second, he gained 18 percent of the presidential vote. The PLRA, with 221,949 votes (20.1 percent), gained nineteen seats in the Chamber of Deputies and ten in the Senate. No other opposition party gained more than two seats in the Chamber or one seat in the Senate. Laíno and the PLRA criticized the government's fraudulent electoral practices. At the end of 1990, the PLRA had two factions: Laíno's majority Liberation for Social Change, and Miguel Abdon Saguier's Popular Movement for Change.

CHRISTIAN DEMOCRATIC PARTY (PARTIDO SOCIAL DEMÓCRATA CRISTIANO—PSDC). Begun as a movement in 1960, the Christian Democratic Party was created in 1965. The party endorsed international Christian Democratic calls for land reform and emphasized the centrality of the family. The Christian Democrats also supported trade union and university autonomy. They advocated nonviolence as the best means for change. The party's largest impact was among the peasants, where they managed to organize rural-based agrarian leagues with some 40,000 members. Party leadership was drawn from young professionals and intellectuals, with support from students, especially at the Catholic University. It also had close ties to the hierarchy of the Roman Catholic Church.

By 1970 the Christian Democrats had become the most outspoken critics of the Stroessner government. The government quieted the party by exiling several party leaders, seizing party records, and barring the party from the 1973 and 1978 elections. In 1979 the party joined the National Accord.

During the 1970s and 1980s, the Catholic Church itself took over the role as the most outspoken critic of the government. The Church excommunicated several government officials over human rights abuses, and Catholic publications and radio broadcasts attacked government policies and repression. The Archbishop of Asunción refused to participate in governmental functions. In return, the government attacked Catholic peasant organizations, expelled foreign priests, and imposed censorship on Catholic communications. The church–state conflict intensified greatly following the militants' takeover of the Colorado Party in 1987.

Weakened by a leadership struggle in 1988, the Christian Democrats received only 1 percent of the vote in the 1989 presidential elections. They elected one deputy and no senators.

COLORADO PARTY (ASOCIACIÓN NACIONAL REPUBLICANA— PARTIDO COLORADO). The Colorado Party, the governmental party under General Alfredo Stroessner, is by far the largest party in Paraguay. The party was organized in the 1870s by General Bernardino Caballero, a hero of the War of the Triple Alliance. He dominated the Colorado governments, which ruled for three decades, until 1904. The Colorados were out of power for the next forty years, but they returned in 1947 when they supported President Higinio Morínigo in thwarting a coup attempt. A year later, some Colorados joined the military in ousting Morínigo. Colorados then participated in a series of unstable governments which terminated in the 1954 coup that brought General Stroessner to power.

Stroessner had not had much contact with the Colorados before the coup, but once he came to power he quickly gained control of the party and appointed loyal supporters to leadership positions. The party lost its autonomy and became Stroessner's personal tool. Colorado party principles facilitated Stroessner's take-over. Officially, the party supports an interventionist state which is to provide order, progress, and equality. In practice, the primary objective often seems to have been merely to stay in power. In addition, the Colorado concept of *coreligionario* calls for preferential treatment for party members. Basically a conservative party— and not a reformist party—it has vague objectives and ideology. As the years passed, Colorado leaders and President Stroessner came to identify the Colorado Party with the state with the slogan: "A Colorado President for all Paraguayans."

Despite Stroessner's control, there was some factionalism in the Colorado Party. A section called the Popular Colorado Movement (MOPOCO) demanded more rights for individuals. Its leaders were forced into exile in 1958.

In the 1980s, a faction called the *colorado ilustrado* (enlightened Colorado) called for democratization and a lessening of Stroessner's personal control. Opposing hard-liners called for toughened attitudes toward political opposition and condemned Stroessner critics, such as U.S. Ambassador Robert White, as Communist sympathizers. The split developed into two factions known as the militants and the traditionalists. The militants included many hard-liners, such as Interior Minister Sabino Montanaro, and longtime leaders of the party who had close personal ties to President Stroessner. Traditionalists, who wanted an opening toward democracy, questioned the continuing rule of President Stroessner. Stroessner sided with the militants, and in 1987 he supported their actions and barred the traditionalists from the party's convention. The militants took full control of all party leadership posts.

The purge of the traditionalists contributed to the 1989 coup. General Rodríguez and some of his military supporters had ties to traditionalists leaders. When Stroessner maneuvered to oust these military officers from positions of power, they staged their coup and assumed control of the government. Rodríguez then ousted leaders of the militant faction from Colorado Party leadership and ran as Colorado presidential candidate in the hastily called May 1989 election. His electoral promises included a pledge to widen the democratic process in Paraguay.

Rodríguez said that one of the reasons behind the coup was the restoration of Colorado Party unity. Throughout 1989 and 1990, he pursued this goal by purging militants (also known as *Stronistas*) from the party. By 1990 a new "democratic" faction had emerged to challenge the traditionalists who had gained control of the party. The democrats included younger leaders, some members who had returned from exile, and some friends of President Rodríguez, for example, Blas Riquelme. By the start of 1991, General Rodríguez, the honorary head of the Colorados, seemed to favor the democratic faction.

Under Stroessner, all military officers were required to be Colorado Party members, but the electoral law was changed under Rodríguez to bar active military from being members of any political party. Nevertheless, the generals continued to attend Colorado Party meetings.

The masses do not take part in Colorado decision making. Their identification with the party is strong, however, due to family tradition, the way in which the party has been presented as representing the nation, and the practical benefits accruing from party membership. The party's branches throughout the country emphasize patron-client and colleague relationships. The party has served as a means for attaining personal favors and benefits, not for making national policy.

The government in Paraguay counts the vote, and it also harasses and outlaws opposition parties. These two facts contribute significantly to Colorado electoral strength. Under Stroessner, the Colorados received from 98.4 percent (1954) to 70.9 percent (1968) of the presidential vote; they polled 90.1 percent (1983) and 88.7 percent (1988) in the last two elections in which Stroessner ran. In the May 1989 election, Colorado candidate Rodríguez continued this tradition by gaining 72 percent of the vote and outpolling the leading opposition candidate by a margin of more than four to one.

COMMUNIST PARTY (PARTIDO COMUNISTA PARAGUAYO—PCP). The Communist Party, founded in 1925, has been illegal throughout almost its entire existence and was still illegal during the 1989 election. During the Stroessner period, the party was actively persecuted; it is estimated that up to 90 percent of its members were forced into exile.

The Sino-Soviet split resulted in the formation of two factions. The pro-Peking faction took the name Paraguayan Marxist-Leninist Communist Party. Communist opposition to the Stroessner government was ineffective, and their calls for a united opposition to his regime were rejected. The other opposition parties barred Communist participation in the National Accord, which was formed in 1979.

The Communist Party's minute size, its factionalism, its rejection by other Paraguayan parties, and its continual persecution by the Stroessner government (some leaders were murdered; others were held in jail for long periods) rendered it ineffective. Julio Rojas, the PCP's president, died in March 1990 in Buenos Aires, where he had lived since 1980. He had spent twenty years in jail during the Stroessner regime.

DEMOCRATIC LIBERAL PARTY (PARTIDO DEMOCRÁTICO LIBERAL—PDL). The Democratic Liberal Party was formed as a result of a split in the Radical Liberal Party over the issue of whether to participate in the 1973 election. After its formation, the PDL was banned from the election.

FEBRERISTA PARTY (PARTIDO FEBRERISTA REVOLUCIONARIO—PFR). A revolt on 17 February 1936 instituted a Febrerista government headed by Colonel Rafael Franco. The Febreristas themselves were, in turn, soon overthrown and forced into exile. Febrerista clubs, with student, worker, and even military supporters, were created, and by the mid-1940s these clubs had established contact with the exiles and were able to create the Febrerista Party at a meeting held in Buenos Aires in 1951. The Febreristas represent a Paraguayan version of the socialistic and nationalistic principles embraced by other parties of Latin America's national democratic left.

The lack of ideological clarity in the Febrerista movement stems from differences found in its two main initial components: veterans of the Chaco War and young intellectuals. Initial differences were compounded in later years by a generation gap in the party and by the long years spent in exile by many of its leaders. Over time, the original leaders, who became more conservative, had to struggle with more activist-oriented younger leaders for control of the party. Some younger members were expelled, and others left to join the Christian Democrats in the 1960s and 1970s. Febreristas were among the 1,000 arrested in the supposed 1974 plot to kill General Alfredo Stroessner.

Febreristas played an important role in both the formation of the National Accord (AN) in 1979 and its later maintenance. As a legal party during the 1980s, the Febreristas served as a focal point within Paraguay for AN activities.

Emerging from the situation caused by the Chaco War, the Febrerista Party was the first party in Paraguay to challenge Liberal and Colorado dominance and to call for social and economic reforms. After their short stay in power, they never regained major strength, owing to imprisonment, exile, fragmentation, and government harassment. The reforms they sought have yet to be implemented. Febrerista weakness is shown by their performance in the 1989 election: they polled only 23,262 votes (2.1 percent) and elected only two deputies and one senator.

LIBERAL PARTY (PARTIDO LIBERAL—PL). The Liberal Party, one of Paraguay's great historic parties, was founded in 1887 and first took power in 1904 as a result of a coup staged against the Colorados. The party remained in power until the Febrerista coup of 1936. During their years in power, the Liberals were often divided into factions revolving around major personalities. Liberal leaders implemented few social or economic reforms.

In 1939 Liberal candidate General José Felix Estigarribia was elected president. His initial moves to allow political freedom were met with strikes and unrest, and he reversed his stance and was made a temporary dictator until a new constitution could be written. When Estigarribia died in an accident, three weeks after the 1940 Constitution was promulgated, this last Liberal president's plans were unfulfilled.

Higinio Morínigo, who succeeded Estigarribia, crushed the Liberal Party and outlawed it in 1942. Many Liberal leaders went into exile, and the party became divided and ineffective. One small faction, the Liberal Renovation Movement, led by Carlos Levi Rufinelli, decided to participate in the 1963 elections and was legally renamed the Liberal Party.

The Liberal majority, then called the Authentic Liberal Party, rejected elec-

494 / POLITICAL PARTIES OF THE AMERICAS

toral participation on the grounds that the elections were a political sham. They returned from exile in 1967. By 1970 most of Levi Rufinelli's Liberal Party followers had been absorbed back into the Authentic Liberal Party grouping, which was renamed the Radical Liberal Party.

In 1977 the small Liberal Party split even further when the majority faction under the Levi Rufinelli brothers left to form the United Liberal Party. Remaining Liberal Party members represented only a tiny fraction of the historic Liberal movement; the Liberal Party, which gained only 4,808 votes in the 1989 election, was unable to elect a single deputy or senator.

MOVIMIENTO DEMOCRÁTICO POPULAR. See POPULAR DEMO-CRATIC MOVEMENT.

MOVIMIENTO POPULAR COLORADO. See POPULAR COLORADO MOVEMENT.

NATIONAL ACCORD (ACUERDO NACIONAL–AN). The Authentic Radical Liberal Party, the Christian Democrats, the Febreristas, and the Popular Colorado Movement created, in 1979, the National Accord, a loose coalition of parties opposed to the Stroessner government. The AN called for mild economic and social reforms, a reduced role for the military, freedom for political prisoners, an end to states of siege, and democratization.

Despite government harassment during the 1980s, including expulsion of leader Domingo Laíno, the AN continued to exist and profess opposition to Stroessner. The Accord often made use of the Febrerista Party's legality to carry out its own activities inside Paraguay. Laíno, who was allowed to return to Paraguay in 1987, coordinated AN activities for the 1988 elections. The police attacked AN demonstrators and broke up their rallies. Shortly before the 1988 election, Laíno and other AN leaders were placed under house arrest. Following the 1989 coup, the Rodríguez government allowed the National Accord to hold a public rally on 11 February, which was broadcast live to the nation. National Accord parties participated in the May 1989 presidential election.

PARTIDO COMUNISTA PARAGUAYO. See COMMUNIST PARTY.

PARTIDO DEMOCRÁTICO LIBERAL. See DEMOCRATIC LIBERAL PARTY.

PARTIDO FEBRERISTA REVOLUCIONARIO. See FEBRERISTA PARTY.

PARTIDO LIBERAL. See LIBERAL PARTY.

PARTIDO LIBERAL RADICAL. See RADICAL LIBERAL PARTY.

PARTIDO LIBERAL RADICAL AUTÉNTICO. See AUTHENTIC RADI-
CAL LIBERAL PARTY.

PARTIDO LIBERAL UNIDO. See UNITED LIBERAL PARTY.

PARTIDO SOCIAL DEMÓCRATA CRISTIANO. See CHRISTIAN DEM-
OCRATIC PARTY.

PARTIDO SOCIALISTA. See SOCIALIST PARTY.

POPULAR COLORADO MOVEMENT (MOVIMIENTO POPULAR COL-
ORADO—MOPOCO). The MOPOCO split from the Colorado movement in
1958 to protest General Stroessner's domination of the party, and, as a consequence of its continued anti-Stroessner stance, it was aggressively persecuted
by the government. Its leaders had to go into exile. In 1978 Stroessner forgave
some MOPOCO members, and many of them returned to Paraguay to rejoin
the Colorados. Persecution eased somewhat after the MOPOCO expelled its
president, Epifanio Méndez Fleitas, a longtime Stroessner foe. In 1979 the
MOPOCO joined the anti-Stroessner National Accord. In the early 1980s, the
colorado ilustrado faction of the Colorado Party favored an amnesty for MOPOCO
members, hoping to reincorporate them into the Colorado Party. Following the
1989 coup, the dominant traditionalist faction welcomed the MOPOCO back
into the Colorado Party. Some former MOPOCO members became active in
the democratic faction of the Colorado Party in 1990.

POPULAR DEMOCRATIC MOVEMENT (MOVIMIENTO DEMOCRÁ-
TICO POPULAR—MDP). The MDP, formed in July 1987, was strongly critical
of the Stroessner regime and attempted to attract lower-class support with a
program to the left of the National Accord parties.

RADICAL LIBERAL PARTY (PARTIDO LIBERAL RADICAL—PLR). President Higinio Morínigo outlawed the Liberal Party and forced its leaders into
exile in 1947. They refused to cooperate in any way with the government, but
in 1962 a small faction of the party, led by Carlos Levi Rufinelli, began to
participate in Paraguayan politics. The government then ruled that this group
could call itself the Liberal Party. As a consequence, when the exiled actual
Liberal leaders returned to Paraguay in 1967, they had to find a new name for
their party. They called themselves the Radical Liberals. By 1970 the Radical
Liberal faction, not the small faction called the Liberal Party, was the dominant
faction of Liberalism and the true continuers of the Liberal Party tradition in
Paraguay. By 1975, however, the Radical Liberals themselves were divided when
various factions disagreed about how best to oppose President Alfredo Stroessner.

In 1975, supported by progressive and youth sections, Domingo Laíno was
elected leader of the PLR. Under Laíno, the Radical Liberals called for an end

to human rights abuses, freedom for political prisoners, and an end to the state of siege, and the party warned against imperialism. Laíno's human rights stance gained international support.

In 1977 the majority faction of the PLR joined the majority faction of the Liberal Party to form the United Liberal Party, which they hoped would come to represent all followers of the Liberal tradition. A court order declaring this new union illegal left the majority factions of both the Radical Liberals and the Liberals without parties, while the minorities controlled both the existing legal parties. When Laíno's majority faction left to form the Authentic Radical Liberal Party, the PLR continued, unsuccessfully running candidates against President Stroessner. In 1989, when the party contested the election against General Andrés Rodríguez, it gained 12,376 votes (1.1 percent) and elected one deputy and one senator.

SOCIALIST PARTY (PARTIDO SOCIALISTA—PS). Established by a group of students and workers in 1920, this party failed to gain any broad support and soon disappeared. Most of its supporters joined the Liberal Party.

UNITED LIBERAL PARTY (PARTIDO LIBERAL UNIDO—PLU). The PLU was created in 1977 by a union of majority factions of both the Liberal Party and the Radical Liberal Party. When a court ruling denied legality to the new United Liberal Party, however, the majority Liberal Party and Radical Liberal Party factions were left without legal standing. In the ensuing confusion, the former Radical Liberals split to form their own party, and the former majority of the Liberal Party took on the name of the United Liberal Party. Controlled by the Levi Rufinelli brothers, the PLU continues to seek an alliance of conservative Liberals.

John T. Deiner

PERU

In area, Peru, with 496,220 square miles, is the third largest country in South America, after Brazil and Argentina. With a coastline of 1,410 miles, Peru is more or less equal in size to the combined territory of the states of Arizona, New Mexico, and Texas. It is divided into three very different geographical regions: the narrow coastal zone, which is a large desert, interrupted by small valleys watered by the rivers that come down from the Andes; the sierra, with its elevated mountain ranges; and the jungle, which is situated to the east of the Andes.

In population, Peru is the sixth largest Spanish-speaking country in the world, after Mexico, Spain, Argentina, Colombia, and the United States. In 1991 it was estimated at 22 million, one fourth of which is concentrated in the greater Lima area. Ethnically, the population is 55 percent mestizo (mixture of Indian and white), 32 percent Indian, 10 percent white, 2 percent black, and 1 percent Chinese and Japanese descendants. Power and wealth in the country are generally monopolized by the whites and a small number of mestizos. A significant percentage of Peruvians, mainly Indians, remain outside the money economy. Like other Latin American populations, about 95 percent of Peruvians identify themselves as Roman Catholics, although millions retain strong vestiges of their pre-Columbian faith.

Peru has been inhabited by humans since at least the ninth millennium B.C. Ancient Peruvians were building their gigantic constructions at about the same time that the Egyptians were building their pyramids. After developing various cultures, they established Tawantinsuyu, the well-organized Inca empire that included most of present-day Peru and Ecuador and parts of Bolivia, Colombia, Chile, and Argentina. The Spaniards conquered Tawantinsuyu in the sixteenth century and established the viceroyalty of Peru in 1544, which was expanded to include almost all of Spanish-ruled South America. In the eighteenth century, the country was drastically reduced in size by the creation of the viceroyalties of New Granada (1717) and Rio de la Plata (1776).

At the beginning of the nineteenth century, two political groups opposed to independence were engaged in a dispute: the conservative defenders of the status quo and the encyclopedists, who called for economic liberalism and better treatment of the Indians. When Spanish military fortunes in America declined and the armies of José de San Martín and Simón Bolívar marched into Peru, the encyclopedists opted, rather apprehensively, for separation from the "mother country." Although San Martín proclaimed the independence of Peru in 1821, it was Bolívar's defeat of the Spanish army at Ayacucho in 1824 that actually secured South America's political autonomy. Since then, until recently, the army has been, most of the time, the dominant political force in the land.

In the newborn republic, Spanish semifeudalism survived, and life for most people continued in about the same manner as during colonial days. The political change, in fact, was in many respects harmful to the Indians, even though they had been the precursors of the struggle for independence and even through they had formed most of the rank and file of the liberating armies. Political autonomy accelerated the process of their exploitation.

As in most of the other Spanish-American countries, Peru experienced during the rest of the nineteenth century a series of uprisings, which, more or less, established a pattern that alternated between dictatorship and chaos. Many army officers believed that the presidency of the republic should be the ultimate achievement of their careers. From 1821 to 1991, the country had seventy rulers, most of them military men, five of whom were not even born in present-day Peru: the Argentine San Martín (1821–1822), the Ecuadorean Antonio José de la Mar (1822–1823, 1827–1829), the Venezuelans Antonio José de Sucre (1823) and Bolívar (1824–1825), and the Bolivian Andrés de Santa Cruz (1826–1827), who was also head of state of the short-lived Peruvian-Bolivian Confederation (1836–1837). Of these seventy presidents, only thirteen were constitutionally elected, and only five abstained from proclaiming themselves dictators: Manuel Pardo (1872–1874, 1875–1876), Eduardo López de Romaña (1899–1903), Fernando Belaúnde Terry (1963–1968, 1980–1985), Alan García Pérez (1985–1990), and Alberto Fujimori (1990–   ). On 6 April 1992, Fujimori suspended the constitution and assumed emergency powers.

The revolution for independence was as incomplete in Peru as it was in most of Latin America; the Spanish forces were defeated but their socioeconomic structure was left almost intact. In this sense, this was an unfinished revolution. The socioeconomic organization of the new republic retained much of the past, which benefited the criollos, the white descendants of the Spaniards born in the Western Hemisphere. Indians, mestizos, and blacks continued to work under wretched conditions. In fact, most people were cast in the role of spectators of national history or cannon fodder of the fraternal and international wars. The patronage system, prejudice, and discrimination flourished and became deeply ingrained.

Peru's crushing defeat in the war against Chile (1879–1883) paved the way for a new type of caudillo and oligarchy. Of the two groups that emerged, one adhered to old-fashioned economic practices while the other allied itself to foreign entrepreneurs and investors, thus creating a new bourgeoisie. Both groups courted army officers and alternated with them in holding on to the reins of government. This arrangement kept the country tightly controlled by the criollo families, which were gradually being strengthened by intermixture with prosperous European immigrants. The process of national domination, moreover, was influenced by regional dynamic forces: northern sugar and cotton barons, southern gentry, and Andean landlords and mineowners. Furthermore, during the nineteenth century, the right to vote was exercised by very few citizens. The 1828 Constitution granted the right to vote to those literate men twenty-one years of age and older with a minimum yearly income of 800 pesos—an unthinkable wage for the majority of mestizos, Indians, and blacks. The result was that only a few thousand Peruvians were eligible to vote. In the 1851 elections, for example only 4,250 people voted out of a total population of nearly three million.

Civilian caudillo Nicolás de Piérola's defeat of General Andrés Avelino Cáceres in a bloody civil war that ended in 1895 ushered in twenty-five years of relative peace and prosperity under the ruling of the privileged few. Afterward, Lima workers, northern sugar plantation laborers, Andean miners, and peasants began to agitate in favor of better working conditions. None of them, however, was able to challenge seriously the established system of domination. Augusto B. Leguia's rule (1908–1912, 1919–1930) was the longest civilian administration in the country's republican history; the governments of Great Marshall Ramón Castilla (1845–1851, 1855–1862), Marshall Oscar R. Benavides (1914–1915, 1933–1939), General Manuel A. Odría (1948–1956), and General Juan Velasco Alvarado (1968–1975) were among the longest military regimes.

Peru did not have a political mass movement before the founding of the Peruvian Aprista Party (PAP) in 1930. Most of the political parties that had been established before 1930 had been formed around a caudillo in response to a group's special interests, without a well-sustained ideology and without popular support. These parties were harshly assessed by Manuel González Prada (1844–1918) as "syndicates of evil ambitions, electoral clubs, and mercantile societies." It is, therefore, no wonder that Mariano Nicolás Valcárcel, toward the end of the nineteenth century, could state accurately that all the members of any political party of Peru could fit into one railroad car.

The most important parties founded in the country during the nineteenth century were the Civilista Party (1871), the Democratic Party (1884), and the Constitutionalist Party (1884); all of them were personalist organizations. Among the many parties created in the twentieth century, only two obtained individually—not in coalition with others—either more than 1 million votes, or more than 50 percent of the votes, in the national elections: the PAP (1980, 1985, and 1990) and the Popular Action (AP) (1980).

The history of Peru, since Leguia's second administration (1919–1930), is intimately related to the history of the PAP. Víctor Raúl Haya de la Torre, its founder, was defeated by Commander Luis M. Sánchez Cerro, candidate of the

Revolutionary Union (UR), a Fascist-like party, in the 1931 general elections. After the new military regime outlawed the PAP, imprisoned many of its leaders, and placed Haya de la Torre in solitary confinement, Aprista activists revolted on 7 July 1932 in Trujillo. In the midst of bloody persecution of the PAP, the dictator Sánchez Cerro was assassinated in 1933. General Benavides succeeded him and governed by force until 1939, when he placed in power as "constitutional president" Manuel Prado, the winner of the 1939 elections during which the PAP was still outlawed. This civilian administration (1939–1945) catered to the special interests of the oligarchy and continued persecution of the Apristas. It bore with pride the name of "Peruvian Stalin" given to Prado by his Communist collaborators.

The victory of the allied forces in World War II permitted the triumph in 1945 of José Luis Bustamante y Rivero, candidate of the Democratic Popular Front, in which the Apristas, who were prevented from running their own presidential candidate, played a major role. However, in 1948 Bustamante himself outlawed the PAP and, shortly afterward, he was unceremoniously deposed by General Odría, who governed dictatorially for the following eight years. In 1956 Prado again became president, succeeding Odría, but this time he served as a true constitutional president, elected with Aprista support in exchange for the restoration of human rights after his inauguration.

The PAP reorganized its ranks and participated in the 1962 general elections. Haya de la Torre received the largest number of votes for the presidency, although he did not reach the one-third minimum required plurality. When a new alignment of forces to solve the impasse was worked out by the Apristas, the armed forces overthrew Prado, installed a military junta, and called for new elections in 1963, in which Belaúnde Terry of the AP was elected. His presidency (1963–1968) ended with the establishment of a Revolutionary Government of the Armed Forces, headed first by General Velasco Alvarado (1968–1975) and then by General Francisco Morales Bermúdez (1975–1980).

In 1978 a constituent assembly, presided over by Haya de la Torre, was convened. Shortly after he signed the new 1979 Constitution, he died. Partially because of an internal struggle in the PAP ranks, Belaúnde Terry was reelected president in 1980 with 1,870,864 votes. The official results of the elections of that year showed that Armando Villanueva, the Aprista presidential candidate, had received 1,129,991 votes. Of the total of 5,307,465 votes cast, 775,423 were voided and 408,244 were declared blanks. The National Electoral Board proclaimed 18 Apristas elected to the 61-member Senate and 58 Apristas elected to the 180-member Chamber of Deputies. Notwithstanding the official results, the PAP was still the largest party in the country, because the votes for Belaúnde were cast mainly by a coalition of anti-Aprista and anti-militarist voters affiliated to the extreme leftist parties, the Christian Popular Party (PPC), and independents, in addition to the members and sympathizers of Belaúnde's AP party. Furthermore, by then the left had split up into more than forty separate political organizations, most of which had a short existence.

During the second Belaúnde administration (1980–1985), there was a general tendency to move away from state protectionism. The government adopted a liberal economic policy that included the reduction of import restrictions and tariff and the completion of the marginal highway, a personal pet project of President Belaúnde. Among the major accomplishments of this regime were the construction of low-income housing and the expansion of domestic demand largely by the growth of imports, especially of intermediate and final consumption goods as well as luxury automobiles, perfumes, and items for the upper ruling classes. As consumption spending of the government increased, investment declined, affected by smaller income available from abroad. Unfortunately, mining, metallurgy, and petroleum remained depressed, affected by low international prices for their products. Meanwhile, the prices of agricultural commodities, which make up the wholesale price index, kept increasing, seriously affecting the majority of the population who saw their real salaries drastically reduced by inflation, unemployment, and recession. The financial situation of most public enterprises also deteriorated. The total foreign debt had risen to US$13 billion by 1985; a significant percentage of that was attributable to accumulated arrears on service payments. According to Manuel Ulloa, former chairman of the Council of Ministers and a prominent member of the ruling AP, the economic crisis was the worst the country had faced since 1883, when the war between Peru and Chile ended.

In great measure because of the economic crisis and the general negative evaluation of the second Belaúnde administration, the PAP obtained 53.10 percent of the valid votes, more than the combined vote of all the other parties, in the 1985 elections. The United Left (IU), the coalition of Marxist parties allied to the Socialist Revolutionary Party (PSR), received 21.25 percent of the votes, the second highest. The PPC, allied to the Movement of Haya Bases (Movimiento de Bases Hayistas), received 12 percent. Belaúnde's AP won only 6 percent. The rest of the participating parties received less than 1 percent, including General Morales Bermúdez's Democratic Front of National Unity (Frente Democrático de Unidad Nacional). Apparently, the architect of the Aprista victory was its presidential candidate, Alan Garcia Pérez. Repeating his slogan, "My commitment is to all Peruvians," his victory was a landslide.

When he took office on 28 July 1985, García became the youngest (born 1949) elected president in the history of Peru and one of the youngest constitutional rulers in the world. During his administration (1985–1990), the number of Mirage 2000 jets ordered from France by the Belaúnde administration was reduced; at the same time, a proposal was made to freeze the regional purchase of armaments. García initiated an economic program to check inflation by controlling prices, limiting government expenditures and the rate of interest, and setting different exchange rates with the dollar. An intense moralization campaign was launched. The new government began to reorganize the police by dismissing thirty-seven generals on charges of corruption or failure to perform their duties. The government dealt crushing blows to the drug-trafficking mafias.

Deep in the jungle, government forces assaulted the largest drug-trafficking complex discovered thus far in Latin America—a complex including sophisticated laboratories for the preparation of cocaine hydrochlorate, a network of illegal airports, modern communications equipment, and light aircraft furnished with computerized gear for landings and takeoffs in areas of dense vegetation and changing atmospheric conditions.

One of the most controversial policies set in motion by Alan García was probably his decision to allocate no more than 10 percent of the total proceeds from Peruvian exports to servicing the foreign debt. This bold decision raised the eyebrows of the creditors even though Belaúnde had already ceased payment of the interest on the US$14 billion owed to foreign governments and banks. This unilateral decision generated intense debate abroad and made many reflect upon the burdensome problem of the foreign debt and the way it had become the major destabilizing factor of both the economy and the society of the developing countries.

The decline of revenues from the export of ores, fuels, and nontraditional products, as a result of depressed external prices, combined with soaring import of foodstuffs and inputs for agriculture and manufacturing, wiped out the trade surplus. The economic policy to stabilize consumer prices and, at the same time, to revitalize production and to redistribute income to benefit the urban and rural poor failed in great measure because of rampant inflation and general recession.

The economic crisis again predisposed the electorate to mistrust traditional politicians. The 1989 and 1990 polls gave Mario Vargas Llosa, the leader of the campaign against President García's attempt to nationalize the banks and insurance companies, a substantial lead over the Aprista Luis Alva Castro, the socialist Alfonso Barrantes, and other presidential candidates in the 1990 general elections. However, Vargas Llosa, the Democratic Front's presidential candidate, was unexpectedly defeated by Alberto Fujimori, the leader of Change 90, a recently constituted political organization. Change 90's elected senators and deputies formed the third largest block in Congress, after the Democratic Front and the PAP. Fujimori, after more than a year in office, suspended the constitution and assumed emergency powers on 6 April 1992, interrupting Peru's democratic order.

Bibliography

Robert J. Alexander, ed. *Aprismo: The Ideas and Doctrines of Víctor Raúl Haya de la Torre.* Ohio, Kent State University Press, Kent, 1973.
Jorge Basadre. *Historia de la República del Perú: 1822–1933.* 10 vols. Editorial Universitaria, Lima, 1983.
François Bourricaud. *Power and Society in Contemporary Peru.* Praeger, New York, 1971.
Eugenio Chang-Rodríguez. *Opciones políticas peruanas.* 2d ed. Editorial Normas Legales, Trujillo, 1986.
———. *La literatura política de González Prada, Mariátegui y Haya de la Torre.* Ediciones de Andrea, Mexico City, 1957.

Eugenio Chang-Rodríguez and Ronald Hellman, eds. *APRA and the Democratic Challenge in Peru*. City University of New York, The Bildner Center, New York, 1988.

Francisco Guerra-García. *Velasco: Del estado oligárquico al capitalismo de estado*. CEDEP, Lima, 1982.

Harry Kantor. *The Ideology and Program of the Peruvian Aprista Movement*. 2d ed. Octagon, New York, 1966.

Peter Klarén. *Modernization, Dislocation, and Aprismo: Origins of the Peruvian Aprista Party, 1870–1932*. University of Texas Press, Austin, 1973.

Cynthia McClintock and Abraham F. Lowenthal, eds. *The Peruvian Experiment Reconsidered*. Princeton University Press, Princeton, N.J., 1983.

Roger Mercado U. *Los partidos políticos en el Perú: El APRA, el P.C.P. y Sendero Luminoso. Síntesis historiográfica*. 2d ed. Ediciones Latinoamericanas, Lima, 1985.

Fredrick B. Pike. *The Politics of the Miraculous in Peru: Haya de la Torre and the Spiritualist Tradition*. University of Nebraska Press, Lincoln, 1986.

Jorge Rodríguez Beruff. *Los militares y el poder: Un ensayo sobre la doctrina militar en el Perú*. Mosca Azul, Lima, 1983.

Raúl P. Saba. *Political Development and Democracy in Peru: Continuity and Change in Crisis*. Westview Press, Boulder, Colo., 1987.

Luis Alberto Sánchez. *Apuntes para una biografía del APRA*. 3 vols. Mosca Azul, Lima, 1978–1982.

Steve Stein. *Populism in Peru: The Emergence of the Masses and the Politics of Social Control*. University of Wisconsin Press, Madison, 1980.

Political Parties—Active

ACCIÓN POLÍTICA SOCIALISTA. *See* SOCIALIST POLITICAL ACTION.

ACCIÓN POPULAR. *See* POPULAR ACTION.

CAMBIO 90. *See* CHANGE 90.

CHANGE 90 (CAMBIO 90). This political organization was created several months before the general elections of 1990 by some small industrialists, evangelists, professors of the National Agrarian University, and middle-class citizens hoping to elect agronomist Alberto K. Fujimori senator, although he ran both for the presidency and the Senate, as permitted by the electoral statutes.

Unexpectedly, the Cambio 90 candidate won the presidency by a landslide, over Mario Vargas Llosa of the Democratic Front (FREDEMO). Cambio's elected senators and deputies constitute the third largest bloc in Congress after the representatives of the FREDEMO and the Peruvian Aprista Party. In a startling reversal of his electoral campaign, President Fujimori put forth a free-market blueprint, drawn up by a team of economists who studied at Oxford, determined to combat hyperinflation and recession, reduce the budget deficit, and make the country attractive to foreign investors.

After the 1990 elections, Víctor Honma Saito was replaced by Andrés Reggiardo, as Cambio's secretary-general. In 1991, Luz Salgado, a close friend of President Fujimori, became the new secretary-general. Among the important members of the party are Máximo San Román, first vice president of the republic and president of the Senate (1991–   ); Victor Paredes, president of the Chamber of Deputies (1991–   ); Wilfredo Alvarez Valer, coordinator of Cambio's parliamentary cell; Pablo Correa, member of Cambio's national executive committee (CEN) and of the Chamber of Deputies (1991–   ); Oscar Cruzado, Cambio's secretary of organization; Santiago Roca, former head of Cambio's commission of government planning; Pedro Vílchez, also member of the party's CEN; Guillermo Yoshikawa, member of the Chamber of Deputies (1990–   ); and Carlos García García, second vice-president of the republic (1991–   ), whose influence in President Fujimori's inner circles diminished after Víctor Honma was replaced as secretary-general. Fujimori's seizure of power in April 1992 interrupted Peru's democratic order, creating an uncertain situation.

CHRISTIAN DEMOCRATIC PARTY (PARTIDO DEMÓCRATA CRISTIANO—PDC). The PDC was founded in 1956 by Héctor Cornejo Chávez, in his native Arequipa, in order to adapt to Peru Christian humanism and the papal encyclicals Rerum Novarum (1891) and Quadragesimo Anno (1931).

In the 1956 general elections, the PDC supported Fernando Belaúnde Terry, the presidential candidate of Popular Action (AP). Although Belaúnde was defeated, the PDC won most of the Arequipa congressional seats. Because the PDC received only 2.88 percent of the votes in the 1962 elections, the party formed an AP–PDC alliance, which won the general elections in 1963. Several PDC members became cabinet ministers in the first Belaúnde administration (1963–1968). In 1966 the party split. The most conservative wing, led by Luis Bedoya Reyes, left the PDC to establish the Christian Popular Party (PPC). The remaining membership, led by Cornejo Chávez, became radicalized, and in 1967 it withdrew its support to the ruling AP. When General Juan Velasco Alvarado overthrew President Belaúnde in 1968, the PDC supported the coup and collaborated with the First Phase of the Revolutionary Government of the Armed Forces (1968–1975). General Francisco Morales Bermúdez's administration (1975–1980), on the other hand, rejected PDC collaboration.

By the 1978 elections, the prestige of the PDC had greatly declined, and it elected only two members to the Constituent Assembly, one of whom was Cornejo Chávez. In the 1980 elections, the party was unable to elect a single candidate. Shortly after the official results were known, Cornejo Chávez announced his retirement from politics. Two years later, Carlos Blancas Bustamante was elected president of the party. The PDC supported Alan García Pérez's presidential candidacy and collaborated with his administration (1985–1990). Blancas became García's first minister of justice. As a result of its small constituency, the PDC played only an insignificant role in the 1990 elections.

CHRISTIAN POPULAR PARTY (PARTIDO POPULAR CRISTIANO—PPC). The PPC, which began as a splinter party of the Christian Democratic

Party (PDC), was established in 1966, under the leadership of Luis Bedoya Reyes. In 1963 Bedoya was Fernando Belaúnde Terry's minister of justice; from 1964 to 1968, he served as the elected mayor of Lima and won the reputation of being an efficient, charismatic administrator. It may have been the abstention of the Popular Action from participating in the 1978 elections that made it possible for the PPC to win 25 of the 100 seats in the 1978–1979 Constituent Assembly. This would explain why, in 1980, the PPC elected only 6 senators out of a total of 60 and 9 deputies out of a total of 180. After losing the presidential election, the PPC accepted President Belaúnde's invitation to form a broad-based government.

The PPC and the Movement of Hayistas Bases (Movimiento de Bases Hayistas—MBH) created the Democratic Convergence (Convergencia Democrática—CD) to participate in the 1985 elections. The CD candidates for the presidency and first and second vice presidencies were Luis Bedoya, Andrés Townsend Ezcurra, and Esteban Rocca. Subsequent poor results in regional, provincial, and municipal elections induced the PPC to join Mario Vargas Llosa's Democratic Front (FREDEMO) in 1988 to partake in the 1990 presidential elections.

COMMUNIST PARTY OF PERU (PARTIDO COMUNISTA DEL PERU—PCP [SENDERO LUMINOSO—SL]). This underground political party is better known as the Sendero Luminoso (Shining Path), a name rejected by Abimael Guzmán, the founder, and his followers. The Sendero began in January 1964, when a new Communist Party was established by the pro-Chinese members of the main PCP. The breakaway faction elected the lawyer Saturnino Paredes Macedo as secretary-general, thanks in part to the assistance rendered by Abimael Guzmán, head of the original PCP committee in Ayacucho and a philosophy professor at the University of Huamanga. Bandera Roja (red flag), the official journal of the new PPC, served to distinguish it from the pro-Moscow faction, which published the weekly Unidad. The splinter group, the PCP–BR, proposed studying the ideology of José Carlos Mariátegui and launching an armed struggle.

The country's guerrilla experience of 1965 generated internal problems for the PCP–BR. Guzmán, in charge of Bandera Roja editorials, tried to distance himself from the internal fights in the party leadership until he presided over the Second Plenary Session of the PCP–BR Central Committee in February 1970. The PCP–BR then split into two camps: one controlled by Paredes; the other by Guzmán. The Paredes faction kept the control of the organization linked with the Chinese Communist Party. The Guzmán faction retained Bandera Roja and entrenched itself in the universities. One of its most active organizations was the Revolutionary Student Front (Frente Estudiantil Revolucionario—FER), which used a letterhead with the slogan: "Por el Sendero Luminoso de Mariátegui" (through Mariátegui's shining path), which led to their unofficial name.

From the moment that the PCP–SL was established, its most distinguished and undisputed leader has been Guzmán, who started his organizational work principally out of the Huamanga University. Losing no time in calling for armed struggle, he sent cadres to the Ayacucho rural zones to convert the peasants and to train them in revolutionary violence. At the same time, other cadres proselytized teachers, university students, and young boys and girls of the lower economic classes. From the very beginning, Sendero's policy was based on clandestine action and rejection of any kind of legal order, following Maoist experience closely.

In 1974 Guzmán's followers lost control of the Student Federation and the Executive Council of the University of Huamanga. This loss of influence was compensated for by increased proselytization of the peasants, the urban and rural lower classes, and the Indian communes. They placed special emphasis on schools for the indoctrination of adolescents. Most of their political activity, however, remained hermetically closed to the general public.

Because, in their view, in a revolutionary situation, the struggle to reform no longer matters—it only dulls the true revolution—Sendero preaches abstention in all elections organized by the bourgeois state. On 17 May 1980, the eve of the national elections, the Sendero began armed attacks, the first of 219 terrorist acts that were perpetrated that year.

The most daring of the Sendero exploits occurred on 2 March 1982, when 500 Senderistas occupied Huamanga, the capital of the Department of Ayacucho, and liberated 304 prisoners, among them the celebrated guerrilla fighter Edith Lagos. After availing themselves of an ample supply of arms, they abandoned the city. Subsequent to this temporary and sensational occupation of that city of 80,000 people, the guerrilla offensive was increased. High-tension towers were dynamited; bridges were destroyed; and police stations, barracks, banks, and business establishments were attacked. Many actions were conducted against the government buildings and offices of the ruling party. During this military phase, the Sendero vanguard briefly occupied small villages, where often they meted out punishment to policemen, soldiers, and civil authorities whom they accused of war crimes. Their personnel were armed with equipment captured from the police, from the armed forces, and from haciendas and mines, as well as their own homemade arms.

By the end of 1987, the Peruvian government calculated that there were between 3,000 and 5,000 Sendero militants and 20,000 active supporters. The officers of the antisubversive war found that the actions of the women who participated in these terrorist actions were important, original, ingenious, and disconcerting. Documents captured by the police reveal that, between 1983 and 1985, three women had headed the Sendero's Political Bureau of Metropolitan Lima: Laura Zambrano (Comrade Meche), Fiorella Montaño (Comrade Lucía), and Margie Clavo Peralta. Sendero women are accused of being extremely dangerous; their responsibilities include "finishing off" their victims. They come from all social classes and regions of the country, especially from the Andean zone. The list of prominent female guerrilla fighters is rather long. Many have died while discharging their daring exploits and while engaged in fierce combat with the police and the armed forces. Hundreds of others have been captured.

Undoubtedly, Sendero Luminoso is the most radical movement in the history of Peru. Economic reasons—including overpopulation, unemployment, extreme poverty, internal migration, lowering of the standard of living, corruption, and so on—have failed to explain satisfactorily the generalized violence in almost the entire country, which is causing thousands of deaths and costing billions of dollars. The conceptual approach to the problem perhaps lies in historical and ideological answers as well as in the acute socioeconomic crisis.

DEMOCRATIC FRONT (FRENTE DEMOCRÁTICO—FREDEMO). The Democratic Front was created by Mario Vargas Llosa in 1988, after he organized the Liberty Movement (Movimiento Libertad) to oppose President Alan García Pérez's attempt to nationalize the banks and insurance companies. FREDEMO's allies include Fernando Belaúnde Terry's Popular Action, Luis Bedoya Reyes's Christian Popular Party, and a group of independent politicians. Mario Vargas Llosa, the FREDEMO's presidential candidate, was unexpectedly defeated by Alberto Fujimori in the 1990 elections. Fujimori's front obtained the highest number of seats in the Chamber of Deputies and in the Senate, but it failed to gain control of either house of the congress. After the results were known, Vargas Llosa courageously opposed his fellow members' outburst of racial prejudice against President-elect Alberto Fujimori and his fellow Peruvians of Japanese ancestry, and then he flew abroad to resume his writing career away from politics.

FREDEMO. See DEMOCRATIC FRONT.

FRENTE DEMOCRÁTICO. See DEMOCRATIC FRONT.

FRENTE NACIONAL DE TRABAJADORES Y CAMPESINOS. See NATIONAL FRONT OF WORKERS AND PEASANTS.

FRENTE OBRERO CAMPESINO ESTUDIANTIL Y POPULAR. See POPULAR FRONT OF WORKERS, PEASANTS, AND STUDENTS.

IZQUIERDA UNIDA. See UNITED LEFT.

LIBERTY MOVEMENT (MOVIMIENTO LIBERTAD). See DEMOCRATIC FRONT.

MOVEMENT OF THE REVOLUTIONARY LEFT (MOVIMIENTO DE LA IZQUIERDA REVOLUCIONARIA—MIR). The MIR had its origins in the Aprista Committee on the Defense of Doctrinaire Principles and Internal Democracy, a group of disenchanted younger leaders of the Peruvian Aprista Party, who were opposed to their party's alliance with the second administration of President Manuel Prado (1956–1962). The committee was formally organized on 29 May 1960. The members asserted that their theoretical principles were those to be found in Víctor Raúl Haya de la Torre's *El antiimperialismo y el APRA*, a basic work that Haya de la Torre wrote in 1928 and published in 1936.

In November 1960, this group established a separate party, under the name Rebel Apra (*Apra Rebelde*). Finally, at a national conference of Rebel Apra held on 13 March 1962, the name was changed to the Movement of the Revolutionary Left, under the leadership of Luis de la Puente Uceda, a young lawyer related to the Haya de la Torre family. Influenced by the example and preaching of Fidel Castro and other theoreticians of the Cuban Revolution, and following a visit to Cuba, the founders of MIR organized three guerrilla columns in the Andes in 1965, all of which were defeated by President Fernando Belaúnde Terry's army. De la Puente and Guillermo Lobatón, the commanders of two of the columns, were captured and killed. Many other MIR guerrilla fighters were killed or captured.

The MIR's history has been plagued by internal bickering and multiple splitting of the movement. At one point, it had split into eight organizations, each one of which retained the original name of the organization. Five of them eventually joined forces again and formed the MIR–5 (MIR de la Confluencia-Grupo de los Cinco). Prior to the 1978 elections, the MIR–5 joined the Popular Democratic Unity coalition and was able to elect Carlos Malpica to the Constituent Assembly (1978–1979) and to the Senate (1980–1985). The main publications of the MIR–5 are *Voz Rebelde* and *Izquierda Popular*. Two other MIR organizations were active in the 1980 elections: MIR–EM (El Militante), led by Hugo Avellaneda, and MIR–FUI, led by Carpio Jordán. The MIR–EM also joined the Popular Democratic Unity; the MIR–FUI, as indicated by its acronym, joined the Unity of the Left (Unidad de Izquierda) coalition. At the same time, some of the few remaining MIR members joined the Tupac Amaru Revolutionary Movement (Movimiento Revolucionario Tupac Amaru—MRT), which is, after the Shining Path, the most important guerrilla organization active in the 1980s and 1990s.

MOVIMIENTO DE LA IZQUIERDA REVOLUCIONARIA. *See* MOVEMENT OF THE REVOLUTIONARY LEFT.

MOVIMIENTO LIBERTAD (LIBERTY MOVEMENT). *See* DEMOCRATIC FRONT.

MOVIMIENTO REVOLUCIONARIO SOCIALISTA. *See* SOCIALIST REVOLUTIONARY MOVEMENT.

NATIONAL FRONT OF WORKERS AND PEASANTS (FRENTE NACIONAL DE TRABAJADORES Y CAMPESINOS—FRENATRACA).

FRENATRACA was founded in 1968 by the brothers Roger and Nestor Cáceres Velásquez and Julio Arce Catacora. A minor left-wing party, but with a loyal core, FRENATRACA won 3 seats in the 1978 constituent assembly and attracted several thousand votes in the 1980 and 1985 general elections. Roger Cáceres is the present leader and the party elected 1 senator and 3 deputies in the 1990 elections.

PARTIDO APRISTA PERUANO. See PERUVIAN APRISTA PARTY.

PARTIDO COMUNISTA DEL PERU. See COMMUNIST PARTY OF PERU.

PARTIDO COMUNISTA PERUANO. See PERUVIAN COMMUNIST PARTY.

PARTIDO COMUNISTA REVOLUCIONARIO. See REVOLUTIONARY COMMUNIST PARTY.

PARTIDO DEMÓCRATA CRISTIANO. See CHRISTIAN DEMOCRATIC PARTY.

PARTIDO OBRERO MARXISTA REVOLUCIONARIO (REVOLUTION-ARY MARXIST LABOR PARTY). See TROTSKYISTS.

PARTIDO OBRERO REVOLUCIONARIO (REVOLUTIONARY LABOR PARTY). See TROTSKYISTS.

PARTIDO POPULAR CRISTIANO. See CHRISTIAN POPULAR PARTY.

PARTIDO REVOLUCIONARIO DE LOS TRABAJADORES (REVOLU-TIONARY WORKERS PARTY). See TROTSKYISTS.

PARTIDO SOCIALISTA DE LOS TRABAJADORES (SOCIALIST WORK-ERS PARTY). See TROTSKYISTS.

PARTIDO SOCIALISTA REVOLUCIONARIO. See SOCIALIST REVO-LUTIONARY PARTY.

PERUVIAN APRISTA PARTY (PARTIDO APRISTA PERUANO—PAP or APRA). The Aprista Party, organized in Peru in 1930, was the first mass party in the country's history. It was constituted by outlawed members of the American Popular Revolutionary Alliance (Alianza Popular Revolucionaria Americana—APRA), which had been organized by Víctor Raúl Haya de la Torre in exile in Mexico City in 1924. A few months after President Augusto B. Leguía was ousted in 1930, in the midst of the world depression, the jails were opened and the exiles began to return home. The Peruvian Aprista Party was founded in Lima on 20 September 1930.

The PAP participated in the national elections of 1931. Fraud kept Haya de la Torre from reaching the presidency, but twenty-two of his disciples were elected to the Constituent Assembly. Luis M. Sánchez Cerro expelled the Aprista representatives from the assembly, outlawed their party, and closed the National University of San Marcos in 1932. After the assassination of Sánchez Cerro in 1933, the provisional president Oscar R. Benavides, soon after he assumed power, permitted the Apristas to exercise their constitutional rights. However, after he felt secure in the presidency, Benavides once more outlawed the Aprista Party in 1934, jailed and exiled thousands of its members, and killed scores of them.

The PAP remained underground until 1945 when it was allowed to join the Democratic National Front (Frente Democrático Nacional) and was permitted to elect some senators and deputies of its own. Relations between the Apristas and José Luis Bustamante y Rivero, the president they helped to elect, soon became strained. He used the pretext of the naval revolt of October 1948 to outlaw the PAP. Without a solid and wide popular base, Bustamante was soon overthrown by his former minister of the interior, General Manuel A. Odría. During his entire dictatorship, from 1948 to 1956, Odría persecuted the Apristas with the same intensity as his dictatorial predecessors had. In 1956 Manuel Prado, the only candidate who promised to restore civil liberties and political rights, won the presidential elections with the aid of the outlawed Apristas.

During Prado's second term in office (1956–1962), the PAP was permitted to reorganize its ranks in order to enter in the national elections of 1962. Haya de la Torre, the PAP's candidate, received 32.94 percent of the votes—more than any other candidate, but short of the one-third required by law to win. The ultimate decision rested with the congress. The PAP approached the Popular Action (AP) for an understanding, but when Fernando Belaúnde Terry rejected the offer, the PAP reached an understanding with Odría to break the impasse. The armed forces, thereupon, revolted, installed a military junta, and called for new elections.

In the 1963 general elections, Haya de la Torre received 34.36 percent of the votes, but Belaúnde won with 39.05 percent of the votes. During Belaúnde's first term in office (1963–1968), the coalition of Apristas and Odriístas controlled both houses of the congress. This decision by the PAP's Executive Committee to collaborate with their former enemies aggravated the PAP's internal crisis. In 1968, just before the approaching elections, Belaúnde was ousted.

The Revolutionary Government of the Armed Forces, first presided over by General Juan Velasco Alvarado (1968–1975) and later by General Francisco Morales Bermúdez (1975–1980), adopted some of the reforms advocated by the PAP, but it remained adamantly opposed to the idea of allowing an Aprista electoral victory. Nevertheless, in the 1978 elections for the Constituent Assembly, the PAP emerged with the highest number of votes, 35.34 percent, and Haya de la Torre received the highest number of preferential votes. The founder of Aprismo was elected president of the Constituent Assembly. On 2 August 1979, a few days after he signed the new Peruvian constitution, he died.

The 1980 general elections gave a surprising triumph to Belaúnde with 45.37 percent of the votes. Armando Villanueva, the PAP's presidential candidate, was the runner-up. Notwithstanding, 18 Apristas were elected to the 61-member Senate, and 58 Apristas were elected to the 180-member Chamber of Deputies. In the general elections of 1985, the PAP obtained 49.60 percent of the votes, more than the combined vote of all the other parties. The United Left received 23 percent of the votes, the second highest. The Christian Popular Party, allied to the Movement of Hayista Bases, received 12 percent, and Belaúnde's Popular Action won only 6 percent. The rest of the participating parties received less than 1 percent, including Bermúdez's Democratic Front of National Unity. There is no question that the architect of the Aprista victory was its own presidential candidate, Alan García Pérez.

During President García's administration (1985–1990), he initiated an economic program to check hyperinflation, limited government expenditures, combated drug trafficking and the ever-growing guerrilla forces of the Sendero Luminoso and the Tupac Amaru Revolutionary Movement, and drastically cut the payment of the foreign debt.

In the 1991 elections, Luis Alva, the Aprista presidential candidate, ranked third in the final results, after Alberto Fujimori of Change 90 and Mario Vargas Llosa of the Democratic Front.

PERUVIAN COMMUNIST PARTY (PARTIDO COMUNISTA PERU-ANO—PCP). A controversy surrounds the origin of the PCP. The Communists maintain that José Carlos Mariátegui founded the PCP on 7 October 1928, with the name Socialist Party of Peru, and that, in March 1930, the executive committee of this party changed its name to the Communist Party of Peru. Others affirm that Mariátegui was not the founder of the PCP but that it was established by Eudocio Ravines on 20 May 1930, thirty-three days after Mariátegui's death.

From the very beginning of its political activities, the PCP relied heavily on the General Confederation of Workers of Peru (Confederación General de Trabajadores del Perú—CGTP), which Mariátegui had founded on 17 May 1929. The PCP did not participate in the general elections of 1931. From 1932 to 1939, it was banned; and it was persecuted until 1956, except during Manuel Prado's first administration (1939–1945). The respectability gained by the Soviet Union during World War II permitted the PCP to be tolerated by Prado. Some of its leaders were elected to the congress with government assistance; others were appointed to high government positions. The support that the Communists gave to President Prado, while he persecuted the Apristas, helps explain why Lombardo Toledano called him "the Peruvian Stalin."

The newly gained freedom permitted Jorge del Prado to organize the First

Congress of the Communist Party of Peru in September 1942. Eudocio Ravines, who had remained the secretary-general of the party for twelve years, had left the PCP and had been succeeded by Jorge Acosta, who occupied that position until 1946. In that year, the Second Congress of the party approved its bylaws and a Declaration of Principles.

During Prado's first administration, the PCP was able to take the lead in establishing a new central labor body, the Confederation of Workers of Peru (Confederación de Trabajadores del Perú—CTP), the first secretary-general of which was Juan P. Luna, Communist member of the Chamber of Deputies. However, after the Apristas returned to legality in 1945, they quickly took control of the CTP away from the Communists. From then, until the advent of the reformist military regime in 1968, the PCP remained a secondary influence in the labor movement.

In recent decades, the Communist movement in Peru has been seriously divided. At the Fourth Conference of the PCP, held in January 1964, the supporters of the pro-Chinese faction separated from the main line of the PCP in order to establish another party with the same name—a problem that was occurring in other countries experiencing the repercussions of the Sino-Soviet ideological struggle. Jorge del Prado was ratified as secretary-general of the faction faithful to the Soviet line. In the general confusion caused by the existence of several parties with the same or similar names, unofficially the name of their paper or a distinctive word was added after the name to distinguish one from the other; thus, the pro-Moscow organization was identified as the Peruvian Communist Party-Unidad (Partido Comunista Peruano-Unidad—PCP-U) because the *Unidad* was the official paper of this party. Its first rival Communist organization was the Peruvian Communist Party-Bandera Roja (PCP-BR), whose official mouthpiece was the *Bandera Roja*.

After 1965 the pro-Peking Communists and Castro sympathizers accused President Fernando Belaúnde Terry of having failed to live up to his promises of nationalizing the oil industry and adopting the urgently needed agrarian reforms. The PCP-U, on the other hand, continued to endorse Belaúnde.

When, on 3 October 1968, Belaúnde was overthrown by General Juan Velasco Alvarado, the PCP-U switched its support to the new ruler and became a valuable backer of the First Phase of the Revolutionary Government of the Armed Forces (1968–1975). As a result of receiving government assistance, a new General Confederation of Workers of Peru (Confederación General de Trabajadores del Perú—CGTP) quickly became the largest central labor organization. It was founded by and remains under pro-Moscow Communist leadership.

General Francisco Morales Bermúdez, after ousting Velasco in 1975 and declaring the Second Phase of the Revolutionary Government, declined the support of the Communists. As the division of the radical left continued, support for the PCP-U diminished. In the 1978 elections, the pro-Moscow party obtained 6 of the 100 seats in the Constituent Assembly. In 1980 the PCP-U allied with five other parties and organizations to form the Unity of the Left (Unidad de Izquierda—UI) coalition to participate in the general elections of that year. The UI elected two senators—del Prado and Enrique Bernales—and one deputy—Alejandro Olivera.

Since 1983 the PCP-U forms part of the new United Left (IU) coalition. It remained with the IU after del Prado failed to maintain the unity of the coalition, and the Socialist Left (Izquierda Socialista—IS) was established under the guidance of Alfonso Barrantes in 1989.

POPULAR ACTION (ACCIÓN POPULAR—AP). This right-of-center party was founded in 1956 by Fernando Belaúnde Terry, the son of Rafael Belaúnde—a minister of President José Luis Bustamante—and the nephew of Víctor Andrés Belaúnde, a well-known Civilista writer. The AP's success can be attributed primarily to the charismatic personality of its founder—his honesty, gentlemanly behavior, dedication, and intelligence. He rejected all foreign ideologies and proposed to draw one from Peruvian history and reality. His doctrine, as he defines it, is sustained by a pragmatic nationalism and people's cooperation with the government and the construction of a highway in the jungle linking all the regions of the country.

In 1956, the first time he ran for president, Belaúnde placed second to Manuel Prado, the winner of the election that year. In the 1962 presidential elections, Belaúnde again ranked second; this time, Víctor Raúl Haya de la Torre won first place and General Manuel A. Odría, third. However, the National Electoral Board announced that Haya de la Torre had received only 32.94 percent of the total votes cast and, consequently, as no candidate had obtained the one-third plurality required by law, the ultimate decision rested with the congress, where the Haya, Belaúnde, and Odría factions each had approximately one-third of the seats. The Peruvian Aprista Party (PAP) approached the AP for an understanding, but Belaúnde rejected their overtures. When the PAP executive committee reached an understanding with Odría to break the impasse, the armed forces revolted, ousted the constitutional president, installed a military junta, and announced new general elections to take place the following year.

In these army-sponsored elections, Belaúnde won with 39.05 percent, thanks to the aid of the Christian Democrats, Communists, and radical leftists. During the Belaúnde administration, an agrarian reform law was passed, rural development programs were started, and other modest reforms were undertaken. The most serious challenge to his government came from the Movement of the Revolutionary Left (MIR) and the Trotskyist guerillas located in the Andes. Throughout his administration, the president had to deal with a congress controlled by the opposition. In 1968, just a few months before the approaching elections, which, according to Belaúnde, the PAP was going to win, another military coup ousted him and installed a Revolutionary Government of the Armed Forces.

After the coup, the AP split, and ex-Vice-President Edgardo Seoane led a dissident group that endorsed the military regime. However, the Seoane faction soon disappeared. By 1978, the party was again unified under Fernando Belaúnde's leadership. The reconstituted AP refused to participate in the 1978 elections for the Constituent Assembly. However, the 1980 general elections gave a surprising victory to the AP: Belaúnde won the presidency, and the AP won a majority in the Chamber of Deputies and twenty-six of the sixty seats in the Senate.

Some of the best known AP leaders are Sandro Mariátegui, Javier Alva Orlandini, Manuel Ulloa, Fernando Schwalb, Oscar Trelles, Eduardo Orrego Villacorta, and Javier Arias Stella.

In 1988 the AP, the Christian Popular Party, and the Liberty Movement formed the Democratic Front (FREDEMO) under the leadership of Mario Vargas Llosa, who became its presidential candidate in the 1990 general elections. Vargas Llosa lost to Alberto Fujimori, the presidential candidate of Change 90.

POPULAR FRONT OF WORKERS, PEASANTS, AND STUDENTS (FRENTE OBRERO CAMPESINO ESTUDIANTIL Y POPULAR—FOCEP). This political front was actually organized in 1977 and not in 1963 as some of its leaders claim. It became more like a party than like a political coalition. Its members call themselves Marxist-Leninist followers of José Carlos Mariátegui who want to apply his ideas to the current Peruvian situation. From 1977 to 1979, the FOCEP was made up of nine organizations and was able to obtain 12 of the 100 seats in the Constituent Assembly (1978–1979). Personal bickering caused six organizations to abandon its ranks prior to the 1980 elections in which the presidential slate of the FOCEP (Genaro Ledesma for president, Manuel Scorza for first vice president, and Laura Caller for second vice president) received 60,839 votes, and its candidates for the Senate obtained 69,814 votes. Ledesma was the only FOCEP senator elected in 1980.

The FOCEP joined other political parties and fronts to constitute the United Left (IU) on 13 September 1981. When some parties withrew from the IU in 1989 to form the Socialist Left (Izquierda Socialita) coalition, the FOCEP remained with the IU to participate in the 1990 elections.

REVOLUTIONARY COMMUNIST PARTY (PARTIDO COMUNISTA REVOLUCIONARIO—PCR). This party, which was created in 1977, immediately joined with the Popular Democratic Unity electoral alliance. Agustín Haya de La Rosa, nephew of Víctor Raúl Haya de la Torre, is the party's main leader. He was elected to the 1978 Constituent Assembly and to the 1980–1985 and 1985–1990 Chamber of Deputies. *Trinchera Roja* was its first official weekly publication. The PCR strongly influenced the political orientation of the well-known weekly *Marka* and the daily paper *Diario de Marka*. Since 1981 the PCR has been a member of the United Left (IU) alliance.

REVOLUTIONARY LABOR PARTY (PARTIDO OBRERO REVOLUCION-ARIO). *See* TROTSKYISTS.

REVOLUTIONARY MARXIST LABOR PARTY (PARTIDO OBRERO MARXISTA REVOLUCIONARIO). *See* TROTSKYISTS.

REVOLUTIONARY VANGUARD–COMMUNIST PROLETARIAN (VAN-GUARDIA REVOLUCIONARIA–COMUNISTA PROLETARIA). *See* PE-RUVIAN COMMUNIST PARTY.

REVOLUTIONARY VANGUARD–POLITICAL MILITARY (VANGUAR-DIA REVOLUCIONARIA–POLITICO MILITAR). This pro-Peking leftist party was founded in 1976. Its main leader, Javier Diez Canseco, was elected to the 1978–1979 Constituent Assembly, to the 1980–1985 Chamber of Deputies, and to the 1985–1990 and 1990–1995 Senate. It has had a strong voice in the direction and political orientation of the weekly *Marka* and in the daily *Diario de Marka*. In the 1980 elections, this party joined the Popular Democratic Unity (UDP) coalition.

REVOLUTIONARY WORKERS PARTY (PARTIDO REVOLUCIONARIO DE LOS TRABAJADORES). *See* TROTSKYISTS.

SENDERO LUMINOSO. *See* COMMUNIST PARTY OF PERU.

SOCIALIST POLITICAL ACTION (ACCIÓN POLÍTICA SOCIALISTA—APS). The APS was founded in 1971 by Gustavo Mohme Llona and several other politicians. In the 1980 general elections, its presidential slate consisted of Mohme for president, Alfonso Benavides Correa, a former ambassador to Mexico during the Velasco administration, for first vice president, and Enrique de la Cruz Hernández for second vice president. This slate received 11,607 votes; the APS's candidates for the Senate obtained 19,167 votes.

SOCIALIST REVOLUTIONARY MOVEMENT (MOVIMIENTO REVOL-UCIONARIO SOCIALISTA—MRS). The MRS was created to participate in the 1980 general elections. At first, it supported Hugo Blanco of the Revolutionary Workers Party but, immediately prior to the elections, it joined the Popular Democratic Union (UDP) coalition. Most of its supporters are Marxist-Leninists and members of the powerful teachers' union, the SUTEP.

SOCIALIST REVOLUTIONARY PARTY (PARTIDO SOCIALISTA RE-VOLUCIONARIO—PSR). The PSR was founded in 1976 by some of General Juan Velasco Alvarado's followers for the purpose of participating in the 1978 elections for the Constituent Assembly. The most important figure in the party was General Leonidas Rodríguez, one-time head of the Velasco government's

System of Social Mobilization (SINAMOS), which had sought to rally popular backing for the First Phase (1968–1975) of the Revolutionary Government of the Armed Forces. The PSR won 6 of the 100 seats in the Constituent Assembly.

Subsequent to the 1978 election, the party split into the PSR-ML (Marxista Leninista) and the PSR-LR (Leonidas Rodríguez). The first faction played a dominant role in what was left of the National Agrarian Confederation, which had been set up by Avelino Mar during the Velasco administration. *El Socialista* was its weekly periodical.

The second faction, which continued to be headed by General Rodríguez, was part of the Unity of the Left (Unidad de Izquierda—UI) coalition in the 1980 general elections, along with the pro-Moscow Peruvian Communist Party and several other, smaller groups. Rodríguez was the UI's candidate for president. The UI ticket came in fifth in the presidential race and sixth in the contest for congressional seats. In 1981, the PSR joined the United Left coalition, contesting elections in 1985 and 1990.

SOCIALIST WORKERS PARTY (PARTIDO SOCIALISTA DE LOS TRABAJADORES). See TROTSKYISTS.

TROTSKYISTS. The Revolutionary Workers Party (PRT), the Peruvian section of the United Secretariat of the Fourth International, was founded in 1978 through the merger of several Trotskyist groups. The new PRT united the forces that remained from the Revolutionary Labor Party (POR), created by the Marxist Workers Group (Grupo Obrero Marxista—GOM) in 1946. The leaders of the early period included Ismael Frías, Francisco Abril de Vivero, Carlos Howes, and Hernando Aguirre, most of whom were jailed or exiled by dictator Manuel A. Odría in 1952.

The great split in the world Trotskyist movement that took place in the 1950s also affected the Peruvian Trotskyists. When they returned from exile after the downfall of Odría, two POR's appeared on the Peruvian scene: one led by Frías and influenced by France's Michel Pablo and Argentina's Juan Posadas, and the other an orthodox branch led by Félix Zevallos under the strong influence of the Argentine Trotskyist movement. Nahuel Moreno, an Argentine leader, indoctrinated Hugo Blanco, the most prominent Trotskyist leader since the 1960s. Blanco joined the movement in Buenos Aires and acquired trade union experience there while working in a meat-packing plant, after dropping out of his agronomy courses at the University of Buenos Aires.

In 1958 Blanco Trotskyists were active in the protest organized in Lima against the visit of U.S. Vice-President Richard Nixon. From that year until 1962, Blanco was assigned to work with the peasants in Cuzco with money "expropriated" from Lima banks. In 1962 he led the armed struggle of the peasants in the province La Convención near Cuzco. Blanco was captured in May 1963 and kept in prison until December 1970. Nine months later, he was exiled to Mexico. After he moved to Sweden, he married a member of the Swedish

Trotskyist party. In 1978 Blanco was back in Peru helping to organize the PRT, which elected him to the Constituent Assembly. In 1980 the PRT obtained 160,713 votes for their presidential slate, headed by Hugo Blanco, Ricardo Napurí Schapiro, and Enrique Fernández Chacón. The party elected two senators—Napurí and Hipólito Enríquez—and three deputies—Blanco, Fernández, and Emeterio Caledonio.

At least three other smaller Trotskyist parties existed in Peru in the 1980s. The Socialist Workers Party (PST) broke away from the PRT in 1979 as a result of the split in the United Secretariat of the Fourth International, led by Nahuel Moreno. The Revolutionary Marxist Labor Party (POMR) is affiliated with an international faction led by the Lutte Ouvrière group in France. These two fielded candidates on the PRT list in the 1980 elections. Napurí, secretary-general of the POMR, was elected senator in those elections. On 7 March 1982, the majority faction of the POMR joined the PST to form a unified Trotskyist party. There still also remains the Revolutionary Labor Party (Trotskyist), which is affiliated with the Posadas rump Fourth International, which participated in the 1978 elections, when its leader Hugo Blanco obtained the third highest number of votes after Víctor Raúl Haya de la Torre and Luis Bedoya Reyes. Blanco was again elected to the Chamber of Deputies in the 1980 elections and to the Senate in the 1990 elections with a considerably smaller percentage of the votes.

UNITED LEFT (IZQUIERDA UNIDA—IU). The IU was established on 13 September 1981 by a coalition of the Union of the Revolutionary Left (Unión de Izquierda Revolucionaria—UNIR), the Democratic Popular Union (Unión Democrático Popular—UDP), the pro-Moscow Peruvian Communist Party (PCP-U), the Popular Front of Workers, Peasants, and Students (FOCEP), and the Socialist Revolutionary Party (PSR), all Marxist organizations, but the last one. Alfonso Barrantes Lingán, a former Aprista, served as secretary-general from its inception until 1987.

Several attempts to unite the Peruvian leftist organizations preceded the creation of the IU. One of these, the Front of the United Left (Frente de Unidad de Izquierda—FUI), was established in August 1967 to participate in the elections to fill the vacancy in the Chamber of Deputies caused by the death of Ciro Alegría, who had been a member of the ruling Popular Action (AP). Carlos Malpica, a former Aprista, the FUI candidate, obtained 14.35 percent of the votes, following Carlos Cueto Fernandini of the AP, who followed Aprista candidate Enrique Chirinos Soto, the winner.

Another attempt was made on 11 January 1980, when the Union of the Left (Unidad de Izquierda—UI) was created by the FOCEP (without the Trotskyists), the PCP-U, the PSR, and other small organizations. The Revolutionary Alliance of the Left (Alianza Revolucionaria de la Izquierda—ARI) joined provisionally a few days later; however, because the ARI included the UDP, the UNIR, and the Revolutionary Communist Party (PCR)—three Trotskyist parties—and other small political organizations, the FOCEP, still adamantly opposed to the Trotskyist parties, withdrew on 21 February 1980. When the ARI disbanded the following day, the failure of this particular coalition was a reality. When the IU was finally organized in 1981, the new coalition comprised UDP, UNIR, and other forces.

The UDP was founded in 1977 by Alfonso Barrantes, Manuel Dammert, Agustín Haya de la Torre, Edmundo Murrugara, and other representatives of several leftist organizations. When the ARI was dissolved, the UDP participated alone in the 1980 elections, running Carlos Malpica for president, Edmundo Murrugara for first vice president, and César Lévano for second vice president. The UDP received 3.29 percent of the votes. After the elections, the UDP included the following organizations: the Revolutionary Communist Party-Red Trench (Partido Comunista Revolucionario-Trinchera Roja—PCR-TR), the Revolutionary Vanguard–Political Military (VR–PM), the Movement of the Revolutionary Left and of the Confluence (Movimiento de la Izquierda Revolucionaria y de la Confluencia—MIR–5), the Anti-imperialist Revolutionary Forces for Socialism (Fuerzas Revolucionarias Antiimperialistas por el Socialismo—FRAS), the Trotskyist Revolutionary Workers Party (POR-T), the Marxist-Leninist FOCEP, and the Socialist Revolutionary Movement (MRS).

On 13 September 1980, the following parties belonged to the UNIR: the Communist Party of Peru-Red Flag, led by Rolando Breña Pantoja; the Revolutionary Vanguard–Communist Proletarian (VR–PC), the Movement of Revolutionary Left–Peru (Movimiento de Izquierda Revolucionaria–Perú—MIR–Perú), the National Liberation Front (Frente de Liberación Nacional—FLN), and the Revolutionary Communist Party (PCR), led by Manuel Dammert Ego Aguirre.

The IU won the Lima municipal elections in 1983 and placed second in the 1985 general elections. In 1989 the IU lost its moderate wing when the Socialist Left (Izquierda Socialista—IS) was established by Enrique Bernales, Edmundo Murrugara, and Manuel Dammert and their parties. Alfonso Barrantes was the IS presidential candidate in 1990. Weakened by the split and the losses of the Communist parties of the Soviet Union and Eastern Europe, the IU ranked fourth in the 1990 elections, although it was slightly ahead of the IS.

VANGUARDIA REVOLUCIONARIA–COMUNISTA PROLETARIA (REVOLUTIONARY VANGUARD–COMMUNIST PROLETARIAN). See PERUVIAN COMMUNIST PARTY.

VANGUARDIA REVOLUCIONARIA–POLITICO MILITAR See REVOLUTIONARY VANGUARD–POLITICAL MILITARY.

Political Parties—Historical

APRA REBELDE (REBEL APRA). See MOVEMENT OF THE REVOLUTIONARY LEFT.

CHRISTIAN DEMOCRATIC MOVEMENT (MOVIMIENTO DEMOCRÁ-TICO CRISTIANO). *See* CHRISTIAN POPULAR PARTY.

CIVILISTA PARTY (PARTIDO CIVILISTA). The Civilista Party (officially named Partido Civil), the first organized political group of Peru, was founded in 1871 to promote the presidential candidacy of Manuel Pardo and to oppose militarism. It flourished during Pardo's government (1872–1876) and during the two administrations of his son, José Pardo y Barreda (1904–1908, 1915–1919). Augusto B. Leguía, who had governed as Civilista president (1908–1912), split the party and returned to power in 1919 to rule the country for eleven years, completely divorced from traditional *civilismo*. After his downfall in 1930, the Civilista Party vainly attempted a comeback, but by the end of the decade it was largely a party of the past.

CONSTITUTIONALIST PARTY (PARTIDO CONSTITUCIONALISTA). The Constitutionalist Party, established in 1884 by the followers of General Andrés Avelino Cáceres, soon was largely transformed into the general's personal vehicle, especially after he was elected president with the assistance of the Civilistas in 1886. Cáceres imposed as his successor Colonel Remigio Morales Bermúdez, who governed from 1890 until his death in 1894. One year after Cáceres imposed Colonel Justiniano Borgoño as Morales Bermúdez's successor, an uprising, led by the Civilistas and the Democratic Party, ousted the Constitutionalist Party regime. Although Cáceres lived for nearly thirty years more, his party never played a major role after 1894.

DEMOCRATIC PARTY (PARTIDO DEMÓCRATA). The Democratic Party was organized in 1884 by Nicolás de Piérola, who ruled Peru twice (1879–1881, 1895–1899). The Democratic Party never returned to power. It had disappeared by 1920.

LIBERAL PARTY (PARTIDO LIBERAL). The Liberal Party was founded in 1900 by Augusto Durand, a one-time member of the National Union established by Manuel González Prada. Although in 1912 the Liberals supported the candidacy of Guillermo Billinghurst, a populist-oriented millionaire, two years later, they joined forces with other groups to oust him from office. Durand had hoped to become president, but, when this did not happen, he joined forces with José Pardo y Barreda's branch of the Civilista Party. The Liberal Party disappeared with Durand's death in 1925.

MOVIMIENTO DEMOCRÁTICO CRISTIANO (CHRISTIAN DEMO-CRATIC MOVEMENT). *See* CHRISTIAN POPULAR PARTY.

MOVIMIENTO DEMOCRÁTICO PERUANO. *See* PERUVIAN DEMO-CRATIC MOVEMENT.

MOVIMIENTO SOCIAL PROGRESISTA. *See* SOCIAL PROGRESSIVE MOVEMENT.

NATIONAL UNION (UNIÓN NACIONAL). This small political organiza-tion was established in 1891 by Manuel González Prada, Germán Leguía Mar-tínez, Abelardo Gamarra, and the other members of the *Círculo Literario*, an association of positivist writers established by Luis E. Márquez in 1886. The Declaration of Principles of the National Union, drafted by González Prada, favored the federal form of government, compulsory minority representation in the congress, return of land to the Indian communes (*comunidades indígenas*), substitution of the army by militias, and universal suffrage even for alien resi-dents. Reflecting positivist philosophy, it favored European immigration and opposed that from Asia. When, in 1901, some of the National Union's prom-inent members began to back the Liberal Party, González Prada resigned from the National Union in protest. A few years later, the party died out through inactivity.

ODRIISTA NATIONAL UNION (UNIÓN NACIONAL ODRIISTA—UNO). This personalist party was created in 1950 with the name of the Restoring Party (Partido Restaurador) by the associates of General Manuel A. Odría, a de facto president who ran unopposed in the 1950 controlled elections and, of course, won them. In order to launch the candidacy of Odría again in 1962 and in 1963, the UNO adopted its new name. In the 1978 elections, a few years after Odría's death, the UNO elected only 2 out of the 100 members of the Constituent Assembly. In 1980 its position deteriorated further; none of its candidates was elected. After 1980 the party ceased to exist.

ORGANIZACIÓN POLÍTICA DE LA REVOLUCIÓN PERUANA. *See* PO-LITICAL ORGANIZATION OF THE PERUVIAN REVOLUTION.

PARTIDO CIVILISTA. *See* CIVILISTA PARTY.

PARTIDO COMUNISTA REVOLUCIONARIO-TRINCHERA ROJA (REV-OLUTIONARY COMMUNIST PARTY-RED TRENCH). *See* UNITED LEFT.

PARTIDO CONSTITUCIONALISTA. *See* CONSTITUTIONALIST PARTY.

PARTIDO DEMÓCRATA. *See* DEMOCRATIC PARTY.

PARTIDO LIBERAL. *See* LIBERAL PARTY.

PARTIDO RESTAURADOR (RESTORING PARTY). *See* ODRIISTA NATIONAL UNION.

PARTIDO SOCIAL DEMÓCRATA. *See* SOCIAL DEMOCRATIC PARTY.

PARTIDO SOCIALISTA DEL PERU. *See* SOCIALIST PARTY OF PERU.

PARTIDO SOCIALISTA PERUANO. *See* PERUVIAN COMMUNIST PARTY.

PERUVIAN DEMOCRATIC MOVEMENT (MOVIMIENTO DEMOCRÁTICO PERUANO—MDP). This personalist party with little popular support was founded originally under the name of Prado Democratic Movement by a group of bankers, industrialists, and businessmen in order to launch the presidential candidacy of former president Manuel Prado in the 1956 elections permitted by the outgoing dictator, General Manuel A. Odría. Prado won with Aprista help, and immediately after he assumed power, he reestablished human rights and political freedom. During his second administration (1956–1962), the MDP tried to expand its ranks. President Prado was unable to prevent the successful military coup that occurred just weeks before the end of his term of office.

When Prado died in 1967, his party began to disintegrate. It elected only two of its members to the 1978 Constituent Assembly. Two years later, it was unable to elect a single member to the congress. In June 1980, a few days after the official results of the general elections were announced, the MDP executive committee declared the party officially dissolved.

PERUVIAN SOCIALIST PARTY (PARTIDO SOCIALISTA PERUANO). *See* PERUVIAN COMMUNIST PARTY.

POLITICAL ORGANIZATION OF THE PERUVIAN REVOLUTION (ORGANIZACIÓN POLÍTICA DE LA REVOLUCIÓN PERUANA—OPRP). This organization claimed to be the heir to the Juan Velasco Alvarado revolution. The OPRP was founded in 1980 by Javier Tantaleán Vanini, minister of fisheries under President Velasco, to partake in the elections of that year. Its presidential slate, headed by Tantaleán, obtained 17,737 votes. None of the OPRP candidates was elected in 1980, and, since it received less than 1 percent of the total number of votes and could not participate in national elections, it ceased to be active.

RESTORING PARTY (PARTIDO RESTAURADOR). *See* ODRIISTA NA-
TIONAL UNION.

REVOLUTIONARY UNION (UNIÓN REVOLUCIONARIA—UR). The
UR, a Fascist-like party, was founded in 1931 by Commander Luis M. Sánchez
Cerro, Luis A. Flores, Ernesto Byrne, and several former members of the Civilista
Party. Although it never formally adopted party statutes, established a perma-
nent press, or held national congresses, the UR had popular support. Flores, its
most aggressive leader, proudly wore a black shirt and declared himself to be "a
Fascist by conviction and temperament."

Extensive manipulation in the vote count brought about the UR's victory in
the 11 October 1931 general elections. Sánchez Cerro assumed power on 8
December 1931. The following month, he declared a state of emergency and
outlawed the Peruvian Aprista Party (PAP) in February 1932. He then launched
a crusade against the Apristas: Thousands were imprisoned and killed, and
hundreds were exiled. In the midst of the civil war that ensued, Sánchez Cerro
was assassinated in 1933. General Oscar R. Benavides succeeded him in the
presidency, and in the 1936 controlled elections, Flores ran unsuccessfully as
the presidential candidate of his party. From that year on, the party's influence
and power declined rapidly. In 1950 it was declared to be in a state of reorganization, when most of the important members resigned and others were expelled.
The UR's disintegration continued until 1956, when the party took part in
national elections for the last time. It disappeared soon thereafter.

SOCIAL DEMOCRATIC PARTY (PARTIDO SOCIAL DEMÓCRATA).
This party was founded by Luis Antonio Eguiguren in 1933. The outlawed
Peruvian Aprista Party supported the presidential candidacy of Eguiguren in the
1936 elections. When the first results began to give Eguiguren a landslide victory,
the counting of the votes was suspended, and the congress elected General Oscar
R. Benavides to continue three more years in the presidency. The Social Democratic Party disappeared soon thereafter.

SOCIAL PROGRESSIVE MOVEMENT (MOVIMIENTO SOCIAL PRO-
GRESISTA—MSP). This political organization was created in 1955 by a small
group of middle-class intellectuals, among whom were Sebastián and Augusto
Salazar Bondy, Jorge Bravo Bresani, Alberto Ruiz Eldrege, Virgilio Roel, José
Matos Mar, and other social scientists. In their manifesto, published on Christ-
mas Day 1956, they claimed to be humanist, non-Marxist-Leninist revolutionaries who were ready to foster the practical teachings of world socialism.

As the years passed, they came out in support of the Peruvian Revolutionary
Government of the Armed Forces, which entrusted to some of them very important positions in the Ministry of Education. With the death of Salazar Bondy,
the party's most important leader, and with the return of constitutional order

in the country in 1980, the MSP became more a movement of the past than of the present.

SOCIALIST PARTY OF PERU (PARTIDO SOCIALISTA DEL PERU— PSP). This party was founded in 1930 by Luciano Castillo, Hildebrando Castro Pozo, Alberto Arca Parró, and Sinforoso Benítez. The PSP was created when Eudocio Ravines changed the name of the Peruvian Socialist Party to the Communist Party of Peru on 20 May 1930. In the 1931 elections, the PSP elected four of its candidates to the Constituent Assembly. However, the PSP delegates were ousted from the assembly when they protested President Luis M. Sánchez Cerro's proclamation of a state of emergency and his outlawing of the Peruvian Aprista Party in February 1932.

The major base of PSP support was in the Talara region in the north. For many years, it controlled one of the two oil workers' federations there. It participated in all elections in which competing parties were allowed to take part; on several occasions, it succeeded in electing one or more members to the Chamber of Deputies. Castillo was elected to the 1956–1960 Senate. He was his party's unsuccessful presidential candidate in 1962 and in 1980, polling 16,776 and 8,714 votes, respectively. The PSP never belonged to the Socialist International.

UNIÓN NACIONAL. See NATIONAL UNION.

UNIÓN NACIONAL ODRIISTA. See ODRIISTA NATIONAL UNION.

UNIÓN REVOLUCIONARIA. See REVOLUTIONARY UNION.

Eugenio Chang-Rodríguez

PUERTO RICO

The Commonwealth of Puerto Rico, a territorial jurisdiction of the United States, is the smallest and easternmost island of the Greater Antilles. The northern shores of its 111-mile east-to-west length front on the Atlantic Ocean; its southern 36-mile width touches the Caribbean Sea. Three-fourths of its approximately 3,500-square-miles area is made up of hilly and mountainous terrain, which extends across the center of the island.

An estimated 3.5 million people live in Puerto Rico, making it one of the most densely populated territories in the Americas. The capital, San Juan, has over 800,000 residents. Most of the other inhabitants live in towns and cities located on or near coastal areas. Another 1.5 million Puerto Ricans live in the United States, primarily in New York City and other east coast metropolitan centers.

The diverse ethnic composition of the population is the legacy of centuries of Spanish colonization and African slavery. People classified as Caucasians form a minority of no more than 30 percent. Over the past three decades, there has been an additional influx of people from Cuba, from other Caribbean islands, and, in lesser numbers, from the United States.

Spain's Colony

Christopher Columbus claimed the island for Spain in 1493. Originally called San Juan Bautista, it acquired its present name much later. The native population, mostly Arawaks of mainland South American origin, died out quickly as a result of European-transmitted diseases and enslavement. African slaves were introduced early and became an important component of the labor force.

The first Spanish colonists established a pastoral and subsistence agriculture. Eventually, a more extensive export-oriented agriculture was developed in sugar, coffee, tobacco, and rum. These commodities were the mainstay of the economy until well into the twentieth century.

Puerto Rico's primary importance to Spain during the first centuries of colonization, however, was its strategic location. As other European imperialist powers made incursions into the Caribbean, the island became a key defensive base. British, French, and Dutch attacks were repelled; massive fortifications were constructed to guard the entrance to San Juan harbor and provide protection for Spanish shipping.

By the eighteenth century, the strategic and economic ascendancy of Cuba diminished the island's role, and it slipped into a sort of colonial somnolence. The early nineteenth-century proindependence movements that swept through Spain's mainland colonies failed to disturb it; Puerto Rico, along with Cuba, remained the last imperial outpost of Spain in the Americas.

Though the mother country reinforced its hold on the island after the 1820s, developments occurred that gradually awakened nationalist consciousness. The Puerto Rican economy, for example, became increasingly oriented toward the growing North American market. This influenced groups who felt constrained by Spain's economic policies. Small political movements, which sought autonomy and reform, even independence, also emerged. In 1868 several hundred proindependence intellectuals and professionals mounted an unsuccessful rebellion at Lares. Spain responded by somewhat liberalizing its rule, which encouraged the organization of the first political parties.

Two political parties, the Conservative Party and Liberal Reformist Party, were founded in 1870. The Liberal Reformist Party, which took the lead in advocating change, led the drive to abolish slavery in 1873. Ten years later, now known as the Autonomist Party, it persuaded Spain to grant internal autonomy and island representation in the Spanish parliament. The occupation by U.S. military forces in 1898 during the Spanish-American War, however, ended the momentum for internal self-rule.

Puerto Rico and the United States

The Foraker Act, passed by the U.S. Congress in 1900, integrated the Puerto Rican economy into that of the United States and established an American system of government dominated by the new imperial power. The island became an "unincorporated territory" with a minimum of self-government. The ambiguity of its legal definition as neither a colony nor a state quickly resulted in the overriding political question of the twentieth century: What is Puerto Rico's status?

Puerto Ricans disappointed by the American government's failure to grant internal autonomy and self-rule formulated several distinct responses to the status question. In 1904 Luis Muñoz Rivera, a former leader of the Autonomist Party, founded the prostatehood Unionist Party. An Independence Party was organized in 1912, followed by the Socialist Party three years later. Agitation by these parties led to the passage of the Jones Act in 1917, which granted Puerto Ricans U.S. citizenship and a Bill of Rights and established a popularly elected two-house legislature. The governor and other officials, however, continued to be appointed by the U.S. president.

In the 1920s and 1930s, as U.S. investment slowed and the economy was severely affected by the Great Depression, island politics became increasingly divisive. The Unionists split: One faction turned to an autonomist position; the other formed a new independence-minded Nationalist Party. The Socialists, meanwhile, collaborated with a new prostatehood Republican Party. By the end of the 1930s, failure to resolve the status issue satisfactorily resulted in the formation of the Popular Democratic Party (PPD) by Luis Muñoz Marín, son of the former Autonomist leader, who successfully argued that the island's economic and social problems took priority over the status question. The Popular Democrats swept to power in the 1940 elections and remained the dominant party until 1968.

Under the leadership of Muñoz Marín and the Popular Democrats, Puerto Rico experienced significant change. Development policies transformed the economy from agrarian to industrial. A modern transportation, communications, and energy infrastructure was built to support growing urbanization and industrialization. State investments in education, housing, health, and social welfare increased dramatically. Although many objected to the island's continued economic domination by U.S. interests and the failure of even rapid growth to solve employment and other poverty-related problems, Puerto Ricans enjoyed rising material standards in the post–World War II decades.

The status question was dealt with temporarily after the amendment of the Jones Act in 1947, which permitted the popular election of governors. Muñoz was elected the following year; in 1952, at his urging, the electorate overwhelmingly voted for a new constitution that established Puerto Rico as a commonwealth.

The successful development programs of the Popular Democrats had the unintended long-term result of contributing to the appeal of their political opponents. Prosperity and growing economic and cultural ties to the United States influenced many in the emerging middle class to adopt prostatehood sentiments. Dissatisfaction with the long-ruling Popular Democrats, increasingly divisive after the retirement of Muñoz Marín in the 1960s, also was a contributing factor. Declining electoral support convinced the Popular Democrats to undercut their opponents in the Puerto Rican Independence Party (PIP) and the Statehood Republican Party (PER) by holding a plebiscite on the status issue in 1967. A majority voted for commonwealth, but the strong showing—39 percent—by those who favored statehood indicated a growing support for that position. The vote for independence was only 1 percent.

The Statehood Republicans abstained from the plebiscite, but a faction of the party split off to campaign for the prostatehood vote. Out of this movement came a new party, the New Progressive Party (PNP), led by Luis Ferré. In 1968 the New Progressives mounted a vigorous campaign against the divided Popular

Democrats which resulted in Ferré's election as governor and the end of an era in island politics.

Throughout the 1970s and 1980s, the Popular Democrats and the New Progressives alternated in controlling the governorship, legislature, and municipal offices (the PPD won the governorship in 1972, 1984, and 1988; the PNP, in 1976 and 1980). The economic programs of the two parties were almost indistinguishable. Both parties supported development by investment policies based on tax incentives, credits, and infrastructure services. Both promoted exports as crucial to growth. Their social programs also were similar. The essential difference between them was their positions on the status question. By the 1980s, the Popular Democrats advocated an enhanced commonwealth relationship with the United States, which translated into greater autonomy and self-rule for the island. The New Progressives, on the other hand, continued to argue that statehood was the only logical outcome of Puerto Rico's long association with the United States.

Stalemate in the 1980s

In 1980 the New Progressive's Carlos Romero Barceló won the governorship in an election that was virtually a tie between him and Rafael Hernández Colón, the Popular Democratic candidate. The election demonstrated not only the virtual parity between the two parties in their electoral support, but also the deep uncertainty of Puerto Ricans about the future of their land. Although public opinion polls, at the end of the decade, indicated that slightly more people than not favored statehood over continued commonwealth or independence, the numbers were not decisive.

For many non–Puerto Ricans, the ongoing discussion about the island's status appears esoteric and even exasperating. For the people involved, however, from politicians and businessmen to artists and workers and islanders who regularly trek between mainland and homeland, the issue is a real one, and it involves a complex of psychological, cultural, linguistic, and economic questions. Puerto Ricans concerned about their rich Spanish, African, and national heritages ask what the fate of these will be under the impact of further "Americanization." Will their vibrant language survive? Are they Latin Americans, North Americans, or some creative synthesis of the two very different cultures? What is their role in a multinational Caribbean in the throes of nation building and struggling for development? How do they fit into an increasingly internationalized economy?

The status question most directly affects the average Puerto Rican in economic terms. Development programs based on tax incentives for U.S. manufacturers and other investors have transformed the economy, making it the most industrialized in the Caribbean and providing islanders with the highest per capita income in Latin America. Economic growth and rising standards of living have been accompanied by the expansion of cities, the building of suburbs, and the array of services and conveniences associated with modern development. Yet, after four decades of what economists call the "Puerto Rican miracle," per capita income is still less than half that of the poorest state, Mississippi, in the United States. Almost two-thirds of Puerto Ricans live below the U.S.–indicated poverty level; the official unemployment figure hovers around 17 percent; and with most food imported because of the disappearance of mixed farming, the cost of living is higher than on the mainland. Dependency on federal funds is underscored by the transfer of over $5 billion annually, partly in the form of social welfare programs such as food stamps for over 40 percent of the population. Changing philosophies in Washington during the 1980s on the role of government, however, have at least implicitly threatened the fiscal relationship between the federal government and the island, as well as the privileged tax policies Puerto Rico enjoys, thus arousing the insecurity that has elevated the status question to one of major importance. The manner in which the question is resolved will have a direct impact on every Puerto Rican.

In 1988 Governor Hernández Colón won reelection. The narrowness of his victory margin (48.7 percent to 45.8 percent for PNP candidate Baltasar Corrada del Rio and 5.3 percent for PIP candidate Rubén Berrios) undoubtedly was a factor in his decision to call for a plebiscite in 1991. Subsequently, after President George Bush announced his support for a plebiscite (and stated that he personally favored statehood), the U.S. Congress held hearings in 1989 on the issue.

The commonwealth, statehood, and independence positions were presented, but the results indicated that the U.S. Congress itself was divided and uncertain. Congressional representatives balked on supporting an updated commonwealth status that would give the island greater autonomy, and they rejected the idea of "equal sovereignty." Others found that statehood would mean an even greater fiscal burden for the federal government, at least for some years to come. The proposal of the *independentistas*, which would involve the payment of up to $50 billion over a period of years, in order to ease the economic transition to independence, was hardly palatable. Additionally, factors such as language, race, and the implications of a large new "Hispanic bloc" in Congress were considered. Congressmen also certainly were influenced by polls indicating that a majority of mainland Americans do not favor statehood. The final upshot of the hearings was a postponement of congressional action.

The congressional hearings were disturbing for Puerto Ricans. The realization that the island's status is largely controlled by outsiders, a realization generally suppressed during the decades of commonwealth and economic growth, exposed once again Puerto Ricans' dilemma. As a result, the current stalemate over the status question has raised another option which has garnered increasing support across the political spectrum: "free association." Under free association, the island would be tied to the United States in a relationship similar to those of the federal government with Micronesia and the Marshall Islands, in which autonomy is linked to U.S. responsibility for defense. Meanwhile, the debate over Puerto Rico's future continues.

Bibliography

Robert W. Anderson. *Party Politics in Puerto Rico.* Stanford University Press, Stanford, Calif., 1965.

Latin American Regional Reports—Caribbean. Latin American Newsletters Ltd., London, 1979–1991.

Gordon K. Lewis. *Puerto Rico: Freedom and Power in the Caribbean.* Monthly Review Press, New York, 1963.

Alan Weisman. "An Island in Limbo." *New York Times Magazine,* 18 February 1990.

Political Parties—Active

NEW PROGRESSIVE PARTY (PARTIDO NUEVO PROGRESISTA—PNP). The PNP emerged from a faction of the Statehood Republican Party that opposed the decision to boycott the 1967 plebescite on the status question. Led initially by Luis Ferré, the PNP is the primary advocate of statehood. The electoral successes enjoyed by the PNP in the 1970s were not repeated in the 1980s. Although the party continues to attract the second largest number of voters and advocates the statehood of the island, which opinion polls indicate a slight majority now favor, the PNP was beset by difficulties during the past decade that contributed to election defeats.

In 1980 party leader and governor Carlos Romero Barceló won reelection by the narrowest of margins; however, he was unable to carry the legislature with him. The Popular Democrats' majorities in both houses meant that little was accomplished in terms of new programs. Adding to the PNP's woes in the early 1980s was the worst recession to hit the island since the Great Depression. Economic growth rates were negative for several years, unemployment soared to 24 percent, and investment fell sharply. Governor Romero Barceló bore the brunt of public unrest, despite the fact that economic dependency on the United States limited any Puerto Rican administration's options. Finally, a scandal involving a police cover-up of the murder of two "terrorists" was skillfully exploited by the opposition and cast doubt on the competency of the administration.

By the time of the run-up to the 1984 elections, the PNP was in serious disarray. San Juan mayor Hernán Padilla challenged Romero Barceló for the leadership—and the gubernatorial candidacy—of the party, then split to form his own political organization. The result was a serious setback for the PNP at all electoral levels.

Since 1984 the party has been weakened by continued infighting. Romero Barceló challenged new party leader Baltasar Corrada del Rio in 1988, despite the fact that traditionally party leaders are gubernatorial candidates. Corrada del Rio won the nomination, but analysts suggested that the three percentage points difference between the PNP and the winning Popular Democrats' votes indicated that a united party could have won. Following the election, Romero Barceló again emerged as party leader.

The PNP draws most of its electoral support from among the urban middle class, especially in the San Juan area, which appeared during the decades of economic growth following World War II. In the 1980s, however, as the economy faltered and the island's relationship with the United States became both closer and more precarious because of federal financial support and challenges to Puerto Rico's special tax privileges, the party attempted to broaden its appeal by pointing out that statehood would mean more federal welfare benefits for the poor.

The party denies, however, that its goal is to make Puerto Rico a "welfare commonwealth." Its economic argument for statehood is based on the claim that, as a state, the island would receive up to $9 billion annually in federal funds, which would spur development and eventually lead to financial solvency. A modern infrastructure, an educated and skilled work force, and cheap labor would continue to attract investors even without the tax incentives that statehood would exclude.

The PNP's programs and appeal, therefore, are closely tied to the resolution of the status issue. The party's leaders promise, as they have done in virtually every previous electoral campaign, to hold a simple yes or no plebiscite for statehood if they win in 1992 and force the issue in the U.S. Congress.

PARTIDO POPULAR DEMOCRÁTICO. See POPULAR DEMOCRATIC PARTY.

PARTIDO INDEPENDENTISTA PUERTORRIQUEÑO. See PUERTO RICAN INDEPENDENCE PARTY.

PARTIDO NUEVO PROGRESISTA. See NEW PROGRESSIVE PARTY.

POPULAR DEMOCRATIC PARTY (PARTIDO POPULAR DEMOCRÁTICO—PPD). Founded in 1938 by Luis Muñoz Marín, the Popular Democrats became the majority party in 1940 and dominated politics until 1968. During that time, the PPD achieved its goal of commonwealth status for Puerto Rico and it promoted economic development and social change. Suffering electoral defeat for the first time in 1968, the PPD regrouped and recovered its dominant position in the 1980 elections. In 1980 it won both houses of the legislature and most of the municipal posts, even though it lost the governorship by a close vote. In 1984 its gubernatorial candidate, Rafael Hernández Colón, won decisively, and he was reelected in 1988. While the party continues to hold a broad spectrum of viewpoints among its leadership, it has overcome the divisiveness that contributed to electoral defeats in the late 1960s and 1970s.

Since its founding in the late 1930s, the PPD has attracted a multiclass following. Its early programs favored the rural and less privileged sectors of Puerto Rican society, but the success of its development policies has broadened its support. Its electoral base widened and shifted as Puerto Rico became urban and industrialized. As the influence of the old rural political bosses waned, the party also modernized its organization and methods in order to appeal to more sophisticated voters.

The PPD continues to emphasize economic development within a commonwealth framework. In the 1980s, this has meant an updated version of support services and tax incentives to attract investment and promote exports. The severe economic recession of the early 1980s caused the party to downplay the status question and concentrate on economic and social problems. After his election in 1984, Governor Hernández Colón elaborated a plan to encourage multinational manufacturing investment, and he sought trade and cultural agreements with other Caribbean Basin nations.

Uncertainties over continued U.S. support of Puerto Rico's tax incentives and federal fiscal policies, in addition to his narrow reelection victory in 1988, caused Governor Hernández Colón to call for a plebiscite on the status question in 1991. Intense party debate resulted in the PPD's calling for a "modernized" commonwealth relationship, one that would permanently tie Puerto Rico to the United States but would provide for a greater degree of autonomy—equal sovereignty. Hernández Colón argues that the island's cultural heritage, its long-standing ties to the United States, and international economic changes merit such a flexible arrangement. Younger leaders of the party, however, although they currently support its position, appear to be considering the idea of "free association" status, especially since the U.S. Congressional hearings held in 1989.

As the final decade of the century began, the PPD looked back with satisfaction over its achievements of the past fifty years. Its future, meanwhile, remained uncertain as it wrestled again with the status question it first ignored, then believed it had settled in previous plebiscites.

PUERTO RICAN INDEPENDENCE PARTY (PARTIDO INDEPENDENTISTA PUERTORRIQUEÑO—PIP). Founded in 1946 by a group of Popular Democratic Party dissidents dissatisfied with that party's position on the status question, the *independentistas* have championed the third alternative for the island's future. Under the leadership of Rubén Berrios, the PIP has inherited and carried forward the struggle for independence of several past political parties. In the 1980s, it attracted only approximately 5 percent of the voters, down from a high of nineteen percent in 1952, but its support among artists, intellectuals, students, and professionals gave it a high degree of visibility which ensured ample publicity for its programs.

The party has a social democratic orientation and ties to international socialist organizations. It has argued that both commonwealth and statehood reduce Puerto Rico to the humiliating level of a permanent charity case, with continuing dependency on an increasingly unreliable federal government. The PIP has proposed, instead, a gradual transition to independence—first, through "free association" status, similar to the relationships between the United States and

Micronesia and the Marshall Islands, which essentially involves U.S. responsibility for defense combined with self-rule; then, eventually, full independence.

The PIP believes that public support for its position is greater than recent elections indicate. It claims that many vote for the Popular Democrats only to prevent statehood. Puerto Rico, party leaders say, has a level of development that makes it attractive for international investors and the ability to compete in a global economy.

With the status question unresolved, with the existing commonwealth arrangement seemingly at a dead end, and with statehood increasingly remote, the *independentistas* may have the opportunity to enhance their political role in the coming decade.

Political Parties—Historical

AUTONOMIST PARTY (PARTIDO AUTONOMISTA). Organized in 1887, the Autonomists, under the leadership of Luis Muñoz Rivera, allied with the Liberal Party in the Spanish parliament and convinced Spain to grant Puerto Rico a Charter of Autonomy in 1897, which gave the island a large measure of self-rule. The party disbanded at the time of the U.S. occupation in 1898.

COMMUNIST PARTY (PARTIDO COMUNISTA). The Communist Party, organized in 1934 under the leadership of Alberto Sánchez, had strong ties to the Puerto Rican labor movement in the 1930s and 1940s. As a result of official persecution, it virtually disappeared in the 1950s.

CONSERVATIVE PARTY (PARTIDO CONSERVADOR). A late nineteenth-century organization of commercial groups with close ties to the colonial system, the Conservatives supported Puerto Rico's continuing status as a colony of Spain.

FEDERALIST PARTY (PARTIDO FEDERALISTA). Founded by former members of the Autonomist Party in 1898 after the U.S. occupation, the party sought internal autonomy and eventual independence. In 1904 the party merged with dissident Republicans to form the Unionist Party.

LIBERAL PARTY (PARTIDO LIBERAL). A middle-class organization of former Unionists and Republicans, the Liberal Party was organized in 1934 and entered an electoral alliance with the independence-minded Nationalists. The party split over the independence issue and disappeared following an electoral defeat in 1940.

LIBERAL REFORMIST PARTY (PARTIDO LIBERAL REFORMISTA). One of the earliest political groups, founded in 1870, the Liberal Reformists led the fight for the abolition of slavery and the reform of Spain's governance system in Puerto Rico. The party disintegrated after the formation of the Autonomist Party.

NATIONALIST PARTY (PARTIDO NACIONALISTA). Organized in 1922 and led for many years by Pedro Albizu Campos, the Nationalists turned to violence and terrorism after suffering electoral defeats in the early 1930s. Severe repression caused many of its adherents to abandon the party and led to its demise in the 1960s.

PARTIDO AUTONOMISTA. See AUTONOMIST PARTY.

PARTIDO COMUNISTA. See COMMUNIST PARTY.

PARTIDO CONSERVADOR. See CONSERVATIVE PARTY.

PARTIDO DE UNIÓN. See UNIONIST PARTY.

PARTIDO DEL PUEBLO. See PEOPLE'S PARTY.

PARTIDO ESTADISTA REPUBLICANO. See STATEHOOD REPUBLICAN PARTY.

PARTIDO FEDERALISTA. See FEDERALIST PARTY.

PARTIDO LIBERAL. See LIBERAL PARTY.

PARTIDO LIBERAL REFORMISTA. See LIBERAL REFORMIST PARTY.

PARTIDO NACIONALISTA. See NATIONALIST PARTY.

PARTIDO REPUBLICANO. See REPUBLICAN PARTY.

PARTIDO SOCIALISTA. See SOCIALIST PARTY.

PARTIDO SOCIALISTA PUERTORRIQUEÑO. See PUERTO RICAN SOCIALIST PARTY.

PEOPLE'S PARTY (PARTIDO DEL PUEBLO). A short-lived party of the late 1960s and early 1970s that acted as a "spoiler" by contributing to the defeat of the Popular Democrats in the gubernatorial election of 1968.

PUERTO RICAN SOCIALIST PARTY (PARTIDO SOCIALISTA PUERTORRIQUEÑO—PSP). Organized in 1971 by Juan Mari Bras, the proindependence, Marxist-Leninist Socialists, sometimes called the Popular Socialists, were positioned on the far left of the political spectrum. In elections held during the 1970s, the party attracted less than 1 percent of the vote. Internal divisions fractured the party in the early 1980s.

REPUBLICAN PARTY (PARTIDO REPUBLICANO). The original prostatehood party, founded after the U.S. occupation in 1898, the Republicans were a major force in island politics until 1940. Shortly thereafter, the party was reorganized as the Statehood Republican Party.

SOCIALIST PARTY (PARTIDO SOCIALISTA). Puerto Rico's first labor party was organized by Santiago Iglesias in 1915 and, in alliance with affiliated trade unions, played an important role in island politics throughout the 1920s and 1930s. The party supported statehood as the best means of protecting Puerto Rican workers.

STATEHOOD REPUBLICAN PARTY (PARTIDO ESTADISTA REPUBLICANO—PER). As a successor to the Republican Party, the Statehood Republican Party steadily increased its electoral appeal against the dominant Popular Democrats throughout the 1950s and 1960s. The party dissolved soon after it fractured over the plebiscite issue in 1967. Many PER adherents transferred their loyalty to the New Progressive Party.

UNIONIST PARTY (PARTIDO DE UNIÓN). Dissident members of the Republican Party joined with members of the Federalist Party to form this party in 1904. Although the party never developed a consistent position on the status question, it dominated island politics until the mid–1920s. Disagreements over independence versus commonwealth caused the party to split, and the elements reorganized as the Liberal Party in the early 1930s.

Richard E. Sharpless

SAINT KITTS-NEVIS

The insular state of Saint Christopher (usually called Saint Kitts) and Nevis is currently the smallest independent state in the Americas. Its population of under 50,000—all but 12,000 of whom live on Saint Kitts—lives in a territory of just over 100 square miles (of which Saint Kitts makes up two-thirds). Located at the northern end of the Leeward Island group of the Lesser Antilles, Saint Kitts-Nevis is roughly 200 miles southeast of Puerto Rico.

Although Saint Kitts and Nevis are separated from each other by only two miles of sea, their sociopolitical and economic integration is among the lowest of any state in the region. For this reason, the perceived equity of the state's political democracy holds the key to the survival of Saint Kitts-Nevis as a nation-state. To that end, the functions and popular support for the country's political parties play an important role.

Political History

Visited by Christopher Columbus on his second voyage, in 1493, Saint Kitts became the first British colony in the Caribbean in 1624, one year before the British explored Barbados. Frequent battles between Britain and France, however, meant that Saint Kitts and Nevis did not pass firmly into British control until the Treaty of Versailles was signed in 1783.

In 1866 the separate legislatures of the two islands were combined into a Crown Colony form of government with its majority of appointed members. An elected legislative assembly was not again in the ascendancy for seventy-five years. After an eighty-five-year effort made by Britain to confederate the Leeward Island colonies (Saint Kitts-Nevis and Anguilla, Antigua and Barbuda, Montserrat, and Dominica), the installation of an embryonic cabinet system in the late 1950s and early 1960s, and two failed attempts at federation with the larger anglophone Caribbean, Saint Kitts-Nevis and Anguilla became a self-governing Associated State, independent in all areas except external relations, in February 1967.

Full independence was realized in September 1983 although not before Anguilla had unilaterally left the tripartite arrangement (officially in 1980) and, of even greater importance, not before considerable opposition to the proposition of association with Saint Kitts was articulated in Nevis. Despite recent moves made to further interstate integration in the Commonwealth Caribbean, this new integrative spirit is not endorsed by constituents in some individual territories, including Nevis. This tiny island may yet declare its intent to seek independence from Saint Kitts. This serious act, which could have troubling implications both locally and regionally, requires but a two-thirds vote of the Nevis legislature, which is currently dominated by the Nevis Reformation Party (NRP).

While Saint Kitts and Nevis share a legacy of long-term British colonization and African slavery, and also joint administration as a single colony after 1956, differences in soil types, in physical as well as populace size, and settlement and development patterns contributed to the rise of Saint Kitts as the dominant sugar island of the two and led to a major divergence in political culture between the islands. Land plots became available to peasant farmers in Nevis, for example, largely because of the limited suitability of its soil for sugar production. In contrast, as early as 1926, a narrow-gauge railway linked the sugar estates of Saint Kitts to the central sugar factory, creating an islandwide plantation and a greater economy of scale.

These disparities, plus the fact that workers in Saint Kitts were victims of some of the lowest wages and poorest health conditions in the region, led to that island's becoming the first insular Commonwealth Caribbean colony to sustain a labor strike turned insurrection (January 1935). Lives were lost in the confrontation between workers and authorities. The increased consciousness among blacks and workers, in turn, contributed significantly to the development of labor parties in Saint Kitts prior to World War II. This same pattern later occurred in two other Caribbean islands, Jamaica and Barbados, after they experienced labor-management strife in the 1930s. The very divergent development pattern in Nevis accounts for that island's lack of labor strife and its failure to develop a labor politics tradition.

Political Parties and Elections

The labor leader who was largely responsible for ushering in mass political parties in Saint Kitts was the charismatic Robert Llewellyn Bradshaw (1916–1978). Bradshaw also served as the first premier of Saint Kitts-Nevis. He entered politics via the trade union movement, serving as vice president of the Saint Kitts Workers' League, an incipient and unofficial union and political organization, from its founding in 1932. If this less official and less functionally differentiated organization is considered, the Labour party that evolved in Saint Kitts can be said to be the oldest in the region, predating the development of labor parties in Jamaica (1937) and Barbados (1938).

By 1940 Bradshaw, then a clerk in the island's lone sugar factory, led a strike of seven weeks duration against the policies of the factory. This action proved costly to the jobs of Bradshaw and several associates, but the pressure applied by the workers was beneficial in inducing the government to rescind a law that made trade unions illegal. This led to official union and party development in Saint Kitts. Due largely to his leadership in the confrontation, Bradshaw was chosen first secretary of the factory workers' section of the newly formed Saint Kitts-Nevis Trades and Labour Union (SKNTLU). That "labor section" evolved into the present Saint Kitts-Nevis Labour Party (SKNLP).

Union activity was often the first step in party development in the suffrage-restrictive days of the pre–World War II era since, without wage increases, there could be no significant expansion of labor votes or the related election of pro-worker candidates. Thus, many additional strikes were initiated as a motivating force for representation. In 1944 Bradshaw was elected president of the union. The following year, the union reorganized, and the St. Kitts-Nevis-Anguilla Labour Party (SKNALP) emerged, with Bradshaw as president. The new Labour Party, led by Bradshaw, elected a number of black members to the Legislative Council in 1946, including Bradshaw himself. Despite these advances, Bradshaw felt that the opportunities for openness under the Crown colonial system were entirely inadequate; therefore, he continued to utilize agitation and the strike as political weapons in 1948 and especially in 1950 when the primary worker demands were for increased representative government.

In 1952, after universal adult suffrage was granted to the island, Bradshaw again led his party to electoral victory. In the late 1950s, as regional politics mustered increasing attention, Bradshaw became vice president of the West Indies Federal Labour Party, which, in actuality, was a confederation of West Indian labor parties. With the inauguration of the West Indies Federation (WIF) in 1958, Bradshaw became minister of finance in the federal government head-quartered in Trinidad.

With the demise of the WIF in 1962, Bradshaw returned to attend to Labour politics in Saint Kitts. Following Labour's electoral victory in 1966, he became chief minister of the then three-island Crown Colony. On 27 February 1967, associated statehood became a reality, and Robert Bradshaw became premier of the tripartite state. His death in May 1978 brought long-time Labour ally Caleb Southwell to the premiership following an intraparty battle with Lee Llewellyn Moore. Upon the death of Southwell in May 1979, Moore, then leader of the Labour Party, became premier, but his tenure was also brief.

With independence on the horizon, new elections were called in 1980. Labour carried only four of the nine seats in this highly competitive election (which could be termed violent in the milder West Indian sense of the word), losing to the People's Action Movement (PAM), its somewhat more conservative rival which tends to be more closely aligned with business. The PAM, led by Kennedy A. Simmonds, carried only three seats on Saint Kitts but gained control of the government as the result of a coalition effort with the NRP, which had carried the two Nevis seats. Simmonds assumed leadership of the government and acquired the title of prime minister when Saint Kitts-Nevis gained formal independence just three years later. Simeon Daniel, leader of the NRP, claimed the important minister of finance portfolio. The remainder of the government was divided between the PAM–NRP coalition partners.

The 1980 election ended twenty-five years of electoral dominance by Labour, a span of six election periods. The PAM, in concert with the NRP, has also been the victorious party in the postindependence general elections of 1984 and 1989. Simmonds remains prime minister of the joint Saint Kitts-Nevis state in 1991 but, in a bow to Nevisian pride, Nevis has its own premier and vice premier, Simeon Daniel and Ivor Stevens, respectively. One might, in fact, speculate that defeat of the PAM–NRP coalition would severely strain the weak bonds of statehood.

Recent campaigns in Saint Kitts-Nevis have been dominated by economic issues, especially the U.S. cutback in sugar purchases from the Commonwealth Caribbean. Other issues prominent in postindependence campaigns include the questions of expanded Eastern Caribbean integration and the increased militarization of the Eastern Caribbean. The contribution of troops by Saint Kitts-Nevis to the October 1983 intervention in Grenada, although quite small, generated considerable campaign support for the Simmonds government in the May 1984 campaign.

Until the advent of independence, the average electoral turnout in Saint Kitts-Nevis (73.6 percent) was second only to Dominica in the Eastern Caribbean. In the period since, the competitive spirit in this two-island state has remained high, perhaps even overly combative, and, in the words of Gary and Rosemary Brana-Shute, has been filled with "heated invective" (1989).

Bibliography

Gary Brana-Shute and Rosemary Brana-Shute. "The Organization of Eastern Caribbean States," in James M. Malloy and Eduardo A. Gamarra, eds., Latin America and Caribbean Contemporary Record, vol. 7, 1987–1988, B512–14. Holmes and Meier, New York, 1990.

———. "The Anglophone Eastern Caribbean and British Dependencies," in Abraham F. Lowenthal, ed., Latin America and Caribbean Contemporary Record, vol. 6, 1986–1987, B445–47. Holmes and Meier, New York, 1989.

Patrick A. M. Emanuel. General Elections in the Eastern Caribbean. Institute of Social and Economic Research, University of the West Indies, Cave Hill, Barbados, 1979.

Percy Hintzen and W. Marvin Will. Saint Kitts-Nevis biographies in Robert J. Alexander, ed., Biographical Directory of Latin America and Caribbean Political Leaders, 412–13, ff. Greenwood Press, Westport, Conn., 1988.

S B. Jones-Hendrickson. "St. Kitts-Nevis," in Jack W. Hopkins, ed., Latin America and Caribbean Contemporary Record, vol. 2, 1982–1983, 746–781. Holmes and Meier, New York, 1984.

Charles H. Kunsman, Jr. "The Origins and Development of Political Parties in the British West Indies." Ph.D. diss., University of California, Berkeley, 1963.

Bonham C. Richardson. "Saint Kitts-Nevis," in Robert J. Alexander, ed., *Political Parties of the Americas*, vol. 2, 624–28. Greenwood Press, Westport Conn., 1982.

W. Marvin Will. "A Nation Divided: The Quest for Caribbean Integration." *Latin American Research Review* 26, 2, 1991, pp. 3–37.

Political Parties—Active

NEVIS REFORMATION PARTY (NRP). Founded in 1970 as a secessionist party, the NRP has been led by Nevisian attorney Simeon Daniel since its inception. Founded just in time for the 1971 election, the NRP was successful in securing one of Nevis's two seats in its initial effort. By 1975 it polled more than 80 percent of the Nevisian vote and won both of the island's seats. The electoral appeal of the NRP remained strong partly because of the secession of Anguilla in the late 1970s.

The NRP opposed independence as a joint state with Saint Kitts on the basis that it meant domination by Saint Kitts. Threats of separate independence for Nevis remain real, but they may have been put on hold by the victory of its Saint Kitts ally, the People's Action Movement (PAM) in 1980, which led to a PAM–NPR coalition government. The PAM–NPR coalition has compiled a streak of three general election victories and currently rules the two-island state. During this time, the number of Nevisian seats has increased from two to three. Simeon Daniel, who continues as leader of the NRP, also serves as a member of the government and as the premier of Nevis.

PEOPLE'S ACTION MOVEMENT (PAM). The PAM was founded on 16 January 1965 as a party opposed to Labour's political domination and a party that would provide alternative leadership more representative of business and smaller island perspectives. Dr. William Herbert was chosen leader and Kennedy A. Simmonds, secretary. Simmonds was a local activist who had just returned from Jamaica (1964) where two years earlier he had graduated from the University of the West Indies. Although Simmonds was defeated in the 1966 general elections, the PAM captured two seats, one in Anguilla (then part of the Crown Colony) and one in Nevis. Simmonds, who had returned from graduate study in the United States, assumed leadership of the PAM upon William Herbert's death in 1976.

When premier and Labour leader Caleb Southwell died in May 1979, Simmonds and the PAM successfully campaigned for his long-held Labour seat. It was a signal of the PAM's growing support, and the converse for Labour, partly because of the deaths of two Saint Kitts-Nevis Labour Party premiers within a one-year period and partly because of the advancement of Lee Moore, a leader with a less prestigious reputation. In the 1980 general elections, a coalition of the PAM and the Nevis Reformation Party (NRP) defeated Labour for the first time in twenty-five years. Thus, when Saint Kitts-Nevis gained independence three years later, Simmonds became the first prime minister of this two-island state. In the elections held in 1984, the PAM won six of seven Kittitian seats; its ally, the NRP, secured all of the Nevis seats, which had increased from two to three. The PAM–NRP team also won the 1989 elections, and it governs the country in the early 1990s.

PEOPLE'S LIBERAL PARTY (PLP). The PLP was founded by its present leader, Dr. James Sutton, in 1988. Shortly after establishing the PLP, Sutton was suspended without pay from his state position as a medical officer. The future for the PLP (and Sutton) is uncertain.

SAINT KITTS-NEVIS LABOUR PARTY (SKNLP). The SKNLP has had several titles. Prior to the secession of Anguilla from its tripartite status with Saint Kitts and Nevis in the late 1970s, the party was formally called the Saint Kitts-Nevis-Anguilla Labour Party; currently, it is informally known as the Saint Kitts Labour Party (for its primary base). The SKNLP was formally founded in 1940 as part of the Saint Kitts-Nevis Labour Union. Its roots, however, extend back to the incipient Saint Kitts Worker's League founded in 1932 and the worker insurrection of 1935. This makes the SKNLP the oldest party in the Commonwealth Caribbean.

The guiding spirit and long-term leader, from 1944 to 1978, of the SKNLP was Robert Llewellyn Bradshaw. Until his death in May 1978, the only break in Premier Bradshaw's leadership of the Labour Party occurred when he left Saint Kitts-Nevis to serve as finance minister of the West Indies Federation during its brief tenure (1958–1962). Upon Bradshaw's death, Caleb Southwell assumed leadership of the SKNLP for the second time and became the second premier of the Associate State of Saint Kitts-Nevis. Lee Llewellyn Moore advanced to leadership of the SKNLP a year later and assumed the role of premier upon the death of Southwell in May 1979. Moore's tenure as premier was also short-lived; in 1980, Labour lost its first election in twenty-five years, a span of six election periods. Labour has now lost three successive general elections, including a massive loss in 1984. The SKNLP is currently the "loyal" opposition.

Political Parties—Historical

PEOPLE'S POLITICAL MOVEMENT (PPM). The PPM contested one general election, the election of 1961. Maurice Davis was its leader.

SAINT KITTS DEMOCRATIC PARTY (SKDP). The SKDP was established as early as 1948, but it did not field candidates in any campaign except the general election of 1957.

SAINT KITTS-NEVIS-ANGUILLA LABOUR PARTY. See SAINT KITTS-NEVIS LABOUR PARTY.

UNITED NATIONAL MOVEMENT (UNM). The UNM was a Nevis-based party that later became the Saint Kitts-Nevis-Anguilla Labour Party affiliate in Nevis. Led by Nevisian barrister Eugene Walwyn, the UNM first appeared on the electoral scene in 1961, at which time it was successful in winning both of the Nevisian parliamentary seats. In 1966 the UNM won only one seat, and it has since then ceased to exist.

W. Marvin Will

SAINT LUCIA

Saint Lucia, a 238 square mile island, is located in the Windward Island group between Saint Vincent and France's Overseas Department of Martinique. One of the most militarily contested territories of the European colonizers, Saint Lucia changed hands between Britain and France as many as fourteen times. The French controlled the island 90 percent of the time between 1659 and 1814, which contributed to a considerably different political culture than that found in the colonies that were in English hands for much longer unbroken periods: the Bahamas, Barbados, and Jamaica. This is evidenced in speech patterns—nearly all Saint Lucians speak French patois as well as the official English—in religion, and in countless other ways, including cultural approaches toward development (see Romalis 1970).

Saint Lucia was a sugar-producing island during most of its colonial period. The vast majority of the estimated 150,000 population of the island reflects the African heritage of workers brought as slaves to work the sugar. Saint Lucia currently leads the Eastern Caribbean in the export of bananas, the crop that has surpassed sugar as the island's most important export. Plantation agriculture, however, continues to have an impact on the island's economy. Unfortunately, like sugar, bananas are a vulnerable crop. In 1979 Hurricane Allen virtually wiped out Saint Lucian production.

Light industry is increasing in this island state, as is tourism, but the economy of Saint Lucia remains skewed and aid dependent. In addition, half the population of the island is under age sixteen. As a result, the island has a relatively low per capita income that trails all but Saint Vincent among the smaller Eastern Caribbean states.

Political History and the Development of Political Parties

Saint Lucia had a legislative council as early as 1832 but, as could be expected, that initial council was heavily dominated by nonelected members. By 1936 the number of elected council members had increased to five of twelve, and property and income requirements had been somewhat relaxed. This change, induced in part by the popular insurrections sweeping over neighboring Trinidad, Barbados, and Saint Vincent, was significant in laying the groundwork for the creation of mass economic and political institutions in Saint Lucia.

By 1939 the Saint Lucia Workers' Union (SWU) had been organized; by 1940, it was officially registered. The SWU significantly increased the number of union leaders elected to the legislative council. With the expansion of suffrage in 1951, the path was opened for the development of party politics in Saint Lucia. Shortly before the initial election held under universal adult suffrage, not one but two political parties were established: the Saint Lucia Labour Party (SLP) and the People's Progressive Party (PPP). Both organizations were progressive, and both displayed a sympathetic attitude toward labor.

In 1967, following the collapse of the West Indies Federation and the abrogation of the so-called Little Eight federation effort, Associate Statehood status was offered to Saint Lucians. Under the domestic home rule this status afforded, and with the international environment favoring decolonization, the next constitutional step for Saint Lucia was to seek independence. This milestone was reached in 1979.

Contemporary Political Parties and Elections

Long before independence, Saint Lucians had come to expect considerable political openness and order. This expectation included party-influenced elections on a regular basis and a minimum of short-lived minor parties such as have long persisted in Saint Vincent and, more recently, in Grenada. But, indicative of life on the political margin, personality politics is alive and well in Saint Lucia and often, as the youth lament, the electoral choices are not greatly different. Independence, as a result, would usher in a period of much greater governmental and party uncertainty than Saint Lucia had known, and voter fallout would be almost a certainty.

The SLP, supported by from 47 to 61.5 percent of the electorate, controlled the first four elections in this island state. Opposition, although not legion, was ever present and ranged from the PPP to the SLP–United Front (SLP–UF). The United Workers Party (UWP), launched in 1964, came to power and controlled the Saint Lucian government from 1964 to 1979, but the SLP was again victorious in 1979, when it secured a 71-percent share of the vote and twelve parliamentary seats. By this time, the nearby Grenadian Revolution and the worsening economy were making a major impact on Saint Lucians, especially on the youth. The resultant ideological divisions were reflected by Saint Lucia's political parties.

The SLP government elected in 1979, led by Allan Louisy, resigned in April 1981 following a budget defeat. In addition, Louisy was undermined by George Oldum, his deputy prime minister and foreign minister, in part on ideological grounds. Oldum left the SLP to form his own group, the Progressive Labour

Party (PLP). A divisive intragovernmental battle, lasting twenty-one months, ensued. Even civil servants took sides in the feud.

Winston Cenac, who formed a new SLP government in May 1981, succeeded Louisy as prime minister of Saint Lucia, but his government lost to the UWP in the 1982 general election. This ex-SLP party and government leader crossed the aisle to join the UWP government in 1987, complaining of "ungratefulness" and broken promises by the SLP. In compensation, Cenac was awarded the foreign ministry portfolio. Saint Lucia is still governed by the UWP, under the leadership of John Compton, although with a very slim margin. Many young people on the island, especially those associated with the Oldum-led PLP, consider Compton and his UWP conservative. Interestingly, this is not the case if, for example, one applies the term conservative in its U.S. context, or even if Compton is compared to Eugenia Charles of Dominica or Edward Seaga of Jamaica.

In reality, Saint Lucia has three progressive labor parties, which, in the 1980s, differed primarily in their approach to President Ronald Reagan's foreign policy. With the administrative change in Washington, with the Grenada crisis fading from the perceptive screen, and with Cuba losing its ability to play a power game in the Eastern Caribbean, differences among the parties of Saint Lucia have become less pronounced. Compton remains a firm supporter of increased regional integration, along with Mitchell of Saint Vincent and the new National Democratic Congress government in Grenada. In Saint Lucia, as in so many neighboring Caribbean states, finding a way to work through adverse problems— economic scale and transport, among others—is not only the interest of local governments but, for the 1990s and beyond, it is also the major problem with which the country's political parties must grapple.

Bibliography

Robert J. Alexander. "Saint Lucia," in Robert J. Alexander, ed., *Political Parties of the Americas*, vol. 2, 629–34. Greenwood Press, Westport, Conn., 1982.

Gary Brana-Shute and Rosemary Brana-Shute. "The Organization of Eastern Caribbean States," in James M. Malloy and Eduardo A. Gamarra, eds., *Latin America and Caribbean Contemporary Review*, vol. 7, 1987–1988, B514–17. Holmes and Meier, New York, 1990.

———. "The Anglophone Eastern Caribbean and British Dependencies," in Abraham F. Lowenthal, ed., *Latin America and Caribbean Contemporary Review*, vol. 6, 1986–1987, B431–34. Holmes and Meier, New York, 1989.

Patrick A. M. Emmanuel. *General Elections in the Eastern Caribbean*. Institute of Social and Economic Research, University of the West Indies, Cave Hill, Barbados, 1979.

Percy Hintzen and W. Marvin Will. Biographical essays of political leaders from Saint Lucia, in Robert J. Alexander, ed., *Biographical Directory of Latin American and Caribbean Political Leaders*, 116–17, ff. Greenwood Press, Westport, Conn., 1988.

S. B. Jones-Hendrickson. "St. Kitts-Nevis," in Jack W. Hopkins, ed., *Latin America and*

Caribbean Contemporary Record, vol. 2, 1982–1983, 746–81. Holmes and Meier, New York, 1984.

Coleman Romalis. "Barbados and St. Lucia: A Comparative Analysis of Social and Economic Development in Two West Indian Islands." Ph.D. diss., Washington University, Saint Louis, Mo., 1970.

Lindel Smith. "St. Lucia Elections, 2nd July 1979." *Bulletin of Eastern Caribbean Affairs* 5, 3, July/August 1979.

Political Parties—Active

PROGRESSIVE LABOUR PARTY (PLP). The PLP was founded in 1981 by youthful and generally more radical dissidents from the Saint Lucia Labour Party, principally the Oldum brothers. Just twenty-seven miles south of Saint Lucia, the Grenada Revolution was under way. The influence on the highly unionized Saint Lucia was considerable.

George Oldum is still the leader of the PLP. At the time of his defection from Labour, he was not only a sitting member of parliament but also foreign minister in the Labour government. Prior to the 1984 election, George Oldum held a PLP seat, but neither he nor his party won a seat in the 1984 or the 1989 general election.

SAINT LUCIA LABOUR PARTY (SLP). The SLP, the island's oldest active party, was founded in 1949. It was an affiliate of the Saint Lucia Workers' Union (SWU), which was established in 1939. Organizers of the party included Allen Lewis (later Sir Allen, who was chancellor of the University of the West Indies and governor general of Saint Lucia until the late 1980s); George Charles; and Carl La Corbinire, president of the SWU. Clive Compton, H. B. Collymore, Gilbert Mason, and J.M.D. Bousquet also played instrumental roles (Emmanuel 1979).

Charles, who was elected general secretary of the SWU in 1949, was selected leader of the Saint Lucia Labour Party in 1957 and retained that position for more than a decade, albeit not without rancor from younger laborites who defected to form the National Labour Movement (NLM) in 1961. Charles became first chief minister of Saint Lucia in 1960, a position he retained until 1964. Upon his replacement as union leader in 1968 and as party leader in 1969, Charles sought office under the banner of the SLP–United Front.

The SLP reached its nadir in the early 1970s under the leadership of Kenneth Foster, who was later forced from office by rebellious new members led by George Oldum and Allan Louisy. Louisy, a Crown attorney and a judge in the Commonwealth Caribbean for nearly three decades, replaced Foster as leader of the SLP in 1974. He became prime minister when Labour came back electorally in 1979, with 71 percent of the vote, to win twelve seats to five seats for the United Workers Party (UWP). Four of the newly elected parliamentarians were trade union leaders. As a result of intraparty conflict and a parliamentary defeat of his budget, the Louisy government resigned in April 1981.

Winston Cenac assumed the SLP leadership role, and in May 1981 he formed a new SLP government. His government fell in the general election of 1982 when the UWP proved victorious. SLP leadership now moved to Julian Hunte. In 1987 Cenac crossed the aisle to join the UWP government, complaining of "ungratefulness" and promises broken by the SLP, and he received the foreign ministry portfolio as compensation. Some SLP loyalists feel the real factors perpetrating the shift were the prestige and financial reward that accrued to Cenac. The election fallout from this defection is likely to impact the UWP more negatively than the SLP.

The SLP has been a national party throughout much of Saint Lucia's history. It controlled the Saint Lucian government consistently from the initial election under universal suffrage in 1951 until 1964, at which time it was replaced by the UWP. The SLP was returned to power in 1979. Currently, it is the loyal opposition party.

UNITED WORKERS PARTY (UWP). The UWP was founded in 1964 by defectors from the Saint Lucia Labour Party (SLP), who formed the National Labour Movement (NLM), which then joined forces with the smaller People's Progressive Party (PPP). The SLP parliamentary defection following the general election in 1961 included John Compton, who was chosen president of the UWP; Dr. Vincent Monrose; and Maurice Mason. John Compton, who currently remains in the post of party leader, served as prime minister following the general elections of 1982 and 1988. (There were actually two elections in 1988 as a result of Compton's unsuccessful attempt to increase his narrow one-seat majority over the SLP.) Former PPP leader, George Mallet, serves as Saint Lucia's deputy prime minister. The state of the Saint Lucian economy, together with Compton's success in negotiating improvements in trade and regional integration, will be key factors in future electoral success for the UWP.

Political Parties—Historical

NATIONAL LABOUR MOVEMENT (NLM). The NLM was established in 1961 by dissident Saint Lucia Labour Party legislators John Compton, Vincent Monrose, and Maurice Mason (Alexander 1982). The NLM gave way to the United Workers Party in 1964.

PEOPLE'S PROGRESSIVE PARTY (PPP). The PPP was created in 1950 as a more business-oriented counterweight to the Saint Lucia Labour Party. It fielded electoral teams from 1951 to 1961, running full slates in the 1957 and 1961 general elections. Founders of the PPP included John Pilgrim, a principal campaigner for universal suffrage; E. J. Carasco; Garnet Gordon; W. St. C. Daniel; C.H.R. King; Lucius Mason; Ives G. John; A. L. Theodore; and Matherson Mathews (Emmanuel 1979). The PPP won representation in parliament in the elections of 1951, 1954, 1957, and 1961 with between 10 and 13 percent of the ballots, but the party won only one seat per election, albeit from three different constituencies. The PPP continued as the opposition party until 1964 when it merged with the National Labour Movement to form the United Workers Party.

ST. LUCIA LABOUR PARTY–UNITED FRONT (SLP–UF). The SLP–UF was the party label under which former SLP chair George Charles and Jean Reynold sought election in 1969. This electoral attempt followed the removal of Charles as leader of the SLP in 1969 and as leader of the SLP parent organization, the Saint Lucia Workers' Union, the previous year.

W. Marvin Will

SAINT PIERRE
AND MIQUELON

Saint Pierre and Miquelon is a French territory made up of islands located just south of the Canadian province of Newfoundland. In the mid-1970s, it was officially an Overseas Department of France, but it was converted by the French parliament in December 1984 into a "territorial collective." Under the new system, there is a prefect named by the French government and a nineteen-member General Council, composed of fifteen representatives from Saint Pierre and four from Miquelon, who are chosen by universal adult suffrage. The change in status was designed, in part, to allow the area to receive investment from the European Economic Community but to limit the EEC's exploitation of the territory's offshore fishing areas.

During the 1980s, there were two turbulent issues in the politics of Saint Pierre and Miquelon. One was a declaration dating from 1976, whereby Canada imposed a 200-nautical-mile economic zone around its frontiers, which encompassed Saint Pierre and Miquelon. Thereupon, France proclaimed a similar limit around its tiny territory. A deadlock ensued, and in February 1988 Senator Albert Le Pen and Deputy Gérard Grignon declared a hunger strike to protest the situation. This controversy was temporarily resolved in March 1989 by an agreement negotiated by Enrique Iglesias, president of the Inter-American Development Bank, a mutually acceptable mediator. This agreement provided quotas for the amount of Atlantic codfish that could be caught in the Saint Pierre and Miquelon area by French and Canadian fishermen until the end of 1991.

The second controversy centered on the dispatch in January 1989 of two factory fishing ships from Saint-Malo, France, to the Saint Pierre and Miquelon area. After strong protests from the region, the French government agreed to withdraw one of the two vessels.

Political parties came to dominate the territory's politics after World War II. During the 1980s there was a considerable movement to the left in the local elections, although this was not so clear in the elections for the French parliament and presidency. In 1981 Socialist Le Pen was reelected to the French

National Assembly. The next year, the Socialists and their allies won an unopposed election for the General Council, campaigning on the issue of changing the territory's relationship with France.

In the March 1986 French general election, Le Pen, the Socialist deputy, was reelected, and six months later, he was the uncontested candidate for the French Senate. In November, Grignon of the Union for French Democracy (UDF) was elected to Le Pen's seat in the assembly. He was reelected in June 1988. In the French presidential election of 1988, the right-wing candidate, Jacques Chirac, won 58 percent of the votes in the territory.

In the September-October 1988 local elections, the Socialists won thirteen of the nineteen seats in the General Council; the UDF won the other six. Marc Plantagenet, a Socialist, was elected president of the council. In the March 1989 municipal elections, the Socialists won control of twenty-three municipalities, and the center right took six. Le Pen was reelected mayor of Saint Pierre.

Bibliography

Europa World Year Book 1990. Europa Publications, Ltd., London, 1990.
Keesings Record of World Events. London.

Political Parties

CENTER OF SOCIAL DEMOCRATS (CENTRE DES DEMOCRATES SOCIAL). This small party is allied with the Socialist Party.

CENTRE DES DEMOCRATES SOCIAL. *See* CENTER OF SOCIAL DEMOCRATS.

PARTI SOCIALISTE. *See* SOCIALIST PARTY.

RALLY FOR THE FRENCH REPUBLIC (RASSEMBLEMENT POUR LA RÉPUBLIQUE FRANÇAISE). The local branch of the neo-Gaullist party of Jacques Chirac, it is overshadowed on the right in Saint Pierre and Miquelon by the Union for French Democracy, and it has not been able to elect any member to the French parliament. It has had only meager representation in local elected bodies.

RASSEMBLEMENT POUR LA RÉPUBLIQUE FRANÇAISE. *See* RALLY FOR THE FRENCH REPUBLIC.

SOCIALIST PARTY. (PARTI SOCIALISTE). The most influential party in the territory, its predecessor, the French Socialist Party (SFIO), was the first party to be organized in the territory after World War II. During most of the existence of the General Council, the Socialists have enjoyed a majority and the party controls most of the municipalities, including the capital, Saint Pierre. During most of the period since World War II, members of the party were the representatives of Saint Pierre and Miquelon in both houses of the French legislature, although, since 1986, the party has not had the deputy's seat in the National Assembly. The Socialists control the major labor group in the territory, Force Ouvrière.

UNION FOR FRENCH DEMOCRACY. (UNION POUR LA DÉMOCRATIE FRANCAIŞE—UDF). The local branch of the party led in France by former French president Valery Giscard d'Estaing, the UDF is the second strongest party in the territory. Since 1986 a member of the UDF has been the deputy in the French National Assembly. The UDF also had the minority in the territory's General Council and controlled about one-third of the municipalities during the 1980s and early 1990s.

UNION POUR LA DÉMOCRATIE FRANCAIŞE. *See* UNION FOR FRENCH DEMOCRACY.

Robert J. Alexander

SAINT VINCENT AND THE GRENADINES

The state of Saint Vincent and the Grenadines is part of the Windward Island chain. It is sandwiched between Saint Lucia and Grenada, just 27 miles southwest of Saint Lucia and approximately 100 miles west of Barbados. Bequia, Canauan, Mayreau, Mustique, Prune Island, Petit Saint Vincent, and Union Island make up the Vincentian portion of the Grenadines; the remaining islands belong to Grenada. Saint Vincent alone makes up roughly 90 percent of the total 150 square miles of this multi-island state, and nearly all of its territory is wrapped around the volcano Mount Soufrière. Soufrière, with a cone approximately one mile in diameter, is one of the largest volcanos in the region. When it erupted in 1979, it severely damaged the local economy.

Of the total population of just over 100,000 in Saint Vincent and the Grenadines, more than 95 percent are of African descent (black and mixed), but there is also a small minority of whites, Amerindians, and Asians. With a per capita gross domestic product of just US $1,463 in 1989, Saint Vincent ranks as the poorest country in the Organization of Eastern Caribbean States (OECS). Similar to other small eastern Caribbean islands, it suffers from major outmigration—and resultant brain drain—due to the usually high unemployment. Largely because of these factors, economic development and related regional integration are the major goals of the government of the prime minister, James Fitz Allen "Son" Mitchell.

After it was explored by the Spaniards in 1498, Saint Vincent, much like its neighbors Saint Lucia and Grenada, alternated between French and British control. It finally became British after 1783 and experienced the colonial pattern typical of the British West Indies: initial heavy-handed control during the British wars with France; a period of shared power with the white planters; a shift to Crown Colony status, with its largely appointed legislature (1877); some gradual democratization, which was capped with semicabinet government in 1957; and home-rule Associate State status in 1969, which culminated in independence in October 1979.

Unlike some of its neighbors, Saint Vincent was not dominated by a sugar culture partly because of its mountainous terrain and partly because, early in the twentieth century, many of its large estates were subdivided and sold to peasant operators. Saint Vincent's primary exportable resources today are bananas, arrowroot, and other agricultural crops. Nonetheless, Saint Vincent experienced much the same pattern of labor unrest in the 1930s as did British Honduras (Belize), Saint Kitts, Jamaica, and neighboring Barbados and Trinidad. The primary protests in Saint Vincent came from the wharf workers, but during October 1935 the unrest expanded from Camden Park to Kingstown, the capital. This confrontation between workers and authorities, which left four dead, had a significant impact on the development of the colony's politics.

Political History

Agitation for franchise expansion in Saint Vincent had occurred soon after World War I, when the Saint Vincent Representative Government Association was established by brown and black business-class individuals led by Ebenezer Duncan and Robert Anderson. Following the 1935 disturbances, a Workingmen's Association, which embodied both union and party functions, was launched by George McIntosh. Official unions continued to be banned by the planter-influenced government, and, as in Grenada, political party development awaited the advent of a popular leader and expanded suffrage; these arrived together in 1951. The Vincentian who emerged as party builder was Ebenezer Theodore Joshua, a leader with charismatic qualities.

In May 1951, Joshua established the United Workers, Peasants and Rate-Payers Union (UWPRU), with major input from a fellow labor leader, George Charles, as well as from several professionals and farmers. The UWPRU was a loosely structured organization that was sympathetic to labor and had an important party function, the nomination and fielding of candidates for office. In the October 1951 election, it put forth a team of candidates, called the Eighth Army of Liberation, to contest each of the eight parliamentary seats in Saint Vincent. The UWPRU's "army" secured all eight seats and, as Patrick Emmanuel has observed, "was St. Vincent's first mass-based political grouping." In 1952 Joshua formally organized these elected parliamentarians into the People's Political Party (PPP), which was truly the colony's first political party. Despite the lack of the familiar word "labor" in its title, the PPP became the de facto labor party in Saint Vincent. The PPP won only three seats against a strong group of independent candidates in 1954, but the party won the succeeding three elections before it lost to its new rival, the Saint Vincent Labour Party (SVLP), in the crucial 1967 statehood election.

The rival SVLP was organized in 1955 by barristers Robert Milton Cato and Rupert John and businessman O. D. Brisbane. Cato, a local sports hero who had been captain of the colony's Cricket Association and had also served as an officer in the Canadian Army in World War II, was elected as the group's first president, a post he retained for more than two decades.

Such a trenchant rivalry developed between the PPP and the SVLP that elections frequently were not clear-cut. A cultural characteristic prevalent among Vincentians, which has directed considerable support toward small transient parties and independents, has intensified this discord. Associate State status was not granted to Saint Vincent in 1967 as intended, for example, but was withheld until 1969 because the government was nearly immobilized after the disputed election of August 1966, which was won by the PPP (five to four) despite being edged by 503 votes in the popular vote. When one PPP member finally crossed the aisle, the government was deadlocked, and new elections were forced. The general election which followed in May 1967 was won by the SVLP, and Britain extended full cabinet government to the colony. Thus, Cato rather than Joshua, became the first premier of Saint Vincent.

In 1972 the PPP and the SVLP again faced off, this time to elect members to an expanded parliament. Once more the voters split, giving six seats to each of these major parties and one seat to independent candidate Mitchell from the island of Bequia, who had won his first seat in parliament in 1967 as a member of Cato's SVLP. The popular "out islander" was selected premier of Saint Vincent as a compromise choice of the deadlocked parties. His tenure lasted two and one-half years before his administration faced a no-confidence vote, and the fragile government fell. Again Saint Vincent went to the polls, this time with an ill-conceived coalition between Joshua's PPP and Cato's SVLP, the two major parties.

This 1974 coalition plan, which was the beginning of the end for the PPP, appeared to be a pact with the devil to many younger, unemployed, or underemployed Vincentians. It seemed to anticipate the Machiavellian 1980s—the Likud-Labor coalition in Israel and the equally opportunistic domination of the nominee process by Blaize's Grenada National Party in Grenada's 1984 party confederation. In the case of Saint Vincent in 1974, Cato, too, negotiated the predominant share of the candidate slate for his party (eleven), leaving only three slots for the PPP. Each major party in the coalition had one losing candidate in the election of 1974, which resulted in a ten-to-two division favoring the SVLP. Again, one seat went to Mitchell, this time under the banner of the Mitchell/Sylvester Faction (Emmanuel, 1979). Cato became Saint Vincent's first prime minister.

Current Electoral Politics

Elections and politics in Saint Vincent during the remainder of the 1970s and throughout the 1980s and early 1990s have continued to reflect change, including a high level of political and labor confrontation in the 1980s. In the 1979 election, immediately following independence, the discredited PPP was shut out. Although leadership of the PPP had evolved to the shoulders of Clive

Tannis, he could not reverse the party's electoral slippage. When Tannis died prior to the next election in 1983, the PPP died with him.

In 1979 Cato and the SVLP won eleven seats to just two for the opposition, which was now the New Democratic Party (NDP), a newly created party led by the recent premier, Mitchell. The NDP was just one of several new parties that were formed in Saint Vincent, partly by renegades from the PPP. This activity was fueled by an attitude that there was little left to distinguish between the two coalition partners of 1974 and by a growing popular unrest. This unrest was especially evidenced in the secessionist revolt on Union Island in December 1979 (forestalled with the aid of Barbadian troops) and by labor unrest that was at times violent in Saint Vincent during 1981.

In 1980 the Saint Vincent National Movement (SVNM) was founded by Gideon Cordice. Another party arriving on the scene was the Progressive Democratic Party (PDP), formed in 1982 by Randolph Russell. One of the larger minor parties, the United People's Movement (UPM), was formed in 1982 as an alliance of the Democratic Freedom Movement, the leftist Youlou United Liberation Movement (YULIMO), and the rural group, Arwee, which is also considered leftist. The leader of the UPM was left-leaning Dr. Ralph Gonsalves, a social scientist at the University of the West Indies. Although considered sympathetic to the Grenadian Revolution of this period, Gonsalves may not have been sufficiently leftist for the UPM; he was dislodged from the leadership of the party he had founded by his assistant, Renwick Rose, in November 1982. Gonsalves has now formed his own more moderate party, the Movement for National Unity (MNU).

Ideological differences between the NDP and the UPM, as in the case of Antigua, initially blunted the development of a viable opposition to Cato's government. "Personal feuds and egos," Rosemary and Gary Brana-Shute note (1988), prevented electoral cooperation, although a few parties did merge. Calder Williams, for example, dissolved his group, the Working People's Party (WPP), to join Mitchell's NDP, and Russell urged opposition parliamentarians and voters to close ranks to oust the Cato regime. Nevertheless, on the eve of the 1984 election, Saint Vincent was fast winning the reputation battle with Grenada for the most parties per capita in the region. With the opposition so divided, Cato appeared to be unbeatable.

The Rise of New Democratic Politics

The 1984 general election defied many experts. Although it was contested by eight parties, the election was a smashing victory for Mitchell and the NDP, who won ten seats to Labour's three. Cato, the ailing leader of the SVLP, resigned from both the party and parliament following the loss. His position was soon filled by Vincent Beache. Despite the economic problems of the 1980s, the 1989 election in Saint Vincent was even more smashing: Mitchell and the

NDP took every seat and shut out the opposition in this the most multiparty system in the area.

Mitchell's victory was applauded by many since he has developed considerable support not only in Saint Vincent but also in the Eastern Caribbean where he is the acknowledged leader of the integration moves being promoted at the decade's end. Mitchell also has a strong following in the United States. The economy remains the big concern in Saint Vincent. Mitchell perceives inte-gration as a means of boosting economic development. Support from opposition parties both at home and abroad is not likely, however, since a party that is small in a Saint Vincent or Grenada would be miniscule or nonexistent in a two-to-four island state. Therefore, this issue faces an uphill struggle as major as any in the region. Mitchell is also a regional leader in opposing the militar-ization of the Eastern Caribbean, its "Central Americanization," in the words of Michael Erisman (1989). Mitchell holds a major advantage in Vincentian politics as a result of his high personal support and the fact that Saint Vincent today experiences a good deal less corruption than under the previous regime.

Bibliography

Robert J. Alexander. "Saint Vincent," in Robert J. Alexander, ed., *Political Parties of the Americas*, vol. 1, 639–44. Greenwood Press, Westport, Conn., 1982.

Gary Brana-Shute and Rosemary Brana-Shute. "The Organization of Eastern Caribbean States," in James M. Malloy and Eduardo A. Gamarra, eds., *Latin America and Caribbean Contemporary Record*, vol. 7, 1987–1988, B517–21. Holmes and Meier, New York, 1990.

———. "The Anglophone Eastern Caribbean and British Dependencies," in Abraham F. Lowenthal, ed., *Latin America and Caribbean Contemporary Record*, vol. 5, 1985–1986, B432–34. Holmes & Meier, New York, 1988.

Rosemary Brana-Shute and Gary Brana-Shute. "The Anglophone Eastern Caribbean and British Dependencies," in Abraham F. Lowenthal, ed., *Latin America and Caribbean Contemporary Record*, vol. 6, 1986–1987, B434–36. Holmes and Meier, New York, 1989.

———. "St. Vincent and the Grenadines," in Jack W. Hopkins, ed., *Latin America and Caribbean Contemporary Record*, vol. 3, 1983–1984, 893–901. Holmes and Meier, New York, 1985.

———. "Saint Vincent and the Grenadines," in Jack W. Hopkins, ed., *Latin America and Caribbean Contemporary Record*, vol. 1, 1981–1982, 617–21. Holmes and Meier, New York, 1983.

Caribbean Development Bank. *Annual Report, 1990*. Coles Printery, for the CDB, St. Michael, Barbados, 1991.

Patrick A. M. Emmanuel. *General Elections in the Eastern Caribbean*. Letchworth Press, Ltd., for ISER (EC) of the University of the West Indies, Barbados, 1979.

H. Michael Erisman. "The Caricom States and U.S. Foreign Policy: The Danger of Central Americanization." *Journal of InterAmerican Studies* 31, 3, Fall, pp. 141–82. 1989.

Percy C. Hintzen and W. Marvin Will. Biographies of political leaders in Saint Vincent,

560 / POLITICAL PARTIES OF THE AMERICAS

in Robert J. Alexander, ed., *Biographical Dictionary of Latin American and Caribbean Political Leaders*, 294–95 ff. Greenwood Press, Westport, Conn., 1988.
W. Marvin Will. Interviews with various political leaders in Kingstown, Saint Vincent, in May 1990.

Political Parties—Active

MOVEMENT FOR NATIONAL UNITY (MNU). The MNU was formed in November 1982 by academic Ralph Gonsalves following his eviction earlier that year from the increasingly Marxist United People's Movement, which he also established.

NEW DEMOCRATIC PARTY (NDP). Formed by James F. "Son" Mitchell in 1975, the NDP is the only party formed since the 1950s that has attracted a truly national following. It is the governing party in Saint Vincent in the early 1990s by virtue of winning its first victory (ten to three) in 1984 with an 89-percent electoral turnout and by sweeping all thirteen seats in the 1989 general election, an almost unheard of feat in the Commonwealth Caribbean. Prior to these elections, the NDP had never controlled more than two seats.

The demise of the People's Political Party (PPP), with which Mitchell worked closely in 1972, coincided with the meteoric rise of the NDP. There is no doubt that the party of the former PPP–backed premier gained substantially from the membership ranks of the abrogated PPP. Mitchell's rockbed of support remains the voters of the Grenadines who recall his opposition on their behalf to a Cato-led independence move they feared would bring domination by Saint Vincent. Mitchell is a well-published author on agricultural development, which does not weaken his support among the Vincentian rural sectors.

Finally, Mitchell's support for regional integration and for economic development over arms build-ups ("Who are we going to fight?" he asks) and, perhaps most important, his reputation for honesty in succeeding a government that floundered in scandal have all been instrumental in his personal rise as well as that of his party.

PROGRESSIVE DEMOCRATIC PARTY (PDP). The PDP was formed in 1982 by its current chair, Randolph Russell. Prior to the 1984 election, Russell advocated that opposition parliamentarians and voters close ranks in an attempt to oust the Cato-led regime.

SAINT VINCENT LABOUR PARTY (SVLP). The SVLP was organized in 1955 by barristers Robert Milton Cato and Rupert John and businessman O. D. Brisbane. Cato was selected to serve as the party's president, a position he retained for nearly three decades until the SVLP's massive defeat by the New Democratic Party in 1984. Although the SVLP tended to divide almost equally election victories with the PPP and its predecessor during the first two decades of party politics in Saint Vincent, Cato's timing was such that he was both Saint Vincent's first premier in 1969 and its first prime minister in 1979.

Following its coalition with the People's Political Party in the 1974 general election, the SVLP dominated the Vincentian political scene for the remainder of the decade. Despite the SVLP's use of the word labor in its title, the SVLP is, in fact, closer to business interests than to labor interests (Alexander, 1982). In the end, its antiworker policy led to numerous strikes and also to the indictment and conviction of members of Cato's cabinet for financial abuse. These factors have contributed to the reversals experienced in the SVLP's electoral support.

SAINT VINCENT NATIONAL MOVEMENT (SVNM). The SVNM was founded in 1980 by its current leader, Gideon Cordice.

UNITED PEOPLE'S MOVEMENT (UPM). The UPM was created in early 1982 by Dr. Ralph Gonsalves, a University of the West Indies academic, through the merger of three leftist groups: the Democratic Freedom Movement, the Youlou United Liberation Movement, and Arwee, a small rural organization. Gonsalves was dislodged from leadership of the UPM in November 1982 by Renwick Rose, second in command of this the second largest of Saint Vincent's opposition parties, possibly because Gonsalves was discussing strategies with the non-Marxist James F. Mitchell for developing a closer working relation between Mitchell's New Democratic Party and the UPM.

Leadership changes have continued in the UPM; first Oscar Allen succeeded to that position, and now, at the beginning of the 1990s, Adrian Sanders heads the party. Meanwhile, after his ouster as leader of the UPM, Gonsalves formed a second party called the Movement for National Unity. The Marxist UPM remains weak, but it has the potential to increase in strength as the Vincentian economy worsens.

Political Parties—Historical

DEMOCRATIC FREEDOM MOVEMENT (DFM). The DFM was formed by Kenneth John in 1974 as a party banner under which he and a colleague could contest the general election held in December of that year. In 1982 the DFM was one of three groups that joined in an alliance to form the second largest opposition party in Saint Vincent, the United People's Movement.

MITCHELL/SYLVESTER FACTION. The Mitchell/Sylvester Faction, the first stage in what was to become the governing New Democratic Party, was organized to contest the 1974 general election. James Mitchell was the only successful candidate.

PEOPLE'S LIBERATION MOVEMENT (PLM). The PLM was founded in 1957 by Herman Young, who had been elected to parliament in 1951 as a member of the Eighth Army of Liberation of the United Workers, Peasants and Rate-Payers Union and again in 1954 as a member of its successor, the People's Political Party. The PLM was made up of a group of independents who formed this party to provide a banner under which to compete electorally. The PLM dissolved following the 1957 election.

PEOPLE'S POLITICAL PARTY (PPP). Following the election of 1951, Ebenezer Theodore Joshua organized the elected parliamentary members into the colony's first real political party, the People's Political Party, which he formally presented in 1952. All of the founding parliamentarians had been elected the preceding year as candidates for the United Workers, Peasants and Rate-Payers Union's Eighth Army of Liberation. Despite the lack of the term labor in its name, the PPP was the primary Saint Vincent labor party. Joshua was to remain the PPP leader for three decades.

After closely competing with the Saint Vincent Labour Party (SVLP) for two decades, a decision was made in 1974 to form a coalition with the SVLP. This decision proved to be a disaster for the PPP, which had ceased to exist by May 1983, almost simultaneously with the death of its new leader, Clive Tannis. With the demise of Saint Vincent's most progressive party, many PPP members apparently joined the ranks of the New Democratic Party (NDP) of James F. Mitchell, a party Mitchell worked with initially during his short tenure as premier from 1972 to 1974.

UNITED WORKERS, PEASANTS AND RATE-PAYERS UNION'S EIGHTH ARMY OF LIBERATION. The Eighth Army of Liberation was the name given to the eight candidates who contested the 1951 general election for the United Workers, Peasants and Rate-Payers Union (UWPRU). The UWPRU was formed by labor leaders Ebenezer Theodore Joshua and George Charles, with assistance from professionals and agricultural leaders, such as Julian and Rudolph Baynes, Clive Tannis, Sam Slater, Herman Young, and Evans Morgan. It was a loosely structured organization that was supportive of labor.

There was a party dimension in the UWPRU that put forth the Eighth Army of Liberation team of candidates for the 1951 general election. All eight candidates were successfully elected to parliament. In 1952, under the leadership of Joshua, these parliamentarians formed the nucleus of Saint Vincent's first real political party, the People's Political Party.

WEST INDIAN NATIONAL PARTY (WINP). The West Indian National Party was formed by a founder of the United Workers, Peasants and Rate-Payers Union, George Charles, as a vehicle for contesting the 1974 election.

WORKING PEOPLE'S PARTY (WPP). The WPP enjoyed a degree of electoral success in the late 1970s and early 1980s, but it dissolved in 1984 when its leader, Calder Williams, joined James F. Mitchell's New Democratic Party

(NDP). This merger was one of the building blocks that produced a national majority for the NDP.

YOULOU UNITED LIBERATION MOVEMENT (YULIMO). The YULIMO was organized as a reaction to the no-confidence vote that ousted Premier James F. Mitchell in 1974. Its youthful "scientific socialist" founders, as Robert Alexander (1982) calls them, perceived the People's Political Party and the Saint Vincent Labour Party, at that time the dominant parties, as bankrupt organizations that offered no meaningful choice. Ralph Gonsalves and Renwick Rose were two of the founders who organized the party on this basis.

In the 1979 election, the YULIMO was the second best organized party in Saint Vincent and received more than 14 percent of the electoral vote. In the aftermath of the Grenadian Revolution, the YULIMO has been called a Marxist group. In 1982 the YULIMO merged with two other opposition parties—the Democratic Freedom Movement and the Arwee—to form the United People's Movement.

W. Marvin Will

SURINAME

Suriname, a former colony of the Netherlands, achieved its independence in 1975. It is located on the north coast of South America, between the Co-operative Republic of Guyana and French Guiana, and encompasses an area of 63,020 square miles. It has a population of slightly more than 400,000 and a 1987 per capita gross national product of $2,360. When it became independent, it had a democratic parliamentary regime similar to that of the Netherlands.

In February 1980, the elected government of Minister President Henck Arron was overthrown by a military coup led by noncommissioned and junior officers. An eight-man National Military Council (MNR), headed by ex-sergeant Desire (Desi) Bouterse, was formed as the effective ruling body.

President Johan Ferrier refused to allow the MNR to be the supreme power, and he appointed a civilian administration headed by Henck Chin A. Sen, a leader of the Nationalist Republic Party (PNR). In August, after Bouterse staged a second coup, he replaced Ferrier with Chin A. Sen, dissolved the legislature, and declared a state of emergency. In February 1982, Bouterse ousted Chin A. Sen, who went to the Netherlands, where he formed the Movement for the Liberation of Suriname in January 1983.

The vice president of the Supreme Court, L. Fred Ramdat Misier, was made interim president by Bouterse. Then, following an unsuccessful coup attempt against Bouterse, a twelve-member cabinet with a civilian majority was appointed, with moderate economist Henry Neyhorst as prime minister. The failure of Bouterse to fulfill the promises he had made to trade union leaders and left-wing politicians made them turn against him and join in the demand for a return to constitutional government.

In October 1982, after the arrest of Cyriel Daal, leader of the country's largest trade union, Die Moederbond, caused strikes and demonstrations, Bouterse promised new elections and a new constitution by March 1983. But, in December 1982, the army burned down a number of buildings used by the opposition, which provoked renewed demonstrations. The army rounded up and killed fifteen leading civilians, including Cyriel Daal. An attempted coup in January 1983 led to the dismissal of two-thirds of the officers of the armed forces.

In February 1983, Dr. Errol Alibux, a former minister of social affairs, was made prime minister. His formation of a cabinet of members of the Progressive Workers and Farmers Labor Union and the Revolutionary People's Party lifted the state of siege.

A year later, in February 1984, another interim government, headed by Wim Udenhout, a former adviser of Bouterse, was established to plan a gradual return to constitutional government. It included nominees of trade unions and the business community.

Meanwhile, Bouterse had established the Standvaste (25 February Movement), in November 1983, to rally civilian support. In January 1985, a nominated National Assembly, with representatives of the Standvaste, trade unions, and businessmen, was established, and a new cabinet was formed by Udenhout. In April, three of the four trade union members of his cabinet resigned.

In June 1985, a new cabinet was organized with people with ties to the old parties, and in November the ban on parties was ended. In November 1985, Henck Arron of the Suriname National Party (NPS), Jaggernath Lachmon of the Progressive Reformed Party (VHP), and Willy Soemita of the Indonesian Peasants Party accepted invitations to join the National Military Council, which was renamed the Supreme Council. In July 1986, there were only two military men still in the Supreme Council when Bouterse appointed a new fourteen-member cabinet, with representatives of the business community, the labor unions, political parties, and Standvaste. Pretaap Radhikishun, a member of the VHP, became prime minister. The cabinet drafted a new constitution, which, when it was submitted to a referendum in September 1987, received the support of 93 percent of the voters.

The new constitution provided for a president elected by a fifty-one-member, elected National Assembly, and a vice president, similarly elected, who would serve as prime minister. The president was presumably head of the government, chief of the armed forces, and chairman of the Council of State (the successor to the Supreme Council), which was authorized to assume all power in case of "war, state of siege or exceptional circumstances determined by law." The constitution declared the army "the vanguard of the people."

In the elections held on 25 November 1987, the old parties were victorious, and the National Democratic Party (NDP), the name Bouterse's Standvaste had assumed in the middle of the year, received only three seats in the new National Assembly. Forty of the fifty-one seats were won by the Front for Democracy and Development—a coalition of the VHP, the NPS, and the Party for National Unity and Solidarity (KTPI)—which had contested only forty-one seats.

On 25 January 1989, Ramsewak Shankar was elected president by the new National Assembly, and Henck Arron was chosen as vice president and prime minister (minister-president). However, relations between the new, elected government and the armed forces, still led by Bouterse, remained tense.

The major issue of dispute between the civilian government and the army leaders was the handling of guerrilla movements in the interior. Attacks by the Surinamese Liberation Army (SLA), a Bush Negro rebel group, had begun in July 1986, under the leadership of Ronnie Brunswick.

The Bush Negroes, descendants of black slaves who had fled to the interior in colonial days, had been very unhappy for some time. During the 1960s, large hydroelectric projects, built to provide power for the bauxite industry, the country's principal export, had resulted in the creation of two large lakes, which displaced many of the Bush Negroes from areas they had long inhabited. Although they had formed a party and participated in the country's parliamentary and political life, they felt themselves abused and neglected by the rest of the community.

The SLA guerrillas at various times interfered with the bauxite mining and the electricity system; for short periods, they even occupied some of the mining centers. In April 1988, a Committee of Christian Churches sought to mediate between the government and the SLA. Meanwhile, the International Commission of Jurists had accused the Suriname army of murdering between 150 and 200 civilians between June 1986 and August 1987 during its antiguerrilla activities.

In August 1988, negotiations held in Kouru, French Guiana, between the elected government and the SLA resulted in an agreement to end the guerrilla war, even though Commander Bouterse and the army leadership expressed their opposition to that agreement. Meanwhile, a dissident Bush Negro group, known as the Mandela Bush Negro Liberation Movement, and an Amerindian guerrilla group, known as Tucayana Amazonica, made their appearance. Both of these groups were reported to be backed by the army.

There were other sources of conflict between the elected civilian government and the armed forces. In April 1988, there was a five-day police strike against army interference in police efforts to arrest military men accused of arson. On 5 May 1989, there was a general strike of the four largest trade unions against the high cost of food and the extent of unemployment.

The tension between the army and the government culminated in yet another military coup on 24 December 1990. Commander Ivan Graanoogst, a leading ally of Bouterse, announced that the army had taken power and dismissed the president, vice president, and cabinet. Shortly afterward, the army named Johan Kraag, a onetime leader of the NPS, as interim president, and Jules Wijdenbosch, a leader of Bouterse's NDP, as vice president and prime minister. A new cabinet of eight soldiers and three civilians, of the NDP, was named.

Since the inception of party politics in Suriname, most of the parties have been organized along ethnic lines. About 35 percent of the population is of East Indian origin, 31 percent is creole (wholly or partly of African descent), and 15 percent of Indonesian origin; the rest are Bush Negroes and small numbers of Europeans, Chinese, and Amerindians. The parties have reflected these divisions of the population.

Bibliography

The Europa World Year Book 1990. Europa Publications, Ltd., London, 1990.
Facts on File. Facts on File, New York.
Keesings Record of World Events. London.
Personal contacts of the writer.
The Times of the Americas, Miami, Florida.

Political Parties

COMMUNIST PARTY OF SURINAME (KOMMUNISTISCHE PARTIJ VAN SURINAME). An orthodox, pro-Soviet Communist Party, it is a fringe group in national politics. Although the party offered candidates under the label of Democratic People's Front in the 1977 election (none of them won), it seems to have played little or no role in the turbulent events of the 1980s. If it ran any nominees in the 1987 election, none of them was successful.

INDONESIAN PEASANTS PARTY (KAUM-TANI PERSUATAN INDO-NESIA). *See* PARTY FOR NATIONAL UNITY AND SOLIDARITY.

KAUM-TANI PERSUATAN INDONESIA (INDONESIAN PEASANTS PARTY). *See* PARTY FOR NATIONAL UNITY AND SOLIDARITY.

KERUKANAN TULODO PRANATAN INGIL. *See* PARTY FOR NA-TIONAL UNITY AND SOLIDARITY.

KOMMUNISTISCHE PARTIJ VAN SURINAME. *See* COMMUNIST PARTY OF SURINAME.

NATIONAL DEMOCRATIC PARTY (NDP). The NDP was established by the military and led by Desi Bouterse to contest the 1987 election. Bouterse had first launched the Standvaste (25 February Movement) to garner civilian support for the military regime in November 1983. With the approach of elec-tions, the Standvaste was converted into the NDP in the middle of 1987. It won only three seats in the fifty-one-person National Assembly in that year's election. With the overthrow of the civilian regime again by the military in December 1990, Jules Wijdenbosch, a leading figure in the NDP, was installed as vice president and prime minister.

NATIONALE PARTIJ SURINAME. *See* SURINAME NATIONAL PARTY.

NATIONALIST REPUBLIC PARTY (PARTIJ NATIONALISTISCHE RE-PUBLIK—PNR). A left-wing, nationalist party, the PNR was established in 1963 under the leadership of Eddy Bruma. Although the PNR placed five members in the Staten (the parliament of the time) in the early 1970s, it lost all of these seats in the 1977 election. After the military coup in February 1980, Bruma was reported to be a close adviser to Desi Bouterse. A member of the PNR, Chin A. Sen, was first named to head a civilian cabinet and, then, in August, was made president by the military. However, in February 1982, Bouterse removed Chin A. Sen, who fled to the Netherlands, where he organized the Movement for the Liberation of Suriname, which plotted from afar for the overthrow of the military regime. The party was revived when the ban on political parties was ended in November 1985, but it failed to elect anyone to the National Assembly in the November 1987 election.

PARTIJ NATIONALISTISCHE REPUBLIK. *See* NATIONALIST REPUBLIC PARTY.

PARTY FOR NATIONAL UNITY AND SOLIDARITY (KERUKANAN TULODO PRANATAN INGIL—KTPI). The KTPI was formed in 1985, after the relegalization of political parties, by a merger of two predominantly Indonesian parties: the Indonesian Peasants Party and the Pendawa Lima. The Indonesian Peasants Party, founded in 1947, has been the principal political representative of the Indonesian population of Suriname. It is headed by Willy Soemita. The Pendawa Lima is headed by Salam Paul Somohardjo. During the military regime, when political parties were relegalized, Soemita accepted a post in the Supreme Council, named by Commander Desi Bouterse.

In the election held in November 1987, the KTPI was part of the antimilitarist Front for Democracy and Development, along with the principal creole and East Indian parties. It elected ten of the fifty-one members of the new National Assembly.

PENDAWA LIMA. *See* PARTY FOR NATIONAL UNITY AND SOLIDARITY.

PROGRESSIEVE ARBEIDERS EN LANDBOUWERS UNIE. *See* PROGRESSIVE WORKERS AND FARMERS LABOR UNION.

PROGRESSIEVE BOSNEGER PARTIJ. *See* PROGRESSIVE BUSH NEGRO PARTY.

PROGRESSIEVE NATIONALE PARTIJ. *See* PROGRESSIVE NATIONAL PARTY.

PROGRESSIEVE SURINAME VOLKSPARTIJ. *See* PROGRESSIVE SURINAME PEOPLE'S PARTY.

PROGRESSIVE BUSH NEGRO PARTY (PROGRESSIEVE BOSNEGER PARTIJ). Founded in 1968, this party became the principal political organization representing the Bush Negro population. The Bush Negroes fully entered national politics in the 1970s when their traditional way of life was threatened by the construction of the hydroelectric projects that formed two large lakes that flooded much of the area in which they had lived. The party, led by Jarien Gadden, does not appear to have played an active role during the military regime of the 1980s. However, in the election held in November 1987, although the party was not a member of the antimilitarist Front for Democracy and Development coalition, it elected four members to the fifty-one-member National Assembly.

PROGRESSIVE NATIONAL PARTY (PROGRESSIEVE NATIONALE PARTIJ). A predominantly creole party, led by Jules Sedney, the Progressive National Party represents conservative middle-class interests. For four years following 1969, Sedney served as minister president (prime minister), but in the 1973 election the party lost its eight seats in the Staten and it had no members in that body at the time of the 1980 military coup. When parties were relegalized in preparation for the 1987 election, the Progressive National Party was reestablished; however, it was unable to elect anyone to the National Assembly.

PROGRESSIVE REFORMED PARTY (VOORUITSTREVENDE HERVORMINGS PARTIJ—VHP). Since its inception in the late 1940s, the VHP has been the principal political organization of the people of East Indian descent. Under its longtime leader Jaggernath Lachmon, the party opposed independence for Suriname but did finally accept it. The VHP was the core of the opposition to the Suriname National Party government in the late 1970s.

With the end of the military regime's ban on political parties in November 1985, Lachmon accepted an invitation to become a member of the regime's Supreme Council. Also, in July 1986, Desi Bouterse installed a leader of the VHP, Pretaap Radhikishun, as prime minister.

In the election held in November 1987, the VHP joined with the principal creole party, the Suriname National Party, and the major Indonesian group, the Party for National Unity and Solidarity, to form the antimilitarist coalition, Front for Democracy and Development, which won the election. The VHP won sixteen seats in the National Assembly, the largest representation of any party. An East Indian, Ramsewak Shankar, was elected president of the republic by the National Assembly; Lachmon became chairman of the National Assembly.

PROGRESSIVE SURINAME PEOPLE'S PARTY (PROGRESSIEVE SURINAME VOLKSPARTIJ). This predominantly Catholic creole party was established in 1946. It was represented in the cabinet of Minister-President Henck

Arron at the time of the military coup in 1980. It does not appear to have played a significant role during the military regime of the 1980s, and, although it was reorganized when the military's ban on political parties was lifted in 1985, it did not win any seats in the National Assembly in the November 1987 election.

PROGRESSIVE WORKERS AND FARMERS LABOR UNION (PROGRESSIEVE ARBEIDERS EN LANDBOUWERS UNIE). Led by Iwan Krous, this is a relatively small, left-wing party. It was aligned with the opposition to the government of Henck Arron before the overthrow of the civilian regime by the military in 1980. Between February 1983 and February 1984, the party participated in the cabinet of Dr. Errol Alibux, organized by the military. In the election of 1987, it succeeded in placing four members in the National Assembly.

REVOLUTIONARY PEOPLE'S PARTY (REVOLUTIONNAIRE VOLKSPARTIJ). This small party made its appearance in the 1980s. Between February 1983 and February 1984, it participated in the cabinet of Dr. Errol Alibux, established by the military. It did not succeed in placing anyone in the National Assembly in the 1987 parliamentary election.

REVOLUTIONNAIRE VOLKSPARTIJ. See REVOLUTIONARY PEOPLE'S PARTY.

SURINAME LABOR PARTY. A new party, established in 1987, it is associated with the C-47 trade union group. Described as being of social democratic orientation, the party is led by Fred Darby. It did not elect anyone to the National Assembly in 1987.

SURINAME NATIONAL PARTY (NATIONALE PARTIJ SURINAME—NPS). A predominantly creole party, one of the oldest in the country, the NPS was founded in 1946. It dominated national politics during much of the period between the end of World War II and the military coup of 1980. Its leader, Henck Arron, was minister-president when the civilian regime was overthrown by the armed forces.

When the military ended the ban on political parties in November 1985, Arron accepted the invitation to become a member of the regime's Supreme Council. In the election held in November 1987, the NPS joined with the Party for National Unity and Solidarity and the Progressive Reformed Party to form the antimilitarist coalition, the Front for Democracy and Development, which triumphed at the polls. The NPS won fourteen seats in the National Assembly, which elected Henck Arron as vice president of the republic and prime minister.

After the December 1990 military coup, a onetime leader and cabinet member of the NPS, Johan Kraag, was named by the military to serve as interim president.

VOORUITSTREVENDE HERVORMINGS PARTIJ. *See* PROGRESSIVE RE-
FORMED PARTY.

Robert J. Alexander

TRINIDAD AND TOBAGO

The Republic of Trinidad and Tobago is situated in the southern Caribbean just off the coast of Venezuela. Discovered by Christopher Columbus, Trinidad was ruled by Spain until the British captured the island in 1797. Tobago was disputed by the Dutch, French, and English until it was ceded to the British in 1814. The islands were administratively joined in 1888. After the abolition of slavery in 1833, the African and European population was augmented by immigrants from India entering under a system of indentureship that lasted until 1915. Today, the population of 1.2 million (1988) is, according to the 1980 census, divided evenly between Africans (41 percent) and East Indians (40.8 percent); the rest are European descendants, Chinese, Syrian, Lebanese, and persons of mixed origin. Economically, Trinidad and Tobago is one of the most industrialized Caribbean countries. Until recently, it was also the wealthiest, with an economy based primarily on oil and sugar. However, the downturn in oil prices produced a severe deterioration of the economy in the 1980s and early 1990s.

Politically, Trinidad and Tobago was governed by Britain as a Crown Colony until 1962. However, in the 1930s the growth of the labor movement and attendant social unrest forced the British to address the concerns of the workers and also to change the political system by increasing the number of elected (as opposed to nominated) members of the legislature and by introducing universal suffrage in 1946. There followed a period of political individualism, characterized by a proliferation of personalistic groups, parties in name only. Finally, in 1956, the first mass party was formed by Dr. Eric Williams, a former Oxford-educated professor of history at Howard University in Washington, D.C. Williams was a former secretary of the Caribbean Commission, which had been established by Britain and the United States to strengthen social and economic cooperation in the Caribbean during World War II. This nationalist, anticolonial party, the People's National Movement (PNM), won a majority in the 1956 general election and remained in power for the next thirty years. Meanwhile, in 1956, Trinidad and Tobago became self-governing. In 1958 it became a member of the short-lived West Indies Federation, and in 1962 Trinidad and Tobago gained its independence from Britain. In 1976 the islands became a republic within the British Commonwealth.

Despite a superficial heterogeneity, the PNM's support base has been the black masses, especially those who live along what is known as the "East-West corridor," the crowded northern section of Trinidad. As a counterpoint to this, the Democratic Labour Party (DLP) was formed in the late 1950s, with a support base in the East Indian population. Until 1970 the DLP, which under the winner-take-all system could win only in the geographically circumscribed East Indian–dominated areas, was the official parliamentary opposition, occupying about one-third of the seats in parliament. In 1970 Trinidad and Tobago experienced a period of social and political unrest that culminated in an aborted military coup. This unrest had its origins in the failure of the "open economy" development model adopted by the PNM and the resulting high level of unemployment, especially among the youth.

The deputy prime minister of the PNM, A.N.R. Robinson, left the PNM to create the Action Committee for Dedicated Citizens (ACDC). Seeking to harness the discontent of the youth, he campaigned heavily for the extension of the vote to eighteen-year-olds. In his campaign, he was joined by a faction of the DLP, and both groups boycotted the 1970 general elections in protest over the PNM resistance to their demands. As a result, the PNM was returned to power, winning all thirty-six constituencies on the basis of a voting turnout of only 32.9 percent and a vote of only 28 percent. Thus, the East Indian element lost its voice in parliament. Instead, a token parliamentary opposition was formed by two members of the PNM who defected in 1972.

The problems of 1970 also spawned the United Labour Front (ULF), a party grounded in three labor unions, which drew its main support from the East Indians of the sugar belt. Its program could be described as socialist. At the same time, Robinson, a Tobagonian by birth, formed the Democratic Action Congress (DAC) in Tobago. A certain cultural distinction, resentment because of the excessive centralization of decision making in Trinidad, and the perception of economic and social neglect by the PNM central government had, over the years, contributed to the widening gap between Trinidadians and Tobagonians. The DAC therefore devoted itself to fighting for self-government for Tobago, a goal which was eventually achieved, although not entirely to the satisfaction of the DAC, in 1980. Four years earlier, in 1976, general elections had again returned the PNM to power, but the ULF won ten seats (roughly the same ones that had been controlled by the DLP), and the DAC won the two seats assigned for Tobago.

Several important developments took place in the early 1980s. In 1981 Williams, the PNM's charismatic leader and the country's prime minister since independence (and chief minister-premier since 1956), died, leaving the PNM with much weaker leadership. By this time, the country, which had experienced an extraordinary economic boom during the years of high oil prices, was at the beginning of an economic downturn. Moreover, after twenty-five years in power, the PNM's patronage network had grown to cumbersome proportions and there was perceived to be widespread corruption within the party, including some highly publicized cases of illegal activities undertaken by high government officials.

Under the circumstances, the opposition seized the opportunity to enter into the politics of alliance in time for the 1981 general elections. Three groups—the ULF, the DAC, and the Tapia House Movement (THM) (a minor party founded in the 1970s with a base of support in the intellectual community)—allied to form the Trinidad and Tobago National Alliance (TTNA). These elections were also contested, separately, by the newly formed Organisation for National Reconstruction (ONR), led by Karl Hudson-Phillips, a former PNM minister whose popular appeal was limited by the fact that, during the disturbances of 1970, he had sought to impose a restrictive public order act that was vetoed after public outcry. The ONR, which had the support of business and elite elements, was viewed as conservative. A third party, the National Joint Action Committee (NJAC), which originated in the so-called black power events of 1970, also entered conventional politics for the first time on a platform that was heavily nationalist and Africanist.

Despite its perceived handicaps, the PNM won the 1981 elections decisively, primarily because the economy was still relatively strong and because there was popular suspicion of the opposition. The ONR was seen as dominated by "neo-colonial" creole (local white business) elements, and its leader was too closely identified with earlier repressive tactics. The ULF–dominated coalition was suspect because of African fears of East Indian domination. The PNM won 53 percent of the vote (compared to 53.57 percent in 1976), but the other parties received significant support: 22.3 percent for the ONR, and 20.7 percent for the TTNA. Although the TTNA received a smaller percentage of the vote than the ONR, it became the official opposition: The ULF had eight seats, and the DAC retained its two Tobago seats.

Before local elections were held in 1983, the opposition groups managed to unite, despite their quite different platforms. In their first test, the local elections, this "accommodation" (ONR–TTNA parties) won the majority of the local districts, all but one of the county councils, and several city and borough councils. In November 1984, the DAC routed the PNM (eleven seats to one) in elections for the Tobago House of Representatives. (The House was already dominated by the DAC, eight seats to four.)

It was clear by now that the opposition had gained significant strength and would for the first time be able to mount a major challenge to the PNM in the general elections of 1986. However, the size of the PNM's eventual defeat could not have been predicted. The National Alliance for Reconstruction (NAR) was launched in 1984 as a reconstituted TTNA. In 1985 the ONR joined the alliance, and the alliance emerged as an officially unified party. From the start, it was clear that this was an uneasy merger of disparate groups, united only in their desire to remove the PNM from power. The difficult issue of leadership was resolved in favor of Robinson, the DAC leader who was perceived to be most acceptable nationally. Led by Robinson, and campaigning on a platform of ethnic unity ("one love"), better economic management, and an improved social climate, the NAR was enthusiastically received by a people who were tired of the long-lived PNM. The NAR swept to power, winning all but three parliamentary seats and securing 65 percent of the vote (compared to 43 percent for the PNM in the comparable benchmark elections of 1956) on the basis of the highest voting turnout since 1956 (65.3 percent compared to 80 percent in 1956).

The defeat of the PNM was attributable to the public's desire for change, the weak leadership of the PNM and its conduct of a lackluster campaign full of gaffes and mistakes, the popular perception that corruption had become endemic to the society, the mismanagement of the state-run sector, the decline of the economy, and the growth of various social ills (unemployment, drugs, crime, homelessness).

The NAR had promised to initiate various corrective measures within ninety days of election, but, instead, within a year, had embarked on few substantial new policies and was embroiled in factionalization as a result of disagreements among the three coalition partners. In June 1987, some Tapia House members, including the leader Lloyd Best, withdrew from the alliance, dissatisfied because of the NAR's seeming lack of a coherent policy. In December, after months of highly publicized intracabinet wrangling that contravened the principle of collective responsibility inherited under the Westminster system, Prime Minister Robinson asked his entire cabinet to resign. The country was in crisis, without a government for some hours, until the cabinet was reconstituted exactly as before, except for one outspoken member, John Humphrey.

Not long after, a damaging article in one of the country's daily newspapers, in the form of an interview with a highly placed technocrat, revealed that the NAR's difficulties stemmed from a "grab for power" by the ULF, the East Indian (Hindu) faction of the NAR. The article served to heighten racial tension in a country where African political dominance has had to be carefully balanced against increasing Indian demographic and economic power and social assimilation. Tensions between Africans and Indians had been muted under PNM rule because of the party's overwhelming dominance, co-optation of some Indians into leading positions in its hierarchy, and its ability, in the favorable economic climate of the 1970s, to open up economic and social opportunities to all segments of the population. However, the NAR's victory, for the first time, brought political and administrative power within reach of the East Indians. The subsequent Indian demands for more bureaucratic posts seem to have precipitated the crisis.

In February 1988, Robinson dismissed the leader of the ULF, Basdeo Panday, and two of his supporters. These former cabinet members (who were subsequently also dismissed from their party) formed a group called "Club 88" which was eventually launched as a political party, the United National Congress (UNC) in 1989. The UNC, with five members in parliament, outnumbered the PNM, but chose to remain an unofficial opposition until September 1990, when, at the UNC request and according to constitutional procedures, the president of the republic appointed them as the official opposition.

The NAR continued to be beseiged by difficulties: racial antagonisms, the limited economic effectiveness of its structural adjustment policies, rising resentment on the part of the beleaguered lower classes, an increase in crime and drug abuse (despite harsh legislation against drug traffickers), increased unemployment, and popular hostility toward Prime Minister Robinson, who was widely perceived as arrogant. Meanwhile, the government concentrated on discrediting the previous regime and on recovering some of the monies lost through individual corruption.

On 27 July 1990, during the conduct of a parliamentary debate on the subject of corruption, the parliament was stormed by a group of Black Muslims attempting to overthrow the government. This group, the Jamaat-al-Muslimeen, felt personally aggrieved because of the government's attempt to recover lands to which they claimed squatters' rights. They were also moved by social concern for the plight of the poor. Apparently seeking to establish a Muslim state, or at least to control the government, the Muslimeen held seventeen parliamentarians (including the prime minister) hostage for six days. Hostages were also held at the television and radio stations. Twenty-five people were reportedly killed and scores were injured in the coup attempt, most during the widespread looting that took place in the business district of the capital city. Prime Minister Robinson was shot and severely beaten during the ordeal, which finally ended with the surrender of the Muslimeen.

The attempt to overthrow the NAR government did not generate a backlash of support for the regime and, in fact, aggravated popular anxiety about the capacity of the NAR to govern and to guarantee the safety and security of citizens. In the wake of the coup, tensions appeared within the governing party between the parliamentarians who had been held hostage and the parliamentarians who, having fortuitously been absent from parliament on 27 July, ran the government in the absence of the prime minister. One newspaper described the problem as the "ONR grab for power" (reminiscent of the earlier ULF "grab for power"). The general elections, constitutionally due by March 1992, in Trinidad and Tobago, will involve a three-way contest between the NAR, a substantially revived and reorganized PNM, and the UNC.

Bibliography

Gordon K. Lewis. *The Growth of the Modern West Indies.* MacGibbon and Kee, London, 1968.

Selwyn Ryan, ed. *The Independence Experience 1962–1987.* Institute of Social and Economic Research, University of the West Indies, Saint Augustine, Trinidad, 1988.

Trinidad under Siege: The Muslimeen Uprising, Six Days of Terror. Daily Express, Port-of-
Spain, Trinidad, 1990.
Eric Williams. *Inward Hunger: The Education of a Prime Minister.* Andre Deutsch, London,
1969.
Personal contacts of author and local newspaper sources.

Political Parties—Active

DEMOCRATIC ACTION CONGRESS (DAC). The DAC was formed in 1971
by A.N.R. Robinson, a Tobago-born former deputy prime minister under the
People's National Movement (PNM). In 1970 Robinson left the PNM and
called for a boycott of the general elections, which resulted in an overwhelming
PNM victory at the polls, based on a 33-percent voting turnout. Robinson's
DAC has subsequently dominated Tobago's politics; it won both of Tobago's
seats in 1976 and in 1981. After Tobago was granted self-government in 1980,
the DAC won eight of twelve House of Assembly seats. In November 1984,
the DAC increased its strength by winning all but one assembly seat. In 1981
the DAC joined with the United Labour Front and the Tapia House Movement
in an electoral alliance, the Trinidad and Tobago National Alliance (TTNA),
which won ten seats in parliament (including the two DAC Tobago seats). In
1984 the TTNA was reconstituted as the National Alliance for Reconstruction
(NAR), and in 1985 it merged with the Organisation for National Reconstruction to form a unified party. The NAR won thirty-three of thirty-six seats in
the general elections of 1986, including the two traditional DAC seats in Tobago. In November 1988, it also won the eleven seats in the Tobago House of
Assembly that had been held by the DAC since 1984.

DAC leader Robinson was chosen to lead the NAR, and he became prime
minister of the country in 1986. The DAC has been concerned primarily with
improving the social and economic status of Tobagonians, especially in view of
what was considered to have been years of neglect by Trinidad. This special
interest in Tobago has been continued by the NAR.

FARGO HOUSE MOVEMENT (FHM). The FHM was formed in 1980 by Dr.
Winston Murray, a former parliamentary representative who broke away from
the Democratic Action Congress. The party espoused a program of autonomy
for Tobago within the limits set by the central administration in Trinidad. Its
name derives from a major Tobagonian political personality of the 1950s, A.P.T.
James, known also as "Governor Fargo." The FHM has been eclipsed by the
DAC–National Alliance for Reconstruction and has never won any seats in the
Tobago House of Assembly.

MOVEMENT FOR SOCIAL TRANSFORMATION (Motion). Motion was
created in 1989 out of the Committee for Labour Solidarity, an amalgam of the
strongest trade union groups. Although it draws most of its support from the

unions, it seeks to be a broad-based people's party, with an emphasis on participatory democracy and a mixed economy. Most of the party hierarchy, including current leader David Abdulah, were associated at one time with the United Labour Force.

NATIONAL ALLIANCE FOR RECONSTRUCTION (NAR). The NAR was formed in 1986 by a merger of four parties: the Democratic Action Congress, the United Labour Front, the Tapia House Movement—which had previously allied to form the Trinidad and Tobago National Alliance—and the Organisation for National Reconstruction. A.N.R. Robinson, who was chosen leader, became prime minister when the party won the 1986 general elections by an overwhelming majority of the vote. The NAR's unity was primarily based on opposition to the then-ruling People's National Movement; the groups that merged to form the party had varying political agendas. The NAR's overall platform has been a conservative one. In power, the party favored the business elite and promoted divestment of state holdings, a reduction in the state sector, and other structural adjustment measures.

NATIONAL JOINT ACTION COMMITTEE (NJAC). The NJAC began in February 1970 as a federation of disparate organizations based at the University of the West Indies in Trinidad. Eschewing conventional politics, the black power group mobilized society by massive demonstrations against foreign corporations and against the perceived domination of the economy by local whites. At the same time, the NJAC promoted cultural nationalism and unity between East Indians and Africans. NJAC actions, coupled with an aborted military coup, in February-April 1970, almost toppled the People's National Movement government. After periods of detention, the leadership, headed by Geddes Granger, turned to institutionalizing the party, through the creation of a trade union, cultural organizations, and research institutions. The NJAC devoted much of its effort to promoting African culture (its members adopted African names), and its National Action Cultural Committee became well-known and respected for its efforts to enhance local culture. The NJAC's earlier thrust for economic nationalism also bore fruit when the government responded by playing a greater role in the economy.

The NJAC entered conventional politics in the 1981 general elections, in which the party secured 3.3 percent of the vote and no seats in parliament. In the 1986 election, it won a 1.49-percent share of the vote. Despite its limited support base, it is viewed as performing a useful role in stimulating debate on the major issues. Its agenda remains nationalist and Africanist, but the NJAC is now perceived as rather moderate and conventional. Its leader remains Makandal Daaga, formerly Geddes Granger.

ORGANISATION FOR NATIONAL RECONSTRUCTION (ONR). This party emerged in 1981 and won 22 percent of the vote (but no parliamentary seats) in that year's general elections. Formed by Karl Hudson-Phillips, a former attorney general in the People's National Movement administration, the ONR, a party of the right, was supported by the business elite and the middle to upper classes. The ONR merged with several other parties to form the National Alliance for Reconstruction in 1985.

PEOPLE'S NATIONAL MOVEMENT (PNM). The PNM was the first mass party in Trinidad and Tobago. Founded in 1956 by Dr. Eric Williams, a widely respected historian, the party dominated Trinidad and Tobago's politics for thirty years. In 1956 the PNM won thirteen of the twenty-four seats in the legislative council; in 1961, twenty seats in an expanded thirty-seat House of Representatives; in 1966, twenty-four seats in a legislature that had again been expanded, this time to thirty-six; and in 1970, all thirty-six seats because of a boycott called by the opposition parties. In that year, civil disturbances had led to the resignation of Williams, but he later withdrew his resignation and continued to serve as prime minister until his death in 1981. The PNM won twenty-four seats in the 1976 elections and two more in 1981, before being defeated thirty-three to three seats by the National Alliance for Reconstruction in 1986.

The PNM was founded as a nationalist, anticolonial party, with a particular appeal to the masses, although its hierarchy has always been solidly middle-class, and it has in practice been supported by a wide cross-section of the society. However, despite efforts to appear heterogeneous, its ethnic base is rooted in the African population. After independence, the party adopted a pro-Western foreign policy and an "open economy" model of development. The failures of this model led to popular demands for economic nationalism in the early 1970s, demands which were met to some degree by the government. The PNM, long committed to industrialization and social and educational development, was able to undertake major development projects in the 1970s as a result of the oil boom initiated by OPEC. However, the decline of the economy and society in the 1980s, disclosures of official corruption, and the desire of the populace for change contributed to the downfall of the party in 1986. The party has since reorganized under younger leadership, and its current political leader, Patrick Manning, is committed to "development with a human face."

PEOPLE'S POPULAR MOVEMENT (PPM). The PPM was formed in 1980 from three small community organizations. Led by a young trade unionist, Michael Als, its appeal has been primarily to the youth and working classes. Its socialist program calls for ownership and control of national resources, social justice, cooperatives, and a "people's democracy." The party contested the 1986 general elections, fielding some very youthful candidates, but won a mere 0.14 percent of the vote. Some of its members were previously associated with the United Labour Front; since 1986, some have moved over to the United National Congress.

PEOPLE'S REPUBLICAN PARTY (PRP). This minor party was formed only to participate in the 1981 elections.

TAPIA HOUSE MOVEMENT (THM). The Tapia group, named after a mud dwelling that used to be common in the country, has its foundations in the New World Movement formed in the late 1960s by intellectuals from the University of the West Indies who were influenced by various Third World ideological currents. The THM became a political unit after the 1970 disturbances in the country.

The party contested the elections held in 1976, when it won 3.81 percent of the vote; and in 1981, in alliance with the Democratic Action Congress (DAC) and the United Labor Front (ULF), when it secured 2.26 percent of the vote. Its support comes mainly from the intellectual community.

Tapia's leader, Lloyd Best, a university professor, served in the Senate along with three other Tapia members, when he was appointed in 1974 by the Leader of the Opposition (at the time, the only recognized opposition member) who had defected from the People's National Movement. In 1984 Tapia merged with the DAC and the ULP to form the National Alliance for Reconstruction (NAR). In 1987 Lloyd Best and several other Tapia members withdrew from the NAR. Tapia's program stresses localization of the economy and self-reliance.

TRINIDAD LABOUR PARTY (TLP). This minor party was formed only to participate in the 1981 elections.

UNITED LABOUR FRONT (ULF). The ULF was formed in 1976 by the leaders of three powerful unions: the All Trinidad Sugar Estates and General Workers Union, led by Basdeo Panday; the Oilfield Workers' Trade Union, led by George Weekes; and the Trinidad Island-wide Canefarmers Trade Union, led by Raffique Shah. Panday had been associated with the Workers and Farmers Party in 1966 and with the Action Committee for Dedicated Citizens–Democratic Labour Party in 1971 before he became the political leader of the ULF. Raffique Shah was a former army lieutenant who had participated in the abortive coup of 1970. He went on to serve as ULF leader between August 1977 and April 1978, after a split in the party led to the removal of the more moderate Panday. Panday returned to the position of Leader of the Opposition and the party in 1978.

The ULF, which had a nationalistic program that included workers' participation in management, won ten seats in the House in 1976, and eight in 1981. In 1984 it merged with the Democratic Action Congress and the Tapia House Movement to form the National Alliance for Reconstruction (NAR), which was later joined by the Organisation for National Reconstruction. Panday became deputy leader of the NAR, and later he served as minister of external affairs. Intracabinet disagreements led, in 1988, to the prime minister's dismissal of Panday and other former ULF members from the cabinet. They were subsequently dismissed from the party, and in 1989 they formed the United National Congress (UNC).

UNITED NATIONAL CONGRESS (UNC). Formed by dissidents who had been dismissed from the National Alliance for Reconstruction (NAR), the UNC was launched in April 1989. The party hierarchy consists of former United Labour Front members disenchanted with NAR policies and leadership. (The ULF merged with others to form the NAR in 1985–1986.) Like the ULF, the UNC draws its main support from the East Indians of the sugar belt, traditionally followers of UNC leader Basdeo Panday.

The UNC won a local council by-election in May 1989. In 1990 one of its founding members and a former NAR parliamentarian, John Humphrey (who is of French creole heritage), claimed publicly that there was racism (anti-Indian) in the party, a charge that was dismissed after an independent review.

The UNC has focused on the perceived discrimination against East Indians in employment, in administration, and in politics, and also on the effects of the government's structural adjustment policies on the workers. In 1990 the UNC became the official opposition in parliament, since its elected members outnumbered those of the PNM.

WEST INDIAN POLITICAL CONGRESS MOVEMENT (WIPCM). This minor party was formed only to participate in the 1981 elections.

Political Parties—Historical

ACTION COMMITTEE FOR DEDICATED CITIZENS (ACDC). The ACDC was formed in 1970 by A.N.R. Robinson, former deputy leader of the People's National Movement. The ACDC was joined by a faction of the Democratic Labour Party (DLP) in seeking electoral changes, including extension of the vote to eighteen-year-olds. The ACDC–DLP boycotted the 1971 elections. The ACDC was superseded by the Democratic Action Committee.

AFRICAN NATIONAL CONGRESS (ANC). This party, which contested elections in 1961 and 1971, merged with several other parties to form the United Democratic Labour Party (UDLP). It is led by John Broomes.

BRITISH EMPIRE WORKERS, PEASANTS AND CITIZENS HOME RULE PARTY (HOME RULE PARTY OR BUTLER PARTY—BP). Established by Uriah Butler, an early champion of the rights of workers, after World War II, the BP disappeared with the rise of the People's National Movement.

CARIBBEAN NATIONAL LABOUR PARTY (CNLP). This party contested only the 1956 elections.

CARIBBEAN PEOPLE'S DEMOCRATIC PARTY (CPDP). The CPDP contested only the 1956 elections.

CARIBBEAN SOCIALIST PARTY (CSP). The CSP was organized in 1947 under the leadership of Victor Bryan; it disappeared after 1956.

DEMOCRATIC LABOUR PARTY (DLP). The major opposition party between 1961 and 1970, the DLP's support base was primarily East Indian. The party was succeeded by the United Democratic Labor Party and the Social Democratic (Labour) Party.

DEMOCRATIC LIBERATION PARTY (DLP). Formed to contest the 1971 elections, this party was the main electoral opposition to the PNM in that year. It was headed by political "boss" Bhadase S. Maraj. It won no seats in parliament.

LIBERAL PARTY (LP). Established in 1966 by three former members of the Democratic Labour Party, the LP joined the United Democratic Labour Party in 1976.

LIBERATION ACTION PARTY (LAP). This splinter party was formed in the 1970s by dissident members of the West Indian National Party. The LAP contested only the 1976 elections on a vague platform.

NATIONAL DEMOCRATIC PARTY (NDP). The NDP was allied with the Trinidad Labour Party in the 1956 elections.

NATIONAL FREEDOM PARTY. See UNITED FREEDOM PARTY.

NATIONAL TRINIDAD AND TOBAGO PARTY. This party contested the 1976 elections on a limited platform.

PARTY OF POLITICAL PROGRESS GROUPS (POPPG). This party was the personal vehicle of trade unionist Albert Gomes, who was the unofficial leader of the government in the early 1950s. The POPPG was considered conservative and probusiness.

PEOPLE'S DEMOCRATIC MOVEMENT (PARTY) (PDM, PDP). This East Indian–based party, established in the early 1950s, merged with the Democratic Labour Party.

PEOPLE'S DEMOCRATIC PARTY (PDP). Formed in 1966 by dissident members of the Democratic Labour Party, the PDP disappeared in the late 1960s.

SEUKERAN INDEPENDENT PARTY (SIP). This personalist party was centered on Lionel Seukeran, who won election as an independent in 1956 and on the Democratic Labour Party ticket in 1961. Both of the SIP's candidates lost the 1966 election, and Seukeran ran unsuccessfully on the Democratic Liberation Party ticket in 1971.

SOCIAL DEMOCRATIC (LABOUR) PARTY (SDLP, SDP). This unofficial faction of the Democratic Labour Party, which broke away after the split of 1972, disappeared after the 1976 election.

TRADE UNION PARTY (TUP). Organized to participate in the 1950 elections, the TUP disappeared shortly thereafter.

TRINIDAD LABOUR PARTY (TLP). The TLP, the country's first political party, was established in 1933. It survived through 1956 but not long after.

UNITED DEMOCRATIC LABOUR PARTY (UDLP). This coalition resulted from the merger, in 1976, of the official faction of the Democratic Labour Party with three other parties: the United Progressive Party, the Liberal Party, and the African National Congress. The UDLP disappeared after 1976.

UNITED FREEDOM PARTY. This party was formed by international lawyer Ramdeo Sampath Mehta in order to contest (unsuccessfully) the 1976 elections; the party became known as the National Freedom Party in the 1981 general elections.

UNITED NATIONAL INDEPENDENCE PARTY (UNIP). Formed in 1970, with a support base at the University of the West Indies, the UNIP merged in 1976 with the United Labour Front.

UNITED PROGRESSIVE PARTY (UPP). Formed in 1971 by a dissident People's National Movement parliamentarian, it merged with several other parties to form the United Democratic Labour Front.

WEST INDIAN INDEPENDENCE PARTY (WIIP). This left-wing, nationalist party contested only the 1956 elections.

WEST INDIAN NATIONAL PARTY (WINP). The WINP, formed in 1942 with labor support, disappeared by 1956. It was the first of two parties to use the same name.

WEST INDIAN NATIONAL PARTY (WINP). This party, formed in the mid-1970s, disappeared after unsuccessfully contesting 1976 elections.

WORKERS AND FARMERS PARTY (WFP). Formed in 1966 to oppose the People's National Movement, the WFP was led by Stephen Maharaj. The party disappeared in the late 1960s.

YOUNG PEOPLE'S NATIONAL PARTY (YPNP). This party contested only the 1976 elections.

Jacqueline Anne Braveboy-Wagner

TURKS AND CAICOS ISLANDS

The Turks and Caicos Islands are a group of eight larger and about forty smaller tropical islands located southeast of the Bahamas, totalling about 166 square miles and supporting a population of approximately 10,000. The economy is based on fishing, tourism, and offshore banking and licensing.

The government of the Turks and Caicos is virtually identical to the other Crown Colonies of the United Kingdom. A British-appointed governor chairs the Executive Council, which is composed of three members appointed by the governor, the chief minister who represents the Legislative Council, and three members from the Legislative Council chosen by their colleagues. The Legislative Council contains thirteen members elected by universal adult suffrage. Queen Elizabeth II is the head of state, and since 1987 she has been represented locally by Governor Michael J. Bradley. The head of government is Chief Minister Oswald O. Skippings, the leader of the People's Democratic Movement (PDM), who has been serving since 1988.

Skippings was chief minister for the first time briefly in 1980, when he succeeded J.A.G.S. McCartney, the founder of the PDM and the first chief minister of the colony (1976), who died in a plane crash while travelling in the United States in 1980. The PDM, which had campaigned under a proindependence banner, lost the 1980 elections to the Progressive National Party (PNP), which favored continued colonial status. In the 1984 elections, the PNP under Norman Saunders repeated its earlier victory, winning eight of the then eleven elective seats (the Legislative Council was expanded to thirteen elected members in 1988).

In 1985 Chief Minister Saunders and two of his ministers were implicated in a narcotics smuggling scheme and barred from office by Governor Bradley. However, even with three PNPers in jail, the party still controlled the Legislative Council by a margin of five to three and selected Nathaniel Francis, the PNP minister of communications, as chief minister. Nevertheless, the political turmoil was such that the British took the unusual step of imposing direct British rule through the office of the governor during 1987 and 1988. In the elections of 1988, Skippings was able to lead the PDM back to power against a seriously damaged PNP.

The Turks and Caicos are the poorest of the British dependencies. No real difference exists among the three existing political parties, and there is no independence movement. In fact, in one bizarre example, prominent business leaders offered the Turks and Caicos to Canada in the late 1980s and asked to become the "sunshine province." The Canadians declined the offer. The islands have recently been plagued by incidents of narcotics transshipping.

Bibliography

Robert J. Alexander. "Turks and Caicos Islands," in Robert J. Alexander, ed., *Political Parties of the Americas*. Greenwood Press, Westport, Conn., 1982.

Central Intelligence Agency. *The World Factbook, 1990*. Central Intelligence Agency, Washington, D.C., 1990.

Latin American and Caribbean Contemporary Record. Holmes and Meier, New York and London. Published annually since 1983 under various editors; an extremely useful annual compendium of political, economic, and social reportage and analysis. Various authors have covered all the British dependencies except Bermuda.

Political Parties

NATIONAL DEMOCRATIC ALLIANCE (NDA). Under the leadership of Ariel Missick, the NDA became active during the 1980s. It holds no seats in the Legislative Council.

PEOPLE'S DEMOCRATIC MOVEMENT (PDM). Founded in 1976 by J.A.G.S. McCartney, the PDM originally took a proindependence stance. Losing both its founder and the election in 1980, the PDM went into a hiatus for most of the decade of the 1980s. It returned to power under Oswald O. Skippings in 1988, winning eleven of thirteen seats, after certain leaders of its principal rival, the Progressive National Party, became embroiled in a narcotics smuggling scheme. It generally looks to the development of the fishing and tourist industries, in order to improve education and health care and overcome the islands' isolation.

PROGRESSIVE NATIONAL PARTY (PNP). Formed in 1976, the PNP exercised power from 1980 to 1988. In the 1988 elections, it captured only two seats, yielding power to the People's Democratic Movement (PDM) after its leader and the chief minister, Norman Saunders, was barred from political office for his role in a narcotics smuggling scheme. At the present time, Dan Malcolm heads the party and is the Leader of the Opposition in the Legislative Council.

Its position on economic and social issues, linked to fishing and tourism, is similar to that of the PDM, the present majority party.

Gary Brana-Shute
Rosemary Brana-Shute

URUGUAY

The Origins of the Modern Party System

For most of the twentieth century, Uruguay was considered to be the most democratic nation in Latin America. An integral aspect of its politics was an entrenched two-party system which developed shortly after Uruguayan independence and had few serious third-party challengers until 1971. The nation's so-called traditional parties, the Blancos (officially called the National Party) and the Colorados, originated in mid-nineteenth century civil wars and owe their names to the colors adopted by the rival armies.

After a period of extreme government instability, the Colorados emerged victorious in 1865. Since that time, the party has lost control of the executive only three times (1958, 1962, and 1989), a length of dominance unmatched in Latin America. Civil strife did not come to an end, however, until 1904, one year after the National Assembly chose Colorado José Batlle y Ordóñez as president. The most influential political figure in modern Uruguayan history, Batlle laid the foundation of a welfare state whose benefits fueled Colorado dominance until the country's post–Korean War economic crisis.

Despite their minority status throughout the first half of this century, the Blancos retained a stake in the political system through what was termed "co-participation." From 1918 to 1933, executive power was divided between the president (always a Colorado) and a Council of Government with guaranteed minority representation. The 1951 Constitution established a strictly collegial two-party executive that functioned from 1952 to 1966, when the country returned to the presidential system. Parliament has been elected through proportional representation, thereby ensuring adequate minority party representation.

As the state sector of the economy grew substantially, both traditional parties were guaranteed a share of patronage in the many state enterprises. Political tranquillity in the first half of this century was also facilitated by an implicit bargain on fundamental economic issues. The National Party, and the powerful ranchers allied with it, accepted the welfare state and import substituting industrialization (ISI)—both largely financed by wool and meat export revenues—while the Colorados did not challenge the landlords' control over the country's most critical resource by attempting land reform.

The Uruguayan Electoral System

Coalition politics has been further promoted by Uruguay's rather unique electoral system. Within each party (legally termed a *lema*), different political factions may present rival presidential candidates and competing lists of parliamentary candidates. Through a system called the double simultaneous vote (DSV), the voters choose both a presidential candidate and an associated parliamentary list within their favored party. The presidency is not necessarily awarded to the candidate with the most votes, but rather to the leading candidate of the party that finishes first. Thus, in the critical 1971 presidential election, the Blancos' Wilson Ferreira Aldunate received the most votes but lost because the combined Blanco vote trailed the Colorado total. Representation in the thirty-member Senate and ninety-nine-member National Assembly is determined by a modified d'Hondt form of proportional representation.

Voting is mandatory, and turnout has been in the region of 90 percent in recent years. This forced mobilization of apathetics probably favors the traditional parties. The DSV used to be thought to favor them also, but this is not so clear. The electoral system has reinforced factionalism and programmatic incoherence within the two traditional parties. Colorado and Blanco factions have historically been built around the leadership of party bosses (known as caudillos after the nineteenth-century military strongmen) and have been cemented through patronage. At the same time, however, the DSV can facilitate alliances between smaller parties. From 1971 the system permitted a number of leftist parties to combine their electoral strength under the Broad Front coalition.

Colorados and Blancos: A System of Catch-All Parties

While the Colorados and Blancos derive, respectively, from the liberal and conservative movements of the nineteenth century, neither party now exhibits a consistent ideology. In the first half of the twentieth century, the Colorados' Batlle dynasty (founded by José Batlle and passed on to his son and nephew) was identified with a generous welfare state, progressive labor legislation, and ISI. Most Blancos at that time were less statist and more clerical, staking out a position to the right of center.

During the 1971 election, however, shifts in the factional balance in both parties led them to switch places ideologically. Wilson Ferreira, a left-of-center senator, assumed the leadership of the Blancos' majority wing. As the Blancos shifted toward the left, the Colorados—under presidents Jorge Pacheco Areco and Juan María Bordaberry—moved sharply to the right. In 1984 the Colorados returned to the center, although they were still to the right of the dominant

Blanco faction, Ferreira's "For the Fatherland." Following Ferreira's death in 1987, the Blancos' conservative (Herrerist) wing reasserted its traditional dominance in that party. During the 1989 election, the leading presidential candidate in each traditional party called for further privatization of state enterprises and a reduction in the size of the vast state bureaucracy.

In short, ideological labels are useful for identifying certain party factions, but they cannot be applied very well to the traditional parties as a whole. The Colorados' and Blancos' clientelistic, factionalized structures have helped make them classic catch-all parties which appeal to voters across ideological lines. The traditional parties tend to span geographical and class lines as well, but family ties still play a significant role in voter choice. Historically, the Colorados have been strongest in Montevideo and the surrounding region; the Blancos' greatest strength has been in the interior. In the 1984 election, the Colorados overtook the Blancos in the interior and maintained their lead in Montevideo. The Blancos, however, reestablished their lead outside Montevideo in the 1989 election and came second behind the Broad Front in the capital.

The Challenge of the Broad Front

In the 1971 national election, the left-wing Broad Front mounted the first serious challenge to two-party dominance. Able to garner from 18 to 21 percent of the national vote in the last three national elections (and a higher proportion in Montevideo), the Broad Front has transformed Uruguay into a three-party system. While the Broad Front has been more ideologically well-defined than the traditional parties, it too started as a somewhat heterogeneous alliance. In the 1971 and 1984 elections, the coalition brought together moderate leftists, the Christian Democratic Party (PDC) and a breakaway social democratic faction of the Colorados, and orthodox Marxists, the Socialist Party (PS), the Communist Party (PCU), and independent leftists. In 1989 the non-Marxist elements left to form the New Space.

Broad Front support is more geographically concentrated than is the vote for the two major parties. In the last election, the coalition finished first in Montevideo but remained weak in the interior. Although the left has the support of Uruguay's Interunion Workers Assembly/National Workers Confederation labor federation, surveys show no correlation between left voting and low income. The Broad Front's strength is greatest among voters under the age of forty. Counterintuitively, its support is correlated with education.

The Travail of Uruguayan Democracy

During the 1960s, Uruguay's democratic order began to unravel. The exhaustion of the import substitution model, the failure of the sheep and cattle ranching sectors to remain internationally competitive, and the existence of an oversized state bureaucracy contributed to economic stagnation and severe inflation. The nation's living standards, once on a par with much of Western Europe, declined substantially. Growing economic strains contributed to a societal polarization, which was manifested in escalating labor-industrial conflicts, increased electoral support for Marxist opposition parties, and the rise of the *Tupamaro* urban guerrilla movement.

Uruguay's political parties bear a major share of the blame for the breakdown of democracy, in as much as they failed to formulate constructive policies to deal with the political and economic crisis. During the Pacheco administration (1968–1971) and the first two years of the Bordaberry administration (1971–1973), civil liberties eroded, and the armed forces increasingly intruded into national politics. On 27 June 1973, the military closed the parliament and established a military-dominated dictatorship. Bordaberry remained president in name only.

Military rule brought the repression of labor unions and strict controls over the nation's political, educational, and cultural institutions. Although the number of people killed by the Uruguayan government was far lower than that in Argentina or Chile, repression was extremely intense in other respects. During the late 1970s, Amnesty International estimated that Uruguay had one of the world's highest per capita populations of political prisoners. Torture and other forms of intimidation were common. As in all bureaucratic-authoritarian regimes, party activity was repressed. The parties of the Broad Front were dismantled, and leaders, such as former General Liber Seregni, the coalition's 1971 presidential candidate, were imprisoned. The traditional parties remained legal, but their activities were suspended.

In 1976 the regime cancelled elections, installed a new puppet president (Aparicio Méndez), decreed leftist parties permanently illegal, and prohibited 15,000 politicians from holding office for fifteen years. Yet, despite the repression, the military professed a commitment to the eventual restoration of two-party democracy. Civilians continued to hold the presidency (though not always much power) until 1981 when a retired general, Gregorio Alvarez, assumed the post. Perhaps the strongest testimony to the underlying legitimacy of Uruguay's party system was the reaction of the armed forces command to a then secret memorandum sent to them in 1976 by President Bordaberry. In it, he suggested that all political parties be permanently abolished and a corporatist regime be established. The military remained loyal to the traditional parties and removed Bordaberry from office.

The Transition from Military Rule

One year after rejecting Bordaberry's proposal, the armed forces announced a timetable (*cronograma*) for restoring the country to limited democracy. The plan called for a national plebiscite in November 1980 on a new constitution to be written by the military. Assuming a positive vote on that document, the reins of government were to be turned over subsequently to an elected civilian government.

While the *cronograma* seemed to be a step in the direction of redemocratization, in fact the proposed constitution, unveiled shortly before the plebiscite, provided a legal basis for continued military intervention in the nation's political life. It also lacked many of the safeguards on civil liberties contained in the 1967 constitution and thereby facilitated further repression of perceived subversives. Opposition to its provisions rekindled political activity by party activists. Despite severe campaign restrictions, the opposition was able to convince 57.2 percent of the voters to reject the constitution and its associated timetable. Rarely had an authoritarian regime experienced such a stunning rebuke. The regime suffered further ignominy in November 1982, when it sponsored primary elections for the two traditional parties. Antimilitary factions won over 70 percent of the Colorado vote and more than 80 percent of the Blanco vote.

By 1984 the military was forced to negotiate its exit from power with opposition party leaders and to establish with them a new set of political rules. Loyal to their jailed leader, Ferreira, the Blancos boycotted the negotiations, ultimately putting themselves at a disadvantage. As part of the so-called Naval Club Pact, elections were set for November, many important leftists were released from jail or allowed to return from exile, and the parties of the Broad Front were legalized. By allowing the Front to run candidates, the military reduced the electoral chances of its implacable Blanco opponents, who otherwise would probably have received most of the leftist votes.

The Restoration of Democracy and the 1984 National Election

Karen Remmer (1989) points out that extended military rule in Latin America has frequently transformed national party systems. This may mean the decline or demise of old parties, the emergence of new ones, or a significant shift in party strength or alignments. Nevertheless, although Uruguayan political repression was among the most extended and severe in the region, Remmer notes that its party system was one of the least transformed by the military interlude. More careful analysis of the 1984 and 1989 elections, however, suggests both continuity and change.

The overall results of the 1984 race were remarkably similar to those of 1971. Once again, the Colorados carried the presidency and a plurality of the parliament. Because Ferreira's uncompromising opposition to political repression contrasted so sharply with the collaboration of former Colorado presidents Bordaberry and Pacheco with the military, the Blancos had anticipated victory. With Ferreira barred from running, however, his stand-in, Alberto Sáenz de Zumarán, was unable to lead the party to victory. Military maneuvering, Ferreira's flawed strategic decisions, and internal Blanco difficulties all contributed to the party's defeat.

The Colorado presidential candidates collectively earned 41.2 percent of the vote, virtually identical to their 1971 share (41.0%). With only 31.2 percent of the national vote cast for him personally, their front-runner, Julio María Sanguinetti, was elected president. Blanco support declined from 40.1 percent (in 1971) to 35.0 percent. The Broad Front registered the only significant gain (from 18.3 to 21.2 percent). Its growth was particularly noteworthy given the previous decade of repression when so many of its supporters had been forced into exile.

Behind this relatively static picture of overall party support lay important changes in the strength of internal factions, the nature of party leadership, and the ecological base of the vote. Within the Colorado Party, Sanguinetti's centrist wing outdistanced Pacheco's rightist faction, which had controlled the party prior to 1973. Broad Front voters also moved toward the center; the moderate List 99 emerged as the Front's largest parliamentary faction at the expense of the hard-line Independent Democratic Left, the successor to the Patria Grande list of 1971. Thus, the electorate clearly expressed two sentiments: a preference for political moderation and a rebuke of the factions that had collaborated with the military. In the wake of the election, the leaders of Uruguay's three major parties—including Sanguinetti, Ferreira, and Seregni—tried to identify themselves with a center-left or center position.

Not surprisingly, given the long hiatus between elections, there was a major infusion of new leadership in all three parties; over 70 percent of the elected deputies were serving in parliament for the first time. According to Juan Rial (1984), the new generation also seemed less inclined toward traditional clientelistic politics. While the Colorados garnered an identical percentage of the vote in 1971 and 1984, they gained outside of Montevideo at the expense of the Blancos, but lost votes to the Broad Front in the capital. To be sure, the most important change in the ecology of the vote was the growth of Broad Front strength in Montevideo and among first-time voters. Since elections had not been held for thirteen years, first-time voters included all citizens under thirty-one years of age.

The 1989 Election: The Blancos Return to Power

During the late 1980s, Uruguay's major political parties and alliances experienced several important shifts. After great controversy, 1986 saw the enactment of a special statute of limitations to prevent trials of military officers for past human rights violations. In the National Party, the decision of Ferreira's For the Fatherland movement to vote for the law led to the end of its long-standing alliance with Carlos Julio Pereyra's National Rocha Movement. At the same time, the reunification of the Blanco's Herrerist factions strengthened the party's right. The Blanco's progressive wing was further weakened the following year by Ferreira's death. Running on a platform of privatization and a scaled-down welfare state in the 1989 presidential election, Herrerist Senator

Luis Alberto Lacalle led the party to its first electoral victory since 1962. In total, the Blancos polled 39 percent of the vote, up four points from 1984. In the tradition of Uruguayan coparticipation, Lacalle formed a coalition cabinet with the Colorados. In return for four minor ministerial posts, they agreed to support much of the president's economic program in the National Assembly.

The incumbent Colorado party lost substantial ground in 1989 and finished with only 30 percent of the national vote, its poorest showing of the century. Its leading presidential candidates, Jorge Batlle and Jorge Pacheco, were neck and neck. Batlle's faction, Unity and Reform (List 15), itself part of a larger group called United Batllism, continued to move away from its traditional support of Uruguay's welfare state in a neoconservative direction. In 1984 it successfully backed Sanguinetti who, under Uruguayan law, could not run again until 1994. In 1989 Battle, the heir to Uruguay's most revered family name, was hurt by the unpopularity of the Colorado administration and factional feuding among the Batllists. He also failed to distinguish his platform from Lacalle's and ran a poor campaign. Meanwhile, the renovator wing of Batllism (Enrique Tarigo's Freedom and Change, List 85) almost evaporated, and the party's left Social Action Movement to all intents and purposes disappeared. By contrast, the right of the party (Pacheco's Colorado Batllist Union and Pablo Millor's Crusade '94) made a dramatic recovery from its slump in 1984.

Early in the race, long-standing tensions between the Broad Front's Marxist and moderate wings led to the defection of the Christian Democrats and the social democratic Party for the Government of the People (PGP, or List 99). The two allied with the centrist Civic Union to form the New Space. The Broad Front was again led by its standard-bearer since 1971, Liber Seregni, who had been prohibited from running in 1984. Despite the loss of its non-Marxist wing, the Broad Front achieved the same vote share as it had in 1984 (21.2 percent nationally and 34.5 percent in Montevideo). Because Colorado strength in the capital declined sharply, Front candidate Tabaré Vázquez was elected mayor. His victory gave the left its first prestigious executive post and cemented its position as the third party. Though List 99 had been the Front's most popular faction in the 1984 election, New Space attracted only 9 percent of the vote in 1989 behind its presidential candidate, Hugo Batalla.

Conclusions

Although the party system's resilience in the face of authoritarian repression demonstrates Uruguay's strong democratic political culture, the persistence of certain electoral features seems troublesome. The retention of the double simultaneous vote continues to produce presidential victors who lack a clear mandate to rule. Typically, the winning party wins approximately 40 percent of the vote, while the victorious presidential candidate personally receives less. In 1989 Lacalle was elected with under a quarter of the national vote. As Luis González (1988) has noted, proportional representation and DSV reduce the possibility of a single party majority in either the legislative or the executive branches and increase tendencies toward party fragmentation. Although democracy seems once again to be on firm footing in Uruguay, the nation still lacks an electoral system that can produce an effective party government.

Bibliography

Angel Cocchi. "Los partidos políticos y la historia reciente." *Cuadernos de Orientación Electoral*, no. 2. Peitho, Montevideo, 1989.

Paul Drake and Eduardo Silva, eds. *Elections and Democratization in Latin America, 1980–85*. University of California, San Diego, La Jolla, Calif., 1986. (See chapters on Uruguay by Charles Gillespie, Howard Handelman, and Juan Rial.)

Charles Guy Gillespie. "Party Strategies and Redemocratization: Theoretical and Comparative Perspectives on the Uruguayan Case." Ph.D. diss., Yale University, 1987.

———. "Uruguay's Transition from Collegial Military-Technocratic Rule," in Guillermo O'Donnell et al., eds., *Transitions from Authoritarian Rule*. Johns Hopkins University Press, Baltimore, 1986.

Charles Guy Gillespie and Luís Eduardo González. "Uruguay," in Larry Diamond et al., eds., *Democracy in Developing Countries: Uruguay*. Lynne Rienner, Boulder, Colo., 1989.

Charles Guy Gillespie et al., eds. *Uruguay y la democracia*, vols. 1–3. Banda Oriental, Montevideo, 1984–1985.

Luis E. González. "Political Structures and the Prospects for Democracy in Uruguay." Ph.D. diss., Yale University, 1988.

Howard Handelman and Thomas Sanders, eds. *Military Government and the Movement toward Democracy in South America*. Indiana University Press, Bloomington, 1981.

Karen Remmer. *Military Rule in Latin America*. Unwyn Hyman, Boston, 1989.

Juan Rial. *Partídos políticos, democracia y autoritarismo*. CIESU-Banda Oriental, Montevideo, 1984.

Juan Rial and Jaime Klaczko. "Tendencias del electorado: Resultado de las elecciones 1925–1989." *Cuadernos de Orientación Electoral*, no. 4. Peitho, Montevideo, 1989.

Juan Rial and Carina Perelli. "El fin de la restauración: La elección del 26 de noviembre de 1989." *Cuadernos de Orientación Electoral*, no. 10 Peitho, Montevideo, 1990.

Martin Weinstein. *Uruguay: Democracy at the Crossroads*. Westview Press, Boulder, Colo., 1988.

Political Parties—Active

ADVANCED DEMOCRACY (DEMOCRACIA AVANZADA). The Communist Party ran under this name in the 1984 and 1989 elections.

ARTIGUIST TENDENCY (VERTIENTE ARTIGUISTA). This democratic socialist alliance was formed in 1989 by nonanarchist elements of the Independent Democratic Left and dissident Blancos. It won 3 percent of the vote in 1989.

BLANCO PARTY (PARTIDO BLANCO). *See* NATIONAL PARTY.

BROAD FRONT (FRENTE AMPLIO). The Broad Front is not a party per se, but rather a coalition of leftist parties which has now been given the legal status of a *lema* by the Electoral Court. Founded in 1971, its most prominent original members were the Communist Party (PCU), the Socialist Party (PS), the Christian Democratic Party (PDC), and the social democratic List 99 faction, which had defected from the Colorado Party and is now known as the Party for People's Government (PGP). Despite severe persecution under the military and an internal split in 1989, it has maintained its position as a strong third party with the support of over 20 percent of the electorate.

Following the return of democracy, the Broad Front adopted a more accommodationist position than that previously held, and in 1984 it received a large segment of its vote from individuals who consider themselves centrists (Rial in Drake and Silva 1986, 267–68). In 1989, however, the Front's non-Marxist coalition parties, the Christian Democrats and the PGP, left to form the New Space coalition. Following this, the former *Tupamaros* urban guerrilla movement, which has renounced violence, was admitted to the Front under the name Movement for Popular Participation.

CHRISTIAN DEMOCRATIC PARTY (PARTIDO DEMÓCRATA CRISTIANO—PDC). The most left-wing Christian Democratic party in Latin America during the early 1970s, the PDC participated in the 1971 and 1984 elections as a member of the Broad Front. In 1984 it suffered from internal conflicts and performed very poorly. The party left the Front in 1989 to help form the New Space coalition, but its total vote fell by over one-fifth to 1.6 percent.

CIVIC UNION (UNIÓN CÍVICA—UC). A small Catholic party, the UC was founded in 1912. In 1962 it changed its name to the Christian Democratic Party and moved left, causing conservatives to leave. In 1982 conservative Catholics refounded the UC. In 1989 it joined the center-left New Space, but its vote collapsed.

COLORADO PARTY (PARTIDO COLORADO). For the past century, this multiclass party has dominated Uruguayan politics. Although the Colorados created Uruguay's welfare state and its extensive bureaucratic structure, during the last twenty-five years its leading factions have been centrist or rightist. In the 1989 national election, the party lost to the Blancos nationally and to the Broad Front in Montevideo. The following major factions were represented in the 1989 national election:

1. United Batllism (Batllismo Unido). The dominant *sublema* of the party in 1984, it is itself a coalition of centrist groups which backed presidential winner Julio María Sanguinetti in 1984 and loser Jorge Batlle in 1989. Its major lists are Unity and Reform (List 15), by far the largest; Freedom and Change (List 85); and Independent Batllist Current (List 89).

2. Colorado Batllist Union (Unión Colorada y Batllista—UCB). Still led by former

President Jorge Pacheco Areco, this faction constitutes the party's right wing. Its major lists are Raumar Judé's List 123 and Pablo Millor's Crusade '94.

3. Social Action Movement (Movimiento de Acción Social—MAS). This progressive faction was organized for the 1989 election behind the candidacy of Labor and Social Security Minister Hugo Fernández Faingold, but it did very poorly.

COMMUNIST PARTY (PARTIDO COMUNISTA DEL URUGUAY— PCU). Countering geopolitical trends, the PCU has been growing in recent years and dominates the trade union movement. It has been a member of the Broad Front coalition since 1971. From 1962 to 1971, it ran under the label of the Left Front for Liberation (FIDEL), and in 1984 and in 1989 as Advanced Democracy. Although the party adopted a moderate stance during the negotiation of the 1984 democratic transition pact, it maintains an orthodox Marxist ideology. A slick, less dogmatic campaign helped it to almost double its vote in 1989 to nearly 10 percent.

DEMOCRACIA AVANZADA. See ADVANCED DEMOCRACY.

FRENTE AMPLIO. See BROAD FRONT.

MOVEMENT FOR POPULAR PARTICIPATION (MOVIMIENTO DE PARTICIPACIÓN POPULAR—MPP). The MPP was formed in 1989 by the *Tupamaros* and the Party for the Victory of the People; it polled 2 percent of the vote in 1989.

MOVIMIENTO DE PARTICIPACIÓN POPULAR. See MOVEMENT FOR POPULAR PARTICIPATION.

NATIONAL PARTY (PARTIDO NACIONAL or PARTIDO BLANCO). One of the two traditional parties, the Blancos have usually been in opposition. Though stronger in the interior, like the Colorados they have a broad geographical, class, and ideological base. Once considered to be the more conservative of the traditional parties, it moved to the Colorados' left in the late 1960s but returned to the center right in the late 1980s. It won a plurality in 1989, polling 39 percent of the vote. The following dominant factions were represented in the 1989 elections:

1. The Herrerists (Herrerismo). In the late 1980s, this faction was reunited following the fusion of various splinter groups representing the party's right wing. It is led by Luis Alberto Lacalle Herrera, grandson of longtime party boss Luis Alberto Herrera. In 1989 the Herrerists won 22.5 percent of the vote, enough to elect Lacalle president under the double simultaneous vote system.

2. For the Fatherland (Por la Patria—PLP). During the 1970s and early 1980s, the PLP was the dominant wing of the party. It was led by Wilson Ferreira Aldunate until

his death in 1987. In 1989 its presidential candidate was Alberto Sáenz de Zumarán, who had run as Ferreira's proxy in 1984, but the party's vote collapsed to 5 percent.

3. National Rocha Movement (Movimiento Nacional de Rocha—MNR). This faction terminated its alliance with Por la Patria in 1986 and backed Carlos Julio Pereyra for the presidency in 1989. This left-of-center faction opposed the 1986 law ending trials of military officers for past human rights violations. With the Popular Blanco Union (a schism from the PLP), it polled 11 percent of the vote in 1989.

NEW SPACE (NUEVO ESPACIO). This coalition was formed by the Party for People's Government, the Christian Democratic Party, and the Civic Union in 1989. It polled 9 percent nationally in the 1989 elections.

NUEVO ESPACIO. See NEW SPACE.

PARTIDO BLANCO (BLANCO PARTY). See NATIONAL PARTY.

PARTIDO COLORADO. See COLORADO PARTY.

PARTIDO COMUNISTA DEL URUGUAY. See COMMUNIST PARTY.

PARTIDO DE LOS TRABAJADORES. See WORKERS' PARTY.

PARTIDO DEMÓCRATA CRISTIANO. See CHRISTIAN DEMOCRATIC PARTY.

PARTIDO NACIONAL. See NATIONAL PARTY.

PARTIDO POR EL GOBIERNO DEL PUEBLO. See PARTY FOR PEOPLE'S GOVERNMENT.

PARTIDO POR LA VICTORIA DEL PUEBLO. See PARTY FOR THE VIC-TORY OF THE PEOPLE.

PARTIDO SOCIALISTA. See SOCIALIST PARTY.

PARTY FOR PEOPLE'S GOVERNMENT (PARTIDO POR EL GOBIERNO DEL PUEBLO—PGP). The PGP had its genesis in the 1960s as a social democratic faction (List 99) of the Colorado Party. In 1971 it joined the leftist Broad Front: in 1984, it was the Front's strongest faction. Five years later, it left the Front, along with the Christian Democratic Party, to form the non-Marxist New Space. Its vote fell one point to 7 percent nationwide in the 1989 elections.

PARTY FOR THE VICTORY OF THE PEOPLE (PARTIDO POR LA VIC-TORIA DEL PUEBLO—PVP). The PVP is a militant, anarchist group which joined the Independent Democratic Left in 1984 and the Movement for Popular Participation in 1989.

SOCIALIST PARTY (PARTIDO SOCIALISTA—PS). In 1971, 1984, and 1989, the PS ran as a member of the Broad Front. After declining in the 1960s, it has recently recovered as a strong Marxist alternative close to the Communist Party. It won 5 percent in 1989 and provided the winning candidate of the Broad Front for mayor of Montevideo, Tabaré Vázquez.

UNIÓN CÍVICA. See CIVIC UNION.

VERTIENTE ARTIGUISTA. See ARTIGUIST TENDENCY.

WORKERS' PARTY (PARTIDO DE LOS TRABAJADORES—PT). The current Trotskyist party, it has only negligible support.

Political Parties—Historical

CATHOLIC PARTY (PARTIDO CATÓLICO). A forerunner of the Civic Union from 1872 to 1912, it never achieved any influence.

CHRISTIAN CIVIC MOVEMENT (MOVIMIENTO CÍVICO CRISTIANO—MCC). This name was used in 1966 by the conservative Christians.

FEDERACIÓN ANARQUISTA URUGUAYA. See URUGUAYAN FEDERATION OF ANARCHISTS.

FRENTE IZQUIERDA DE LIBERACIÓN (FIDEL). See LEFT FRONT FOR LIBERATION.

GREAT FATHERLAND (PATRIA GRANDE). This sublema of the Broad Front was formed in 1971 by various ultraleft factions, including the sympathizers of the Tupamaros urban guerrillas.

INDEPENDENT DEMOCRATIC LEFT (IZQUIERDA DEMOCRÁTICA INDEPENDIENTE—IDI). Successor to the Great Fatherland list of 1971, the IDI was the most radical component of the Broad Front in 1984. Prior to the 1989 elections, however, it split. Its anarchist wing joined with the Tupamaros to form the Movement for Popular Participation; the remainder joined the Artiguist Tendency.

INDEPENDENT NATIONAL PARTY (PARTIDO NACIONAL INDEPENDIENTE). These anti-Herrerista Blancos opposed the 1933 coup and left the party. They rejoined the Blancos in 1958.

IZQUIERDA DEMOCRÁTICA INDEPENDIENTE. *See* INDEPENDENT DEMOCRATIC LEFT.

LEFT FRONT FOR LIBERATION (FRENTE IZQUIERDA DE LIBERACIÓN—FIDEL). The Communist Party ran under this banner in 1966 and 1971.

MOVEMENT OF THE REVOLUTIONARY LEFT (MOVIMIENTO IZQUIERDISTA DE REVOLUCIÓN—MIR). This tiny Maoist group existed in the late 1960s.

MOVIMIENTO CÍVICO CRISTIANO. *See* CHRISTIAN CIVIC MOVEMENT.

MOVIMIENTO IZQUIERDISTA DE REVOLUCIÓN. *See* MOVEMENT OF THE REVOLUTIONARY LEFT.

MOVIMIENTO REVOLUCIONARIO ORIENTAL. *See* ORIENTAL REVOLUTIONARY MOVEMENT.

MOVIMIENTO 26 DE MARZO. *See* 26TH OF MARCH MOVEMENT.

ORIENTAL REVOLUTIONARY MOVEMENT (MOVIMIENTO REVOLUCIONARIO ORIENTAL—MRO). This pro-Cuban group existed in the 1960s. Since Uruguay was once Argentina's eastern province, "oriental" here means Uruguayan.

PARTIDO CATÓLICO. *See* CATHOLIC PARTY.

PARTIDO COLORADO RIVERISTA. *See* RIVERIST COLORADO PARTY.

PARTIDO NACIONAL INDEPENDIENTE. *See* INDEPENDENT NATIONAL PARTY.

PARTIDO OBRERO REVOLUCIONARIO. *See* REVOLUTIONARY LABOR PARTY.

PARTIDO REVOLUCIONARIO DE LOS TRABAJADORES. *See* WORKERS' REVOLUTIONARY PARTY.

PATRIA GRANDE. *See* GREAT FATHERLAND.

PATRIOTIC UNION (UNIÓN PATRIÓTICA). This party, which had some military support, lost its leader in the 1984 campaign and withered.

POPULAR UNION (UNIÓN POPULAR). This *sublema* was formed by the Socialists and dissident Blancos in the 1960s.

RADICAL CHRISTIAN UNION (UNIÓN RADICAL CRISTIANA). This name was used by the conservative Catholics in 1971.

REVOLUTIONARY LABOR PARTY (PARTIDO OBRERO REVOLUCIONARIO). This main, but small, Trotskyist group existed in the 1950s and 1960s.

RIVERIST COLORADO PARTY (PARTIDO COLORADO RIVERISTA). The main faction of the Colorado Party, it was formed by opponents of José Batlle y Ordóñez in the early 1920s.

26TH OF MARCH MOVEMENT (MOVIMIENTO 26 DE MARZO). This schism from the *Tupamaros*, under the military regime, gravitated toward orthodox Marxism-Leninism and the Communist Party.

UNIÓN PATRIÓTICA. *See* PATRIOTIC UNION.

UNIÓN POPULAR. *See* POPULAR UNION.

UNIÓN RADICAL CRISTIANA. *See* RADICAL CHRISTIAN UNION.

URUGUAYAN FEDERATION OF ANARCHISTS (FEDERACIÓN ANARQUISTA URUGUAYA). A tiny group, it was active prior to 1973 when it joined the Independent Democratic Left in 1984.

WORKERS' REVOLUTIONARY PARTY (PARTIDO REVOLUCIONARIO DE LOS TRABAJADORES). This Trotskyist group existed from 1969 to 1973.

Charles Gillespie
Howard Handelman

VENEZUELA

There were approximately 19 million people living in Venezuela in 1990 in an area of 352,143 square miles located at the northern tip of South America. In the mid-1980s, Venezuela demonstrated to the world that it retains the Western Hemisphere's largest proven oil reserves and, including the extra-heavy oil of the Orinoco Belt, perhaps one of the largest in the world. The focus of Venezuelan politics since 1936 has been "sowing" this oil wealth to produce a modern and just nation.

The name Venezuela comes from the early Spanish explorers who thought that the Lake Maracaibo Indian villages built on stilts reminded them of Venice, hence the name "little Venice." Independence was achieved in 1821, but its liberator, Simón Bolívar, continued to fight to dislodge the Spanish from all of South America and to create one large nation—Gran Colombia, which included the present nations of Colombia, Ecuador, Panama, and Venezuela. Bolívar's lieutenant, Jośe Antonio Páez, separated Venezuela from Gran Colombia in 1830.

Venezuelan politics from 1830 to 1935 was warlord or caudillo politics. In 1898 caudillos from the Andean mountain region replaced those from the plains states. The last of the traditional caudillos was Juan Vicente Gómez who ruled in a highly personalist fashion from 1908 to his death in December 1935. The great wealth that flowed into his regime from the foreign oil companies after 1920 was one of the key reasons that his rule survived twenty-seven years.

The contemporary political party system had its origins in a 1928 student uprising against the Gómez regime. The development of these political parties was influenced by the climate of the mid-1930s. The world at that time was wracked by global depression, the rise of Fascism, and the false promise of Stalinism. The student rebels of 1928 became the "generation of '28." One of them, Rómulo Betancourt, organized what is today Venezuela's largest political party, the Democratic Action (AD), in 1941. A second leader of the "generation of '28," Jóvito Villalba, became the leader of the Democratic Republican Union

(URD), which was influential in the 1950s and 1960s. José Pio Tamayo created the Communist Party of Venezuela (PCV) in 1931.

Other, more conservative and Catholic-oriented students, the "generation of '36," such as Rafael Caldera, were to organize the Social Christian Party (COPEI) in 1946. COPEI has become Venezuela's second largest party since 1958. The tense political reality of the period between 1936 and 1957 accentuated the ideological conflict between the AD and COPEI. By the mid-1950s, the leadership of both the AD and COPEI had moved toward reconciliation and joint opposition to the personalist dictatorship of Colonel Marcos Pérez Jiménez. Since the present establishment of representative democracy in 1958, the AD and COPEI have become the pillars of the contemporary political establishment and "friendly" rivals in the electoral process.

In 1936 General Eleazar López Contreras (1936–1941) took power following the death of Gómez and sought to guide Venezuela through a period of constitutional transition. The "generation of '28," Betancourt and Villalba, were first allowed to organize an active political opposition, but, after a bitter December 1936 general strike which paralyzed the oil industry, López Contreras outlawed the opposition movement. Nevertheless, he modernized the politics of Venezuela in drafting the 1936 Constitution, and Caldera supported his labor reform.

The more liberal General Isaías Medina Angarita (1941–1945) allowed Betancourt and others to create the AD as a legal party in 1941. Villalba drew close to Medina, as did some young Communists, given the climate of World War II. The AD opposition and Communist supporters of the Medina administration were in a heated competition to control urban labor unions and to control the beginnings of agrarian modernization and reform.

Following failed efforts at reconciliation between the AD and the Medina administration, the AD's leaders joined with young military officers in overthrowing the Medina administration in October 1945. The AD's participation in the October 1945 coup remains controversial today, forty-five years after the fact.

During the next three years, 1945 to 1948, called the "Trienio," the AD dominated the government and carried out fundamental reforms of the political system. Universal adult suffrage was made the basis of a mass-based electoral system, and the AD's mobilization of peasants became a new fact of political life.

Betancourt was the AD's primary leader. Villalba became the leader of the URD, the moderate opposition party created in 1946, and Caldera created the more strident COPEI, which became the Social Christian COPEI Party. The public polemic and occasional violence between AD and COPEI supporters weakened the stability of the AD–dominated regime.

In November 1948, perhaps influenced by the start of the cold war, the same military men who helped the AD into power in 1945 overthrew it. The AD was outlawed. The URD and COPEI originally cooperated with the military regime (1948–1950). However, the assassination of moderate Colonel Carlos

Delgado Chalbaud ended this cooperation. Colonel Pérez Jiménez created his personalist dictatorship in 1951 and prevented the November 1952 election of Villalba of the URD.

The oil boom of the 1950s helped Pérez Jiménez stay in power. As competitive Arab oil came on the market, the world price weakened as did the dictator's popularity. In 1957 Betancourt of the AD, Caldera of COPEI, and Villalba of the URD met to plan joint action against the dictator and to plan for a reestablished democracy. The military, the business elite, and the political parties joined in a 23 January 1958 overthrow of Pérez Jiménez.

The leaders of the AD, URD, and COPEI returned to Venezuela and, in an understanding called the Punto Fijo Pact, they agreed on moderate reforms and the moderation of the partisan conflicts that had separated them. Punto Fijo also called for a broad-based AD–URD–COPEI government for the period from 1959 to 1964 regardless of the results of the December 1958 elections.

Party Politics: 1958–1984

The AD's Betancourt was elected president in the December 1958 elections. The rise of Cuba's revolutionary leader, Fidel Castro, in January 1959, and the hope of many youths in the AD, the URD, and the PCV to emulate the Cuban example shattered the hopes of the Punto Fijo Pact. Many in the AD and some PCV youths formed guerrilla forces and a new radical party, the Movement of the Revolutionary Left (MIR), in 1962. Between late 1960 and 1965, the focus of Venezuelan politics was the suppression of revolutionary violence.

In 1967, following the defeat of the guerrillas, two factions in the AD clashed to control the party's post–cold war destiny. One, headed by Jesús Angel Paz Galarraga, the secretary-general, wanted the AD to resume its reformist program. Party founder Betancourt wanted the AD to remain moderate and pragmatic. The AD split into two, and the radical reformers created the Popular Electoral Movement (MEP).

COPEI's Caldera was elected president for the period from 1968 to 1974 because of the AD–MEP split. The early 1970s was a time of Third World ideological ascendancy with the U.S. defeat in Vietnam looming and the 1973 Arab-Israeli conflict. A dynamic leader, Carlos Andrés Pérez took command of the AD and won the 1973 presidential elections. Venezuela nationalized its oil industry in 1975 and tried to use the oil bonanza to buy its way into modernity.

The easy money of the oil bonanza years caused much corruption and mismanagement in both the AD administration of Pérez (1974–1979) and that of its COPEI successor, Luis Herrera Campíns (1979–1984). Herrera won the 1978 elections by asking the voters, "Where has all the money gone?" However, his administration failed to discipline public spending and popular consumerism. Venezuela's international debt stood at US$34 billion in 1983, and its economy was in shambles.

The death of Betancourt in 1981 allowed Pérez to take command of the AD once again. His friend, Jaime Lusinchi of the AD, was elected president in 1983 with 56 percent of the vote. Lusinchi's administration was noted for its lack of control over the police and military. The war against poverty promised by the AD during the years of Pérez (1974–1979) became associated with an alleged war against the poor. Lusinchi's administration also failed to develop a consistent economic policy.

Post–1984 Political Discontent and Reform

Political discontent was on the rise in the mid-1980s. Lusinchi first attempted a Social Pact (*Pacto Social*) between labor and business as a means of controlling inflation, but this effort failed. The economic and social crisis deepened. Venezuela's currency was rapidly being devalued. Unemployment and inflation were on the rise. It became necessary to consider a basic and profound reform of the political system. Politics had to do more than provide government employment and patronage. In response to this growing discontent, Lusinchi in late 1984 created a high-level Presidential Commission for Reform of the State (COPRE). The creation of COPRE was an admission that the Venezuelan government needed a profound reform, not just a minor tinkering with its civil service.

One of COPRE's primary goals was to sponsor a major modification of the electoral system, which implied a basic criticism of the highly centralized and over-ossified political party system. The proposed direct election of governors, in off-year elections, and the creation of an elected strong mayor for Venezuela's municipalities highlighted the political reform agenda of COPRE. A major assault on the closed nature of Venezuela's political party system began.

Within the AD, Peréz, the former president, began his successful challenge of President Lusinchi for control of the party and the party's presidential nomination. Within COPEI, the youthful, forty-eight-year-old party secretary-general, Eduardo Fernández, succeeded in wresting control of the party and its 1988 presidential nomination from the party founder, Caldera. Pérez won the popularity contest for president with 52.7 percent of the vote to 40 percent for Fernández. Teodoro Petkoff of the Movement to Socialism (MAS) received most of the remaining votes. The legislative ballot vote for the AD was, however, well below that of Pérez at 43.3 percent. The AD was not to control the national legislature from 1989 to 1993.

The national congress in early 1989 passed the political reform aimed at lessening the overly centralized nature of Venezuelan politics and at strengthening its civil society. This Organic Law of Decentralization authorized the direct election of state governors and strong mayors.

This reduction of state centralism in favor of strengthened federalism was coordinated with a major effort at privatizing the vast number of autonomous state enterprises considered responsible for much of Venezuela's fiscal mismanagement and poor economic performance. President Pérez, in a pun concerning the reform of the Soviet economic system, called the Venezuelan effort at privatization, "Pérez-Stroika."

The Venezuelan Political System

Representative democracy with its periodic competitive elections and political party system must share decision-making power with two other political subsystems or political styles. Powerful private sector business groups, especially those associated with big family networks—the Cisneros family, the Mendoza family, and the Vollmer family—use their economic power to be represented by means of a nonpartisan planning dialogue. Some scholars utilize the label corporatism to describe this political style. The influence in Venezuela of both the International Monetary Fund (IMF) and the World Bank is also quite independent of the political party system.

There is also the politics of representational and revolutionary violence, which has been a fact of Venezuelan political life since 1830. Although the revolutionary violence that wracked the nation from 1960 to 1965 is a fading memory, there were some small, isolated guerrilla bands still in existence in the early 1980s. The military and national guard also continue to act free from constitutional constraint. The 1988 El Amparo shooting of fourteen fishermen and the tragic rioting that took place from 17 February to 11 March 1989, which left 300 dead, illustrate the continuing existence of a politics of violence, or praetorian politics. The drug traffickers in Venezuela are also a source of continuing violence.

These drug traffickers have allegedly bought political protection by electoral campaign contributions. There is also evidence that congress and the executive branches fail to investigate allegations that key military and police units have periodically been paid to look the other way regarding the drug trade.

Growing unemployment and an uncontrolled inflation, combined with a growing public weariness with continuing government corruption, led to a sharp rise in public discontent with the political party system and, even, with democracy in early 1990. Several scandals rocked confidence in the government party, the AD. By July 1990, several former AD leaders associated with the Lusinchi administration (1984–1989) were in hiding, and the courts issued arrest warrants for them. The most notorious of these scandals involved the public agency (Recadi) charged with managing the nation's international debt. The leadership of the AD appeared to have been decapitated by charges of corruption.

In July 1990, rumors of an imminent military coup swept through the nation. President Pérez was obliged to dismiss the defense minister and order the retirement of 143 military officers. Public confidence in the government plummeted. Regardless of the true nature of the threat of a military coup, the government relaxed its austerity measures in order to avoid additional public demonstrations. In June 1990, a decision to increase the price of gasoline was reversed in the face of popular discontent.

The August 1990 Iraqi invasion of Kuwait and the earlier agreement reached between Venezuela and several private banks to reduce Venezuela's international debt by 20 percent reversed the slide of Venezuelan politics into chaos. The debt agreement limited Venezuela's annual debt service payments to a manageable US$1.4 billion; the doubling of the world price of oil should earn Venezuela an additional $1 billion in 1990.

The immediate political impact of the Persian Gulf crisis of 1990–1991 and Venezuela's ability to increase its oil production by 25 percent has been to rescue the political image of President Pérez and to end any talk of a possible military coup. (On 4 February 1992, a brief, unsuccessful military uprising occurred.)

In late June 1991, it appears that a number of recent global events will impact on the future of Venezuela's political party system in ways that defy easy analysis. The collapse of communism will change the ideological perspective for the classification of parties. The configuration of the Venezuelan party system presented by David J. Myers (1986) has been overtaken by these events. The utility of a cold war–oriented left-right continuum in the 1990s is questionable. The new emerging ideological dimension in Venezuelan politics appears to be between those who seek a closer link for Venezuela with the United States' economic, cultural, and political orbit and those who seek a more flexible global link.

Key to a closer U.S. relationship is the strengthening of the position of the AD and COPEI as the twin, bland, pragmatic pillars of a two-party system. Key to the maintenance of close ties with Europe is the continued strengthening of alternative programmatic political parties and movements of a multiparty system.

The 1990 electoral victory of Alberto Fujimori in Peru and the fact that the other serious presidential candidate, Mario Vargas Llosa, was also a political independent suggests a potential collapse of the present party system: Independent, nonparty, presidential candidates have historically done well in Venezuela's cities. Venezuela is now over 80 percent urban. Both of Venezuela's two major establishment parties, the AD and COPEI, started as rural-based protest movements and have spent the last twenty years adjusting to the emerging urban reality.

The implementation of the electoral reforms of COPRE in 1989 meant that the grass-roots bases of many of the political bosses of the AD and COPEI were destroyed by the successful gubernatorial races of both radical and independent candidates. In many ways, the future of Venezuela's political party system will depend on the relative success or failure of the two radical governors of the key industrial states of Aragua and Bolívar. Can they carry out a meaningful progressive program, or was their election in December 1989 only a reflection of a short-lived situation and movement?

In Peru, Guatemala, and to a lesser degree Ecuador, a religious dimension—that of a Catholic–Evangelical Protestant difference—was a key factor in recent presidential elections. There is little evidence in 1991, however, that such a religious factor will be important in Venezuela over the next decade.

Elections in Venezuela in the 1990s will most likely resemble an annual shareholders meeting of a large corporation. The citizen-owners of this corporation will have the right of voice and will vote in the selection of which team of competitive "top managers" will be promoted to run the very powerful national presidency. This analogy to a large corporation is very relevant to Venezuela because, since 1975, this nation of 19 million inhabitants has depended on the success of one public corporation, Petroleum of Venezuela, Inc. (PDVSA) for over 70 percent of government revenue and 90 percent of foreign exchange earnings.

The fragility of this political relationship can be illustrated by thinking of a triangle resting on one of its points rather than on its longest side or on the hypotenuse. On one hand, grass-roots democracy in Venezuela cannot force Saudi Arabia to lower its oil production, even if the Organization of Petroleum Exporting Countries survives the challenges of the 1990s. On the other hand, Venezuela was wise to allow the PDVSA to invest heavily in oil refineries and gas station networks in the United States, Germany, and Sweden as a means of securing markets even if domestic needs were neglected.

Venezuela's oil and foreign ministers played a key role in organizing the July 1991 Paris meeting between oil exporter and consumer nations. Only after the personal intervention of the socialist president of France, François Mitterrand, did the United States send an observer to this meeting (New York Times, 3 July 1991, p. c4). Venezuelan Foreign Minister Armando Durán insisted that some interference with the free-market flow of oil was necessary. Such a dialogue over the world's oil production and distribution has been a key goal of Venezuela since 1946.

Regardless of the results of the 1993 elections, substantial changes should be expected to transform the Venezuelan party systems described below. Many of the political parties considered active in 1990 will not survive until the year 2000. Unless there is a sharp change in direction, the political party system itself could become a marginal factor in the Venezuela of the year 2000. And the military remains a persistent threat, as an abortive coup on 4 February 1992 demonstrated.

Bibliography

Robert J. Alexander. The Communist Party of Venezuela. Hoover Institution, Stanford, Calif., 1969.

David E. Blank. Venezuela: Politics in a Petroleum Republic. Praeger, New York, 1984.

———. Politics in Venezuela. Little, Brown and Company, Boston, 1973.

Steve Ellner. Venezuela's Movimiento al Socialismo: From Guerrilla Defeat to Innovative Politics. Duke University Press, Durham, N.C., 1988.

Judith Ewell. Venezuela: A Century of Change. Stanford University Press, Stanford, Calif., 1984.

Donald Herman and David J. Myers. "The Venezuelan Election," in Howard R. Penniman, ed., *American Enterprise Institute Election Yearbook–1983*. Duke University Press, Durham, N.C., 1985.

———. *Christian Democracy in Venezuela*. University of North Carolina Press, Chapel Hill, 1980.

John D. Martz. *Acción Democrática: Evolution of a Modern Political Party in Venezuela*. Princeton University Press, Princeton, N.J., 1966.

David J. Myers. "The Venezuelan Party System: Regime Maintenance under Stress," in John D. Martz and David J. Myers, eds., *Venezuela: The Democratic Experience—Revised Edition*. Praeger, New York, 1986.

Howard R. Penniman, ed. *Venezuela at the Polls: The National Election of 1978*. American Enterprise Institute, Washington, D.C., 1980.

Political Parties—Active

ACCIÓN DEMOCRÁTICA. *See* DEMOCRATIC ACTION.

COMMUNIST PARTY OF VENEZUELA (PARTIDO COMUNISTA DE VENEZUELA—PCV). The PCV, Venezuela's oldest political party, was founded in 1931. In 1958 the PCV gained 10 percent of the congressional vote and was part of the coalition which supported Admiral Wolfgang Larrazábal. In 1962 it sacrificed this political legitimacy by joining in the Castro-inspired guerrilla war. It was relegalized in 1967, only to suffer the defection of the Movement to Socialism (MAS) faction in 1970.

In the 1970s and 1980s, the PCV seemed to exist only to block the political career of Teodoro Petkoff of the MAS. By 1988 nearly all of its distinguished members had left the party and, shocked by Mikhail Gorbachev's perestroika, the PCV elected only one congressman. Its vote in 1988 was so low that the party must revalidate its status as a political party by 1993. The collapse of communism may doom the party.

DEMOCRATIC ACTION (ACCIÓN DEMOCRÁTICA—AD). In 1990 the AD is Venezuela's primary political party and the principal pillar of the political establishment. The reason for this success is the vibrant, starlike, charismatic personality of President Carlos Andrés Pérez, who, in December 1988, became the first ex-president to win reelection. The 1988 presidential election was a personal triumph for Pérez, who defeated the youthful candidate of the Social Christian COPEI Party, Eduardo Fernández, by 52.7 percent of the vote to 40 percent.

That Pérez would take control of the AD, in the 1986 to 1988 period, away from a former president, Jaime Lusinchi, and win reelection in 1988 is surprising because, in 1978, Venezuelan voters threw out the AD in a clear castigation of the corruption and mismanagement of the first Pérez administration (1974–1979). In fact, in 1981, COPEI had the Venezuelan congress morally censor ex-president Pérez for his alleged role in one of the many scandals associated with his government, the so-called Sierra Nevada case. The extent to which the AD was being castigated by the voters in the late 1970s was illustrated by the fact that, in the first off-year municipal elections of 1979, the AD's vote was reduced to a paltry 30 percent.

The reason for the political rehabilitation of Pérez and for the political comeback of the AD in the mid and late 1980s can be found in the disastrous administration of the COPEI president, Luis Herrera Campíns (1979–1984). When Pérez and the AD left office in 1979, the oil bonanza was still keeping Venezuela afloat, and the people were more or less content. The 1983 plummeting world oil prices made Herrera Venezuela's most unpopular president. The AD, during the Lusinchi administration (1984–1989), was able to uncover much corruption and mismanagement associated with the Herrera administration.

The beginning of Pérez's second term as president was most inauspicious. On 17 February 1989, a dispute over an increase in bus fares led to an outbreak of riots which cost 300 lives before coming under control in early March 1989. This tragedy occurred weeks after Pérez's lavish inauguration party and days after his government publicly announced an austerity program as part of its seeking financial relief from the International Monetary Fund.

The populist Pérez, who, in the years from 1974 to 1979, was largely responsible for building Venezuela's version of "state capitalism" with the creation of many poorly managed state enterprises, in 1990 was promising a profound restructuring, seeking to privatize most of these enterprises, and attempting to make the country attractive to foreign investors. The fact that Central Bank president Pedro Tinoco appears to be a principal adviser to President Pérez, has alienated many in the AD from his administration. AD congressional leaders, and others, have publicly blamed Tinoco for causing the tragic February 1989 rioting.

The AD labor leadership in control of the Confederation of Venezuelan Labor (CTV) broke ranks with the Pérez administration in 1989. On 18 May 1989, the CTV organized an unprecedented general strike to protest the government's economic policies. CTV president Juan José Delpino, who led the May 1989 demonstration, has since left the CTV to join the "renewal" faction in the AD seeking to clean up the party in time for the 1993 elections. Luis Piñerua, AD's unsuccessful 1978 presidential candidate, and Luis Raúl Matos, a former planning minister, are the other leaders of this faction. Delpino appears to be considering running for the presidency in 1993.

The present CTV president, Antonio Rios, has also indicated a degree of autonomous action. The CTV has organized protests against the proposed economic restructuring and the influence of businessmen in the Pérez administration in 1990.

A deeply felt personal feud between former president Lusinchi and President Pérez has further shaken the AD. Although Pérez and Lusinchi had been close allies in the 1970s, and although Lusinchi was Pérez's candidate for the party nomination in 1978, in 1989 a number of key AD ministers of Lusinchi were subjected to a criminal investigation. Lusinchi's former private secretary and companion, Blanca Ibáñez, has stayed in Miami, Florida, rather than face either party expulsion or public investigation.

The ongoing economic hardship and party divisions led to what most observers call a harsh defeat for the AD in the December 1989 gubernatorial and mayoral elections. The AD bosses and local political machines won 11 of the 21 state gubernatorial races and 154 of the 274 mayoral races. One AD leader was elected governor of Guárico State despite the fact that he had already been named a target of a criminal investigation; however, in nine populated and highly urbanized states, these AD bosses lost their grass-roots power bases.

In 1991 it appeared that the AD party bosses were resorting to an increased use of economic pressure and political harassment in order to maintain their local power bases. If political party patronage and the resultant preferences in the granting of contracts and jobs were important to maintaining the AD in power in a time of economic abundance, it appears to be more important in a prolonged period of economic scarcity. And it may not be able to hang on. In the aftermath of the failed coup on 4 February 1992, observers expressed concern that Pérez would finish his term.

DEMOCRATIC REPUBLICAN UNION (UNIÓN REPUBLICANA DEMOCRÁTICA—URD). Created in 1946 by progressive supporters of the overthrown president, Isaías Medina Angarita, the URD attracted one of the most respected leaders of the "generation of '28": Jóvito Villalba. Villalba, who became the leader of the URD, probably had been elected president in 1952 before dictator Marcos Pérez Jiménez cancelled the electoral vote count.

In 1958 the URD supported Admiral Wolfgang Larrazábal, who came in second. Villalba and the URD continued to play a key political broker role from 1958 to 1968, but the party was clearly losing its electoral base.

In 1960 the URD left the Betancourt coalition to protest the beginning cold war violence. In 1964 it joined the Democratic Action (AD) to maintain political stability. It also expelled its left wing, including José Vicente Rangel, in 1964.

In 1973 Villalba expected to be the candidate of the New Force Coalition, an alliance proposed between the Popular Electoral Movement (MEP) and the URD. Both the MEP and the URD suffered and declined as a result of their failure to form an effective "new force." This alliance may have been the basis for its designation as being on the left by David J. Myers (1986). However, in 1978, the URD supported Luis Herrera Campíns, the Social Christian COPEI Party's candidate.

Following the death of Villalba, his widow, Ismenia de Villalba ran as Venezuela's first female presidential candidate in 1988. Her electoral impact was most disappointing. In the 1989 gubernatorial campaigns, the URD supported the winning AD candidate in six states and was not a part of any of the nine winning opposition alliances. The URD is not likely to survive the 1990s.

DEVELOPMENTALIST MOVEMENT (MOVIMIENTO DESARROLLISTA). In 1968 Pedro Tinoco, a director of Chase Manhattan Bank's Venezuelan subsidy and a longtime lawyer and spokesman for the U.S. oil companies, created the Developmentalist Movement with the aim of spreading the doctrine of efficient management and economic realism to combat the romantic leftist ideologies of the political parties. He announced his support of the Social Christian COPEI Party's Rafael Caldera in 1968, and he became minister of finance and served in that position from 1969 to 1972. In 1973 he considered organizing the political return of Marcos Pérez Jiménez, the former dictator, but he ran for president himself; he received less than 1 percent of the vote.

Tinoco became one of the businessmen advisers to President Carlos Andrés Pérez and was named to head the Presidential Commission for the Comprehensive Reform of Public Administration. In 1990 he was the powerful president of the Central Bank of Venezuela. Tinoco, after 1974, apparently no longer needed a political party base in order to be an influential actor in the Venezuelan government.

LIGA CAUSA "R." See RADICAL CAUSE.

MOVEMENT OF NATIONAL INTEGRATION (MOVIMIENTO DE INTEGRACIÓN NACIONAL—MIN). In 1978 popular television personality Renny Ottolina decided to run for president as a protest against party rule. In a campaign speech he stated that "[t]he country no longer believed in political parties." In March 1978, he was killed in a plane crash, but his widow, Rhona de Ottolina, has kept his party alive. The Ottolina campaign of 1978 appeared to reflect that of an independent conservative, Arturo Uslar Pietri, who ran in 1963.

MOVEMENT OF THE REVOLUTIONARY LEFT (MOVIMIENTO DE IZQUIERDA REVOLUCIONARIO—MIR). The MIR was created in 1960 when the radical youth of the Democratic Action broke with the old-guard leadership in order to bring about a violent revolutionary change. The two principal leaders of the MIR's guerrillas were Américo Martín and Moisés Moleiro. The MIR continued its guerrilla war until 1969. In 1973, as a legal party, it elected only one member to congress; nonetheless, the MIR emerged as a force in the student movement of several universities in the late 1970s.

In the 1980s, Moleiro brought his faction of the MIR into association with the Movement to Socialism; the Martín faction joined the other minor parties of the left behind José Vicente Rangel.

The young men who wanted to emulate the experience of Cuba's Fidel Castro in the early 1960s appear to be irrelevant in the Venezuela of the 1990s.

MOVEMENT TO SOCIALISM (MOVIMIENTO AL SOCIALISMO—MAS). The real beginning of the MAS can be traced to the 1968 Soviet invasion of

Czechoslovakia and the repudiation of that act by the Italian Communist Party (PCI). Two factions within the old Communist Party of Venezuela (PCV) were fed up with the blind, pro-Soviet stance of the aged party old guard controlled by the Machado brothers. Teodoro Petkoff, the former guerrilla leader, publicly attacked the Soviet invasion as did party Secretary-General Pompeyo Márquez. In 1970 Petkoff and Márques broke away from the PCV to create the MAS.

In the 1970–1990 generation, the MAS has prospered while other militant leftist parties have faded. The assistance of the independent PCI may have been crucial for this relative success. As part of its break with the Soviet Union, the PCI had popularized the writings of Antonio Gramsci who had died in one of Benito Mussolini's prisons in 1937. Gramsci had questioned the relevance of the 1917 Soviet revolution to the Communist parties of the democratic West. The rise of Joseph Stalin had also prevented a democratic unity from successfully resisting the rise of fascism in Europe. Gramsci insisted that the Communist strategy at that time was a mistake and that Western Communists must prove their loyalty to pluralist democracy. Gramsci also appealed to Catholic Venezuela by suggesting that the anticapitalism inherent in Catholic communitarian values is compatible with liberal socialism.

Petkoff, who in 1960 pushed the old PCV into participating in guerrilla warfare, emerged in the late 1970s as a mature political leader. He pushed the MAS into a political convergence with the establishment. By 1980, the German Social Democratic Party's foundation, the Friedrich Ebert Foundation, included the MAS, along with the Democratic Action (AD) and the Popular Electoral Movement, as its Venezuelan affiliate.

The MAS and Petkoff were aided by the fact that many university-based intellectuals have been associated with the movement. One additional reason for the ascendancy of the MAS between 1979 and 1984 was that the Social Christian COPEI Party administration may have secretly helped the MAS and Petkoff financially with the aim of the MAS taking votes away from the AD.

Between 1970 and 1983, Márquez resisted Petkoff's efforts to become the president of the MAS. The independent radical, José Vicente Rangel, was the presidential candidate of the MAS in 1973 and 1978. In 1980 when Petkoff was a guest of the prestigious Woodrow Wilson Center in Washington, D.C., he suggested that the label "Eurocommunist," first applied in Italy, no longer applied to the MAS. Some in the MAS even considered replacing the word socialism in the party's name with social justice. The political rivalry for leadership of the left between Petkoff and Rangel was to deny the left a unified candidate in 1983.

A host of small leftist parties, including the PCV and groups such as the Liga Socialista (LS), which allegedly maintained ties to the remaining small guerrilla operations, and one faction of MIR, created a Popular Unity Electoral Alliance (Alianza para la Unidad del Pueblo—AUP) to support the 1983 presidential candidacy of Rangel and to block the ascendancy of Petkoff in the MAS. For his part, Petkoff insisted that he was interested in the MAS, not in leftist unity, and he secured his party's presidential nomination.

The first time Petkoff ran for president, he gained a disappointing 4.1 percent of the vote. His real problem may have been his failure to cross the threshold of trust for the average voter since he had been a guerrilla leader.

Despite his personal setback in the 1983 presidential election, Petkoff secured his leadership of the MAS from 1984 to 1988. He had to beat back a challenge for the 1988 presidential nomination from both Márquez and Freddy Muñoz, a former university student leader. Petkoff was aided in his effort to control the MAS by the gains the party was making in the Confederation of Venezuelan Labor. In 1986 its labor leaders won a surprise victory over those of the AD in the printer's union.

In 1988 Petkoff gained 8.2 percent of the presidential vote, and the MAS gained 10.2 percent of the congressional vote making it clearly Venezuela's third political force. In the 1989 gubernatorial elections, a local MAS leader, Carlos Tablante, won the governorship of the important industrial state of Aragua. Tablante, a progressive businessman and intellectual, was never a guerrilla leader and never a Communist. He may represent a new generation of MAS leaders who might challenge Petkoff in 1998 if not in 1993.

MOVIMIENTO AL SOCIALISMO. *See* MOVEMENT TO SOCIALISM.

MOVIMIENTO DE INTEGRACIÓN NACIONAL. *See* MOVEMENT OF NATIONAL INTEGRATION.

MOVIMIENTO DE IZQUIERDA REVOLUCIONARIO. *See* MOVEMENT OF THE REVOLUTIONARY LEFT.

MOVIMIENTO DESARROLLISTA. *See* DEVELOPMENTALIST MOVEMENT.

MOVIMIENTO ELECTORAL DEL PUEBLO. *See* POPULAR ELECTORAL MOVEMENT.

NATIONAL OPINION (OPINIÓN NACIONAL—OPINA). The OPINA, established in 1962 as a conservative party, supported Arturo Uslar Pietri in 1963 and Miguel Angel Burelli Rivas in 1968. In 1973 Jorge Olavarria, editor of the now defunct, but respected, *Resumen* magazine, appeared to have taken over the OPINA.

Olavarria, who is antiparty, anti–Democratic Action (AD), and anti–COPEI, is not necessarily a conservative. He has fought against human rights abuses as well as against the corruption of the post–1958 governments; he was briefly imprisoned by both president Carlos Andrés Pérez (AD) and Luis Herrera Campíns (COPEI). Rather than a conservative, Olavarria could be considered a political sniper.

NATIONAL RESCUE (RESCATE NACIONAL). Illustrative of the growing political discontent in Venezuela has been the periodic appearance of military and law-and-order candidates for president. In 1983 a former defense minister, General Luis Enrique Rangel Borgoin, organized the National Rescue party as his political vehicle. Rangel Borgoin had been identified with those in Venezuela who expressed the need to press for a favorable resolution of its border claims with Colombia and Guyana and for an enhanced national security consciousness. His 1983 electoral impact was minimal; nevertheless, a significant part of public opinion seems to favor a strong military president.

NEW DEMOCRATIC GENERATION (NUEVA GENERACIÓN DEMO-CRÁTICA—NGD). In June 1981, a group of antiparty, antipopulist young businessmen and executives created the NGD. Like the independent candidacy of Arturo Uslar Pietri in 1963 and the ill-fated campaign of television personality Renny Ottolina in 1978, the NGD opposed the "folkloric" populism of the political establishment and its uniquely inept blend of socialism and capitalism. In early 1983, the NGD considered retired General Castro Hurtado to be its presidential candidate. Hurtado had resigned his commission in 1979 to protest the extensive amnesty given to former guerrilla leaders.

The core of the party was to be the political ambition of Vladimir Gessen (party secretary-general) and José Marsicobetre (party president). Gessen, as the NGD congressional delegate, was to receive international publicity for his highly publicized charges that populist Venezuela had become a major element of the Latin American–U.S. drug connection. However, when he became apprehensive about his own safety, he apparently fled to Panama.

In 1989 Gessen announced that a right-wing, conservative congressional bloc had been created by one senator and ten national deputies. In addition to the NGD, this bloc included Rhona Ottolina of Formula Uno, the remnant of her late husband's Movement of National Integration, and the Authentic Renovating Organization (Organización Renovadora Auténtica).

In the 1989 gubernatorial elections, the NGD was listed as supporting successful candidates of the Democratic Action in four states—Lara, Táchira, Monagas, and Apure—and a successful candidate of the COPEI in one state—Zulia.

In 1991 President Carlos Andrés Pérez named Gessen to be in charge of the government's official tourist promotion effort. This appointment was seen to be an indication of the new "economic liberal" look of the Pérez administration.

NUEVA GENERACIÓN DEMOCRÁTICA. See NEW DEMOCRATIC GENERATION.

OPINIÓN NACIONAL. See NATIONAL OPINION.

PARTIDO COMUNISTA DE VENEZUELA. *See* Communist Party of Venezuela.

POPULAR ELECTORAL MOVEMENT (MOVIMIENTO ELECTORAL DEL PUEBLO—MEP). The MEP resulted from the most serious division of the Democratic Action (AD), which occurred in 1967. In 1967 and 1968, two old-guard AD leaders competed for the party's 1968 presidential nomination. Progressive Luis Beltran Prieto apparently won a confusing primary vote. Party founder Rómulo Betancourt vetoed the Prieto nomination because he feared the radicalism of party Secretary-General Jesús Angel Paz Galarraga.

In 1968 the MEP was created and Prieto gained 19.3 percent of the presidential vote. The 1973 decision of Paz Galarraga to create a New Force coalition, including the Communist Party (PCV), proved to be a disaster. Many of the labor leaders who had left the AD to join the MEP in 1967 returned to the AD fold in 1973. Paz ran as the MEP's presidential candidate, but he gained only 5.09 percent of the vote. By 1978 the MEP was nearing extinction although its aged leader, Prieto, had become a respected elder statesman. The implication of some MEP labor leaders in the 1982–1983 Bank of the Venezuelan Workers scandal further weakened the MEP.

In 1988 the MEP and the PCV created a Moral Movement (Movimiento Moral) to fight corruption. The anticorruption candidate nominated by the MEP–PCV Moral Movement was a former president of Central University, Edmundo Chirinos. Although the MEP elected two congressmen on the national quotient, its 1988 vote was low enough that it must revalidate its formal party registration in order to retain permanent party status for 1993. In 1989 the MEP was a small part of many of the anti–AD electoral alliances which contested the first direct election of governors and strong mayors.

The individual elected in December 1989 as governor of the oil-producing state of Anzoategui, Ovidio González, appears to have MEP membership, but he was also supported by the Movement to Socialism, the Social Christian COPEI Party, and the PCV.

RADICAL CAUSE (LIGA CAUSA "R"). In the 1970s, many Venezuelan radicals moved to the new, planned industrial city, Guayana City, which was being built as part of Venezuela's most significant regional development. The state-owned steel industry of Guayana employed over 16,000 workers in 1980, and Guayana City, which had close to 250,000 inhabitants, was a real working-class city.

A small group of radicals headed by Alfredo Maneiro and Andrés Velásquez created the Radical Cause in 1971. By 1979 they won the union election to represent the steel workers. The response of the Democratic Action–Social Christian COPEI Party establishment was to intervene in this local union and nullify its elections. The Radical Cause fought back and gained broad national support. The Radical Cause won 70 percent of the vote in the Steel

Workers Union in 1988, and in 1989 Velásquez was elected governor of Bolívar state, in which Guayana City is located. Velásquez did not form any electoral alliance in his 1989 gubernatorial race. The Radical Cause differs from other leftist parties inasmuch as it engages in building grass-roots organizations in working-class neighborhoods rather than personal careers in Caracas.

By mid-1991, it appeared that the Velásquez governorship had survived in Bolívar state. Both he and his grass-roots supporters are engaged in keeping the Orinoco Steel Company a public enterprise in the face of tremendous pressure to privatize it. He has attempted to place the blame for the failure of the thirty-year-old Guayana Regional Development effort on the AD leadership of the Venezuelan Guayana Corporation.

RESCATE NACIONAL. *See* NATIONAL RESCUE.

SOCIAL CHRISTIAN COPEI PARTY (PARTIDO SOCIAL CRISTIANO—COPEI). In 1990 the COPEI remains the second pillar of the political establishment. In a bitter struggle for party control, the aged party founder, Rafael Caldera, lost a 1988 party convention vote to the youthful party secretary-general, Eduardo Fernández. In the 1988 campaign, Fernández portrayed himself as a young tiger, *El Tigre*, ready to devour the problems afflicting Venezuela and to defeat the "corrupt" generation of Carlos Andrés Pérez.

His defeat and, in his campaign, his attack on the performance of COPEI's last president, Luis Herrera Campíns (1979–1984), have caused a bitter personal feud in the COPEI. Herrera has joined forces with Caldera in a bitter generational battle with the Fernández group in charge of the COPEI. The appeal of Fernández remains his youth; he was forty-eight years old in 1988.

The five COPEI governors elected in 1989 appear to be representative of a new generation of COPEI leaders whose rise to political prominence has been independent of the highly centralized and personalist rule of Caldera. One of these elected COPEI governors, Oswaldo Alvárez Paz, of the oil-rich state of Zulia, may in fact emerge to be the compromise COPEI presidential candidate in 1993.

COPEI's leaders are more involved in theoretical disputes involving various interpretations of Catholic social doctrines than are the pragmatic leaders of the Democratic Action (AD). The extent of the theoretical dispute lies in the difference between members of Opus Dei, a secretive, elitist, and technocratic Catholic group in COPEI, and those associated with liberation theology and its proposed communitarian restructuring of Venezuela.

The winning COPEI candidates in many of the 1989 state and municipal campaigns were able to form a broad, multiparty alliance against the AD candidate. This was especially true regarding the Movement to Socialism (MAS) and the Popular Electoral Movement (MEP). The Venezuelan press has indicated that the personal friendships among local COPEI, MAS, and MEP leaders have been largely responsible for the formation of these alliances rather than any national party strategy. It is not inconceivable that, in 1993, the COPEI will try to move to the left of the AD in order to maximize its electoral chances.

UNIÓN REPUBLICANA DEMOCRÁTICA. *See* DEMOCRATIC REPUBLICAN UNION.

Political Parties—Historical

AGRARIAN SOCIALIST PARTY (PARTIDO SOCIALISTA AGRARIO). *See* SOCIALIST PARTIES.

AGRUPACIÓN CÍVICA BOLIVARIANA. *See* BOLIVARIAN CIVIC GROUP.

BOLIVARIAN CIVIC GROUP (AGRUPACIÓN CÍVICA BOLIVARIANA). During the administration of President Eleazar López Contreras (1935–1941), government-sponsored candidates in legislative elections used the Bolivarian Civic Group label. The Bolivarian Civic Group was organized as a party in 1941 and officially launched the candidacy of López Contreras for reelection in 1945, shortly before the October overthrow of President Isaías Medina Angarita.

CAUSA COMÚN. *See* COMMON CAUSE.

COMMON CAUSE (CAUSA COMÚN). The Common Cause was organized in April 1973 for the purpose of mobilizing independent support for the presidential candidacy of Carlos Andrés Pérez of the Democratic Action (AD). In 1978 Diego Arria, Common Cause's founder, launched his own presidential candidacy using Common Cause. One of the also-ran candidates, his candidacy appeared to have hurt the AD.

CONSERVATIVE PARTY (PARTIDO CONSERVADOR). Founded in 1840 by followers of José Antonio Páez, the party was friendly with the Catholic hierarchy. No attempt was made to revive the Conservative Party after the death of Juan Vicente Gómez in 1935.

CRUZADA CÍVICA NACIONALISTA. *See* NATIONALIST CIVIC CRUSADE.

DEMOCRATIC SOCIALIST PARTY (PARTIDO SOCIALISTA DEMOCRÁTICO). *See* SOCIALIST PARTIES.

FRENTE ELECTORAL INDEPENDIENTE. *See* INDEPENDENT ELECTORAL FRONT.

FRENTE NACIONAL DEMOCRÁTICA. *See* NATIONAL DEMOCRATIC FRONT.

FUERZA DEMOCRÁTICA POPULAR. *See* POPULAR DEMOCRATIC FORCE.

INDEPENDENT DEMOCRATIC MOVEMENT (MOVIMIENTO DEMO-CRÁTICO INDEPENDIENTE—MDI). In 1966 Alirio Ugarte Pelayo broke with Jóvito Villalba and the Democratic Republican Union to form the MDI, but he committed suicide before the party could take shape. The remnant of the MDI supported Rafael Caldera, the candidate of the Social Christian COPEI Party, in 1968.

INDEPENDENT ELECTORAL FRONT (FRENTE ELECTORAL INDEPEN-DIENTE—FEI). The FEI was organized in 1951 by followers of Colonel Marcos Pérez Jiménez when the military dictator decided to hold elections in 1952. When the first election returns were reported after the 30 November poll, it was clear that the FEI was losing. As a result, Pérez Jiménez ordered a recount of the vote and announced that the FEI had won the majority of votes. Subsequent efforts by some of the FEI officials to keep the party alive after November 1952 were thwarted by the Pérez Jiménez government.

INDEPENDENT NATIONAL ELECTORAL MOVEMENT (MOVIMIENTO ELECTORAL NACIONAL INDEPENDIENTE—MENI). This minor party, established in 1958, supported Wolfgang Larrazábal in 1958, Jóvito Villalba in 1963, and Miguel Angel Burelli Rivas in 1968. It did not receive enough votes in 1968 to continue to be a legal party.

LIBERAL PARTY (PARTIDO LIBERAL). The Liberal Party was established by Leocadio Guzmán in 1840 to oppose José Antonio Páez. His son, Antonio Guzmán Blanco, reestablished the party as the Liberal Union in 1886. The last use of the word liberal occurred in 1899, when the caudillo, Cipriano Castro, called his group the Restoring Liberal Cause (Causa Liberal Restauradora). Juan Vicente Gómez liquidated all political parties, and any attempts to revive the Liberal Party after the death of Gómez in 1935 failed (Alexander 1969). However, according to Donald Herman (1980), a small Liberal Party supported Rafael Caldera, of the Social Christian COPEI Party, in 1968.

MOVEMENT FOR NATIONAL RENEWAL (MOVIMIENTO RENOVA-DOR NACIONAL—MORENA): Leonardo Montiel Ortega, a former leader of the Democratic Republican Union, used MORENA in 1978 to run for president.

MOVIMIENTO REPUBLICANO PROGRESISTA. *See* SOCIALIST PARTIES.

MOVEMENT OF NATIONAL ACTION (MOVIMIENTO DE ACCIÓN NA-CIONAL—MAN). The MAN was founded by a right-wing journalist, Germán Borregales, in 1960. Borregales was elected as the party's only member in the Chamber of Deputies in 1963. The MAN failed to elect anyone in 1973 and 1978.

MOVIMIENTO DE ACCIÓN NATIONAL. See MOVEMENT OF NA-TIONAL ACTION.

MOVIMIENTO DEMOCRÁTICA INDEPENDIENTE. See INDEPENDENT DEMOCRATIC MOVEMENT.

MOVIMIENTO ELECTORAL NACIONAL INDEPENDIENTE. See INDE-PENDENT NATIONAL ELECTORAL MOVEMENT.

MOVIMIENTO RENOVADOR NACIONAL. See MOVEMENT FOR NA-TIONAL RENEWAL.

NATIONAL AGRARIAN PARTY (PARTIDO AGRARIO NACIONAL—PAN). The PAN was founded in 1937 by Rodolfo Rojas, a friend of President Eleazar López Contreras. Arturo Uslar Pietri was also a leader of the party. The PAN does not appear to have survived the López Contreras era.

NATIONAL DEMOCRATIC FRONT (FRENTE NACIONAL DEMOCRÁ-TICA—FND). The FND was organized following the 1963 independent pres-idential campaign of Arturo Uslar Pietri. Uslar's Independents for a National Front (IPFN) had its foundation in the fear of the business community that the 1958 Rómulo Betancourt coalition had been shattered and that the urban middle class needed to find its own voice in politics. Uslar won 42 percent of the vote in metropolitan Caracas in 1963, but he had little following outside of the large cities.

In 1963 Uslar was considered too close to the family of Isaías Medina Agarita, who was overthrown by the Democratic Action (AD) and others in 1945. Other leaders of the FND were Martín Vegas, Pedro Segnini La Cruz, and a former leader of the AD, Ramón Escovar Salóm.

In 1964 Uslar, believing he could influence President Raúl Leoni of the AD regarding the need for a conservative policy on oil, joined in an Ample Based Coalition with the AD and Jóvito Villalba's Democratic Republican Union. Leoni won only 32 percent of the 1963 vote. Many IPFN supporters rejected this reconciliation with the AD, and, in 1966, the FND left the coalition. In 1968 it joined another electoral coalition, which supported the independent, Miguel Angel Burelli Rivas. In 1973 Segnini ran on the FND ballot for president, but he received only 0.14 percent of the vote. No one was elected to the congress on the FND ballot. Soon afterward, the party went out of existence.

NATIONALIST CIVIC CRUSADE (CRUZADA CÍVICA NACIONAL-ISTA—CCN). Organized in 1965 by followers of the former dictator, Marcos Pérez Jiménez, the leader of the CCN was P. Salas Castillo. In 1968 the CCN ran the former dictator, who had been convicted, sentenced, and released from prison for economic crimes, for senator in the national capital, Caracas. Pérez Jiménez received the highest vote on the CCN ballot, but he was disqualified by the courts from taking his seat, "on grounds that he had not been present in the country to campaign for the post." The CCN alternate became senator. Nationwide, the CCN gained an impressive 10.9 percent of the legislative vote in 1968.

The political establishment, led by the Democratic Action and the Social Christian COPEI Party, moved to amend the constitution to disqualify anyone "who had been convicted of misusing a public post to enrich himself" from running for public office. The CCN supported attempted public demonstrations and a publicized disruption of congress in order to have Pérez Jiménez seated in the Senate. In 1973 the CCN again sought to run Pérez Jiménez for president. Finding himself comfortably situated in Spain, however, the former dictator opted not to renew his Venezuelan political career. The CCN sought to run his daughter for president, but this too failed. As the nostalgia for the former dictator ebbed in the days of the oil bonanza, the CCN disappeared.

NATIONALIST REVOLUTIONARY PARTY. See REVOLUTIONARY PARTY OF NATIONALIST INTEGRATION.

PARTIDO AGRARIO NACIONAL. See NATIONAL AGRARIAN PARTY.

PARTIDO CONSERVADOR. See CONSERVATIVE PARTY.

PARTIDO DEMOCRÁTICO VENEZOLANO. See VENEZUELAN DEMO-CRATIC PARTY.

PARTIDO LIBERAL. See LIBERAL PARTY.

PARTIDO REVOLUCIONARIO DE INTEGRACIÓN NACIONALISTA. See REVOLUTIONARY PARTY OF NATIONALIST INTEGRATION.

PARTIDO REVOLUCIONARIO NACIONALISTA (PRN). See REVOLU-TIONARY PARTY OF NATIONALIST INTEGRATION.

PARTIDO SOCIALISTA AGRARIO. See SOCIALIST PARTIES.

PARTIDO SOCIALISTA DEMOCRÁTICO. See SOCIALIST PARTIES.

PARTIDO SOCIALISTA DE TRABAJADORES. See SOCIALIST PARTIES.

PARTIDO SOCIALISTA VENEZOLANO. *See* SOCIALIST PARTIES.

POPULAR DEMOCRATIC FORCE (FUERZA DEMOCRÁTICA POPU-LAR—FDP). The 1960 youthful dissidents from the Democratic Action who created the Movement of the Revolutionary Left (MIR) divided over the question of participating in guerrilla warfare against the Betancourt government. In 1962, led by deputy Jorge Dager, those in the MIR who rejected the road of armed struggle and revolution created the FDP. The party attracted Admiral Wolfgang Larrazábal to its leadership when the FDP made him its candidate for the 1963 presidency. He gained 9.4 percent of the vote. In 1968 the FDP backed the independent, Miguel Angel Burelli Rivas. In the 1973 and 1978 elections, the remnants of the FDP appeared to be absorbed into the Social Christian COPEI Party, and the FDP has supported COPEI's presidential candidates ever since.

POPULAR NATIONALIST VANGUARD (VANGUARDIA POPULAR NACIONALISTA). *See* REVOLUTIONARY PARTY OF NATIONALIST INTEGRATION.

PROGRESSIVE REPUBLICAN MOVEMENT (MOVIMIENTO REPUBLICANO PROGRESISTA—MRP). *See* SOCIALIST PARTIES.

REVOLUTIONARY PARTY OF NATIONALIST INTEGRATION (PARTIDO REVOLUCIONARIO DE INTEGRACIÓN NATIONALISTA—PRIN). The PRIN was organized in the early 1960s by leaders of the second split in the Democratic Action (AD) in 1962. After 1963 this group formed the Nationalist Revolutionary Party (PRN). The left wing of the Democratic Republican Union, led by José Vicente Rangel, had been expelled in 1964 and formed the Popular Nationalist Vanguard (VPN). Domingo Alberto Rangel, the former leader of the AD and the Movement of the Revolutionary Left, was also looking for a political home.

In August 1966, the Rangel faction of the MIR, the PRN, and the VPN joined to form the PRIN. Its president was Raúl Ramos Gimínez of the PRN, a former AD leader. In 1968 the PRIN supported Luis Beltran Prieto of the Popular Electoral Movement for president. In 1969 the party began to disintegrate, and Rangel moved to the Movement to Socialism.

SOCIALIST PARTIES. Two small parties have used the name socialist since the years of the Trienio (1945–1948). The Agrarian Socialist Party (PSA), established in 1945, pledged its support to the revolutionary Democratic Action (AD) government. In 1946 a group broke away from the PSA to form the Socialist Workers Party (PST). The PST organized the first oil worker union in El Tigre, a major center in the eastern oil production region.

In 1958 the PSA became the Venezuelan Socialist Party (PSV) and supported

Rafael Caldera, of the Social Christian COPEI Party, in 1958 and Jóvito Villalba, of the Democratic Republican Union, in 1963. It changed its name to the Democratic Socialist Party (PSD) in 1967.

In 1973 the PSD backed General Martín García Villasmil, who was considered to be friendly to former dictator Marcos Pérez Jiménez. The party received only 0.27 percent of the vote.

In 1961 the PST merged with several other groups to form the Progressive Republican Movement (MRP), headed by Ramón Escovar Salóm. The MRP supported Arturo Uslar Pietri in 1963 and disappeared soon afterward. The PST was reestablished, but it disappeared in 1973 when it merged with National Opinion.

Neither the PSA nor the PST ever joined the Socialist International. In fact, only the AD and its breakaway, the Popular Electoral Movement, have ever been associated with the International.

SOCIALIST WORKERS PARTY (PARTIDO SOCIALISTA DE TRABA-JADORES—PST). See SOCIALIST PARTIES.

VANGUARDIA POPULAR NACIONALISTA (VPN). See REVOLUTION-ARY PARTY OF NATIONALIST INTEGRATION.

VENEZUELAN DEMOCRATIC PARTY (PARTIDO DEMOCRÁTICO VE-NEZOLANO—PDV). Two parties created after 1936 have used the name Venezuelan Democratic Party. The first was organized in 1937 by General José Rafael Gabaldon, "an old caudillo who had long fought the Gómez dictatorship." It was an attempt to find a legal vehicle for those who had participated in the parties outlawed by the López Contreras government in February 1937. Many of its leaders, for example, Juan Pablo Pérez Alfonzo and Luis Beltran Prieto, were to become top leaders of the Democratic Action. Because they had been associated with subversive parties, however, the PDV was never legally recognized.

The second PDV was launched by President Isaías Medina Angarita in 1943. Designed to mobilize political support for his government, it was originally called by the clumsy name of Partisans of the Policy of the Government (PPG). With the 1945 election to choose a successor to Medina approaching, the PDV nominated the minister of agriculture, Angel Biaggini. Many future leaders of the Democratic Republican Union, such as Jóvito Villalba, Luis Hernández Solis, and Alirio Ugarte Pelayo, were once members of the PDV. The October 1945 coup effectively ended the existence of the PDV.

VENEZUELAN SOCIALIST PARTY. See SOCIALIST PARTIES.

David E. Blank

VIRGIN ISLANDS OF THE UNITED STATES

The Virgin Islands consist of approximately 100 islands and cays under the jurisdiction of the United States and Britain. Located east of Puerto Rico, between the Atlantic Ocean and the Caribbean Sea, they are the northernmost of the island chain known as the Lesser Antilles. The larger western islands of Saint Croix (80 square miles), Saint Thomas (32 square miles), and Saint John (20 square miles) are territories of the United States.

The estimated permanent population of the three U.S.–controlled islands is 112,000. During the winter months, the population rises to as high as 135,000 due to an influx of workers for the tourist industry. Most of the people live on Saint Thomas and Saint Croix, which is located in the Caribbean 40 miles south of Saint Thomas–Saint John. Two-thirds of thinly populated Saint John is a national park.

During the 1960s and 1970s, rapid economic growth attracted immigrants from other West Indian islands, including Puerto Rico, and the U.S. mainland. By 1990 only about 42 percent of the U.S. islands' population was native born. Thirty percent were West Indian, 20 percent were from the mainland, and 8 percent were Puerto Rican. Ethnically, people of at least some African ancestry account for about 70 percent of the population. Those classified as white constitute the largest minority, or about 20 percent.

Historic Antecedents

The islands were named by Christopher Columbus when he came upon them during his 1493 voyage. Settlements were established by the English and French in the mid-seventeenth century, but possession changed hands frequently among various European colonial powers until Denmark finally acquired the islands in the late seventeenth and early eighteenth centuries. The United States purchased the islands for $25 million in 1917, primarily to provide a strategic safeguard for the Atlantic approaches to the Panama Canal.

The early economy of the islands was based on plantation agriculture, with sugar as the principal export crop. The familiar Caribbean social pattern of a small, white bureaucratic-merchant-planter class dominating a mass of dark-skinned, mostly slave workers was established during the first decades of permanent settlement. By the time the United States took ownership, the plantation system was in permanent decline. Stagnation plagued the islands until post–World War II affluence in the United States made them an attractive destination for tourists.

Under Danish rule, the creole merchant and planter elite gained representation through colonial councils. Limited franchise ensured domination of island politics by conservative local economic interests. There were no political parties; the politics of the council representatives was personalist and parochial.

The Islands Under U.S. Rule

Danish administrative structures continued during the first years of U.S. control, when the U.S. Navy exercised jurisdiction. Actions of the local councils were subject to influence and even veto by the American presidential-appointed governors; the councils, which continued to represent local elite interests, were content to work within the framework of Navy paternalism and subordination to executive rule.

In 1927 Virgin Islanders were granted U.S. citizenship; an Organic Act of 1936 revised administrative structures and provided for universal suffrage. During the final months of the Hoover administration, jurisdiction was transferred to the federal Department of the Interior. As a result of these changes, political clubs were organized to represent the new voters and to contend for participation in various New Deal programs. The clubs were strongly Democratic in orientation; they were led by men of primarily lower-middle-class origin who challenged the big landowner-merchant elite. By the 1940s they formed the core of a new colored political elite which effectively dominated local legislatures and electoral offices.

Clubs such as the liberal Progressive Guide were the forerunners of political parties in the 1940s. The Democratic and Republican parties were formally recognized as the result of the Election Code of 1962. The Democrats enjoyed a three-to-one voter registration advantage over the Republicans (now the Progressive Republicans) and the newer Independent Citizens Movement, but they could not translate that into a permanent political supremacy. The factious Democrats lost the governorship (made an elective office in 1970) several times, and were not able to consolidate their hold on the unicameral fifteen-seat legislature until 1976.

Issues in the 1980s

The post–World War II tourist boom transformed the economy of the Virgin Islands. The building of a modern infrastructure to support tourism also provided a base for limited industrialization. Oil refining, mineral processing, and pharmaceutical and other manufacturing plants were built by mainland companies enticed by tax incentives and credits granted by local governments. Federal funds for infrastructure development and social programs in the 1960s also contributed to prosperity. Employment soared and per capita income rose steadily.

Economic growth, however, was accompanied by increasing social tensions. The influx of large numbers of generally impoverished people from other West Indian islands to work in the labor-short construction and tourism industries aroused local hostility. A black power movement in the early 1970s resulted in some racial violence. Multinational corporations, with their profit-maximization mentality, contributed to labor unrest and aroused environmental concerns. Added to these problems—and linked to them—was the fact that offshore interests and a relatively small group of white and colored residents controlled a disproportionate share of the available wealth. The politically powerful black and mulatto monied groups, with ties to the dominant economic interests, appeared increasingly remote from the concerns of the lower classes to whom they were ethnically related. Furthermore, the status of the islands as an unincorporated territory of the United States meant that they were hostage to the shifting policies of the U.S. Congress, thus limiting the options of local administrations in dealing with the problems.

A deepening economic crisis in the 1980s added to the islands' woes. Recession, a relatively high-wage labor force, and a shifting global economy resulted in the closing or reduction of several major industries, leading to unemployment, loss of governmental revenues, and cutbacks in public sector jobs. Additionally, changing congressional priorities meant lower federal subsidies. Throughout the decade, island administrations were faced with growing deficits and were forced to curtail expenditures in the economically important public sector.

Tourism continued to expand, however; by 1989, it accounted for 70 percent of the gross domestic product and employment. On the other hand, it also brought problems: inflated land prices, monopoly of the higher paying jobs by the better educated mainland whites, and environmental concerns related to uncontrolled development. Resentment and even occasional violence against tourists occurred, yet dependence on the industry required its further promotion. For hard-pressed public administrations, continued growth of tourism, and the taxes it provided, was the only short-term means of funding programs to alleviate social tensions.

The islands' difficulties have brought the political status question to the forefront. Dependency on the mainland, combined with limited options for local governments, has raised the demand for greater autonomy among both political leaders and a large part of the population. Yet various efforts to amend the Organic Act of 1954 in order to give local governments more authority have failed. Affluent whites have resisted reduced congressional authority because they fear increased taxation by local governments which would fund programs primarily of benefit to the lower socioeconomic groups. Virtually all sectors of the population oppose the added taxation that increased autonomy would require. Though the Congress did, during the 1980s, somewhat expand the ability of islanders to affect legislation, this has not seriously altered the islands' status. In the 1990s, efforts to deal with economic and social problems will necessarily require dealing with the islands' future political status.

Bibliography

Gordon K. Lewis. *The Virgin Islands.* Northwestern University Press, Evanston, Ill., 1972.

Edward A. O'Neil. *The Rape of the American Virgins.* Praeger, New York, 1972.

"U.S. Virgin Islands." *Latin America and Caribbean Review.* World of Information, NTC Business Books, Saffron Walden, Essex, UK, 1986–1990.

Political Parties—Active

DEMOCRATIC PARTY. The Democrats continued their hold on a majority of the islands' voters throughout the 1980s. The party's historically liberal orientation, with its emphasis on economic development and social welfare programs and its appeal to upwardly mobile colored groups, was sorely tested, however, by changing circumstances during the decade. Recession in the early 1980s, cutbacks in federal assistance, party factionalism, and challenges from independent political groups undermined the party's hold on power and its ability to implement its programs. New issues that affected the Democrat's traditional political base included the related impacts of immigration, employment, and land ownership. Finally, the party was faced with the question of the islands' future political status.

The party won the governorship in 1986 with the candidacy of Alexander Farrelly, who was strongly supported by business groups, but the Democrats elected only seven candidates to the fifteen-seat legislature, further evidence of the party's eroding base. Nevertheless, the Farrelly administration moved vigorously to deal with the severe fiscal crisis by cutting the budget, reducing the public sector work force, and increasing taxes. These necessary but highly unpopular measures, departures from the Democrats' traditional policies, resulted in a very contentious political atmosphere. By the end of the administration's first term, the budget was narrowly in balance, and concessions were obtained from the federal government that contributed to a more attractive climate for future investment. A promised referendum on the status question was not held, however, thus delaying any significant efforts to restructure the islands' taxation system or gain control over immigration.

As the 1990s began, the Democrats were faced with the necessity of formulating new policies in order to retain their majorities during an era of fiscal restraint, economic restructuring, heavy dependence on one industry, and challenges from nationalist groups.

INDEPENDENT CITIZENS MOVEMENT. Organized in the late 1960s by dissident Democrats and liberals protesting the alleged corruption of Democrat-controlled governments, the movement appealed primarily to lower-class groups who felt excluded from the prevailing patronage-based political system. It achieved success in electing members to the legislature throughout the 1970s and 1980s. One member, Juan Luis, won the governorship in 1978 and was reelected in 1982.

In the 1980s, the movement, which from its founding had a populist cast, adopted a somewhat more radical and nationalist stance in response to growing social and economic inequities in the islands. Its 1986 candidate for governor, Adelbert Bryan, a former Saint Croix policeman, ran on a platform emphasizing the rights of native Virgin Islanders. Even though he was attacked by his opponents for being both antiwhite and antibusiness, he won 36 percent of the vote and brought the issues of immigration and islanders' control of their economic future to the forefront of discussion. By the end of the decade, the movement had not only become the second most important political party, it had tapped into the growing discontent of the islands' poor. It forced the ruling Democrats to address problems that had been largely ignored, including the Virgin Islands' role in an awakening Caribbean community.

PROGRESSIVE REPUBLICANS. The success of party leader Melvin Evans, governor from 1970 to 1974, in refurbishing—and renaming—the former Republican Party as an organization with broader appeal than to the old conservative white landowning and business groups did not carry through in the 1980s. Though the party managed to attract support among both middle-class colored groups and immigrant whites, it could not develop the mass base required to win more than a few legislative seats. By the 1980s the party, like its rival Democrats affiliated with the similarly named mainland party, was attempting to reconcile a free-market orientation with the need for progressive social attitudes. It also had not yet successfully formulated a position on the islands' future political status. As a result, it remains the islands' second minority party.

Political Parties—Historical

PEOPLE'S PARTY. A party of the 1950s, the People's Party represented Puerto Rican immigrant groups, primarily on Saint Croix.

PROGRESSIVE GUIDE. As the first true political party in the islands, the Progressive Guide represented the interests of the colored lower middle and working classes in the late 1930s and 1940s. Many of its adherents joined the Unity Party after 1952.

REPUBLICAN PARTY. Originating as a political club in the 1930s, the Republicans represented the interests of white businessmen and landowners. Later the party incorporated affluent colored groups and immigrants from the mainland. In an effort to change its conservative image, the party was renamed Progressive Republican in the late 1960s.

UNITED PEOPLE'S PARTY. This small party, which failed to gain widespread popular support, was the islands' manifestation of the black power movement of the late 1960s and early 1970s.

UNITY PARTY. In existence between 1952 and 1962, the liberal, nationalist Unity Party originally sought commonwealth status for the islands. It dissolved after its members took control of the Democratic Party.

Richard E. Sharpless

APPENDIX

CHRONOLOGY

ANGUILLA

1980   Formal recognition of Anguilla's status as a separate dependent territory of the United Kingdom

1981   Formation of Anguilla People's Party by J. Ronald Webster, who became chief minister following June elections

1984   Webster retires following electoral defeat; Émile Gumbs of Anguilla National Alliance becomes chief minister

1989   Gumbs retains parliamentary leadership in February election; new constitution proclaimed

ANTIGUA AND BARBUDA

1981   Independence achieved on 1 November

1984   Antigua Labor Party (ALP) sweeps general election, continuing its long domination under the leadership of Vere Bird, Sr., and his sons

1989   General election in March won easily by ALP, despite charges of corruption

ARGENTINA

1981   General Leopoldo Galtieri assumes power, continuing Argentina's military rule

1982   Falklands/Malvinas War; General Galtieri forced to step down

1983   Civilian rule restored, with election of Raul Alfonsín of the Radical Party (UCR) as president

1985   General Jorge Videla and other military officers convicted and imprisoned for human rights violations during the "dirty war" (1976–1979)

1989   Alfonsín completes term; succeeded by Carlos Saúl Menem of the Justicialist Party (Peronist) in a free, democratic election

1990   Nationalist military leaders, the *carapintadas*, fail in coup attempt

ARUBA

1981   Electoral Movement of the People (MEP), Aruba's principal party, withdraws from the Netherlands Antilles government

1983   Agreement reached providing for separation of Aruba from the Netherlands Antilles; the MEP wins elections and Gilberto (Bertico) Croes becomes head of government

1985   Aruban People's Party (AVP) forms new government following November election and MEP defeat

1986   Aruba obtains full autonomy in internal affairs as part of the Dutch realm and separates from the Netherlands Antilles; J.H.A. Eman of the AVP becomes Aruba's first prime minister

1989   Following January elections, the MEP regains control of government; Bertico Croes dies in auto accident; Nelson Oduber becomes prime minister

THE BAHAMAS

1973   Independence of Commonwealth of the Bahamas; Progressive Liberal Party in power, and its leader Lynden O. Pindling becomes prime minister

1987   Most recent general election in June; Progressive Liberal Party wins, as it has every parliamentary election since 1972; Prime Minister Pindling firmly in control despite allegations of improprieties

BARBADOS

1981   Barbados Labour Party (BLP) wins control of government; J.M.G.N. "Tom" Adams becomes prime minister

1985   Death of Prime Minister Tom Adams; Bernard St. John becomes prime minister and head of the BLP

1986   Democratic Labour Party (DLP) soundly defeats BLP in general election; Errol Barrow becomes prime minister; New Democratic Party (NDP) formed and replaces BLP as official opposition party

1987   Errol Barrow dies in June, and is succeeded by Erskine Sandiford as prime minister and head of the DLP

1991   Sandiford and DLP retain control of government in January general elections, but BLP makes a comeback, and NDP fades significantly

BELIZE

1981	Belize becomes independent; People's United Party (PUP) in control of government, with leader George Price serving as prime minister
1984	First general elections following independence; United Democratic Party (UDP) sweeps PUP from office; Manuel Esquivel becomes prime minister
1988	Belize and Guatemala reach a joint accord establishing a permanent commission to resolve long-standing territorial dispute
1989	The PUP wins close general election; Price regains premiership; UDP remains strong opposition party

BERMUDA

1968	New constitution establishes universal adult suffrage and cabinet-style government
1980	United Bermuda Party (UBP), continuing its domination since 1968, wins parliamentary elections; David Gibbons of the UBP continues as premier
1982	Gibbons steps down as premier and is succeeded by John W. D. Swan; National Labour Party (NLP) is formed
1985	UBP and Swan win early elections decisively
1989	UBP suffers a loss of eight seats in parliamentary elections to the Progressive Labour Party (PLP), Bermuda's principal opposition party since 1963

BOLIVIA

1980	Seizure of power by General Luis García Meza, after third presidential election, which had assured Hernán Siles Zuazo of victory
1982	Transitional military government restores Siles Zuazo to his rightful place as president
1985	Coalition of Nationalist Revolutionary Movement (MNR) and Democratic Nationalist Action (ADN) wins presidential and congressional elections; Víctor Paz Estenssoro becomes president for the fourth time in his career
1989	Though running third in the popular balloting, Jaime Paz Zamora of the Movement of the Revolutionary Left (MIR) was named president by the congress

BRAZIL

1978	General Joâo B. Figueiredo elected president for 1979–1985 term; military regime begins phasing out power held since 1964
1979	Military regime enacts legislation designed to preserve government party and to create multiple parties within the opposition

1982   Elections at every level except the presidential are a setback for the regime; despite efforts to manipulate voting procedures to favor the government party—the Democratic Socialist Party (PDS)—opposition parties make substantial gains

1984   "Direct Elections Now" amendment defeated; further setback for military regime's efforts to control presidential succession, as Brazil prepares for restoration of democratic rule

1985   Electoral College names Democratic Alliance (opposition) candidates Tancredo Neves and José Sarney president and vice president, respectively; Neves dies before taking office, leaving Sarney to complete full term

1986   In February President Sarney announces Cruzado Plan designed to overcome inflation; elections in November for national congress and state governments; congress to serve as a constituent assembly for drafting a new constitution; transition to full electoral democracy

1988   New constitution proclaimed on October 5

1990   Fernando Collor de Mello becomes Brazil's first popularly elected president in almost thirty years; congressional and state elections confirm weakness of political party system in Brazil

BRITISH VIRGIN ISLANDS

1977   New constitution establishes virtually complete internal self-government

1979   H. Lavity Stoutt of the Virgin Islands Party (VIP) forms new government following parliamentary elections

1983   Independent Cyril B. Romney forms coalition government after the VIP and the United Party (UP) each win four seats in the 1983 elections

1986   Stoutt and the VIP return to power

CANADA

1980   Liberal Party returns to power under Pierre Elliot Trudeau as prime minister

1982   New constitution proclaimed

1984   Trudeau resigns as prime minister and is replaced by John Turner, who calls a federal election; Conservatives achieve sweeping triumph in federal election; Brian Mulroney becomes prime minister

1987   Reform Party established in Calgary as protest against Mulroney government

1988   Conservatives repeat victory in federal election, but with a reduced majority; Mulroney continues as prime minister

1990   Failure of the Meech Lake Constitutional Accord (designed to give Quebec "special status" within a federalist framework) revived goal of the Parti Québécois for an independent Quebec

CAYMAN ISLANDS

1959   Cayman Islands become a separate (from Jamaica) dependency under the British crown

1980   Unity Team wins elections and Jim Bodden becomes chief minister

1984   Amid charges of improprieties, Unity Team loses elections; Dignity Team and independents form coalition government under Benson Ebanks

1988   Ebanks and Dignity Team continue coalition government after new elections

1991   BCCI scandal places Cayman Islands offshore banking sector under scrutiny

CHILE

1973   Overthrow and death of President Salvador Allende; installation of military dictatorship under General Augusto Pinochet; all political parties outlawed

1980   President Pinochet decrees new constitution which provides for an eventual restoration of democracy

1983   Christian Democratic Party continues to function underground, organizing demonstrations against the Pinochet regime

1988   Defeat of plebiscite authorizing Pinochet to continue in the presidency; opponents of Pinochet regime form broad coalition, La Concertación, to defeat plebiscite

1989   La Concertación candidate, Christian Democrat Patricio Aylwin, wins presidential election and restores Chilean democracy

COLOMBIA

1978   Liberal Party candidate Julio César Turbay Ayala narrowly elected president

1982   Belisario Betancur elected president (though the candidate of the Conservative Party, Betancur organized the National Movement, a coalition of Liberals and Conservatives disenchanted with their respective parties); amnesty law passes and truce is arranged with principal revolutionary groups

1984   Dialogue between "truce revolutionaries" and national administration

1985   M-19 guerrillas occupy Palace of Justice; resulting carnage terminates "national dialogue" peace process

1986   Liberal Party returns to power with the election of Virgilio Barco as president; government takes tougher stand against guerrillas and drug traffickers

1988   Nation beset by guerrilla attacks, drug-related killings, terrorism, and death squad activity; President Barco's peace plan, including amnesty for rebels and possible extradition of drug dealers, fails

1989   Luis Carlos Galán, Liberal candidate for president, assassinated, allegedly by gunmen of the Medellín drug cartel

| 1990 | Two more presidential candidates assassinated; new Liberal Party candidate César Gaviria Trujillo elected president; 60 percent of the electorate abstains from voting |
| 1991 | Gaviria administration moves to overcome violence, including peace negotiations with guerrilla forces and judicial leniency toward drug traffickers who cooperate; support for election of a constituent assembly to draft a new constitution and to reorganize political and judicial system |

COSTA RICA

1982	Luis Alberto Monge Alvarez, of the dominant National Liberation Party (PLN), elected president
1985	Social Christian Unity Party (PUSC), replacing the Unity coalition, formally organized under the leadership of Rafael Angel Calderón Fournier
1986	PLN's Oscar Arias Sánchez upsets Calderón Fournier to win the presidency
1987	Arias wins the Nobel Peace Prize for his efforts to achieve peace in Central America
1990	Calderón Fournier (PUSC) narrowly wins presidency on third try; former president José Figueres dies in June

CUBA

1980	Mariel boat exodus; indications of internal discontent stimulates Rectification Process, an abandoning of pragmatism and a return to ideological rigidity
1986	Fidel Castro declares intention "to build socialism"
1989	Execution of General Arnaldo Ochoa for treason (corruption and drug trafficking)
1990	Castro implements policies to go it alone to achieve the survival of socialism under hostile conditions

DOMINICA

1978	Dominica becomes independent
1979	Government of Dominica Labour Party under Patrick R. John ousted
1980	Eugenia Charles of Dominica Freedom Party (DFP) becomes prime minister
1983	Charles, as chair of the Organization of Eastern Caribbean States, supports U.S. intervention in Grenada
1985	DFP easily wins elections, and Charles remains prime minister
1990	DFP and Charles repeat as winners in elections, but economic hard times reduce majority

DOMINICAN REPUBLIC

1982   Salvador Jorge Blanco of the Dominican Revolutionary Party (PRD) wins presidency

1986   Former President Joaquín Balaguer (heading the newly formed Social Christian Reformist Party) wins extremely close election over the PRD's Jacobo Majluta

1989   Majluta quits PRD and founds Independent Revolutionary Party (PRI)

1990   Balaguer reelected despite deteriorating economic conditions and amidst charges of vote fraud; Balaguer and Juan Bosch seem to go on forever

ECUADOR

1979   Jaime Roldós Aguilera of the Concentration of Popular Forces elected president

1981   Roldós dies in plane crash; Vice President Osvaldo Hurtado Larrea of the Popular Democracy completes his term

1984   León Febres Cordero, representing the Front for National Reconstruction, wins presidency in runoff election, upsetting Rodrigo Borja Cevallos of the Democratic Left (ID)

1988   Though forced into a runoff, Borja (ID) wins presidency on his third try

1990   ID defeated in midterm elections; Borja loses congressional majority

EL SALVADOR

1979   General Carlos Humberto Romero overthrown in October; reformist civil-military junta in power for two months

1980   Christian Democratic–military junta installed amid continuing violence from right and left; José Napoleón Duarte of the Christian Democratic Party (PDC) named president of the junta in December; Popular Social Christian Movement (MPSC) founded by Rubén Zamora and other former PDC leaders who break with Duarte over junta participation; Farabundo Martí Front for National Liberation (FMLN) created and undertakes military operations; Democratic Revolutionary Front formed as political side of revolutionary forces

1981   Emergence of extreme right-wing political party, the Nationalist Republican Alliance (ARENA)

1982   Elections for a constituent assembly to draft new constitution

1984   Duarte elected president in runoff election against ARENA's Roberto D'Aubuisson

1987   Establishment of the Democratic Convergence (CD), comprising three democratic left parties and led by Guillermo Manuel Ungo (National Revolutionary Movement, MNR) and Zamora (MPSC)

1989   Alfredo Cristiani of ARENA wins presidency; seeks to soften ARENA's image

1990   Cristiani government and FMLN enter into peace negotiations

1991   Assembly and mayoral elections; ARENA loses its majority, with PDC second largest party, and CD coming in third, gaining 12 percent of the vote

FALKLAND ISLANDS

1982   Argentine forces invade islands in April; British forces defeat Argentines and regain control in June

1983   Falkland Islands Development Corporation founded to develop and diversify economy

1985   New constitution approved providing for eight elected members of a Legislative Council and islanders' right to self-determination

1988   Formation of the Desire for the Right Party, the first and only political party on the islands

1989   Legislative Council election; all eight seats won by independents espousing "no links with Argentina"

FRENCH GUIANA

1982   Executive power of the prefect, named by the French government, transferred to the locally elected General Council

1983   Regional Council elections won by left coalition

1986   French National Assembly election; Guiana elects two deputies; left coalition again successful in Regional Council elections; Georges Othely of the Guyanese Socialist Party (PSG) reelected president of the Regional Council

1988   Left coalition victorious in General Council elections; Elie Castor of the PSG elected president of the General Council

1989   Othely expelled from the PSG; wins seat in French Senate as candidate of the right

GRENADA

1979   New Jewel Movement (NJM), led by Maurice Bishop, carries out coup against regime of Eric Matthew Gairy; establishes People's Revolutionary Government (PRG)

1983   Rival PRG faction under Bernard Coard overthrows and executes Bishop on 19 October; U.S. forces invade Grenada on 25 October; PRG deposed; Nicholas Brathwaite becomes interim prime minister

1984   Founding of the New National Party (NNP) as an amalgamation of the Grenada National Party (GNP), the National Democratic Party (NDP), and the Grenada Democratic Movement (GDM); NNP easily wins 1984 election and its leader Herbert Blaize (GNP) becomes prime minister

1987   Founding of the National Democratic Congress (NDC) by breakaway elements of the NNP, specifically, George Brizan (NDP) and Francis Alexis (GDM)

1989   Further splintering of the NNP, as Prime Minister Blaize forms The National Party (TNP); Blaize dies in December; Ben Jones serves as TNP leader and acting prime minister

1990   NDC achieves plurality in parliamentary election; forms coalition government, with Brathwaite (NDC) as prime minister

GUADELOUPE

1982   Executive powers formerly exercised by appointed prefect transferred to popularly elected General Council; establishment of direct elections for Regional Council (formerly appointed)

1983   First popular elections for Regional Council; right-wing coalition wins majority

1984   Caribbean Revolutionary Alliance carries out terrorist bombings

1985   Socialist–Communist alliance wins General Council elections; Socialist leader Dominique Larifla becomes General Council president

1986   Socialist–Communist alliance wins Regional Council elections, Socialist Party leader Félix Proto chosen Regional Council president, and leftist parties repeat victories in General Council elections; Armed Revolutionary Organization engages in terrorist bombings; Communist Ernest Moutoussany and Socialist Frédéric Jalton elected to French Chamber of Deputies, and both are reelected in 1988

1989   French National Assembly approves amnesty for terrorist acts in Overseas Departments, including Guadeloupe

GUATEMALA

1978   General Romero Lucas García wins presidency in fraudulent election

1979   Manuel Colom Argueta and Alberto Fuentes Mohr, two leading democratic and progressive political leaders, are assassinated

1982   General Aníbal Guevara declared victor in fraudulent presidential election; election moot when junior officers stage coup against President Lucas and install General Efraín Ríos Montt as chief of state

1983   Military coup removes Ríos Montt and replaces him with General Oscar Humberto Mejía Víctores; army condemned for human rights violations

1984   Elections held for a constituent assembly

1985   Vinicio Cerezo Arévalo of the Christian Democratic Party elected president

1990   Jorge Serrano Elías of the Solidarity Action Movement wins presidency in a runoff election that manifested voter apathy and general disdain toward traditional parties

GUYANA

1980   New constitution establishes presidential form of government; Linden Forbes Burnham of the People's National Congress (PNC) elected nation's first executive president; Walter Rodney, leader of the Working People's Alliance, murdered

1985   President Burnham dies and is succeeded by Vice President and Prime Minister Hugh Desmond Hoyte; Hoyte elected president in national elections; PNC retains control over National Assembly; opposition parties form umbrella organization, the Patriotic Coalition for Democracy in hope of challenging PNC control more effectively

1991   National elections held

HAITI

1983   New constitution proclaimed in August

1986   Constitution suspended in February

1987   New constitution approved in March; election day massacre in November

1988   Leslie Manigat wins army-controlled presidential election in January; army removes President Manigat and suspends constitution in June; second coup follows in September; General Prosper Avril assumes presidency

1989   Constitution reinstated in March

1990   President Avril resigns in March and Ertha Pascal-Trouillot named provisional president; Council of State formed; presidential election held in December and Jean-Bertrand Aristide, representing the National Front for Change and Democracy (FNCD), an electoral alliance, is elected president

1991   President Aristide is ousted on 30 September in a military coup

HONDURAS

1980   Elections for a constituent assembly to draft a new constitution and restore democratic rule

1981   New constitution in place; Roberto Suazo Córdoba of the Liberal Party is elected president

1984   Internal military coup removes General Gustavo Alvarez Martínez, the country's real power

1985   Special electoral formula awards presidency to Liberal Party candidate José Azcona del Hoyo, despite fact he received only 27.5 percent of the vote

1989   Rafael Leonardo Callejas of the National Party wins presidency in a campaign marked by mudslinging rather than issues

1990   Inauguration of Callejas in January marks first democratic transfer of power between competing political parties in nearly sixty years

JAMAICA

1980   Jamaica Labour Party (JLP) returns to power, winning parliamentary election decisively; Edward Seaga becomes prime minister

1983   Prime Minister Seaga calls early election; People's National Party (PNP) boycotts election; JLP wins all parliamentary seats

1989   PNP easily wins election; Michael Manley returns as prime minister

1992   Manley resigns as prime minister, citing ill health; P.J. Patterson named to succeed him.

MARTINIQUE

1982   Executive powers formerly exercised by appointed prefect transferred to popularly elected General Council; establishment of direct elections for Regional Council (formerly appointed)

1983   First popular elections for Regional Council held; Aimé Césaire of the Martinican Progressive Party (PPM) becomes president

1985   General Council elections held; coalition of left-wing parties makes gains

1986   Césaire elected to French National Assembly

1988   Césaire resigns as president of the Regional Council and is succeeded by Camille Darsières (PPM); General Council elections held and coalition of left-wing parties achieves majority, but Émile Maurice of the Rally for the Republic continues as president; left-wing coalition takes all four seats in French National Assembly

MEXICO

1982   Miguel de la Madrid Hurtado of the Institutional Revolutionary Party (PRI) wins presidential election; 72 percent winning percentage is lowest for a PRI presidential candidate in thirty years

1985   Midterm elections; PRI margin in Chamber of Deputies is 72 percent

1988   Carlos Salinas de Gortari of the PRI wins presidency with only 51 percent of the vote; Cuauhtémoc Cárdenas of the breakaway National Democratic Front wins 31 percent; PRI's margin in Chamber of Deputies shrinks to 52 percent

1989   Formation of the Party of the Democratic Revolution, emerging from the electoral coalition of 1988

1991   Midterm elections; PRI makes strong comeback in Chamber of Deputies

MONTSERRAT

1978   John A. Osbourne of the People's Liberation Movement (PLM) becomes chief minister

1983   The PLM and Osbourne win elections; Osbourne objects that British-appointed governor will not permit him to send a peace-keeping force to Grenada

1987   The PLM and Osbourne continue in power; formation of the National Development Party under Bertrand Osbourne

NETHERLANDS ANTILLES

1979   Elections for the Staten (parliament) result in a coalition government headed by Domenico F. Martina of the New Antilles Movement (MAN)

1982   Parliamentary elections; Martina continues as minister president

1984   Cabinet resigns; Maria Liberia-Peters of the National United People's Party (PNP) forms government

1985   The PNP wins most of the seats in the Staten, but Liberia-Peters is unable to form government; Martina returns as minister president of coalition government

1986   Aruba secedes

1988   Cabinet resigns; Liberia-Peters returns as minister president at head of a new coalition

1990   General elections; Liberia-Peters continues as minister president at head of yet another coalition

NICARAGUA

1978   Pedro Joaquín Chamorro Cardenal, principal opposition leader against Somoza regime, assassinated

1979   Anastasio Somoza Debayle ousted; five-member junta in control and Sandinista National Liberation Front (FSLN) exercises majority

1980   Violeta Barrios de Chamorro and Alfonso Robelo Callejas, non-Sandinista members, resign from junta

1981   Counterrevolutionary (Contra) movement begins against Sandinistas, including preparations for military operations

1982   State of emergency declared and civil and political rights curtailed

1983   Political Parties Law enacted to oversee political party activity

1984   Electoral Law decreed and elections set for November; Daniel Ortega Saavedra of the FSLN wins presidency; FSLN wins overwhelming control of the National Assembly

1985   Contra war continues; FSLN reimposes state of emergency; opposition deputies temporarily withdraw from the National Assembly

| 1987 | Esquipulas peace accords, signed in August, are designed to achieve negotiated settlement of Contra war; new constitution adopted |
| 1990 | National elections held in February; Barrios de Chamorro of the National Opposition Union, a coalition of groups and parties opposed to the Sandinistas, unseats Ortega as national president |

PANAMA

1978	New Canal treaty with the United States, passing ultimate control to Panama and abolishing Canal Zone immediately, ratified by both countries
1981	General Omar Torrijos dies in plane crash
1982	National Guard deposes President Aristides Royo and replaces him with Vice President Ricardo de la Espriella
1983	New sixty-seven-member Legislative Assembly created, to be elected popularly every five years; National Guard renamed the Panama Defense Forces (FDP)
1984	General Manuel Antonio Noriega becomes head of FDP and replaces President de la Espriella with Vice President Jorge Illueca; national elections held and Nicolás Ardito Barletta of the National Democratic Union, an electoral coalition, wins presidency with help of Noriega
1985	Noriega removes Barletta and replaces him with Eric Delvalle
1988	Delvalle tries to dismiss Noriega as head of the FDP; Noriega ousts Delvalle and replaces him with Manuel Solís Palma; United States continues to recognize Delvalle as president and imposes economic sanctions against Panama
1989	National elections held in May; Noriega nullifies election apparently won by Guillermo Endara of the Democratic Opposition Civic Alliance, a coalition of parties in opposition to Noriega; Noriega installs Francisco Rodríguez as president; U.S. forces invade Panama on 20 December; Endara installed as president; Noriega extradited to the United States to stand trial on criminal charges involving drug trafficking

PARAGUAY

1954	General Alfredo Stroessner seizes power
1979	Formation of the National Accord, a coalition of anti-Stroessner parties
1983	Stroessner reelected president with 90.1 percent of the vote
1987	Ruling Colorado Party shows signs of splintering as Stroessner ages and succession becomes an issue
1988	Stroessner reelected president with 88.7 percent of the vote
1989	General Andrés Rodríguez overthrows Stroessner in February; Rodriguez elected president in May

PERU

1978	Election of constituent assembly
1979	New constitution proclaimed restoring democratic rule; Victor Raúl Haya de la Torre, founder of the Aprista movement, dies
1980	Fernando Belaúnde Terry of the Popular Action elected president
1982	Shining Path (*Sendero Luminoso*) guerrillas temporarily occupy Huamanga
1985	Alan García Pérez of the Peruvian Aprista Party elected president
1990	Alberto K. Fujimori of Change 90, a new political organization created only months before the general election, elected president over Mario Vargas Llosa, the popular author and candidate of the Democratic Front
1992	President Fujimori suspends constitution in April and assumes dictatorial power.

PUERTO RICO

1980	Carlos Romero Barceló of the New Progressive Party reelected governor
1984	Rafael Hernández Colón of the Popular Democratic Party elected governor
1988	Governor Hernández Colón wins reelection; calls for plebiscite in 1991 on the status question

SAINT KITTS-NEVIS

1980	Parliamentary election held; People's Action Movement (PAM) in coalition with the Nevis Reformation Party (NRP) gains control of government; Kennedy Simmonds becomes premier
1983	Saint Kitts-Nevis becomes independent; Simmonds assumes title of prime minister
1984	PAM–NRP retains control in first postindependence election; Simmonds continues as prime minister
1989	Parliamentary elections held; PAM–NRP and Simmonds retain control

SAINT LUCIA

1979	Saint Lucia becomes independent; Saint Lucia Labour Party (SLP) wins parliamentary elections; Allan Louisy (SLP) becomes prime minister
1981	Louisy government resigns; Winston Cenac forms new SLP government

1982 United Worker's Party (UWP) wins general elections; John Compton becomes prime minister

1988 General elections held; UWP retains control and Compton continues as prime minister

SAINT PIERRE AND MIQUELON

1976 Saint Pierre and Miquelon becomes an Overseas Department of the French Republic

1982 Socialists and allies win unopposed election for the General Council

1984 French parliament converts islands into a "territorial collective" in a move to protect offshore fishing areas

1988 Socialists continue to control General Council elections; Marc Plantagenet of the Socialist Party elected president of the council

SAINT VINCENT AND THE GRENADINES

1979 Saint Vincent and the Grenadines becomes an independent state; Saint Vincent Labour Party (SVLP) wins first postindependence elections; SVLP leader Robert Milton Cato becomes new nation's first prime minister

1984 New Democratic Party (NDP) wins general elections handily; James F. Mitchell becomes prime minister

1989 NDP sweeps parliamentary election; Mitchell continues as prime minister

SURINAME

1975 Suriname becomes independent

1980 Government of Minister President Henck Arron overthrown; National Military Council (MNR) led by ex-sergeant Desire (Desi) Bouterse assumes control

1985 Ban on political parties and activities lifted

1986 Bloody guerrilla warfare conducted in the interior; International Commission of Jurists condemns Suriname Army for its brutality (1986–1987)

1987 Voters approve new constitution in referendum; parliamentary elections held and Front for Democracy and Development, an antimilitary coalition, wins election; Ramsewak Shankar of the Progressive Reformed Party elected president of the republic by the National Assembly; Bouterse still in control of armed forces

1990 Commander Ivan Graanoogst, a leading ally of Bouterse, stages coup; army names Johan Kraag of the Suriname National Party interim president

TRINIDAD AND TOBAGO

1962   Trinidad and Tobago achieve independence

1976   Islands become a republic within the British Commonwealth

1981   Death of Eric Williams, leader of the People's National Movement (PNM) party and prime minister since independence; PNM retains control in 1981 general elections; George Michael Chambers becomes prime minister

1986   National Alliance for Reconstruction, a coalition of opposition parties, sweeps PNM from power in general elections; A.N.R. Robinson of the Democratic Action Committee, a coalition member party, becomes prime minister

1987   Cabinet crisis; Robinson reorganizes government

1990   Parliament building seized and held for six days by the Jamaat-al-Muslimeen (a Black Muslim group); Prime Minister Robinson shot and severely beaten during the siege

TURKS AND CAICOS ISLANDS

1980   Chief Minister J.A.G.S. McCartney of the People's Democratic Movement (PDM) dies in a plane crash; Oswald O. Skippings succeeds him, but Skippings and the PDM are defeated in subsequent elections by the Progressive National Party (PNP); Norman Saunders of the PNP becomes chief minister

1984   Saunders and the PNP continue in power

1985   Saunders is implicated in a drug-smuggling scheme and barred from public office; Nathaniel Francis of the PNP succeeds him

1987   British government suspends constitution and imposes direct rule

1988   Constitution is restored; PDM dominates Legislative Council elections; Skippings becomes chief minister again

URUGUAY

1976   Military removes President Juan María Bordaberry from office; Aparicio Méndez installed as puppet president

1977   Military announces a timetable (*cronograma*) for restoring democratic order

1980   National plebiscite rejects constitution providing for continued military intervention in political affairs

1981   Gregorio Alvarez, a retired general, assumes presidency

1984   Military negotiates its exit from power in the Naval Club Pact and national elections are set for November; national elections are held; civilian rule is restored; Julio María Sanguinetti, a Colorado Party candidate, is elected president

1989 Blancos return to power in national elections for first time since 1962; because of Uruguay's unique balloting system, Luis Alberto Lacalle is elected president with only 22.5 percent of the vote

VENEZUELA

1978 Luis Herrera Campíns of COPEI elected president

1981 Death of Rómulo Betancourt, former president and founder and longtime leader of Democratic Action (AD)

1983 Jaime Lusinchi of AD elected president

1988 Carlos Andrés Pérez of the AD, president from 1974 to 1979, wins presidency again

1989 Rioting in Caracas from 17 February to 11 March leaves 300 dead

1992 Army uprising fails in attempt to assassinate and remove Pérez from power, but Venezuelan democratic order shaken.

VIRGIN ISLANDS OF THE UNITED STATES

1982 Juan Luis of the Independent Citizens' Movement reelected governor

1986 Alexander Farrelly of the Democratic Party elected governor

1990 Alexander Farrelly reelected governor

INDEX

MEP. *See* Electoral Movement of the People; Popular Electoral Movement

MERECEN. *See* Centrist Republican Stable Movement

Mexican Communist Party, 419–21, 430

Mexican Democrat Party, 421

Mexican Democratic Party, 433

Mexican Ecologist Party, 421–22

Mexican Popular Party, 420, 422

Mexican Socialist Party, 419–21, 422, 428

Mexican Workers' Party, 422

Michaux-Chévry, Lucette, 329, 330

MID. *See* Movement of Integration and Development

MIDA. *See* Democratic Integration Movement

MIDH. *See* Movement for Installing Democracy in Haiti

Miguel, Lorenzo, 31

Milián, Arnaldo, 228

Militant Workers' Revolutionary Party, 215

MIM. *See* Independence Movement of Martinique

MIN. *See* Movement of National Integration; National Integration Movement

Miolán, Angel, 253

MIR. *See* Movement of the Revolutionary Left, various Tentries

Miranda Bengochea, Bonifacio, 469, 470

MIR-Bolivia Libre. *See* MIR-Free Bolivia

MIR-Free Bolivia, 97

Mitchell, James Fitz Allen ("Son"), 555, 557, 558, 559, 560, 561, 562, 563

Mitchell, Keith, 309, 314, 316, 317, 320, 321

Mitchell/Sylvester Faction, 557, 561

Mitre, Bartolemé, 21, 35, 41, 45

M-LIDER. *See* Liberal Democratic Revolutionary Movement

MLN. *See* National Liberation Movement

MLR. *See* Rodista Liberal Movement

MNP-28. *See* National Patriotic Movement of 28 July

MNR. *See* National Reformist Movement; Nationalist Revolutionary Movement; New Republic Movement; Revolutionary National Movement

MNRI. *See* Nationalist Revolutionary Movement of the Left

MNU. *See* Movement for National Unity

Mobilisation pour le Developpement National. *See* Mobilization for National Development

Mobilization for National Development, 365

MODELH/PRDH. *See* Democratic Movement for the Liberation of Haiti/ Revolutionary Democratic Party of Haiti

Mohme Llona, Gustavo, 515

Moleiro, Moisés, 615

Molina, Armando, 288

MOLIRENA. *See* National Liberal Republican Movement

MONARCA. *See* Nationalist Rafael Callejas Movement

Monge Alvarez, Luis Alberto, 209, 210, 211, 216

Montalvan, Wilfredo, 472

Montás, Luis Adolfo ("Pin") 250, 251

Montero, Juan Esteban, 182

Moore, Lee Llewellyn, 539, 542

MOP. *See* Movement for the Organization of the Country

MOPOCO. *See* Popular Colorado Movement

Mora Valverde, Manuel, 208, 211, 213, 218

Morales, Manolo, 468, 471

Morales Bermúdez, Francisco, 500, 510

MORENA. *See* Movement for National Renewal

Morena, María Eugenia Rojas de, 200

Moreno, Nahuel, 37

Moreno Martínez, Alfonso, 258

Morínigo, Higinio, 486, 490, 493

Morones, Luis, 433

Mottley, E.D., 73

Moutoussany, Ernest, 328

Movimiento 26 de Marzo. *See* 26th of March Movement

MPC. *See* Popular Christian Movement

MPD. *See* Democratic Popular Movement; Dominican Popular Movement

MPGI. *See* Popular Movement for an Independent Guadeloupe

MPN. *See* Neuquen Popular Movement

MPP. *See* Movement for Popular Participation

MPSC. *See* Popular Social Christian Movement

MRO. *See* Oriental Revolutionary Movement

MRP. *See* Peronist Revolutionary Movement; Progressive Republican Movement

MRS. *See* Socialist Revolutionary Movement

MSN. *See* Movement of National Solidarity

MSP. *See* Social Progressive Movement

M-26-7. *See* Twenty-sixth of July Movement

Mulroney, Brian, 160, 162

Muñoz Ledo, Porfirio, 406, 415, 425, 439

Muñoz Marín, Luis, 527, 531

Muñoz Rivera, Luis, 526, 533

Munroe, Trevor, 390

MUR. *See* United Revolutionary Movement

Murray, Winston, 578

Musa, Said, 86

Muslimeen, Jameat-al-, 577

NAR. *See* National Alliance for Reconstruction

National Accord, 486, 490, 493, 494

National Action Party (Dominican Republic), 255

National Action Party (El Salvador), 299

National Action Party (Mexico), 403, 405, 407, 408, 409, 423–25

National Advancement Front, 342

National Agrarian Industrial Party, 366

National Agrarian Party (Mexico), 402, 433

National Agrarian Party (Venezuela), 623

National Alliance for Democracy and Progress, 366

National Alliance for Reconstruction, 575, 576, 577, 579

National Alliance Front, 366

National Autonomist Party, 41

National Catholic Party, 433

National Center Party, 33

National Christian Alliance, 215

National Christian Party. *See* Christian Democratic Party (Chile)

National Civic Crusade, 478

National Civic Union, 263–64

National Congress of Democratic Forces, 366

National Conservative Party, 460, 464

National Democratic Action, 51

National Democratic Alliance, 588

National Democratic Congress, 309, 314, 315, 316, 317, 319–20, 321

National Democratic Front (Guyana), 352, 353

National Democratic Front (Mexico), 406, 415, 425–26, 428

National Democratic Front (Nicaragua), 460, 464

National Democratic Front (Venezuela), 623

National Democratic Movement, 347

National Democratic Party (Antigua), 18

National Democratic Party (Argentina), 42

National Democratic Party (Grenada), 313, 321–22

National Democratic Party (Guyana), 357

National Democratic Party (Suriname), 566, 567, 568

National Democratic Progressive Party of Haiti, 367

National Democratic Union (Cuba), 231

National Democratic Union (Panama), 477, 481, 483, 484

National Development Party, 435, 436

Partido de Integración de América
Central. *See* Central American Party
of Integration
Partido de Integración Democrática. *See*
Democratic Integration Party
Partido de la Democracia Cristiana. *See*
Christian Democratic Party (Bolivia)
Partido de la Izquierda Revolucionaria.
See Party of the Revolutionary Left
Partido de la Liberación Dominicana. *See*
Dominican Liberation Party
Partido de la Revolución Democrática.
See Party of the Democratic
Revolution
Partido de la Revolución Guatemalteca.
See Party of the Guatemalan
Revolution
Partido de la Unión Republicana
Socialista. *See* Party of the Republican
Socialist Union
Partido del Frente Cardenista de
Reconstrucción Nacional. *See*
Cardenista Front Party for National
Reconstruction
Partido de los Trabajadores. *See* Workers'
Party, various entries
Partido del Progreso. *See* Progressive
Party
Partido del Pueblo. *See* People's Party,
various entries
Partido del Pueblo Civilista. *See* Civil
People's Party
Partido del Pueblo Costarricense. *See*
Costa Rican People's Party
Partido del Pueblo Cubano—Ortodoxo.
See Cuban People's Party
Partido del Trabajo. *See* Labor Party
(Mexico)
Partido Demócrata. *See* Democratic
Party, various entries
Partido Demócrata Conservador Popular.
See Popular Conservative Democratic
Party
Partido Demócrata Cristao. *See* Christian
Democratic Party (Brazil)
Partido Demócrata Cristiano. *See*
Christian Democratic Party, various
entries

Partido Demócrata Cristiano de
Honduras. *See* Christian Democratic
Party of Honduras
Partido Demócrata Mexicano. *See*
Mexican Democrat Party
Partido Demócrata Nacional. *See*
National Democratic Party
Partido Demócrata Nacionalista. *See*
Nationalist Democrat Party
Partido Demócrata Progresista. *See*
Progressive Democratic Party
Partido Democrático. *See* Democratic
Party (Guatemala)
Partido Democrático Constitucional. *See*
Constitutional Democratic Party
Partido Democrático de Cooperación
Nacional. *See* Democratic Party of
National Cooperation
Partido Democrático Liberal. *See*
Democratic Liberal Party
Partido Democrático Mexicano. *See*
Mexican Democratic Party
Partido Democrático Popular. *See* Popular
Democratic Party
Partido Democrático Revolucionario
Dominicano. *See* Dominican
Democratic Revolutionary Party
Partido Democrático Social. *See*
Democratic Social Party
Partido Democrático Trabalhista. *See*
Democratic Labor Party
Partido Democrático Venezolano. *See*
Venezuelan Democratic Party
Partido de Orientación Popular. *See* Party
of Popular Orientation
Partido de Unidad Nacional. *See*
National Unity Party
Partido de Unificación Anti-Comunista.
See Anti-Communist Unification Party
Partido de Unión. *See* Unionist Party
Partido Dominicano. *See* Dominican
Party
Partido do Movimento Democrático
Brasileiro. *See* Brazilian
Democratic Movement Party
Partido dos Trabalhadores. *See* Workers'
Party (Brazil)

SI. *See* Socialist Independent
Siles Suazo, Hernán, 93, 97, 98, 99
Silfa, Nicolás, 253, 259
Silva Cimma, Enrique, 182
Simmonds, Kennedy A., 539, 540, 541, 542
Singh, Marcellus Felden, 355
Sint Maarten People's Movement, 442
Sisniega Otero, Leonel, 339
SKDP. *See* Saint Kitts Democratic Party
Skippings, Oswaldo O., 587, 588
SKNALP. *See* Saint Kitts-Nevis-Anguilla Labour Party
SKNLP. *See* Saint Kitts-Nevis Labour Party
SL. *See* Sendero Luminoso
SLP. *See* Saint Lucia Labour Party
SLP-UF. *See* Saint Lucia Labour Party-United Front
Social Action Movement, 597, 600
Social Christian Conservative Party. *See* Christian Democratic Party (Chile)
Social Christian Copei Party, 606, 607, 620–21
Social Christian Party (Brazil), 129
Social Christian Party (Ecuador), 269, 270, 279–80
Social Christian Party (Nicaragua), 444, 448, 451, 465, 471–72
Social Christian Popular Alliance, 345
Social Christian Reformist Party, 246, 247, 257–58
Social Christian Revolutionary Party, 246, 258
Social Christian Unity Party, 209, 210, 211, 212, 219
Social Conservative Party, 187, 188, 193, 196, 202–3
Social Credit, 134, 135, 136, 140, 143, 147, 148, 152, 162–64
Social Democracy, 37
Social Democracy Party, 182–83
Social Democratic Alliance Party, 258
Social Democratic Party (The Bahamas), 58
Social Democratic Party (Bolivia), 102
Social Democratic Party (Brazil), 129

Social Democratic Party (Costa Rica), 222
Social Democratic Party (Nicaragua), 448, 451, 465, 472–73
Social Democratic Party (Peru), 522
Social Democrat Party (El Salvador), 284, 289, 298
Social Independiente. *See* Socialist Independent
Socialist Action Party, 213, 222
Socialist Alliance, 37
Socialist Federation of Martinique, 393, 397, 398
Socialist Independent, 442
Socialist Labor Party. *See* Communist Party of Chile
Socialist Party (Argentina), 45
Socialist Party (Bolivia), 100
Socialist Party (Guadeloupe), 330
Socialist Party (Guatemala), 348
Socialist Party (Martinique), 394, 397–98
Socialist Party (Panama), 484
Socialist Party (Paraguay), 496
Socialist Party (Puerto Rico), 526, 527, 535
Socialist Party (Saint Pierre and Miquelon), 552–53
Socialist Party (Uruguay), 593, 599, 602
Socialist Party of Chile, 169, 170, 183–85
Socialist Party of Peru, 523
Socialist Party of the Southeast, 402, 434
Socialist Party of the Workers. *See* Revolutionary Party of the Workers (Argentina)
Socialist Political Action, 515
Socialist Revolutionary Movement, 515
Socialist Revolutionary Party, 515–16
Socialist Workers' Party (Argentina), 45
Socialist Workers' Party (Mexico), 413, 431
Socialist Workers' Party (Panama), 478, 479, 480, 482
Socialist Workers' Party (Peru), 516, 517
Socialist Workers' Party (Venezuela), 625, 626
Social Progressive Movement, 522–23